Single Text

Hamlet

The Great Gatsby

Introduction

What is the Single Text?

The Single Text is Section I on the Leaving Certificate English – Higher Level – Paper 2. It is worth 60 marks.

You must answer **one** question from Section I, The Single Text. There are questions on **five** Single Texts on the examination paper, but you must answer only **one** of these. There are **two** questions within each option, but you must answer only **one** of these.

The options are identified by the first five letters of the alphabet (A–E), by the title of the text and by the author's name. On the front page of the examination paper, there is an index of Single Texts, identifying each. You must locate your chosen text from this index and go immediately to the relevant page. Ignore all other texts and questions within Section I, The Single Text.

The five texts prescribed for Higher Level students are listed in alphabetical order by author's surname, as given by the NCCA in its **List of prescribed texts for the Leaving Certificate English examination of 2017**. In 2017, the five texts prescribed for Higher Level students, as they will appear on the examination paper, are:

- *Emma* by Jane Austen
- *The Great Gatsby* by F. Scott Fitzgerald
- *A Doll's House* by Henrik Ibsen
- *Death and Nightingales* by Eugene McCabe
- *Hamlet* by William Shakespeare.

As noted in all Chief Examiner's Reports, and most recently in 2013: 'In Paper 2, Section I, The Single Text, Shakespeare proved to be by far the most popular single text studied, almost to the exclusion of the four other options.' The 2013 report also noted: 'Other texts which appeared occasionally in candidates' answers included … Fitzgerald's *The Great Gatsby*' and 'very few candidates' presented answers on the remaining texts. Based on these figures, this textbook offers comprehensive study aids on both William Shakespeare's *Hamlet* and F. Scott Fitzgerald's *The Great Gatsby*.

IMPORTANT: The text you have chosen as your Single Text must **not** be used again as a text in Section II, The Comparative Study. For the purposes of this textbook, this means that if *Hamlet* is your Single Text, you can select **any one** of the three Comparative Study options to accompany it, but if *The Great Gatsby* is your Single Text, you **must** select Comparative Study Option Two – *Othello*, *Rear Window*, *The Fault in Our Stars* – to accompany it, since 'at **Higher Level** a play by Shakespeare **must be one of the texts chosen**'. This can be studied on its own or as an element in a comparative study. (NCCA **List of prescribed texts for the Leaving Certificate English examination of 2017**.)

Leaving Certificate Higher Level

Excellence in English Literature

Paper 2

Cathy Sweeney

First published 2015

Educate.ie

Walsh Educational Books Ltd

Castleisland

Co. Kerry

Ireland

www.educate.ie

The publisher reserves the right to change, without notice, at any time, the specification of this product, whether by change of materials, colours, binding, format, text revision or any other characteristic.

ISBN: 978-1-910052-90-7

Design and Cover: Kieran O'Donoghue

Layout: Compuscript

Printed and bound in Ireland: Walsh Colour Print, Castleisland, Co. Kerry

Contents

How *Excellence in English Literature* works

Excellence in English Literature is a **multimedia** concept. Students are provided with:

- A hard-copy textbook
- An electronic version of the textbook
- Dedicated digital resources.

Three icons are used throughout the textbook to indicate the availability of material on *www.educateplus.ie*:

Audio lecture

Further material

Guide to answering examination questions

The textbook is divided into three main sections:

1. **Single Text**
2. **Comparative Study**
3. **Poetry**

Each part is modelled on a **READ–ANALYSE–MAKE** method, whereby students **read** texts, **analyse** texts and **make** texts themselves. Audio lectures , further material and guides to answering examination questions are available on *www.educateplus.ie* to support student learning.

Part 1: Single Text covers two options:

- *Hamlet* by William Shakespeare
- *The Great Gatsby* by F. Scott Fitzgerald

Each option offers an introduction to the text (discussing its setting and distinctive features), a plot outline, and analyses of the major characters, themes and stylistic features.

Part 2: The Comparative Study covers three options:

- Option 1: *All My Sons* by Arthur Miller, *Juno* (film) and *Foster* by Claire Keegan
- Option 2: *Othello* by William Shakespeare, *Rear Window* (film) and *The Fault in Our Stars* by John Green
- Option 3: *A Doll's House* by Henrik Ibsen, *The King's Speech* (film) and *The Uncommon Reader* by Alan Bennett.

Option 2 is designed for students who do *not* opt to study *Hamlet* as their Single Text.

Each option offers a comprehensive summary of the texts, a detailed discussion of each in relation to the modes of comparison set for 2017 – Theme, General Vision and Viewpoint, and Literary Genre – as well as a guide to answering examination questions on each of the modes.

Part 3: Poetry provides text and notes on all the poems set for each of the 2017 prescribed poets: Elizabeth Bishop, Eavan Boland, John Donne, Paul Durcan, T.S. Eliot, Gerard Manley Hopkins, John Keats and Sylvia Plath. It also gives a detailed discussion of the characteristic themes and stylistic features of each poet, as well as a comprehensive guide to unseen poetry and a glossary of poetic terms.

What Questions are on the Examination Paper?

There are **two** questions on each Single Text. You must answer **one** of these. Each question consists of a critical quotation on some aspect of the text and an invitation to agree or disagree with this assessment, or otherwise to discuss its merits. It is vitally important for you to understand that you are *not* being asked merely to reproduce what you *know* about the text, but rather to use what you know to assess the merits of a critical quotation. Therefore your essay is an exercise in the language of argument – thesis, reasons, supporting discussion and evidence, in the forms of quotations and reference – and *not* an exercise in the language of information – facts, synopsis, outline.

If you understand this, it will help you to avoid the damaging error that the Chief Examiner draws attention to year after year – 'unfocused narrative', or simply outlining the events in a text, without reference to the question set. 'Students should be aware of the dangers of unfocused narrative particularly in their response to a Single Text question. It is important to move beyond mere description of content' (*Chief Examiner's Report,* 2008). And, 'it is important that the question set is the question answered' (*Chief Examiner's Report*, 2013).

Single Text questions may be set on **CHARACTERS**, **THEMES**, including the world of the text, **STYLISTIC FEATURES**, such as imagery or symbolism, dramatic techniques or narrative techniques, and **INDIVIDUAL SCENES OR EPISODES**, the discussion of which can refer to characters *and* themes *and* stylistic features.

For example, Question E(i) in 2012 – 'Hamlet's madness, whether genuine or not, adds to the fascination of his character for the audience.' Discuss this statement, supporting your answer with suitable reference to the play, *Hamlet*. – was a question on **CHARACTER**, while Question E(ii) the same year – 'Shakespeare uses a variety of techniques to convey a world of corruption in the play, *Hamlet*.' Write your response to this statement, supporting your answer with suitable reference to the text. – is a question on **STYLISTIC FEATURES** guided by the **THEME** of corruption.

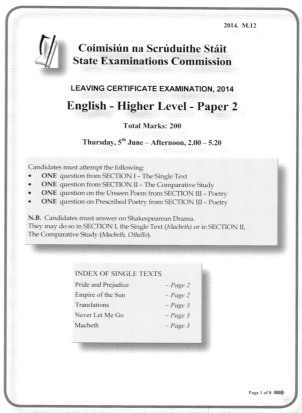

In 2013, Question B(i) – 'Readers of *The Great Gatsby* are greatly influenced by the narrator, Nick Carraway.' Discuss this statement, supporting your answer with suitable reference to the text. – is on **STYLISTIC FEATURES**, specifically narrative technique, guided by an understanding of the **CHARACTER** of Nick Carraway, and Question B(ii) – 'Readers often find aspects of *The Great Gatsby* attractive but ultimately the world of the novel is not admirable.' Discuss this view, supporting your answer with suitable reference to the text. – is on **THEMES**, inviting a judgement on the world of the text.

How much Time should I Spend on each Question?

The general rule for English Higher Level Paper 2 is to allocate one minute of writing time for each mark available. Section I, The Single Text is worth 60 marks, and you should therefore spend 60 minutes answering it.

How should I use this Textbook to Prepare for the Examination Questions?

In this textbook, the two most popular texts prescribed for Higher Level students are treated separately, in order of popularity: *Hamlet* and *The Great Gatsby*.

Each section contains:

- a guide to the background of the text, including its fictional and historical settings,
- a detailed outline of the plot, supported by frequent **MAKE** tasks for revision purposes,

- comprehensive analyses of the major **CHARACTERS**, main **THEMES** and notable **STYLISTIC FEATURES**.

At the end of each section, there are two links: one to a guide on how to use all this material to answer examination questions and write examination essays, and one to further material – lists of DVDs, books and websites – relating to the text.

Hamlet
by William Shakespeare

Background

Although it is impossible to date the writing and first performance of *Hamlet* accurately, the existing evidence points strongly to it being in 1599 or 1600 in London. The play was immediately popular, and there were further performances in the English universities and abroad. It's not an original story. In fact, an earlier version, also called *Hamlet* and also a revenge tragedy, had been popular almost twenty years earlier, but this text is now lost.

In 1600, Queen Elizabeth was on the throne of England, although her right to reign had just been challenged from within by her former favourite the Earl of Essex and from without by the King of Spain. Obviously, it was a very different world from today. Although extensive research into the period is not required for a full appreciation of *Hamlet*, there are certain features of this world – the belief in ghosts, the role of the monarchy, the conditions in the playhouses and the conventions of revenge tragedy – that you need to be familiar with.

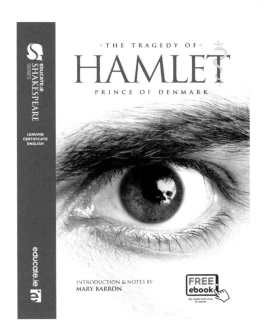

Ghosts

Ghosts were a conventional dramatic device in the theatre of Shakespeare's time. They were part of a literary tradition dating back hundreds of years, rather than reflections of contemporary social beliefs. Sometimes, the Ghost can be seen by all characters and sometimes, as in *Hamlet*, Act III, Scene iv, it is seen only by a single individual and may therefore be a figment of that individual's fevered imagination. One way or the other, a ghost is almost always a murder victim who returns to the world of men seeking justice or vengeance.

Single Text

Monarchs

Today, Britain has a constitutional monarchy. The power of the monarch has been restricted by the British parliament over a number of centuries, so that the monarch has no power to create or change any law. Things were very, very different in Shakespeare's time and, in order to fully appreciate *Hamlet*, you need to make an effort to understand just how different – just how essential a king or queen was to a society and just how easily that society could slide into chaos if the monarch was challenged and rebelled against.

The Shakespearean scholar, A.L. Rowse, in his book *The England of Elizabeth*, put it succinctly: 'kingship … was the normal mode, along with religion, of holding society together in the sixteenth century'. It follows that regicide – the killing of a king – was a heinous crime, threatening the destruction of an entire society, it was not just the assassination of an individual, as it is now. For Shakespeare's contemporaries, this understanding of regicide must have applied as much to Hamlet, whose task it is to kill a king, as it did to Claudius, who *did* kill a king. In part, this accounts for Hamlet's necessary hesitation. It also follows that an inept or corrupt king, such as Claudius, was also a threat to the entire society. In part, this explains why Hamlet, despite his reservations, must kill the king.

Playhouses

We don't have playhouses any more. We have concert venues, cinemas, sports stadia and theatres. The Elizabethan public – people who lived during the reign of Elizabeth I – had the open-air playhouse, the first of which, the Red Lion, was built in 1567. Other famous theatres were the Theatre, the Curtain and the Globe. There were also some indoor theatres, used by child actors, and plays were performed in great halls and at court, as *The Murder of Gonzago* is in *Hamlet*. In all locations, though, production conditions were similar and, again, a basic understanding of these will really improve your appreciation of *Hamlet*.

As you can see from the illustration, Shakespeare's plays were produced in day-time on a bare stage, with little or no scenery (that is, fixed backdrops to indicate a location), no lighting effects, no special effects and very few props (that is, portable equipment, such as swords and daggers). Costumes were used extensively to provide colour, visual appeal and character insights (noble characters wore rich clothing, for instance) but other than that, the language carried everything – descriptions of locations, descriptions of characters, descriptions of thoughts and feelings … and what a rich language it is as a consequence.

Of all the differences between our world and Shakespeare's, this is perhaps the greatest. Enchanted by the marvels of technology in films and television and computers today, we tend to approach stories primarily as visual experiences. The Elizabethans experienced a play primarily as language. There were bits of action and spectacle, just as there is dialogue in modern blockbusters, but the major effects were achieved by the words, just as the major impact of a modern film lies in the images. Can we get back to concentrating on the words? If you can, you'll arrive at the best of all possible approaches to *Hamlet*.

Revenge Tragedy

In English cultural and theatrical traditions, revenge is a morally ambiguous activity because in seeking it, an individual rejects the code of law in his own society and threatens its stability, a dilemma that Shakespeare fully exploited and explored in *Hamlet*. Again, in part, this explains Hamlet's necessary delay in the play. By the time Shakespeare wrote *Hamlet*, around 1600, the revenge tragedy had been established in the English theatre for about fifteen years – Shakespeare had written his first, *Titus Andronicus*, in 1594, and explored revenge as a motif in several other works. He went much further in *Hamlet*, because as well as using the conventions of the revenge tragedy, this play also critically questions them. Hamlet's delay, therefore, is essentially a refusal to accept mere revenge as the solution.

Setting

Nominally, the setting of *Hamlet* is Denmark in the late Middle Ages, roughly the fourteenth or fifteenth century. Most of the action takes place in and around the royal castle at Elsinore – on its battlements, in its hallways and state rooms, and in the private chambers of king, queen and councillors. The exception is Act V, Scene i, which is set in a graveyard. There are references to other significant locations of the period, such as the neighbouring countries of Norway and Poland, and the universities at Wittenberg, in what was then Saxony and is now Germany, where Hamlet studied, and at Paris in France, where Laertes studied. There are also references to significant military disputes of the time, such as that between Denmark and Norway, which becomes an element in the play's plot.

Hamlet is not a historical drama, however. That is, it makes no attempt to represent faithfully the culture or politics of the period in which it is nominally set. The society that is depicted is actually much closer to the England of Shakespeare's own time than to Denmark of the Middle Ages. Travelling players, theatrical performances at court, court conspiracies, acting styles, the philosophical understanding of man's place in the universe, the moral ambiguity of revenge … these are all distinctive features of Shakespeare's England around 1600.

Hamlet, then, uses the setting of medieval Denmark to explore moral, social and philosophical issues that were of vital importance to his own contemporaries.

Summary

Single Text

READ

Act I, Scene i

We are on the battlements of the Danish royal palace at Elsinore. The state is on a war footing, preparing for a retaliatory strike by young Fortinbras of Norway, whose father was recently slain by King Hamlet of Denmark, who has since been killed himself. Nervous sentries insist to the student Horatio that they have seen the ghost of King Hamlet walking the battlements. Even as they are talking, the Ghost reappears, but refuses to speak. They all resolve to tell the former king's son, young Prince Hamlet.

Act I, Scene ii

Claudius, the current King of Denmark and old King Hamlet's brother, holds court. Essentially, he delivers the official version of recent events that everyone else must now believe. He says that it was with a heavy heart, still mourning his dead brother, that he married his brother's widow, Queen Gertrude, but life must go on. Then he settles efficiently to business. He sends ambassadors to Norway to curb Fortinbras' threatening moves. He grants a favourite – young Laertes, son of his councillor Polonius – permission to return to his studies in France. This is a show of magnanimity, after the show of strength and the show of sensitivity. It's very important for a leader that he appears to his people as he is supposed to be.

Claudius then turns to his remaining problem – Prince Hamlet, who is dressed in black, still mourning his dead father, and who has been glowering in the background all this time. Claudius encourages him to look more manly. Hamlet insists to his mother that he is not interested in mere appearances, but nonetheless agrees to her request, prompted by Claudius, to remain in Elsinore and not return to his studies in Germany. Left alone when the others exit to prepare to celebrate the marriage of Claudius and Gertrude, Hamlet reflects with horror and disgust, and a little self-hatred, on his mother's behaviour. His friend Horatio arrives to tell him the news of his father's ghost and Hamlet agrees to stand watch with the sentries on the battlements that night.

Act I, Scene iii

The action follows Polonius and Laertes after their audience with Claudius. At their home, Laertes warns his younger sister Ophelia not to trust Hamlet as a suitor, and insists that Hamlet is trifling with her affections. Laertes then leaves to return to France, after enduring endless lectures of advice from his father. Polonius then repeats Laertes' warning to his daughter Ophelia, but much more crudely, and forbids her to communicate with Hamlet.

Act I, Scene iv

On the battlements that night, as the noise of drunken celebration echoes in the background, much to Hamlet's disgust, the ghost of Hamlet's father reappears and beckons his son away from the others. Hamlet follows, against the advice of Horatio.

Act I, Scene v

When they are alone, the Ghost reveals to Hamlet that he did not die of a snake bite, as the official version has it, but that he was murdered in his sleep, poisoned by his brother Claudius, who had already seduced Gertrude. The Ghost urges Hamlet to avenge his murder, but to spare Gertrude, as the proper way of 'remembering' his father. Hamlet vows to do this, suggesting that he will move swiftly. The Ghost vanishes and Horatio and the sentries catch up with Hamlet. He doesn't tell them what the Ghost revealed, but he does swear them to secrecy. Hamlet also hints to them that he may pretend to be mad as part of his strategy.

Single Text

MAKE

Act I

1. Name a contemporary film that opens with the same tension as *Hamlet*. How is the tension achieved in the film? Refer to the effects of dialogue, action and music. Why is the tension created, both in the film you have chosen and in *Hamlet*?

2. Not many people really believe in ghosts anymore, whereas the belief in their existence and power was firm at the time *Hamlet* was written. On the other hand, many of today's films, such as *Lord of the Rings*, *The Matrix* and *Harry Potter*, rely on an acceptance of supernatural powers. How do you respond to the appearance of a ghost in a drama?

3. Write a short note on the character of Hamlet in Act I, Scene ii. Do you think we are meant to sympathise with him or not?

4. Trace the imagery of clothes throughout Act I, Scene ii and comment on how it reveals characters and expresses themes.

5. Claudius is obviously an accomplished statesman or politician. How much do you find to admire in him? What is there to be wary of about him?

6. Laertes and Polonius lay down a lot of rules for Ophelia in Act I, Scene iii. How relevant would any of them be today?

7. Trace the imagery of money and trade through Act I, Scene iii and comment on its purpose.

8. 'Hamlet is a man of feeling, a man of thought and a man of action.' Discuss briefly with reference to Act I.

9. Evaluate Hamlet's responses, behaviour and plans throughout Act I, Scene v and briefly discuss whether he should or could have done anything differently.

READ

Act II, Scene i

Polonius, in his usual long-winded style, instructs one of his servants to spy on his son Laertes in Paris. As the servant leaves, Ophelia comes in, in distress, and agitatedly describes how Hamlet burst in on her in her private rooms and behaved weirdly, apparently mad. Polonius decides that her rejection of him has actually driven Hamlet insane and he immediately drags Ophelia off to tell Claudius.

Act II, Scene ii

Claudius and Gertrude are receiving Rosencrantz and Guildenstern, student friends of Hamlet, who have been summoned from Wittenberg to spy on him, although the official story is that they are to care for him in his depression. With the two spies sent about their duties, Polonius arrives with the returning ambassadors to Norway. They report that Fortinbras has been rebuked by his king and has turned his aggression against Poland rather than Denmark. Pleased, Claudius and Gertrude then listen, though with diminishing patience, to Polonius' tediously delivered theory that Hamlet has gone mad from frustrated love for Ophelia. Claudius is hopeful that this is the case – as he fears that Hamlet may otherwise suspect the truth about King Hamlet's murder – but he needs proof, so they all agree to set up an 'accidental' encounter between Hamlet and Ophelia while they are watching secretly. At this point, Hamlet morosely wanders in and Claudius and Gertrude retire, leaving Polonius alone with the young prince, who insults the old man endlessly, under the guise of madness, and speaks crudely, even threateningly, of Ophelia.

Polonius retires when Rosencrantz and Guildenstern turn up. Hamlet very quickly forces them to acknowledge that they were sent to spy on him, and very openly tells them of his disillusionment with life. He brightens when he hears from them that a troupe of actors have arrived in court and he comes to life when they are escorted in by Polonius. Hamlet gets their chief tragedian to recite a speech about the destruction of Troy by the Greeks and the lament of Hecuba for her slaughtered husband, King Priam, and then manoeuvres to be left alone with this actor while Polonius brings the others to their quarters. Hamlet arranges to have the troupe perform the play *The Murder of Gonzago*

in front of Claudius and the court, but including some additional material written by himself. Alone again after the actor leaves, Hamlet berates himself for his delay in 'remembering' his dead father, contrasts his own lack of action with the intensity of the actor merely playing a part, but he decides that by observing Claudius during the performance of *The Murder of Gonzago*, the plot of which more or less mirrors the murder of King Hamlet, he will be able to determine whether or not Claudius is actually guilty.

Act II

1. Hamlet is a man who loves puns and riddles and jokes, loves playing with the sounds and the sense of words – 'Look after the sense and the sounds will look after themselves', as the Mad Hatter advises in *Alice in Wonderland*. Hamlet loves poetry and drama and all complex forms of verbal expression. Why does he say nothing at all to Ophelia in Act II, Scene i? This is a world where many of the characters – Claudius and Polonius, in particular – just love the sound of their own voices. Briefly discuss why Hamlet is reduced, not to silence, because he sighs and moans, but to *non-verbal* expression.

2. Referring only to Act II, Scene ii, discuss briefly:

   (a) How evil is Claudius?

   (b) How caring is Gertrude about Hamlet?

   (c) How evil is Polonius?

   (d) How mad is Hamlet?

   (e) How honest is anybody?

MAKE

Single Text
READ

Act III, Scene i

Rosencrantz and Guildenstern tell Claudius and Gertrude that they have nothing to report. Claudius is obviously displeased; Gertrude is obviously concerned. Getting rid of everyone else, Claudius hides with Polonius to spy on Ophelia's contrived encounter with Hamlet. Hamlet wanders in, reflecting deeply on suicide, the fear of death and the justifications for action. When he spots Ophelia, he somewhat loses his composure in the surprise, and hysterically attacks her lack of faithfulness and virtue. Then, suspecting that he's in a trap, his attack intensifies, before he storms off. Emerging from their hiding place, and more or less ignoring the deeply distraught Ophelia, Claudius disagrees with Polonius' stubborn theory that Hamlet is love-sick and resolves to get the dangerous prince out of the way to England. For his part, to get further information, Polonius offers to spy on a meeting between Hamlet and Gertrude.

Act III, Scene ii

Before the performance of *The Murder of Gonzago*, Hamlet instructs the actors on technique and interpretation. After they have left to prepare, Hamlet reveals to Horatio the real purpose of the performance and asks him to keep an eye on Claudius' reactions during it. The court arrives to watch the play, in which a Player Queen swears eternal fidelity to a Player King, but then gets her lover Lucianus to poison him. At this point, Claudius jumps out of his chair, demands lights and storms away, with the court in disarray behind him, and Hamlet and Horatio now convinced of his guilt. Rosencrantz and Guildenstern return to summon Hamlet to Gertrude, who is astonished and probably troubled by her son's behaviour, and then Polonius, typically, arrives with exactly the same summons.

Act III, Scene iii

Claudius is scared by what he has just experienced. Hamlet obviously knows the truth and is taunting him with it. He instructs Rosencrantz and Guildenstern to take Hamlet to England at once. He hears from Polonius that Hamlet is on his way to see Gertrude, in whose bedroom Polonius will hide and spy.

When he is alone, Claudius kneels to ask forgiveness for his brother's murder, although he is unwilling, or unable, to relinquish the benefits of that murder, namely Gertrude and the crown. Unseen by him, Hamlet slips in behind him. Here is the perfect opportunity to avenge his father's murder. But Hamlet decides against it. Why send the villain to heaven while he's praying, he reasons, instead of damning him to hell while he's sinning? Ironically, as soon as Hamlet leaves, the king rises from his knees to reveal that he hasn't been able to pray.

Act III, Scene iv

Polonius arranges with Gertrude to hide behind the arras, or wall hanging, in her private rooms. Hamlet arrives and so aggressively attempts to force his mother to see the truth that she thinks he's about to kill her. She cries out, alerting Polonius, who also cries out. Not unnaturally, Hamlet assumes it's Claudius hiding behind the arras and stabs impetuously, hinting at his father's murder to Gertrude before discovering that he has killed Polonius.

He then feverishly attempts to show his mother how far she has fallen in choosing Claudius over King Hamlet, becoming so enraged in expressing his disgust that he is on the point of losing self-control, until the Ghost, unseen by Gertrude, reappears to remind Hamlet not to be distracted from his revenge. Gertrude, on the point of admitting her own errors and guilt, now reverts, rather conveniently, to believing that Hamlet is mad, since she watches him talking to thin air (as far as she is concerned) before he lugs Polonius' corpse away like a sack. Before he goes, Hamlet extracts from her a promise to stay out of Claudius' bed – in other words, to detach herself morally and physically from Claudius – and though she agrees, she has done so only to placate Hamlet and save herself, which seems a good strategy when Hamlet immediately changes his mind again and comes up with a new plan that actually involves Gertrude sharing a bed with Claudius.

MAKE

Act III

1. In relation to the advice 'judge characters by what they do, not by what they say', discuss each of the following with reference to Act III, Scene i:

   (a) Claudius

   (b) Polonius

   (c) Ophelia

   (d) Hamlet.

2. At the beginning, Hamlet's task had three parts: (a) how to discover the truth; (b) how to reveal the truth; and (c) what to do about it. By Act III, Scene ii, the first two have been

achieved. Explain briefly how they have been achieved and then discuss briefly what you think Hamlet should now do about the problem. Be reasonable and show an awareness of the situation in which Hamlet finds himself.

3. Act III, Scene iii is a very complex and interesting scene that gives rise to two fascinating discussion points:

   (a) Hamlet hates Claudius so intensely that he wants to condemn him to hell. Merely taking his life is not enough. Firstly, is this consistent with Hamlet's character as you know it up to now? Secondly, do you sympathise with Hamlet's desire to damn Claudius?

   (b) Imagine a different version of the action. Claudius kneels down to pray after his long speech. Hamlet comes in and immediately stabs him in the back. How do you think you'd respond to Hamlet doing this?

4. Work quickly back through the play from Act III, Scene iv and locate *three* instances where the past is described as having been better than the present. *One* of these must refer to the entire society, *one* to Hamlet himself and the *third* to a topic of your choice.

Act IV, Scene i

As it happens, Gertrude goes immediately to Claudius to tell him that the mad Hamlet has just killed Polonius. This offers Claudius the perfect justification for what he is about to do. He summons Rosencrantz and Guildenstern and instructs them to apprehend Hamlet. He then leads Gertrude away to supposed safety, telling her that they are the endangered ones.

Act IV, Scene ii

Rosencrantz and Guildenstern catch up with Hamlet, but he mockingly refuses to tell them where he has put Polonius' body.

Act IV, Scene iii

Hamlet is brought before Claudius, who struggles to contain his fear and fury in the face of the prince's mocking taunts. But contain them he must because, as he admits when alone, if he moves publicly against Hamlet, who is very popular with the people, then his reputation as a good guy will go up in smoke. After revealing where Polonius' body is hidden, Hamlet is led away under arrest, and Claudius prays that England will solve this problem for him. In other words, Claudius is arranging to have Hamlet killed in England and to make it look like an act of treachery by the English.

Act IV, Scene iv

Fortinbras' army crosses Danish territory by permission of the agreement between the two countries. On his way to England, Hamlet encounters this army and reflects self-critically on the difference between Fortinbras' assured and decisive ambition, and his own slow-burning, contorted revenge.

Act IV, Scene v

Gertrude is told that Ophelia has gone mad since her father's death. Although Gertrude is reluctant to see the girl, she is encouraged to do so by Horatio, and Ophelia is summoned, but she distractedly sings inappropriately bawdy songs to both Gertrude and Claudius when she arrives. After she wanders off again, Claudius bemoans his own fate and blames it all on Hamlet, before Laertes, who has just come back from France, bursts in at the head of a mob with the intention of killing Claudius as revenge for his father's death. Two things distract Laertes from his mission. Firstly, he listens to Claudius, who is an accomplished politician, able to sway the minds of weaker creatures. Secondly, he witnesses his sister's insanity, as she wanders in again singing heart-breakingly of fathers and death and lovers. His rage deflected, his mind convinced that Hamlet is the culprit, Laertes agrees to be commanded by Claudius.

Act IV, Scene vi

Horatio receives a letter from Hamlet in which Hamlet describes escaping in a pirate ship from his captivity and returning alone to Denmark.

Act IV, Scene vii

Claudius, too, receives a letter from Hamlet to the same effect and conspires with Laertes, who is now his ally, to kill Hamlet in a fencing match and make it look like an accident. The tip of Laertes' sword will be uncovered for the bout and dipped in poison. In case this fails, a cup of poisoned wine will be ready to offer to Hamlet when he needs refreshment in the contest. As they finalise their plot, Gertrude arrives with news that the mad Ophelia has drowned in a river. Laertes' rage returns with the news and Claudius has to struggle again to bring him under control.

MAKE

Act IV

1. Examine the relationship between Gertrude and Claudius, with particular reference to Act IV, Scenes i–iii, but briefly looking back over the previous action as well. Do they love one another? Does either love Hamlet? Is it a strong relationship? Consider these and other factors.

2. Act IV, Scene iv is the last time we see Hamlet before the final Act. Take a quick look back over the play and discuss briefly whether or not he has changed since we first met him. Explain what, if any, changes have occurred. If you do not think he has changed, demonstrate in detail how he has remained the same.

3. With reference to Act IV, Scene v, compare in detail both the words and the actions of Laertes and Hamlet in the aftermath of their respective fathers' deaths, paying particular attention to the language they both use to express their grief and outrage. The decisions they make reflect their separate characters, of course, but which, in your opinion, takes the wiser course?

4. Examine Act IV, Scene vii in detail and mark the occurrences of the following streams of imagery:

   (a) falsity

   (b) disease, corruption, poison.

Act V, Scene i

READ

As two gravediggers are joking while they work, Hamlet and Horatio arrive in the graveyard. Also jocular at first, Hamlet's mood becomes more serious when he discovers that one of the skulls in the ground belonged to Yorick, who was a court jester when Hamlet was a boy. It leads him to reflections on mortality, which are interrupted by the arrival of a funeral procession led by Claudius and

Gertrude. Hamlet conceals himself, but on learning that it is Ophelia who is being buried as a suicide, he openly matches Laertes' grief with his own, to the point of physically struggling with him. When they are parted and Hamlet leaves with Horatio, Claudius advises Laertes to hold his patience so that their plot can succeed.

Act V, Scene ii

Hamlet describes to Horatio how he unsealed the letter to the King of England that was being carried by Rosencrantz and Guildenstern, discovered that it contained instructions for Hamlet's execution, and then substituted another letter ordering the execution of the bearers. After this, he jumped ship.

A courtier named Osric arrives with Laertes' challenge to a fencing match, which Hamlet accepts, despite his misgivings. The court assembles for the duel. As they shake hands before the duel, Hamlet offers friendship to Laertes, who feigns acceptance. Hamlet scores the first hit, and is offered refreshment from the poisoned cup by Claudius, but refuses it. After Hamlet scores the second hit, Gertrude unknowingly takes a drink of the poisoned wine.

Laertes cuts Hamlet with the poisoned rapier while they should be resting between bouts, which incenses Hamlet, and, in the ensuing violent struggle, they exchange rapiers. Hamlet scores another hit against Laertes, but this time with the poisoned sword.

As he dies, Laertes identifies Claudius as the one to blame for everything. Gertrude, too, realises this as she faints and dies. Hamlet stabs Claudius with the poisoned sword and forces him to drink the poisoned wine. Hamlet and Laertes exchange forgiveness.

Hamlet prevents Horatio from adding himself to the casualties, hears the approach of Fortinbras' army returning from Poland, prophesies that Fortinbras will be the next King of Denmark and then dies. Fortinbras arrives, takes control of the situation and arranges a military funeral for Hamlet.

Act V

1. In relation to the following topics, discuss how Hamlet has changed or matured by Act V, Scene i, from the beginning of the play:

    (a) his attitude to women

    (b) his attitude to death

    (c) his attitude to the struggles of life.

2. With reference to Act V, Scene ii, how well do you think the play resolves:

    (a) the plot, the basis of which is Hamlet's need to revenge his father's murder?

    (b) the main theme, which is the restoration of health to a corrupt society?

Characters

Single Text

ANALYSE

Hamlet

Our first experience of every character in this play is influenced by our awareness that there is a restless ghost on the move and that everything is not well in the state of Denmark. Hamlet is dressed in black – 'Cast thy nighted colour off' (I.ii), his mother encourages him, referring both to his appearance and his expression – while the other members of court are colourfully dressed for the coronation of Claudius. Hamlet is isolated, unhappy, brooding, not a part of the celebrations. You can play him as either a sulky adolescent unable to come to terms with life or as a deeply disturbed young man unwilling to accept the corruption of others. The latter obviously offers a more rewarding interpretation.

Hamlet is not solitary by nature, though. He likes company. Witness his enthusiastic reception of his old friend Horatio, his initial welcome for Rosencrantz and Guildenstern, his joy at the Players' arrival and his involvement in the drama. His pleasure is always short-lived, however. He quickly expresses his bitterness to Horatio: 'We'll teach you to drink deep ere you depart' (I.ii). It doesn't take him long to discover that Rosencrantz and Guildenstern are not true friends, but spies. And his pleasure in play acting is diminished by his need to put the performance to practical use.

Most significant of all in this regard is his response to Ophelia and his treatment of her. He is as capable of love as he is of friendship, but he is also wary of it, as he is suspicious of almost everything and everyone in Denmark. Friendship makes you vulnerable. If he had accepted Rosencrantz and Guildenstern on face value, he would have been led by them to his death. Love makes you even more vulnerable. And so, while the loss of the two faithless friends means little to him, the loss of Ophelia – used as pawn, or as bait, by others – hurts him deeply. So deeply that he cannot even express it in words. 'He took me by the wrist and held me hard … He raised a sigh so piteous and profound/As it did seem to shatter all his bulk/And end his being' (II.i).

It is only in the final Act, when he has come to an acceptance of life's inadequacies and death's inevitability, that he is comfortable again with others. By then, he knows who he can trust and who he should not, and he knows that his love is dead and can make no more impossible demands on him.

Hamlet is not perfect, of course – he thinks he can trust Laertes, for instance – but in the final action sequence of the duel, he is an active participant, a central part, of the court of Denmark. This contrasts sharply with his isolation and ineffectiveness in the same situation at the beginning of the play. The development of Hamlet through the play is his progression from isolation to participation, or, if you like, from inaction to action.

Why are Hamlet's pleasures and joys so short-lived? The circumstances, of course – 'his father's death and our o'erhasty marriage' (II.ii) as Gertrude puts it – explain much of his melancholy. But, undoubtedly, he is temperamentally inclined that way anyway. He is a young man of deep thought, always raising the unanswerable questions of life. You'll find his reflections and his tendencies in his soliloquies, which you should be very familiar with. In the first, we encounter his desire to end it all, escape from everything. He is plainly suicidal. 'O that this too too sallied flesh would melt … Or that the Everlasting had not fixed/his canon 'gainst self slaughter' (I.ii). (In the opening line, 'sallied', meaning 'assailed', is emended in some editions to 'sullied', meaning 'contaminated', or 'solid', meaning 'fat'.) This wish for oblivion is repeated as the play advances and his problems deepen. Then there is disgust at and weariness of life in general. 'How weary, stale, flat and unprofitable/Seem to me all the uses of this world' (I.ii). He tends to see life as innately corrupt: ''tis an unweeded garden/That grows to seed. Things rank and gross in nature possess it merely' (I.ii). Again, this disgust is expressed time and again in the later soliloquies.

But he's wrong. The world, although it contains decay, is not *only* populated by corruption. It also contains much beauty. And in his error, we can understand the most revealing aspect of his nature before the final Act – he tends to overreact.

In a philosophical sense, this means that if he encounters one bad thing in the world, he dismisses the entire world as hopelessly rotten: 'Things rank and gross in nature possess it merely' (I.ii). If he deals with one evil man, he condemns all men. If he encounters one unfaithful woman, he damns all women: 'frailty, thy name is woman' (I.ii). This is an extremely dangerous tendency. It has the ability to make someone severely depressed, if it is encouraged. And encourage it is exactly what Hamlet does. In fact, there are times when he *wallows* in it.

In relation to doing things, this same tendency to overreact makes Hamlet rash and impetuous, instead of calculating. When he has time to think – most notably in the scene where he comes across Claudius kneeling with his back to him and has the chance to finish him off – his conclusion is always, *What's the point?* He has different reasons for this conclusion at different times, but the end position is always the same. *What's the point?* When he has no time to think – most notably in the scene where he kills Polonius – he acts too hastily and with poor judgement.

These two aspects might seem like a contradiction – too much thought and too hasty action – but in fact they derive from the same tendency to overreact. Mixed within the same character, as they are here, they lead to deep problems.

Hamlet has few releases from his problems. The pressures on him, from within and without, are consistent and intense. He is obviously comfortable with Horatio. And he clearly takes great delight in the company of the Players. Otherwise, he seeks a kind of wacky refuge in playing with words, and indeed in playing around generally. He's not mad. And he's not frivolous or childish. But a person under so much stress must surely find a release somewhere. He achieves it with puns, jokes, odd words and clowning.

Hamlet believes that there *was* – the past tense is vital – goodness, beauty, love and order in the world. These all thrived during his father's reign. This seems to have much truth in it, although the perfection is exaggerated. But he also believes that all these qualities died with his father. Forever. And this, while understandable, is plainly not true. Again, the first soliloquy expresses it neatly: 'So excellent a king, that was to this/Hyperion to a satyr' and 'My father's brother, but no more like my father/than I to Hercules' (I.ii).

In the final Act, there is a maturity about Hamlet that was absent earlier in the play. We don't witness any moment when he suddenly changes, suddenly grows up, but there are signs of a new composure and resolve in both his final soliloquy – 'How all occasions do inform against me' (IV.iv) – when he meets the army of Fortinbras, and in his letter to Horatio. In relation to the points being discussed, what does this maturity consist of? Well, he no longer condemns all women for the sins of one. 'I loved Ophelia', he says finally (V.i). He no longer acts too hastily or with poor judgement. We can all rant over our losses, he says to Laertes; it means nothing. He no longer thinks the world is a place where only corruption grows, but now sees the truth of human existence: it is a thing of beauty, of joy, of pleasure … that ends inevitably in corruption. This is captured in his address to the skull: 'Now get you to my lady's chamber and tell her, let her paint an inch thick, to this favour she must come' (V.i). This is not a morbid reflection on death, as many of the earlier ones were, but a calm acceptance of its inevitability.

Claudius

Most importantly, Claudius is the source of all the corruption in Denmark's society. This is stressed repeatedly at important stages of the play. It is expressed in words, for the benefit of all, in Laertes' final accusation: 'The king, the king's to blame' (V.ii). This, for us and for Hamlet, is merely an echo of the Ghost's words in Act I, Scene v: 'The serpent that did sting thy father's life/Now wears his crown.' Note the religious imagery of the serpent here, suggesting an association with the devil. In between these, the same revelation is made – twice – in *The Murder of Gonzago*, the play that Hamlet has the Players perform. These timely reminders are no accident, of course. We are meant to keep the horror of the truth constantly in front of us.

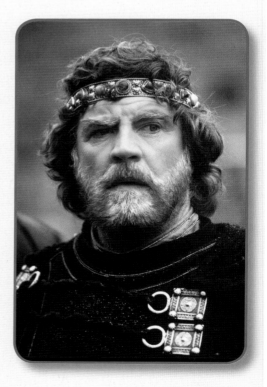

Claudius is an accomplished politician and manipulator. Study Claudius' behaviour in Act I, Scene ii, when we first meet him. He's smooth – with words, with actions, with flattery, with favours. He's in control. He's self-satisfied. The entire opening speech – 'Though yet of Hamlet' (I.ii) – should be considered in detail. However, even here, he doesn't seem to know how precisely to deal with Prince Hamlet. The young man obviously makes him uncomfortable. Claudius asks him to stay in Denmark, but when Hamlet assents, you get the impression that Claudius is not quite sure whether or not this is a good thing, whether or not he's made the right move.

These two aspects of Claudius the politician – his domination of the rest of the court and his uneasiness with Hamlet – never change throughout the play. He twists Polonius, for instance, any way he wants him. But he never gets to grips with Hamlet. Should he keep him in sight or send him away? Should he kill him? No, the people would revolt. Imprison him? Same result. Placate him? The man is beyond that. Things are no different in the final Act. Claudius manipulates Laertes as easily as he did the young man's father, but he still can't get to Hamlet and simultaneously save himself. Whatever he does to Hamlet, he does to himself also. This strange fact is expressed in the wonderful image from Act IV, Scene iii: 'Like the hectic in my blood he rages.' Hamlet is Claudius' disease, infecting his bloodstream. You should think more about this.

Claudius is selfish, self-centred and self-absorbed. He is a man who professes love easily – particularly for Gertrude – and regard, for anyone who happens to be near. But let's judge by actions and not by words. His behaviour tells us that saving his own skin is of the greatest importance to him. In Act IV, Scene i, after Hamlet kills Polonius and Gertrude tells Claudius of her fears, Claudius' response is entirely selfish: 'It had been so with us, had we been there.' Does he ever consider anyone else throughout the entire play? Given what we experience of him, it's easier to believe that he married Gertrude, while attracted to her, primarily for selfish reasons in order to get his hands on the throne.

Claudius understands the horrors of his own crimes. Study in detail the speech in Act III, Scene iii where he kneels to pray. He knows exactly the nature of what he has done: 'O, my offence is rank, it smells to heaven.' Curiously, he uses exactly the same imagery as Hamlet does – *rank* – to describe his crimes. But it is fear that motivates his guilt – fear of Hamlet immediately and then of the afterlife – not repentance. To stress a point that needs to be made in relation to all aspects of the play – repentance has to be expressed in deeds, not just words. And Claudius is not willing to relinquish what he has gained by murder. In fact, he is eager to kill again to hang on to his gains. This is why, without him being too much bothered about it, he simply gives up on the effort of praying for forgiveness. His interest is in the pleasures of this life. As he puts it himself, 'my thoughts remain below' (III.iii).

Gertrude

We simply do not have enough information about Gertrude to judge her with any certainty. Consider the following questions. Was she having an affair with Claudius before her husband died, as the Ghost claims? Was she involved in the plan to murder her husband? Did she even know about the plan? Did she do whatever she did for love (of Claudius)? Does she believe what Hamlet says? Does she betray Hamlet to Claudius, or is she trying to protect him?

We cannot, with certainty, know the answers to these questions. You must use what you know of Gertrude to make your own judgements.

Perhaps the best way to approach her is to apply to her alone Hamlet's general condemnation of women, which arises, in any case, when he's thinking of his mother: 'Frailty, thy name is woman' (I.ii). Gertrude is frail. She is morally weak. She doesn't seem to have a clear idea of what is right and what is wrong. She is always more interested in what the safest, the most beneficial thing to do is. This places her much closer in spirit to Claudius than to Hamlet. And, indeed, it is to Claudius that she runs whenever there's a problem. She has, therefore, pitched her lot in with Claudius and this choice always dominates her actions. You might like to consider again the questions asked in the first paragraph in light of this.

Gertrude is at her most accomplished, and most comfortable, in public, social situations, when the court is in session and where her natural beauty and graceful command can dominate. There are indications that she is also blissfully happy in Claudius' bed. This is all she wants of life: public esteem and domestic pleasure. Anything beyond these – particularly Hamlet's insistence on moral matters – simply confuses her.

Polonius

Polonius is funny – he's long-winded, flowery, prone to silly errors, full of his own self-importance, bumbling and the butt of endless jokes, mostly cracked by Hamlet – but he is funny in a very sinister way. His values are entirely expressed in the modern phrase *look after number one* – his advice to his son Laertes in Act I, Scene iii is 'to thine own self be true'. Polonius, Laertes and Claudius all believe that you should look out for number one, be practical, look good on the outside and get as much of the good things of life as you can. Hamlet, on the other hand, is clearly struggling with the belief that there's got to be more to life than all that, there has to be something more authentic than making good, something more human than selfishness.

Polonius' way to the top of the tree is to serve the king. To carry this through, he will stoop to the most disgusting tactics: spying on everyone, including his own family; informing on everyone; lying; using his own daughter as bait; and snooping and setting traps for others. Polonius is corrupt. In the context of a society, corruption has many meanings. One of them is exposed in Act II, Scene i, when Polonius sends a servant to spy on Laertes in Paris. Nobody trusts anybody else, not even their own sons. Everybody spies on everybody else, including their own sons. Everybody tells lies about everybody else, including their own sons.

Polonius is at once comic (so long-winded and pompous and self-important that he's ridiculous), pathetic ('let him ply his music' (II.i)) and disgusting. Most of all disgusting. He is, remember, Claudius' right-hand man. He is the moral level of the regime. In Act II, Scene ii, while plotting with Claudius to trap Hamlet, he says, 'I'll loose my daughter to him.' This is a grotesque image, derived from hunting. Ophelia is to be used as bait. Does the man have any standards? Other than self-interest and serving the king, the answer is no.

Polonius is sinister and evil, not just a bumbling old fool. This is something that Hamlet himself knows well and expresses openly, under the guise of madness. 'You are a fishmonger,' he says (II.ii). When the play was written, this was slang for a pimp, someone who acquired women for clients in return for money, which is what Polonius is attempting with Ophelia, his own daughter. In the end, Polonius suffers an ignominious death, mistakenly stabbed for someone else while hiding and snooping.

Laertes

Because he must also avenge a wrong done to his father, Laertes offers us an obvious, and significant, comparison and contrast with Hamlet. His actions give us a deeper understanding of Hamlet's inaction. In Act IV, Scene v, having just returned from Paris with his head filled with rumours about Polonius' death, Laertes bursts into the private chambers of Claudius and Gertrude at the head of a riotous mob. He is convinced that he knows the truth about what happened, certain that Claudius is the culprit. He is determined on action – on revenge – and raises a sword to Claudius' neck. However, within minutes, his impressionable mind is corrupted by the lies and half-truths and smarmy flattery of Claudius, and Laertes comes to believe the opposite of everything he had thought. This is what happens when you're overhasty – when you rush to judgement and rush to action, you get things wrong.

In Act IV, Scene vii, when Laertes is expressing his acceptance of Claudius' version of events, his first line says it all: 'It well appears.' Meaning, what you say appears to be the truth. By this point in the play, we know to distrust appearances. Accepting those appearances as truth, Laertes' genuine grief is now corrupted and he is seduced into becoming a calculating murderer. His reaction to the news of his sister's death is also revealing. This is a young man who a short time before was on fire with anger, resentment and grief. Now, he does not know how to react, and Claudius, who has corrupted him, fears that a natural reaction will wreck all their plans again.

Although he contributes to the trickery almost to the end, with poisoned sword tips, drugged drinks and other deceptions, Laertes does redeem himself finally. It is his public cry in Act V, Scene ii, 'The king, the king's to blame' that finally exposes everything, and in particular the true source of the evil.

Ophelia

Ophelia is one of only two female characters in the play – the other is Gertrude, of course – and yet, *Hamlet* is a drama obsessed with the treatment and the role of women. In Act I, Scene ii, Hamlet says of his mother, 'Frailty, thy name is woman' (I.ii). He is extremely critical of Claudius *as an individual*, but accuses his mother *as a representative of her gender*. There were great men before Claudius – his father resembled Hyperion and Hercules – but: 'Frailty, thy name is woman.'

In Act I, Scene iii, the gentle and passive Ophelia is brutally lectured to by both her brother and her father. The advice is the same: forget about Hamlet. From the beginning, the imagery of flowers is associated with her, a suggestion of tenderness and innocence that is scoffed at by the other characters – Polonius calls her 'a green girl' – because it also suggests frailty to them. Is Ophelia too weak to support Hamlet, though they clearly love each other? In Act II, Scene i, she reports to Polonius, 'as you did command, I did repel his letter and denied his access to me', and the blow is too much for Hamlet. Or is it that tenderness, innocence and love cannot survive without being corrupted and destroyed in the brutal society created by Polonius? Ophelia, a passive, obliging young woman, is helplessly caught in the middle. She's doomed.

Look at Polonius' line, in Act II, Scene ii: 'I'll loose my daughter to him.' In Act III, Scene i, although she is the bait in the trap, Ophelia says nothing in the early part of the scene. She is obviously reluctant – otherwise her father wouldn't drag out the encouraging speech about everybody lying – but she never objects. She finally speaks only when Hamlet leaves her. Ironically, while lamenting Hamlet's madness, she expresses exactly the same despair as he did. The pressures of living in a corrupt world are driving her in the same direction. But she and Hamlet will not meet each other, for Hamlet is only pretending insanity. This is their tragedy: they can't understand that they are suffering the same agonies and that they are soul-mates.

As regards the harsh judgement on the frailty of all women, Act IV, Scene v offers a significant contrast between the two women in the play: the self-absorbed and insensitive Gertrude and the oversensitive, vulnerable Ophelia. One is culpable; the other is not. Ophelia is the first major innocent casualty of the corrupt society that Claudius and Gertrude have engendered, and the imagery of flowers – tenderness, sweetness, fragility – that has long been associated with her, reaches its fullest and saddest expression in Act IV, Scene v, when she sings in her madness.

Horatio

We meet Horatio early, on the battlements in Act I, Scene i, before we encounter Hamlet or any of the other major characters. He is simultaneously presented to us as both a perfect model of reason and intelligence, and utterly wrong. He insists that the guards are hallucinating about seeing a ghost and suggests that, in any case, such things do not exist – 'Horatio says 'tis but our fantasy', Marcellus reports, while Horatio himself brushes it all aside with a 'Tush, tush, 'twill not appear' – seconds before the Ghost reappears.

Throughout the play, Horatio remains rational, philosophical and conventionally ethical, qualities that are splendid and admirable, but inadequate in themselves when dealing with the murkiness and complexity of real affairs, a judgement explicitly made by Hamlet in his slightly exasperated admonition in Act I, Scene v: 'There are more things in heaven and earth, Horatio,/Than are dreamt of in your philosophy.'

Horatio is a 'scholar', as Marcellus says, a philosopher, a man of thought. The very opposite of the intemperate Laertes and the decisive Fortinbras, for instance, he is forever cautioning against action. He knows the history of ghosts, the motivation of ghosts, the circumstances in which ghosts appear. He even knows the correct formula for addressing ghosts: 'If thou hast any sound or use of voice,/Speak to me' (I.i). But all his knowledge is useless. The Ghost simply ignores him.

Single Text

In Act I, Scene v, he cautions Hamlet against following the Ghost: 'Do not, my lord.' In the same scene, after Hamlet's encounter with the Ghost, Horatio is unable to grasp what has happened: 'These are but wild and whirling words, my lord.' Significantly, Hamlet employs Horatio as an *observer* when putting on *The Murder of Gonzago* before Claudius: 'Give him heedful note' (III.i). Equally significantly, Hamlet praises Horatio as a man elevated above the corruptions of life, 'not passion's slave' and 'not a pipe for Fortune's finger' (III.iii). But Hamlet also understands the inadequacy of that elevation, no matter how much he admires it. He has to act, and Horatio is always cautioning against action. Even at the end, in Act V, Scene ii, Horatio cautions against the fencing match with Laertes – 'I will … say you are not fit' – and once again, and for the last time, we see the contrast between the man of detached thought, who is Horatio, and the man of thoughtful action, who is Hamlet, when the latter responds that 'the readiness is all' (V.ii).

This is not to ignore the fact that Horatio represents the personal and social virtues that the play, and Hamlet, holds up against the corrupt society run by Claudius – the resilience, honesty, rationality, lack of flattery, openness, lack of interest in money and self-advancement that Hamlet explicitly praises in Act III, Scene ii – or to ignore the fact that Horatio's friendship, support and loyalty are vital for Hamlet. It is simply to acknowledge that Hamlet must act – 'Revenge his foul and most unnatural murder' (I.v), the Ghost commands – and Horatio stoically endures 'the slings and arrows of outrageous fortune' (III.i).

To the end, Horatio remains a commentator on life, an interpreter of life – 'Let me speak to th' yet unknowning world/How these things came about' (V.i) – one who reports the world, rather than one who changes the world.

Themes

ANALYSE

Certainty, Knowledge, Truth, Reality, Falsity, Appearance, Deception

The play opens with a series of nervous, clipped exchanges between the jittery sentries on the battlements of the royal castle, but the first speech of any duration, delivered by Marcellus (I.i), invites us to consider questions other than military ones – what you can believe, whether you should believe your own eyes, ghosts and the afterlife, and the power of reason (Horatio's scepticism) against the power of fear ('this dreaded sight' (I.i)). The introduction of these related themes is no accident. They are the main concerns of the play.

Let's start with the implied tension between appearance and reality. This is immediately developed in Act I, Scene ii when Claudius' first speech is long and formal and full of conventional paradoxes, and Polonius is long-winded, flowery and formal. Without the tension of the first scene, these speeches might make us think Denmark is a dull, boring and politically stable place. But the tension on the battlements undermines the appearance of security and comfort, making it look more like concealment than reality – what, in political terms today, we would call a 'cover-up'. This is one of the play's main themes: falsity or phoniness, the difference between the fake and the genuine, and how to be certain which is which.

This entire display in Act I, Scene ii, including the permission for Laertes to leave, is set up to make Claudius look good. It works, too … until Hamlet starts playing around with language – not saying what he means, and yet making his meaning obvious – and then reacting angrily to his mother's use of the word 'seems'. Hamlet draws a distinction between what appears to be ('seems') and what actually is – a distinction that is crucial to an understanding of both Hamlet himself and the play. It is worth noting also that Hamlet's obsession with this problem is experienced entirely in relation to language at this stage. He deals in puns and definitions – and, of course, in colours, since he dresses in mourning black while everyone else is in festive costume for the coronation of Claudius.

However, when he encounters his father's ghost in Act I, Scene v, and the Ghost describes Gertrude as 'my seeming-virtuous queen', Hamlet has to do something more than merely dress differently. His task is threefold, he has to work out:

1. how to confirm the truth

2. how best to reveal it

3. what to do afterwards.

None of these tasks is simple or straightforward. Hamlet's first reaction, as always, is to buy time by playing with language – 'there's never a villain … but he's a knave'. His behaviour, after the Ghost leaves, indicates his uncertainty. His one plan, for the moment, is to pretend not to know that his father has been murdered. Fairly wise, really, since he would probably be killed otherwise – this is the point of the oath he gets the others to swear and of his indication that he may act strangely or oddly in the future – but that word 'seems', which the Act I has played with, takes on even more meaning.

Throughout Act II, Hamlet sets about the first of his tasks: how to confirm the truth. This is not easy in a world where everybody – including the supposedly mad Hamlet – pretends to be other than who they are: from Claudius, who conceals the crime of regicide, through the devious Polonius, who lies about everything, to the two friends pretending to have turned up out of the blue, and right down to the Player, who fakes emotions that he does not feel. The Player has a good motive for deception. So has Hamlet, of course. As for the rest …

But with so much deception around, how can you make accurate assessments and judgements? To put this another way: you might lunge at the actor because you hate the character he's playing, in which case you have made a terrible mistake.

It is only when Hamlet is alone in Act II, Scene ii that we can get away from the stifling atmosphere of deception, pretence and falsity. As always, his soliloquy is worth considering in detail, because it touches on so many of the play's themes and issues: falsity and pretence, of course ('this player here, in a fiction, in a dream of passion'), the need for action to improve things ('Am I a coward?'), the uselessness of words, insults and curses ('like a whore … fall a-cursing') and the usefulness of words and falsity ('I'll have these players play something like the murder of my father.') All in all, the soliloquy is a very complex exploration of the play's themes, particularly the related ones of certainty, knowledge, fakery, truth and proof. There are no simple answers or formulae provided. Just as there is no simple course of action for Hamlet himself.

In Act III, Scene i, Claudius privately expresses guilt and disgust at his own actions. Typically, his feelings are expressed while the language further explores the theme of falsity. He is like a whore, he says, all bright make-up on the outside, rotten on the inside. But is his conscience lashed, as he puts it, because he recognises the wrong of what he has done or because Hamlet's behaviour is making him increasingly nervous? You cannot answer this question because you cannot see beyond Claudius' exterior, into his mind and soul (unless he reveals himself in soliloquy). Hamlet attempts to answer it, though, and gets it all wrong, again.

In Act III, Scene iii, after the play-within-a-play has revealed his guilt, Claudius is kneeling, his eyes closed, when Hamlet comes in silently behind him. Hamlet hesitates. As he sees it, Claudius will be absolved of his sins and will go to heaven if he dies while praying. Hamlet leaves. But Claudius is not praying. He is only mouthing words. And in this play, words and appearances are valueless. Time and again, we are reminded that we must judge characters by what they do and not by what they say. After all, anybody can *say* anything. Anyone can pretend. Indeed, it is Polonius' cynical advice to Ophelia – make a 'show' of reading a prayer book, he instructs her because 'with devotion's visage … we do sugar o'er/The devil himself' – that precedes Claudius' attack of guilt in Act III, Scene i.

Because all this trickery is not arrested by Hamlet – whose inaction even after confirming the truth enables it to flourish – it persists right to the end of the play, with fake duels and poisoned sword tips, drugged drinks and other deceptions, until Laertes' public cry, ironically – 'The king, the king's to blame' – exposes everything, in particular the true source of the evil. Freed of the burden of being the only one holding the truth, Hamlet finally acts and kills Claudius.

Action and Inaction, Procrastination, Delay

This theme is really a development from the third part of Hamlet's task: what to do after confirming the truth. It is therefore related to the themes of certainty, appearance and reality, deception, and so on. After all, acting out of ignorance, or error, is a mistake, and can have terrible consequences.

Like all the play's other themes, this one is introduced at a very early stage, in this case in Hamlet's soliloquy in Act I, Scene ii, where it is linked, not only to falsity – his mother's unfaithfulness to his father's memory – but to questions about whether life is worth living at all, and whether or not anything can or should be done to improve it. For Hamlet, then, the choice of action or inaction is influenced not only by deception, appearances and the rest, but also by the emotional bonds between people (the effect his actions will have on Ophelia and Gertrude in particular), by psychological strength of character (is he mentally strong enough?) and by moral considerations (is it right or wrong to do this?). At one point or another, Hamlet is slowed up by each of these considerations.

The Ghost has left him with the well-nigh impossible task of moving against Claudius without harming Gertrude. As late as Act III, Scene iv, after the play scene, Hamlet is still trying to calm himself before confronting his mother. But he is not calm. Still intensely excited after the revelation at the performance of the play, Hamlet has just stopped himself from stabbing Claudius in the back. He is still trying to calm down, but his relationship with his mother is passionate and complex. Immediately, their meeting turns into a vehement exchange of accusations and insults, twisting the nerves to breaking point. Everyone panics. Hamlet lashes out. We judge his actions – the killing of Polonius is, in a practical sense, a terrible error, leading to all sorts of complications, and it is morally wrong – but we must also understand them. Claudius' crime, by contrast, was cold-blooded, calculated and for his own gain. It is not simply a question of acting or not acting, in other words. It is a matter of motivation.

The other characters are different from Hamlet in this regard. They act decisively in their own interests, particularly Claudius, Polonius and Gertrude. As a way of dealing with life, this is a lot simpler. But is it better – not only morally, but practically as well? How does Polonius end up? As a dead spy in a woman's chamber. How do the others fare? Gertrude finally understands that she has been betrayed all along and Claudius squeals for his life to be spared.

It's not, then, simply a case of Hamlet being indecisive and a procrastinator. This is far too simplistic an interpretation, apart from the fact that he acts impetuously – too quickly – a number of times, such as following the Ghost on the battlements and stabbing Polonius. Early in the play, in Act I, Scene iii, the emergence of two dominant and conflicting attitudes to life, two philosophies, two value systems, is apparent. Polonius, Laertes and Claudius believe that you should look out for number one ('to thine own self be true'), be practical, look good on the outside and get as many of the good things in life as you can. Hamlet, on the other hand, is clearly struggling with the belief that there's got to be more to life than all that, that there has to be something more authentic than making good, something more human than selfishness.

He struggles with it throughout the play. In one soliloquy (IV.iv), he wonders what a man *is*. It's a central concern of the drama. What makes us truly human? What makes our life as humans worth living? What values should we hold? How should we live? How should we act? There are many, many more ways of formulating the question. Man, Hamlet reflects, must have some goal beyond merely feeding and sleeping. This reflection is prompted by the sight of an army marching towards its objectives, which leads him to consider his own goal. The tragic thing is, that the army's goal is useless. Men may expend themselves, even kill themselves, pointlessly. And although his own task is more just and infinitely more significant, it too will end in waste. Surely there are better things to devote your life to, but, unfortunately, Hamlet's fate has trapped him. He accepts this now. The tone of this soliloquy is less excited than his earlier ones. He is beginning to accept the consequences of what he has to do.

For the self-interested, action is a simple matter. You always act in your own best interest, regardless. But for all the appearance of self-absorption, Hamlet is deeply concerned about issues larger than his own self-interest – truth, justice, order, love, loyalty and fidelity. For such a man, action is *never* a simple matter. Even at the end, as he is dying in Act V, Scene ii, he is insisting that there are some things worth struggling for – the restoration of political order in Denmark, stability, and a just and rightful ruler.

Disease, Corruption, Poison, Disturbance, Disorder, Decay

The source of all the corruption, of all that is rotten in the state of Denmark, is the poison poured into old King Hamlet's ear by his brother Claudius. From this murderous act, the poison spreads out to infect the entire court and country. Poison and its consequences, disease and disorder, are aspects of the same evil. They infect individuals, families, institutions and states. Like all the other major themes, this one is developed quickly very early in the play.

In Act I, Scene i, starting with Horatio's observation, 'This bodes some strange eruption to our state', note how the various forms of disturbance are introduced separately: inner or psychic disturbance ('sick at heart'), universal or cosmic disturbance (Ghost appearing), military disturbance ('young Fortinbras … to recover from us'), and political disturbance ('a little ere the mightiest Julius fell'). Denmark is threatened from within and without, from above and below.

It is important to understand that the Elizabethans (Shakespeare's period of history) saw a link between all living things, from the lowest animal to the highest being, which they understood as God. The king was God's earthly representative. To put it simply, a good king ruled over a stable society, therefore because there is so much disorder here, it indicates that there is a serious illness or evil somewhere. It is something that Hamlet recognises and expresses throughout Act I, particularly in his soliloquy, suspecting its source, but having no proof: ''tis an unweeded garden/ That grows to seed, things rank and gross in nature possess it merely' (I.ii).

The psychological sickness of Hamlet, the corruption of Polonius, the disturbances in heaven (the Ghost walking) and the psychological imbalance in Ophelia all develop from the same source: the poisoning of King Hamlet and the incestuous marriage between his brother Claudius and his wife Gertrude. The disorder becomes comprehensive, infecting the spiritual, political and individual realms.

The corruption has many forms. One of them is exposed in Act II, Scene i, when Polonius sends Reynaldo to Paris to snoop on Laertes. Nobody trusts anybody else, not even their own sons. Everybody spies on everybody else, including their own sons. Everybody tells lies about everybody else, including their own sons. Polonius, remember, is the king's right-hand man, the moral level of the regime.

This is why Hamlet detests him so much. He stands for the opposite of Hamlet's own values, which are listed in his expression of admiration for Horatio in Act III, Scene ii – resilience, honesty, rationality, lack of flattery, openness, and a lack of interest in money and self-advancement. These are the personal and social virtues that the play and Hamlet hold up against the present, corrupt society. They not only offer an important contrast, they also show that Hamlet, for all his despair, retains a positive, if not optimistic, attitude to life.

On the other hand, the longer Claudius hangs on to the throne, the more and more disordered everything becomes. In Act I, Scene ii, Gertrude, Polonius, Laertes, Ophelia and others all contributed to the show of stability orchestrated by Claudius, but by Act IV, Scene v, Polonius is dead, Ophelia is mad, Gertrude is on the point of hysteria, relationships at court are at best strained, the populace is restless and unhappy, the state is threatened by outside forces and Laertes is at the head of a riotous mob, clamouring for revenge. As the poison works its way through the entire society, it finally exhausts itself in Act V, Scene ii, but at the cost of the deaths of so many, the innocent (Hamlet), the duped (Laertes), the blind (Gertrude) and the guilty (Claudius). All the tainted end up being physically poisoned. Those who are left – Horatio and Fortinbras – were untouched by the initial crime.

The term 'decay' deserves additional attention, because it means the disintegration of something that was once whole, and this is a major theme in the play. Note how often the verb 'remember' in all its forms is used throughout the play, from its use by the Ghost – 'Remember me' (I.v) – in its command to Hamlet. There was a time, it is suggested, when Denmark was a stable, healthy, moral society, a judgement that is echoed by Hamlet's sustained contrast between his father and Claudius in Act I, Scene ii: 'So excellent a king; that was, to this,/Hyperion to a satyr.' In case anyone forgets this, versions of 'remember' occur eighteen times in the play, and the word 'memory' is used ten times.

The obligation to remember is a heavy duty: 'Adieu, adieu! Hamlet, remember me' (I.v), the Ghost commands Hamlet; 'farewell, Ophelia, and remember well what I have said to you' (I.iii), Laertes commands Ophelia; 'My lord, I have remembrances of yours' (III.i), Ophelia reminds Hamlet; 'together with remembrance of ourselves' (I.ii), Claudius fittingly captures his own self-interest, in a phrase echoed by Fortinbras, another acquisitive military man, at the end of the play, 'I have some rights of memory in this kingdom' (V.ii). In fact, the obligation is so heavy that it can drive a person insane: 'There's rosemary, that's for remembrance; pray,/love, remember' (IV.v), Ophelia rambles in her madness; 'His madness is poor Hamlet's enemy' (V.ii), Hamlet tries to convince Laertes; 'Do not forget' (III.iv), the Ghost upbraids Hamlet when he reappears in Act III, Scene iv – because to forget that there were ever such things as virtue and loyalty and honesty and order and rationality … that is far worse.

Death

From the earliest stages of the play, Hamlet dwells on and considers death. His first soliloquy demonstrates his suicidal tendencies. This is not just an individual's unrelated depression, however, but arises directly out of the circumstances of the play. He is in this situation because of the death, indeed the murder, of his father.

So death is a natural concern, contemplated in all its aspects by Hamlet, from the play's beginning to its end. This is consistent, because at the start of the drama Hamlet has been left with the *mystery* of his father's death – its cause, its circumstances, its reality for his father, its consequences. Life cannot be understood without an understanding of death, a philosophical insight that Hamlet articulates in Act V, Scene i, as he looks at Yorick's skull: 'Now get you to my lady's chamber and tell her, let her paint an inch thick, to this favour she must come.' And with this acceptance of death's inevitability comes a final acceptance of life's compromises, complexities and possibilities, and of life itself.

Before this point, Hamlet often thought that death might help him solve or evade the profound problems that life has presented to him, the problems of establishing and living the truth. What draws him back from the attraction of suicide is a belief in an afterlife, where the sins and failings of this life have to be atoned for, a reality brought home to him by the Ghost's graphic descriptions of his sufferings in the afterlife in Act I, Scene v: 'confined to fast in fires/Till the foul crimes done in my days of nature/Are burnt and purged away.' Simultaneously, the Ghost explains the mystery of its life: 'Revenge his foul and most unnatural murder.' And simultaneously, Hamlet is drawn *towards* death because this revenge can only be accomplished by the killing of Claudius.

Hamlet's most complex reflections on death are in his soliloquy in Act III, Scene i, in the centre of the play: 'To be or not to be …' In it, he concludes that fear of the afterlife is what fundamentally motivates human choices and action or inaction.

Perhaps the best way to understand Hamlet's profound complexity is to contrast the reactions of other characters to the deaths of those close to them, and therefore to death itself. Following what must have been the highly suspicious death of her husband, Gertrude adopts an almost indifferent stoicism – death is 'as common as any the most vulgar thing' (I.ii), as Claudius lectures Hamlet in Act I, Scene ii. She marries again quickly and gets on gaily with life. A response that testifies to her shallowness. Claudius thinks Hamlet's mourning is 'unmanly grief' (I.ii) and proclaims a similarly facile life-must-go-on philosophy, but clings pathetically to his empty life, even as he is dying: 'I am but hurt' (V.ii), are his final words. Her father's death brings madness to the delicate Ophelia and rage and intemperance to her brother Laertes. Instead of promoting self-reflection, the death of Polonius reinforces Gertrude's superficiality – according to her, Hamlet 'in this brainish apprehension kills the unseen good old man' (IV.i) – and Claudius' self-interest – his first reaction is to think that it might have been him: 'It had been so with us, had we been there' (II.i). Only Hamlet arrives at, articulates and represents the profound truth that the entire play explores: life cannot be understood without an understanding of death.

Kingship and Power

In Martin Scorcese's 2002 film *The Gangs of New York*, Amsterdam Vallon, played by Leonardo di Caprio, asserts: 'When you kill a king, you don't stab him in the back. You kill him where the entire court can watch him die.' If you kill a king secretively – as Claudius did his brother by pouring poison in his ear – it leaves your power vulnerable to rumour, conspiracy, distrust, uncertainty, disrespect and moral opposition. In Act III, Scene iii, Hamlet rejects the opportunity to exact his revenge in this manner by stabbing Claudius in the back, ostensibly because Claudius might be praying and go to heaven if killed in that instant, but actually, we suspect, because such an act, as base as his own father's murder, is abhorrent to Hamlet's morality and sense of justice, and would leave him exposed to opposition

afterwards, not least from his own mother. Hamlet must expose Claudius as a criminal and a murderer, and then punish him in public.

The fact that Hamlet is not an accomplished politician, an accomplished statesman or an accomplished warrior is almost crippling, and contributes to his long delay, but it isn't the most difficult of his many dilemmas. His greatest problem is that he is obliged to kill, not merely a man, and not merely the man his mother loves, but the king. To avenge the crime of regicide – the killing of a king – he must also commit regicide.

As mentioned on page 6, it is impossible to understand the full moral, philosophical and political weight of this injunction without understanding that kingship was the mode 'of holding society together in the sixteenth century' (A.L. Rowse). Kill a king and you risk plunging an entire society into chaos. Murder a king, as Claudius does, and you establish a criminal empire, poisoned by fear, intimidation and paranoid surveillance, not a healthy society. Execute a king – which the English actually did in 1649, fifty years after *Hamlet* was written, with Charles I, whose last words were that 'liberty and freedom consist in having government [a king], not in having a share of government' – and you embark on the uncertainties of a secular, parliamentarian system.

There is no easy solution, no easy way to kill a king in seventeenth-century England. But perhaps there is a *right* way. In 1648, parliament established a separate court for Charles I's unprecedented trial – and this is the way that Hamlet seeks throughout the play. He cannot proceed until Claudius' guilt is publicly established, which finally happens only with Laertes' dramatic and morally unambiguous testimony in Act V, Scene ii – 'the king, the king's to blame' – a judgement immediately echoed by the lords attending the fencing match – 'Treason, treason!' Fifty years later, Charles I was convicted and executed for the same crime of treason, separating forever the secular, democratic European world that we all now live in from the England of Shakespeare, which believed in, but was bold enough to question, the divine right of kings.

Style

Language

Shakespeare's plays were performed on a predominantly bare stage that was lit only by daylight, a constriction – or a freedom, whichever way you want to look at it – that forced the dramatic language of the period to become incredibly rich in the creation of character, situation, action and tension.

The opening of *Hamlet* is a perfect example of how the language carries everything in one of these plays. Without lighting effects or elaborate scenery available, it is the language that quickly establishes the time, the weather and the nervous atmosphere. This is achieved not only by the imagery – 'bitter cold … sick at heart … struck twelve … not a mouse stirring' – but also by the rhythm of the short, tense exchanges.

In the middle of a bright afternoon, because plays were performed at about three o'clock, this opening scene is shrouded in threatening darkness because of the richness of the language, which also contains references that suggest the opposites to darkness, insecurity and terror – the dawn, birds singing, the morning light, keeping evil spirits away – since these conflicts are among the major themes of the play.

Dialogue and **soliloquy** are the specific uses of language for the creation of dramatic characters, and **imagery** is the specific use of language for atmosphere and the treatment of themes, but in a Shakespeare play, language is also used, perhaps surprisingly, for the presentation of action sequences. Consider the number of times that characters *describe* events that the audience does not otherwise witness: the Ghost recounting its own murder and subsequent sufferings in the afterlife; Ophelia telling her father of Hamlet's apparently insane intrusion into her chamber; the Player recreating Hecuba's grief at the death of her husband, King Priam, after the siege and sack of Troy; Hamlet telling Horatio how he gave Rosencrantz and Guildenstern the slip and escaped on a pirate ship.

Today, no producer or director would pass up the opportunity for the spectacular action sequences that these passages offer – but hasn't something been lost in the contemporary preference for visual storytelling? Doesn't the reliance on language bring the events to life *in* the imagination of the audience rather than bringing them to life on a screen *outside* the imagination of the audience?

But there is more to this reliance on language for reporting certain events than the relationship with an active rather than a passive audience. Consider how Hamlet's actions are reported in Act II, Scene i, rather than directly shown. As always, this is an interesting dramatic choice in itself. And it *is* a choice, for keep in mind that certain other actions – the play-within-a-play, for instance, and the fencing duel at the end – are shown and not reported. Firstly, the fact that Hamlet's actions are reported by a credible character in Ophelia enables us to believe the description. After all, we are reluctant to take the words of other characters, such as Claudius or Polonius, at face value. Secondly, the fact that it *is* an individual's version gives rise to questions, not of authenticity in this case, but of interpretation – Polonius thinks Hamlet is actually mad ('mad for thy love', he says, and 'ecstasy of love' (II.i), where the word 'ecstasy' means madness), Ophelia is confused and distraught, and we are left with much to reflect on. Is Hamlet actually mad, already feigning madness (as he forewarned Horatio and the others in Act I, Scene v), or so traumatised by his situation and his inevitable loss of Ophelia that his pain is beyond words and beyond composure? We don't quite know, because we haven't seen it for ourselves, and our uncertainty becomes an essential part of our experience of the play.

Dialogue

How a character speaks to other characters is, of course, a standard device for creating those characters in a stage play, but its use is particularly subtle and accomplished in *Hamlet*.

Consider the character of Claudius and how the man's diminishing power is wonderfully expressed in the changing nature of his dialogue. In Act I, Scene ii, when he is addressing the court, he is in total control. He speaks, uninterrupted, for a lengthy period, in a polished, assured delivery – 'So much for him./Now for ourself' – commanding the entire audience, which of course includes ourselves, and listening to others only when he invites them to speak, after defining what they may talk about – 'And now, Laertes, what's the news with you?'

But this only holds up to a point. When he tries the same controlling trick with Hamlet, the young prince immediately interrupts him, and Claudius' control begins to waver – 'But now, my cousin Hamlet, and my son—' (I.ii), he begins, obviously intending to launch into a leisurely lecture, but Hamlet instantly disrupts the smoothness with a muttered barb, 'A little more than kin, and less than kind' – which means, *you're not my father, so don't go around claiming that I'm your son, and your motive is not one of kindness, so stop pretending that it is.* After this, as Gertrude pitches in and Hamlet reacts impatiently to her, the dialogue, and the court, descend into a form of unseemly squabbling, and by the time Claudius regains control, sarcasm has replaced condescension in his attitude to others – ''Tis sweet and commendable in your nature, Hamlet' – insults have replaced compliments – ''tis unmanly grief … 'tis a fault to heaven' – and veiled threats have replaced generous favours – 'remain/Here in the cheer and comfort of our eye'.

It's the beginning of the end for Claudius, and the cracks first appear in his control of dialogue. After this, his exchanges with others – Gertrude, Polonius, Rosencrantz, Guildenstern, Laertes and Hamlet – become increasingly pressurised, fractured, impatient, even desperate, more marked by expressions of uncertainty and helplessness ('O heavy deed!' (IV.i)) and strained questions ('Where is he gone? (IV.i)) and frantic orders ('Pluck them asunder' (V.i)) than royal command.

Revealingly, Hamlet's first line of dialogue – 'A little more than kin, and less than kind' – is a play on words, and it is this playing around with language – not saying what he means, and yet making his meaning obvious – that so unsettles and disrupts Claudius. A moment later, Hamlet reacts angrily to his mother's use of the word 'seems'. He draws a distinction between what appears to be ('seems') and what actually is, a distinction that is crucial to our understanding of the character and the play. But it is interesting to note that Hamlet experiences this problem entirely in relation to language at this stage. He deals in puns and definitions. The style defines his dialogue. Not knowing who to trust and who to be wary of, it's how he handles social interaction with others – Polonius ('you are a fishmonger' (II.ii)), Rosencrantz and Guildenstern ('The body is with the king, but the king is not with the body' (IV.iii)), and Claudius ('Farewell, dear mother' (IV.iii)), among others. Just as Claudius' disintegrating power is expressed through his increasingly fractured dialogue with others, so Hamlet's progression from weakness to strength, from despair to acceptance, is expressed in the changing character of his humour. His jesting with the gravediggers in Act V, Scene i, and with Osric in Act V, Scene ii, is light and composed, exposing the absurdities of human life, but without the acidity and self-defensive aggression of his earlier quips.

Soliloquy

The word 'soliloquy' comes from the Latin for 'to speak (*loqui*) alone (*solus*)'. While dialogue reveals the cracks in the social personae of characters and accelerates the tensions between them, the great soliloquies of *Hamlet* dramatise both a character's speculation about the human condition and his or her deep emotional or psychological disturbance, in addition, they sometimes slow the play's pace to one of profound contemplation, and they are justly famous for these achievements.

There are eight soliloquies in the play and all are worth detailed attention. Apart from Claudius' soliloquy in Act III, Scene iii – 'O, my offence is rank: it smells to heaven' – they are spoken by Hamlet.

The first, in Act I, Scene ii – 'O that this too too sallied flesh would melt' – as well as dramatically expressing Hamlet's suppressed emotions in its exclamations of pain, tortured questions and repetitions, concisely introduces and defines all of the play's major themes: life is corrupted and diseased (incest, frailty, decay, the loss of a perfect past); whether life's worth living at all (suicide, life as stale and flat); whether anything can be done or should be done ('I must hold my tongue'); and falsity (Gertrude's unfaithfulness to the memory of King Hamlet, whose ghost will shortly reappear and command Hamlet, 'remember me'). In the opening line of this soliloquy, 'sallied', meaning 'assailed', is emended in some editions to 'sullied', meaning 'contaminated', or 'solid', meaning 'fat'.

The second soliloquy, in Act I, Scene v, immediately after the Ghost's revelations – 'O all you host of heaven, O earth – what else?', also has exclamations of disgust, fevered questions and bewildered repetitions. It perfectly expresses the turbulence and confusion within Hamlet at this point. Neither of these first two soliloquies is reflective; both function as eruptions of Hamlet's pent-up feelings.

In the third, in Act II, Scene ii – 'Now I am alone' – Hamlet finally, though briefly, escapes the stifling atmosphere of deception and pretence and surveillance. He is further on from the immediate shock of learning that his father was murdered and this soliloquy is a more considered and complex update on the themes already touched on: falsity and pretence ('this player here, in a fiction, in a dream of passion'); the need for action ('Am I a coward?'); the uselessness of words ('like a whore … fall a-cursing'); the usefulness of words and falsity ('I'll have these players play something like the murder of my father').

As an insight into Hamlet's character, his most famous soliloquy – 'To be or not to be' – in Act III, Scene i, reveals how desperately low he has sunk, seeing human endeavour as pointless and longing for death. Or perhaps not. When Hamlet is speaking these lines, he is *not* actually alone. Ophelia is also on stage, waiting for him, and Claudius and Polonius are hiding behind an arras. If Hamlet is aware of *any* of these three, then what he says may be calculated for effect, and not an expression of his true being.

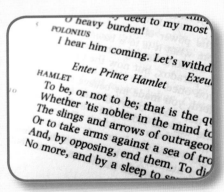

This is a play about appearances, in which the validity of everything is questioned. In this case, the dramatic device of the soliloquy, because it is not technically a soliloquy at all, questions itself.

Either way, this soliloquy is not an examination of a personal crisis – the pronoun 'I' is not used – but a general reflection on man – 'to say we end … when we have shuffled off … who would bear? … who would fardels bear?' – so much so that the meaning of the famous opening 'question' remains unclear. Is it whether a man's life is worth living, whether his own life is worth living or whether he should kill Claudius? Similarly, Hamlet is not alone on stage for his sixth soliloquy, in Act III, Scene iii, where he is standing behind the kneeling Claudius, or for his final soliloquy, in Act IV, Scene iv, where his guards are still present if a little apart.

The soliloquies advance the plot, encapsulate the major themes and provide insights into Hamlet's emotional state at various times, but one needs to be wary of interpreting them as self-conscious explorations of Hamlet's inner being. In this play, nothing is what it initially 'seems', including the apparent 'soliloquies'.

Imagery

It's very important to avoid treating the imagery in a Shakespeare play as mere ornament, instead it should be discussed as being integral, both as a method of advancing the action and an expression of the themes and characters that unfold as the action progresses.

One of the most dominant strands of imagery in *Hamlet* is that of poison, simply because the corruption and disease that overwhelm the state of Denmark have their origins in the poison that Claudius uses to kill King Hamlet, as the Ghost describes in Act I, Scene v. The poison that is poured into the old king's ear is not only a physical poison that kills an individual man, but also a spiritual poison that corrodes a whole society. (Note 'the whole ear of Denmark is … rankly abused' (I.v)). This surely explains why Hamlet's task becomes so complicated. To revenge the killing of a single man might be straightforward. To heal a corrupt state ('something is rotten in the state of Denmark' (I.iv)) is something else altogether.

Nevertheless, there are hints, in the imagery of **freshness**, **light** and **sweetness**, here in Act I, Scene v – 'methinks I scent the morning air' – and throughout the play, that this is possible.

The above quotation is followed, of course, by a very detailed and gruesome description of the effects of poison on a living body. The detail is deliberate. It describes the corrupted, decayed mess that the state of Denmark now is. It should be noted again that the Elizabethans saw connections between things that we no longer see, and that one of the main ones was that between the health of the human body, particularly the human body of the king, and the health of the entire society (the 'body politic', as it is sometimes referred to, a reference that makes sense of Hamlet's quip to Rosencrantz and Guildenstern 'The body is with the king, but the king is not with the body' (IV.iii)).

Whenever Claudius wants to present his usual justification for things – whatever is happening, it's Hamlet's fault – he, too, draws on the imagery of poison. This goes so far in Act IV, Scenes i–iii, that Claudius, in his imagery, accuses Hamlet of being the source of all the poison – 'his poisoned shot … diseases desperate grown … like the hectic in my blood he rages'. Every mention of poison, of course, is merely another reminder to the audience that Claudius himself is the source of the corruption.

In Act IV, Scene vii, when Claudius and Laertes are plotting to murder Hamlet and pass it off as an accident, the most significant imagery, again, is that of poison. The corruption began with poison in the King's ear and, at this point, it has spread throughout the entire society and is about to overwhelm it. However plausible or implausible you may think the multiple ruses to kill off Hamlet are, there is a metaphorical point in the accumulation of poison, on the sword and in the drink, in that it represents the overwhelming of a society.

As the poison works its way through, it finally exhausts itself in Act V, Scene ii, though at the cost of so many lives.

Other significant strands of imagery in the play include: that of **flowers**, suggestive of tenderness and innocence, associated with Ophelia from Act I, Scene iii, which finds its fullest expression in Act IV, Scene v when she gives flowers as uncomfortable gifts to others in her madness; that of **money** and **trade**, most associated with the practical Polonius and his son Laertes; that of **falsity** or **deception**, mostly used by Hamlet, particularly against the female characters, Ophelia – 'God hath given you one face, and you make yourselves another' (III.i) – and Gertrude – 'blurs the grace' (III.iv); and finally that of **decay** and **corruption**, in all its forms, from nature – 'ah, fie, 'tis an unweeded garden/That grows to seed' (I.ii) – to the body – 'blister … mildewed ear' (III.iv) – to marriage – 'stewed in corruption … rank corruption' (III.iv) and to the life of man – 'To what base uses we may return, Horatio' (V.i).

Dramatic Technique

Hamlet is a play of great formal design within which there is apparent chaos.

The formal design is obvious. For example, Hamlet, Fortinbras and Laertes are three young men of different temperaments who share an unusual fate – their fathers have been violently killed, and each character is taxed with the burden of revenge. Each is thwarted: Hamlet by inclination and circumstances; Fortinbras by command from his king; and Laertes by being misled. The parallels are neat.

The apparent chaos is equally obvious. There's a ghost abroad, a mad prince running around the castle, an older woman frantically trying to hold on to her warring son and husband, a young woman who goes insane and seemingly kills herself, a young man who causes a riot, and a king's councillor who spends much of his time spying on other people.

The dramatic device that Shakespeare most often uses to create this sense of chaos is the interruption of the action. Nothing is allowed to settle, no pattern is permitted to develop. Everything is fractured, unfinished, unsettled. It's extremely effective in establishing a world that is out of control, or 'out of joint' as Hamlet phrases it.

In Act I, Scene i, the sentries are just settling down, after a nervous changing of the guard, to telling the story of how a ghost appeared the night before when … the Ghost appears, disrupting the account and throwing them into fearful confusion. It happens *twice* in the opening scene.

In Act I, Scene ii, Claudius is in full flow when Hamlet's pointed interruption sends the court into a squabbling spin, and, in Act I, Scene iii, Laertes is on the point of leaving for France when Polonius turns up to hurry him on his way and detains him for another ten minutes with a tedious lecture.

The most dramatically significant of the interruptions is that to the play-within-a-play, because it is caused by Claudius, unable to contain the explosion of his own guilt. The hectic activity after his departure – all that rushing around, all those wild words and puns, all those urgent exits and entrances – captures both the excitement that Hamlet feels at completing the second part of his mission (getting proof) and the fear and chaos that spreads through the court.

Even the solemn funeral of Ophelia, already truncated and hurried because her death was considered a suicide, is further disrupted by her brother and suitor leaping into her grave in competition with one another. And in the end, of course, things are resolved more by accident than design, chaotically, in the fencing match between supposedly friendly rivals that turns into a deadly battle, a mess that is interrupted – for the final time in the play – by the sudden arrival of Fortinbras at the head of an army.

The other main dramatic technique used is the creation of atmosphere. The tension of the opening, the paranoia of the court and the near-hysteria of Hamlet's relationships with Gertrude and Ophelia have all been referred to in earlier sections. In Act V, Scene i, however, there is a freshness in the scene that is absent from the rest of the play and it heralds a major shift in the drama and in Hamlet's development.

This scene is set in a graveyard, which might be considered gruesome, but it has a tone of acceptance that was absent before – an acceptance of the inadequacies of life, of the inevitability of death, of the tasks and duties and burdens that are laid on us. The scene is in the open air, in daylight, not stuck inside the claustrophobic rooms of the court, which are full of spies, or on the chilly battlements, haunted by ghosts. The two gravediggers are down-to-earth (so to speak) characters, with no phoniness about them. Hamlet is dressed differently, possibly wearing his 'sea gown' described in Act V, Scene ii. He is calmer, more open. Indeed, the accusation that he is mad, from both Claudius and Gertrude, is patently absurd. He carries this new assurance and acceptance with him to the end of the play, dictating, as he couldn't do before, the atmosphere of the Danish court.

MAKE

Since the introduction of the new syllabus, *Hamlet* has been prescribed as a Single Text in 2001, 2002, 2005, 2011 and 2012. The following questions were on the examination paper in 2012.

(i) 'Hamlet's madness, whether genuine or not, adds to the fascination of his character for the audience.'

Discuss this statement, supporting your answer with suitable reference to the play, *Hamlet*.

OR

(ii) 'Shakespeare uses a variety of techniques to convey a world of corruption in the play, *Hamlet*.'

Write your response to this statement, supporting your answer with suitable reference to the text.

The Great Gatsby
by F. Scott Fitzgerald

Background

First published in April 1925, *The Great Gatsby* received mixed reviews and sold poorly. Its author, Francis Scott Fitzgerald, died in 1940 believing himself to be a failure and his work forgotten. However, the novel experienced a revival during the following decades and, today, it is widely considered a literary classic. One reason for the growing status of the novel is that, in many ways, it was prescient. Fitzgerald's portrait of the corruption at the heart of the Jazz Age foreshadowed the Wall Street Crash of 1929, while the modern world – technological, consumerist, driven by leisure – is seen here in one of its first fictional representations.

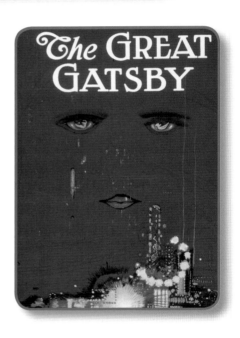

The Author

Fitzgerald was born in 1896 and raised in St Paul, Minnesota. Despite being a mediocre student, he managed to enrol at Princeton but never graduated. He enlisted in the army in 1917, as the First World War neared its end. Fitzgerald was stationed at Camp Sheridan in Montgomery, Alabama, where he met and fell in love with a wild seventeen-year-old beauty named Zelda Sayre. Zelda finally agreed to marry him, but her desire for wealth, fun and leisure led her to delay their wedding until Fitzgerald had attained some financial success.

Many of the events from Fitzgerald's early life appear in *The Great Gatsby*, his most famous novel. Like Fitzgerald, Nick Carraway is a thoughtful young man from the Midwest, educated at an Ivy League school, who moves to New York

after the war. Also similar to Fitzgerald, however, is Jay Gatsby, a sensitive young man who idolises wealth and luxury and who falls in love with a beautiful young woman while stationed at a military camp in the South.

The Jazz Age

Fitzgerald was the most famous chronicler of 1920s America, a time when the economy soared. He referred to the era as 'the Jazz Age'. The chaos and violence of the First World War left the country in a state of shock, and the generation that fought the war turned to wild and extravagant living to compensate. Prohibition, the ban on the sale and consumption of alcohol, was brought into law in 1919 and remained in force until 1933. It made millionaires out of bootleggers, who supplied alcohol illicitly, and an underground culture of private parties and secret clubs thrived. It is hinted in the novel that Gatsby's wealth is due, in part at least, to his involvement with bootlegging.

The Language of Film

It is interesting to note how the structure of the novel is influenced by the language of film. The 1920s was an important decade in cinema history, with directors making great advances in technique, and novelists, including Fitzgerald, were quick to learn from their innovations. *The Great Gatsby* is full of abrupt transitions, similar to the way a cut is used to switch scenes in a film. The novel's visual immediacy also reminds us that this was the age when photography began to be popular. Structurally, the novel is built around a series of images – Gatsby stretching his arms out to the green light, the panorama of the great party, the car crash, Gatsby's body in the pool.

Real Events

Another great strength of the novel is Fitzgerald's fusion of real historical occurrences such as the murder of Rosy Rosenthal – an actual event recalled by the character Wolfsheim in Chapter 4 – with the stuff of romance. He registers some of the social realities of the 1920s, such as the rise of gangsters, and at the same time reveals one of the main themes of the novel – how the material world and an ideal world coexist.

Title and Epigraph

Fitzgerald was never fully satisfied with the title *The Great Gatsby* and tried to change it to *Under the Red, White and Blue* at the last minute, but he was too late. The epigraph to the novel is a poem written by Fitzgerald but attributed to Thomas Parke D'Invilliers, a character in his first novel, *This Side of Paradise*.

In 1922, Fitzgerald wrote to his editor that he wanted to write something '*new* – something extraordinary and beautiful and simple and intricately patterned'. In *The Great Gatsby*, he certainly achieved his aim.

Setting

Set in prosperous Long Island, New York, in 1922, *The Great Gatsby* provides a critical social history of America during the Roaring Twenties. That era, known for unprecedented economic prosperity, the evolution of jazz music, youth culture, bootlegging and other criminal activity, is plausibly depicted in Fitzgerald's novel.

The main action of the novel takes place in New York. However, there are flashbacks and many references to the Midwest, the area from which the main characters in the book all originate. The narrator, Nick Carraway, describes the narrative as: 'a story of the West … Tom and Gatsby, Daisy and Jordan and I, were all Westerners'.

The Midwest of America is associated with a conservative lifestyle and traditional values. By the 1920s, Midwestern society had remained unchanged for generations. Nick describes his home city as one where 'dwellings are still called through decades by a family's name'. The West, associated with the frontier, holds a special place in the American psyche – it is the fresh start, the new beginning. George Wilson's dream, expressed to Tom Buchanan in Chapter 7, is to go West with his wife, and to begin life anew; but it *is* just a dream and one that will never be realised.

Significantly, Nick and Gatsby both reside in the New York suburb of West Egg. It is less fashionable than nearby East Egg, but its name carries with it connotations of the westward movement that characterised America's frontier past. The suggestion is that both Nick and Gatsby preserve American ideals which have been lost in the sophisticated cities of the East. This is, of course, ironic, as both Eggs are located on the east coast.

Nick had been educated in New England and had been to Europe during the First World War. When he came back, the Midwest seemed to him 'like the ragged edge of the universe'. However, after becoming disgusted with the immorality of the East, he comes to appreciate his native region. He recalls how much he enjoyed the 'sharp wild brace' of the cold air when returning home at Christmas. After his involvement with the events of summer 1922, Nick turns his back on the East. Gatsby also comes from the Midwest, specifically North Dakota, a relatively poor, agricultural area on the northern edge of the Midwest. He has also abandoned it in favour of the more glamorous East.

Gatsby's house in West Egg is obviously new, something that is a negative feature because it means it has a lack of heritage, something Tom mocks Gatsby for when he calls him 'Mr Nobody from Nowhere'. Nick's house, which Tom mocks as a 'small eyesore', is also in West Egg. However, Nick has admitted that his family are 'well-to-do' and his poverty is only assumed. When he describes his little house as 'squeezed between two huge places', this foreshadows Nick being caught in the emotional crossfire between Gatsby and the Buchanans. Daisy and Tom Buchanan live in East Egg, which is much more exclusive. The phrase 'indiscernible barbed wire' used in Chapter 8 sums up the social barrier between the two 'Eggs', which even money cannot penetrate. While East Egg is expensive and luxurious, it is also beautiful – 'the white palaces of fashionable East Egg glittered along the water'.

In the novel, New York represents a modern lifestyle with moral values that are more liberal than in the Midwest. At first, Nick embraces the freedom that life in New York seems to offer, but he later rejects it. He describes a scene from one of his 'fantastic dreams' in which four well-dressed men are carrying a stretcher on which lies a drunken woman in a white evening dress whose hand 'sparkles cold with jewels'. They take her to 'the wrong house. But no one knows the woman's name and no one cares'. This vision sums up the basic heartlessness of New York society in which Nick has detected a moral vacuum. This is the society that attends Gatsby's parties, but ignores his funeral. In the final chapter, Nick admits that 'even when the East excited me most … even then it had always for me a quality of distortion'.

The 'valley of ashes' lies between Long Island and New York, and George and Myrtle Wilson live on the edge of this area. It is a desolate industrial wasteland, bounded on one side by 'a small foul river'. Fitzgerald uses an agricultural image to stress its barren nature through contrast – 'a fantastic farm where ashes grow like wheat into ridges and hills and grotesque gardens'. The 'spasms of bleak dust' that drift over the area turn everything grey so the men who work on the railroad there are themselves 'ash-grey'. The imagery of dust and ashes recalls death – the people who are condemned to live and work there inhabit a kind of living death, shut out from the wealth that more privileged people, such as the Buchanans, enjoy.

The description of the 'valley of ashes' recalls the bleak spiritual landscape of T.S. Eliot's poem 'The Waste Land', published in 1922, the year in which *The Great Gatsby* is set. That poem responds to the horrific violence of the First World War and also to the spread of materialistic, consumerist values in modern society. As well as revealing the huge gulf between the haves and have-nots in America in the 1920s, in the valley of ashes Fitzgerald also hints at the spiritual barrenness of American society, which is materialistic and lacking in morals and decency. Nick says he always finds the area 'vaguely disquieting', reflecting his feelings about the moral decay that it suggests.

Summary

Chapter 1

The novel opens with the narrator, Nick Carraway, in philosophical mood, looking back on the events of the past. He considers himself to be a man 'inclined to reserve all judgements' but, since coming back from the East the previous autumn, he has less tolerance for the world. Nick mentions Gatsby. He provides the reader with no concrete information but says 'there was something gorgeous about him, some heightened sensitivity to promises of life'. Nick compares Gatsby to a seismograph, 'one of those intricate machines that registers earthquakes ten thousand miles away'. Nick finishes this musing with a reference to the 'foul dust' that preyed on Gatsby.

Nick then gives an account of his own background and the events that led him to leave the Midwest. At the beginning of his story, in the spring of 1922, he has moved to New York to 'learn the bond business' and is renting a 'cardboard bungalow' in West Egg, Long Island, twenty miles from the city. Next door to him is a mansion inhabited by a man named Gatsby.

Shortly after arriving, Nick visits Daisy and Tom Buchanan's 'Georgian colonial mansion' in 'fashionable' East Egg. Daisy is Nick's 'second cousin once removed' and he knew Tom in college. He meets Jordan Baker, a friend of Daisy. The four converse and have dinner on the porch but, during the course of the evening, tensions arise. There's a phone call for Tom, and Daisy follows him into the house as he goes to take it. Jordan tells Nick: 'Tom's got some woman in New York.'

At one point in the evening, Jordan mentions that Nick must know Gatsby, and Daisy asks: 'What Gatsby?' She receives no answer, because just at that moment dinner is announced. The chapter ends with Nick back in West Egg, watching Gatsby standing in darkness in his garden, his arms outstretched towards a green light at the end of a dock across the water.

MAKE

Chapter 1

1. In this chapter, the reader is introduced to all the main characters in the novel through the narration of Nick Carraway. Write briefly about how Nick describes Tom Buchanan, Daisy Buchanan, Jordan Baker and Jay Gatsby.

2. Based on the account he offers the reader about himself at the start of the chapter, and on his narration of the story, what kind of person do you think Nick Carroway is?

READ

Chapter 2

'Halfway between West Egg and New York' is a desolate area of land called the 'valley of ashes'. The train to New York often stops there when the drawbridge over 'a small foul river' is up to let barges through. A gigantic billboard, displaying the eyes and yellow glasses of Doctor T. J. Eckleburg, dominates this landscape.

One Sunday, travelling by train to New York, Nick is 'forced' from the carriage by Tom, who wants him 'to meet my girl'. His 'girl' is Myrtle Wilson, the wife of George Wilson, who owns an 'unprosperous' garage in the valley of ashes. After a brief conversation with her husband, Tom tells Myrtle to get on the next train.

In New York, Myrtle buys a puppy from a man in the street and Nick, Tom and Myrtle take a cab to 'a long white cake of apartment-houses' on 158th Street. A party ensues. Neighbours called the McKees arrive as well as Myrtle's sister, Catherine. Nick tells the reader he has 'been drunk just twice in my life. The second time is this afternoon'. When Nick mentions to Catherine that he lives at West Egg, she says she was 'there at a party about a month ago. At a man named Gatsby's'. She adds, 'they say he's a nephew or a cousin of Kaiser Wilhelm's'.

During the course of the evening, Myrtle tauntingly shouts Daisy's name a number of times and Tom breaks her nose 'with his open hand'. The night ends with Nick in Pennsylvania Station waiting for the four o'clock train.

MAKE

Chapter 2

1. Describe the 'valley of ashes'. What does it look like and what does it represent?

2. In this chapter, we meet George Wilson and Myrtle Wilson and we learn more about Tom Buchanan and Nick Carroway. Write a brief note on each character based on your reading of Chapter 2.

Chapter 3

The chapter opens with Nick describing the opulent parties held in Gatsby's mansion 'through the summer'. The first night he goes to Gatsby's house he is 'one of the few guests who had actually been invited'. Nick sees Jordan Baker at the party and they spend the evening together. The atmosphere is one of hedonistic pleasure. Rumours of Gatsby's past abound. A girl tells Jordan that he 'killed a man once' while another says 'he was a German spy during the war'.

Jordan and Nick look for Gatsby. They enter a 'Gothic library' where a man 'with enormous owl-eyed spectacles' exclaims with surprise that the books are real. Back outside, Nick finds himself at a table with a man 'about my own age' who asks him if he was 'in the First Division during the war'. Nick replies that he was in the Twenty-Eighth Infantry. The man says he was in the Sixteenth and he and Nick chat. When his companion leaves after a butler tells him that there is a call for him from Chicago, Nick is surprised to discover that the man is Gatsby. Later, Jordan tells Nick that Gatsby once told her he was 'an Oxford man' but that she doesn't believe him.

The butler informs Jordan that Gatsby would like to speak with her alone. When she returns, she tells Nick that she has 'heard the most amazing thing'. She then parts from Nick telling him to contact her at her aunt's house.

As Nick leaves, he sees that a new coupé has gone into a ditch and is blocking the cars behind it. The driver is Owl Eyes, the man Nick met in the library earlier.

The chapter finishes with a reflective passage. Nick tells the reader that what he has written so far is 'merely casual events in a crowded summer'. He describes New York as having a 'racy, adventurous feel' at this time, as well as 'haunting loneliness', and reveals that he spent time with Jordan over that summer and realised she was 'incurably dishonest', despite which his feelings for her intensified and he saw that he needed to get out of that 'tangle back home'. As the chapter ends, Nick confides in the reader that he sees himself as 'one of the few honest people I have ever known'.

Chapter 3

MAKE

1. In this chapter, Nick finally meets Gatsby. Describe Gatsby the first time Nick sees him. What rumours have been circulating about Gatsby? What does Nick think of Gatsby after meeting him?

2. At the end of the chapter, Nick says that he is one of the few honest people he knows. Do you think he is honest?

Single Text

Chapter 4

READ

Continuing in reflective mode, Nick recalls having written down, in the empty spaces of a timetable, the names of those who came to Gatsby's house during that summer of 1922. The timetable is now old, he tells us, but he can still read the names. After listing the names, which are of people from all walks of life, he resumes his narrative.

One morning in late July, Gatsby drives up to Nick's door and insists on taking him to lunch. During the course of the drive to the city, Gatsby tells Nick about his life. He says he is 'the son of some wealthy people in the Middle West' who are all dead now and that he was educated at Oxford. He adds that he spent time travelling in Europe 'trying to forget something very sad that happened to me long ago', before accepting a commission as first lieutenant and fighting in the war. Nick finds this story 'incredulous', and is annoyed when Gatsby confides that he wishes to make a request of Nick and that Jordan Baker will speak to Nick about it when they meet later that afternoon for tea.

Nick and Gatsby have lunch in a cellar on Forty-Second Street. Gatsby introduces Nick to his friend Mr Wolfsheim, a 'small, flat-nosed Jew', who Gatsby later reveals was 'the man who fixed the World's Series back in 1919', referring to a scandal in baseball. Over lunch, Wolfsheim recalls the murder of his friend Rosy Rosenthal at the Metropole Hotel and asks Nick if he is looking for a 'business gonnegtion', but Gatsby tells him that 'this isn't the man'. Towards the end of lunch, Nick sees Tom Buchanan across the crowded room and goes over to say hello to him. When he turns to introduce Gatsby, he's 'no longer there'.

Single Text

Later that afternoon in the tea garden at the Plaza Hotel, Jordan Baker tells Nick of the circumstances surrounding Daisy's marriage to Tom Buchanan. The story begins in Louisville in October 1917 when Daisy Fay was eighteen. Jordan, who is two years younger, saw Daisy one day sitting in her car with a young lieutenant and recalls that they were 'engrossed in each other'. The young lieutenant was Jay Gatsby. Jordan tells Nick that although she didn't see much of Daisy after that, she heard wild rumours about her – that her mother caught her packing her bag one night to go to New York to say goodbye to a soldier who was going overseas.

The following autumn, Daisy 'was gay again' and by summer she was engaged to Tom Buchanan of Chicago. The day before the wedding was due to take place, Jordan found Daisy drunk in her room. She told Jordan to 'Tell 'em all Daisy's change' her mine'. Jordan and a maid got her into a cold bath to sober her up. Daisy had a letter from Gatsby in her hand which she wouldn't let go of. The next day, Daisy married Tom and when Jordan next saw her, she thought she'd 'never seen a girl so mad about her husband', but shortly after that Tom was involved in a car crash and there was a chambermaid from the hotel in the car with him. The following year, Daisy had a little girl, Pammy, and the Buchanans moved around before finally settling in East Egg.

Nick and Jordan leave the Plaza Hotel and drive through Central Park, where Jordan finally reveals Gatsby's request. Gatsby wants Nick to invite Daisy to tea in Nick's house. Gatsby bought his mansion to live across the bay from Daisy and he wants her to see it when she visits Nick. The chapter ends with Nick holding Jordan in his arms.

Chapter 4

MAKE

1. How does Nick describe Meyer Wolfsheim? What do you think his role in the novel is?

2. Write an account of the story Jordan Baker tells Nick about Daisy's life back in Louisville when she was a young woman. What does the story of her marriage reveal about Daisy?

READ

Chapter 5

When Nick arrives home that night, Gatsby walks across his lawn to speak with him. They agree that Nick will invite Daisy to tea. Gatsby attempts to make Nick a business proposition, but Nick cuts him off.

Rain falls on the day that Daisy is expected for tea. Gatsby oversees all arrangements, delivering 'a greenhouse' of flowers to Nick's house and having the grass cut. Daisy arrives at four. When Gatsby enters the living room, there isn't 'a sound'. Both Daisy and Gatsby are extremely nervous and Gatsby knocks a clock off the mantelpiece, but manages to catch it in his 'trembling fingers'. Nick leaves the couple alone and takes shelter from the rain under a 'huge black knotted tree' in his garden. When he returns to the living room, the mood has changed. Daisy's face is 'smeared with tears', while Gatsby glows.

Nick, Daisy and Gatsby go to Gatsby's house. Daisy admires various aspects of the garden. Gatsby points out to her that if it wasn't for the mist, they would be able to see her house across the bay with its 'green light' at the end of the dock. The interior of Gatsby's mansion is opulent. In Chapter 3, Owl Eyes compares Gatsby to the theatrical director, David Belasco, and indeed the mansion is not a home but an extravagant prop. Inside, Gatsby seems 'dazed'. In his bedroom, he takes out 'a pile of shirts' and begins 'throwing them, one by one'. Daisy bends her head into the shirts and begins crying at their beauty.

Nick notices a large photograph of 'an elderly man in yachting costume'. Gatsby says it is Dan Cody, his 'best friend years ago'. Gatsby also has newspaper clippings about Daisy that he has collected over the years. In the music room, Klipspringer, a pianist who lives in Gatsby's mansion, plays for them. He and his guests drink Chartreuse, a bright green liquor. Nick notices an 'expression of bewilderment' on Gatsby's face and reflects that nothing 'can challenge what a man can store up in his ghostly heart'. Gatsby and Daisy, 'possessed by intense life', are barely aware of Nick's departure.

It is worth noting that this chapter is a major turning point in the novel since Gatsby's dream of being reunited with Daisy becomes a reality. It is significant that the reunion is interrupted by a phone call that seems to be from one of Gatsby's business partners. The past Gatsby is desperately trying to recapture is already being affected by the present. In the course of the chapter, he is described as 'an over-wound clock', seeking the future by trying to relive the past.

Single Text

MAKE

Chapter 5

1. Write a brief note on the descriptions of the weather in this chapter. How do these descriptions relate to the plot?

2. Daisy and Gatsby say very little to each other in this chapter. The intensity of their feelings is instead conveyed in gesture and action. Find examples of how Daisy and Gatsby express themselves either in what they do or in their body language.

READ

Chapter 6

The chapter opens with another reflective passage, in which Nick reveals the truth about Gatsby's background, adding that 'he told me all this very much later'.

Gatsby's real name was James Gatz, and he had been born the son of 'shiftless and unsuccessful farm people' from North Dakota. By the time he was seventeen, he had spent over a year along the shore of Lake Superior doing any work that brought him bed and board. His life transformed when he rowed out one day to inform the owner of a yacht that it was anchored in a dangerous place on the lake. The owner was a millionaire named Dan Cody, who took the seventeen year old to work for him. Gatz changed his name to Gatsby and spent five years working for Dan Cody in various capacities until Cody died. Nick informs us that although Gatsby did not get the inheritance Cody had left him, his new identity had been created. Nick then resumes his narrative.

Because Nick is busy spending time with Jordan in New York, he doesn't see Gatsby for several weeks. When he eventually goes over to his house one Sunday, Tom Buchanan also arrives. Buchanan is with a man named Sloane and 'a pretty woman'. They have dropped in for a drink after being out riding. At first Gatsby is uneasy in Tom's company, but he soon gains confidence. The woman invites Nick and Gatsby to supper. Nick declines but Gatsby accepts the offer, not realising that it's not genuine. While Gatsby is getting ready, the others leave without waiting for him.

The following Saturday, Tom accompanies Daisy to one of Gatsby's parties. Nick feels 'an unpleasantness in the air'. Although Daisy and Gatsby dance and spend time alone together, Daisy does not enjoy the party and, at the end of the night, Nick guesses at Gatsby's 'unutterable depression'. Gatsby wants Daisy to tell Tom that she never loved him. He wants her to return to Louisville with him and 'be married from her house', in the Southern tradition, just as if it's five years earlier.

Nick tells Gatsby: 'You can't repeat the past.'

Gatsby replies: 'Why of course you can!'

Chapter 6

1. Why does Nick decide to relate the story of Gatsby's background at this point in the text when he was not actually told the story until later in the summer?

2. During the course of Gatsby's party, Nick is by turns an objective observer, a faithful reporter and an active participant, as well as an imaginative writer. Write a brief note on each of his narrative roles in this part of the chapter.

Chapter 7

Quite suddenly, Gatsby stops hosting parties on Saturday nights. Soon afterwards, he replaces his servants with 'some people Wolfsheim wanted to do something for'. He tells Nick that it's because 'Daisy comes over quite often'.

On the hottest day of the summer, Gatsby invites Nick to lunch at Daisy's house. Jordan is already there. Tom Buchanan is taking a call from Wilson about selling him a car and Daisy thinks that he is talking to his 'girl'. Before lunch, Gatsby is taken aback at meeting Daisy's daughter, Pammy. Afterwards, Daisy tells Gatsby, 'you look so cool', and Tom realises that a relationship exists between them.

The group decide to go to town. On Tom's insistence, he and Gatsby swap cars, although Daisy still opts to go with Gatsby in Tom's coupé, leaving Nick and Jordan to travel with Tom in Gatsby's Rolls-Royce. Tom stops at Wilson's garage to get gas and Wilson tells him that he and Myrtle are going West. Tom promises to sell him his car. As they leave, Nick notices Myrtle, who is Tom's mistress, in a window above the garage and realises that she has mistaken Jordan for Daisy.

Single Text

In New York, the group engage a suite in the Plaza Hotel. The room is 'hot and stifling' and the atmosphere soon becomes tense. Buchanan challenges Gatsby about his background. Gatsby tells Tom that Daisy never loved him, but Tom fights back by making allegations about the source of Gatsby's wealth and reminding Daisy of times when they were close. Daisy becomes upset and tells Gatsby: 'I did love him once – but I loved you too.'

At Tom's suggestion, Daisy and Gatsby leave the hotel to travel back together, this time in Gatsby's yellow Rolls. Nick remembers that it's his birthday. He and Jordan travel back with Tom in the coupé.

At this point, Nick interrupts his own narrative to piece together events that he didn't witness, but heard about later. Michaelis, a 'young Greek' who ran a 'coffee joint' next to Wilson's garage had had a conversation with Wilson earlier that had surprised him, with Wilson telling him that he had locked up his wife and that they were going to move away. Michaelis remembered this because a little after seven, he heard Myrtle shouting before she ran out onto the road and was killed.

In Nick's resumed narrative of his own experiences, as he and Tom and Jordan pass Wilson's garage on the way back from the city, they see a commotion and stop. Myrtle, they hear, has been killed by the driver of a yellow car that didn't stop. Myrtle's body is laid out on a bench and Wilson is distraught.

At the Buchanans' house, Nick declines Jordan's offer to go inside. While he is walking towards the gate to wait for a taxi, he meets Gatsby. In the conversation that ensues between them, Nick discovers that Daisy was driving Gatsby's car when it killed Myrtle. Gatsby is waiting to make sure Daisy is not bothered by Tom about the 'unpleasantness' that afternoon. Nick goes back to the house and checks. Tom and Daisy are sitting at the kitchen table together, with chicken and ale in front of them. Nick leaves Gatsby 'watching over nothing'.

Chapter 7

MAKE

1. Write a brief note on the interaction between Tom, Daisy and Gatsby in the Plaza Hotel. What do they say to each other?

2. The narrative technique of *The Great Gatsby* – the entire story being the memoir of one of the characters – requires that occasionally Nick uses sources outside of his own direct experience to tell the story. What source does he use in order to accurately relay the events surrounding Myrtle's death?

Chapter 8

Nick is unable to sleep. Towards dawn, he hears a taxi going up Gatsby's drive. He dresses and walks across to Gatsby's mansion, where he and Gatsby both hunt for cigarettes. Nick advises Gatsby to leave New York for a week or two, but Gatsby declines. Instead, he tells Nick 'the strange story' of his youth with Dan Cody, how he fell in love with Daisy, 'did extraordinarily well' in the war, received the letter telling him Daisy was married while he was at Oxford, and, penniless, made a miserable journey to Louisville and stayed there a week when he returned to America.

Gatsby and Nick have breakfast and Gatsby tells the gardener not to drain the pool yet. Reluctantly, Nick leaves to catch a train to New York. He shouts back to Gatsby across the lawn: 'They're a rotten crowd … You're worth the whole damn bunch put together.'

In the city, Nick is unable to work. He takes a phone call from Jordan, but there is little communication between them and the phone is hung up with a sharp click.

Travelling past Wilson's garage on the train home, Nick crosses to the other side of the carriage. Again, he interrupts his own narrative to piece together events that he didn't witness, but heard about later. After the accident, Michaelis had sat with Wilson until dawn. Realising that Myrtle had been having an affair, Wilson became convinced that she was murdered by the driver of the yellow car. While staring at the eyes of Doctor T. J. Eckleburg, he claimed he 'had a way of finding out' since 'God sees everything'. After six o'clock, Michaelis went home to get some rest. When he returned four hours later, Wilson was gone. Afterwards, eye-witness accounts traced Wilson's movements to Gad's Hill, after which he disappeared for three hours. At half-past two, he was seen again in West Egg, where he asked someone the way to Gatsby's house.

Resuming his own narrative, Nick describes how he rushes to Gatsby's house and how he, the chauffeur, the butler and the gardener find Gatsby dead, floating on a mattress in his pool with 'Wilson's body a little way off in the grass'.

MAKE

Chapter 8

1. What do you think Nick means when he says to Gatsby 'They're a rotten crowd … You're worth the whole damn bunch put together'?

2. George Wilson looks out at an advertising hoarding erected by an optician and believes the bespectacled eyes of Doctor T. J. Eckleberg to be the eyes of God. What is Fitzgerald telling the reader about symbols?

READ

Chapter 9

The days become 'an endless drill of police and photographers and newspaper men in and out of Gatsby's front door'. At the inquest, Myrtle's sister Catherine swears that her sister was 'into no mischief whatever', and it is accepted that Wilson was simply a man 'deranged by grief'.

Gatsby's affairs are left entirely to Nick to sort out. He tries to phone Daisy but she and Tom have 'gone away … and taken baggage with them'. Gatsby's father, Henry C. Gatz, arrives from Minnesota for the funeral, having read about the death in a newspaper. Nick goes to see Meyer Wolfsheim and asks him to come to Gatsby's funeral, but Wolfsheim refuses. Gatsby's father shows Nick an old book of Gatsby's into which, as a teenager, he wrote a daily schedule and a list of things he should do to improve himself. The only mourners at Gatsby's funeral are Nick, Gatsby's father and 'the man with the owl-eyed glasses' whom Nick had met in Gatsby's library once.

Nick muses that his story is 'a story of the West, after all – Tom and Gatsby, Daisy and Jordan and I were all Westerners'. After Gatsby's death, the East is 'haunted' for Nick and he decides to return home, amid vivid memories of coming back West from prep school as a boy, and later college as a young man, at Christmas-time. Before he leaves, he meets Jordan, and 'half in love with her and tremendously sorry', he ends the relationship.

On Fifth Avenue one afternoon in October, Nick meets Tom Buchanan. He refuses to shake Buchanan's hand and asks him what he said to Wilson on that fateful afternoon. Tom stares at Nick without a word and Nick realises he has guessed right about those missing hours. Tom admits telling Wilson where Gatsby lived and feels justified in his actions. He believes Gatsby was driving on the night that Myrtle was killed and that Gatsby 'never even stopped his car'. The meeting ends in a handshake as Nick accepts that there's no point telling the truth, since Tom and Daisy are just 'careless people'.

The novel ends with Nick recalling his last evening in West Egg, how he had gone over to Gatsby's house and thought about what the first settlers saw when they had reached America, and about Gatsby's dream, and about all our quests to reach the future even as we are 'borne back ceaselessly into the past'.

MAKE

Chapter 9

1. What do you think Nick means by his comment that his story is 'a story of the West, after all – Tom and Gatsby, Daisy and Jordan and I were all Westerners'?

2. The novel ends with Nick standing on the beach imagining the first settlers' vision of America as a new world. How does this vision relate to both the character of Gatsby and to the exploration of the American dream in the novel?

Characters

Nick Caraway

It is important to recognise that *The Great Gatsby* is first and foremost a book about a man writing a book. This frames the presentation of all the other characters in the story, and the relationships between them.

Originally from Minnesota, Nick travels to New York in 1922 to learn the bond business. He is a young man – he turns thirty that summer – a Yale graduate and veteran of the First World War. Nick rents a 'cardboard bungalow' in the West Egg district of Long Island, next door to the mansion of a man named Jay Gatsby. Nick is Daisy's 'second cousin once removed' and he knew Tom Buchanan in college. This enables him both to facilitate and observe the love affair that rekindles between Daisy and Gatsby. As a result of his relationship to these two characters, Nick is the perfect choice to narrate the novel, which functions as a personal memoir of his experiences in the summer of 1922.

Nick is also well suited to narrating *The Great Gatsby* because of his temperament. As he tells the reader in Chapter 1: 'I'm inclined to reserve all judgements.' Because of this, people talk to him and tell him their secrets. Gatsby, in particular, comes to trust him and treat him as a confidant. Nick generally assumes a secondary role throughout the novel, preferring to describe and comment on events rather than dominate the action. His position, established at the outset of the novel, as a writer, enables him to meditate deeply on events and to use highly descriptive language. Fitzgerald has attributed to him a certain amount of self-consciousness as a writer. But the mystery at the heart of the novel remains unresolved – What drives a solid Midwesterner, with apparently old-fashioned values, to write a lyrical account of a man tragically obsessed with a youthful love affair?

In Chapter 3, Nick says: 'I am one of the few honest people that I have ever known.' This self-proclaimed honesty is something readers should question. He may not consciously depart from telling the truth, as he sees it, but he has blind spots and seems to suppress or play down certain aspects of events to suit his own purpose.

From the opening page of the novel, Nick is riven with a powerful internal conflict. On the one hand, Gatsby represents for him 'everything for which I have an unaffected scorn' while, on the other hand, he says of Gatsby that 'there was something gorgeous about him'. This internal conflict exists is all aspects of Nick's life – in his attitude to the East, in his enthusiasm for his job and in his relationship with Jordan Baker. In Chapter 2, after drinking heavily, Nick describes himself as 'within and without, simultaneously enchanted and repelled by the inexhaustible variety of life'. He is conflicted until the end of the novel when, having gained maturity and insight, he returns to Minnesota in search of a quieter life structured by more traditional moral values. Despite his dismay at his thinning hair and diminishing prospects, Nick finds purpose in his own life and devotes himself to the creative task of writing the story of Jay Gatsby.

Jay Gatsby

The title character of *The Great Gatsby* is a young man, around thirty years old, who rose from an impoverished childhood in rural North Dakota to become fabulously wealthy. However, it appears that he achieved this lofty goal by participating in organised crime. Though Gatsby has always wanted to be rich, his main motivation in acquiring his fortune was his love for Daisy Fay, whom he met as a young military officer in Louisville before leaving in 1917 to fight in the First World War. Gatsby immediately fell in love with Daisy's aura of luxury, grace and charm, and lied to her about his own background in order to convince her that he was good enough for her. Daisy promised to wait for him when he left for the war, but married Tom Buchanan in 1919, while Gatsby was studying at Oxford after the war. From that moment on, Gatsby dedicated himself to winning Daisy back, and his acquisition of millions of dollars, his purchase of a gaudy mansion on West Egg, and his lavish weekly parties, are all merely means to that end.

Gatsby's reputation in the novel precedes him – he does not appear in a speaking role until Chapter 3 when Nick first meets him. Gatsby uses the Anglophile term 'old sport', which he affects throughout the novel. Nick notes that Gatsby has 'one of those rare smiles with a quality of eternal reassurance in it'. But he also perceives a rough reality beneath his cultivated charm and even a risk of absurdity in the precariousness of his image. It is Gatsby's 'extraordinary gift for hope' that ultimately draws Nick to him. Fitzgerald contrasts the energy of Gatsby's desire with the apathy and cynicism of those around him. Daisy, still in her early twenties, complains that she has 'been everywhere and seen everything and done everything'.

Fitzgerald initially presents Gatsby (through Nick's account) as the aloof, enigmatic host of the unbelievably opulent parties thrown every week at his mansion. He appears surrounded by spectacular luxury, courted by powerful men and beautiful women. He is the subject of a whirlwind of gossip throughout New York and is already a kind of legendary celebrity before he is ever introduced to the reader. Fitzgerald propels the novel forward through the early chapters by shrouding Gatsby's background and the source of his wealth in mystery. As a result, the reader's first, distant impressions of Gatsby strike quite a different note from that of the lovesick, naïve young man who emerges during the later part of the novel.

Fitzgerald uses this technique of delayed character revelation to emphasise the theatrical quality of Gatsby's approach to life, which is an important part of his personality. Gatsby has literally created his own character, even changing his name from James Gatz to Jay Gatsby to represent this reinvention of himself. As his relentless quest for Daisy demonstrates, Gatsby has an extraordinary ability to transform his hopes and dreams into reality; at the beginning of the novel, he appears to the reader just as he desires to appear to the world. This talent for self-invention is what gives Gatsby his quality of 'greatness'. Even the title – *The Great Gatsby* – carries a suggestion of the stage magicians who practise an art of illusion.

As the novel progresses, Gatsby reveals himself to be an innocent, hopeful young man who stakes everything on his dreams, not realising that his dreams are unworthy of him. Gatsby invests Daisy with an idealistic perfection that she cannot possibly attain in reality and pursues her with a passionate zeal that blinds him to her limitations. His dream of her disintegrates, revealing the corruption that wealth causes and the unworthiness of the goal.

Daisy Fay Buchanan

Daisy is a beautiful young woman from Louisville, Kentucky. She is Nick's cousin and the object of Gatsby's love. As a young debutante in Louisville, Daisy was extremely popular among the military officers stationed near her home, including Jay Gatsby. Gatsby won Daisy's heart, and they fell in love before Gatsby left to fight in the war. Daisy promised to wait for Gatsby but, in 1919, she chose instead to marry Tom Buchanan, a young man from a wealthy, aristocratic family.

After 1919, Gatsby dedicated himself to winning Daisy back, making her the single goal of all of his dreams and the main motivation behind his acquisition of immense wealth. To Gatsby, Daisy represents perfection. Her voice is repeatedly referred to as holding the key to her character and, in Chapter 7, Gatsby notes that her voice is 'full of money'. In reality, however, Daisy falls far short of Gatsby's ideals. She is beautiful and charming, but she is also shallow. Nick characterises her as a careless person who smashes things up and then retreats behind her money. Daisy proves her real nature when she chooses Tom over Gatsby in Chapter 7, then allows Gatsby to take the blame for killing Myrtle Wilson even though she herself was driving the car. Finally, rather than attend Gatsby's funeral, Daisy and Tom move away, leaving no forwarding address.

In Fitzgerald's conception of America in the 1920s, Daisy represents the amoral values of wealth. She is in love with money, ease and material luxury. She is capable of affection – she seems genuinely fond of Nick, occasionally seems to love Gatsby sincerely and, according to Jordan Baker, was in love with Tom after they married. She is, however, incapable of sustained loyalty or care.

Tom Buchanan

Powerfully built and coming from a wealthy old family, Tom is an arrogant, hypocritical bully. His social attitudes are laced with racism and sexism, and he never even considers trying to live up to the moral standard he demands from those around him. In Chapter 1, he draws support for his racist views from a recently published book, Goddard's *The Rise of Coloured Empires* and, in Chapter 6, he remarks: 'I may be old-fashioned in my ideas, but women run around too much these days to suit me.' Tom has no moral qualms about his own extramarital affair with Myrtle, but when he begins to suspect Daisy and Gatsby of having an affair, he becomes outraged and forces a confrontation. In Chapter 1, Daisy refers to Tom as 'hulking', which seems an appropriate word to describe a man whose characterisation is developed from the initial description of him in the first chapter as having 'a cruel body'.

Pammy Buchanan

Pammy is the three-year-old daughter of Tom and Daisy Buchanan. Little mention is made of her, but she represents the children of the Jazz Agers. In Chapter 1, Daisy tells Nick what she felt when Pammy was born: 'I hope she'll be a fool – that's the best thing a girl can be in this world, a beautiful little fool.'

Jordan Baker

Jordan is a friend of Daisy. They grew up together in Louisville. Jordan is two years younger than Daisy and so at the time the novel is set, she is twenty-one. A competitive golfer, she represents one of the new young women of the 1920s – cynical, boyish and self-centred. Jordan is beautiful and modern and her name combines the names of two makes of car. During the course of the novel, Jordan becomes romantically involved with Nick. In Chapter 3, Nick remembers a news report concerning Jordan cheating at golf, and concludes: 'She was incurably dishonest.'

Myrtle Wilson

Myrtle is the wife of George Wilson and the mistress of Tom Buchanan. When Nick meets her in Chapter 2, he describes her as 'in the middle thirties, and faintly stout, but she carried her flesh sensuously, as some women can'. She and her husband live in relative poverty in the 'valley of ashes' but, through her affair with Tom, she gains entry into the world of the rich, and the change in her personality as a result is remarkable. She conducts a secret life with Tom, wherein she exhibits all the power and dominance she finds lacking in her everyday life. She eventually suffers a tragic end when she is killed by a car driven by Daisy.

George Wilson

George is Myrtle's husband. He runs an 'unprosperous' garage and gas station in the 'valley of ashes' and seems resigned to a life of misery. He is described as 'a blond, spiritless man, anaemic and faintly handsome'. When he discovers that his wife is having an affair, his response – to lock her in her bedroom – helps drive her to her death. Distraught at what happens, Wilson becomes Fitzgerald's way of expressing the despair prevalent in the seemingly trapped lower-middle class.

Catherine

Catherine is Myrtle's sister. She is aware of her sister's secret life and willing to partake in its benefits. The description given of her in Chapter 2 is a perfect example of Fitzgerald's mastery in characterisation: 'The sister, Catherine, was a slender, worldly girl of about thirty, with a solid, sticky bob of red hair, and a complexion powdered milky white. Her eyebrows had been plucked and then drawn on again at a more rakish angle but the efforts of nature towards the restoration of the old alignment gave a blurred air to her face.'

Meyer Wolfsheim

Meyer Wolfsheim is Gatsby's business associate. Nick and Gatsby have lunch with him in Chapter 4. A professional gambler, Wolfsheim is attributed with fixing the 1919 World Series. Wolfsheim helped build Gatsby's fortune, although the wealth came through questionable means.

Michaelis

Michaelis is the Wilsons' young Greek neighbour who 'ran the coffee joint beside the ashheaps'. He comforts George Wilson after Myrtle is killed and is one of the few charitable people to be found in the novel.

Ewing Klipspringer

Klipspringer is convivially known as Gatsby's 'boarder'. He plays the piano for Gatsby and Daisy in Chapter 5. He is a quintessential leech, a representative of the people who frequented Gatsby's parties. After Gatsby's death, he phones the house to request that a pair of shoes he left behind be forwarded to him. Nick hangs up the phone.

Dan Cody

Dan Cody was Gatsby's wealthy mentor. They met when Gatsby, a young drifter, swam out to tell him that his yacht was anchored in a dangerous spot on Lake Superior. Cody took Gatsby under his wing and taught him much about living adventurously and pursuing dreams.

Henry C. Gatz

Henry C. Gatz is the father of Jay Gatsby. He reads about his son's death in a newspaper and comes from the Midwest to attend the funeral. Gatz serves as a very tangible reminder of Gatsby's humble roots. He also provides Nick with a poignant insight into Gatsby, the teenager who wanted so much to make something of himself.

Themes

ANALYSE

On the most straightforward level, *The Great Gatsby* can be read as a love story. On another level, it can also be read as a social satire, mocking the shallowness, hypocrisy and greed of the Jazz Age. In 1945, yet another level was opened up by the American literary critic Lionel Trilling, who argued that Jay Gatsby stands for America itself.

The novel therefore has a wide range of themes including love, idealism and the American dream, and memory and the past.

Love

The Great Gatsby does not offer a definition of love, or a contrast between love and romance, but it does suggest that what people believe to be love is often only a dream. Gatsby thinks he loves Daisy when, in fact, he loves a memory of her. Daisy, too, thinks she loves Gatsby, but she really loves

being adored. Our narrator, Nick Carraway, is 'half' in love with Jordan at the end of the novel, but recognises the impossibility of being with her. Love is also a source of conflict in *The Great Gatsby*, driving men to fight and ultimately causing three deaths. This novel seems to argue that there is a violence and destruction inherent in love.

Connected to the theme of love is another – that of vision, the ability to see clearly. Doctor T. J. Eckleburg's advertising hoarding is a powerful symbol of this. The billboard assumes significance at the end of the novel, when George Wilson mistakes the eyes for those of an omniscient God. Fitzgerald seems to suggest that materialism has blinded people to real values in modern America, including love.

Idealism and the American Dream

The American literary critic Lionel Trilling argued that, in a sense, Gatsby is America, and it is certainly the case that an overarching concern of the novel is the condition of America in the early twentieth century. Fitzgerald is examining the fate of American ideals during a period when the aspirations expressed in the Declaration of Independence were under threat from the pressures of modern life. He depicts a society that is riven by class distinctions, dramatically rendered in the different fortunes of Tom Buchanan, residing in fashionable East Egg, and George Wilson, trapped in the dismal 'valley of ashes'. The conception of America nurtured by Thomas Jefferson was of an agrarian society, but the census of 1920 showed that America had become a predominantly urban nation for the first time.

Also, America was to be a peace-loving nation, but Fitzgerald stresses the significance to his characters of the First World War. *The Great Gatsby* portrays a society in which individuals have become regimented during wartime, and subjected to prohibition laws during peacetime. We are told in Chapter 8 that, as a young officer, Jay Gatsby, 'was liable at the whim of an impersonal government to be blown anywhere about the world'. More generally, the novel shows the emergence of a mass society with pressure placed upon individual integrity from such sources as advertising and fashion, through images spread by cinema and magazines.

Fitzgerald portrays the 1920s as an era of decayed social and moral values, evidenced in its cynicism, greed and empty pursuit of pleasure. The reckless jubilance that led to decadent parties and wild jazz music – epitomised in *The Great Gatsby* by the opulent parties that Gatsby throws every Saturday night – resulted ultimately in the corruption of the American dream, as the unrestrained desire for money and pleasure surpassed more noble goals.

As Fitzgerald saw it – and as Nick explains in Chapter 9 – the American dream was originally about discovery, individualism and the pursuit of happiness. In the 1920s depicted in the novel, however, easy money and relaxed social values have corrupted this dream, especially on the east coast. The main plotline of the novel reflects this assessment, as Gatsby's dream of loving Daisy is ruined by the difference in their respective social statuses, his resorting to crime to make enough money to impress her and the rampant materialism that characterises her lifestyle. The idealism of the Founding Fathers has mutated into a consumerist ideology – 'liberty' and 'the pursuit of happiness' have become a series of choices about where to play golf or what shirts to buy.

Gatsby attributes to Daisy a kind of idealised perfection that she neither deserves nor possesses. His dream is ruined by the unworthiness of its object, just as the American dream in the 1920s is ruined by the unworthiness of its object – money and pleasure. Like 1920s Americans in general, fruitlessly seeking a bygone era in which their dreams had value, Gatsby longs to recreate a vanished past – his time in Louisville with Daisy – but is incapable of doing so. When his dream crumbles, all that is left for Gatsby to do is die, and all Nick can do is move back to Minnesota where American values have not decayed.

Memory and the Past

The speculation about Gatsby's past is part of a larger thematic concern in *The Great Gatsby* with reconstruction of past events. It is evident from the novel that recollection is inextricably linked to point of view. So, the past may exist in different versions according to whose memory is involved.

The novel deals at great length with issues of the past, present and future. In love with a girl from his past, Gatsby is unable to have her again in the present. He wants a future with her, but only if she will lie to erase the marriage in her past. The narrator indicates in the final lines of the text that nobody can ever reach the future – it is a beacon of light that calls to us, but even as we try to reach it, we are beaten back into the past. The manipulation of time in the narrative adds to this theme. Nick tells the whole tale with a tone of nostalgia, beginning the text with mention of his father's advice to him in his youth.

In Chapter 6, when Nick tells Gatsby: 'You can't repeat the past', Gatsby replies: 'Why of course you can!', illustrating a capacity to delude himself. Gatsby envisages his future in terms of an event that is irretrievably in the past. He envisages a future time when he can live perpetually in the intensity of that moment when he fell in love with Daisy. Fitzgerald suggests a parallel between that self-deluding obsession and a sense of the past that is evident in American culture more generally. The ideal American future has been cast frequently as a return to that simple but pure past when the first settlers arrived on the continent, encountering, as Nick describes it at the end of the novel, 'a fresh, green breast of the new world'. The final words of the novel compare people to boats struggling against the current, 'borne back ceaselessly into the past'. However strong our desire, we cannot arrest the inexorable passage of time.

Style

Narration

As narrator of the novel, Fitzgerald employs Nick Carraway, who is a participant in the story, but is more of a spectator than an actor. This creates a complex point of view which involves the reader in acts of interpretation that necessarily extend to making judgements about the narrator. The character of the protagonist, Jay Gatsby, is filtered through Nick's narration at a pace that sustains our interest without dispelling an element of mystery. So as we are piecing together the puzzle of Gatsby, we are inevitably adjusting our sense of the man who is telling Gatsby's story.

By making Nick a writer, Fitzgerald combines an authorial capacity to comment and to pass judgement with the involved immediacy of the first-person voice. So we find him making carefully formulated and considered remarks such as: 'Instead of rambling, this party had preserved a dignified homogeneity, and assumed to itself the function of representing the staid nobility of the countryside – East Egg condescending to West Egg and carefully on guard against its spectroscopic gaiety' (Chapter 3). Then, a few pages after this wry commentary, we find Nick thoroughly caught up in events: 'I was enjoying myself now. I had taken two finger-bowls of champagne, and the scene had changed before my eyes into something significant, elemental, and profound.'

Nick is still concerned to impress upon us the importance of events occurring in the narrative, but his seriousness is lightened by the image of his own light-headedness, and by the immediate sense of his own pleasure.

However, although the point of view held by Nick Carraway dominates the novel, we are not allowed to forget that other viewpoints are possible. Tom Buchanan's view of Gatsby and Henry C. Gatz's view of his son are included in the account, for example, and show how different the views of a single individual may be.

Dialogue

Narrating the story from Carraway's point of view, Fitzgerald must have been acutely aware of certain dangers. For example, the voice of the narrator might have become monotonous, his manner of expression too insistent and self-conscious. Fitzgerald avoids this pitfall by having Nick create dramatic exchanges in dialogue. As he writes his account, he mimics the idiosyncrasies of a range of voices. For example, Gatsby has the affectation of a nervous Anglophile, while Wolfsheim's voice is blatantly stylised as stereotypically Jewish: 'I understand you're looking for a business gonnegtion.'

Symbolism

Through the wealth of detail provided by Nick's narrative, Fitzgerald has created an atmosphere of symbolism in which any object may resonate with additional significance. So, a shirt is not just a functional item of clothing, but is made to carry the weight of social class and of cosmopolitan sophistication. Similarly, a car is not just a vehicle, it is also a symbol of social mobility, with large, flamboyant automobiles declaring the superiority of their drivers over the owners of more mundane ones. This kind of symbolic value is by no means an exclusively literary device – it is the essence of advertising, that modern practice of generating desires, which features centrally in the novel.

Fitzgerald was also interested in the way that symbolism could produce a kind of magical transformation in which the physical world might, through an act of imagination, come to assume the quality of the ideal. So, towards the end of *The Great Gatsby*, when Gatsby's aspirations have been shattered by events, he sees the world no longer filtered through symbolism and so robbed of its power of enchantment. Nick remarks: 'He must have looked up at an unfamiliar sky through frightening leaves and shivered as he found what a grotesque thing a rose is and how raw the sunlight was upon the scarcely created grass.'

There are numerous symbols in the novel – the most prevalent being the eyes of Doctor T. J. Eckleburg, the green light and the 'valley of ashes'.

The Eyes of Doctor T. J. Eckleburg

The eyes of Doctor T. J. Eckleburg are a pair of fading, bespectacled eyes painted on an old advertising billboard over the valley of ashes. They may represent God staring down upon and judging American society as a moral wasteland, though the novel never makes this point explicitly. Instead, throughout the novel, Fitzgerald suggests that symbols only have meaning because characters give them meaning. The connection between the eyes of Doctor T. J. Eckleburg and God exists only in George Wilson's grief-stricken mind. This lack of concrete significance contributes to the unsettling nature of the image. Thus, the eyes also come to represent the essential meaninglessness of the world and the arbitrariness of the mental process by which people invest objects with meaning. Nick explores these ideas in Chapter 8, when he imagines Gatsby's final thoughts as a depressed consideration of the emptiness of symbols and dreams.

The Green Light

Fitzgerald also uses the familiar associations of symbols in ironic ways. Green symbolises nature, fertility and growth. But that symbolic resonance is used ironically when Fitzgerald writes of a green electric light at the end of the Buchanans' dock. The green light represents Gatsby's hopes and dreams for the future. He associates it with Daisy, and, in Chapter 1, he reaches towards it in the darkness as a guiding light to lead him to his goal. Because Gatsby's quest for Daisy is broadly associated with the American dream, the green light also symbolises that more generalised ideal. In Chapter 9, Nick compares the green light to how America, rising out of the ocean, must have looked to early settlers of the new nation.

The Valley of Ashes

First introduced in Chapter 2, the 'valley of ashes' between West Egg and New York City consists of a long stretch of desolate land created by the dumping of industrial ashes. It represents the moral and social decay that results from the uninhibited pursuit of wealth, as the rich indulge themselves without regard for anything but their own pleasure. The valley of ashes also symbolises the plight of the poor, like George Wilson, who live among the dirty ashes and lose their vitality as a result.

Imagery

The novel is written in highly descriptive language. There are numerous image patterns – the most prevalent being colour, light and weather.

Colours – notably green, white and gold – recur regularly, often applied to very different objects. The familiar associations of these colours are modified as the images appear in differing contexts. Thus, white is the colour of the 'palaces' of the wealthy, of the 'ashen dust' that coats George Wilson's clothes and of Daisy's 'white girlhood' in Louisville.

Light creates a poetic effect in the novel. Short, descriptive passages punctuate the narrative, creating atmosphere in the same way a film director might do with lighting: 'I sat on the front steps with them while they waited for their car. It was dark here; only the bright door sent ten square feet of light volleying out into the soft black morning. Sometimes a shadow moved against a dressing-room blind above, gave way to another shadow, an indefinite procession of shadows, that rouged and powdered in an invisible glass' (Chapter 6).

The novel also develops a contrast between natural and artificial light. Gatsby's meeting with Daisy in Chapter 5 is poetically organised around an interplay between real and artificial light. When Nick returns, Daisy and Gatsby have had their chat: 'He literally glowed; without a word or gesture of exultation a new wellbeing radiated from him and filled the little room.' And when it stops raining, Gatsby 'smiled like a weather man, like an ecstatic patron of recurrent light'. Later Gatsby declares: 'My house looks well, doesn't it? … See how the whole front of it catches the light.' Meanwhile the buttons on Daisy's dress 'gleamed in the sunlight'. The key question about Gatsby is being posed – is he a natural being, a genuine bringer of sunshine, or is the light that he brings to Daisy and Nick artificial, an effect produced by money rather than personality?

Weather is also used in the novel as a signifier of the emotional tone of the story. Gatsby and Daisy's reunion begins amid pouring rain, creating an atmosphere of melancholy, while their love reawakens just as the sun begins to come out. Gatsby's climactic confrontation with

Tom Buchanan occurs on the hottest day of the summer, under the scorching sun. On the first day of autumn, despite a palpable chill in the air, Gatsby floats in his swimming pool, symbolising his desire to stop time and restore his relationship with Daisy to the way it was five years earlier, in 1917. Ironically, it's also the day Wilson kills him.

Poetic Language

In *The Great Gatsby*, Fitzgerald uses language in a heightened way to intensify the atmospheric quality of the novel. The following techniques are particularly notable.

Alliteration

'Under the **d**ripping bare **l**ilac-trees a **l**arge open car was coming up the **d**rive. It stopped. **D**aisy's face, tipped sideways beneath a three-cornered **l**avender hat, **l**ooked at me with a bright ecstatic smile.' (Chapter 5)

Simile

'A damp streak of hair lay **like** a dash of blue paint across her cheek.' (Chapter 5)

Metaphor

'This is a **valley of ashes** – a fantastic farm where **ashes** grow like wheat into ridges and hills and grotesque gardens; where **ashes** take the forms of houses and chimneys and rising smoke and, finally, with a transcendent effort, of ash-grey men who move dimly and already crumbling through powdery air.' (Chapter 2)

Foreshadowing

On leaving Gatsby's party in Chapter 3, Nick witnesses a car accident: 'In the ditch beside the road, right side up, but violently shorn of one wheel, rested a new coupé.' This foreshadows the accident that kills Myrtle in Chapter 7.

Since the introduction of the new syllabus, *The Great Gatsby* has been a prescribed as a Single Text in 2013, 2015 and 2016. The following questions were on the examination paper in 2013.

(i) 'Readers of *The Great Gatsby* are greatly influenced by the narrator, Nick Carraway.'

Discuss this statement, supporting your answer with suitable reference to the text.

OR

(ii) 'Readers often find aspects of *The Great Gatsby* attractive but ultimately the world of the novel is not admirable.'

Discuss this view, supporting your answer with suitable reference to the text.

Comparative Study

Option 1: All My Sons
Juno
Foster

Option 2: Othello
Rear Window
The Fault in Our Stars

Option 3: A Doll's House
The King's Speech
The Uncommon Reader

Introduction

What is the Comparative Study?

The Comparative Study was introduced into the Leaving Certificate syllabus to bring variety to the manner in which texts are studied at Leaving Certificate level and to give students another perspective on the potential of literature in their lives. Studying texts comparatively invites students to interact with the different imaginative worlds encountered and to make discriminations and evaluations. The Comparative Study is worth 70 marks out of 200 on Paper 2.

In answers to comparative questions, students may compare and/or contrast – address similarities and/or differences in – both the content and style of their chosen texts. In shaping their responses to the questions set on the Comparative Study, it is expected that students will be involved in some/all of the following kinds of activities:

- Description/analysis of the text(s) in the light of the modes for comparison.
- Making general observations about the texts in relation to each other.
- Making connections between similar aspects of texts.
- Recognising differences between texts.
- Showing that similarities/differences need to be qualified.
- Demonstrating awareness of themselves as readers, their reaction/responses/involvement.

Three texts are selected from a prescribed list of plays, novels, autobiographies and films for study according to set comparative modes. The modes of comparison for Higher Level Leaving Certificate 2017 are:

- Theme or issue
- The general vision and viewpoint
- Literary genre.

Theme or Issue

This mode invites the student to select *one* theme that has some commonality to all three texts that the student has chosen to study, and to compare and contrast the treatment of that theme in the texts. It is important to consider how exploring a particular theme adds to the impact of a text and allows for interesting comparisons.

A *theme* is a unifying idea or motif repeated or developed throughout a work. This means that it must be one of the **central concerns** of the text. At its simplest, an *issue* means a topic of interest or discussion, but clearly what is meant is a topic that is consistently treated throughout the text. For the purposes of the Leaving Certificate examination, the terms *theme* and *issue* are understood to mean the same thing. Popular themes that students select to explore include: deception, romantic love, family, identity, humanity, power, self-realisation and relationships.

The General Vision and Viewpoint

Vision and viewpoint refers to the broad outlook on life presented in the text. The most essential question relates to how the text ends. Does the text end on an optimistic or pessimistic note? You can then consider how this ending relates to the beginning of the text. Have we advanced? Have we regressed? Has the author suggested that society/people can or cannot change? This mode explores the general messages about life that texts communicate to us. Many of these messages are the same, even among texts with very different plots. Some common messages in texts are:

- The triumph of the individual against adversity.
- Love conquers all.
- The destruction of the individual by society.
- The truth will prevail.
- You reap what you sow.

Be aware of the fact that not all texts have a coherent vision and viewpoint. Literature and films are the product of the world from which they come. Texts that date from before the First World War often have more coherent messages since the philosophical understanding of the world then was of a place of structure and order. Hence Shakespearean plays or novels by Jane Austen tend to carry a coherent vision, whether it be that the truth will always prevail or that love conquers all. Texts written in the twentieth and twenty-first centuries – after world wars, the Holocaust, environmental destruction and technological revolution – tend to be far less coherent in terms of their vision, often carrying messages that contradict each other. For example, in *A Doll's House* by Henrik Ibsen the general vision and viewpoint is both bleak – depicting the subservient position of women in society – and hopeful – Nora's departure from home signifying an impending change in the position of women in society. Remember also that the way the reader/viewer responds to the vision of a text is not something the author/director can control. For example, a reader/viewer may not like romantic comedies. He may think they are formulaic, predictable, simplistic and saccharine. So, even though the person who created it might want the reader to respond positively to the vision they are offering, the reader probably won't.

The general vision and viewpoint of a text is communicated through style – imagery, symbols, foreshadowing, camera angles, music, etc. – as well as setting, character and plot.

Literary Genre

This mode focuses on the ways that texts tell their stories. The word *genre* simply means *kind*, *category* or *sort*. So, in discussing literary genre, we are asking and answering the following questions:

- How is the story told? (Who tells it? When and where is it told?)
- Why is the story told in this way?
- Is there one plot or many plots? How do these relate?
- What are the major tensions in the texts? Are they resolved or not?
- Is the story humorous or tragic, romantic or realistic?
- To what genres to the texts belong?
- How do the experiences of encountering a novel, a play and a film differ?

What kind of work is this? What category does it fall into? Initially, the best way to understand the whole concept is to apply it to something that you're already very familiar with, for example, television soaps or detective fiction or western films or situation comedy or pantomime. These are all immediately recognisable genres in contemporary culture. In our society, a child could distinguish between them and would not confuse one with the other. No one watching *Coronation Street* is either going to refer to it as a western or, more importantly for our purposes, going to discuss it in the same terms that they would use to discuss a western. Further, if you ask yourself what makes one genre so distinct from another, you will be well on the way to providing yourself with all the materials you need to discuss literary genre.

Each genre – or type of text – has some technique available to it that is either not available to or not quite as important in other genres. For instance, films tells their stories largely through flickering images on a screen, stage plays tell their stories almost entirely through the spoken word or dialogue, and prose works (novels, short stories and memoirs) rely on their access to a character's thoughts or reflections to advance and deepen the story. In writing an essay on literary genre as part of the Comparative Study, you are exploring the various **techniques**

Comparative Study

employed by the author/director in order to create a text, and how these techniques are both similar and different to each other. Remember that different techniques often produce similar effects. For example, in a novel an author may create setting with a descriptive passage, while in a play the playwright may create setting through stage directions, while finally in a film the director may create setting with a long panning shot over a scene.

How much Time should I Spend on each Question?

The general rule for English Higher Level Paper 2 is to allocate one minute of writing time for each mark available. Section II, The Comparative Study, is worth 70 marks, and you have 70 minutes to answer it. If you choose to answer the two-part question, you should allocate 30 minutes for the 30-mark question and 40 minutes for the 40-mark question.

Remember, you are not expected to use all of the time writing your answers. You also need time to read the questions carefully and to plan your answers.

How should I Use this Textbook to Prepare for the Examination Questions?

In this textbook, nine of the prescribed texts for Comparative Study 2017 have been selected and grouped into options as follows:

- Option 1: *All My Sons* by Arthur Miller, *Juno* (film), *Foster* by Claire Keegan

- Option 2: *Othello* by William Shakespeare, *Rear Window* (film), *The Fault in Our Stars* by John Green

- Option 3: *A Doll's House* by Henrik Ibsen, *The King's Speech* (film), *The Uncommon Reader* by Alan Bennett

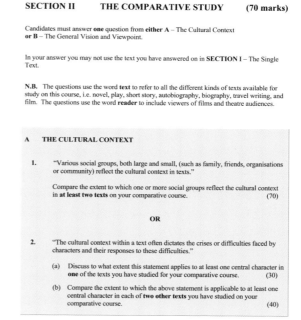

SECTION II   THE COMPARATIVE STUDY   (70 marks)

Candidates must answer **one** question from either **A** – The Cultural Context or **B** – The General Vision and Viewpoint.

In your answer you may not use the text you have answered on in **SECTION I** – The Single Text.

N.B. The questions use the word **text** to refer to all the different kinds of texts available for study on this course, i.e. novel, play, short story, autobiography, biography, travel writing, and film. The questions use the word **reader** to include viewers of films and theatre audiences.

A   THE CULTURAL CONTEXT

1.   "Various social groups, both large and small, (such as family, friends, organisations or community) reflect the cultural context in texts."

Compare the extent to which one or more social groups reflect the cultural context in **at least two texts** on your comparative course.   (70)

OR

2.   "The cultural context within a text often dictates the crises or difficulties faced by characters and their responses to these difficulties."

(a)   Discuss to what extent this statement applies to at least one central character in **one** of the texts you have studied for your comparative course.   (30)

(b)   Compare the extent to which the above statement is applicable to at least one central character in each of **two other texts** you have studied on your comparative course.   (40)

You should select **one** option to study. **Note, however, that Option 2 is designed for students who do not opt to study *Hamlet* as their Single Text.**

Each option offers a comprehensive summary of the texts, a detailed discussion of each in relation to the modes of comparison set for 2017 – Theme, General Vision and Viewpoint and Literary Genre – as well as a guide to answering examination questions on each of the modes and a link to further material – lists of DVDs, books and websites relating to the texts – at www.educateplus.ie.

Things to Remember when Preparing for the Comparative Study Essay

You must have a detailed knowledge of your three texts. In other words, you must know the following in relation to each:

- the genre, or category, that the text falls into (e.g. biography, realistic fiction, Shakespearean stage drama, etc.)
- the historical setting – where and when the action takes place
- what exactly happens and in what sequence it happens
- the names and personalities of the main characters
- the relationships between the main characters.

Your task is to write an integrated essay-style answer in which you note with consistent reference to the question, the similarities and differences between the texts and link them using examples from the texts. The best way of doing this is to focus on key moments in the texts. Key moments are extracts from texts that you choose to study in a detailed way (a few paragraphs, a speech, 3–4 minutes of film). Key moments are often found in the opening of texts (exposition), at the high point of texts (climax) and at the end of texts (resolution).

The most important things to remember are:

- understand clearly your modes of comparison
- you must plan your answer before you begin
- open each paragraph with a topic sentence relating to some aspect of the question
- compare your texts in each paragraph
- don't summarise your texts – refer to key moments to support your points.

Remember, it is important not to over-simplify the connections you make between texts. Similarities/differences between texts may need to be qualified. Also, demonstrate an awareness of yourself as a reader. What did you think of the texts?

Throughout your discussion, you can use the following terms to demonstrate to the examiner that you are consistently comparing and contrasting the texts:

Comparative Study

TERMS USED TO DENOTE SIMILARITY	TERMS USED TO DENOTE DISSIMILARITY
Likewise	By contrast
Similarly	On the other hand
In the same way	However
Also	Whereas this is black, the other is blue
There is a parallel between	There is a distinct difference
There is a resemblance between	There is no comparison between
There is an analogy between	As different as chalk and cheese
They are alike	Totally dissimilar
Identical	Totally unlike
Equivalent to	The antithesis of
Corresponds with	The reverse of
Equally	The opposite of
One and the same	At variance with

Writing a Comparative Study Essay

- Keep your introduction short – answer the question, define the mode, introduce your texts and give a brief outline of your intentions.
- The rest of the essay consists of paragraphs, and paragraphs are developed from topic sentences, each of which relates both to some aspect of the question being discussed and some aspect of the mode being explored, such as narrative technique in a literary genre essay, for instance, or presentation of theme in the exposition in a theme essay.'
- In each paragraph analyse the texts in relation to the topic sentence, drawing comparisons and contrasts as you move between texts.
- Be consistent in addressing the question you are answering.
- Offer a brief synopsis of your points in the conclusion and offer a personal opinion of the texts, in relation to the mode you are discussing.

Film Studies

'Every time I go to a movie, it's magic, no matter what the movie's about.'

Steven Spielberg

The study of film as a comparative element is an option in the English syllabus. There are seven films on offer for the 2017 Leaving Certificate, ranging from the Alfred Hitchcock classic *Rear Window* to the 2007 American 'Indie' film *Juno*. Film studies is an exciting component of the syllabus and is relevant in a world saturated with visual imagery. The Comparative Study invites an approach to studying film that explores the technical side of the medium as well as regular elements of story-telling.

The films on the Leaving Certificate syllabus span a variety of genres. An awareness of the conventions associated with particular genres will help you in the study of your chosen film, as will an understanding of how these genres are constantly being subverted and transformed.

Films tell their stories through a system of signs and images that film-makers have developed over the past one hundred years into what might be called a visual language. These signs and images are called codes.

Personal codes apply to drama as well as film. They are the codes communicated to us by the actors through action, gesture, costume, facial expression and body language. Personal codes are essential aspects of story-telling within film, which is why the close-up shot is so powerful. Personal codes are vital in how we interpret the film narrative. **Technical codes** involve camera, time, lighting, colour, sound, movement, and so on.

Sound is an essential part of the way a film communicates. Music has become a code for telling the story, whether through a specially composed score or a carefully chosen soundtrack. Music and other sound effects, like voices and noises, can be labelled under two headings – diegetic, which means they have their source on-screen, and non-diegetic, which means they seem to come from a source off-screen. There are different ways in which music can be built into a film. It may be background or incidental or it may be specifically chosen as a way of explaining what the film is about. Music may even act as an ironic counterpoint to the action of a scene. Music may also be used to create a smooth transition between scenes in a film. Voiceover is a technique in which one of the characters speaks directly to the audience.

The **camera** is the essential tool of film-making. We cannot see what the camera does not show us, and in this sense it functions as an omniscient narrator. The director focuses on the scenes which are relevant to the story by using a variety of shots. A long shot is often used to establish setting and offers a panoramic view of a scene, whereas a close-up shot offers an intimate portrait of a character. Camera angle is also decisive in how a scene is interpreted. A high-angle shot places the camera above the character, creating the illusion of vulnerability, whereas a low-angle shot achieves the reverse effect.

Comparative Study

Mise-en-scène is a French term and originates in the theatre. It means, literally, 'put in the scene'. In film, it refers to all that exists within the frame. Everything inside the frame is the result of a choice and, as an audience, we are being 'positioned' to read what we see on screen in a particular way. This forces us to imagine other details that are often outside the frame. In this way, suspense and tension are created.

Colour, light and dark exist within film texts in order to create atmosphere and depth. They are frequently used by directors in a symbolic way. The connotations are archetypal. Gentle piano music is good; scratchy violin is bad. Red stands for lust or violence; black is ominous. Light is positive; darkness is menacing. Of course, the objective of good narrative is to unsettle as well as entertain, and many directors use classical symbols in new ways to subvert audience expectation.

Temporal codes suggest the passing of time in a story. The choice of code – dissolve, fade, cut, titles – also affects how the story is communicated. Movement codes also influence our interpretation of a film text. What we take as movement when we watch a film is really an optical illusion. What we actually see is a series of still images punctuated by darkness. Twenty-four frames a second produce what we accept as natural movement. Slow motion and fast motion are signals for the audience to bring an alternative interpretation to a scene.

All My Sons by Arthur Miller

Summary

READ

Comparative Study

Act One

It's 1947, a few years after the conclusion of the Second World War. We're in the backyard of the Keller home, on the outskirts of an unspecified American town. It's early Sunday morning, in August.

Joe Keller, a dedicated father and husband in his late fifties, is sitting reading the Sunday paper while chatting at various points with his neighbours, Dr Jim Bayliss and Frank Lubey, and their wives, Sue and Lydia. An apple tree has fallen in a storm during the night and its upper trunk and branches lie toppled beside the stump. The tree was planted in honour of Larry, Keller's older son, whose plane went down in China in the war and who is still listed as Missing in Action. Later, when the neighbours have left, Keller and his younger son Chris, who also served in the war but who came home safely, discuss the fallen tree, betraying their anxiety about how Kate Keller, Joe's wife, will react to it. Chris also reveals his feelings for Ann Deever, their former next-door neighbour, who is visiting the Kellers for the first time since moving to New York. Chris wants to marry her. Joe Keller likes Ann, but discourages the engagement because of how Kate will react. Kate Keller believes that her son Larry is still alive, that Ann is 'Larry's girl' and that she is waiting for his return with the same conviction as herself – therefore Chris has no right to marry Ann.

As soon as she appears and speaks for herself, however, it is obvious that Ann is ready to move on and build a life with Chris. She looks to the Kellers as a symbol of how happy her family life was in the past. During the exchanges, it emerges that Ann's father, Steve Deever, is in jail. Keller ran an engineering business supplying aircraft parts to the military during the war, and Deever was his employee. One batch of cracked cylinder heads was produced, passed as fit to use and sold by the factory, but the cylinder heads were not fit for use and caused the deaths of twenty-one pilots. Keller and Deever were arrested. Keller was cleared of criminal negligence, but Deever was convicted. Now his daughter Ann has cut all ties with him. Keller urges her to be more understanding, saying: 'The man was a fool, but don't make a murderer out of him.' Ann asks him to forget about it, suggesting that she has her mind made up on the matter, and Keller proposes that they should all dine out later to celebrate her visit.

When Chris is finally alone with Ann, he confesses his love for her. She responds enthusiastically: 'Oh, Chris, I've been ready for a long, long time!' He shares with her his sense of guilt at surviving the war and prospering in his father's business and she tells him that he has a right to whatever he has. Just when their future seems assured, Ann receives a mysterious and unsettling phone call from her brother George, who has just visited his father in prison for the first time and is now urgently on his way to the Kellers. This news makes Joe Keller suspicious and frightened. While Chris and Ann are on a drive, he betrays his fears to his wife. She warns him to 'be smart now', but he loses his composure and storms out, leaving her sitting there, wondering what secrets will be revealed.

Act Two

Twilight falls. It's the evening of the same day. We remain in the backyard of the Keller home.

Apprehension over George's impending arrival affects many of the characters. Joe Keller sleeps to relieve the stress, his wife busies herself with making cool drinks, Chris starts sawing the fallen tree. Kate warns Chris that the Deever family hates the Kellers, and points out that Ann is a member of that family. She asks Chris to protect them from what George might do. Chris believes his father to be an honourable man and tells her not to worry, while simultaneously assuring Ann when she arrives that he will tell his mother about their engagement when she's 'in a better mood'.

When Chris leaves, Ann is greeted by Sue Bayliss, the next-door neighbour who occupies Ann's old house. Sue is irritated by the effect that Chris' 'phoney idealism' has on her doctor husband, making him dissatisfied with his modest career, and she tells Ann that the Keller family is not as holy as it appears, given that 'Everybody knows Joe pulled a fast one to get out of jail'. When he returns, Chris reassures Ann that his father is innocent, that there is nothing to fear from George, and that there is nothing 'wrong' for her in the Keller home. Joe Keller arrives just as Chris and Ann are embracing. He shares his plan to find George a position in a local law firm, which pleases Ann, and then to offer Steve Deever a job after his prison term, a proposal that annoys both Ann and Chris.

The tensions increase when George arrives and gives Steve Deever's version of the fatal events that occurred in Keller's factory. When he saw the defective cylinder heads, Deever rang Keller, his boss, who told him to patch them up and ship them out, with the assurance that Keller would take responsibility for the decision. At the trial, Keller denied that the phone call had taken place, and Deever was convicted. With this information, George tries to persuade or force Ann to leave. She and Chris insist that the trial evidence is the true version of events and plead with George not to further distress  Kate Keller, who is ill, with arguments. Kate enters into this tense stand-off. For a while, her warmth almost persuades George to abandon his attempt to expose Keller, particularly when she dangles in front of him the prospects of a good job, a comfortable marriage, a happy return to his childhood neighbourhood. Joe Keller appears with the reminder that George's father has a history of blaming others for his own mistakes. George accepts this and is on the point of admitting that he's in the wrong, when Kate unwittingly says that Joe was never sick a day in his life. George now realises that Keller was lying about his supposed pneumonia. He presses Keller to reveal the truth. But they are interrupted by Frank Lubey rushing in and declaring that, according to his horoscope, Larry must still be alive. Chris thinks the whole astrology theory is insane, but his mother desperately clings to hope. At Ann's insistence, George leaves, angry that Ann plans to remain engaged to Chris. Confronting his mother's belief that Larry is not dead, which forms her resistance to the marriage, Chris insists that Larry *is* dead. However, she responds: 'Your brother's alive, darling, because if he's dead, your father killed him.'

So the truth is out. Kate knows that Joe Keller allowed the cracked cylinders to be shipped out. She believes that if Larry is in fact dead, then his blood is on her husband's hands. When Chris comprehends this, he accuses his father of murder. Joe Keller futilely defends himself, claiming that he thought the military would catch the mistake. He also explains that he did it for his family, disgusting Chris even more. Outraged and disillusioned, Chris yells at his father: 'What the hell do you mean you did it for me? Don't you have a country? … What must I do?'

He pounds his father's shoulder. Then he covers his hands and weeps.

Act Three

It's two o'clock the following morning, about five hours later. We remain in the backyard of the Keller home.

Chris has run off and his mother waits anxiously for him. Returning from a house call, Dr Bayliss assures her that Chris will come back, describing how he once unsuccessfully tried to leave his own dutiful life behind. He also reveals that he knows the truth about Joe's crimes. As he departs, Keller enters and he and Kate discuss what should be done to achieve a reconciliation with Chris. Kate believes that Joe should offer to admit his guilt to the authorities. She does not believe that Chris would allow his father to turn himself in. However, she thinks that by making the offer, it will help Chris adjust to the truth. This idea exasperates Joe. He does not understand why he needs forgiveness. He argues that his actions were justified because he did what he did for his family, and he unfavourably contrasts Chris' scruples with his dead son's pragmatism.

Ann comes from the house and explains that she has no plans to reveal Keller's guilt. In return, she wants Kate Keller to release Chris from guilt by admitting that his brother is dead, so that Ann and Chris can build a life together. After telling her husband to return to the house, Kate still insists that Larry is alive and that Ann will leave alone in the morning. Now, as the last resort, Ann produces a letter that Larry wrote to her shortly before he died. Reading it, Kate moans in dismay.

Chris returns at this stage and declares that he intends to move away alone, without Ann, since it's pointless punishing one man when the whole society is corrupt. Keller comes back out and challenges his son to throw away all his money, if he feels bad about how he came to have it. Insisting that he is judging him as a *father*, Chris struggles to get Keller to accept his guilt and turn himself in, but Keller still refuses to admit full responsibility and claims that everyone does everything for money. In desperation, Ann now gives Chris Larry's letter, which he reads aloud, revealing that Larry was so distraught about his father's murderous greed and inhumanity that he deliberately crashed his plane, committing suicide. Finally, Joe Keller understands the disastrous implications of his actions. He reflects on the twenty-one airmen who died because of him, saying quietly of his dead son: 'I think to him they were all my sons. And I guess they were.' Then Keller enters the house, apparently to get ready to turn himself in. Moments later, a gunshot is heard. Joe Keller has shot himself, leaving Ann, Chris and Kate stunned and grief-stricken.

Mode: Theme of Family

Understanding of 'Family'

All My Sons concerns the intersected lives of a group of families – the Kellers, the Deevers, the Baylisses and the Lubeys. Family is the basic unit of society and in this text it refers to the 'nuclear family', a term used to define a family group as consisting of a married heterosexual couple and their children. The nuclear model was widely accepted as the only foundation of family in mid-twentieth-century America, the time and place when the text

is set. When Lydia discovers that Annie is staying with the Kellers she asks: 'She going to get married?', and, in fact, Annie *has* come back to marry Chris. Despite the complications of his mother seeing Annie as 'Larry's girl', Chris tells his father: 'I want a family, I want some kids, I want something I can give myself to.'

Reality of Family Life

Family is seen as the source of all value and meaning for the characters in this text. When Sue explains to Annie that Chris makes Jim feel unfulfilled in his work, she says: 'My husband has a family, dear.' In other words, family takes precedence over private ambitions, and, more ominously, over moral scruples as well. Joe Keller has committed the crime of allowing faulty cylinder heads to leave his factory, resulting in the deaths of twenty-one men. He justifies his actions on the grounds that everything he did was for his family. He is shocked at the end of the play to find out how wrong his justification was: 'I thought I had a family here. What happened to my family?' Miller exposes the reality of the 'all-American' family with its mythology of picket fences and apple pie, and its rotten value system underneath. All of the married couples in the play bicker. Most of the discord is trivial, such as Frank sniping at Lydia in Act One: 'I don't know why you can't learn to turn on a simple thing like a toaster!' But some of it is serious, such as Jim telling Kate in Act Three that since he married he lives in 'the usual darkness' and that although he is a good husband 'it's even hard sometimes to remember the kind of man I wanted to be'. Family, in Miller's view, is only as good as the individuals in it. Kate's words in Act Two demonstrate this: 'Honest to God, it breaks my heart to see what happened to all the children. How we worked and planned for you, and you end up no better than us.'

Role of Money in Family Life

Money plays a powerful role in family life in this text. Joe has put all his energies into making money and building up his business. He was determined to keep his factory's production line running, even when it caused the deaths of twenty-one pilots through faulty airplane parts.

At the end of Act Two, when Chris realises that Joe is responsible for the pilots' deaths, Joe says he did it for the business: 'What could I do! I'm in business, a man is in business; a hundred and twenty cracked, you're out of business …' In Joe's mind, this is not selfish, as he did everything for Chris: 'Chris, I did it for you, it was a chance and I took it for you.' Horrified, Chris demands: 'Is that as far as your mind can see, the business?' *All My Sons* presents us with a value system in which love is equated with money. In Keller's mind, he is a good father because he provides financial comfort for his family. And the next generation share the same views. When Annie accepts Chris' proposal of marriage, he says: 'Oh Annie, Annie … I'm going to make a fortune for you.'

Effect of Family on Individuals

Ultimately the treatment of the theme of family in *All My Sons* offers a negative perspective. Miller presents us with an institution that is corrupt but full of nostalgia about the past. The characters in this play idealise the past, such as when Joe tells Jim: 'That was a very happy family used to live in your house, Jim.' It is the reality of the past that the characters cannot face. When Chris disappears, Kate finally tells Joe what she thinks of his crime: 'It don't excuse it that you did it for the family.' He replies: 'I'm his father and he's my son, and if there's something bigger than that I'll put a bullet in my head!' But of course there is something bigger, as expressed by Chris in Act One – 'A kind of – responsibility. Man for man.' – and when Joe finally sees this at the end, his earlier words foreshadow the play's tragic resolution.

MAKE

Write a short essay in which you consider which of the four aspects – understanding of family, reality of family life, role of money in family life or effect of family on individuals – is the *most* important for a discussion of the theme of family in *All My Sons*. Give reasons for your answer and refer to key moments in the text in support of your points.

Comparative Study

Mode: General Vision and Viewpoint

The general vision and viewpoint of *All My Sons* is pessimistic.

Vision of Society

The play exposes the American dream as something that has been corrupted by money. In other words, the core values that American society prides itself on – freedom, honesty, loyalty – have become fragile myths that crumble away under pressure. Miller's vision of America is a bleak one in which idealism is dead and has been replaced by a Darwinian society in which the modus operandi is 'the survival of the fittest'. In Act Three, Chris offers a savage indictment of his country: 'This is the land of the great big dogs, you don't love a man here, you eat him!'

Another ideal on which America was founded was 'the pursuit of happiness'. Yet Miller in *All My Sons* presents a world that is devoid of any real happiness, as it has come to be equated entirely with money. In Act One, Ann says of Joe 'He just wants everybody happy' – but to achieve this Joe has told lies, betrayed his friend, and created a metaphorical jail for his wife and son to live in. While Chris sees his job as one in which he has to 'grub for money all day long', he tells Ann that he will 'make a fortune' for her. Happiness, and even love, have becomes synonymous with making money.

View of Identity

The characters in *All My Sons* are either disillusioned or deluded. The doctor, Jim Bayliss, says of his son Tommy, 'Over my dead body he'll be a doctor', while in Act One, Keller says, 'I ignore what I gotta ignore'. Dishonesty, in one form or another, has infected all their lives and is at the root of the vision of the play. Keller is caught in a web of deceit. Chris is dishonest with himself and is told so by George in Act Two – 'Oh Chris, you're a liar to yourself' – while Kate colludes in her husband's dishonesty. As a moral yardstick for many of the characters, exoneration in court has replaced a concern for the truth. Keller tells Chris that he is not guilty of gross negligence because 'there was a court paper in my pocket to prove I wasn't'.

Vision of Individual Responsibility

Miller's play makes a strong statement about an individual's responsibility to society as a whole. As a member of society, Joe Keller bears responsibility towards others. He is bound not to undertake any action that may knowingly harm others. But he has broken this social contract by placing personal gain above all else, and thus forsaken his duty. He is not the only one. Steve Deever is also culpable since, instead of relying on his own judgement about the faulty cylinders, he allowed Keller to make a decision for him. Likewise, Kate is complicit in her husband's deception, as are others. Jim and Sue Bayliss are aware that Keller's account of events is untruthful but they continue to be friendly with him, as do the people who spend every Saturday night 'playin' poker in this arbour'.

Finally, in Act Three, Joe has to confront the implications of his actions. In words that foreshadow his end, he says of Chris: 'I'm his father and he's my son, and if there's something bigger than that I'll put a bullet in my head!' As the play shows, there is something bigger than that. So when Joe finally does face up to his crime, he does the only thing that he feels he can do, which is to extinguish his life. The sense of waste is overwhelming – not just of Joe's life, but of all the other lives that have been lost or torn apart because of the pursuit of profit: the twenty-one airmen, Steve and the rest of the Deever family, Larry, Chris and Kate.

View of the Past

Miller's vision in the text is one that is present in much of literature – that the past cannot be escaped. Thus, the characters in *All My Sons* are haunted by the past, as articulated by Kate in Act One: 'Everything that happened seems to be coming back.' The play works by the logic that a misdeed committed in the past is inescapable and must eventually be rectified. Beyond the strong ethical stance put forward in the play, this is perhaps Miller's most poignant message. Kate and Joe Keller are punished for their failure to face up to their past, and particularly for their prolonged and concerted efforts to suppress it.

All My Sons comes to a shocking conclusion with the sound of a gunshot from the house, when Keller shoots himself. His act is prompted by Larry's letter, which is in effect a suicide note, and these actual suicides are a culmination of several threatened suicides throughout the play. In a text so concerned with acceptance of guilt and retribution, the resolution is deeply ambiguous. In some ways, Keller's retribution is absolute – he has paid with his life – but the question is raised as to whether his death actually represents atonement for his crime. In *All My Sons*, the curtain falls on Chris weeping with guilt over his father's death, and there is a sense that his guilt will hang like a shadow over the marriage between him and Ann, if indeed it still takes place. Thus, the ramifications of Joe's crime do not end with his death, but go on indefinitely.

MAKE

Write a short essay in which you consider which of the four aspects – vision of society, view of identity, vision of individual responsibility or view of the past – is the *most* important for a discussion of the general vision and viewpoint in *All My Sons*. Give reasons for your answer and refer to key moments in the text in support of your points.

Comparative Study

Mode: Literary Genre

Genre

All My Sons is an exemplar of the realist dramatic tradition. It recreates a setting that closely resembles reality, has characters that are believable and recognisable to the audience as ordinary people, and the events of the play are plausible.

Narrative Technique and Characterisation

Without an omniscient narrator, plays rely on dialogue for both characterisation and delivery of plot. Conversation dominates *All My Sons* and, in keeping with the realist tradition, the dialogue is plain and natural. The characters use colloquial language and discuss everyday topics, but Miller meticulously constructs their speech to reveal both their personalities and the underlying tensions in their relationships. Diction, the pacing of speech, the level of emotion in speech and pronunciation all combine to create distinct and memorable characters. Diction refers to the way characters use words, such as Joe Keller's use of abbreviated sentences and dropped letters in his speech, for instance 'Gonna rain tonight' or 'What's doin?'. Pacing is created by stage directions, such as ['He pauses'] or by ellipses that often appear in characters' speeches. Emotion is also conveyed by stage directions, such as ['emotionally'] or ['with increasing demand'], both referring to Kate's speeches. Pronunciation refers to how characters pronounce words, such as Keller saying 'brooch' when he means to say 'broach'.

Miller also uses stage directions to enhance his story, endowing the stage set and the characters' movements with symbolic significance. Non-verbal information plays a major role in telling the story. Consider the final exchange between Keller and Kate at the end of Act One:

> [KELLER, in hopeless fury, looks at her, turns around, goes up to porch and into house, slamming the screen door violently behind him. Mother sits in chair downstage, stiffly, staring, seeing.]

Structure and Setting

The structure of *All My Sons* is designed to enhance the story being told. With Miller's decision to divide the play into three Acts, he has only two major pauses with which he can create a sense of suspense and tension, aside from the close of the play in Act Three. He uses these pauses to full effect. Act One closes with Kate and Keller's panicked conversation about George's imminent arrival.

Act Two closes with Keller's admission of guilt and Chris' total repudiation of his father. Act Three closes with the reading aloud of Larry's letter and Keller's suicide. Without scene breaks within

ANALYSE

Comparative Study

the Acts themselves, Miller uses the characters' entrances and exits from the stage to introduce different tones and subjects for discussion. He also runs conversations into each other to make the transitions between different conversations smooth and natural. To accomplish these smooth shifts, Miller designed a set that enabled free movement. The major characters enter and exit the backyard and house with no restrictions while the minor characters are on familiar enough terms with the Kellers to make their entering the house or yard without knocking plausible.

All My Sons is modelled loosely on Greek tragedy. In such plays, the hero's downfall is inevitable because of a flaw in their character – such as Keller's dishonesty – while the unfolding of events is commented on by a chorus – much like the input given by Sue and Jim Bayliss.

The setting is far more than just a device dictated by the structure of the play. The choice of a single setting for the entire play situates all the action in a community setting, a semi-private yard. In this way, it complements the moral and ethical messages of the play as it is a symbol of the involvement of the community in the Keller family crisis.

Language and Imagery

Miller employs imagery and symbolism to great effect in *All My Sons*. The most prominent symbol in the play is the apple tree planted in memory of Larry Keller. The frequent references to the fallen tree in the early stages of the play emphasise its symbolic importance in the lives of all the characters. The tree serves as a constant reminder of Larry's death and the characters are unable to exorcise his memory from their minds. In the stage directions, the tree is described as 'slender' and with 'fruit still clinging to its branches', suggesting that Larry has been cut down while still young and full of potential. At the opening of Act Two, Chris chops up the remains of the tree and hauls the timber out of view, foreshadowing his confrontation with the past later in the play. But the past returns again, represented by a different symbol – Larry's letter to Ann. Other symbols in the play include Larry's baseball glove, which represents him as he was before the war: a carefree adolescent, and the hat that George wears, which represents him as he was before the incident at the factory: an upstanding business man. There is also religious imagery in the play, which points to its underlying moral message, and clothing imagery, which highlights the theme of deception.

Foreshadowing is also employed by Miller to add drama to the text. The episode with Bert is a presage of Keller's suicide, according to the principle of drama theory known as 'Chekhov's gun', after Russian playwright Anton Chekhov. The theory holds that if a gun is hanging on the wall in the first act, it should be used in the next. Thus, when Keller mentions the gun in his house, he is signaling that it will be used by the end of the play.

MAKE

Write a short essay in which you consider which of the three aspects – narrative technique and characterisation, structure and setting, or language and imagery – is the *most* important for a discussion of literary genre in *All My Sons*. Give reasons for your answer and refer to key moments in the text in support of your points.

Juno directed by Jason Reitman

Summary

Juno, a film directed by Jason Reitman, was released in 2007.

The story opens in 'AUTUMN', with a girl remembering making love with her boyfriend. We follow her into a drugstore where we learn her surname – MacGuff – and where she picks up a pregnancy test kit, goes to the toilet and confirms that she is pregnant. She walks home in fading light and from her cluttered, somewhat-childish bedroom, rings her best friend, Leah, on her hamburger phone. She is Juno, a sixteen-year-old high-school student.

She tells her boyfriend, known only as 'Bleeker' at this point. Bleeker is also a high-school student and he is one of the athletes on the school running team. He is too stunned to react in any meaningful way, even when she tells him, in an apparently casual manner, that she is considering an abortion. In the meantime, they both get on with day-to-day school work.

At home, Juno rings a local abortion clinic for an appointment and tells us (the audience) about her family history. Her parents separated when she was five and she now lives with her father and his partner, Bren. After breakfast, Juno goes to the clinic, but when she gets there, she bumps into a school friend who is holding a placard and campaigning against abortion. Inside, Juno becomes hyper-sensitive to the noises being made by other waiting clients and she bolts from the place.

She tells Leah that she is 'staying pregnant' and will give the baby to 'someone who totally needs it'. Leah suggests looking at the adoption ads, where they find 'Mark and Vanessa Loring', a 'beautiful couple', according to Juno.

Later that evening, Juno, supported by Leah, tells her parents that she is pregnant. Though surprised at first, particularly when they hear that the father is Paulie Bleeker, they immediately offer unquestioning support and advice.

Mac, Juno's dad, accompanies her on her first visit to the Lorings' affluent home. Initially, the Lorings' attorney suggests an open adoption, which means that Juno would be entitled to updates and contact with the baby, but Juno says she would prefer a closed adoption, and to have no further contact with the baby. Vanessa says that she 'was born to be a mother', but it is obvious from his cooler responses that her husband, Mark, is not quite as committed. He seems to be going through with it primarily to keep his wife happy. Mark is a former rock-band member who has a 'room of his own' in the house for his stuff. He doesn't seem to have fully grown up, and is more comfortable sneaking off to play a duet with the sixteen-year-old Juno than negotiating with the adults downstairs.

Time passes and 'WINTER' comes. Juno is now noticeably pregnant, although Paulie seems to have no involvement at all in the pregnancy. Juno goes for an ultrasound scan and sees images of her baby, although she doesn't want to know its gender. When the female technician makes disparaging remarks about teenage pregnancies, Bren defends her step-daughter aggressively.

Juno revisits the Lorings to show them the images from the scan. Only Mark is at home. Again, they hang out as if they were both teenagers. When Vanessa comes home, she shows Juno all the baby equipment she has already bought and she confides anxiously that they went through this process unsuccessfully before. Vanessa seems uneasy generally. Back home, when Juno tells Bren how she spent the afternoon, Bren is also uneasy. She obviously doesn't trust Mark. Later, when Juno tells Paulie the same story, he too wonders if it's 'normal'. They wonder if they should 'get back together', or even if they were ever together. When the focus returns to the Lorings, we again see that Vanessa wants to 'nest' – prepare for the baby – while Mark isn't really interested – 'yet', he says. Vanessa's maternal nature is again revealed when Juno meets her at the Mall and Vanessa talks ecstatically to the baby.

Time passes, once more, and 'SPRING' comes. Juno, heavily pregnant, rings Mark to talk music, and then learns from Leah that Paulie Bleeker is asking another girl to the prom. It leads to a row between Juno and Paulie at the school lockers, demonstrating that they at least still care about each other. Still annoyed, Juno calls on Mark. They dance intimately, until Mark reveals that he's leaving Vanessa. This horrifies Juno, for her baby's sake. Finally, Mark admits, 'I don't think I'm even ready to be a father' and 'Vanessa and I are not in love anymore'. Vanessa arrives as Juno is about to leave and the gap between her and Mark comes into the open. While they are arguing, Juno leaves, crying as she drives home. She pulls over, writes a note, and drives back to the Lorings to deliver it.

Back home, Juno seeks reassurance, about love and relationships, from her father. He advises her to find someone who loves you, regardless. Juno says she thinks she has someone like that. It is, of course, Paulie Bleeker, whose mail box she fills to overflowing with his favourite treat, orange tic tacs, as an expression of her love. They meet at the school track, where Juno confesses that she's in love with him. They kiss.

The next scenes are of the frantic dash to the hospital when Juno goes into labour. Not wanting to distract Paulie from his race, she doesn't tell him. However, after he has won his race, when he realises she's not in the stands watching, Paulie senses what has happened and jogs to the hospital to be with Juno. Helped by her mother and her best friend, Juno has given birth to a baby.

Vanessa comes to the hospital to collect the baby, and the content of the note Juno drove back to leave for her is finally revealed:

Vanessa

If you're still in, I'm still in.

Juno

The final scenes are of 'SUMMER'. Juno cycles to Paulie Bleeker's house and they play a guitar duet – 'Anyone Else But You' – on the front lawn.

Mode: Theme of Family

Understanding of 'Family'

In *Juno*, family is presented as a unit in society that takes many different forms. Juno's family is made up of her father (Mac), her stepmother (Bren) and her half-sister (Liberty Bell). Bren and Mac have been together for ten years. Juno's mother and three half-siblings live in Arizona. Juno finds it strange that her mother sends her a cactus every year for St Valentine's Day, which indicates that there is little relationship between Juno and her birth mother. In the film, Juno is supported and loved unconditionally within her blended family. Juno herself does not see family in conventional terms. When she initially considers adoption she says to her friend, Leah: 'I just, like, don't want to give the baby to a family that describes themselves as "wholesome".' And when Mark Loring separates from Vanessa, Juno sends Vanessa a note which reads: 'Vanessa: If you're still in, I'm still in. —Juno.' Juno does not dismiss Vanessa as a suitable adoptive parent for her child just because she is single, and when Vanessa goes to the hospital and picks her son up for the first time, she asks, 'How do I look?', Bren answers 'Like a new mom'. The most important aspect of family, as shown in the film, is the love that exists between people within the family unit, whether they are step-parent and step-child, or a single adoptive mother and her infant.

Reality of Family Life

Family, as demonstrated by the MacGuffs, offers love and support to each of its members, even in times of adversity and conflict. When Juno tells Mac and Bren that she is pregnant they are shocked, but very supportive of Juno's decision to have the baby. Bren gets vitamins for Juno, schedules a doctor's appointment and consoles Mac, saying: 'Somebody is going to get a precious blessing from Jesus out of this garbage dump of a

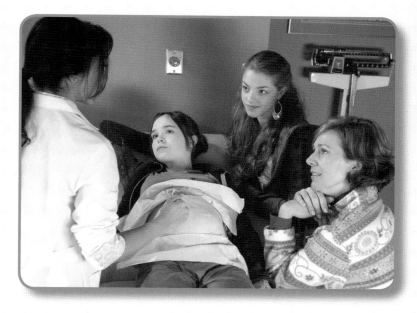

situation.' Mac goes with Juno to visit the Lorings. Later in the film, he tells her that he'll always be there to love and support her. When Bren takes Juno for her ultrasound appointment, she gets very angry at the technician who refers to teenage parenthood as 'poisonous' and defends Juno. However, there is conflict in the MacGuff family life, too. When Juno returns from hanging out with Mark, Bren warns her about keeping 'boundaries' and 'the dynamics of marriage'. Juno does not appreciate Bren's advice and they have a row. Bren tells Juno that she has sacrificed a lot for her (Bren cannot have a dog because Juno is allergic to their saliva). The row between Juno and Bren shows that that the relationship between them is honest. Bren voices her opinion because she wishes to protect Juno and is ultimately proved correct in her concerns.

Role of Money in Family Life

The MacGuffs live in a pleasant suburb of Minnesota. Both parents work hard to provide a comfortable standard of living for the family. Mac used to be in the army but now works as a heating maintenance engineer and Bren owns a nail salon. The Lorings serve as a sharp contrast to the MacGuff family. Mark and Vanessa Loring live in an affluent neighbourhood in St Cloud, a city in Minnesota. Vanessa works in business and Mark writes music for commercials. They are wealthy in comparison to Juno's family, but their relationship is built on dishonesty. Initially, Mark appears to be content in his marriage and positive about his upcoming role as an adoptive father but, as Juno's pregnancy progresses, Mark's behaviour regresses. He speaks about Vanessa in a less than respectful way – 'She just hates when I sit around watching movies and "not contributing"' – and his conduct towards Juno when they dance is inappropriate. He tells her he is leaving Vanessa. When Vanessa arrives home, he says: 'That it [the pregnancy] feels a little like bad timing.' Mark has not been honest with himself or Vanessa about what he wants from life and this causes the marriage to end. The text presents us with an understanding that money does not equate with happiness. Juno does not want any financial compensation for allowing her baby to be adopted. She simply wants her baby to well cared for and loved.

Effect of Family on Individuals

In *Juno*, the treatment of the theme of family offers a positive perspective. Family exists as bonds of love between people rather than just biological ties or legal arrangements. When Juno returns from the Lorings having discovered that Mark is leaving Vanessa, she says: 'I never realise how much I like being home unless I've been somewhere really different for a while.' Juno has lost meaningful contact with her mother, but receives the support she needs to cope with her unplanned pregnancy from her father and stepmother. In contrast, the Loring family, based on dishonesty, is presented in the text as a legal arrangement that can be undone easily, as seen in the final exchange between Mark and Vanessa:

> Mark: I called Gerta Rauss. She says she can represent both of us. They call it 'collaborative divorce.' It's apparently all the rage right now. And it's easy because we don't have children.
> Vanessa: No, it's fine. Thanks for making the call, I guess.

MAKE

Write a short essay in which you consider which of the four aspects – understanding of family, reality of family life, role of money in family life or effect of family on individuals – is the *most* important for a discussion of the theme of family in *Juno*. Give reasons for your answer and refer to key moments in the text in support of your points.

Comparative Study

Mode: General Vision and Viewpoint

The general vision and viewpoint of *Juno* is optimistic.

Vision of Society

The importance of love and friendship in human society is an aspect of the vision and viewpoint in this text. When Juno discovers that she is pregnant, the first person she turns to is her friend, Leah. In a telephone conversation, the exchange between the two girls is heartfelt and honest:

> Leah: Oh my GOD. Oh shit! Phuket, Thailand!
> Juno: There we go. That was kind of the emotion that I was searching for on the first take.

Leah is at Juno's side throughout her pregnancy, supporting her when she has to tell Mac and Bren the news, accompanying her to her ultrasound appointment, staying with her as she gives birth. Her friendship is a vital source of support for Juno.

The ability of love to triumph and flourish in difficult situations is the most powerful message in *Juno*. When she returns from the Lorings after Mark has revealed his intention to leave Vanessa, Juno tells Mac: 'I'm just like losing my faith with humanity.' When Mac asks her to narrow that down, Juno says: 'I just need to know that it's possible that two people can stay happy together forever.' Mac responds by telling her: 'The best thing you can do is find a person who loves you for exactly what you are.' Juno realises she loves Paulie Bleeker and proceeds to tell him so by putting a hundred boxes of orange tic tacs in his mailbox. At the end of the film, Juno tells us: 'As far as boyfriends go, Paulie Bleeker is totally boss. He is the cheese to my macaroni.'

View of Identity

The formation of identity is another aspect of the vision and viewpoint of *Juno*. When she discovers that she is pregnant, Juno's whole world changes. She presumes that she will have an abortion but instead decides to have the baby and give it up for adoption. She imagines that the experience will be relatively straightforward: 'And what ah 30 or odd weeks, we can just pretend that this never happened.' But the reality is totally different. Juno has to learn some difficult lessons about adult life and relationships. She has to discover the truth of her own feelings. She has to face the pain of giving up the baby she has given birth to. Early in the film, when Mac says 'I thought you were the kind of girl who knew when to say when', Juno responds: 'I don't know what kind of girl I am.' During the course of the film, Juno finds out that she is very much as Bren described her in the beginning of the film: 'Well, you're a brave young lady. You're made of stronger stuff than I thought. You're a little Viking!'

Comparative Study

Vision of Individual Responsibility

Juno MacGuff is a typical teenager, interested in music and enjoying life, except that she becomes pregnant as a result of having sex once with her friend, Paulie Bleeker. She is faced with the very adult problem of an unplanned pregnancy. Juno phones an abortion clinic and makes an appointment but, after visiting the clinic, changes her mind and decides to continue with the pregnancy and have the baby adopted. This is a courageous decision. Juno is an admirable character, not because of the decisions she makes but because she has the courage to follow through on what she believes in. She is forced to grow up during the course of the film as she struggles to understand her own feelings and to do what she believes is right.

When she comes back from witnessing the break-up of the Loring marriage, her father asks her where she has been. She replies: 'Oh, just out dealing with things way beyond my maturity level.' The film offers a strong vision of individual responsibility as something each character must discover for themselves. Mark Loring decides that he is not yet ready to be a father and also that he is unfulfilled in his current life. It is easy to make judgements about such characters, but the text suggests that an important aspect of individual responsibility is to oneself, and this requires honesty in relation to one's own needs as well as responsibility to others.

View of the Past

During the course of the text, Juno learns the value of honest communication. The strength of her bond with Paulie overcomes all adversity, even the loss of the baby they conceived together. In the hospital, Paulie lies on the bed beside Juno, holding her and comforting her in her distress. In the resolution of the text, they accept what has happened and continue to live. It is possible for Juno to overcome the trauma of being pregnant at such a young age and giving birth and putting her baby up for adoption because she is supported in her choices throughout the text. The vision of the film is that adversity can be triumphed over so long as an individual is supported and loved.

The past does not cast its shadow over Juno or Paulie. They accept the painful experience that they have been through and recover from it. Their baby has brought great joy into another's life, as depicted in the shot of Vanessa feeding her son at the end of the film, with the note Juno put under her door framed on the nursery wall. The seasonal settings of the text enhance the film's positive message about journeying through difficult periods during the course of life. Winter is a universal symbol for struggle but, in the resolution of the text, it is summer and Juno cycles to Paulie's house where they play guitar and sing the joyful duet 'Anyone Else But You'.

> **MAKE**
>
> Write a short essay in which you consider which of the four aspects – vision of society, view of identity, vision of individual responsibility or view of the past – is the *most* important for a discussion of the general vision and viewpoint in *Juno*. Give reasons for your answer and refer to key moments in the text in support of your points.

Mode: Literary Genre

Genre

Juno is a dramatic comedy film about coming of age. It explores the serious subject of unplanned teenage pregnancy in a warm and humorous way. Because of its huge crossover appeal – to both adults and teens – *Juno* became Fox Searchlight's first film to surpass $100 million at the box office. When considering the literary genre of *Juno*, it is worth remembering that films tell their stories through a system of signs and images called codes.

Narrative Technique and Characterisation

In *Juno*, as in all films, the camera functions as an omniscient narrator. This creates an impression of neutrality in the telling of the story but it is important to remember that, at all times, the director both decides what images to show the audience and manipulates the audience to read those images in a particular way. When we watch a pregnant Juno walking along a corridor in school and see the other students moving back from her, we realise she is being ostracised, and when we see her driving along a barren, industrial road in Minnesota and pulling the van in on the verge, we understand that she is on a difficult journey in metaphorical terms.

Her occasional voiceovers also position Juno as a first-person narrator. Through the use of different camera shots and angles, as well as other codes, Reitman brings Diablo Cody's screenplay to life according to his interpretation of the story. The mise-en-scène, for example, plays a big role in establishing the tone and genre of the film. The opening sequence of the film shows Juno walking through suburban USA with shiplap houses, mailboxes and local shops, such as the guitar shack, the beauty parlour and the drug store. These elements set up her small world. She also walks past a tree with falling leaves that establish the time of the year. An interesting effect used in the opening sequence is the animation technique of rotoscoping, creating animated sketches that are traced over live footage. It establishes the look and feel of *Juno* as an independent-style movie, as well as allowing the audience to get a sense of Juno's unique, quirky view of the world.

Dialogue is also an important aspect of characterisation in *Juno*. What the characters say, as well as how they say it, creates their personality. Leah, Juno's best friend, speaks in the same youth vernacular as Juno, saying 'What? Honest to blog?' when Juno tells her she is pregnant or 'It's probably just a food baby. Did you have a big lunch?'. Paulie Bleeker, on the other hand, whom Juno says is not like anyone else, has a more reticent style of speech. When Juno confronts him about taking Katrina De Voort to the prom he says: 'You're being really immature … You have no reason to be mad at me, I mean, you know, you broke *my* heart. I should be royally ticked off at you.'

However, other personal codes, such as action, gesture, costume, facial expression and body language are essential aspects of story-telling within film, which is why the close-up shot is so powerful.

Structure and Setting

Setting and structure are vital aspects of literary genre. The setting of *Juno* is the fictional town of Dancing Elk in Minnesota, where Juno lives, and St Cloud, where the Lorings live. The contrast between the two places emphasises the differences that exist between the two families. *Juno* is a forward-moving text and the timeline – communicated to the audience in hand-drawn captions that read 'Autumn', 'Winter', 'Spring' and 'Summer' – is one year. The natural landscape of each season is presented on screen in rich imagery which, as well as evoking the passage of time, also suggests the cycle of life.

Another code that is an essential part of the way a film communicates is sound and in *Juno* the carefully chosen sound track assists in telling the story. The album features several songs performed by Kimya Dawson and her bands Antsy Pants and The Moldy Peaches. The soundtrack creates the warm tone of the film while the lyrics, such as those in the Lou Reed song 'I'm Sticking With You', echo the sentiment of the text.

Language and Imagery

The most distinctive aspect of literary genre in *Juno* is the dialogue. The screenplay won an Academy Award for originality. It is marked by the use of a witty youth vernacular delivered at a fast pace by all the cast, but particularly by Ellen Page playing Juno. Consider the exchange of dialogue between Rollo, the drugstore clerk, and Juno:

> Rollo: So what's the prognosis, Fertile Myrtle? Minus or plus?
> Juno: I don't know. It's not seasoned yet.
> [grabs products]
> Juno: I'll take some of these. Nope … There it is. The little pink plus sign is so unholy.
> [shakes pregnancy tester]
> Rollo: That ain't no Etch-A-Sketch. This is one doodle that can't be un-did, Homeskillet.

Other image patterns – such as light, dark and colour – are used by Reitman to great effect in the text. Juno is always in the light and can be clearly seen in each scene, except the scene where she finds out that she is pregnant. This foreshadows that everything will turn out all right in the end. The use of colour in the film is also bright and cheerful. Colours like orange, lime-green and yellow serve to lighten the mood and emphasise the humour of the text.

MAKE

Write a short essay in which you consider which of the three aspects – narrative technique and characterisation, structure and setting, or language and imagery – is the *most* important for a discussion of literary genre in *Juno*. Give reasons for your answer and refer to key moments in the text in support of your points.

Foster by Claire Keegan

Summary

Claire Keegan's *Foster* is a long short story written in seven chapters. It won the Davy Byrnes Irish Writing Award in 2009 and was subsequently published in book form. It is set in rural Wexford in 1981 and is narrated by a young girl who is fostered out to her aunt and uncle, the Kinsellas, for the summer months.

The story begins with an unnamed young girl narrator telling us what happened at the beginning of summer: 'Early on a Sunday, after first mass in Clonegal, my father, instead of taking me home, drives deep into Wexford towards the coast where my mother's people came from.'

The girl is taken to stay with relatives, her aunt and uncle, John and Edna Kinsella. Edna is the sister of the girl's mother. It is not entirely clear why this has been arranged, but the girl's mother, Mary, is due to have another baby and her father, Dan, comments, 'It's the feeding them that's the trouble', so we assume that the girl has been fostered out for the summer to ease the strain on her family. After having something to eat, the girl's father leaves, forgetting to take her suitcase from the car.

And so begins the girl's stay with the Kinsellas. From the outset she observes details of their life that contrast with that of her own family: 'But this is a different type of house. Here there is room, and time to think. There may even be money to spare'.

The aunt bathes the girl and gives her spare clothes to wear – trousers and a plaid shirt. She tells the girl that 'There are no secrets in this house' and takes her out through the farmyard, over a stile, along a path through a field, and to the well. The woman holds the girl over the well so that she won't fall in and tells her to 'Be careful'.

That night the aunt puts the girl to bed. She asks about the girl's mother and why the hay isn't in yet. The girl says that her mother 'hasn't enough money to pay the man' and the aunt says 'God help her'. The aunt tells the girl: 'If you were mine, I'd never leave you in a house with strangers.'

During the night the girl wets the bed but when the aunt discovers the wet mattress she says it is an old mattress and is 'weeping' and does not scold the girl. Later, the uncle says that 'another striker is dead'. He is referring to one of the IRA men who died on hunger strike in the Maze Prison in 1981. The aunt and girl do chores in the house during the day while the uncle works outside. In the afternoon, the uncle times the girl as she runs to the post box and back to pick up any letters. The aunt gives the girl dry Weetabix to eat and, when she wakes in the morning, she has not wet the bed.

The days pass, each one similar to the previous one. At night, people come to the house to play cards and talk. One afternoon, the uncle comes into the kitchen while the aunt and the girl are preparing gooseberries for jam. He says the girl must be taken into Gorey to get some clothes. When the aunt says 'Sure isn't she clean and tidy?', the uncle replies: 'You know what I'm talking about, Edna'. In the bathroom, the girl realises that her aunt has been crying but she doesn't know why. The three of them go into Gorey where the aunt buys new clothes for the girl and the uncle gives her a pound note to spend.

When they arrive home, a woman is on the front step. She is a neighbour and asks the uncle to help dig a grave for a relative of hers called Michael who has passed away. Later, the aunt takes the girl to the wake – a celebration of a dead person's life that usually takes place in the home – because she doesn't want to leave her on her own, but after a while agrees to let her neighbour, Mildred, take the girl to her house. On the way to her house, Mildred tells the

girl that the Kinsellas had a son who drowned. The girl realises that she has been wearing the dead boy's clothes and sleeping in his room. Just after Mildred reaches her house, the Kinsellas arrive and take the girl home with them. The girl tells the Kinsellas what Mildred told her.

Later, John Kinsella takes the girl for a walk to the strand. He calls the girl 'Petal' and they run in the waves, the girl on her uncle's shoulders, and walk as far as the 'place where the cliffs and rocks come out to meet the water'. The uncle talks to the girl. He tells her that his wife 'trusts people, hoping she'll not be disappointed' and that women can sense things that are going to happen. The girl doesn't understand fully what he is saying but she feels close to him.

At the end of the summer, on a Thursday, a letter comes from the girl's mother saying that the new baby is a boy and asking that the girl be brought home at the weekend to get ready to go back to school. The girl feels like crying.

The next day, the girl prepares to return home. A car pulls into the yard and a neighbour says that 'Joe Fortune needs a hand pulling a calf'. The uncle is in the milking parlour so the aunt goes to fetch him and tells the girl she will finish the milking herself. Left on her own, the girl goes to the well to fetch water and falls in. She imagines 'another hand, just like mine seems to come out of the water and pull me in.' The girl does not drown. She returns to the house soaked to the skin and is put to bed and nursed by the aunt.

On Sunday, although she still has a cold, the girl returns home. The house 'feels damp and cold'. The girl's sisters look at her as though she is 'an English cousin'. The new baby is 'pink and crying'. The aunt and uncle sit with the family and drink tea and eat bread. The girl's father arrives but doesn't eat anything as he says he had 'a liquid lunch' (drank alcohol). The girl's father questions her about her cold but the girl says nothing. The Kinsellas give the girl's mother jam and potatoes before saying goodbye and getting into their car. They say the girl is welcome to stay with them anytime. When they are gone the girl's mother asks 'What happened at all?', but the girl replies 'Nothing'. And then, suddenly, the girl rushes after the car and catches up with it where the uncle has stopped to open and close the gate. The girl jumps into his arms. The aunt is crying in the car 'not for one now, but for two'. The story finishes with the girl calling her uncle 'Daddy'.

Mode: Theme of Family

Understanding of 'Family'

In *Foster*, Keegan shows family to be a complex place. It is not simply a matter of biology. The bonds that connect children to parental figures are more complex than that, as they are based on love, trust and care, rather than on blood relationships. The young girl learns this over the months she spends with the Kinsellas, people who are initially strangers to her, and she is, in effect, a stranger when she finally returns home to her family of origin.

Reality of Family Life

The girl's parents send her away for the summer to stay with her aunt and uncle, who are strangers to the girl. Her aunt, Edna, says to the girl: 'The last time I saw you, you were in the pram.' The girl is aware that her parents do not want her at home, as she overheard her mother saying to her father that the Kinsellas could 'keep her as long as they like'. She is in a strange house with strange people and naturally finds the situation difficult: 'I take big breaths so I won't cry.' However, as the summer passes, the young girl becomes attached to her aunt and uncle and when the time comes for the young girl to return home, she is upset: 'I stand there and stare at the fire, trying not to cry.'

Keegan presents the reader with two sharply contrasting pictures of Irish family life.

The Kinsellas are warm and caring. The first meeting between the young girl and Edna is significant. Edna kisses the girl and tells her that the last time she saw her, she was in a pram. When the girl says that her brother used the pram as a wheelbarrow and broke it, Edna laughs and 'licks her thumb and wipes something off the girl's face'. She is happy to have the girl staying with her and her husband, John. She calls the girl 'Leanbh', which is the Irish for child, and says to the girl's father, 'She's welcome here'. Likewise, John Kinsella is friendly and kind to the young girl. He times her as she races to collect the post and gives her the nickname 'Petal'.

Edna cares for the girl. On the girl's first night staying with them, she bathes her and gives her clean clothes and warns her to be careful of the well. She checks on the girl during the night, sitting on her bed and saying: 'If you were mine, I'd never leave you in a house with strangers.' When the girl wets the bed, Edna says that the mattress is weeping to save the girl from being embarrassed. As the summer progresses, Edna and the girl work together harmoniously, cooking and doing housework, and when a woman in a shop in Gorey says that it'll be a relief when the children go back to school, Edna tells her: 'It's only missing her I'll be when she is gone.'

John, too, becomes very fond of the girl, and when he takes her hand on a night-time walk to the shore the girl is struck with feeling as she realises that her father has never once held her hand.

On the other hand, the girl's relationship with her parents is very different. When her father leaves the girl with the Kinsellas, he forgets to take her suitcase out of the car and simply tells her

not to 'fall into the fire'. Throughout the story, the father is presented as deficient in care and responsibility for his family. He lost the 'red Shorthorn' in a card game in Shillelagh and tells the Kinsellas 'it a great year for the hay all the same' when the hay has not been cut because there is no money 'to pay the man'. The young girl wonders why her father lies. When the girl has to return home at the end of the summer, the father arrives late and says he has had a 'liquid supper [drunk alcohol]… down in Parkbridge'. This causes tension as the girl's mother 'changes the subject'. The girl's relationship with her mother is also strained. The girl says 'With my mother it is all work', and describes her later as being 'too busy'. At the end of the summer when the girl returns home, her mother is suspicious rather than loving, telling the girl 'You've grown' and giving her a 'deep look'.

Role of Money in Family Life

Money is presented in the text as having a powerful influence on family life. The young girl is sent to stay with her aunt and uncle for the summer. It is not entirely clear in the text why this arrangement is made but it is likely that the arrangement was put in place to save the girl's family the expense of keeping her. The girl's father tells the Kinsellas: 'It's the feeding them that's the trouble.' The Kinsellas, by contrast, are financially comfortable. They take the young girl to Gorey and buy her clothes and books. John also gives the girl money to spend, something she is not used to. The comfort of the Kinsellas' home with its freezer and vacuum cleaner and 'Kimberley biscuits' contrasts starkly with the girl's home, where: 'Inside, the house feels damp and cold. The lino is all tracked over with dirty footprints.'

In this text, money is shown to be a vital ingredient in a positive experience of family life. While the Kinsellas are not wealthy, they have enough money to be free of financial worry. The girl's parents, on the other hand, are plagued with financial difficulties and the shadow of poverty looms over the family. It is hinted at in the text that their money problems may be linked to the girl's father's consumption of alcohol. Whatever the root cause of their financial difficulties, the girl's mother cannot afford to have the hay cut and is worn down from stress and over-work.

Effect of Family on Individuals

In *Foster*, Keegan presents family as both a place of nurture and a site of struggle and, significantly, as a bond between people rather than a social institution. The young girl flourishes in the care of the Kinsellas. At first, she keeps 'waiting for something to happen', for the 'ease' she feels to end, but 'each day follows on much like the one before'. She stops wetting the bed and learns new skills and improves her reading. The girl's first impression of the Kinsellas' house proves correct: 'But this is a different type of house. Here there is room, and time to think. There may even be money to spare.' At the end of the story when the girl runs after the Kinsellas, she hears Edna in the car 'sobbing and crying'. The girl too is heartbroken, holding on to Kinsella and calling him 'Daddy'. It is an inconclusive ending as the reader does know what will happen next, but the sentiment of the ending of *Foster* is clear – the girl has formed familial bonds of love with the Kinsellas which transcend physical separation.

MAKE

Write a short essay in which you consider which of the four aspects – understanding of family, reality of family life, role of money in family life or effect of family on individuals – is the *most* important for a discussion of the theme of family in *Foster*. Give reasons for your answer and refer to key moments in the text in support of your points.

Mode: General Vision and Viewpoint

ANALYSE

The general vision and viewpoint of *Foster* is both pessimistic and optimistic.

Vision of Society

The story offers a miniature portrait of rural Irish life in the early 1980s. It is a confined world in which human nature is both full of generosity and mean spirited. When two men call to the Kinsellas' house selling lines in a raffle towards building a new roof for the local school, Kinsella invites them in saying, 'Just 'cos I've none of my own doesn't mean I'd see the rain falling in on anyone else's'; but when Edna entrusts the young girl to a neighbour, Mildred, the girl is subjected to a barrage of intrusive questions and told about the death of the Kinsellas' son without any sensitivity.

Ireland was experiencing an economic depression during the period in which the text is set, and although there are no explicit references to this in the story, an atmosphere of deprivation hangs over the girl's family. Political disturbance is also referenced in the text with John's mention of the death of another hunger striker. This is a society that is under pressure and that pressure is characterised by a complex vision of language in this text. It is a site of struggle. When the young girl describes disharmony between her parents she says: 'Words had passed between them.' Language itself is problematic. It leads to misunderstandings. When Edna tells the girl that there are no secrets in the house, the girl doesn't want to answer back but feels she has to. When she replies with 'Yeah', Edna tells her to say 'Yes', but when she returns home, her mother says '"Yes", is it?' The young girl is navigating a world she finds difficult to understand and comes to realise that words themselves can be dangerous, carrying meanings beyond dictionary definitions. When she first arrives at the Kinsellas she says: 'I feel at such a loss for words but this is a new place, and new words are needed.'

Silence marks the social interaction between the Kinsellas and the girl's family. When her father has tea with the Kinsellas, there is a 'patchy silence', and in the girl's home 'A little bit of talk starts up'. On the walk with Kinsella, he tells the girl 'You don't ever have to say anything', and when her mother quizzes her about what happened at the Kinsellas the girl realises: 'It is my perfect opportunity to say nothing.' In this text, silence is as powerful a communication as language.

Comparative Study

Comparative Study

View of Identity

The formation of identity is another aspect of the vision and viewpoint of *Foster*. The young girl is in the process of forming her identity and, in the story, the world around her is depicted as playing a huge role in that process. At the visit to the well with Edna, the girl waits until 'I see myself not as I was when I arrived, looking like a tinker's child, but as I am now, clean, in different clothes', and later she realises: 'Everything changes into something else, turns into some version of what it was before.' In this text, selfhood is seen as malleable and childhood is presented as a vulnerable time. The formation of a strong sense of identity in childhood is presented in *Foster* as being reliant on nurture and love. Only in an environment of acceptance and care can the girl prosper and flourish, both physically and mentally. The Kinsellas encourage the girl to read and to develop confidence. This is not the same experience she has had in her family of origin. It is worth noting that the word 'foster' refers to helping something grow and develop, and not just the care adults might provide for a child who is not biologically their own.

Vision of Individual Responsibility

The vision and viewpoint of *Foster* is one in which responsibility is communal rather than individual. The responsibility for the girl is shared between her own parents and the Kinsellas. The responsibility for their son's death is shared equally by the Kinsellas. The responsibility for the workings of the community in rural Ireland is shared by everyone – John helps dig a grave for a dead neighbour, helps another neighbour to pull a calf, and Edna helps her sister by giving her farm products and money to pay to get the hay cut. In a world where people work hard to make ends meet, the emphasis lies in helping each other rather than in cultivating individuality.

View of the Past

Truth is revealed as being complex in *Foster*. Edna tells the girl that 'there are no secrets in this house', but she doesn't tell her that she and John had a son who drowned and that the bedroom the girl is sleeping in and the clothes she is wearing used to belong to the dead boy. When the girl finds out the truth later in the story, she is shocked but instinctively understands that Edna did not tell her of the tragedy simply because the loss she has suffered is too painful to talk about. Truth in this text is not black and white.

How people deal with the past is an important aspect of the general vision and viewpoint of *Foster*. The Kinsellas have lost their only child in a drowning accident and have found a way to live with their grief that has not destroyed them. The ultimate message here is powerfully optimistic – that love is stronger than even the most awful tragedy. The Kinsellas love each other and, even more importantly, they trust each other. Neither one holds negative feelings towards the other in relation to their son's death. Despite their suffering, they accept what has happened and continue to live. The visit of the girl opens up painful memories for both Edna and John. Edna is upset when John says the girl must get new clothes in Gorey as she has obviously been deriving comfort from seeing the girl wearing her son's clothes. John is suffering too. When he takes the girl for a walk on the strand, she tells us: 'And that is when he puts his arms around me and gathers me into them as though I were his.' The text offers a vision in which the pain of the past must be felt and accepted if it is to be transformed into something positive.

MAKE

Write a short essay in which you consider which of the four aspects – vision of society, view of identity, vision of individual responsibility or view of the past – is the *most* important for a discussion of the general vision and viewpoint in *Foster*. Give reasons for your answer and refer to key moments in the text in support of your points.

Mode: Literary Genre

ANALYSE

Genre

Foster is a short story. Although it contains chapters and is longer than the average short story, its use of inference and imagery to convey a narrative is characteristic of the short story form rather than the novella. It is written in the genre of social realism as it depicts a society at a particular place and time – the rural east of Ireland in 1981 – and has credible characters and a plausible plot. It also contains elements of fable since its plot involves secrecy, superstition and repetitions.

Narrative Technique and Characterisation

Foster is narrated in the first person by an unnamed young girl. This choice of narrative technique impacts powerfully on the story. The girl is naïve. She observes the world around her carefully but there is much that she cannot make sense of. This creates a complex layering of meaning for the reader. We empathise with the child's perspective but also read 'between the lines' to work out what is actually happening in the adult world. This kind of narrative technique offers a rich experience for the reader because the story being told demands interpretation rather than simply being delivered. Although *Foster* is written in the continuous present, it is a memory piece – this is significant as it allows the narrative voice to move freely between the language repertoire of a young girl and that of a linguistically dexterous adult. The girl's voice is enticing. She speculates and reflects on the world around her as well as reporting events, such as when she wonders why her father 'lied about the hay'. Here and there, however, small details in the story remind us that this is the voice of a young girl, such as when she doesn't understand the word 'offended' and when she says 'Aunt Acid' instead of antacid, a digestive remedy.

Dialogue is a vital aspect of characterisation in *Foster*. It is reported verbatim by the girl narrator and each of the adults – John, Edna, Dan and Mary – is thus represented as much by their voice as their actions and the descriptions of them. John is warm in his manner – 'Dan. What way are you?' – while Dan is taciturn, merely replying with the terse greeting, 'John'. Edna is straight talking – 'Have ye not the hay cut?' – while Mary is evasive – 'He went out there earlier, wherever he's gone'. Colloquial language, the use of real place names and the odd Irish word such as 'Leanbh' add authenticity to the story.

Comparative Study

Structure and Setting

Foster is set in the rural east of Ireland in the summer of 1981. The narrative is linear since it begins at a particular point in time – 'Early on a Sunday, after first mass in Clonegal, my father, instead of taking me home, drives deep into Wexford towards the coast where my mother's people came from' – and ends at another point in time a few months later with the girl 'in Kinsella's arms, holding on'. Although it is a long short story, *Foster* is organised in nine chapters each detailing another aspect of the unfolding experiences of the girl. Unlike many novels, the plot of *Foster* is slight – one girl's experience of a summer spent staying with relatives – but, in keeping with the short-story genre, there is great depth to the story. It immerses the reader in a world that is rich in atmosphere and suggestion, and leaves them, in the end, with more questions than answers.

Language and Imagery

Claire Keegan has been praised as a writer of great descriptive ability and her use of imagery in *Foster* is evocative. Her description of the natural landscape is at times poetic in its ability to conjure both visual images and atmosphere. Consider the following description of the wind from Chapter 5: 'The wind is high and hoarse in the trees, tearing fretfully through the dry boughs, when their leaves rise and swing.' Although written as prose, the sentence contains features that we associate more with poetry, such as personification, assonance, alliteration and cadence. Keegan also employs sensory imagery, which heightens the reader's involvement in the world of the text. When the girl first enters the Kinsellas' kitchen, we are told that under 'the smell of baking there's some disinfectant, some bleach' and when the girl picks up shells from the beach on her walk with Kinsella, we are told that they 'feel smooth and clean and brittle'.

Another aspect of Keegan's use of language that is worth noting is her highly original pairings of adjectives and nouns. A breeze is described as 'queer' and 'ripe' and when Edna shouts at the dog, it is in an 'iron voice'. The unusual choice of words is arresting. They force the reader to pay attention to a world that is familiar and yet unfamiliar, to experience the world as the young girl does. Keegan also employs similes that are unexpected, such as 'eyes like picks' in Chapter 5.

Symbolism is also used to great effect in *Foster*. The 'weeping willow' trees in the Kinsellas' drive represent the sorrow they have experienced, while dressing the girl in their dead son's clothes symbolises their unspoken joy at having a child in the house once more. Light and dark are also used to evoke mood, such as when the girl tastes something 'darker in the air' as she walks to the wake in a neighbour's house.

MAKE

Write a short essay in which you consider which of the three aspects – narrative technique and characterisation, structure and setting, or language and imagery – is the *most* important for a discussion of literary genre in *Foster*. Give reasons for your answer and refer to key moments in the text in support of your points.

ANALYSE

Comparative Study

Comparative Study: Theme of Family

UNDERSTANDING OF 'FAMILY'

	All My Sons	*Juno*	*Foster*
Key Points	A 'nuclear' family – that is, a heterosexual, married couple with children.	Family takes different forms, including that of a single adoptive mother with an infant.	Familial bonds are based on love, trust and care, and not simply on biology.
Key Moments	Act One: The section in which Mother asks Ann about her parents: '… she's not getting a divorce, heh?'	Resolution: The scene where Vanessa holds her son in the hospital and Bren tells her that she looks, 'Like a new mom.'	Resolution: The final paragraph in which the girl, in Kinsella's arms, sees her father and calls out: '"Daddy", I keep calling him, keep warning him. "Daddy."'
Comparisons	The understanding of family in *All My Sons* is very different from the understanding of family in *Juno* and *Foster*. In *All My Sons*, family is presented as an institution within society that has a very specific make-up, whereas in both other texts, family is presented as the bonds of love that exist between people within a home. In *Juno*, the family is a blended one, while, in *Foster*, the girl is nurtured by her aunt and uncle, the Kinsellas. *Foster*, however, has some similarity to *All My Sons*, as the girl's family of origin, like the Kellers, is a traditional one.		

REALITY OF FAMILY LIFE

	All My Sons	*Juno*	*Foster*
Key Points	Exposes the myth of the perfect 'all-American' family.	Family relationships difficult but redeemed by honesty.	Family can be warm and caring – for instance, the Kinsellas – but also strained and tense – for example, the girl's family of origin.
Key Moments	Act Three: The section in which Jim delivers a speech about his life as a husband and father: '…now I live in the usual darkness.'	The scene in which Bren supports Juno through her labour: 'Hey, can we get my kid the damn spinal tap already?'	Chapter One: This dramatises the girl's knowledge of the strained relationship between her parents: 'Words had passed between them.'
Comparisons	*All My Sons* is different from both *Juno* and *Foster*, as family is indicted within the text. The Keller family is depicted as corrupt under the respectable surface, much like Miller's view of America itself. In *Juno* and *Foster*, the MacGuff and Kinsella families respectively are presented as warm and supportive. Disagreements, such as those between Bren and Juno and between Edna and John, are resolved through honest communication and love. *Foster*, however, has some similarity to *All My Sons*, as the girl's family, like the Kellers, is characterised by unresolved tensions.		

ROLE OF MONEY IN FAMILY LIFE

	All My Sons	*Juno*	*Foster*
Key Points	Financial provision is equated with familial love, but is ultimately inadequate.	Money does not necessarily equate with happiness in family life.	Financial comfort adds to quality of family life, while financial worry places a huge strain on it.

Key Moments	Act Three: The section in which Keller begins to recognise the true cost of his profiteering. He challenges his wife: 'You wanted money, didn't you?'	There are many shots in the film of the luxurious interior of the Lorings' home in an affluent suburb of St Cloud.	Chapter 2: When the girl confides in Edna regarding the financial strain her mother is under: 'She hasn't enough money to pay the man.'
Comparisons	There is some similarity between *All My Sons* and *Foster* with reference to the role of money in family life. Money is at the root of the difficulties in both the Keller family in *All My Sons* and the girl's family in *Foster*. The difficulties, however, are different. In *All My Sons*, Joe's acquisition of wealth at the expense of higher values, such as honesty, destroys his family while, in *Foster*, it is financial hardship that puts a strain on the girl's family. *Juno* is different from *All My Sons* and *Foster* in this respect, as within the text money is shown to have little or no correlation to family happiness. The Lorings are wealthy but this does not prevent their marriage from collapsing. There is some similarity between *Juno* and *Foster*, as both the MacGuff family and the Kinsellas, while not rich, are not under financial pressure and are both depicted as loving units.		

EFFECT OF FAMILY ON INDIVIDUALS			
	All My Sons	*Juno*	*Foster*
Key Points	Family is depicted as a corrupt institution that causes suffering, and even death.	Familial bonds of love create a supportive environment.	Family is presented as a site of both struggle and nurture.
Key Moments	Resolution: In which the stage directions convey the horror of the denouement: [*A shot is heard in the house. They stand frozen for a brief second …*]	In the scene where Juno has a 'heart-to-heart' with Mac, he gives her valuable advice: 'Look, in my opinion, the best thing you can do is find a person who loves you for exactly what you are.'	Chapter 6: At the end of the summer, the girl does not wish to return home. She asks Edna: 'I have to go back then?'
Comparisons	*All My Sons* is different from both *Juno* and *Foster* in that it portrays the effect of the family on individuals as devastating. The lives of both Chris and Larry are destroyed as a consequence of their father's actions. *Juno* is similar to *Foster* as both *Juno* and the girl are well cared for, the former in her blended family and the latter by the Kinsellas. *Foster* is different from *Juno* in one crucial respect, however, as the reader of *Foster* is left with the strong impression that the girl may not thrive in her family of origin.		

Tip: When you are answering a question worth 70 marks, your task is to write an essay-style answer in which you compare and contrast all three comparative texts.

Answer the following **Theme** question from Leaving Certificate 2013 using the guide below to structure your answer.

'Studying a theme or issue enables a reader to form both personal and universal reflections on that theme or issue.'

Compare both the personal and universal reflections that you formed on a common theme or issue in two or more texts from your comparative course. (70)

Guide to Answering 2013 Theme Question

In your introductory paragraph, it is essential to answer the question: do you agree, partially agree or disagree with the quotation you are being offered? You must also tell the examiner what the particular theme is that you have explored and which three texts you have studied – give the title of each text and the name of its author or director. It is also advisable to offer a 'blurb' or 'snapshot' of each of your texts – where and when is it set and what is the essence of the plot – but confine this to one sentence per text. Finally, outline your intention to compare and contrast the texts in relation to the stance you have adopted with reference to the quotation offered in the question.

The main body of your essay will consist of a series of paragraphs relating to the question you are answering. Begin each paragraph with a topic sentence – a sentence that outlines the main point you intend to discuss in that paragraph, with reference to the question you are answering. Compare and contrast all three of your texts in each paragraph. Remember, the most important element of a good comparative study is sensitivity to the material you are discussing. Avoid generalisations and remember that comparisons may be qualified – sometimes texts are both similar to and different from each other. There is no set number of comparisons you should make in an answer – sometimes one complex comparison requires an entire paragraph to elucidate clearly, at other times a series of comparative points may be made in quick succession.

In this instance, you may use the following points to construct the main body of your essay, remembering to keep the question to the forefront of your answer at all times.

- Understanding of 'family' in the texts.
- Reality of family life as presented in the texts.
- The role of money in family life as presented in the texts.
- The effect of family on individuals in the texts.

Finally, include a concluding paragraph. The objective of a conclusion in a comparative study is two-fold – firstly, to provide a general summary of your answer and, secondly, to demonstrate your personal opinion in relation to the treatment of the theme in each of your texts. What did you admire? What didn't impress you? It is important throughout Paper 2 to present yourself as a critical reader of texts.

A complete answer to a comparative study question in the Leaving Certificate exam should be approximately 1,000 words in length.

Comparative Study: General Vision and Viewpoint

ANALYSE

Comparative Study

GENERAL VISION AND VIEWPOINT

	All My Sons	Juno	Foster
Key Points	Pessimistic	Optimistic	Pessimistic and optimistic

VISION OF SOCIETY

	All My Sons	Juno	Foster
Key Points	The 'American dream' has been corrupted. The pursuit of happiness, enshrined in the constitution, has been replaced by the pursuit of money.	Love and friendship are presented as the most important values in society.	A troubled domestic and social world – financial depression and political unease – is reflected in a complex language of silence, in which problems are not acknowledged or addressed.
Key Moments	Act Three: The section in which Chris expresses his disgust at American society: 'This is the land of the great big dogs …'	The scene in which Leah learns that Juno is pregnant and tries to support her friend: 'Oh my GOD.'	Chapter 2: When the girl is left with the Kinsellas, she does not know how to communicate with them: '… new words are needed.'
Comparisons	All My Sons is different from Juno as the texts present opposing visions of America. All My Sons offers a negative vision of a society that has been corrupted by money, while Juno offers a positive vision of a society in which people talk openly to one another, thereby strengthening their bonds of love and friendship. The vision of society in Foster, however, is different from that in Juno, as the Ireland of the 1980s that is depicted is one in which real communication is rare. Foster has some similarity to All My Sons, since the silence that pervades the short story is similar to the frozen moment following the gunshot is the final scene of the play.		

VIEW OF IDENTITY

	All My Sons	Juno	Foster
Key Points	Characters are disillusioned or deluded. Intrinsic moral judgement has been replaced with external parameters, such as the legal system.	The individual is seen as capable of discovering inner strength in times of adversity.	The text presents childhood as a vulnerable time in terms of the formation of individual identity. A child requires love and nurture in order to thrive.
Key Moments	Act One: The section in which Keller tells Chris that he is not guilty of gross negligence, because 'there was a court paper in my pocket to prove I wasn't'.	The scene in which a distraught Juno lies on a hospital bed having given birth to a baby boy. She is comforted by Mac and then by Paulie.	Chapter 2: Going to bed the first night in the Kinsellas, the girl realises: 'Everything changes into something else, turns into some version of what it was before.'
Comparisons	All My Sons is different from both Juno and Foster as the view of identity in the text is a pessimistic one. The characters in the play lack agency and a secure sense of self. Juno is different from All My Sons in that the protagonist, a sixteen-year-old girl, discovers great inner strength when faced with the crisis of an unplanned pregnancy. Foster is different from both All My Sons and Juno, as the main character is a child and so her identity is not yet formed.		

VISION OF INDIVIDUAL RESPONSIBILITY			
	All My Sons	*Juno*	*Foster*
Key Points	Individual responsibility has been sacrificed to personal gain, resulting in terrible consequences.	Individual responsibility is a personal journey in which the goal is to be true to oneself.	In a harsh world, communal responsibility is as important as individual responsibility.
Key Moments	The broken tree in the Kellers' yard, visible from the opening scene, symbolises the stunted lives of the characters as a result of evasion rather than honesty.	The scene in which Juno tells Mac and Bren that she is pregnant and has decided to give the baby up for adoption.	Chapter 7: Kinsella goes to help a neighbour, Joe Fortune, who 'needs a hand pulling a calf'.
Comparisons	*All My Sons* is different from *Juno* as all the characters in the play, in varying degrees, have abdicated personal responsibility, whereas in *Juno* the young protagonist faces up to the responsibility of remaining true to herself in challenging circumstances. *Foster* is different from the other two texts as the short story depicts a world in which individual responsibility, to a large degree, is not as vital as communal responsibility. Co-operation in farming, as well as in child rearing, is essential to the survival of the community.		

VIEW OF THE PAST			
	All My Sons	*Juno*	*Foster*
Key Points	The past is inescapable.	Difficult experiences in the past can be recovered from, if an individual is loved and supported.	People can continue to live healthily after traumatic events, if truth and pain are accepted.
Key Moments	Resolution: In which the curtain falls on Chris weeping with guilt over his father's death, while his mother 'begins sobbing'.	In the final scene of the film, it is summer and Juno cycles to Paulie's house where they play guitar and sing the joyful duet, 'Anyone Else But You'.	Chapter 4: The evening habits of the Kinsellas – supper, the walk to the well, the nine o'clock news, as well as the occasional visitors to play cards – evidence the continuance of life in the aftermath of tragedy.
Comparisons	*All My Sons* is different from both *Juno* and *Foster*, as the play offers a pessimistic view of the past in which its repercussions are felt long into the future. *Juno* and *Foster*, on the other hand, both offer a much more optimistic vision in relation to the past. In the film, Juno recovers from her experience of giving her baby up for adoption while in the short story, John and Edna continue to live and to love each other after the tragic death of their son.		

Comparative Study

Tip: When you are answering a question that is split into two parts, take care to follow the instructions of the question carefully. You will be discussing one text in (a) and comparing and contrasting that text with at least one of your other two texts in (b). Both (a) and (b) will consist of essay-style answers.

Answer the following **Vision and Viewpoint** question from Leaving Certificate 2014 using the guide below to structure your answer.

MAKE

(a) 'The extent to which a reader can relate an aspect of a text to his or her experience of life, helps to shape an understanding of the general vision and viewpoint of that text.' Discuss this view in relation to your study of one text on your comparative course. (30)

(b) With reference to the text you referred to in 1. (a) above and at least one other text from your comparative course, compare how two other aspects of the texts (excluding the aspect discussed in 1. (a) above) influenced your understanding of the general vision and viewpoint of those texts. (40)

Guide to Answering 2014 Vision and Viewpoint Question

In your introductory paragraphs to both (a) and (b), it is essential to answer the question: do you agree, partially agree or disagree with the quotation you are being offered? You must also tell the examiner what vision and viewpoint means – the broad outlook on life presented in the text – and which three texts you have studied – give the title of each text and the name of its author or director. It is also advisable to offer a 'blurb' or 'snapshot' of each of your texts, but confine this to one sentence per text. Finally, in (b) only, outline your intention to compare and contrast the texts in relation to the stance you have adopted with reference to the quotation offered in the question.

The main body of your essays in both (a) and (b) will consist of a series of paragraphs relating to the question you are answering. Begin each paragraph with a topic sentence – a sentence that outlines the main point you intend discussing in that paragraph, with reference to the question you are answering. In (b) only, compare and contrast all three of you texts in each paragraph. Remember, the most important element of a good comparative study is sensitivity to the material you are discussing. Avoid generalisations and remember that comparisons may be qualified – sometimes texts are both similar to and different from each other. There is no set number of comparisons you should make in an answer – sometimes one complex comparison requires an entire paragraph to elucidate clearly, at other times a series of comparative points may be made in quick succession.

In this instance, you may use the following points to construct the main body of your essay in both (a) and (b), remembering to keep the question to the forefront of your answer at all times. In this question, you should discuss one point in (a) and that point along with two other points in (b).

- Vision of society in the texts.
- View of identity in the texts.
- Vision of personal responsibility in the texts.
- View of the past in the texts.

Finally, include a concluding paragraph in both (a) and (b). The objective of a conclusion in a comparative study is two-fold – firstly, to provide a general summary of your answer and, secondly, to demonstrate your personal opinion in relation to the vision and viewpoint of each of your texts. What made an impression on you? What engaged you less? It is important throughout Paper 2 to present yourself as a critical reader of texts.

A complete answer to a comparative study question in the Leaving Certificate exam should be approximately 1,000 words in length.

Comparative Study: Literary Genre

ANALYSE

GENRE

	All My Sons	*Juno*	*Foster*
Key Points	Realist drama	Dramatic comedy film	Short story
Key Moments	The opening stage directions: 'The back yard of the Keller home in the outskirts of an American town.'	Camera shots of Juno's suburban neighbourhood and scene where Mac, Bren, Juno and Liberty Bell share a family meal.	Exposition, in which a young girl is left with people who are strangers to her: 'There's a moment of darkness …'
Comparisons	Although the three texts are different in terms of genre, they all embody the characteristics of social realism. Each text depicts a setting that closely resembles reality, credible characters that are recognisable as ordinary people to the audience or reader, plausible events and believable plots. *Foster*, however, is different from the other two, as it also contains elements of fairytale.		

NARRATIVE TECHNIQUE AND CHARACTERISATION

	All My Sons	*Juno*	*Foster*
Key Points	The story is told through dialogue and stage directions. Characters are brought to life by means of distinctive dialogue and non-verbal communication.	The camera functions as an omniscient narrator, but the director's choice of angles, shots and music heavily influences the telling of the story. Juno acts as first person narrator in occasional voiceovers. Characters are created through dialogue and personal codes.	The story is told in first-person, continuous present tense, by a child narrator. Characters are created through description and dialogue.
Key Moments	The combination of stage directions and dialogue throughout, for instance, in Act One: 'Keller [looking up]: Yeah, nice.'	Juno's voiceover in the exposition of the text, telling us, 'It started with a chair' – and again, later in the film, 'It ended with a chair.'	The opening paragraph: 'Early on a Sunday, after first mass in Clonegal, my father, instead of taking me home, drives deep into Wexford …'
Comparisons	There are some similarities in the narrative techniques of *All My Sons* and *Juno*, since, in both plays and films, the story is communicated largely through dialogue. Film, however, also employs a wide range of personal and technical codes to communicate the director's vision to the audience. In addition, the camera always functions as an omniscient narrator in film, since we cannot see what it does not show us. This is different from a stage play as, in the latter, the audience is watching a three-dimensional stage, not a flat screen. It is also similar to some extent since, in both mediums, the audience's viewpoint is confined at all times to a mise-en-scène. In this respect, Foster is different from both *All My Sons* and *Juno*, as the story is narrated in first-person by a child. As in the other two texts, however, dialogue is an essential part of how the story is told.		

STRUCTURE AND SETTING

	All My Sons	*Juno*	*Foster*
Key Points	The play is divided into three acts and the action takes place over twenty-four hours on one stage set, a back yard of a suburban house in America in August 1946.	The film is set in two suburbs of Minnesota in the mid-2000s. Captions on screen tell us that the time-frame is one year, autumn through to summer.	The short story is set in rural east Ireland in 1981 and takes place over one summer. It is told chronologically in nine chapters.

Comparative Study

Key Moments	Stage directions Act Two: 'As twilight falls, that evening.' Stage directions Act Three: 'Two o'clock the following morning.'	The seasonal appearances of Paulie's high school cross-country team running across the screen convey passage of time in a humorous way.	Chapter 3: Kinsella says, 'They said on the early news that another striker is dead.' This reference to the IRA hunger strikes of 1981 is the only direct allusion to time in the text.
Comparisons	There is some similarity between all three texts, as they are all forward-moving narratives, organised by acts, captions or chapters. *All My Sons* is different from both *Juno* and *Foster*, since the action takes place in one stage set and is condensed into twenty-four hours. *Juno* has some similarity to *All My Sons*, in that it is also set in suburban America, as communicated in the animated opening sequence in which Juno walks through her neighbourhood. *Foster* is different from the other two texts, not only in that its setting is rural Ireland rather than suburban America, but also because the location is described in prose rather than depicted in visuals.		

LANGUAGE AND IMAGERY

	All My Sons	Juno	Foster
Key Points	Miller uses symbols, such as the broken apple tree, to communicate the themes of the play. Ominous foreshadowing is also employed to create tension. Diction and idiom are used to add realism to the dialogue.	As in all films, the use of light to brighten the atmosphere, darkness to cloud it and vibrant colours to enhance it, is a key technique. Positive foreshadowing is used to keep the text firmly within a comedic genre. Youth vernacular is employed to great effect in the dialogue.	The short story is replete with descriptive imagery and symbols, such as a weeping willow tree. Repetitions in the patterning of the plot – children, wells, clothes, water – add intensity to the short story, while colloquial dialogue adds to the realism of the text.
Key Moments	The opening stage directions: 'In the left corner, downstage, stands the four foot-high stump of a slender apple-tree whose upper trunk and branches lie toppled beside it, fruit still clinging to its branches.'	In the opening sequence, Juno seems to walk into an animated world. The music is jaunty: 'All I want is you, will you be my bride / Take me by the hand and stand by my side.' Leaves lie underfoot and birds fly across the sky. The sequence sets the tone for the film – quirky and light-hearted.	Chapter 1: 'At the end of the lane there's a long, white house with trees whose limbs are trailing the ground.'
Comparisons	All three texts employ imagery as part of their story-telling repertoire. *All My Sons* is replete with symbols and, like *Foster*, uses a tree to represent disturbance in the lives of the characters. In this respect, *Juno* has some similarity to the other texts, although since film is a visual medium, Reitman relies more on light – brightness, darkness, colour – than on physical objects to evoke atmosphere. Foreshadowing is used to great effect in both *All My Sons* and *Juno*. In *Foster*, on the other hand, Keegan relies more on patterns of repetition to tell the story. All three texts contain vernacular dialogue, promoting naturalism as well as distinctive characterisation.		

MAKE

Tip: When you are answering a question worth 70 marks your task is to write an essay-style answer in which you compare and contrast all three comparative texts.

Answer the following **Literary Genre** question from Leaving Certificate 2010 using the guide below to structure your answer.

'The unexpected is essential to the craft of story-telling.'
Compare how the authors of the comparative texts you have studied used the unexpected in their texts. You may confine your answer to key moments in the texts. (70)

Guide to Answering 2010 Literary Genre Question

In your introductory paragraph, it is essential to answer the question: do you agree, partially agree or disagree with the quotation you are being offered? You must also tell the examiner what literary genre means – the ways that texts tell their stories – and which three texts you have studied – give the title of each text and the name of its author or director. It is also advisable to offer a 'blurb' or 'snapshot' of each of your texts, but confine this to one sentence per text. Finally, outline your intention to compare and contrast the texts in relation to the stance you have adopted with reference to the quotation offered in the question.

The main body of your essay will consist of a series of paragraphs relating to the question you are answering. Begin each paragraph with a topic sentence – a sentence that outlines the main point you intend discussing in that paragraph, with reference to the question you are answering. Compare and contrast all three of you texts in each paragraph. Remember, the most important element of a good comparative study is sensitivity to the material you are discussing. Avoid generalisations and remember that comparisons may be qualified – sometimes texts are both similar to and different from each other. There is no set number of comparisons you should make in an answer – sometimes one complex comparison requires an entire paragraph to elucidate clearly, at other times a series of comparative points may be made in quick succession.

In this instance, you may use the following points to construct the main body of your essay, remembering to keep the question to the forefront of your answer at all times.

- Genre.
- Narrative technique and characterisation.
- Structure and setting.
- Language and imagery.

Finally, include a concluding paragraph. The objective of a conclusion in a comparative study is two-fold – firstly, to provide a general summary of your answer, and secondly, to demonstrate your personal opinion in relation to the treatment of the literary genre of each of your texts. What did you enjoy? What did you find dull or clichéd? It is important throughout Paper 2 to present yourself as a critical reader of texts.

A complete answer to a comparative study question in the Leaving Certificate exam should be approximately 1,000 words in length.

Comparative Study

Othello by William Shakespeare

Summary

Act I

Scene i: The scene is Venice, a city at the centre of the Christian Empire. It's night. For the moment, all is peaceful. But the ensign Iago, a commissioned officer of low rank, is enraged that his Moorish general, Othello, has made Cassio his second-in-command instead of Iago himself. To begin his revenge, he has the love-struck, foolish Roderigo awaken the Venetian senator Brabantio to tell him that his daughter, Desdemona, has eloped with Othello. Horrified, Brabantio raises a hue and cry.

Scene ii: Iago goes to meet Othello, pretending to be his ally and warning him against Brabantio's rage. Cassio arrives with a summons to Othello from the Duke. Brabantio turns up, wildly accusing Othello of having bewitched and seduced his daughter. Othello remains calm and they all depart for the palace.

Scene iii: In the council chamber, members of the government of Venice discuss their preparations for dealing with the hostile Turkish fleet heading for Cyprus. Othello enters and is ordered immediately to Cyprus, but Brabantio intervenes with the accusation that Othello has seduced and stolen his daughter. While Desdemona is sent for to speak on her own behalf, Othello colourfully explains how he courted her, by recounting his adventures in the wars, and how this aroused her compassion and her love. Desdemona confirms this when she arrives and the inconsolable Brabantio rejects her bitterly. Since no one wants Desdemona to continue living at her father's house, arrangements are made to allow her to follow Othello to Cyprus under Iago's escort. Left with Roderigo, Iago convinces him that his best option is to follow the fleet and work on seducing Desdemona. Alone, Iago hatches a devious plan that will utilise the weaknesses of others in order to get revenge on Othello.

Act II

Scene i: The scene is Cyprus. While anxiously scouring the seas for the attacking Turkish fleet, Montano (the governor) receives news that it was wrecked at sea by a violent storm. Cassio arrives from Venice in one ship, worried about the safety of Othello, who was travelling in another ship and became separated from the convoy. Desdemona, Iago, Emilia (Iago's wife) and Roderigo arrive next. Iago slyly watches the friendship between Desdemona and Cassio, which he's convinced he can use to make trouble for everyone. Othello finally arrives safely and is lovingly reunited with his wife. Alone with Roderigo, Iago convinces him that Desdemona loves Cassio, and outlines a plan to set up Cassio by picking a fight with him that night. Alone, Iago puts a few finishing touches to his plan.

Scene ii: A civil celebration in honour of Othello's marriage and the scattering of the Turks is announced.

Scene iii: As Othello and Desdemona retire to bed, leaving Cassio in charge of the garrison, Iago quickly gets Cassio drunk and prompts Roderigo to pick a fight with him. Roderigo is pursued by Cassio, who is stopped by Montano. Cassio and Montano start fighting. The alarm bell rouses Othello, who quells the brawl and tries to find out who started it. Pretending to defend Cassio, Iago actually lays the blame on him, and Othello, without seeking other proof, strips Cassio of his rank and job, before again retiring to bed with Desdemona. Alone with Iago, Cassio bemoans the loss of his reputation. Iago advises him to get Desdemona on his side secretly. Left to himself, Iago wallows in his own cleverness and hypocrisy. When Roderigo arrives, complaining that Iago has done nothing for him, he is easily fobbed off and reassured. Alone once more, Iago plans to get his wife to plead for Cassio to Desdemona and then to have Othello spy on Cassio's approach to Desdemona. He is hoping to make Othello believe that Desdemona is having a secret affair with Cassio.

Act III

Scene i: The next morning, Cassio arrives at Othello's apartments, hoping for an interview with Desdemona. Iago turns up and promises to keep Othello out of the way.

Scene ii: Othello arranges to meet Iago at the citadel.

Scene iii: Desdemona promises Cassio to plead with her husband on his behalf. When Cassio slips away discreetly as the others approach, Iago draws Othello's attention to this apparently suspicious behaviour. It doesn't put Othello in the best frame of mind for receiving Desdemona's petition. When they are alone again, Iago keeps hinting to Othello that Desdemona may be having an affair with Cassio, and offers to help the increasingly tortured Othello to verify this. Left alone, Othello convinces himself that Desdemona *is* unfaithful. When she returns to remind him of his official duties, he's torn between faith in her and doubting her, and aggressively brushes away the handkerchief she offers him to cool his brow. Emilia recognises this as the first gift Othello gave Desdemona and as the handkerchief Iago has been asking her to get for him. She gives it to her husband. Othello returns, in turbulence, convinced of Desdemona's affair with Cassio, but demanding proof. Iago offers to supply it, saying that he has seen Cassio with her handkerchief. They swear a pact on their knees. Iago will kill Cassio, Othello with kill Desdemona.

Scene iv: While Desdemona is resuming her plea on Cassio's behalf, Othello asks her for the handkerchief. When she admits she has lost it, he tells her that this is a fatal omen and storms off. After informing Cassio and Iago, when they arrive, that Othello is out of humour, Desdemona speculates that he must be troubled with official matters, and goes after him.

Act IV

Scene i: Iago tells Othello that Cassio has boasted of sleeping with Desdemona. Othello falls into a fit. When he wakes again, Iago sets up a situation where Othello can spy on Cassio talking to Iago. Cassio starts laughing about having fun with his own lover, Bianca, but Othello is convinced that he is talking about Desdemona. Othello and Iago renew their pact, with Iago convincing Othello to strangle his wife. Ludovico arrives from Venice with orders for Othello to return, leaving Cassio in charge. Infuriated, Othello strikes Desdemona, astonishing Ludovico.

Scene ii: Othello dismisses Emilia's objections, calls his wife a whore and storms off. In tears, Desdemona pleads with Iago to help. When the women leave, Roderigo turns up to accuse Iago of leading him on, but Iago convinces him that Desdemona wants him to kill Cassio.

Scene iii: Desdemona, instructed by Othello to retire to bed at once, does so with a heavy heart, mournfully singing a sad song about a forsaken lover.

Act V

Scene i: Iago sets Roderigo on to attack Cassio, who is only wounded and repels Roderigo in the ensuing fight. Hearing Cassio's cries, Othello thinks he is dead and goes to Desdemona. Iago pretends to help separate the brawlers, but kills Roderigo to keep him quiet, and orders Emilia to let Othello know what has happened.

Scene ii: Othello arrives at Desdemona's chamber. Kissing her, he tells her she is about to die, and though she protests her innocence, he smothers her. He admits Emilia, who brings the news that Cassio is only wounded. Desdemona regains consciousness, insists Othello was not her killer, and then dies. Othello confesses, however. Emilia calls for help and confronts Iago about the tales he's been telling. When Othello mentions the handkerchief as evidence, Emilia reveals the truth about this, and is killed by Iago, who escapes an attack by Othello because of the intervention of the others. Othello bewails his fate and produces another sword to stab Iago when he is brought back a prisoner. Cassio appears to confirm everything. Othello asks his pardon, vainly tries to get the now silent Iago to explain his motives, and then kills himself with a dagger, kissing Desdemona as his last act. Cassio is appointed governor of Cyprus. Iago is condemned to torture and death.

Mode: Theme of Romantic Love

Treatment of Romantic Love in the Exposition

In the exposition of the text, Othello and Desdemona have eloped, and it appears that they are deeply in love despite the differences between them. He is older, black and a military general, while she is a young, white, privileged Venetian woman. In the Senate chamber in Act 1, after Brabantio has charged Othello with using drugs and magic to seduce Desdemona, the First Senator has a crucial question for Othello:

Did you by indirect and forced courses
Subdue and poison this young maid's affections?
Or came it by request and such fair question
As soul to soul affordeth?

This interrogation indirectly defines true love, which is understood as imploring ('request') and as mutual, since it flourishes in conversation ('fair question') that is both honest and respectful ('as soul to soul affordeth'). In response, Othello delivers a long speech which makes it clear that his relationship with Desdemona *is* respectful and mutual. He ends by saying: 'She loved me for the dangers I had pass'd/And I loved her that she did pity them.'

Shortly after this, Desdemona requests permission to accompany Othello to Cyprus. She tells the Senate:

> My heart's subdued
> Even to the very quality of my lord.
> I saw Othello's visage in his mind,
> And to his honours and his valiant parts
> Did I my soul and fortunes consecrate.

Desdemona is asserting that she is one with her husband and belongs with him, even in war. If she is left behind, she will be desolate. It is a powerful depiction of romantic love. At the end of the scene, however, when Roderigo and Iago are alone, we get a much more cynical view. Having lost in love, Roderigo tells Iago: 'I will incontinently drown myself.' Iago responds by saying that love is merely a 'lust of the blood' and a 'permission of the will', and keeps on talking until he wins Roderigo over to his way of thinking.

Treatment of Romantic Love in the Complication

Later in the play, Iago embarks on the first step in his plot for revenge. He convinces Othello that Venetian women, such as Desdemona, are notoriously unfaithful. After Iago leaves, Othello laments: 'O curse of marriage, that we can call these delicate creatures ours, and not their appetites!'

In this description of marriage as a curse, the earlier association of love with sinister witchcraft – 'indirect and forced courses' – is reinforced. In addition, Othello's implicit desire to possess both Desdemona's body and mind reveals an alarming insight about the nature of love – that lovers wish to possess their partner entirely.

Before Iago deceives him, love intoxicates Othello to the point of euphoria. Speaking of his happiness with Desdemona, he exclaims: 'I cannot speak enough of this content … it is too much of joy.' However, it does not protect him from the hazardous snare of jealousy. Even as we celebrate that euphoric emotion called 'love', we are reminded of its darker side, which can render us powerless in more sinister ways, filling us with jealous fury, to the point of draining us of life itself. Othello's swift transformation from Desdemona's lover to her murderous enemy illustrates the volatile nature of romantic love.

Treatment of Romantic Love in the Climax

Approaching the climax of the drama, Othello tells Desdemona that he would tolerate 'all kinds of sores and shames', but that he cannot endure the pain in his heart, 'the fountain from which my current runs or else dries up'. Shakespeare uses two layers of metaphor in this speech – a fountain as a metaphor for the heart, and the heart as a metaphor for love. Positioning love within the heart is significant because the heart is a vital organ. Othello implies that he either lives or dies according to love. In a literal sense, if the heart stops pumping blood like a fountain, then Othello's veins will dry up and he will die. Figuratively, because Othello incorrectly believes that Desdemona slept with Cassio, she obstructs the flow of his heart's fountain, drying up both his love and his desire to live. By likening love to a vital organ such as the heart, Shakespeare highlights the tremendous suffering that can arise when love is wounded.

Treatment of Romantic Love in the Resolution

In the last scene of the play, Othello looks upon the sleeping Desdemona and tries to ready himself to kill her. He tells himself that he will do so because it is the just thing to do, but then he kisses her and says:

> Ah balmy breath, that dost almost persuade
> Justice to break her sword! One more, one more.
> Be thus when thou art dead, and I will kill thee,
> And love thee after.

One kiss leads to another, and then another, so that, eventually, he has to remind himself that she must die. He tries to resolve his inner struggle by saying that if she looks as beautiful when she's dead as she does now, he'll love her after he kills her. Othello feels completely justified in killing Desdemona, believing her to be unfaithful. When Desdemona wakes and Othello demands 'Think on thy sins', she answers, 'They are loves I bear to you'. Even in death, Desdemona remains true in her love for Othello but, in the end, he wrestles her down and smothers her, calling her a 'strumpet'.

In the finale of the play, having discovered the truth of Iago's machinations, Othello resolves to commit suicide. He dies asking to be remembered as 'one that loved not wisely but too well'. But the question remains: Can a passion which leads to murder be called 'love'? The answer is no. Othello did not love too well, at all. He loved inadequately. He believed justice to be more important than love. It was Desdemona who loved 'too well'. *Othello* suggests that romantic love is subjective and fragile, rather than all-encompassing and strong.

MAKE

Write a short essay in which you consider which of the four explorations of romantic love – in the exposition, complication, climax or resolution – is the *most* important for a discussion of this theme in *Othello*. Give reasons for your answer and refer to key moments in the text in support of your points.

Comparative Study

Mode: General Vision and Viewpoint

The general vision and viewpoint of *Othello* is primarily pessimistic.

Vision of the World

The action of *Othello* moves in Act II from the city state of Venice to the island of Cyprus. This movement has major implications in terms of the general vision and viewpoint of the text. It is a movement from a secure social order, which Venice embodies, to the random and uncertain conditions which prevail in Cyprus. The arrival of Othello and Desdemona in Cyprus is heralded by a storm, a metaphor for the passage from relative security to relative chaos, at social as well as psychological levels. The atmosphere of the play following the move to Cyprus is claustrophobic. The critic A.C. Bradley referred to the mood in Cyprus as that of 'a close-shut murderous room'. In addition, following the destruction of the Turkish fleet, there is very little for the characters to do. All of these factors – isolation, uncertainty, boredom – play into the hands of Iago and help his plans – and ultimately contribute to the tragedy of the play.

View of Human Nature

Tragic drama necessarily takes a bleak view of the human condition and of the possibility of human happiness, and in *Othello*, the focus is almost entirely on the success of an evil and clever man in absorbing all those around him in his depraved vision of life. Iago's mental torture of Othello and the subsequent humiliation inflicted on Desdemona by her husband, culminating in his murder of her, make *Othello* one of the most depressing of Shakespeare's tragedies. The vision of human nature presented in the play is deeply pessimistic. All of the principal characters – Othello, Desdemona, Cassio, Roderigo, Emilia – allow themselves to be manipulated by 'honest

Iago'. They are, at best, naïve and, at worst, gullible and stupid. The only hint of optimism in the play comes from the fact that Iago does not triumph without cost to himself. In the resolution of the text, Emilia acts out of basic human decency to defend Desdemona's virtue and to expose evil-doing. She does, however, pay for her valour with her life.

Vision of Suffering and Struggle

Discovery or recognition on the part of the protagonist is often regarded as the essential tragic experience. This comes through suffering. It is, however, only when the play has almost run its course that Othello achieves a recognition of the truth about the evil in the world – but even at this point, his awareness of his own responsibility for the catastrophe is very imperfect. Only at the very end of the text does he reach a degree of understanding of the elements of his own nature that have contributed to his downfall and to the wrong he has done Desdemona. In his final speech, Othello recognises the terrible truth of his foolishness: '… as one whose hand,/Like the base Indian, threw a pearl away/Richer than all his tribe.'

Though not entirely to blame, he does assume full responsibility for his action and proceeds to inflict on himself the terrible penalty that he wrongfully imposed on Desdemona. The text presents us with a vision of suffering that is particularly bleak since it is, for the most part, self-imposed.

View of Truth

In the genre of dramatic tragedy, truth is always recognised too late, and so it is with *Othello*. It is only when a terrible price has already been extracted from the tragic hero that Emilia valiantly insists on revealing the truth in Act V, Scene ii. She tells her husband: 'I will not charm my tongue; I am bound to speak.' But, by then, it is too late for most of the characters. Desdemona lies dead, smothered by Othello. This is the nature of tragedy, which invariably presents a vision of the world that is dark. The characters, blinded by their emotions – in this case jealousy – cannot see the truth until all is lost.

MAKE

Write a short essay in which you consider which of the four aspects – vision of the world, view of human nature, vision of suffering and struggle, or view of truth – is the *most* important for a discussion of the general vision and viewpoint in *Othello*. Give reasons for your answer and refer to key moments in the text in support of your points.

Mode: Literary Genre

ANALYSE

Genre

Othello is a Shakespearean tragedy. A key feature of this genre is the movement of the tragic hero from prosperity to adversity, a journey of intense suffering leading to awareness and perception. The protagonist's passage from good fortune to bad is usually seen as the outcome of some fundamental error – a false step, a miscalculation, a defect of character – but, in the case of Othello, there is no consensus as to the precise nature of his tragic fall or its cause. Those who see his proneness to jealousy as the essential reason for his fall must contend with Othello's own claim that he is 'not easily jealous'. A more rewarding way of thinking about *Othello* is perhaps to consider Shakespeare's exploration of the incompatibility of military heroism and love.

Narrative Technique and Characterisation

A play consists primarily of dialogue and stage directions, However, Shakespeare also employs other techniques in order to tell the story of the play. *Othello* exploits **dramatic irony** more relentlessly than any other Shakespearean play, letting us know of 'honest' Iago's treachery from its opening scene, but denying that knowledge to the rest of the cast until the final Act. For instance, we know that Iago wants the handkerchief as evidence that Desdemona is having an affair. However, even Emilia, who has picked up the handkerchief, has no idea he is using it for this reason. We also know that the conversation between Cassio and Iago about a woman is designed to enrage Othello, but Cassio has no idea about this. And even when Desdemona goes to speak to Othello towards the end of the play, we know he intends to kill her, but she is unaware of this. Dramatic irony is often used to make the audience more involved – we know what is happening but feel powerless to do anything – and is a powerful aspect of the narrative technique of *Othello*.

Another vital tool in the telling of the story of the play is Shakespeare's use of the **soliloquy**. Soliloquy is the act of speaking one's thoughts aloud, when no other characters are around to listen. During the Elizabethan era, soliloquy was regarded as an ordinary but convenient way of imparting information to the audience or of developing the action of the play. As used by Shakespeare, however, the real function of soliloquy seems to be self-analysis or self-revelation in order to bring out the inner thoughts of characters. In *Othello*, there are seven soliloquies by Iago and two by Othello, and they are an essential aspect of the narrative technique of the play.

Structure and Setting

Othello is set against the backdrop of the wars between Venice and Turkey that raged in the sixteenth century. Cyprus, which is the setting for most of the action, was a Venetian outpost attacked by the Turks in 1570 and conquered the following year. Shakespeare's information

on the Venetian–Turkish conflict probably derives from *The History of the Turks* by Richard Knolles, which was published in England in the autumn of 1603. The story of *Othello* is also derived from another source – an Italian prose tale written in 1565 by Giovanni Cinzio. The original story contains the bare bones of Shakespeare's plot but the action is compressed into the space of a few days and set against the backdrop of military conflict. The compression of action gives rise to the famous 'double time' effect, whereby the play's events seem at once to take place with terrible swiftness over only two or three days – so that there is no time for Othello to realise the truth – and yet to encompass enough time for Iago's allegations to be plausible. The two locations – Venice and Cyprus – work as symbols within the text, since Venice is a byword for order and civilisation while Cyprus represents a more primitive, less certain world.

Shakespeare originally wrote his plays without Acts. These were added later. The basic unit of all his plays is the scene. Scenes are separated from each other by distinct pauses as one group of characters leaves the stage and is replaced by another. An obvious example occurs at the end of Act I, Scene i when the stage is cleared, so that Act I, Scene ii can begin at Othello's lodgings.

The pause signifies a change of place, but it also creates a tension because the audience now eagerly awaits the confrontation between Brabantio and Othello that Iago has engineered. It is this intricate web of incident and character that makes the play's structure so complex and dramatically effective.

Language and Imagery

In the theatre of Shakespeare's time, the stage contained no scenery, very few props and costumes, and no sophisticated sound or lighting effects. Plays relied entirely on language to communicate not only the action of the drama, but also the setting and atmosphere. *Othello* is considered a poetic drama since many of the speeches are dense with metaphor and simile as well as highly symbolic language. Shakespeare does, however, employ a wide variety of expression in the play, ranging from the poetic to a more natural language, not far removed from that of everyday speech. These variations in style fulfill a dramatic purpose.

In a play like *Othello*, in which formal order is attacked and destroyed, the language reflects the unfolding drama. The basic metre that Shakespeare uses is the iambic pentameter, a combination of five unstressed/stressed syllables in a single line. However, as characters come under pressure, both the rhythm and order of their language break down. Consider, for example, how Othello's speech fragments when he contemplates the adultery of Desdemona and Cassio:

> Pish! Noses, ears and lips.
> Is't possible? Confess? – Handkerchief? – O Devils!

There are many examples in the play of the way in which Shakespeare seeks to convey different levels of emotional response in his characters to the situations in which they find themselves.

Imagery is used in *Othello* both to reveal characters and to highlight differences between characters. Othello and Iago differ almost totally in their usual manner of speech and in the subject-matter of the images they invoke. Othello's distinctive images are heroic and romantic. Waves are 'hills of seas Olympus-high', thunder is 'the Immortal Jove's dread clamours' and life is 'Promethean heat'. In contrast, Iago's imagery is loathsome, vile and disgusting. He sees his fellow men as beasts and insects and the world as a vast menagerie. The depths of Iago's wickedness are suggested by his frequent use of diabolic images. Shakespeare puts imagery to subtle use as a means of depicting the degeneration of Othello's character. From the middle of Act III, his speeches begin to sound like Iago's, as if the latter were gradually gaining control of Othello's mind. From this time until he is fully resolved to murder Desdemona, Othello's speeches abound in animal and demonic images. Desdemona, the fountain from which he draws his life, has become 'a cistern for foul toads to knot and gender in'. In *Othello*, Shakespeare uses imagery as an effective means of both revealing character and depicting the progressive degeneration of the protagonist.

Aside from characterisation, the main function of imagery in *Othello* is to evoke atmosphere and elucidate major themes. Three image-groups in *Othello* deserve particular attention. **Storm and sea imagery** provide symbols of human discord, of massive disruption in the affairs of men. In *Othello*, the storm at sea is presented in all its potential menace and destructive power ('The chiding billow seems to pelt the clouds' … 'The wind-shake'd surge, with high and monstrous

Comparative Study

main' … 'It is impossible they bear it out'). The storm symbolism is also cruelly ironic. On his arrival in Cyprus, Othello tells Desdemona:

> O my soul's joy!
> If after every tempest comes such calmness
> May the winds blow till they have waken'd death!

The winds of Othello's passion will indeed soon blow, bringing death in their trail.

The **imagery of heaven and hell** symbolises the battle between good and evil in the play. The diabolic imagery originates with Iago, but as he gains control over Othello's mind, this imagery becomes a distinctive feature of Othello's speeches. Othello applies images of hell and damnation to Desdemona. He wants swift means of death for 'the fair devil', he finds a 'young sweating devil' in her palm, and he is possessed by the vision of her damnation: 'Ay, let her rot and perish and be damned to-night.'

Animal imagery also abounds in *Othello*. Like imagery of heaven and hell, it originates with Iago, who has a degraded view of human nature, but becomes part of Othello's language from Act III, Scene iii. Othello's use of animal imagery in the second half of the play is, if anything, more repulsive than Iago's, degrading both himself and Desdemona, who is the chief subject of his bestial fantasies. His once 'fair warrior' is now esteemed as chaste as summer flies in the slaughterhouse, 'that quicken even with blowing'.

MAKE

Write a short essay in which you consider which of the three aspects – narrative technique and characterisation, structure and setting, or language and imagery – is the *most* important for a discussion of literary genre in *Othello*. Give reasons for your answer and refer to key moments in the text in support of your points.

Rear Window directed by Alfred Hitchcock

Summary

READ

Rear Window is a 1954 American thriller directed by Alfred Hitchcock. James Stewart stars as the wheelchair-bound L.B. Jefferies, Grace Kelly as his girlfriend, Lisa Carol Freemont, and Raymond Burr as the suspected murderer Lars Thorwald.

News photographer L.B. ('Jeff') Jefferies has sustained a fractured leg while photographing a crash at a car race and is now confined to a wheelchair in his apartment with his leg in plaster. Bored, he spends his time prying through the rear window of his home on his neighbours in the apartments on the other side of the courtyard. It's a hot summer and people have their blinds and windows open. Among these neighbours are a young male piano player/composer, a scantily clad female dancer ('Miss Torso'), and a heavy, thickset salesman (Lars Thorwald)

returning home from work and arguing angrily with his wife, who lies in bed in a negligee and appears to be ill. Afterwards, Thorwald emerges into his back garden, tends his roses and rudely dismisses a female neighbour who attempts to chat.

The insurance company nurse, Stella, arrives for Jeff's physiotherapy session and jokingly warns him about getting into 'trouble' for prying. In the same light-hearted tone, Jeff confesses to her that he's 'just not ready to marry' Lisa Fremont, the model and fashion columnist, a 'perfect' woman whose sophisticated style clashes with his own nomadic, masculine career. Across the courtyard, a newly married couple ('the Newlyweds') arrive in their new home and pull the blinds.

At sunset that evening, Jeff is woken from his dozing by a kiss from Lisa. She has brought a lobster dinner and wine. Lisa suggests that she can help establish him as a fashion photographer, so that he can settle down. He rebuffs the offer. He goes back to prying on the neighbours as she prepares dinner. Across the courtyard, a lonely middle-aged woman ('Miss Lonelyhearts') pretends that she's entertaining a gentleman caller; 'Miss Torso' actually entertains three suitors; and Thorwald serves his nagging wife dinner in bed, during which she tosses away the rose he has placed on her tray and then snoops on his phone conversation, presumably with a mistress, and fights with him about it.

After dinner, Jeff and Lisa argue about the impossibility of a life together. He doesn't want his freedom curtailed; she doesn't fancy his rugged news photographer lifestyle.

After Lisa leaves, Jeff turns back to the night-time courtyard. In the darkness, he hears a woman's scream and the breaking of glass. He dozes. When he wakes, it's raining. He sees

Thorwald leaving his apartment, in which all the blinds have been pulled down. The salesman is dressed in a black raincoat and carrying his samples suitcase. It's almost two in the morning. Forty minutes later, Thorwald returns and almost immediately leaves again, still with the suitcase, and returns again sometime later.

While Jeff is asleep early the following morning, Thorwald leaves his apartment with an unidentified woman. Later, Jeff confides his suspicions about the salesman's behaviour to Stella, the nurse, and they both watch as a dog roots at something in the rose garden, to the obvious anxiety of Thorwald. Through a telephoto lens, Jeff sees Thorwald wrapping a butcher's knife and saw in newspaper. When he establishes that the salesman's wife is no longer in the apartment, he suspects murder.

That night, Jeff attempts to persuade Lisa that Thorwald may have cut up his wife. She argues that any number of things could explain the disappearance of the ill woman. But then they both see Thorwald securing a large chest with rope and Lisa is suddenly intrigued. She goes across the courtyard to read Thorwald's name from his mailbox.

The next morning, Jeff calls in a friend, a detective named Doyle, but, before he arrives, Thorwald's trunk is taken by delivery men. Doyle is sceptical. Later, he returns with the testimony of the buildings superintendent, who says he saw Thorwald leaving with his wife at six, and with the transcript of a postcard saying Mrs Thorwald had arrived safely after her trip.

That night, as Jeff watches the neighbours – the musician has a party, Miss Lonelyhearts dresses up and goes out, Miss Torso rehearses a dance – Thorwald returns with laundered shirts and begins to pack. Jeff fears he may be escaping. Thorwald examines his wife's jewellery from her handbag, something that further arouses Lisa's suspicions when she arrives. Lisa's now willing involvement impresses Jeff and their relationship immediately becomes more assured, with Lisa announcing her intention to stay the night. Doyle returns and is introduced to Lisa and her theories. He dismisses them, revealing that Thorwald's trunk has been examined, that it contained only Mrs Thorwald's clothes, and has since been picked up by Mrs Thorwald herself. He leaves, declaring the case closed.

Dejected, Jeff and Lisa watch Miss Lonelyhearts arriving home with a man and repulsing his crude advances, and they decide that they have been wrong to observe people's private lives. They close their own blinds and settle for a night together.

Suddenly, a woman screams. The little dog who had been rooting among the roses is lying dead in the courtyard, its neck broken. The only one who doesn't come to his window in response is Thorwald, although the glow of the cigarette he is smoking is visible in the darkness of his apartment.

Their suspicions revived, Jeff, Lisa and Stella watch Thorwald cleaning his apartment and packing the next morning. Jeff produces photographs he recently took which show that the flowers in the rose garden are *shorter* than before, proving that the earth underneath was disturbed. He writes a note – 'WHAT HAVE YOU DONE WITH HER?' – which Lisa delivers, barely avoiding being detected. Thorwald reads it and searches desperately for who posted it, as Lisa returns to Jeff's apartment. Jeff speculates that the presence of Mrs Thorwald's wedding ring in her handbag, which her husband still has, would prove his guilt. To get Thorwald out of the way, Jeff rings him, pretending to be a blackmailer setting up a meeting.

Thorwald falls for it. When he leaves, Lisa and Stella dig up the rose garden, but find nothing. Lisa then enters Thorwald's apartment through an open window, to Jeff's great anxiety, and eventually finds Mrs Thorwald's jewellery, just as Thorwald returns. Lisa is trapped. Jeff calls the police. Thorwald discovers and attacks Lisa. Just in time, uniformed officers appear at the front door of Thorwald's apartment. As Lisa is arrested, she gestures behind her back across the courtyard to Jeff, showing him that she has Mrs Thorwald's wedding ring on her finger. Thorwald sees this. He looks across, knowing now where the threat is coming from.

Jeff sends Stella to bail out Lisa from jail and explains the situation over the phone to the detective, Doyle. Immediately after, there's a silent phone call to Jeff, obviously from Thorwald, establishing where his watcher is. Jeff, confined to the wheelchair and alone, now knows that Thorwald is on his way towards him. His door is still unlocked, as it has been throughout. Thorwald's heavy footsteps are heard climbing the stairs. They stop outside. Thorwald comes in. He demands the wedding ring back. When Jeff refuses, he advances menacingly, slowed by Jeff briefly blinding him a few times with photographic flash bulbs, but eventually starts to strangle Jeff, who calls out as he sees Lisa and the police arrive at Thorwald's apartment across the courtyard. Thorwald quickly overpowers Jeff and is about to throw him to his death out the window of his apartment when police officers arrive and subdue Thorwald. Jeff's hold on the window ledge slips anyway, but his fall is broken by two officers. As he lies on the ground in the courtyard, he is embraced by Lisa and declares his love for her, saying how 'proud' he is of the part she played.

The story ends the next morning with workmen redecorating Thorwald's apartment, Miss Lonelyhearts visiting the composer to listen to his new record, Miss Torso enthusiastically welcoming home her chubby soldier husband, and Jeff asleep, with *both* legs now in plaster, while a protective Lisa watches over him.

Mode: Theme of Romantic Love

Treatment of Romantic Love in the Exposition

In its exploration of the theme of romantic love, *Rear Window* focuses on the relationship between two very different personalities – adventurous photojournalist L.B. Jefferies and fashion model socialite Lisa Carol Fremont – against the backdrop of various other relationships that are visible through Jeff's rear window. In the exposition of the text, Jeff has a bleak view of marriage. He pleads with his editor to get him back on the job, telling him: 'If you don't pull me out of this swamp of boredom, I'm gonna do something drastic … like what? I'm gonna get married and then I'll never be able to go anywhere.'

When his editor tells him that it's about time he got married, Jeff responds by saying that he would not want to come home to a 'nagging wife'. Paralleling his conversation about the difficulties of marriage – boredom, nagging and oppressiveness – Jeff watches his grouchy neighbour Thorwald returning home from work and arguing with his nagging, sick wife, who is lying in bed. Later, in the conversation he has with his nurse Stella, Jeff restates his views on marriage as entrapment. Stella, however, has little sympathy with him and expresses a more spontaneous and romantic approach towards marriage: 'Baloney! Once, it was see somebody, get excited, get married. Now, it's read a lot of books, fence with a lot of four-syllable words, psychoanalyse each other until you can't tell the difference between a petting party and a civil service exam.'

Treatment of Romantic Love in the Complication

As Jeff recuperates in his apartment, he becomes obsessed with the events he observes through his rear window. In his first scene with Lisa, while she's enthusiastically discussing her day, Jeff swishes wine around in his mouth, keeps his eyes low to the ground, and musters only fake smiles. It is not the behaviour of a man truly interested in a woman, or in love, but that of a man wishing he were someplace else, out of his cast and touring the world again. This idealised life of adventure, and the cause of his distraction from Lisa, is symbolised by Hitchcock's placement of Miss Torso in the background while Lisa discusses her day. Jeff cannot take his eyes off her. As soon as Lisa shifts focus and asks Jeff to settle down with her – 'Isn't it time you came home?' – Hitchcock moves the camera so that the Newlyweds' window is now in the background to symbolise the idea of marriage. This is expressive use of mise-en-scène. Jeff dismisses the idea of settling down as 'nonsense' and, as Lisa prepares dinner in the kitchen, he returns to gazing out the window, focusing on Miss Lonelyhearts, whom he toasts with his wine glass. The irony is striking – a real, loving woman is right there in his apartment, and yet he's toasting his glass to another woman. Moments later, the two focus on a song being written by the pianist, which they can hear from across the way. 'It's almost as if it were being written especially for us,' Lisa says, to which Jeff shoots back, 'No wonder he's having so much trouble with it'.

Treatment of Romantic Love in the Climax

It is not until the film nears its climax that Jeff's impression of Lisa begins to change. In the scene when she is apprehended by the police after breaking into Thorwald's apartment, she positions herself with her back to the window so that she can be seen from Jeff's rear window, viewed through Jeff's telephoto lens. To signal that she has found the wedding ring belonging to Thorwald's wife, she points to it on her own finger as she waves her hand behind her back. While this reveals that she has  discovered the crucial evidence, it is also an expression of her symbolic wish to be married to Jeff. By wearing the ring she fulfils her own fantasy, and by daringly placing herself in danger, she inspires Jeff towards love, concern and marriage. In *Rear Window*, romantic love is depicted as thriving on excitement and adventure, and withering in everyday domesticity.

Treatment of Romantic Love in the Resolution

In the final scene, the temperature is 72 degrees and the heatwave has broken. The camera makes a wide pan one last time across the courtyard and the framed windows. Miss Lonelyhearts visits the composer in his studio, where he plays his new hit record for her. His beautiful music saved her life and prevented her suicide attempt. Miss Torso opens her door for Stanley, a chubby, spectacled, uniformed soldier boyfriend and true love, returning home and hungry for what's in the refrigerator. The Newlyweds quarrel for the first time because the bridegroom quit his job. In his apartment, Jeff snoozes with his back towards his rear window, facing inwards and presumably having given up spying on others. There is a smile on his face despite his two broken legs in casts. The camera now finds Lisa at the side of her fiancé. The shot pans up her legs, revealing that Lisa is in blue pants and shirt, a significantly masculine style. After noticing that he is asleep and not watching her, she casts off her male image by putting down her adventure-tale reading material, *Beyond the High Himalayas*, and assertively substitutes her own preferred reading material, *Harper's Bazaar*. On the soundtrack is the musician's song, 'Lisa'. This conclusion suggests that romantic love is ultimately a struggle where one person wins.

Write a short essay in which you consider which of the four explorations of romantic love – in the exposition, complication, climax or resolution – is the *most* important for a discussion of this theme in *Rear Window*. Give reasons for your answer and refer to key moments in the text in support of your points.

MAKE

Comparative Study

Mode: General Vision and Viewpoint

The general vision and viewpoint of *Rear Window* is primarily optimistic.

Vision of the World

In the exposition of the film, the protagonist, L.B. Jefferies, is confined to a wheelchair, recuperating in his apartment following an accident in which he broke his leg. By profession, Jeff is a photojournalist used to an active and adventurous way of life and this confinement is torturous to him. Stuck all day sitting in an apartment in a heatwave with nothing to do, he becomes absorbed in the lives of the people living in the apartments beyond his rear window. The world of the text is claustrophobic, adding to the suspense that builds steadily as the narrative unfolds. With nothing healthier to occupy him, Jeff becomes obsessed with finding out what happened to the wife of one of his neighbours, Thorwald. As he gazes out the window, the camera shots employed by Hitchcock position the audience to view a cramped world from Jeff's confined perspective. The viewer becomes conscious of their own uneasy role every time they watch the film, which is that of a voyeur. Hitchcock offers the world as a spectacle.

View of Human Nature

Hitchcock presents the audience with a complex view of human nature in *Rear Window*. While Jeff sees himself as worldly wise and uncompromising in the early stages of the film, he appears to be otherwise by the resolution, a man heading more towards marriage than towards a mission.

Lisa is also complex, a fashion model and socialite who demonstrates heroic courage in the course of the film, by breaking into Thorwald's apartment and surviving an entanglement with him virtually unscathed. In the final scene, Lisa – wearing trousers and a shirt instead of her usual ensemble – lies on a couch beside the sleeping Jeff reading a book about adventure in the Himalayas, which she then swaps for a fashion magazine. This is a composite woman, able to exist in various contexts. Stella is also an interesting character, hard-nosed and sentimental all at once. Likewise the cast of characters on view through Jeff's rear window show themselves to be contradictory and changeable, rather than types. After the killing of her dog, the owner sobs from her balcony: 'You don't know the meaning of the word neighbour!' But the neighbours have in fact been watching over each other – literally. The vision of human nature presented in the text is complex and all too realistic.

Vision of Suffering and Struggle

In keeping with the thriller genre, the protagonist does manage to solve the mystery, but only after paying a price. In *Rear Window*, the price Jeff pays is that of another broken leg. The film, however, is much more than a mere mystery. Running concurrently with the 'who-done-it?' story is the even more intriguing story of Jeff and Lisa's relationship. The premise here is a familiar one: a strong-willed man rejects the commitment of marriage, fearing it will curtail his freedom, only to have his views changed by an even stronger willed woman, intent on marriage. The vision of struggle dramatised in the text is that between the sexes. Hitchcock addresses this in many of his films and, although he has been criticised for his presentation of women on screen, there is no doubt about who is 'wearing the trousers' at the end of *Rear Window*.

View of Truth

Rear Window is a mystery thriller and the convention of such texts is that the truth is always discovered just in time to prevent catastrophe. In the exciting finale, Jeff is left alone in his apartment. When his phone rings, he doesn't wait to hear who the caller is but blurts out, 'Tom, I think Thorwald's left. I don't— Hello …' The phone then clicks off and disconnects. Jeff slowly realises his error. It was not the detective on the other end of the line. He sits in the darkness while Thorwald slowly opens the door and enters. He loads new bulbs and fires the flash on his camera to keep the killer at a distance, but Thorwald reaches him, tries to strangle him, and then throws him out of the wheelchair and through the open window. Jeff's fall towards the courtyard is dramatically broken by detectives, who – in line with the conventions of the genre – arrive just in time to save him, armed with their belated, but not *too* late, understanding of the truth. When they  are reunited, Lisa cradles Jeff's head in her lap as he tells her: 'I'm proud of you.' However, he sarcastically asks Doyle: 'You got enough for a search warrant now?' There is, of course, another truth revealed in the text. All of the danger and excitement of the plot have inadvertently led Jeff to the truth about his feelings for Lisa.

Thus, in relation to truth and its potential for salvation, the vision and viewpoint presented in *Rear Window* is primarily optimistic, despite the real murder that has taken place.

MAKE

Write a short essay in which you consider which of the four aspects – vision of the world, view of human nature, vision of suffering and struggle, or view of truth – is the *most* important for a discussion of the general vision and viewpoint in *Rear Window*. Give reasons for your answer and refer to key moments in the text in support of your points.

Comparative Study

Mode: Literary Genre

ANALYSE

Genre

Rear Window is a 1954 film directed by Alfred Hitchcock that explores the theme of obsessive human curiosity and voyeurism. The screenplay, by John Michael Hayes, was based on Cornell Woolrich's original 1942 short story 'It Had to Be Murder'. Concurrent with the crime-thriller genre of the film is the struggle of the immobile protagonist (played by James Stewart), a magazine photographer, who is confined to a wheelchair while recuperating. He struggles, as he does with his plaster cast, to overcome his noncommittal feelings and reluctance to get married to his high-fashion model fiancée-girlfriend (played by Grace Kelly).

Narrative Technique and Characterisation

In *Rear Window*, as in all films, the camera functions as an omniscient narrator. This creates an impression of neutrality in the telling of the story, but it is important to remember that, at all times, the director both decides what images to show the audience and manipulates the audience to read those images in a particular way. In *Rear Window*, the camera angles are largely from the protagonist's – L.B. Jefferies – own apartment, so the audience sees the inhabitants of the other apartments almost entirely from his point of view. Camera shots of panning and zooming make it even more realistic as it seems as though the audience is viewing the world through Jeff's eyes. There is a good use of different levels throughout, showing the audience that a lot goes on behind closed doors that no one knows about. This is clear when the musician has the social gathering while Miss Lonelyhearts, in a neighbouring apartment, contemplates suicide.

Hitchcock employs natural framing in many of his films and in *Rear Window* many shots are framed by openings such as window frames, door frames and hallways. At the beginning of the film bamboo curtains are shown rising up slowly, similar to that in a theatre, representing an almost cinema-like view of the world for Jeff. He is the spectator of the 'film' going on beyond his rear window as he sits and watches from his wheelchair. Thorwald's entrance into Jeff's apartment during the resolution of the film is extremely dramatic as it is the first time someone Jeff has been watching interacts with him. The final shot of the film is of the window shades rolling down on the audience – the ultimate voyeurs – before the screen fades to black.

Dialogue is also an important aspect of characterisation in *Rear Window*. What the characters say, as well as how they say it, creates their personality. The two leads in *Rear Window* are well matched in terms of strength of personality and verbal wit. This is shown in the frequent exchanges of quick-fire dialogue that pass between them, such as when Lisa challenges Jeff's assertion that his career is not one she could survive in:

Jeff: OK. Now that's your opinion. You're entitled to it. Now let me give you my side …
Lisa: It's ridiculous to say that it can only be done by a special, private little group of anointed people—

Jeff: I made a simple statement, a true statement, but I can back it up if you'll just shut up for a minute!

Lisa: If your opinion is as rude as your manner, I don't think I care to hear it.

Other personal codes, such as action, gesture, costume, facial expression and body language, are essential aspects of story-telling within film, which is why the close-up shot is so powerful in film, such as when Lisa first appears on screen. A shadow – suggesting the negative image on Jeff's table – slowly rises up Jeff's face as Lisa, in close-up, approaches, bends over and then kisses him lovingly.

Structure and Setting

Setting and structure are vital aspects of literary genre. *Rear Window* was made entirely on one set built at Paramount Studios – a realistic courtyard composed of thirty-two apartments at a non-existent address in Manhattan, New York. The tenants in the apartments each offer a comment on male–female relationships as Jeff watches them through his window.

Hitchcock wastes no time in introducing us to this brilliant concept, showing us this rear window frame during the opening credits. Then, in personified camera – the camera acting like an independent pair of eyes – we move out through the window to survey the courtyard and ultimately return back inside the window where we started.

The setting also adds to the suspense of the film as the audience is confined to viewing only Jeff's flat, the courtyard and a small alleyway. By shooting the film through the frame of the rear window, Hitchcock creates a metaphorical film screen. As Jeff watches this 'screen', he decides which neighbours to watch. In doing so, he acts as a director would, cutting from one image to the next. The condensed timeline of the film – all the action takes place over a few days – adds to the suspense of the text, as do familiar tropes from the crime-thriller genre, such as the disbelieving detective, footsteps on the stairs, the anonymous note, and so on.

Language and Imagery

Language, while an important element of film, is only one part of the story-telling repertoire available to directors. So much of what we experience on screen is communicated via personal and technical codes, many of which are used in a symbolic way. Hitchcock gives the audience all the necessary background information in the opening scene of *Rear Window* without using dialogue. He simply shows various images in the apartment. A thermometer at 94 degrees explains why everyone has their windows open. A man wearing a cast with 'L.B. Jefferies' written on it introduces Jeff, the wheelchair-bound protagonist. A photograph of an automobile crash explains how he broke his leg. More action photographs explain his job as a travelling photojournalist, and, the most important image of all, a framed negative and the photograph of a beautiful woman on the front of a fashion magazine, introduces Jeff's girlfriend, Lisa.

Another element that adds to the realistic atmosphere of *Rear Window* is Hitchcock's use of diegetic sound. In the opening scene, we see a man shaving. There is a radio blaring a commercial – 'Men, are you over forty? When you wake up in the morning, do you feel tired and run down? Do you have that listless feeling?' – and we then see the man changing the radio station to one playing music. This is then followed by the noise of an alarm clock, which shifts the attention from one apartment to another. By leading the audience to where each noise is coming from, Hitchcock makes them involved in the scenes.

Although Franz Waxman is credited with the score for the film, his contributions were limited to the opening and closing titles and the piano tune 'Lisa' played by one of the neighbours, a composer, during the film. Popular songs by singers such as Nat King Cole and Dean Martin, also feature on the soundtrack.

MAKE

Write a short essay in which you consider which of the three aspects – narrative technique and characterisation, structure and setting, or language and imagery – is the *most* important for a discussion of literary genre in *Rear Window*. Give reasons for your answer and refer to key moments in the text in support of your points.

The Fault in Our Stars by John Green

Summary

READ

The Fault in Our Stars, a novel by John Green, was published in 2012.

Sixteen-year-old Hazel Lancaster, who has cancer, attends a support group 'to make my parents happy'. There, however, she meets 'a hot boy' named Augustus Waters, who is seventeen, 'had a little touch of osteosarcoma a year and a half ago' (actually he lost a leg to the disease), but is there now to support his friend, Isaac.

After Hazel quotes material from *An Imperial Affliction*, a book written by the reclusive author Peter Van Houten, Augustus tells her she looks like Natalie Portman in *V for Vendetta* and invites

her to his place to watch it. It's the start of a complex and troubled relationship between the two. Hazel admits, 'I really, really, really liked him.' Hazel names *An Imperial Affliction* as her favourite book and Augustus recommends *The Price of Dawn* to her. They agree to meet again the next day.

Because of her potentially fatal illness, Hazel feels slightly disassociated from both her mother and her best friend, Kaitlyn, and starts to read *The Price of Dawn*, and its sequels, to be closer to Augustus. She then starts re-reading *An Imperial Affliction*, a book about a girl named Anna who suffers from cancer, that ends mid-sentence, just as Anna is about to start a new treatment. Afterwards, she and Augustus discuss the books over the phone.

The following day, Hazel calls on Augustus, who is gaming with Isaac in the basement of his home. In the midst of the banter between the three, Augustus admits that he 'can't stop thinking about that book', *An Imperial Affliction*, and Hazel speculates about its mysterious author, Van Houten. A week goes by before they talk again but, again, it's the book that dominates their conversation. Augustus reveals that he has tracked down Van Houten's email address, and that Van Houten revealed that he 'has not written anything else', nor will he. Hazel uses the email address to write to Van Houten herself, asking him questions about the book that 'have haunted' her 'for years'. When Van Houten finally replies, it is to tell her that he will answer her questions only in person, not in writing.

A few days later, Augustus turns up at Hazel's house dressed in a Dutch-themed jersey and takes her to the park to eat Dutch-themed sandwiches. He tells her that he has organised a trip to Amsterdam to meet Van Houten. Although deeply pleased and excited, she subsequently worries about Augustus falling for her – because she is suffering from a fatal disease and he will be hurt badly if he loves her and then loses her. For this reason, she describes herself as 'a grenade', liable to blow up on anyone who comes too near her.

That night, Hazel has a relapse and ends up in the local hospital's intensive care unit. She's there for six days. When she is home again, Augustus visits her, with news that he wrote to Van Houten about her and that Van Houten wrote back. She reads the letter, in which Van Houten has written: 'She wishes to spare you pain, and you should let her.'

The trip to Amsterdam is booked with the help of the Genies (a Make-A-Wish organisation), although Hazel still has to get her doctor's permission to travel.

Eventually, despite Hazel's tears and pessimism, clearance from the doctor comes through and Hazel, her mother and Augustus fly to Amsterdam. On the plane, after chatting and watching a movie, Augustus tells Hazel, 'I'm in love with you.' She experiences it as a 'painful joy'. In Amsterdam, they stay at the Hotel Filosoof, in rooms named after individual philosophers. The young couple tour the city together and enjoy its pleasures, discussing life and death, and, most importantly of all, *An Imperial Affliction*. Again, Hazel is troubled by the danger of being a grenade to anyone she gets really close to.

The only real disappointment of the adventure, however, is Van Houten himself, who turns out to be rude, unwelcoming, insulting and a heavy drinker. He refuses to answer questions about *An Imperial Affliction* and, instead, lectures them about philosophy and philosophers. Hazel knocks the whiskey glass out of his hand, but that doesn't work either. Augustus drags her away and they visit the Anne Frank house instead, where they finally kiss, long and passionately. Back at the hotel, accepting their feelings for one another, they make love.

It has been noticeable to Hazel that Augustus is struggling physically more than usual, and the next day Augustus explains the reason. He has had a recurrence of his cancer and 'lit up like a Christmas tree' when tested. He is now the one threatened with death. He is now the 'grenade'.

Back home, the couple spend a great deal of time together, and with Isaac, until Augustus is admitted to the ER with chest pains. He is kept in hospital and Hazel wheels him on outings to the local park in a period she calls 'late-stage Gus'. When he returns home, it is in a wheelchair because he is too weak to walk. Over the next month, he deteriorates, unable to care for himself. One night, he leaves the house in his car, but his G-tube malfunctions and he has to call Hazel to rescue him. He returns to hospital and is weaker again when he is released once more. Though he is dying and she will soon lose him, Hazel tells him, 'I cannot tell you how thankful I am for our little infinity.'

Augustus dies and, at his funeral service, Van Houten makes an appearance – we learn later this is on Augustus' insistence. But Hazel is no longer interested in Van Houten's explanations. A few days later, Isaac reveals to Hazel that Augustus was writing something for her before he died. Driving towards Augustus' house in an effort to locate this, Hazel is startled to find Van Houten in the back seat of her car. He reveals, at last, that the Anna of *An Imperial Affliction*, was his own daughter, who died of cancer aged eight, and that the book was an attempt to come to terms with her loss.

Hazel cannot find Augustus' writing at his home, or in any of his notebooks but, through Van Houten's assistant, Lidewij, she learns that Augustus sent what he had written to Van Houten, and Lidewij now sends it on to her. The story ends with Hazel reading what Augustus had written, which is really his song of love for her. It ends with: 'I like my choices. I hope she likes hers.' Hazel's response is the final sentence of the novel: 'I do.'

Mode: Theme of Romantic Love

ANALYSE

Comparative Study

Treatment of Romantic Love in the Exposition

The Fault in Our Stars charts the romantic relationship between two teenagers – Hazel Grace Lancaster and Augustus Waters – who meet at a cancer support group. Hazel and Augustus are attracted to each other instantly. When asked by the group facilitator what he fears, Augustus says 'oblivion'. Hazel, who rarely speaks, tells the group: 'There will come a time when all of us are dead. All of us. There will come a time when there are no human beings remaining to remember that anyone ever existed or that our species ever did anything.'

When Hazel is finished speaking, Augustus says: 'Aren't you something else.' Each thinks the other is smart, charming and, of course, physically attractive. Importantly, they are on common ground, as they're both cancer patients, which allows them to talk freely about things such as the so-called 'cancer perks' in a way they might find difficult with someone who has not been through the experience of having cancer. Perhaps more importantly, however, they also get to know each other beyond their experiences with cancer. Augustus makes a point of this when he asks Hazel what her story is, then interrupts when she starts talking about her diagnosis and tells her he means *her* story, not her cancer story. He is determined to distinguish one from the other, and it is from this point on that their relationship begins to develop in a deeper way.

Treatment of Romantic Love in the Complication

The complication that exists in the burgeoning relationship between Hazel and Augustus is fear. Hazel struggles to come to terms with the knowledge that being close to people will cause them a great deal of

pain when she dies. One of the very harsh realities Hazel faces is that she will ultimately die of her cancer and that those close to her will have to deal with the emotional trauma of her death. Looking at Caroline Mathers' online profile and the comments left for her makes this reality more immediate, and Hazel begins describing herself as a 'grenade' that will inevitably blow up and hurt everyone close to her.

Hazel finds herself in a difficult predicament. She wants to be close to her parents and Augustus, but she does not want to hurt them, and she thinks being close to them will do just that. Her reaction is to push them away in order to keep them safe. However, despite her fear that she will hurt Augustus when she dies, Hazel finally lets herself fall completely in love with him. Her defences give way after Augustus comforts her over her sadness about the swing set in her backyard. It is a big step for Hazel emotionally, and it allows her to feel even closer to Augustus. The relationship between Hazel and Augustus finds full expression in the liberating environment of Amsterdam. They share a passionate kiss in Anne Frank's house. It is a sad place but their kiss becomes an affirmation of life in the face of suffering and death – not just as represented by the Holocaust, but also as represented by cancer – and so it makes sense when the onlookers cheer and applaud.

Treatment of Romantic Love in the Climax

A major change occurs in the relationship between Hazel and Augustus with the news that Augustus' cancer has returned. The roles in their relationship are reversed and this causes Hazel to re-evaluate her opinion on getting close to others. Until now, Hazel has been the 'grenade', meaning the one who would hurt everyone around her when she died. Her fear of hurting others has led her to wonder if it was best to maintain her distance from people in order to spare them pain when she finally succumbs to her own cancer. It is the reason she initially hesitated to be anything more than friends with Augustus. Augustus' news, however, suddenly makes him the 'grenade' in their relationship, since his death is almost certain to come before hers, and Hazel is forced to view him the way her loved ones view her. With the change in their roles, she immediately realises that she cannot keep from hurting people when she dies, and that perhaps she shouldn't want to. She recognises that, even though it will be painful when Augustus dies, she would not want to love him any less. This epiphany suggests that Hazel does not want those around her to love her any less, and that she shouldn't keep others at a distance to avoid hurting them later.

Treatment of Romantic Love in the Resolution

In Chapter 21, Augustus dies. Hazel receives a call from his mother in the middle of the night letting her know. She thinks of how her final days with Augustus were spent in recollection, but now the pleasure of remembering is gone since there is nobody to remember with. It is worse than any pain she has experienced from cancer, and she describes it as 'waves tossing me against the rocks then pulling me back out to sea so they could launch me again into the jagged face of the cliff, leaving me floating face up on the water, undrowned'.

Hazel calls Augustus' voicemail, attempting to revisit their magical 'third space', but she finds no comfort in it. The final words of the novel – Hazel's 'I do' – are significant, as they mark the first and only instance of Hazel using the present tense during her narration of the novel. This change in tense is notable because it indicates that Hazel currently loves Augustus. Her love persists in the present. The words are also a prominent feature of wedding vows. The use of these words suggests that Hazel is entering into an agreement with Augustus to continue loving him into the future. It indicates that Hazel does not see Augustus' death as an end to their love for one another. The novel suggests that romantic love is powerful and does not end with death.

MAKE

Write a short essay in which you consider which of the four explorations of romantic love – in the exposition, complication, climax or resolution – is the *most* important for a discussion of this theme in *The Fault in Our Stars*. Give reasons for your answer and refer to key moments in the text in support of your points.

Mode: General Vision and Viewpoint

ANALYSE

Comparative Study

The general vision and viewpoint of *The Fault in Our Stars* is both pessimistic and optimistic.

Vision of the World

Apart from a brief visit to Amsterdam, the action in *The Fault in Our Stars* takes place in specific locations in Indianapolis – the suburban homes of Hazel and Augustus, the basement of a church where their support group meets, and various hospitals. The day-to-day life that Hazel, Augustus and other cancer patients live is very confined and insular. The trip to Amsterdam symbolises the 'great big world'

that the characters are excluded from as a result of their illness. The vision is one of isolation, since the characters inhabit a particular psychological and emotional world that family and friends cannot enter. They experience a sense of 'otherness' that defines cancer victims within society. Their illness is the main feature that other people use to relate to Hazel and Augustus, something that is always apparent when others interact with them. It can be seen, for instance, when Hazel is with her friend Kaitlyn. There is a certain 'unbridgeable distance' between the two girls as they shop for shoes in the mall.

View of Human Nature

Human nature is explored in great depth in *The Fault in Our Stars*. Because both Hazel and Augustus are faced with the reality of death at such a young age, they question how they can find meaning in their lives. In one notable episode following Augustus' death, Hazel recalls her first encounter with him, when she said that the problem of life is not that it leads to oblivion, but that there is no evident meaning in that oblivion. Appropriately, then, there are recurring allusions to existentialist theories and thinkers throughout the novel. For example, the rooms in the hotel in Amsterdam are all named after existentialist philosophers. The metatextual novel

An Imperial Affliction also ties into this motif, since it raises questions about authenticity and value in life.

In *The Fault in Our Stars,* human nature is presented as essentially good, if troubled. The characters are all involved in a search for meaning. Even Van Houten's mean-spirited behaviour is viewed sympathetically by Hazel when she learns that *An Imperial Affliction* is really a fictional account of his daughter, Anna, who died from cancer at a young age.

Vision of Suffering and Struggle

Unsurprisingly for a novel about cancer, suffering is a prominent part of the characters' lives. Hazel, Augustus and Isaac all endure physical and emotional pain, but they come to realise that pain is simply a part of living, and that though it is never desirable, it is always inevitable. This is similar to the worldview of many great philosophers, such as Seneca and Nietzsche. Apart from illness, the most significant form of suffering in the novel is that caused by the death of a loved one. It is this that Hazel worries about most. Over the course of the novel, however, Hazel comes to recognise that even this pain is necessary, and to accept that, in fact, it is part of joy. Hazel touches on this idea in her eulogy for Augustus. The first thing she says to the mourners is that there is a quote hanging in Augustus' house that always gave the two of them comfort: 'Without pain, we couldn't know joy.'

View of Truth

The Fault in Our Stars is a coming-of-age novel written in the genre of social realism. In such texts, the quest of the characters is for truth in terms of universal human experience. Throughout the story, Augustus questions the meaning of his life without any clear answers, but in his letter to Van Houten, he finally seems to draw a conclusion about what makes a life significant. He refers to the marks people leave on the world as 'scars', and says that he is happy about the scar he left on Hazel. He suggests that, because this scar resulted from their love for each other, it means he genuinely mattered, at least to her. Hazel also comes to her own conclusions about meaning and purpose in her life. When Patrick asks her in support group why she continues to live, Hazel stops to consider the question and comes to the conclusion: 'I felt that I owed a debt to the universe that only my attention could repay, and also that I owed a debt to everybody who didn't get to be a person anymore and everyone who hadn't gotten to be a person yet.' After her relationship with Augustus, she sees her purpose as continuing on with her life, not in order to achieve anything extraordinary, but simply to notice what's around her. Living, her thinking suggests, is its own purpose.

Write a short essay in which you consider which of the four aspects – vision of the world, view of human nature, vision of suffering and struggle, or view of truth – is the *most* important for a discussion of the general vision and viewpoint in *The Fault in Our Stars*. Give reasons for your answer and refer to key moments in the text in support of your points.

Mode: Literary Genre

Genre

The Fault in Our Stars is a novel by John Green, published in January 2012. The story is narrated by a sixteen-year-old cancer patient named Hazel Grace Lancaster. The title comes from Act 1, Scene 2 of *Julius Caesar* by William Shakespeare, in which Cassius says to Brutus: 'The fault, dear Brutus, is not in our stars,/But in ourselves, that we are underlings.' There are many literary allusions in the novel as well as metafictional references to a book called *An Imperial Affliction*.

Narrative Technique and Characterisation

The novel is written in first-person point of view from the perspective of the main character, Hazel Grace Lancaster. This point of view is intimate, enabling a reader to connect closely with Hazel, to get inside Hazel's head, thoughts and inner struggles. Because her voice is direct and honest, the reader cares about Hazel. She has a dry sense of humour which is engaging: 'This support group featured a rotating cast of characters in various states of tumor-driven unwellness. Why did the cast rotate? A side effect of dying.' But when she finds out that people are putting inspirational messages on Gus' online wall after he dies, she is angry: '(That particularly galled me, because it implied the immortality of those left behind: You will live forever in my memory, because I will live forever! I AM YOUR GOD NOW, DEAD BOY! I OWN YOU! Thinking you won't die is yet another side effect of dying.)'

It is partly because of her physical constraints that Hazel relies on words, thoughts and feelings to give her the full experience of life. She tells her story in a straightforward manner, but is also often introspective and philosophical as she considers existential questions. The other characters are brought to life through Hazel's descriptions and observations as well as through the use of dialogue. When Hazel first meets Augustus she offers the following highly visual description of him: 'Long and leanly muscular, he dwarfed the molded plastic elementary school chair he was sitting in. He looked my age, maybe a year older, and he sat with his tailbone against the edge of the chair, his posture aggressively poor, one hand half in a pocket of dark jeans.' And when he speaks his voice is distinctive: 'I'm on a rollercoaster that only goes up, my friend.'

Structure and Setting

The novel has twenty-five chapters and the narrative is written chronologically in the past tense, with the exception of the last sentence. The novel also contains an epigraph. It is an excerpt from a fictional book that only exists within the world of the text – *An Imperial Affliction* by Peter Van Houten. The book matters to Hazel in a very real sense and so the epigraph illustrates the importance of fiction in our lives.

The year is never explicitly mentioned, but as is clear from context clues, such as physical setting and technology, the story takes place in Indianapolis, the capital of Indiana, and Amsterdam sometime between 2008 and 2012. Although *The Fault in Our Stars* is set in Indianapolis, it is not the Indianapolis of people who go to work and school each day, but the Indianapolis of the sick. For teenagers like Hazel, Augustus and Isaac, their hometown consists of the places that they can frequent as cancer patients: hospitals, churches hosting support groups, and occasionally each other's homes. Their world is quite isolated and somewhat claustrophobic. Hazel is aware of the limitations of her environment. She describes Indiana as a place where she feels confined: 'It was a cloudy day, typical Indiana: the kind of weather that boxes you in.'

Even when she meets Augustus and they start spending time together, they are limited in where they are allowed to go. The Indianapolis that they know is very small and utterly familiar. Amsterdam provides a brief but liberating contrast to Indianapolis. For Hazel and Augustus, it is not just another country or continent, it is a totally different life. On her arrival in the city, Hazel reflects: 'It looked nothing like America. It looked like an old painting, but real—everything idyllic in the morning light—and I thought about how wonderfully strange it would be to live in a place where almost everything had been built by the dead.'

Both she and Augustus get to sample a world where anything is possible, where they can have a romantic dinner outdoors, climb flights of stairs, and even sneak into each other's hotel rooms. Even Hazel's mother acts differently in Amsterdam, allowing Hazel and Augustus to go off on their own while she tours the city.

Language and Imagery

The language of the novel is for the most part straightforward and conversational as the narrative voice is that of sixteen-year-old Hazel Grace Lancaster. However, Hazel is a bookish teenager and there are many literary allusions within the text. During the course of the novel, poems by both T.S. Eliot and William Carlos Williams are cited. There is also frequent use of figurative language in the text. Hazel uses simile, metaphor and personification to express herself. There are many examples of this:

'I fear oblivion, I fear it like the proverbial blind man who's afraid of the dark.' (simile, Chapter 1)

'My thoughts are stars I can't fathom into constellations.' (metaphor, Chapter 25)

'I remember once early on when I couldn't get my breath and it felt like my chest was on fire, flames licking the inside of my ribs fighting for a way to burn out of my body, my parents took me to the ER.' (personification, Chapter 21)

Other features of the language of the text – the use of brackets for Hazel's thoughts, the use of acronyms such as PDA for 'public display of affection', and the use of italics to emphasise words – all add to the conversational tone of the novel.

There are many image patterns and symbols in the text. Three of these – water, cigarettes and the grenade – are particularly effective in highlighting the themes of the novel.

Water in *The Fault in Our Stars* mostly directly represents suffering, both as a negative and a positive aspect of life. Water symbolises the fluid that collects in Hazel's lungs as a result of her cancer and that causes her a huge amount of suffering. She likens the suffering she feels in that instance to being smashed by waves but unable to drown. At the same time, it's significant that Augustus' last name is Waters. He is Hazel's great love, and his physical deterioration and eventual death cause her an intense amount of pain. However, Hazel would not trade that pain for anything. Also, the novel's epigraph, taken from the metanovel *An Imperial Affliction*, offers another layer of meaning to the symbol of water in the text. It refers to water as 'conjoinder rejoinder poisoner concealer revelator', giving it an omnipotent quality, like a god, and compares water to time, both of which take everything with them in their tide.

The **cigarettes** Augustus often puts in his mouth but doesn't light represent his attempt to deal with and control the things he fears. Though Augustus doesn't say so explicitly, the thing he fears most is cancer. Towards the end of the novel, his incident at the gas station in which he has to call Hazel for help occurs because he's trying to buy cigarettes. In the context of their symbolic value, he is trying to regain control. By this point, his body is failing.

The **grenade** metaphor signifies the suffering a person's death causes to those close to them. Hazel uses the term to describe herself after she reads Caroline Mathers' online profile and sees the effect Caroline's death had on others. She also says Augustus becomes the grenade after his cancer returns and it becomes evident that he will die before Hazel. For Hazel, not hurting others is a major concern. The grenade also turns up in the video game Augustus plays with Isaac. In the game, Augustus heroically throws himself on a grenade to save nearby school children.

After Augustus dies, Hazel reads a letter he sent to Van Houten in which he discusses the idea of the people close to us hurting us. He says people don't get to choose who they hurt, but they can choose who hurts them. The grenade represents the suffering we cause others, but as Augustus shows in the game, in some cases the cause is worth it.

MAKE

Write a short essay in which you consider which of the three aspects – narrative technique and characterisation, structure and setting, or language and imagery – is the *most* important for a discussion of literary genre in *The Fault in Our Stars*. Give reasons for your answer and refer to key moments in the text in support of your points.

Comparative Study

Comparative Study: Theme of Romantic Love

ANALYSE

EXPOSITION

	Othello	*Rear Window*	*The Fault in Our Stars*
Key Points	The romantic love between Othello and Desdemona is seen as respectful, mutual and powerful. A less lofty version of romantic love, however, is presented by Iago – 'merely a lust of the blood'.	Jeff has a negative view of marriage in the opening of the film, seeing it as the death of romantic love. Stella, however, sees marriage as spontaneous and romantic.	Romantic love is presented as a mutual attraction between two individuals, often enhanced by common experience. It is also seen as a desire to know another person intimately.
Key Moments	Act One, Scene iii: The scene in the council chamber in Venice in which Othello and Desdemona give an account of their love for one another.	The opening scene of the film in which Jeff sits in a wheelchair recuperating from his accident, watching the activities of his neighbours through his rear window and talking to his editor on the phone.	Chapter One: The first meeting of Hazel and Gus at a cancer support group. Hazel – 'Look, let me just say it: He was hot.'
Comparisons	Although the three texts offer differing perspectives on romantic love, there is some commonality between them. In both *Othello* and *The Fault in Our Stars*, romantic love is depicted as a powerful attraction between two people. In *Othello*, the old adage 'opposites attract' applies, whereas in *The Fault in Our Stars*, the attraction between Hazel and Gus in based on common experience. More cynical views of romantic love are evinced by Iago in *Othello* and by Jeff in *Rear Window*. In both cases, it is seen as something transitory, a fleeting passion.		

COMPLICATION

	Othello	*Rear Window*	*The Fault in Our Stars*
Key Points	The nature of romantic love is seen as euphoric, but also as having a dark side. As Iago begins pouring 'poison' into Othello's ear, romantic love is seen as intrinsically volatile since it gives rise to powerful feelings, including possessiveness.	There is disharmony between Jeff and Lisa as they have different expectations with regard to romantic love. While they row about a possible future together, Hitchcock depicts various stages of romantic love through Jeff's rear window – Miss Torso, the Newlyweds and Miss Lonelyhearts.	Romantic love can only thrive when obstacles – such as fear – are removed. Hazel allows herself to get close to Gus when her fear of hurting him is abated. In the novel, romantic love is presented as an affirmation of life.
Key Moments	Act Three, Scene iii: Iago begins his scheme to make Othello suspicious of Desdemona and thus destroy his love – 'Ha! I like not that' is Iago's hint to Othello at seeing Cassio take leave of Desdemona.	The scene in which Lisa arrives in Jeff's apartment. Everything she does, from ordering dinner to discussing her day or her dress, is met with disapproval from Jeff while he stares disconsolately out the window.	Chapter 8: Hazel is forced to confront her feelings for Gus when he comes to her house to see her old swing set and tells her – 'You realize that trying to keep your distance from me will not lessen my affection for you.' She replies – 'I guess?'

Comparisons	In all three texts, romantic love is seen as fraught with difficulties. However, in each text, these difficulties take on different characteristics. In *Othello*, the dark side of romantic love is the volatile emotions it can generate. This is different from *Rear Window*, where the downside to romantic love, according to the various depictions of it in the text, is that it does not last. In *The Fault in Our Stars*, the treatment of romantic love is antithetical to both *Othello and Rear Window*, as it is seen as an affirmation of life and – in the resolution – everlasting.

CLIMAX

	Othello	*Rear Window*	*The Fault in Our Stars*
Key Points	The climax in *Othello* is in Act Three, when Othello comes to believe that Desdemona has been unfaithful to him. The text depicts the tremendous suffering that can arise when romantic love is wounded.	The climax in *Rear Window* is the revelation of Thorwald as a murderer. This begins with Lisa breaking into his apartment. In this scene, Jeff's romantic love for Lisa is ignited, illustrating the contention within the text that romantic love thrives on excitement and adventure.	The climax in the *The Fault in Our Stars* is Gus' revelation to Hazel, in Amsterdam, that his cancer has returned. In the text, romantic love is seen as a risk for the individual – of hurting others or of being hurt – but one that cannot be avoided.
Key Moments	Act Three, Scene iv: Othello: 'She's gone. I am abused, and my relief must be to loathe her.'	During the scene in which Lisa breaks into Thorwald's apartment and ends up caught in a tussle with him, Jeff realises how much he really cares for her.	Chapter 13: Gus tells Hazel that his cancer has returned – 'I lit up like a Christmas tree, Hazel Grace. The lining of my chest, my left hip, my liver, everywhere.'
Comparisons	In all three texts, romantic love is seen as a powerful force. In both *Othello* and *The Fault in Our Stars*, this force can bring tremendous suffering, either in the form of jealousy in *Othello* or in the form of loss in *The Fault in Our Stars*. In contrast, the force of romantic love is seen in a positive light in *Rear Window*. It is a sudden and strong surge of deep feelings for another person, revealed under pressure of threat.		

RESOLUTION

	Othello	*Rear Window*	*The Fault in Our Stars*
Key Points	In *Othello*, romantic love is fragile. Othello kills Desdemona. He chooses notions of justice above his love for her. However, from Desdemona's perspective, romantic love is unshakeable. Her love for Othello never diminishes despite his appalling treatment of her.	In *Rear Window*, Hitchcock presents romantic love as a power struggle between two individuals. Lisa and Jeff love each other but have differing views about their future together. One of these, according to the text, will prevail, and in the resolution it appears to be Lisa's.	The depiction of romantic love in the resolution of *The Fault in Our Stars* is powerful. Hazel experiences tremendous suffering as a result of Gus' death, and yet she is strengthened by her love for him. Love does not end with death but continues beyond it.

Key Moments	Act Five, Scene ii: As Desdemona dies, her last words are – 'Commend me to my kind lord: O, farewell!' Othello, on realising the terrible truth, gives a final speech before taking his own life in which he sees himself as a 'base Indian' who 'threw a pearl away/Richer than all his tribe'.	In the final scene of the film, Lisa is with Jeff as he dozes in his apartment. While they seem to have reached a rapprochement in their relationship, scenes of romantic and not-so-romantic love unfold beyond the window, restating the ambivalent attitude to romantic love that characterises the entire text.	The novel ends with Hazel reading the letter Gus wrote to Van Houten about her. In it, Gus says – 'You don't get to choose if you get hurt in this world … but you do have some say in who hurts you. I like my choices. I hope she likes hers.' Hazel's last words in the novel are: 'I do, Augustus. I do.'
Comparisons	There is some similarity between Desdemona's love for Othello in *Othello* and Hazel's love for Gus in *The Fault in Our Stars*. Both are resolute and immoveable, even in the face of death. In *Othello*, Othello declares his intention to love Desdemona after death, but this is ultimately mere words, since he himself is her murderer. *Rear Window* is different from the other two texts, and perhaps closer to a contemporary depiction of romantic love. After their adventure together, Jeff and Lisa face the future. Will they sustain adventure in their life together or fall into the trap of adopting gender roles that leave neither of them satisfied? Hitchcock only hints at an answer to that question.		

MAKE

Tip: When you are answering a question worth 70 marks your task is to write an essay-style answer in which you compare and contrast all three comparative texts.

Answer the following **Theme** question from Leaving Certificate 2013 using the guide below to structure your answer.

'Studying a theme or issue enables a reader to form both personal and universal reflections on that theme or issue.'
Compare both the personal and universal reflections that you formed on a common theme or issue in two or more texts from your comparative course. (70)

Guide to Answering 2013 Theme Question

In your introductory paragraph, it is essential to answer the question: do you agree, partially agree or disagree with the quotation you are being offered? You must also tell the examiner what the particular theme is that you have explored and which three texts you have studied – give the title of each text and the name of its author or director. It is also advisable to offer a 'blurb' or 'snapshot' of each of your texts, but confine this to one sentence per text. Finally, outline your intention to compare and contrast the texts in relation to the stance you have adopted with reference to the quotation offered in the question.

The main body of your essay will consist of a series of paragraphs relating to the question you are answering. Begin each paragraph with a topic sentence – a sentence that outlines the main point you intend discussing in that paragraph, with reference to the question you are answering. Compare and contrast all three of your texts in each paragraph. Remember, the most important element of a good comparative study is sensitivity to the material you are discussing. Avoid generalisations and remember that comparisons may be qualified – sometimes texts are both similar to and different from each other. There is no set number of comparisons you should make in an answer – sometimes one complex comparison requires an entire paragraph to elucidate clearly, at other times a series of comparative points may be made in quick succession.

In this instance, you may use the following points to construct the main body of your essay, remembering to keep the question to the forefront of your answer at all times.

- Treatment of romantic love in the exposition.
- Treatment of romantic love in the complication.
- Treatment of romantic love in the climax.
- Treatment of romantic love in the resolution.

Finally, include a concluding paragraph. The objective of a conclusion in a comparative study is two-fold – firstly, to provide a general summary of your answer and, secondly, to demonstrate your personal opinion in relation to the treatment of the theme in each of your texts. What did you admire? What didn't impressed you? It is important throughout Paper 2 to present yourself as a critical reader of texts.

A complete answer to a comparative study question in the Leaving Certificate exam should be approximately 1,000 words in length.

Comparative Study: General Vision and Viewpoint

GENERAL VISION AND VIEWPOINT			
	Othello	*Rear Window*	*The Fault in Our Stars*
Key Points	Pessimistic	Primarily optimistic	Pessimistic and optimistic

VISION OF THE WORLD			
	Othello	*Rear Window*	*The Fault in Our Stars*
Key Points	From Act Two, the action of the play is confined to Cyprus, an outpost of Venice. This location brings an atmosphere of uncertainty and isolation to the play, as well as boredom, as the destruction of the Turkish fleet at sea removes the threat of military conflict.	After an accident in which he broke his leg, Jeff is confined to a wheelchair in his New York apartment while he recuperates. Bored, he develops a voyeuristic interest in events outside his rear window.	As a cancer patient, Hazel's life is far more restricted than that of a healthy teenager. With the exception of a trip to Amsterdam, her world is confined and quite isolated.

Key Moments	Act Two, Scene i: Cassio describes the coastline of Cyprus as 'guttered rocks and congregated sands'. This description, along with the storm, creates an image of Cyprus as dangerous and wild.	Opening scene: incapacitated and bored, Jeff spends his time watching his neighbours through the window of his apartment. On the phone, he tells his editor: 'You've got to get me out of here.'	Chapter 1: when Hazel decides to go to Gus' house, it is a change from her routine – home, support group, hospital – and she asks her mother to record episodes of *America's Next Top Model* on TV.
Comparisons	The worlds of the three texts are very different – Cyprus in the sixteenth century, 1950s New York, and Indianapolis in the 2000s – and yet there are some similarities between them in terms of vision. In each text, there is a vision of a world that is confined by some restriction – the remoteness of an isolated island, the restraints of being wheelchair-bound in an apartment, the narrowness of a social life because of cancer. The emotional and psychological lives of the characters in the texts are intensified by their confinement. In fact, in *Othello* and *Rear Window*, the behaviour of both Othello and Jeff is no doubt exacerbated by boredom.		

VIEW OF HUMAN NATURE

	Othello	*Rear Window*	*The Fault in Our Stars*
Key Points	*Othello* offers a pessimistic view of human nature, in which people are gullible and easily manipulated. Emilia's decisive action at the end of the play, when she discovers the truth, offer some relief from this vision.	In *Rear Window*, human nature is presented as complex. In line with recent understanding of human psychology, people are seen as both contradictory and changeable in their attitudes and behaviour.	*The Fault in Our Stars* offers an optimistic view of human nature, seeing it as essentially good. People may have to search for meaning in their lives, but they do not deliberately inflict pain on others.
Key Moments	Iago's soliloquies throughout the play demonstrate how easily he can manipulate the other characters: 'The Moor is of a free and open nature … and will as tenderly be led by the nose/As asses are.'	In the resolution of the text, the various characters that Jeff has been observing have changed circumstances. Miss Torso has a boyfriend. Miss Lonelyhearts is friendly with the composer. The Newlyweds have a row.	Chapter 23: Hazel finds out that Van Houten had a daughter, Anna, who died when she was eight, and that this is the reason for his poor behaviour. Van Houten apologises to Hazel and tells her: 'I am trying, I swear.'
Comparisons	The three texts offer different visions of human nature. In *Othello*, the vision is bleak, as the characters are easily manipulated. In *The Fault in Our Stars*, in contrast, the vision of human nature is optimistic, as characters are essentially good. *Rear Window* is different from both the play and the novel, as it offers a vision of human nature that is complex and contradictory, both optimistic and pessimistic.			

Comparative Study

VISION OF SUFFERING AND STRUGGLE

	Othello	Rear Window	The Fault in Our Stars
Key Points	In *Othello*, the vision of suffering is a grim one. It is, for the most part, self-inflicted, as with Othello, or needless, as in Desdemona's case.	In *Rear Window*, Jeff pays a price for solving the murder. He must suffer the pain and inconvenience of another broken leg. This is, however, secondary to the real vision of struggle in the text – that between the sexes.	*The Fault in Our Stars* offers a clear vision of suffering and struggle. They are seen, in a philosophical light, as being an essential part of the experience of living.
Key Moments	Act Five, Scene ii: Othello smothers Desdemona. When Emilia discovers the truth about her husband's evil machinations she tells Othello: 'Nay, lay thee down and roar;/For thou hast killed the sweetest innocent/That ever did lift up eye.'	In the final scene, it appears that Lisa, wearing trousers, is the victor with regard to her relationship with Jeff. The replacement of a travel book with a fashion magazine seems to symbolise the dominance of her wishes.	Chapter 25: In his letter to Van Houten, Gus says: 'You don't get to choose if you get hurt in this world … but you do have some say in who hurts you. I like my choices. I hope she likes hers.'
Comparisons	The three texts offer different views regarding the role of suffering and struggle in life. In *Othello*, the presentation of suffering is deeply pessimistic. Suffering is ultimately self-imposed or needless. This is different from *The Fault in Our Stars*, where suffering is seen as an essential part of human experience, and thus is more positively presented. *Rear Window* offers a traditional vision of suffering as the price one pays for gain. The film, however, also treats struggle, specifically between the sexes, as an inevitable dynamic, showing some similarities to the philosophy espoused in *The Fault in Our Stars* and to the conflict dramatised in *Othello*.		

VIEW OF TRUTH

	Othello	Rear Window	The Fault in Our Stars
Key Points	In *Othello*, truth is recognised, but too late. This is a bleak vision. The characters cannot see the truth until all is lost.	In *Rear Window*, truth – as regards Thorwald – is discovered just in time to prevent disaster. This is an optimistic vision. The film also presents a vision in which true feelings are uncovered in crisis.	The vision of truth in *The Fault in Our Stars* is an optimistic one. Truth is presented as the discovery of personal meaning. For Gus, it is the 'scars' one person leaves on another that matter, while for Hazel, life should be lived for its own sake.
Key Moments	Act Five, Scene ii: finally exposed as a villain, Iago refuses to offer any explanation for his motives: 'Demand me nothing: what you know, you know: /From this time forth I never will speak word.' This is a vision of unrepentant evil, without regard for honesty, and the truth Othello must face is that of his own role in Iago's puppeteering: 'O fool! Fool! Fool!'	In the resolution, Jeff dangles from the window ledge as Thorwald tries to push him to his death. At the last minute, detectives grab Thorwald, but Jeff lets go and falls to the ground below. His fall is partially broken by other detectives. Reunited, Lisa cradles Jeff's head in her lap as he tells her: 'I'm proud of you.' The murderer is apprehended.	Chapter 25: Despite her suffering following the death of Gus, Hazel enjoys a picnic with her parents and reflects: 'All I know of heaven and all I know of death is in this park: an elegant universe in ceaseless motion, teeming with ruined ruins and screaming children.'

Comparative Study

Comparisons	The visions of truth presented in the texts are different, but there are some similarities with regard to the understanding of the nature of truth. In *Othello*, the truth is tangible, but is discovered too late; while in *Rear Window*, truth is also clearly definable, but by contrast, is discovered just in time. In both cases, truth is understood as external, objective and available for discovery. In *The Fault in Our Stars*, in contrast, truth is presented as internal, subjective and created by the individual.

MAKE

Tip: When you are answering a question that is split into two parts, take care to follow the instructions of the question carefully. You will be discussing one text in (a) and comparing and contrasting that text with at least one of your other two texts in (b). Both (a) and (b) will consist of essay-style answers.

Answer the following **Vision and Viewpoint** question from Leaving Certificate 2014 using the guide below to structure your answer.

(a) 'The extent to which a reader can relate an aspect of a text to his or her experience of life, helps to shape an understanding of the general vision and viewpoint of that text.'

Discuss this view in relation to your study of one text on your comparative course. (30)

(b) With reference to the text you referred to in 1. (a) above and at least one other text from your comparative course, compare how two other aspects of the texts (excluding the aspect discussed in 1. (a) above) influenced your understanding of the general vision and viewpoint of those texts. (40)

Guide to Answering 2014 Vision and Viewpoint Question

In your introductory paragraphs to both (a) and (b), it is essential to answer the question: do you agree, partially agree or disagree with the quotation you are being offered? You must also tell the examiner what vision and viewpoint means – the broad outlook on life presented in the text – and which three texts you have studied – give the title of each text and the name of its author or director. It is also advisable to offer a 'blurb' or 'snapshot' of each of your texts, but confine this to one sentence per text. Finally, in (b) only, outline your intention to compare and contrast the texts in relation to the stance you have adopted with reference to the quotation offered in the question.

The main body of your essays in both (a) and (b) will consist of a series of paragraphs relating to the question you are answering. Begin each paragraph with a topic sentence – a sentence that outlines the main point you intend discussing in that paragraph, with reference to the question you are answering. In (b) only, compare and contrast all three of your texts in each paragraph. Remember, the most important element of a good comparative study is sensitivity to the material you are discussing. Avoid generalisations and remember that comparisons may be qualified – sometimes texts are both similar to and different from each other. There is no set number of comparisons you should make in an answer – sometimes one complex comparison requires an entire paragraph to elucidate clearly, at other times a series of comparative points may be made in quick succession.

In this instance, you may use the following points to construct the main body of your essay in both (a) and (b), remembering to keep the question to the forefront of your answer at all times. In this question you should discuss one point in (a) and that point along with two other points in (b).

- Vision of the world.
- View of human nature.
- Vision of suffering and struggle.
- View of truth.

Finally, include a concluding paragraph in both (a) and (b). The objective of a conclusion in a comparative study is two-fold – firstly, to provide a general summary of your answer and, secondly, to demonstrate your personal opinion in relation to the vision and viewpoint of each of your texts. What made an impression on you? What engaged you less? It is important throughout Paper 2 to present yourself as a critical reader of texts.

A complete answer to a comparative study question in the Leaving Certificate exam should be approximately 1,000 words in length.

Comparative Study: Literary Genre

GENRE			
	Othello	*Rear Window*	*The Fault in Our Stars*
Key Points	Shakespearean tragedy.	Crime-thriller film with a romantic subplot.	Novel written as social realism.
Key Moments	The climax is in Act Five, Scene ii, when Othello murders Desdemona.	The climax is in the penultimate scene, when Jeff falls from the balcony and Thorwald is apprehended.	The climax is in Chapter 21, when Gus dies.
Comparisons	Although all three texts, as well as being different media, are also from different genres, they share a classic patterning in the way they tell their stories. All three texts exhibit the following stages – exposition, complication, climax and resolution.		

NARRATIVE TECHNIQUE AND CHARACTERISATION			
	Othello	*Rear Window*	*The Fault in Our Stars*
Key Points	A play consists primarily of dialogue and stage directions, however, Shakespeare also employs other techniques in order to tell the story, such as dramatic irony and soliloquies. Imagery is used as an effective means of both revealing character and depicting the progressive degeneration of the protagonist.	In film, the camera functions as an omniscient narrator. However, in *Rear Window*, camera shots of panning and zooming make it seem as though the audience is viewing the world through Jeff's eyes. Dialogue, as well as personal codes, is used to create character.	The novel is written in first-person point of view from the perspective of the main character, Hazel Grace Lancaster. She tells her story in a straightforward manner, but is also often introspective as she considers existential questions. Description and dialogue are used to create characters.

Key Moments	Dramatic irony is seen throughout the play as Iago is frequently referred to as 'honest'. His actual character is revealed in the crude images he uses, such as when he refers to Desdemona as a 'land carrack'. Under Iago's sway, Othello's language disintegrates and he too uses crude language and animal images in Act Three, Scene iii.	Dialogue is used by Hitchcock to convey character: 'Jeff: Is this the Lisa Fremont who never wears the same dress twice? Lisa: Only because it's expected of her. It's right off the Paris plane. You think it will sell? A steal at $1,100 dollars. Jeff: Eleven hundred? They ought to list that dress on the Stock Exchange.'	Chapter 1: When Hazel first meets Augustus, she offers the following highly visual description of him: 'Long and leanly muscular, he dwarfed the molded plastic elementary school chair he was sitting in. He looked my age, maybe a year older, and he sat with his tailbone against the edge of the chair, his posture aggressively poor, one hand half in a pocket of dark jeans.'
Comparisons	Different media tell their stories in different ways. The story in *Othello* is conveyed through dialogue and stage directions. This is different from *Rear Window* as the camera in a film functions as an omniscient narrator. The narrative technique in *The Fault in Our Stars* is different from the other two texts, as the story is told in the first person by a sixteen-year-old narrator. However, *The Fault in Our Stars* has some similarity to *Othello*, as the soliloquies in a Shakespearean play offer a first-person perspective, and also some similarity to *Rear Window*, as Hitchcock shot the film in such a way as to position the viewer as seeing the world from Jeff's perspective. All three texts use dialogue to create character.		

STRUCTURE AND SETTING

	Othello	*Rear Window*	*The Fault in Our Stars*
Key Points	The action of the play is compressed into two or three days and organised into scenes. The two locations – Venice and Cyprus – work as symbols within the text as well as locations.	The setting adds to the suspense of the film as the audience is confined to viewing only Jeff's flat, the courtyard and a small alleyway. The condensed timeline of the film – all the action takes place over a few days – adds to the suspense of the text.	The novel is written chronologically in chapters in the past tense, with the exception of the last sentence. The novel also contains an epigraph. The two settings – Indianapolis and Amsterdam – work as symbols within the text as well as locations.
Key Moments	Act Two, Scene i: Cassio describes the coastline of Cyprus as 'guttered rocks and congregated sands'. This description, along with the storm, creates an image of Cyprus as dangerous and wild, in contrast to Venice which is civilised and ordered.	The opening shots reveal the view through Jeff's rear window – a realistic courtyard surrounded by thirty-two apartments.	In Chapter 1, Indianapolis is described rather blandly as 'the 137th nicest city in America'. Amsterdam, on the other hand, is described as 'everything achingly idyllic in the morning light'.

Comparisons	All three texts employ chronological narratives to tell their story, but in *The Fault in Our Stars* everything has already happened, since the text is a recollection of past events. *Othello* and *Rear Window*, in contrast, are forward-moving narratives and thus have a lot of suspense. The settings in all three texts add to the atmosphere as each is restricted or confined in some way. In addition, the condensed timelines in *Othello* and *Rear Window*, and the sense of the pressure of time in *The Fault in Our Stars*, also contribute to atmosphere. In both *Othello* and *The Fault in Our Stars,* the locations act as symbols within the text.

LANGUAGE AND IMAGERY

	Othello	Rear Window	The Fault in Our Stars
Key Points	*Othello* is a poetic drama, since many of the speeches are dense with figurative language. Shakespeare does, however, employ a wide variety of expression in the play to reflect the unfolding drama. The text is also replete with imagery.	Hitchcock gives the audience all the necessary background information in the opening scene of *Rear Window* without using dialogue. Diegetic sound adds to the atmosphere of the film, as do the film score and soundtrack.	The language of the novel is for the most part straightforward and conversational as befits a sixteen-year-old narrator. However, there are also literary allusions within the text and it is replete with symbols.
Key Moments	Act Three, Scene iv: Othello's use of language deteriorates: 'Lie with her! Lie on her! We say lie on her, when they belie her. Lie with her! That's fulsome.'	Opening shots: Underneath the credits, jazz music plays as the bamboo shades rise slowly over four rectangular windows in a small apartment. The camera tracks out through the windows, showing the surrounding apartment buildings, lower courtyard and garden. A camera pan follows a miaowing cat up a wide set of steps in the foreground of the courtyard, and then keeps moving up to a wide pan of almost the entire complex.	Chapter 1: When Hazel thinks that Gus is going to smoke a cigarette she says: 'But of course there is always a *hamartia* and yours is that oh, my God, even though you HAD FREAKING CANCER you give money to a company in exchange for the chance to acquire YET MORE CANCER.'
Comparisons	The use of language across the three texts shows fundamental differences. *Othello* is a poetic drama, while both *Rear Window* and *The Fault in Our Stars* employ conversational dialogue. *The Fault in Our Stars* is different from *Rear Window* as the novel contains both a contemporary youth vernacular and literary allusions. *Othello* is different from both *Rear Window* and *The Fault in Our Stars*, in that the play exhibits rare psychological acuity in its language, and particularly in the language employed by the protagonist. As Othello breaks down under Iago's torment, so does his speech. The once-articulate and eloquent general becomes crude in his choice of words and fragmented in his delivery. Both *Othello* and *The Fault in Our Stars* employ imagery to great effect, whereas Hitchcock in *Rear Window* makes wonderful use of both sound and music.		

Comparative Study

MAKE

Tip: When you are answering a question worth 70 marks your task is to write an essay-style answer in which you compare and contrast all three comparative texts.

Answer the following **Literary Genre** question from Leaving Certificate 2010 using the guide below to structure your answer.

'The unexpected is essential to the craft of story-telling.'
Compare how the authors of the comparative texts you have studied used the unexpected in their texts. You may confine your answer to key moments in the texts. (70)

Guide to Answering 2010 Literary Genre Question

In your introductory paragraph, it is essential to answer the question: do you agree, partially agree or disagree with the quotation you are being offered? You must also tell the examiner what literary genre means – the ways that texts tell their stories – and which three texts you have studied – give the title of each text and the name of its author or director. It is also advisable to offer a 'blurb' or 'snapshot' of each of your texts, but confine this to one sentence per text. Finally, outline your intention to compare and contrast the texts in relation to the stance you have adopted with reference to the quotation offered in the question.

The main body of your essay will consist of a series of paragraphs relating to the question you are answering. Begin each paragraph with a topic sentence – a sentence that outlines the main point you intend discussing in that paragraph, with reference to the question you are answering. Compare and contrast all three of your texts in each paragraph. Remember, the most important element of a good comparative study is sensitivity to the material you are discussing. Avoid generalisations and remember that comparisons may be qualified – sometimes texts are both similar to and different from each other. There is no set number of comparisons you should make in an answer – sometimes one complex comparison requires an entire paragraph to elucidate clearly, at other times a series of comparative points may be made in quick succession.

In this instance, you may use the following points to construct the main body of your essay, remembering to keep the question to the forefront of your answer at all times.

- Genre.
- Narrative technique and characterisation.
- Structure and setting.
- Language and imagery.

Finally, include a concluding paragraph. The objective of a conclusion in a comparative study is two-fold – firstly, to provide a general summary of your answer and, secondly, to demonstrate your personal opinion in relation to the treatment of the literary genre of each of your texts. What did you enjoy? What did you find dull or clichéd? It is important throughout Paper 2 to present yourself as a critical reader of texts.

A complete answer to a comparative study question in the Leaving Certificate exam should be approximately 1,000 words in length.

A Doll's House by Henrik Ibsen

Summary

Act One

It's Christmas Eve. Nora Helmer arrives home in high spirits with the Christmas tree and presents. When her husband, Torvald Helmer, hears her, he emerges from his study. He chides her playfully for overspending, calling her his 'little lark'. She reminds him that he's just got a new job and that soon he will have a large salary. He insists that they should live without borrowing. She shows him her purchases, but when he asks her what she wants for herself, she requests more money. Again, he playfully reminds her that she wastes too much money, this time making a mysterious reference to inheriting the trait from her father.

The front doorbell rings. Dr Rank has called, along with a woman named Christine Linde, an old friend Nora hasn't seen for ten years. Mrs Linde's husband died three years earlier, leaving her nothing to live on. Nora feels sorry for her, but can't help talking about her own good fortune, particularly now that her husband has been made bank manager on a large salary. As the two women catch up, we learn that, in the past, Torvald and Nora overworked and that this resulted in the breakdown of Torvald's health, forcing them to spend an entire year recuperating in Italy at enormous expense, the money for which, Nora says, came from her father, who died shortly afterwards. Mrs Linde asks Nora if Torvald can find her employment. In an effort to convince Mrs Linde that she is not the child everyone thinks her to be, Nora now confides her secret. She didn't get the money for Torvald's life-saving trip to Italy from her father. Without Torvald's knowledge, she borrowed it, and is still paying it back in instalments.

A lowly bank official named Krogstad turns up, looking for an interview with Torvald. He is known to Mrs Linde, and makes her uneasy. Torvald appears, is introduced to Mrs Linde, indicates to her that there may be employment for her at the bank and leaves with Dr Rank. When Mrs Linde leaves too, Nora plays with her three children, until she is startled by the reappearance of Krogstad. It emerges when the two are alone again that it was Krogstad who arranged Nora's loan. Now, he says that Mrs Linde appears to be taking his position at the bank and that Nora has to use her influence with her husband to prevent this. Unless this is done, he threatens to tell Torvald of Nora's financial borrowings. Then, he reveals that he has a more powerful hold over her. Her father was supposed to sign as guarantor for the bond for the loan, but Nora forged his signature two days after his death. Krogstad leaves, with Nora clearly agitated. When Torvald returns, Nora does her best to plead Krogstad's case. However, Torvald tells her that Krogstad was guilty of forgery and is the type of person he finds impossible to work with. After this, he returns to his study, closing the door behind him. A terrorised Nora is unable to find peace of mind.

Act Two

It's Christmas Day. Nora is extremely agitated. When the Nurse comes in, we learn that Nora has excluded herself from her children. She considers leaving the home altogether. Mrs Linde arrives. She questions Nora about her relationship with Dr Rank, thinking *he* gave Nora the money. Nora is on the point of revealing all when Torvald appears. In a long exchange between husband and wife, Torvald holds to the belief that his life depends entirely on his reputation. This is why he won't reinstate the sacked Krogstad. Krogstad adopted 'a familiar tone'. Nora challenges Torvald's position as narrow-minded. 'You will see I am man enough to take everything upon myself,' he boasts to her. Torvald leaves and Dr Rank arrives.

The light fades, foreshadowing Rank's revelation that he is a terminally ill man. Nora's initial reaction is one of horror. She is appalled, not by his condition, but by his description of it. 'What an ugly thing to *say*,' she complains. She wriggles away from his honesty by playing Rank in exactly the same way she plays her husband. She flirts with him. She makes herself seem slightly silly and slightly helpless – and totally irresistible. But Rank has admitted that he is dying. He is not interested in charades any more. He explains openly that she 'put him on the wrong track'. She now decides against telling him her secret, after promising to do so. If he helped her, she suddenly realises, then she would have to respond in kind. She gets rid of Rank when she receives news of Krogstad's arrival. Krogstad wants respectability, to be rehired in a better position. He has written a letter to Torvald, explaining everything, expecting it to force Torvald's hand. He places it in the Helmers' letterbox as he leaves. In a panic, Nora asks for Mrs Linde's advice. Mrs Linde follows Krogstad, leaves a note for him, but doesn't expect him to receive it until the next day. As Torvald moves to collects his letters, Nora distracts him by dancing wildly. She displeases him with this violent expression, but she extracts a promise from him that he won't open the letter until after she has danced the tarantella at the party the following night.

Act Three

It's the following night. While the costume party takes place upstairs, Mrs Linde meets Krogstad in the Helmers' living room. We learn that they loved each other in the past, but Mrs Linde married a wealthy man to save her family. Now she is free, and she wants to marry Krogstad, who offers to retrieve his letter from Torvald. But Mrs Linde insists that it should be seen by Torvald. The truth should be revealed. When Nora and Torvald return from the dance, they are both in a state of intense excitement, but for very different reasons. Nora wants to avoid the coming confrontation. Torvald's excitement is because of his wife's stunning performance at the dance.

Dr Rank, who has come to say goodnight, interrupts Torvald's advances. Nora knows that he is also saying goodbye and will soon die. When he leaves, she insists that Torvald reads Krogstad's letter. Torvald is outraged, attacks Nora as a 'hypocrite' and 'liar', and accuses her of destroying his happiness. A letter arrives from Krogstad, returning the contract with Nora's forged signature. Torvald is elated and proposes concealing everything. But Nora refuses to deny the truth that she has just seen: 'You don't understand me, and I have never understood you either – before tonight.' She decides to leave Torvald and her children. 'I must stand alone if I am to understand myself,' she asserts. She walks out. The last sound we hear is of her closing the street door behind her.

Mode: Theme of Self-Realisation

Self-realisation is the fulfilment by oneself of the possibilities of one's character or personality.

Protagonist's Sense of Self in the Exposition of the Text

Nora has a very poor sense of herself at the start of *A Doll's House*, she is too busy trying to be what she thinks other people want her to be. Her total economic dependence on her husband reduces her to 'wheedling' in order to gain influence. Nora is also childish. She conceals the macaroons she has bought because Torvald has forbidden her to eat them and she doesn't want him to know about the purchase. He calls her 'my little skylark' and she tells him: 'Your little squirrel would run about and do all her tricks if you would be nice and do what she wants.' Later, we discover that Nora saved her husband's life by forging a signature on a bond. Later still, we learn that Nora was denied self-expression as a girl by an overbearing father. All her talents and energies seem to be directed into pretending to be what she is not. Quite clearly, Ibsen places the blame for this, not on an individual like Nora, but on society's understanding of the role of women. In the exposition of the play, Nora is disingenuous, shallow and manipulative. Her relationship with her husband is built on deceit, yet she is excited by his new position as it will bring 'heaps and heaps of money'. Nora hopes Torvald will find a position for Mrs Linde if she broaches the subject 'very cleverly'. When Mrs Linde calls Nora 'a child', her description is quite accurate.

Relationship as a Catalyst for Personal Development

Nora's marriage has hindered her from self-discovery. The relationship between Nora and Torvald depends entirely on the two of them continuing to observe their conventional roles. The wife must be dutiful, sentimental and physically attractive. The husband must be strong and independent. We already know, of course, that Helmer's strength and independence are really illusions because he had to rely on his wife to restore his health. How much of the rest is illusion also? Nora's beauty will not last and 'tears and entreaties' will have less and less effect as time passes. When Nora tells Mrs Linde how she borrowed money to save her husband, she unwittingly reveals her frustration and dissatisfaction with her conventional woman's role. 'I was the one responsible for it,' she claims proudly when explaining how she got the extra money to finance the trip abroad. And then: '… it was a tremendous pleasure to sit there working and earning money. It was like being a man.' But, unfortunately, she is also rather scattered and finds it very difficult 'to keep an account' – to do the bookkeeping properly.

Nora is really a bundle of contradictions. On the one hand, as we have seen, she dreams of independence. On the other, she has fantasies of complete female dependence, including the one that involves a rich, old sugar-daddy to look after her: 'Imagine a rich old gentleman had fallen in love with me.'

It is the *breakdown* of relationship that acts as a catalyst for change in this text. While their marriage is functioning, Torvald has no interest in Nora's development as a person. He is invested in her remaining as a 'doll', a silly, flirtatious plaything, as it fulfils his sense of masculinity. It is only when Torvald reveals his true feelings, calling Nora 'a thoughtless woman' and telling her that he doesn't trust her to bring up the children, that Nora faces the truth about her marriage, and herself: 'I must try and educate myself – you are not the man to help me in that. I must do that for myself.'

Development of Selfhood in Crisis

During the course of the play, Nora is the only character who changes, grows, develops and, ultimately, discovers her self. She is the only character who is more complex at the end than at the beginning. She does this in the play by facing the truth about what her marriage actually is. Ibsen exposes the reality that what lies at the core of a relationship, such as the one between Torvald and Nora, is not love, but power, a master-slave contract licensed by society through marriage. 'Am I not your husband?' Torvald reminds Nora when she tries to refuse his sexual advances.

Torvald does not change as a character as the action progresses. He believes that his security depends entirely on his reputation. One aspect of this all-important reputation is the fear of making himself look 'ridiculous' by being influenced by his wife. In the world of the text, any sort of equal partnership between man and wife would be classed as absurd. Nora faces the truth of her own collaboration in her dysfunctional marriage. She traces her adoption of a role rather than personhood back to her relationship with her father: 'He called me his doll child, and he played with me just as I used to play with my dolls.'

She then tells Torvald: 'I have existed merely to perform tricks for you.' Through the crisis of the exposure of the truth, Nora develops suddenly and radically in the play.

Self-Realisation in the Resolution of the Text

By Act Three, Nora is the one who issues the orders. 'Sit down', she says to Torvald. Reflect on how significant these two words are. This is the same woman who tiptoed timidly towards the study door in Act One, terrified of making a noise that might disturb her master. 'Sit down,' she says. 'I have a lot to talk over with you.' What a magnificent maturing of her character these two sentences represent. She instructs Torvald: 'You must simply listen to what I say.' As well as her words, note also her silences in the resolution of the play. She is not quiet because she is wary or lacking in confidence – as she was before – she is silent because she is thinking and wants to communicate in an accurate, honest, straightforward way. Not surprisingly, Torvald becomes 'alarmed'. Nora now expresses openly the truth of what the audience has already experienced while watching the action: 'I must stand quite alone if I am to understand myself and everything about me.'

Nora has made the journey from a 'doll' in a doll's house to a free human being. The play explores what it means and what it involves to discover oneself and become a free individual. Freedom and maturity and responsibility for one's actions are all interlinked, and maturity is only possible – for both men and women – if they put away the childishness of play and face reality honestly. It is a painful journey for Nora and one that involves the loss of her children. But a human being is not a doll, or a little squirrel, or a little songbird.

MAKE

Write a short essay in which you consider which of the four aspects – protagonist's sense of self in the exposition, relationship as a catalyst for personal development, development of selfhood in crisis or self-realisation in the resolution – is the *most* important for a discussion of the theme of self-realisation in *A Doll's House*. Give reasons for your answer and refer to key moments in the text in support of your points.

Mode: General Vision and Viewpoint

ANALYSE

Comparative Study

The general vision and viewpoint of *A Doll's House* is both pessimistic and optimistic.

Vision of Society

To understand the general vision and viewpoint of *A Doll's House*, the audience needs to be aware that it concerns middle-class characters and values. It takes place in an unnamed city in Norway, where banking and law are considered normal and respectable occupations. Banking is the occupation most closely associated with money and the symbol of middle-class goals. In addition, the crimes of the characters – Nora, her father and Krogstad – are monetary ones. In this society, respectability is a core value, more important than authenticity. Krogstad is as obsessed as most of the other characters with social respectability, despite his reputation as 'a diseased moral character'. He must gain, he says, 'as much respect as I can in the town'. His motivation is entirely selfish and conventional – he wants to improve himself socially and economically. Respectability and reputation are everything in the world of this text. Torvald tells Nora: 'Your father's reputation as a public official was not above suspicion. Mine is, and I hope it will continue to be so as long as I hold my office.'

In *A Doll's House,* Ibsen offers an exposé of bourgeois society in Norway in the late 1800s. This is a world epitomised by hypocrisy and conformity. It is no wonder that the play caused consternation when it was first performed and, for years, had a different ending when staged.

View of the Past

The burden of the past and the necessity of truth are other important aspects of the vision and viewpoint of *A Doll's House*. Dr Rank is suffering and dying, not through any fault of his own, but because of his father's sins – his father contracted syphilis. 'To have to pay this penalty for another man's sins!' he laments. Throughout the play, the sins of the parents are visited on the children, and it is this that so frightens Nora when Torvald talks about a deceitful mother inevitably corrupting her children. For Ibsen, the question is not, how we escape our fate – because we cannot do that – but, rather, how we deal with it. Torvald's philosophy is to disguise the truth, and this is why he is so attached to his good name, his reputation and his social position. This, Ibsen suggests, enslaves humans. The only possibility of freedom lies in accepting the truth in all its ugliness and making choices that you believe in. This is the course that Dr Rank has decided on, and this is the course, influenced by his example, that Nora ultimately decides on too. He is the one to show her the way. Thus, the past is presented in the text as something the characters should face honestly and clearly, and not evade or conceal, if they wish to be free of it.

Vision of Individual Agency

A Doll's House is considered a feminist text by many critics, and the vision and viewpoint of this text is one that promotes equality between the sexes. Note that when Nora is expressing her hopes at the end of the play, she does not describe herself as a woman, but declares 'above all else I am a reasonable human being'. This is important because it demonstrates that Ibsen was concerned in the play not with the liberation of women only, but with the liberation of 'human beings', in other words, of men *and* women.

Some commentators maintain that *A Doll's House* is bleak and pessimistic. It is certainly not an optimistic play – it ends with Nora's decisiveness, but without any clue to her future success. The last sound is of the street door closing as Nora leaves. That door, we feel, slams shut on hope and optimism, as well as on Torvald. However, the play is not devoid of hope. The reclaimed relationship between Mrs Linde and Krogstad testifies to that. Without honesty, Ibsen suggests, man is doomed. This is why Mrs Linde insists that Krogstad's letter should be seen by Torvald. The truth must be revealed. Secrets must be exposed. Individual agency – the capacity of *a person* to act independently and to make their own free choices – is possible only when they have confronted the reality of their lives and their own collaboration in that reality.

View of Honesty

A central aspect of the general vision and viewpoint of the play is the importance of honesty and truth in relationships. Ibsen acknowledges that truth can be complex. Was Nora wrong, for instance, to forge her father's signature? She would claim that the motivation is everything: 'I did it for love's sake', she declares proudly.

Essentially, however, the play is unequivocal on the necessity for truth and honesty in relationships. Nora and Torvald have been living a lie. Their marriage is a façade, a pretence that will disintegrate when it is seriously tested. Deep down, Nora realises this. Initially confident that Torvald will support her if Krogstad tells him that she borrowed and still owes money – 'If my husband does get to know about it, he will pay at once.' – this confidence evaporates and turns to fear. Nora lies when Krogstad leaves and Torvald returns: 'No one was here', she claims. Caught out, she immediately lies again. She has no choice, if she wants the marriage to remain stable. And that is the real point. From first to last, the marriage depends on lies, secrets, deceit and suppression for its survival. Deception is presented as insidious in *A Doll's House*, a blight that rots everything that it touches. It is Torvald's selfish reaction to Krogstad's letter that opens Nora's eyes to the truth about her relationship with Torvald, and leads her to rearrange her priorities and her course of action.

Comparative Study

MAKE

Write a short essay in which you consider which of the four aspects – vision of society, view of the past, vision of individual agency or view of honesty – is the *most* important for a discussion of the general vision and viewpoint in *A Doll's House*. Give reasons for your answer and refer to key moments in the text in support of your points.

Mode: Literary Genre

ANALYSE

Genre

The late nineteenth-century theatre movement of which Ibsen was both a part and an inspiration was called 'realism' or 'naturalism'. Before this, there were certain dominant conventions in the theatre. The dialogue was unnatural, the acting style was exaggerated and lines were delivered very loudly and with heightened emotions. The stage sets were also elaborate and colourful. Ibsen was one of the first to change all this. He set out to produce plays about situations that closely reflected the social and domestic problems people experienced in their ordinary, everyday lives, and that emphasised the psychological motivation of the characters. All of these aspects of realism are apparent in *A Doll's House* – the play deals with a common domestic problem, the characters are recognisable as ordinary people, it is set inside a middle-class home and the dialogue approximates to natural speech.

Narrative Technique and Characterisation

Drama is different from prose, as the story of a play is not delivered by a narrator, and different from film, as it is not delivered via a camera. In a theatre, the audience must piece together the story of the play from a number of sources – the script, the personal codes of the actors (such as facial expression and gesture), and the technical codes employed by the director (such as set, lighting and music).

Ibsen wrote *A Doll's House* in what is called a limited third-person point of view. Point of view is 'third person' when the audience has access to speech and action, but not the characters' thoughts, and it is 'limited' when the perspective is almost exclusively confined to a single character, as it is with Nora in *A Doll's House*. Ibsen's point of view for *A Doll's House* can also be categorised as 'a limited third-person narrative with a *near proximity*', because the audience has the opportunity to hear a central character making side remarks. We hear Nora's side remarks in Acts One and Three. In Act One, after Torvald tells Nora that deceitful women poison their homes and their children, leading to immoral human beings like Krogstad, we see Nora pause and hear her whisper to herself: 'No, no … it isn't true. It's impossible; it must be impossible.' A few lines further down, while being 'pale with terror', Nora asks herself: 'Deprave my little children? Poison my home? … It's not true. It can't possibly be true.' This dramatic technique gives the audience an insight into the mind of the protagonist and is an excellent method of characterisation.

Another method of characterisation in *A Doll's House* is the dramatic technique of the formal speech. When a character in this play wants to express his views, he gives a formal speech. 'There can be no freedom or beauty about a home life that depends on borrowing and debt', Torvald declares. This device enables the characters to express their inner lives. In scene after scene, characters talk *at* rather than *to* each other, opining or filling in the back story. The device points to the limitations of realism, as such speeches are far less convincing than techniques such as interior monologue in novels or close-up shots that reveal emotion in films. In drama, characterisation is also achieved by personal codes, including costume, as well as dialogue.

Structure and Setting

A Doll's House is set in a large Norwegian town. The entire drama unfolds on one set, a 'comfortable room' in the Helmers' house that serves both as a drawing room in which to receive guests and as a family room where the children play and where the family sets up its Christmas tree. There is a door to the entryway and another to Torvald's study. Ibsen describes this setting in minute detail in the stage directions, adding to the realism of the play: 'Near the window are a round table, armchairs and a small sofa.'

The timeframe of the play is very compressed and takes place over three days. The five major characters are closely related, and their lives and roles mirror or contrast with each other's. This unity of time, place and characters is constructed to make the audience feel the tension mounting within the play. Another structural technique used by Ibsen is to place many of the significant events in a time before the play opens. Instead of witnessing these events as they occur, the audience finds them revealed and explained in different ways as the play progresses.

Language and Imagery

The language of the play is highly suggestive. Nothing reveals the power dynamic between Torvald and Nora more than his repeated use of the term 'little' in the early part of the play. Initially used as a rather silly and condescending term of endearment ('my little lark' and 'my little squirrel'), it is later used as criticism ('my little spendthrift'), as a put down ('my dear little Nora') and as a soother ('my sweet little skylark'). In other words, the affection shown by Torvald is essentially patronising. Likewise, Nora's words to Torvald – 'Your little squirrel would run about and do all her tricks if you would be nice and do what she wants' – perfectly capture the indignity of Nora's situation, with its image of a performing animal, and a tamed wild one at that.

Ibsen makes use of dramatic symbols in the play. One of these is doors, which are important throughout. For one thing, they separate characters. Notice how Torvald 'lives' in his study and Nora in the more domestic world of the living room. Torvald may pass through the door that divides these worlds, but Nora cannot. The very first time we meet Nora, she is approaching that door cautiously, wary of disturbing her husband. Doors also admit threats and challenges from the outside world, allowing both the encouraging Mrs Linde and the destructive Krogstad to enter. And the play ends with the symbolic slamming of a door.

Krogstad's letter is another dramatic symbol in the play. Dropped into the post box for later retrieval, it becomes the time bomb that ticks while Nora struggles desperately to find a way out of her situation. The return of the wedding rings at the end of the play is also significant. This exchange symbolises, not only that the marriage is effectively dissolved and that Nora and Torvald are to return to being single, but, much more significantly, that the two of them are to become individuals, each responsible for his or her life, each accepting the consequences of their own actions and decisions.

MAKE

Write a short essay in which you consider which of the three aspects – narrative technique and characterisation, structure and setting, or language and imagery – is the *most* important for a discussion of literary genre in *A Doll's House*. Give reasons for your answer and refer to key moments in the text in support of your points.

The King's Speech directed by Tom Hooper

Summary

READ

Comparative Study

The King's Speech, a film directed by Tom Hooper, was released in 2010.

Before the opening credits sequence, in which a microphone looms at us like a threatening weapon, the screen presents us with a title card.

> ### 1925
>
> **King George V reigns over a quarter of the world's people.**
>
> **He asks his second son, the Duke of York, to give the closing speech at the Empire Exhibition in Wembley, London.**

After this, we see Prince Albert (known as 'Bertie' to his family) agonising at the bottom of a stairs over the radio speech he is about to deliver. He is then led to the microphone at a crowded Wembley Stadium like a man fearfully mounting the gallows for his own public execution. His speech is a failure, as he stammers uncontrollably throughout his performance. Following a series of unsuccessful treatments, his wife,

Elizabeth, enlists the help of an unorthodox Australian speech therapist, Lionel Logue. At their first, awkward meeting, the two men take up opposing positions. Logue keeps insisting, 'My castle, my rules', while Bertie is used to being deferred to. Despite Logue getting close to the reason for Bertie's stammer – his unhappy childhood – the consultation seems doomed, especially when Bertie stumbles over the first words of the 'To be, or not to be' speech from *Hamlet*. Logue asks him to try again, this time while very loud music is playing, and he records the results. Judging it 'hopeless', Bertie storms off, terminating the sessions, but taking the recorded disc with him, as a 'souvenir'.

We become aware of the potential disaster ahead of Bertie when we witness him being criticised by his father, King George V, for his failures, and we hear that his older brother,

David, the Prince of Wales is 'shirking his duties' as heir to the throne. Again, however, Bertie fails painfully to read a script for his enraged father. Distraught, Bertie listens in private to the recording he made with Logue and discovers, to his astonishment, that he enunciated Shakespeare's lines almost perfectly. He returns to Logue, but insists, along with his wife, that his problem is merely 'mechanical'. Even though Logue knows that he has to probe deeper than this, into Bertie's childhood experiences, he agrees to the 'mechanics' treatment, and has some modest success in improving Bertie's public speaking.

With the death of King George V, David, ascends the throne. After this, Bertie visits Logue as a friend, and talks freely about his relationship with David and with his father. During this conversation, he reveals how he was 'corrected' and punished as a child, particularly by his first nanny, who 'hated' him. All this is immediately dramatised in an encounter where David, now King Edward VIII, humiliates Bertie at Balmoral before declaring his intention to marry his lover, Mrs Simpson. When Logue tells Albert that he could succeed as king, if necessary, Bertie dismisses this as 'bordering on treason', and the pair argue again. Bertie declares that 'these sessions are over'.

Eventually, David decides to abdicate to marry Mrs Simpson – he cannot remain as king and head of the Church of England if he marries a divorcée. Bertie becomes King George VI. At his accession ceremony, he fails painfully in his speech once again, and imagines in horror the number of similar public speeches he will now be required to make. He returns to Logue, full of fear for the future. Logue reassures him that he is 'very much his own man'.

At the rehearsal for Bertie's coronation at Westminster Abbey, Logue rubs the authorities and the royal advisors the wrong way. They investigate his background and expose the fact that he has no formal qualifications. Despite Logue revealing that he learned his skills treating shell-shocked soldiers, Bertie wants to dismiss him. Instead, by sitting on St Edward's Chair (the 'throne') and dismissing all the 'royal arseholes' who have sat on it, Logue goads Bertie into a rage, during which he shouts, significantly, 'I have a voice!' After this, Bertie rejects the overbearing advice of the Archbishop of Canterbury, and continues with Logue as his therapist. They rehearse, enthusiastically.

Bertie is crowned king, but his coronation coincides with Hitler's rise to power in Germany and his preparations for war. Bertie is thrown into a challenge greater than any other he has faced: he must prepare to lead his people in war. When war is declared, on 3 September 1939, Bertie has to address the nation on radio, and he calls again for Logue's assistance. Amid panicking citizens and the sound of air-raid sirens, Logue arrives at the palace forty minutes before the scheduled broadcast, and rehearses the anxious and at times despairing Bertie through his speech. In the final moments before the broadcast, things look grim, as Bertie stammers when he receives the good wishes and words of encouragement from the leaders of the government. He is then intimidated, and dwarfed by, a giant microphone in the makeshift studio. However, Logue stays with him throughout his ordeal, encouraging him to 'say it to [him] as a friend'. As a result, Bertie's speech to the nation – as the camera allows us to visit homes and pubs and workplaces of the people listening to him – is a profound success, bringing the nation together in the time of its greatest need. Before the end credits, the captions tell us that 'Lionel was with the King for every wartime speech'.

Mode: Theme of Self-Realisation

Self-realisation is the fulfilment by oneself of the possibilities of one's character or personality.

Protagonist's Sense of Self in the Exposition of the Text

Self-discovery is one of the main themes of *The King's Speech*. The film begins in 1925 with Prince Albert, known as Bertie to his family, enduring agonies of embarrassment as he attempts to deliver a speech at Wembley Stadium. He is second in line to the throne of England but has had a speech impediment – a stammer – since early childhood. His position demands that he be able to speak in public, but this is the one thing he cannot do. He has seen numerous specialists but no one has been able to help him.

The breakthrough comes when Bertie's wife, Elizabeth, persuades him to see Lionel Logue, an Australian speech therapist practising in London. From the outset, it is obvious that Bertie's speech impediment is rooted in childhood trauma. When Logue asks Bertie: 'What was your earliest memory?', he answers defensively: 'I'm not … here to discuss … personal matters.' But in order to discover who he is and to move forward with his life, that is exactly what Bertie is going to have to do. Until he faces the reality of his past, he is exactly what Logue unwittingly called him when he thought his name was Mr Johnson, 'an indentured servant'.

Bertie's lack of selfhood is communicated powerfully in the codes used by Hooper in the exposition of the film. In the opening sequence, when Bertie is waiting to enter the recording studio, he is to the side of the frame with dead space taking up the rest of the frame. This indicates to the viewer a lack or void in relation to the protagonist, in this case, of a sense of self. Also, in this shot, Bertie is waiting to ascend a staircase, symbolising the difficult personal journey ahead of him.

Relationship as a Catalyst for Personal Development

The relationship with Lionel Logue functions as a catalyst for change for Bertie. Their first meeting is unpromising. Logue addresses Prince Albert as 'Bertie', a name used only by the prince's family, and when Bertie objects, Logue says: 'My castle, my rules.' Bertie becomes angered by the questions Logue asks him and says that he is 'not here to discuss personal matters'. Logue wagers a shilling that Bertie can recite Hamlet's 'To be, or not to be' speech without trouble while listening to music on headphones. Bertie carries no money so Logue stakes him a shilling. Logue records his performance on a record. Convinced that he has stammered throughout, Bertie leaves in anger, declaring his condition 'hopeless' and dismissing Logue. Logue offers him the recording as a keepsake.

Later, however, when Bertie plays Logue's recording and hears himself unhesitatingly reciting Shakespeare, he decides to return to Logue, where he and Elizabeth both insist that Logue focus only on physical exercises. Logue teaches his patient muscle relaxation and breath control techniques but continues to probe gently and persistently at the psychological roots of the stutter. Bertie eventually reveals some of the pressures of his childhood – a cruel nanny who preferred his brother to him, the death of his brother Johnny, and constant teasing about his stammer – and the two men start to become friends. Thus begins Bertie's journey towards selfhood.

Development of Selfhood in Crisis

As the film progresses, Bertie changes. He reveals some of the pain of his childhood to Logue but the journey into the past is a painful one and the exchanges between the two men are often fraught:

> Logue: What is it about David [Bertie's older brother] that stops you speaking?
> Bertie: What is it about you that bloody well makes you want to go on about it the whole bloody time?

During the abdication crisis, Logue tells Bertie that his place may well be on the throne and that he 'can outshine David'. Bertie retorts furiously, 'That's bordering on treason' and insults Logue by calling him a 'nobody' and terminating the sessions. For a time, the relationship between the two men breaks down. Later, Bertie visits Logue at home and apologises. This is a turning point in his personal development. Bertie has come to realise the value of honest communication and also to accept that he needs Logue, both as a therapist and a friend.

When, during preparations for his coronation as King George VI in Westminster Abbey, Bertie remains unconvinced of his own fitness for the throne, Logue sits in St Edward's Chair and dismisses the importance of monarchy – 'royal arseholes'. Goaded by Logue's seeming disrespect, Bertie surprises himself with his own sudden burst of outrage: 'I have a voice.' Logue tells Bertie that he is 'the bravest man I know' and Bertie decides, against opposition, to retain the services of Logue.

Self-Realisation in the Resolution of the Text

Upon Britain's declaration of war with Nazi Germany in September 1939, Bertie summons Logue to Buckingham Palace to prepare for his upcoming radio address to millions of listeners in Britain and the Empire. Bertie and Logue are left in the room and, with Logue's guidance, Bertie delivers his speech competently. By the end of it, Bertie is speaking freely with little to no guidance from Logue.

Afterwards, Logue tells Bertie that the speech was very good. Bertie thanks him and says: 'Well done, my friend.' Logue responds: 'Well done, your Majesty.' Bertie has become King George VI, not just in name, but in spirit. He embodies the kingly virtues of authority, leadership and integrity.

During his speech, the camera cuts to people all around Britain, including Bertie's mother, listening to the speech and being genuinely moved by it. Bertie has realised his destiny. The film ends with Bertie and his family stepping onto the balcony of the palace to be applauded by the thousands who have gathered. A title card explains that Logue was always present at King George VI's speeches during the war, and that they remained friends for the rest of their lives.

MAKE

Write a short essay in which you consider which of the four aspects – protagonist's sense of self in the exposition, relationship as a catalyst for personal development, development of selfhood in crisis or self-realisation in the resolution – is the *most* important for a discussion of the theme of self-realisation in *The King's Speech*. Give reasons for your answer and refer to key moments in the text in support of your points.

Mode: General Vision and Viewpoint

Comparative Study

ANALYSE

The general vision and viewpoint of *The King's Speech* is primarily optimistic.

Vision of Society

The vision of society in this text presents us with a world that is experiencing great change. As well as economic and political instability in the wider world, Britain in the 1920s and 1930s underwent a technological revolution that had a huge impact on the position of the monarchy. The text explores the introduction of a modern medium of communication [radio] to society and the changes such media brought.

In the film, before giving his Christmas radio message in 1934, King George V says:

This devilish device will change everything … In the past all a king had to do was look respectable in uniform and not fall off his horse. Now we must invade people's houses and ingratiate ourselves with them. This family has been reduced to those lowest and basest of all creatures. We have become actors.

His outburst is accurate. Radio – and later television and the internet – changed the way the monarchy interacted with the public. With the growing power of the media, the royal family was subjected to constant scrutiny and was forced to sacrifice a private life for a public one. Disabilities, such as speech impediments, do not present well in the world of the media. Society now requires a monarch who represents stability and who can also communicate successfully via modern technology.

View of the Past

The film explores the role of the past in both personal conflict (inside the main character, Bertie) and interpersonal conflict (Bertie's conflict with Logue and with his brother, David). Bertie has no desire to be king – in fact, he dreads the prospect. He is, however, mindful and respectful of his duty to accept the title and fulfil the role of king if necessary. Unfortunately for Bertie, this does become necessary when his older brother, David, abdicates.

Throughout the text Bertie struggles with his stammer, and this brings him into an initially conflictual relationship with speech therapist, Lionel Logue. As Bertie begins to trust Logue, he reveals some of the horrors of his treatment as a child. In order to make progress, Bertie is forced to confront the demons of his past. His parents, King George V and Queen Mary, had little involvement in their children's lives and, as was usual among wealthy families, the children were brought up by nannies. As a child, Bertie was treated cruelly by one of his nannies and developed chronic stomach problems as a result. He was also forced to write with his right hand although he was naturally left-handed and he was forced to wear painful corrective splints because he had 'knock knees'.

The general vision and viewpoint of the text is that, in order for an individual to be free of the past, he or she must first confront it with clarity and honesty. When Bertie visits Logue at home, the therapist tells him: 'You don't need to be afraid of the things you were afraid of when you were five.' The general vision and

viewpoint of the film is optimistic in that it shows how, to a large extent, society has improved in its treatment of children. For instance, Logue's boys and Bertie's daughters, Elizabeth and Margaret, are all well-loved by their parents.

Vision of Individual Agency

Individual agency – the capacity of *a person* to act independently and to make their own free choices – is portrayed in this text as a vital aspect of personal development, but also as something that is greatly affected by relationships. Across a great social divide, Prince Albert and Lionel Logue develop a friendship in which Bertie, deeply affected by the first 'ordinary' citizen he has befriended, gains in confidence and humanity.

The first meeting between the two men is unpromising. Logue addresses Prince Albert as 'Bertie', a name used only by his family. When Prince Albert objects, Logue says: 'My castle, my rules.' Bertie becomes angry at the questions Logue asks him and says that he is 'not here to discuss personal matters'. At his next session, Bertie expresses his frustration that his speech has improved while talking to most people, with the exception of his own brother, and he reveals the extent of his brother's involvement with Mrs Simpson, an American divorcée. When Logue insists that Bertie could be a good king instead of his brother, the latter labels such a suggestion as treason and, in his anger, lashes out at Logue, calling him a 'disappointing son of a brewer … a nobody'. The meeting ends with Bertie saying: 'These sessions are over.'

Shortly afterwards, David abdicates and Bertie does become King George VI. When he visits Logue at his home to apologise, Bertie gives him the shilling he owes him as a peace offering and the relationship between the two men resumes. The general vision and viewpoint of the text suggests that Bertie's decision to take on the role of king and put his own mark on that role is greatly influenced by the support he receives from Lionel Logue. In a conversation the two men have in Logue's home, Lionel tells Bertie that he is 'very much your own man'. Title cards at the end of the film tells the audience that 'Lionel was with the King for every wartime speech' and that they 'remained friends for the rest of their lives'.

View of Honesty

The general vision and viewpoint of *The King's Speech* presents honesty as an essential component of relationships – both with oneself and with others. When Bertie first meets Logue, he is shocked at the Australian's forthright manner and honest expression. Bertie is used to a world of deference and respect and Logue's manner, treating Bertie as an equal, is deeply unsettling. However, as the film progresses, it is exactly this quality that makes the relationship develop into a deep friendship.

A crisis occurs prior to Bertie's coronation when he finds out that Logue has 'no training, no diploma, no qualifications'. The issue between the two men is now one of honesty. Bertie tells Logue that he trusted him but that he is no more than a 'fraud'. Logue responds by giving an account of his experience of treating traumatised soldiers returning from the First World War who had lost 'faith in their own voices'. Logue makes the point that he never presented himself as a doctor – the plaque on his door reads 'L. Logue Speech Defects'. He then, in order to provoke Bertie, sits in St Edward's Chair and refers to all the 'royal arseholes' who have sat there before him. His ploy works. Bertie becomes enraged and shouts at Logue: 'I have a voice.' The honesty of the exchange between the two men is the catalyst for personal growth and a release from the demons of the past.

Write a short essay in which you consider which of the four aspects – vision of society, view of the past, vision of individual agency or view of honesty – is the *most* important for a discussion of the general vision and viewpoint in *The King's Speech*. Give reasons for your answer and refer to key moments in the text in support of your points.

Mode: Literary Genre

Genre

The King's Speech is a 2010 British historical film directed by Tom Hooper and written by David Seidler. Colin Firth plays King George VI who, to cope with a stammer, sees Lionel Logue, an Australian speech and language therapist, played by Geoffrey Rush. The film is set in England and Scotland during the years 1925 to 1939, when the British Empire, with the King of England at its head, ruled over a quarter of the world's people.

The text focuses on the lives of the royal family during this period. King George V was on the throne until his death in 1936. His eldest son, David, became King Edward VIII in January of that year but, as a result of his insistence on marrying an American woman – Mrs Wallis Simpson, who had been married twice before – a constitutional crisis ensued. As Head of the Church of England, a monarch may not marry a person who has been divorced. On 11 December 1936, Edward VIII abdicated and his younger brother, Albert (Bertie), became King George VI. The plot of the film centres on Bertie's struggle to overcome his stammer in order to fulfil his duties to his people.

Narrative Technique and Characterisation

In a film, the camera functions as an omniscient narrator. We cannot see what the camera does not show us, but it is important to remember that what we cannot see is sometimes as important as what we can. What we cannot see is known as 'outside the frame' and is similar to the subtext in a novel or something happening 'off stage' in a play.

Although the camera is omniscient, point of view does exist within film texts, as the director may present events from a protagonist's perspective or focus strongly on a protagonist via the close-up shot. Personal codes, such as facial expression, offer a powerful insight into the thoughts and emotions of a character. An example of this occurs in the climax of *The King's Speech* when Colin Firth comes within two inches of a microphone to deliver a speech announcing the outbreak of war. The audience sees Bertie summoning up all his courage to overcome his anxieties and fears successfully and prove his mastery of oratory for this most important of speeches.

In fact, the success of the film comes in part from always being with the king. Emotionally, the audience invests an enormous amount in the character, and that empathy is subtly encouraged by Hooper's use of interesting camera angles. Wide lenses are used very close to Firth's face to accentuate the expression, while camera movement and lighting keep the viewer engaged with the anxious monarch. Dialogue is also an important aspect of characterisation in any text. Humour is used effectively in *The King's Speech* to illustrate personality features of both Bertie and Logue:

Logue: How do you feel?
Bertie: Full of hot air.
Logue: Isn't that what public speaking is all about?

Structure and Setting

The timeline of *The King's Speech* is fourteen years and yet the pace of the film is quite fast, as Hooper focuses on a select number of events. Although it is based on historical events, the chronological delivery of the plot creates suspense and tension. Setting also adds to the tension in the text. The majority of *The King's Speech* was shot indoors, where oblong sets, corridors and small spaces manifest constriction and tightness, in contrast to the usual emphasis on sweep and majesty in historical dramas. This choice of setting conveys a feeling of interiority within the text, the sense that what is unfolding is not so much a political crisis as a personal one inside Bertie's mind.

Hooper also employs a number of cinematic techniques to further evoke Bertie's feelings of constriction. He and cinematographer Danny Cohen used wider than normal lenses to photograph the film as the subtle distortion of the picture helps to convey Bertie's discomfort. In addition, although historical dramas traditionally tend to use soft light, Hooper used a harsher glare, which gives a more contemporary feel, and thus a greater emotional resonance to the text.

Language and Imagery

Language, while an important element of film, is only one part of the story-telling repertoire available to directors. So much of what we experience on screen is communicated via personal and technical codes, many of which are used in a symbolic way.

In *The King's Speech*, Hooper uses frame space to add complexity and depth to the film. He frequently shoots the actors to the far left or right of the frame to capture something significant in the background, often a door, hallway or corridor. A clear example of this use of frame space is

evident in the scene in which Elizabeth first meets Logue in the waiting room of his office. During their conversation, the camera captures Elizabeth to the far right of the frame with an open door behind her at the far left. Although the door is several feet behind Elizabeth, she and the door balance each other in the frame. Elizabeth's venture to the office is fuelled by hope, and the open door behind her, which is just as much a presence in the scene as she is, greatly symbolises this. Elizabeth is hopeful that Logue can cure her husband's stammer and she is open, like the door, to his unconventional method.

Music is also used in a symbolic way in the text. The film's original score was composed by Alexandre Desplat. A sparse arrangement of strings and piano and the repetition of a single note represent the difficulty Bertie has in speaking, however, as the film progresses, growing banks of warm strings code the deepening friendship between him and Logue. The music played during the broadcast of the 1939 radio speech at the climax of the film is from the 2nd movement of Beethoven's 7th Symphony.

MAKE

Write a short essay in which you consider which of the three aspects – narrative technique and characterisation, structure and setting, or language and imagery – is the *most* important for a discussion of literary genre in *The King's Speech*. Give reasons for your answer and refer to key moments in the text in support of your points.

Comparative Study

The Uncommon Reader by Alan Bennett

Summary

The Uncommon Reader is a novella by Alan Bennett published in 2007. It is an imagined account of royal life. A common reader is generally someone who reads for pleasure, but the uncommon reader of the title is none other than Queen Elizabeth II. She begins to read widely and intelligently, and the consequences are surprising, mildly shocking and very funny.

The novella begins at a state banquet with the Queen asking the French president about the French writer Jean Genet. Genet was a social outcast and criminal, and the French president, surprised by the question, knows nothing about him.

We then flashback to the beginning of the Queen's journey into reading when, one day, her corgis stray and she accidentally comes across a mobile library parked at Buckingham Palace. The librarian is a man called Mr Hutchins and he tells the Queen that the library visits the palace every Wednesday. The only other person in the mobile library is a ginger-haired young man who works in the kitchen called Norman Seakins. The Queen has never taken much interest in reading, but she takes out a novel by Ivy Compton-Burnett. The following Wednesday, the Queen visits the library again, mostly to get out of a meeting with her private secretary, Sir Kevin Scatchard. The Queen finished reading the novel by Compton-Burnett, not because she loved it so much, but because she was brought up to finish things. She borrows another book, a novel by Nancy Mitford, and this time the Queen is hooked.

Norman is promoted as *amanuensis* (literary assistant) to the Queen and guides her in her choice of books to read. As time goes on, the Queen finds that 'doors keep opening' from one book to another and that the days aren't long enough for all the reading she wants to do. The Queen thinks about writers she has met in the past and regrets the wasted opportunities to talk to them about their work. She encourages others, such as her chauffeur Summers, to take up reading.

The mobile library is cancelled due to cutbacks but the Queen is undeterred. Other members of the royal household, such as Sir Kevin, do not look approvingly on the Queen's reading but the Queen considers her reading a duty rather than a pleasure as it aids her in understanding people.

On a coach trip to open parliament, the Queen waves to the crowds while reading from a book that is open on her lap. Prince Philip is unhappy and, on the return journey, the book has been confiscated as a suspicious device. The Queen says that books are a 'device to ignite the imagination'.

On her trips around the country, the Queen asks her subjects what they are reading and people begin to give the Queen gifts of books rather than flowers. Sir Kevin is increasingly concerned: 'To read is to withdraw,' he complains. 'To make oneself unavailable.'

The Queen reads without distinction – from a biography of the poet Sylvia Plath to one of the actress Lauren Bacall. She considers herself an opsimath (one who learns late in life). Reading gives the Queen a new-found sense of empathy. She holds a reception for writers but it is not a success, and the Queen concludes that authors are best met within the pages of their books. The Queen begins reading aloud in public. At a tree-planting ceremony she quotes from Philip Larkin's poem 'The Trees'.

We are about halfway through the text at this stage and there is a page-break to indicate a time shift, as we return to the opening of the novella, with the Queen asking the French president about Jean Genet.

On her summer holiday in Balmoral, the Queen reads Marcel Proust. The cold, wet weather suits her. When the prime minister and his wife visit, they are largely ignored. Afterwards the prime minister's special adviser complains to Sir Kevin and, while the Queen is on a trip to Canada, Sir Kevin dispatches Norman to the University of East Anglia. Norman writes to the Queen but she never receives his letter.

After Norman's departure, the Queen begins to write down her thoughts in her notebook more and more. The gulf separating the Queen from the rest of humanity is so great that it is hard for her to understand certain topics, such as class difference in Jane Austen's novels. She persists nonetheless and the royal household runs smoothly, although the equerries (officers of the British royal household who attend members of the royal family) believe that the Queen is showing signs of senility. When the Queen begins giving the prime minister books to read at their weekly meetings, his special adviser again complains to Sir Kevin, who asks an old member of the royal household, Sir Claude, to speak with the Queen. Sir Claude suggests that the Queen considers writing. He intends the suggestion as a way of distracting the Queen from books, but she becomes very interested in the idea. She feels that she has no voice and muses:

> Had she been asked if reading had enriched her life she would have had to say yes, undoubtedly, though adding with equal certainty that it had at the same time drained her life of all purpose.

In the following weeks, the Queen reads less. While at Sandringham, she attends a lunch at the University of East Anglia in Norwich where she is served by Norman. The Queen is seated beside the professor of creative writing who describes Norman as 'very promising'. Afterwards, the Queen meets with Norman. He tells her everything, and Sir Kevin is sacked.

The novella ends with the Queen holding a party for her eightieth birthday. She invites all those who have advised her over the years – the Privy Council. She makes a speech in which she outlines her intention to write a book 'that might stray into literature'. When the prime minister reminds her that the last monarch to do such a thing – Edward VIII – abdicated, the Queen retorts, 'But … why do you think you're all here?'

Mode: Theme of Self-Realisation

Self-realisation is the fulfilment by oneself of the possibilities of one's character or personality.

Protagonist's Sense of Self in the Exposition of the Text

The Queen's odyssey into the world of books begins accidentally. 'It was the dogs' fault', the reader is told, that the Queen discovers the City of Westminster travelling library by chance in the palace grounds one day. The Queen has 'never taken much interest in reading' and is unsure what book to borrow. She reflects that she does not have hobbies, since hobbies involve preferences, and preferences are to be avoided: 'Her job was to take an interest, not to be interested herself.' The Queen also sees herself as a 'doer', and 'reading wasn't doing'. Spotting a name she remembers – Ivy Compton-Burnett – the Queen chooses a book by this novelist and departs.

The exposition of the text reveals the Queen as someone who, although powerful, knows very little about herself. The visit to the library is an inauspicious start to a life-changing journey, but even this seemingly insignificant event shows the Queen as someone who is open to change. She is naturally curious and convivial. She asks Norman about his choice of book and says of the photographer Cecil Beaton: 'I suppose everyone gets written about sooner or later.' Finally, the

Queen is surprised but not offended at being contradicted by Norman in relation to the musical that Cecil Beaton designed. This shows an open mind. In entering the mobile library, the Queen, who has led a life of service and duty for over seventy years, takes her first step towards self-realisation.

Relationship as a Catalyst for Personal Development

The Queen first encounters Norman Seakins in the mobile library parked in the grounds of Buckingham Palace. He is described as a ginger-haired young man and tells the Queen that he works in the kitchens. Norman is taking out a book on the photographer, Cecil Beaton, which surprises the Queen. When the Queen says that Cecil Beaton also designed *Oklahoma*, Norman corrects her, saying: 'I think it was *My Fair Lady*, ma'am.' The following week, when she returns to the library, the Queen meets Norman again. This time Norman is looking at a book of photographs by the artist David Hockney. When the Queen describes a picture as smudged, Norman says: 'I think that was his style then, ma'am.' The Queen is not used to people speaking freely to her. Later, she requests that Norman be promoted, describing him as a young man of some intelligence. Thus begins the unlikely relationship between Norman Seakins and the Queen of England. He becomes her *amanuensis* (literary assistant) and together they embark on a journey into the world of reading. Norman's job is to choose books for the Queen to read. Having no formal education and with his reading tending to be determined by whether an author was gay or not, he makes some unusual reading choices for the Queen, but she is very pleased with him, as he is always himself and seems incapable of being anything else. Norman, on the other hand, initially sees the Queen as an old lady, before 'he woke up to how sharp she was'.

As the Queen becomes more and more absorbed in the world of reading, some of her household – especially her private secretary, Sir Kevin Scatchard – become increasingly suspicious and irritated by her new interest and Norman is seen as a bad influence on the Queen. His close relationship with her also arouses jealousy among some. When the prime minister's special adviser complains to Sir Kevin, he asks: 'Is this bloke Norman a nancy?' Soon after this, while the Queen is in Canada, Sir Kevin removes Norman from his position as the Queen's assistant by arranging for him to attend university in East Anglia. When the Queen fails to respond personally to a long letter that Norman writes to her, he knows that he had been eased out, though whether by the Queen or her private secretary, he isn't sure. The Queen never receives Norman's letter.

The relationship with Norman Seakins is a catalyst for personal development for the Queen for many reasons. Firstly, Norman speaks openly to the Queen and this is a rare experience for her. 'Oddity though he was, Norman was himself and seemed incapable of being anything else.' This honest engagement is beneficial to the Queen and she appreciates it, referring to Norman as 'a find'. Secondly, Norman does not patronise the Queen. He recommends books to her that he finds stimulating himself, such as *My Dog Tulip* by J.R. Ackerley, thus introducing her to the varied and marvellous world of literature. Finally, Norman provides the Queen with support and solidarity in her new-found pleasure.

Development of Selfhood in Crisis

A crisis occurs for the Queen after Norman's departure. Although she feels that she 'was outgrowing him … or rather, out-reading him', they had talked to each other about what they were reading. After Norman's departure, the Queen begins 'conducting lengthier discussions with herself and putting more and more of her thoughts on paper'. This is the turning point in the Queen's journey towards self-realisation. Without someone to communicate with, she is forced to communicate with herself by writing down her thoughts and feelings.

Writing leads the Queen to the painful discovery that she has 'no voice'; in other words, no true identity. From this point on in the novella, the Queen begins to realise herself. She develops empathy for others through reading. Speaking to a professor of creative writing at the University of East Anglia, she muses that 'reading softens you up', while also commenting that 'you have to be tough' to write. The crisis of Norman's departure forces the Queen to dialogue with herself, which in turn leads to her becoming more determined to find her own 'voice'.

Self-Realisation in the Resolution of the Text

The novella ends with the Queen turning eighty and deciding to throw 'a party of her own'. She holds a tea party and invites the Privy Council, which comprised all those who had advised

Comparative Study

her over the years. During the course of the gathering, the Queen announces her intention of writing a book – not a memoir: 'something more radical. More … challenging.' When pressed by the prime minister to be more forthcoming, the Queen delivers a speech that is shocking in its honesty: 'One has given one's white-gloved hand to hands that were steeped in blood and conversed politely with men who have personally slaughtered children.'

The Queen takes a break so that champagne can be served and then continues her speech saying that she hopes her book will, to quote Emily Dickinson: 'Tell all the truth but tell it slant.' At this point, the prime minister intervenes to remind the Queen of her 'unique position', in other words, of the fact that an acting monarch could not publish such a book, and that the Duke of Windsor (King Edward VIII) had already abdicated when he published *A King's Story*. The novella ends with the Queen saying: 'But … why do you think you're all here?'

The Queen has found her voice and claimed for herself a life that is more than simply service and duty. Divested of title, she intends to express herself, and the truth of the world, as she sees it.

MAKE

Write a short essay in which you consider which of the four aspects – protagonist's sense of self in the exposition, relationship as a catalyst for personal development, development of selfhood in crisis or self-realisation in the resolution – is the *most* important for a discussion of the theme of self-realisation in *The Uncommon Reader*. Give reasons for your answer and refer to key moments in the text in support of your points.

Mode: General Vision and Viewpoint

The general vision and viewpoint of *The Uncommon Reader* is primarily optimistic.

ANALYSE

Vision of Society

The vision of society in *The Uncommon Reader* is narrow since the novella is set entirely in the world of the Queen and, ironically, although she presides over the Commonwealth and travels a great deal, her world is very small. During the course of the novella, the Queen resides in London, Windsor, Balmoral and other palaces, as well as visiting, among others places, Norwich and Canada. And yet her world is unchanging. She describes travel as 'a ritual of departure and arrival in which she was just a piece of luggage'. The Queen's world is ordered and hierarchical. Her household – from her personal secretary to the equerries to the kitchen staff – is large and everyone has a place and a clearly defined role. It is telling in the novella that the Queen cannot appreciate the minutiae of class differences that are so important in a Jane Austen novel she is reading. We are told that gender and class differences were 'nothing compared with the gulf that separated the Queen from the rest of humanity'.

The vision of this society is one of extraordinary privilege, but also of great personal restriction. This is an enclosed, almost claustrophobic world. In the novella, the wider society of the late twentieth and early twenty-first century is seen only in tiny comedic glimpses – the Queen's chauffeur reading *The Sun* newspaper, the Archbishop of Canterbury watching *Strictly Come Dancing*, or the footman saying 'Fuck' when the Queen expresses displeasure at the disappearance of her book from the royal carriage.

View of the Past

The past plays a central role in *The Uncommon Reader*. As the Queen becomes more and more involved in the world of books, she experiences regret at the opportunities she has missed. The nature of reading – 'how one book led to another' – is one of journeying, and some of that journey is inevitably into the past. The Queen also experiences sadness at the past. With regard to her reading, she says: 'I have started too late. I will never catch up.' Later, she says: 'Too late. It was all too late.' For the first time in her life, the Queen feels that there is a good deal she has missed. She refers to herself as an 'opsimath' – one who learns only late in life.

Through reading, the Queen becomes interested in history, and tries to involve the prime minister in discussions on the subject. The prime minister, however, does 'not wholly believe in the past or in any lessons that might be drawn from it'. At her party, at the end of the novella, the Queen says that from her long perspective 'things do not occur; they recur'. The Queen, however, certainly does believe in the power of the past to illuminate both the present and the future.

Vision of Individual Agency

The Queen has devoted her entire life to duty and to fulfilling her role as monarch. She acceded to the throne at the age of twenty-five and is in her seventies when the narrative of the novella begins. During her reign, the Queen has 'gone through … ten prime ministers, six Archbishops of Canterbury, eight speakers … and fifty-three corgis'. The general consensus of those surrounding the Queen, and her subjects, is that she has done a good job.

However, when the Queen takes to reading, she is met with hostility. Initially, the Queen is troubled by this. For her, 'pleasure had always taken second place to duty'. When the Queen begins asking her subjects what they are reading, her equerries agree that she is becoming 'a handful'. Sir Kevin objects to her reading as 'selfish' and later, when as a result of her reading the Queen is more honest in her reflections about life, the household mistakes her new sensibility for the onset of 'senility'.

For the Queen, individual agency – the capacity of *a person* to act independently and to make their own free choices – comes with the decision to write and thus to find her own 'voice'. To do this, the Queen must first relinquish the role she has spent her entire life playing – she must give up being the Queen. The journey towards individual agency is not an easy one. The Queen has not expected that reading would result in her being 'drained of enthusiasm for anything else' and there are times 'when she wished she had never opened a book and entered into other lives' because: 'It had spoiled her.' The growth of the self – which is what reading affects – also brings isolation with it, and a new, sometimes painful, sensitivity to the world.

View of Honesty

The Uncommon Reader is about the awakening – emotionally, intellectually, philosophically – of one woman, the Queen, through reading. This awakening is at times painful. At one point, the Queen remarks: 'Had she been asked if reading had enriched her life she would have had to say yes, undoubtedly, though adding with equal certainty that it had at the same time drained her life of all purpose.'

But the Queen has no choice but to continue in her odyssey – 'it was impossible not to do it and at this late stage of her life she had been chosen to read as others were chosen to write'. The awakening in the Queen, brought on by reading, is not a sentimental one, or one in which literature is presented as a force for good. The Queen is awakened emotionally; her empathy is stirred. She asks a professor of creative writing if he agrees that reading 'softens one up'. The Queen is awakened philosophically, writing in her notebook: 'One recipe for happiness is to have no sense of entitlement.' Intellectually, when she turns to writing she realises that like reading it was something 'she was going to have to do on her own'.

The Queen also understood that in some ways writing is the reverse of reading – 'you have to be tough'. The Queen is tough. Being honest – especially with oneself – is tough. The Queen sacks Gerald, the equerry who picked up her notebook, and she sacks Sir Kevin for his deception in relation to Norman. With her increasingly honest perspective on the world, the Queen has less tolerance for mendacity.

On her eightieth birthday, she holds a party to announce her abdication and her intention to write a book that, quoting Emily Dickinson: 'Tells all the truth.' The reaction of the assembled Privy Council is one of deep discomfort – 'the room did not answer'. When, earlier in the novella, the Queen refers to books as a 'device to ignite the imagination', she is not wrong.

MAKE

Write a short essay in which you consider which of the four aspects – vision of society, view of the past, vision of individual agency or view of honesty – is the *most* important for a discussion of the general vision and viewpoint in *The Uncommon Reader*. Give reasons for your answer and refer to key moments in the text in support of your points.

Mode: Literary Genre

ANALYSE

Comparative Study

Genre

The Uncommon Reader is a novella published in 2006. It is an entertaining comic narrative based on the imagined scenario whereby Queen Elizabeth II embarks on a journey into the world of books and reading. The novella is also, however, a serious manifesto for the potential of reading to change lives. Alan Bennett builds his fictional account on a foundation of fact which makes the narrative both amusing and plausible. The title of the novella, *The Uncommon Reader*, is a play on the word 'common', which means 'usual' but also refers to someone who is not of royal or noble heritage.

Narrative Technique and Characterisation

The narrative technique of the novella is interesting. The narrative voice moves between the third person, which offers the Queen's perspective, and a dry, ironic omniscient voice. This seamless shift in voices adds a layer of interest to the story being told as the reader is privy both to the intimate thoughts of the Queen and the opinions of another more distant, slightly bemused observer. The omniscient narrative voice enables the reader access to the thoughts of other characters in the novella, such as Norman, while also offering commentary on events as they occur. When the Queen pretends to have a cold in order to stay in bed reading, we are told 'that this was only the first of a series of accommodations, some of them far-reaching, that her reading was going to involve'. Bennett's narrative technique enables an insight into the protagonist which creates sympathy for her struggle while simultaneously maintaining a more objective view of the world. This depiction of the personal world of the Queen as well as the public world she inhabits adds tension and realism to the text.

Characterisation is also achieved by the use of realistic dialogue, action and reaction, as well as interior monologue. The Queen's reflections on life, inspired by her reading, provide a strong insight into her personality: 'And it occurred to her (as next day she wrote it down) that reading was, among other things, a muscle that she had seemingly developed.'

Structure and Setting

The Uncommon Reader is written in a flashback structure, but not a conventional one. The novella opens *in media res* on 'the evening of the state banquet' in Windsor with the Queen asking the French president about the writer Jean Genet. The narrative then flashes back in time to the day the Queen happened upon the travelling library in the grounds of Westminster Palace and unwittingly began her journey into the world of books and reading.

The structure is unusual, however, in that we arrive back at the state banquet with the Queen questioning the French president, not at the end of the novella, as we might expect, but exactly in the middle of it. The remainder of the story is then told in chronological, forward-moving narrative. This creates suspense in the latter stages of the text. The novella has no chapters. Page breaks are used to convey the passage of time or a change of scene. The lack of formal divisions within the text enables a fluid, fast-paced narration. One thing leads on to the next, much the same way as books do for the Queen – 'one book led to another, doors kept opening'.

Various places provide a setting for the novella – London, Windsor, Balmoral and other palaces, as well as Norwich and Canada. However, there is no distinction between locations. In each case, the Queen's immediate environment remains virtually the same – ordered, comfortable and privileged. The fact that the exterior world is static in the novella is significant as *The Uncommon Reader* is primarily a psychological text, charting as it does the interior life of the Queen over a period of years.

Language and Imagery

In a text that explores the immersion of a character into the world of books and reading, and all the personal transformation such a journey brings, it is only fitting that language is at the heart of the novella. *The Uncommon Reader* is written in a style that self-consciously uses language to illustrate the growth of the Queen's relationship with the written word. In her reading, the Queen discovers new words – '*amanuensis*', 'opsimath' – and relishes them. The journey of the Queen is mirrored in the use of language in the novella. By including passages that contain challenging vocabulary, Bennett seems to be exploring how art mirrors life. Sir Kevin is described as 'a young(ish) man who would sweep away some of the redundant deference and more flagrant flummeries that were monarchy's customary accretions'.

Pleasure in words is part of the Queen's new world. While the novella, for the most part, is written in a matter-of-fact style, much like what the reader might imagine the Queen's writing style to be, it also contains some poetic passages. While the Queen reads Proust, Balmoral is described as follows: '… while in the wet butts on the hills the guns cracked out their empty tattoo and the occasional dead and sodden stag was borne past the window.'

At other times, the language of the novella is more robust, especially in the dialogue: 'Shit,' said Gerald. 'Shit. Shit. Shit.'

Finally, as one might expect in a text whose theme is reading, there are copious literary allusions throughout the novella, from Jean Genet to Philip Larkin, from Sylvia Plath to Alice Munro. These allusions enrich the text by adding a layer of realism to it, and, as Alan Bennett presumably hoped, sparking curiosity about the authors to which reference has been made!

MAKE

Write a short essay in which you consider which of the three aspects – narrative technique and characterisation, structure and setting, or language and imagery – is the *most* important for a discussion of literary genre in *The Uncommon Reader*. Give reasons for your answer and refer to key moments in the text in support of your points.

ANALYSE

Comparative Study

Comparative Study: Theme of Self-Realisation

PROTAGONIST'S SENSE OF SELF IN THE EXPOSITION

	A Doll's House	The King's Speech	The Uncommon Reader
Key Points	Nora has a very poor sense of herself at the start of the play, as she is too busy trying to be what she thinks other people want her to be. She is childish and economically dependent on her husband.	Bertie's lack of selfhood is communicated through film codes at the start of the text. Until he faces the reality of his past, he is unable to discover who he is or to address his speech impediment.	The exposition of the text reveals the Queen as someone who, although powerful, knows very little about herself. The accidental visit to the mobile library is an inauspicious start to a life-changing journey.
Key Moments	Act One: Torvald repeatedly refers to Nora as his 'little skylark' and she plays along with his image saying: 'You haven't any idea how many expenses we skylarks and squirrels have.'	In the opening sequence Bertie is at the bottom of steps, waiting to be called to make a speech. He is presented to us in tight close-up, which shows clearly the sense of dread in his eyes at the arduousness of the task that faces him.	At the beginning of the text, when the Queen visits the library, she has no idea what book to borrow. She muses: 'One had no preferences. Her job was to take an interest, not to be interested herself.'
Comparisons	In the expositions of all three texts, there are some similarities between the protagonists – Nora, Bertie and the Queen – in that each lacks a secure sense of self. Nora considers herself a 'doll' rather than a person, Bertie is still struggling to assert himself outside of the negative influence of his family and the Queen has devoted her life to duty at the expense of personal development. Their circumstances are different but, in each case, their upbringing has been a factor in their arrested development.		

RELATIONSHIP AS A CATALYST FOR DEVELOPMENT

	A Doll's House	The King's Speech	The Uncommon Reader
Key Points	Nora's marriage has hindered her from self-discovery. The relationship between Nora and Torvald depends entirely on the two of them continuing to observe their conventional gender roles.	The relationship with Lionel Logue functions as a catalyst for change for Bertie. Logue treats Bertie as an equal and encourages him to talk about his personal life, particularly his childhood.	The unlikely relationship between Norman Seakins and the Queen of England begins when they meet in the library. He becomes her *amanuensis* and together they embark on a journey into the world of reading.
Key Moments	Act Three: Nora faces the truth about her marriage, and herself: 'I must try and educate myself – you [Torvald] are not the man to help me in that. I must do that for myself.'	In the scene where Bertie, following the death of his father, visits Logue, the two men engage in a frank conversation. Bertie reveals some of the pressures of his childhood. Thus begins Bertie's journey towards selfhood.	Norman speaks openly to the Queen and this is a rare experience for her. At the beginning of the text, the Queen is surprised, but not offended, at being contradicted by Norman in the library. Norman provides the Queen with support and solidarity in her journey into reading.

Comparisons	In both *The King's Speech* and *The Uncommon Reader*, the protagonists enter a relationship that proves to be a catalyst for change in their lives. Bertie attends Lionel Logue to improve his stammer and the Queen promotes Norman Seakins to be her literary assistant. In both cases, the relationships challenge the protagonists to re-evaluate their sense of self. *A Doll's House* is different from the other texts as Nora does not experience personal growth within a relationship, and certainly not in her marriage. She has to leave her husband and children in her quest for selfhood.

DEVELOPMENT OF SELFHOOD IN CRISIS

	A Doll's House	*The King's Speech*	*The Uncommon Reader*
Key Points	Through the crisis brought about by the exposure of the truth about her past, Nora develops suddenly and radically. She does this by facing the truth of what her marriage actually is – a master–slave contract licensed by society through marriage.	During the abdication crisis, when Logue tells Bertie that his place may be on the throne, the relationship between the two men breaks down. Later, Bertie accepts responsibility for this and apologises to Logue. This is the turning point in Bertie's development, as he comes to realise the value of honest communication.	A crisis occurs for the Queen after Norman's departure. Without someone to communicate with, she is forced to communicate with herself by writing down her thoughts and feelings. Writing leads the Queen to the painful discovery that she has no true identity.
Key Moments	Act Three: Believing his reputation to be under threat, Torvald turns on Nora, calling her a 'thoughtless woman' and telling her that she shall not be allowed to bring up their children. This crisis forces Nora to act.	In the scene in the park during the abdication crisis, Logue tells Bertie that his place may well be on the throne and that he 'can outshine David'. Bertie retorts furiously – 'That's bordering on treason' – and insults Logue by calling him a 'nobody' and terminating the sessions.	Writing down her thoughts and feelings leads the Queen to the painful discovery that she has 'no voice'.
Comparisons	In both *A Doll's House* and *The King's Speech*, the protagonists face crises in the external world. In *A Doll's House*, Nora's dealings with Krogstad come to light, and in *The King's Speech*, Bertie has to accede to the throne when his brother abdicates. In both texts, this external crisis forces the development of selfhood. *The Uncommon Reader* is different from the other two texts, as the Queen does not face an external crisis, but instead faces up to a crisis within herself in terms of personal identity. The Queen chooses to acknowledge her inner struggle and thus creates a minor constitutional crisis herself when she abdicates at the end of the text.		

Comparative Study

SELF-REALISATION IN THE RESOLUTION

	A Doll's House	The King's Speech	The Uncommon Reader
Key Points	By the end of the play, Nora has made the journey from a 'doll' in a doll's house to a free human being. It is a painful journey, and one that involves the loss of her children.	Bertie has become King George VI, not just in name, but in spirit. During his speech at the outbreak of war, the camera cuts to people all around Britain, including Bertie's mother, listening to the speech and being genuinely moved by it.	The novella ends with the Queen abdicating. She has found her voice and claims for herself a life that is more than service and duty. Divested of title, she intends to express herself, and the truth of the world, as she sees it.
Key Moments	Act Three: At the end of the play Nora is the one who issues the orders. She instructs Torvald to sit down, saying: 'I have a lot to talk over with you.' She communicates in an accurate, honest, straightforward way.	The film ends with King George VI and his family stepping onto the balcony of the palace to be applauded by the thousands who have gathered.	The novella ends with the Queen announcing her intention of writing a book – not a memoir but: 'something more radical. More … challenging.'
Comparisons	In all three texts, the protagonists achieve self-realisation. A Doll's House is different from The King's Speech and The Uncommon Reader, in that Nora has to pay a high price for selfhood. She loses her children. There is some similarity between The King's Speech and The Uncommon Reader, as both Bertie and the Queen gain self-realisation without having to make any terrible personal sacrifice. In the case of both The King's Speech and The Uncommon Reader, however, the protagonists' journeys towards selfhood are at times painful ones. Bertie has to uncover traumatic memories of childhood, while for the Queen there is the bittersweet knowledge that she has started her journey 'too late'.		

Tip: When you are answering a question worth 70 marks your task is to write an essay-style answer in which you compare and contrast all three comparative texts.

Answer the following **Theme** question from Leaving Certificate 2013 using the guide below to structure your answer.

'Studying a theme or issue enables a reader to form both personal and universal reflections on that theme or issue.'

Compare both the personal and universal reflections that you formed on a common theme or issue in two or more texts from your comparative course. (70)

Guide to Answering 2013 Theme Question

In your introductory paragraph it is essential to answer the question: do you agree, partially agree or disagree with the quotation you are being offered? You must also tell the examiner what the particular theme is that you have explored and which three texts you have studied – give the title of each text and the name of its author or director. It is also advisable to offer a 'blurb' or 'snapshot' of each of your texts, but confine this to one sentence per text. Finally, outline your

MAKE

Comparative Study

intention to compare and contrast the texts in relation to the stance you have adopted with reference to the quotation offered in the question.

The main body of your essay will consist of a series of paragraphs relating to the question you are answering. Begin each paragraph with a topic sentence – a sentence that outlines the main point you intend discussing in that paragraph, with reference to the question you are answering. Compare and contrast all three of your texts in each paragraph. Remember, the most important element of a good comparative study is sensitivity to the material you are discussing. Avoid generalisations and remember that comparisons may be qualified – sometimes texts are both similar to and different from each other. There is no set number of comparisons you should make in an answer – sometimes one complex comparison requires an entire paragraph to elucidate clearly, at other times a series of comparative points may be made in quick succession.

In this instance, you may use the following points to construct the main body of your essay, remembering to keep the question to the forefront of your answer at all times.

- Protagonist's sense of self in the exposition of the text.
- Relationship as a catalyst for personal development.
- Development of selfhood in crisis.
- Self-realisation in the resolution of the text.

Finally, include a concluding paragraph. The objective of a conclusion in a comparative study is two-fold – firstly, to provide a general summary of your answer and, secondly, to demonstrate your personal opinion in relation to the treatment of the theme in each of your texts. What did you admire? What didn't impressed you? It is important throughout Paper 2 to present yourself as a critical reader of texts.

A complete answer to a comparative study question in the Leaving Certificate exam should be approximately 1,000 words in length.

Comparative Study: General Vision and Viewpoint

GENERAL VISION			
	A Doll's House	*The King's Speech*	*The Uncommon Reader*
Key Points	Pessimistic and optimistic	Primarily optimistic	Primarily optimistic

VISION OF SOCIETY			
	A Doll's House	*The King's Speech*	*The Uncommon Reader*
Key Points	The play examines middle-class characters in Norway in the late 1800s. The society is one in which money and reputation are valued above all. It is a world epitomised by hypocrisy and conformity.	The text explores the introduction of radio to Britain in the 1920s and the changes such media bring. This is a society that requires a monarch who can communicate successfully via modern technology.	The vision of society in the novella is narrow since it is set entirely in the world of the Queen of England in the 2000s and, ironically, although she presides over the Commonwealth and travels a great deal, her world is very small.

ANALYSE

Comparative Study

Key Moments	The opening stage directions provide a visual representation of a typical middle-class home of this period: 'A room furnished comfortably and tastefully but not extravagantly … Between the doors stands a piano.'	Before the 1934 radio broadcast of the King's Christmas message, King George V says: 'This devilish device will change everything … In the past all a king had to do was look respectable in uniform and not fall off his horse. Now we must invade people's houses and ingratiate ourselves with them. We have become actors.'	The descriptions of the Queen's travels make clear the tedious and repetitive nature of such undertakings: 'So in due course Her Majesty went to Wales and to Scotland and to Lancashire and the West Country in that unremitting round of nationwide perambulation that is the lot of the monarch.'
Comparisons	The three texts offer different visions of society. In *A Doll's House* the world of the text is one of bourgeois values and it is rife with hypocrisy. This is different from *The King's Speech*, where the vision of the world is one of impending change. *The Uncommon Reader* has some similarity to *A Doll's House*, in that it too offers a vision of a world that is narrow and restrictive, but it is different from *The Uncommon Reader*, since the Queen can choose to break free of this world without undue sacrifice. *The King's Speech* shares some commonality with *The Uncommon Reader* as both texts are set in the world of the British royal family.		

VIEW OF THE PAST

	A Doll's House	*The King's Speech*	*The Uncommon Reader*
Key Points	The burden of the past and the necessity of truth are important aspects of the vision and viewpoint of the play. Ibsen suggests that the only possibility of freedom lies in accepting the truth of the past and making choices that one believes in.	The film explores the role of the past in both personal and interpersonal conflict. In order for an individual to be free of the past, the text suggests, he or she must first confront it with clarity and honesty.	The past plays a central role in the text. As the Queen becomes more and more involved in the world of books, she is inevitably drawn into a reconsideration of her own past.
Key Moments	Act Three: Nora traces her adoption of the role that prevents her maturing as an individual back to her relationship with her father: 'He called me his doll child, and he played with me just as I used to play with my dolls.'	In a session with Logue, Bertie confronts the demons of his past, including the early death of one of his brothers. As a child, he was also treated cruelly by one of his nannies.	The nature of reading is one of journeying, and some of that journey is inevitably into the past. With regard to her reading, the Queen says: 'I have started too late. I will never catch up.' Later she says: 'Too late. It was all too late.'
Comparisons	There is a similarity between *A Doll's House* and *The King's Speech* with regard to the view of the past. Both texts espouse a vision whereby the past must be confronted in order for the individual to be free of it. Both Nora and Bertie have issues in terms of their upbringing: Nora's father treated her like a 'doll' while Bertie's childhood was traumatic. Both achieve personal freedom when they acknowledge the truth of the past. *The Uncommon Reader* is different from the other two texts. The Queen has no difficult events to confront in her past. Instead, her journey into reading has brought with it a keen awareness of the passage of time and, by necessity, a re-evaluation of her own past.		

VISION OF INDIVIDUAL AGENCY

	A Doll's House	*The King's Speech*	*The Uncommon Reader*
Key Points	The play promotes equality between the sexes. Individual agency is possible only when the reality of one's life and one's own collaboration in that reality are confronted.	Individual agency is portrayed in this text as a vital aspect of personal development, but also as something that is greatly affected by relationships.	The journey towards individual agency is not an easy one for the Queen. The development of the self brings isolation with it, and a new, sometimes painful, sensitivity to the world.
Key Moments	Act Three: Nora faces the truth about her marriage, and herself: 'I must try and educate myself – you [Torvald] are not the man to help me in that. I must do that for myself.'	In the scene where Bertie, following the death of his father, visits Logue, the two men engage in a frank conversation. Bertie reveals some of the pressures of his childhood. Thus begins Bertie's journey towards selfhood.	Norman provides the Queen with support and solidarity in her journey into reading. After his departure, the Queen is forced to communicate with herself by writing down her thoughts and feelings.
Comparisons	The three texts all offer a vision in which individual agency is essential to personhood. In *A Doll's House,* individual agency is presented as being possible only when a character, in this case Nora, confronts the reality of her life and dismantles gender constructions. *The King's Speech* is different from *A Doll's House*, as individual agency is presented in the film as something that is developed within a relationship, rather than in isolation, as in the play. Bertie gains selfhood, to a large extent, in his interaction with Logue. *The Uncommon Reader* has some similarities to both *A Doll's House* and *The King's Speech*. In the novel, the Queen, like Bertie in the film, is stimulated into journeying towards individual agency by her relationship with another, although after Norman's departure she continues her journey in isolation, like Nora in *A Doll's House*.			

Comparative Study

Comparative Study

VIEW OF HONESTY

	A Doll's House	The King's Speech	The Uncommon Reader
Key Points	A central aspect of the vision of the play is the importance of honesty. Ibsen acknowledges that truth can be complex, but the play is unequivocal on the necessity for honesty in relationships.	The vision of the film presents honesty as an essential component of relationships. The honesty of the exchanges between Bertie and Logue is the catalyst for personal growth and a release from the demons of the past.	The novella is about the awakening of a woman – the Queen – through reading. This awakening is not always easy and requires a great deal of emotional honesty on the part of the Queen.
Key Moments	Act Three: Nora honestly confronts the reality of her marriage: 'Torvald – it was then it dawned upon me that for eight years I had been living here with a strange man and had borne him three children.'	In the scene where Bertie is confronted about his relationship with his brother, the exchanges between himself and Logue are honest: Logue: What is it about David that stops you speaking? Bertie: What is it about you that bloody well makes you want to go on about it the whole bloody time?	At her tea party to celebrate her eightieth birthday, the Queen delivers a speech that is shocking in its honesty: 'One has given one's white-gloved hand to hands that were steeped in blood and conversed politely with men who have personally slaughtered children.'
Comparisons	All three texts offer a similar vision of the necessity of honesty in life, both with self and with others. In *A Doll's House*, it is Nora's honest appraisal of her marriage that sets her free. This has some similarity to *The King's Speech* where it is Bertie's honest recollection of the past that frees him from it. In both texts, the protagonists are forced to be honest with others as well as themselves. *The Uncommon Reader* has some similarity to both *A Doll's House* and *The King's Speech*, in that the Queen has to honestly re-evaluate her life in the light of the personal journey reading has taken her on.		

MAKE

Tip: When you are answering a question that is split into two parts, take care to follow the instructions of the question carefully. You will be discussing one text in (a) and comparing and contrasting that text with at least one of your other two texts in (b). Both (a) and (b) will consist of essay-style answers.

Answer the following **Vision and Viewpoint** question from Leaving Certificate 2014 using the guide below to structure your answer.

(a) 'The extent to which a reader can relate an aspect of a text to his or her experience of life, helps to shape an understanding of the general vision and viewpoint of that text.'

Discuss this view in relation to your study of one text on your comparative course. (30)

(b) With reference to the text you referred to in 1. (a) above and at least one other text from your comparative course, compare how two other aspects of the texts (excluding the aspect discussed in 1. (a) above) influenced your understanding of the general vision and viewpoint of those texts. (40)

Guide to Answering 2014 Vision and Viewpoint Question

In your introductory paragraphs to both (a) and (b), it is essential to answer the question: do you agree, partially agree or disagree with the quotation you are being offered? You must also tell the examiner which vision and viewpoint means – the broad outlook on life presented in the text – and which three texts you have studied – give the title of each text and the name of its author or director. It is also advisable to offer a 'blurb' or 'snapshot' of each of your texts, but confine this to one sentence per text. Finally, in (b) only, outline your intention to compare and contrast the texts in relation to the stance you have adopted with reference to the quotation offered in the question.

The main body of your essays in both (a) and (b) will consist of a series of paragraphs relating to the question you are answering. Begin each paragraph with a topic sentence – a sentence that outlines the main point you intend discussing in that paragraph, with reference to the question you are answering. In (b) only, compare and contrast all three of your texts in each paragraph. Remember, the most important element of a good comparative study is sensitivity to the material you are discussing. Avoid generalisations and remember that comparisons may be qualified – sometimes texts are both similar to and different from each other. There is no set number of comparisons you should make in an answer – sometimes one complex comparison requires an entire paragraph to elucidate clearly, at other times a series of comparative points may be made in quick succession.

In this instance, you may use the following points to construct the main body of your essay in both (a) and (b), remembering to keep the question to the forefront of your answer at all times. In this question, you should discuss one point in (a) and that point along with two other points in (b).

- Vision of society.
- View of the past.
- Vision of individual agency.
- View of honesty.

Finally, include a concluding paragraph in both (a) and (b). The objective of a conclusion in a comparative study is two-fold – firstly, to provide a general summary of your answer and, secondly, to demonstrate your personal opinion in relation to the vision and viewpoint of each of your texts. What made an impression on you? What didn't engage you? It is important throughout Paper 2 to present yourself as a critical reader of texts.

A complete answer to a comparative study question in the Leaving Certificate exam should be approximately 1,000 words in length.

ANALYSE

Comparative Study

Comparative Study: Literary Genre

GENRE

	A Doll's House	The King's Speech	The Uncommon Reader
Key Points	Realist drama that deals with the domestic life of middle-class Norwegians in the late 1800s.	British historical drama film based on the life of King George VI.	Novella based on an imagined scenario in which Queen Elizabeth II, embarks on a journey into the world of reading.
Key Moments	The opening stage directions provide an accurate visual representation of a typical middle-class home of this period: 'A room furnished comfortably and tastefully but not extravagantly … Between the doors stands a piano.'	The title card in the opening scene provides factual background information: '1925. King George V reigns over a quarter of the world's people. He asks his second son, the Duke of York, to give the closing speech at the Empire Exhibition in Wembley, London.'	The novella begins at a state banquet with a fictional version of Queen Elizabeth II asking the French president a question: 'I've been longing to ask you about the writer Jean Genet.'
Comparisons	Although the three texts are different in terms of genre, they all embody the characteristics of social realism. Each text depicts a setting that closely resembles reality, and has credible characters that are recognisable as ordinary people to the audience or reader, plausible events and believable plots. While *A Doll's House* is entirely fictional, *The King's Speech* and *The Uncommon Reader* are similar in that they both base their plots on the lives of real people, one as a historical drama and the other as an imagined scenario.		

NARRATIVE TECHNIQUE AND CHARACTERISATION

	A Doll's House	The King's Speech	The Uncommon Reader
Key Points	Ibsen wrote *A Doll's House* in what is called 'a limited third-person narrative with a near proximity', since the audience has the opportunity to hear Nora making side remarks. Characterisation is achieved by personal codes as well as dialogue, and Ibsen also made use of the dramatic technique of the formal speech.	In a film the camera functions as an omniscient narrator, but point of view does exist within film texts as the director may present events from a protagonist's perspective via the close-up shot. The success of *The King's Speech* comes in part from Hooper doing just this – keeping the camera on Bertie.	In the novella, the narrative voice moves seamlessly between the third person, which offers the Queen's perspective, and a dry, ironic omniscient voice. Characterisation is achieved by the use of realistic dialogue, action and reaction, as well as interior monologue.

Key Moments	Act One: After Torvald tells Nora that deceitful women poison their homes and their children, we see Nora pause and hear her whisper to herself: 'No, no … it isn't true. It's impossible; it must be impossible.' A few lines further down Nora asks herself: 'Deprave my little children? Poison my home? … It's not true. It can't possibly be true.'	In the climax scene, Bertie comes within two inches of a microphone to deliver a speech announcing the outbreak of war. The audience sees Bertie summoning up all his courage to successfully overcome his anxieties and fears to prove his mastery of oratory for this most important of all speeches. Empathy is subtly encouraged by Hooper's use of interesting camera angles.	Following her meeting with Sir Claude, the Queen muses: 'Had she been asked if reading had enriched her life she would have had to say yes, undoubtedly, though adding with equal certainty that it had at the same time drained her life of all purpose.'
Comparisons	Different media tell their stories in different ways. The story in *A Doll's House* is conveyed primarily through dialogue and stage directions. This is different from *The King's Speech* as the camera in a film functions as an omniscient narrator. The narrative technique in *The Uncommon Reader* is different from that of the other two texts, as the story is told in a mixture of third person and omniscient narrative voice. However, there is a similarity between all three texts. Their stories are all told from the perspective of the protagonist. Ibsen does this by employing third-person point of view with near proximity. Hooper does it by keeping the camera on Colin Firth playing Bertie. Bennett does it through the use of interior monologue.		

STRUCTURE AND SETTING

	A Doll's House	*The King's Speech*	*The Uncommon Reader*
Key Points	The entire play unfolds on one set. The action takes place over a period of three days. The five major characters are closely related, and their lives and roles mirror or contrast with each other. This unity of time, place and characters is constructed to make the audience feel the tension mounting within the play.	The timeline of *The King's Speech* is fourteen years and yet the pace of the film is quite fast, as Hooper focuses on a select number of events. Although it is based on historical events, the chronological delivery of the plot creates suspense and tension. Setting also adds to the tension in the text as the majority of *The King's Speech* was shot indoors.	The novella is written without chapters in a mixture of flashback and chronological, forward-moving narrative. Various locations provide a setting for the novella but there is no real distinction between them, since the novella is primarily a psychological text.

Key Moments	Act Two: Tension within the play – Nora persuades Torvald to watch her practise the tarantella in order to prevent him opening Krogstad's letter. He tries to rein in her wildness with his instructions, but she ignores his comments and dances ever more wildly, her hair coming loose.	The music played during the broadcast of the 1939 radio speech at the climax of the film is from the 2nd movement of Beethoven's 7th Symphony and hugely adds to the tension of the scene.	Reflective passage: 'All readers were equal, and this took her back to the beginnings of her life. As a girl, one of her greatest thrills had been on VE night, when she and her sister had slipped out of the gates and mingled unrecognised with the crowds. There was something of that, she felt, to reading.'
Comparisons	Both *A Doll's House* and *The King's Speech* employ forward-moving, chronological narratives, which add to the tension in the texts. The timeframe of *A Doll's House* is very short, but Ibsen intensifies the action by including references to potentially destructive events from the past. *The King's Speech*, on the other hand, has a longer time-frame and so omits all but the crucial events. *A Doll's House* is divided into Acts, while *The King's Speech* uses title cards to communicate information to the audience. *The Uncommon Reader* is different from the other texts as it written without chapters in a mixture of flashback and chronological, forward-moving narrative. This text, therefore, has less suspense and a more reflective tone.		

LANGUAGE AND IMAGERY

	A Doll's House	*The King's Speech*	*The Uncommon Reader*
Key Points	The language of the play is highly suggestive. Torvald's pet names for Nora – squirrel, skylark, songbird – are often prefaced by 'little', showing that he sees her as a child. Ibsen also makes use of dramatic symbols in the play such as doors, letters and rings.	Language, while an important element of film, is only one part of its story-telling repertoire. Hooper uses frame space to add complexity and depth to the telling of the story. Music is also used in a symbolic way in the text.	While the novella, for the most part, is written in a matter-of-fact style, it also self-consciously illustrates the growth of the Queen's relationship with the written word. The text contains numerous literary allusions as well as some fine poetic passages.
Key Moments	Act One: The power dynamic between Torvald and Nora is powerfully suggested in his repeated use of the term 'little'. Initially used as a rather silly and condescending term of endearment – 'my little lark' and 'my little squirrel' – it is later used as criticism ('my little spendthrift'), as a put-down ('my dear little Nora') and as a soother ('my sweet little skylark').	The film's original score was composed by Alexandre Desplat. A sparse arrangement of strings and piano and the repetition of a single note represent the difficulty Bertie has in speaking but, as the film progresses, growing banks of warm strings code the deepening friendship between him and Logue.	While staying at Balmoral, the Queen and Norman read Proust, and the landscape is described as follows: '… while in the wet butts on the hills the guns cracked out their empty tattoo and the occasional dead and sodden stag was borne past the window.'

Comparisons	The three texts use language and imagery in different ways. In *A Doll's House*, Ibsen uses suggestive language both to convey character and to create atmosphere. This is different from *The King's Speech* where Hooper uses the language of music both to heighten atmosphere and to add depth to characterisation. *The Uncommon Reader* is different from both *A Doll's House* and *The King's Speech*, as Bennett uses language itself to demonstrate Wittgenstein's theory that 'the limits of my language are the limits of my mind'. As the Queen becomes more embroiled in the world of books, her vocabulary, as well as her thoughts, are stretched. Both *A Doll's House* and *The King's Speech* employ symbols effectively, whereas in *The Uncommon Reader* Bennett uses poetic passages to enrich the narrative.

MAKE

Tip: When you are answering a question worth 70 marks your task is to write an essay-style answer in which you compare and contrast all three comparative texts.

Answer the following **Literary Genre** question from Leaving Certificate 2010 using the guide below to structure your answer.

'The unexpected is essential to the craft of story-telling.'

Compare how the authors of the comparative texts you have studied used the unexpected in their texts. You may confine your answer to key moments in the texts.

Guide to Answering 2010 Literary Genre Question

In your introductory paragraph, it is essential to answer the question: do you agree, partially agree or disagree with the quotation you are being offered? You must also tell the examiner what literary genre means – the ways that texts tell their stories – and which three texts you have studied – give the title of each text and the name of its author or director. It is also advisable to offer a 'blurb' or 'snapshot' of each of your texts, but confine this to one sentence per text. Finally, outline your intention to compare and contrast the texts in relation to the stance you have adopted with reference to the quotation offered in the question.

The main body of your essay will consist of a series of paragraphs relating to the question you are answering. Begin each paragraph with a topic sentence – a sentence that outlines the main point you intend discussing in that paragraph, with reference to the question you are answering. Compare and contrast all three of your texts in each paragraph. Remember, the most important element of a good comparative study is sensitivity to the material you are discussing. Avoid generalisations and remember that comparisons may be qualified – sometimes texts are both similar to and different from each other. There is no set number of comparisons you should make in an answer – sometimes one complex comparison requires an entire paragraph to elucidate clearly, at other times a series of comparative points may be made in quick succession.

Comparative Study

In this instance, you may use the following points to construct the main body of your essay, remembering to keep the question to the forefront of your answer at all times.

- Genre.
- Narrative technique and characterisation.
- Structure and setting.
- Language and imagery.

Finally, include a concluding paragraph. The objective of a conclusion in a comparative study is two-fold – firstly, to provide a general summary of your answer and, secondly, to demonstrate your personal opinion in relation to the treatment of the literary genre of each of your texts. What did you enjoy? What did you find dull or clichéd? It is important throughout Paper 2 to present yourself as a critical reader of texts.

A complete answer to a comparative study question in the Leaving Certificate exam should be approximately 1,000 words in length.

Comparative Study

Poetry

Unseen Poem

Prescribed Poets

Introduction

What is Poetry?

Before you embark on the journey, please pause for a moment to consider the question – what is poetry? Over the years, students have offered the following kinds of answer to this question: 'writing divided into lines', 'a complicated way of saying things', 'a painful experience'. This is hardly surprising. The truth is that poetry, as it is experienced in many classrooms, *is* painful. It is not the fault of the teacher or the student or the syllabus, but rather a result of not reflecting enough on this essential question – what is poetry?

The fact is that poetry is something completely different from all the other elements that make up the Leaving Certificate English syllabus and, as such, requires a completely different learning methodology. Why? Because poetry comes from an oral tradition – it is the earliest form of literature in all cultures and it is composed primarily to be heard. In its beginnings, poetry was linked with prophecy and religious ritual, and the exalted states of mind these generate. This is a medium that lives and breathes somewhere in the space between words and music, in the sensory perception of the individual imagination, and not as a silent typeface of the page of a book – which is, by and large, the only place that students find it. So, before you decide that you dislike poetry or that it is hard to understand, think about this – although many people will never read poetry after they leave school, even now, in the twenty-first century, we need it. When someone dies or gets married or when a president is inaugurated, we reach for a poem as the best way to mark such significant occasions. Why? Because poetry is the most intense form of language we have. A good poem contains every single component of communication available – musical components, such as rhythm, rhyme and sound effects, and language components, such as imagery, description and interesting words. And this is just the tip of the iceberg! In a good poem, all these things coalesce to create a compact bomb of communication.

This is what good poetry is – feelings – the sense of being emotionally awakened. Feelings are expressed less in imagery than in movement, in the inner rhythm of the language. When a poet is genuinely animated, you can hear it in the way the lines move. This is why poetry and music are similar. The rhythm – the way the sounds combine, separate, recombine – is the vehicle for the feeling. The critic Al Alvarez says it is possible to hear a poem before you know what it is about, to get the movement before you get the words, as though the movement were a dimly lit wake-up call or the first faint stirring of something waiting to be expressed. A line of poetry may contain no visual elements at all but if you listen properly, you can hear it stir and pause and breathe.

Poetry

Glossary of Poetic Terms

Language

argumentative: characterised by systematic reasoning, as in Donne's debates with lovers, Donne's and Hopkins' debates with their God, Keats' debates with himself; implies logical and analytical techniques

cerebral: relating to the brain, characterised by the use of the intellect rather than emotion or intuition; Boland's 'Sleep in a world your final sleep has woken' ('Child of our Time') deliberately invites the reader's mind to engage with its meaning

colloquial: used in everyday conversation, not formal; Eliot uses colloquial language ironically, as dialogue to reveal character, and Bishop and Durcan use it directly as a poetic language

dynamic: characterised by constant change or progress; Plath's language is particularly dynamic in its sudden shifts, as is Hopkins' and Donne's, though Durcan's anecdotes tend to derive their strength from developing predictably

innovative: featuring new methods, original; few poets redefine poetic language, but there are two examples on your course – Eliot, who did it in a way that others could use after him, and Hopkins, who did it in ways that remain unique to him

intense: passionate, ardent, fervent, vehement, usually in the expression of emotion; Donne's 'The Flea' is playfully ardent, while Plath's 'Poppies in July' is intensely serious

literal: without metaphor or exaggeration, words in their most basic sense; not common in poetry – where words are intended to mean more than themselves – but successfully adopted as a characteristic manner by Durcan

lyrical: expressing the writer's emotions, usually spoken in the present tense; the very titles of Boland's 'This Moment', Donne's 'Sweetest love, I do not go,/For weariness of thee', Keats' 'Bright star! would I were steadfast as thou art' and Plath's 'Morning Song' are examples

personal: relating to one's private life, relationships and experiences; Eliot's language is deliberately **impersonal** – he developed a theory of 'impersonal poetry' which insisted that great works do not express the personal emotion of the poet – whereas Plath's language is deliberately personal, though it achieves the same universality

plain: unadorned, undecorated, homely, clear; at the end of her poem about a 'homely' fish ('The Fish'), Bishop's statement of six everyday monosyllabic words – 'And I let the fish go' – is a perfect example of her plain style

reflective: both deeply thoughtful and providing a reflection of something; best applied to poetry reconsidering past events, as in almost all of Boland's work and some of Durcan's

satiric: using **irony** (the full significance of the speaker's words in Bishop's 'Filling Station' are apparent to the reader, but not the speaker), **sarcasm** (Plath's description of modern times as 'tidy' in 'The Times Are Tidy') or **ridicule** (the judge's words and values are plainly absurd in Durcan's 'Wife Who Smashed Television Gets Jail') to expose human folly – respectively, prejudice, suppression and hypocrisy

sensuous: appealing to or relating to the senses, subdivided as **visual**, **auditory**, **tactile**, **olfactory** and **gustatory**; used by all poets, but most richly by Keats, who often combined the senses to make **synesthetic imagery**, as in the combination of visual, auditory and gustatory images in 'Tasting of Flora and the country green,/Dance, and Provençal song, and sunburnt mirth!' ('Ode to a Nightingale')

Imagery

allusion: reference to another text; common with most poets, who are inevitably readers also, but Eliot's 'The Love Song of J. Alfred Prufrock' and 'The Waste Land' turn it into an element of the style

conceit: an unlikely and elaborate **metaphor** (q.v.) or comparison; occasionally used by all poets, but a characteristic feature of the poetry of Donne, who compared parting lovers to the legs of a mathematical compass ('A Valediction: forbidding Mourning')

hyperbole: exaggeration for effect; Hopkins' 'Thrush's eggs look little low heavens' ('Spring') is an unusually delicate example, since hyperbole, by definition, tends to go for the big effect

metaphor: an imaginative implied comparison that is not literally applicable; the fabric of all poetry, a claim that is itself metaphoric, since poetry is not cloth

personification: a form of metaphor whereby inanimate objects are attributed human qualities; the entire Keats poem 'Ode on a Grecian Urn' is an extended exercise in personification; also referred to as **anthropomorphism** and **pathetic fallacy**

simile: an imaginative direct comparison that is not literally applicable; our everyday language is littered with them – *like two peas in a pod* and *as clear as mud* – although 'littered' is a metaphor, because it doesn't use 'like' or 'as', but still compares language to a landscape

symbol: words or images signifying more than they literally represent, differing from **metaphor** and **simile** in that the signified meanings tend to be more permanent, holding in all contexts – such as the national plant symbols of shamrock (Ireland), thistle (Scotland) and maple leaf (Canada) – whereas a metaphor can change meaning from poem to poem

Poetry

Sound

alliteration: the use of words with the same initial letter in sequence or proximity, usually with the intention of capturing a distinctive quality of the subject; the most impressive examples come from Hopkins, including his description of the majestic windhover, 'king-/dom of daylight's dauphin, dapple-dawn-drawn Falcon' in 'The Windhover'

assonance: the effect created from placing words with the same vowel sounds but different consonants in close proximity; the thin 'i' or 'e' sounds can communicate discomfort, the broader 'o' or 'a' sounds evoke fullness or strength

cadence: the natural **rhythm** (q.v.) of speech, rather than the rhythm of poetic **metre** (q.v.); Bishop often hits it perfectly: 'even then I knew she was/a foolish, timid woman' ('In the Waiting Room')

caesura: a pause within a line, usually indicated by some punctuation mark, that helps control the **rhythm** of the delivery, and therefore the expression of the emotion; Donne uses it extensively in building his arguments: 'Let not to this, self murder added be,/And sacrilege, three sins in killing three.' ('The Flea')

enjambment: continuing a sentence across a line break, also known as **run-on**, an element that helps control the **rhythm** (q.v.) of delivery, and therefore the expression of the emotion; in Plath's 'Pheasant', after a series of clipped line endings, the run-on 'it isn't/As if I thought it had a spirit.' is particularly expressive

metre: the pattern of stressed and unstressed syllables in a line of poetry, identified by the number of feet in a line, where a foot contains one stressed and any number of unstressed syllables; the most common form in traditional English poetry is **iambic pentameter** – a pattern of five unstressed/stressed feet, such as 'When I have fears that I may cease to be' (Keats); most modern poetry is irregular in metre, with the emphasis more on rhythm as the element expressive of emotion: 'I know the bottom, she says. I know it with my great tap root:/It is what you fear.' (Plath)

onomatopoeia: sound in a word imitating sound in the world; '"Jug, Jug" to dirty ears' from Eliot's 'The Waste Land' imitates a nightingale's call

rhyme: the chiming of similar vowel sounds – 'mend … bend … end … defend' from Donne's 'Batter my heart' – primarily to create the music of poetry, but often also to associate previously unconnected terms and thoughts, and to add stress and emphasis, and therefore importance, to certain words

rhythm: movement, **beat**; expressive of thought or emotion; determined by standard patterns in **metrical verse**, but more by the theme in **free verse**

tone: dominant emotion in a phrase, line or poem; **mood**

Form

aubade: a poem in celebration of dawn, although Donne's take on it in 'The Sun Rising' is typically humorous – why would you want to *celebrate* anything that tries to get you out of bed in the morning?

ballad: traditionally, a narrative poem or song with each **stanza** (q.v.) a **quatrain** (q.v.) and the second and fourth lines rhyming; Keats' 'La Belle Dame Sans Merci' injects horror, mystery and incantation into what can be a dull form

couplet: two-line **stanza** (q.v.) or poem; Durcan's poetry contains a number of examples of this concise, pithy form

dramatic monologue: a poem narrated by a character, as in a stage play; Eliot's 'The Love Song of J. Alfred Prufrock' and 'Journey of the Magi' are brilliant examples (see **personal** above), as are Durcan's 'Six Nuns Die in Convent Inferno' and Bishop's 'In the Waiting Room'

lyric: a personal poem expressive of emotion and written in the present tense; Plath and Boland are the most obvious exponents on your course

narrative: a poem that tells a story; the favourite form of Durcan, but also used by Keats, Bishop and Boland

ode: from the Greek for 'song' and developed from classical Greek theatre, a **lyrical** (q.v.), exalted celebration of something with standard rhyming and **stanza** (q.v.) schemes; its greatest, and effectively last, exponent in English poetry is John Keats

quatrain: a section or stanza of four lines

sestina: a form consisting of six **stanzas** (q.v.) of six lines each, with the last word in each line from the first stanza being repeated in a different order in each subsequent stanza; Bishop, whose 'Sestina' is on your course, was fond of its odd containment

sonnet: fourteen-line poem, usually in iambic pentameter, divided either octave (8)/ sestet (6) – Petrarchan sonnet – or quatrain(4)/ quatrain(4)/quatrain(4)/ couplet(2) – Shakespearean sonnet

stanza: section of a poem separated from other sections by line spacing

The Examination Paper

Poetry is Section III on English, Higher Level, Paper 2. It is worth 70 marks in total. It consists of two parts:

- A: Unseen Poem (20 marks)
- B: Prescribed Poetry (50 marks)

The general rule for English Higher Level Paper 2 is to allocate one minute of writing time for each mark available. You should therefore spend 20 minutes answering Unseen Poem and 50 minutes answering Prescribed Poetry.

Unseen Poem

You are presented with a poem that you will not have studied before and which you may not have seen before. Sometimes, an introduction to the poem is provided. Don't ignore or disregard this. It can provide valuable insights and valuable material for answering the questions. You will be set questions on: the **language** of the poem, either in the poem as a whole or in selected lines or phrases; the **imagery** of the poem; the moods and emotions of the poem, particularly as expressed through **sound**; and the **theme**, experience or content of the poem.

You can choose between:

1. two separate questions dealing with specific aspects of the poem (10 marks each)
2. a single question on the entire poem (20 marks).

SECTION III   **POETRY**   **(70 marks)**

Candidates must answer **A** – Unseen Poem **and B** – Prescribed Poetry.

A   **UNSEEN POEM** (20 marks)

Read the following poem by Seamus Heaney from his collection, *Door into the Dark*, and answer **either** Question **1 or** Question 2 which follow.

The Peninsula

When you have nothing more to say, just drive
For a day all round the peninsula.
The sky is tall as over a runway,
The land without marks, so you will not arrive

But pass through, though always skirting landfall.
At dusk, horizons drink down sea and hill,
The ploughed field swallows the whitewashed gable
And you're in the dark again. Now recall

The glazed foreshore and silhouetted log,
That rock where breakers shredded into rags,
The leggy birds stilted on their own legs,
Islands riding themselves out into the fog,

And drive back home, still with nothing to say
Except that now you will uncode all landscapes
By this: things founded clean on their own shapes,
Water and ground in their extremity.

Seamus Heaney

1. (a) In the above poem Seamus Heaney recommends driving "all round the peninsula". Based on your reading of the poem, explain why you think the poet recommends undertaking such a journey. (10)

   (b) Choose two images from the poem that appeal to you and explain your choice. (10)

   OR

2. Discuss the effectiveness of the poet's use of language throughout this poem. Your answer should refer closely to the text. (20)

Page 6 of 8

Prescribed Poetry

'Students at Higher Level will be required to study a representative selection from the work of eight poets: a representative selection would seek to reflect the range of a poet's themes and interests and exhibit his/her characteristic style and viewpoint. Normally the study of at least six poems by each poet would be expected.' (DES English Syllabus, 6.3)

The eight prescribed poets on the 2017 course are: Elizabeth Bishop, Eavan Boland, John Donne, Paul Durcan, T.S. Eliot, Gerard Manley Hopkins, John Keats and Sylvia Plath.

Four of these poets will appear on the examination paper. **One** question will be set on each of the chosen four. Each question will consist of a critical assessment of the poet's work in the form of a quotation and an invitation to agree or disagree or otherwise discuss this assessment, supporting your answer with reference to both the themes and language in the poetry on your course. You must answer **one** of these questions.

To be mathematically certain of being able to answer a question, therefore, you must prepare **five** of the prescribed poets.

Unseen Poem

In its annual guidelines to examiners correcting Leaving Certificate English scripts, the State Examinations Commission offers the following general observations on the Unseen Poem.

> 'Students should be able to … read poetry conscious of its specific mode of using language as an artistic medium.' (DES English Syllabus, 4.5.1)

> 'Note that responding to the unseen poem is an exercise in aesthetic reading. It is especially important, in assessing the responses of the candidates, to guard against the temptation to assume a "correct" reading of the poem. Reward the candidates' awareness of the patterned nature of the language of poetry, its imagery, its sensuous qualities, and its suggestiveness.' (SEC Higher Level Marking Scheme)

In discussing the patterns of **sound**, keep in mind that sounds can be hard, harsh, jarring and cacophonous or soft, sweet and melodious. To achieve either effect, poets might use **assonance**, **alliteration**, **metre** and **rhyme**. The word **tone**, which has an emotional content, may be used when discussing the 'feel' of a particular sound. All the sounds together create the **rhythm** of a poem, and rhythm, as in music, may be fast or slow, but more precisely, a million things in between those poles, such as excited, intense, frantic, languorous, seductive, reflective …

A technique very often used to control rhythm is the **caesura**, a pause inside a line, mostly because it gives the rhythm the movement of informal speech, which many modern poets strive for. All these terms are further explained and illustrated in the **Glossary of Poetic Terms** given on page 195.

In discussing the patterns of **imagery**, keep in mind that the term refers to the images stimulated in the imagination by the language used, and has its origins in the essential human activity of comparing one thing to another. We use images all the time in everyday speech, usually without thinking about them. When we call someone a clown, for instance, we don't mean that they're a clown, literally. Imagery is therefore **figurative language**, not **literal language**. In poetry, images are selected very carefully and used very precisely, usually in patterns, where one image is linked to another to enrich the effect and the meaning. Think of the imagery of poison in *Hamlet*, beginning with the deadly stuff poured into old King Hamlet's ear, which then spreads through the whole of Denmark, until it infects and kills everyone – Hamlet, Laertes, Claudius, Gertrude – at the end. The main technical terms for discussing imagery are **simile** – a direct comparison, using as or like, as in Horatio's description of the Ghost hearing the morning cock crow, 'And then it started, like a guilty thing/Upon a fearful summons' – and **metaphor** – an implied or indirect comparison, as when Hamlet calls the world 'an unweeded garden'. Hamlet develops the metaphor at length in his soliloquy, which makes it a **controlling metaphor** or **extended metaphor**.

The best verb to use when you are discussing an image is that *it suggests* … All these terms are further explained and illustrated in the **Glossary of Poetic Terms** on page 195.

Unseen Poem 1

Leaving Certificate 2005, English Higher Level Paper 2, Unseen Poem

Answer **either** Question **1** or Question **2**.

READ

Back Yard

Shine on, O moon of summer.
Shine to the leaves of grass, catalpa and oak,
All silver under your rain to-night.

An Italian boy is sending songs to you to-night from an accordion.
A Polish boy is out with his best girl; they marry next month;
      to-night they are throwing you kisses.

An old man next door is dreaming over a sheen
      that sits in a cherry tree in his back yard.

The clocks say I must go – I stay here sitting on the back porch
      drinking white thoughts you rain down.

      Shine on, O moon,
Shake out more and more silver changes.

Carl Sandburg

Exemplar: Questions on 'Back Yard'

1. (a) Do you like the world that the poet describes in this poem? Give reasons for your answer supporting them by reference to the text. (10)

The world created in 'Back Yard' is pleasant, and therefore very attractive. It is dominated by the imagery of soft light: 'Shine … moon … shine … silver … sheen … white … shine … silver.' The very first word – 'Shine' – is heavily stressed and suggests energy and power as well as brightness. This is the 'moon of summer' that the poet is urging to shine on, and summer is a time of warm nights. With the repetition of 'shine' in line two and then the use of 'silver' in the next line to capture the rain on the vegetation, the impression of something sparkling, glittering – and valuable – is developed. 'Songs' and 'kisses' are then thrown in to add to the warm celebratory atmosphere, which the poet is naturally reluctant to leave, because he's so much at ease, enjoying himself so much, 'sitting on the back porch' and 'drinking' in the 'white' splendour of the rain falling through the light of the moon. The entire world of the poem is sparkling and pleasurable – the opposite of the mechanical, duty-obsessed world suggested by 'the clocks' – and one that is therefore very appealing to me.

201

(b) Choose a line or two that you find particularly appealing and explain why. (10)

The line that is most suggestive and most effective in my opinion is: 'The clocks say I must go – I stay here sitting on the back porch.' Firstly, because there is a great sense of rebelliousness, independence and freedom in the second part of the line. It has almost a childish boldness about it: 'I stay here sitting …' It resists the authoritarian tones in 'must go' and strikes a little blow for enjoyment instead of duty. The second thing I like about the line is the rhythm. The first part – 'The clocks say I must go' – actually sounds like the mechanical ticking of a clock, because each syllable is short and clipped. However, the second part – 'I stay here sitting on the back porch' – is more drawn out because of the longer syllables, and is at a more relaxed pace, which is appropriate. Finally, what I like is the contrast in the images, between the mechanical 'clocks' and their bossy commands and the relaxation of the 'back porch', which is where you put your feet up.

2. Write a personal response to the poem 'Back Yard'. (20)

On a first reading, the most striking feature of this poem, 'Back Yard,' is the imagery of soft light: 'Shine … moon … shine … silver … sheen … white … shine … silver.' It's introduced on the first line, in the very first word, 'Shine', which is heavily stressed and which suggests energy and power as well as brightness. This is the 'moon of summer' that the poet is urging to shine on, and summer is a time of warm nights. With the repetition of 'shine' in line two and then with the use of 'silver' in the next line to capture the rain on the vegetation, the impression of something sparkling, glittering – and valuable – is developed. 'Songs' and 'kisses' are then thrown in to add to the warm celebratory atmosphere, which the poet is naturally reluctant to leave, because he's so much at ease,

enjoying himself, 'sitting on the back porch' and 'drinking' in the 'white' splendour of the rain falling through the light of the moon.

Generally, in studying the poems and novels and plays on our course, I have found that the more significant the experience being explored, then the greater impact the work has on me. Sylvia Plath's poetry, for instance, which deals with the rawness of her own emotional and psychological life, meant the most to me. In this respect, the present poem, 'Back Yard,' has a less than profound impact on me. It is a pleasant, laid-back celebration of relaxation and the pleasures of life – songs, love, dreams and rest – but it doesn't go any deeper than this. When Sandburg repeats his opening in the last two lines – 'Shine on, O moon' – it now has a contented feel to it, and it is probably difficult, generally, to get excited about an evocation of contentment, although 'Back Yard' remains an enjoyable, accomplished poem.

ANALYSE

1. (a) Start your response by answering the question – 'the world … is attractive'. Everything that is the poem, including its world, is created by sound and imagery. You may open with either, and then include the other. This answer begins with imagery – 'of soft light' – and refers to sound in support – 'stressed … energy … repetition'. Illustrations are given. Some of these are selected for more detailed discussion, commenting on what the images *suggest* and what feelings the sounds *express*. As with all responses to tasks on English Paper 2, the focus throughout is on answering the set question, from the beginning – 'the world … is attractive', through the middle – 'the warm celebratory atmosphere' – to the end – 'the entire world is sparkling and pleasurable … and appealing to me'.

1. (b) Start your response by answering the question – 'the line that is most effective is …'. Everything that is a line of poetry is created by sound and imagery. You may open with either, and then include the other. This answer begins with sound – 'rebelliousness … tones … rhythm …' – and refers to imagery in support – 'the contrast in the images'. Illustrations are given. Some of these are selected for more detailed discussion, commenting on what feelings the sounds *express* and what the images *suggest*. As with all responses to tasks on English Paper 2, the focus throughout is on answering the set question, from the beginning – 'the line that is most effective in my opinion' – through the middle – 'the second thing I like' – to the end – 'Finally, what I like …'.

2. Everything that is a poem consists of sound, imagery and theme. You may open a personal response or general assessment with any of these, although it is best to leave theme until last. A poem *is* something, and not *about* something, and if you start with theme, you tend to neglect the very thing the examiners are instructed to reward you for – 'the patterned nature of the language of poetry'. Language is sound and imagery. This answer begins with imagery as the most 'striking' feature – 'the imagery of soft light' – and refers to sound in support – 'stressed … energy … repetition'. Illustrations are given. Some of these are selected for more detailed discussion, commenting on what the images *suggest* and what feelings the sounds *express*. As with all responses to tasks on English Paper 2, the focus throughout is on answering the set question, in this case a personal response to the poem, from the beginning – 'the most striking feature of this poem', through the middle – 'a less than profound impact on me' – to the end – 'an enjoyable, accomplished poem'.

Unseen Poem 2

Read the following poem by the American writer John Berryman from his collection *The Dream Songs* and answer **either** Question 1 **or** Question 2 which follow.

READ

Dream Song 14

Life, friends, is boring. We must not say so.
After all, the sky flashes, the great sea yearns,
we ourselves flash and yearn,
and moreover my mother told me as a boy
(repeatingly) 'Ever to confess you're bored
means you have no

Inner Resources.' I conclude now I have no
inner resources, because I am heavy bored.
Peoples bore me,
literature bores me, especially great literature,
Henry bores me, with his plights & gripes
as bad as achilles,

who loves people and valiant art, which bores me.
And the tranquil hills, & gin, look like a drag
and somehow a dog
has taken itself & its tail considerably away
into mountains or sea or sky, leaving
behind: me, wag.

John Berryman

MAKE

1. (a) The mood of this poem, quite obviously, is one of boredom. Briefly explain how it is conveyed. Make reference to the text in your answer. (10)
   (b) Choose a line or phrase from the poem that appealed to you. Explain your choice. (10)

   OR

2. Discuss the poet's use of language in 'Dream Song 14'. Your answer should make close reference to the text. (20)

Unseen Poem 3

Read the following poem by Katie Donovan and answer **either** Question 1 **or** Question 2 which follow.

READ

Yearn On

I want you to feel
the unbearable lack of me.
I want your skin
to yearn for the soft lure of mine;
I want those hints of red
on your canvas
to deepen in passion for me:
carmine, burgundy.
I want you to keep
stubbing your toe
on the memory of me;
I want your head to be dizzy
and your stomach in a spin;
I want you to hear my voice
in your ear, to touch your face
imagining it is my hand.
I want your body to shiver and quiver
at the mere idea of mine.
I want you to feel as though
life after me is dull, and pointless,
and very, very aggravating;
that with me you were lifted
on a current you waited all your life to find,
and had despaired of finding,
as though you were wading
through a soggy swill of inanity and ugliness
every minute we are apart.
I want you to drive yourself crazy
with the fantasy of me,
and how we will meet again, against all odds,
and there will be tears and flowers,
and the vast relief of not I,
but us.
I am haunting your dreams,
conducting these fevers
from a distance,
a distance that leaves me weeping,
and storming,
and bereft.

Katie Donovan

Poetry

MAKE

1. (a) What, in your opinion, is the dominant emotion in this poem? Briefly explain how it is conveyed. Make reference to the text in your answer. (10)

    (b) Choose two images from the poem that appealed to you and explain your choice. (10)

    OR

2. Discuss the poet's use of language in 'Yearn On'. Your answer should make close reference to the text. (20)

Poetry

Unseen Poem 4

Read the following poem by Li-Young Lee and answer **either** Question 1 **or** Question 2 which follow.

READ

A Story

Sad is the man who is asked for a story
and can't come up with one.

His five-year-old son waits in his lap.
Not the same story, Baba. A new one.
The man rubs his chin, scratches his ear.

In a room full of books in a world
of stories, he can recall
not one, and soon, he thinks, the boy
will give up on his father.

Already the man lives far ahead, he sees
the day this boy will go. *Don't go!*
Hear the alligator story! The angel story once more!
You love the spider story. You laugh at the spider.
Let me tell it!

But the boy is packing his shirts,
he is looking for his keys. *Are you a god,*
the man screams, *that I sit mute before you?*
Am I a god that I should never disappoint?

But the boy is here. *Please, Baba, a story?*
It is an emotional rather than logical equation,
an earthly rather than heavenly one,
which posits that a boy's supplications
and a father's love add up to silence.

Li-Young Lee

MAKE

1. (a) From your reading of this poem, explain your understanding of the title, 'A Story'. (10)
   (b) Choose one image from the poem that appealed to you. Explain your choice. (10)

OR

2. Write a personal response to this poem, highlighting the impact it makes on you. Your answer should make close reference to the text. (20)

Poetry

Prescribed Poetry

How Should I Use this Textbook to Prepare for the Examination Questions?

Every poet has individual experiences, recurring interests, a particular vision of the world and a characteristic style, with favoured images and references and effects. Each poet writing in English is different from all other poets writing in English, though they share a common language. The opening section on each poet – **The poetry of** … – identifies the unique **thematic** and **stylistic** features of the relevant poet. Style is always considered under the four headings: **language**, **imagery**, **sound** and poetic **forms**. The subsequent analyses of individual poems illustrate and develop the observations in this overview, which is then expanded on in broader discussions at the end of the analysis of the poems.

The reason for this approach is straightforward – every question on the prescribed poetry in the Leaving Certificate examination asks you to discuss the unique thematic and stylistic features of a poet's work. For instance, the question on Sylvia Plath in 2014 asked candidates to discuss the view that 'Plath makes effective use of language to explore her personal experiences of suffering and to provide occasional glimpses of the redemptive power of love'. In this case, 'effective language' is the stylistic feature, 'suffering' and 'love' are the themes. Much of this book, therefore, is designed to equip you with the *content* required for answering examination questions.

The rest of the book will help you to develop the *techniques* required for using that content within an essay-length response to the critical assessment that you are asked to discuss. Two aids are provided – the MAKE tasks in the textbook and the GUIDES on www.educateplus.ie. Two MAKE tasks – usually, one on theme and one on style – follow each poem. They are challenging, to encourage you to write material that you will later incorporate into a full-length essay. Each of the GUIDES at www.educateplus.ie demonstrates how to interpret and respond to examination questions on a prescribed poet, and each provides two additional MAKE tasks, in the form of further examination questions.

Exemplar: Prescribed Poetry Essay

Elizabeth Bishop wrote of her own poetry, 'The greatest challenge for me is to try and express difficult thoughts in plain language.'

Discuss this assessment by Bishop of her own poetry, supporting your answer with reference to both the themes and the language found in the poetry of Elizabeth Bishop on your course.

In relation to the above question, the correctors marking the exam papers would be issued with the following guidelines:

'Reward responses that show clear evidence of engagement with "difficult thoughts" and "plain language" (though not necessarily equally) in Bishop's poetry.'

Code **DT** for difficult thoughts

Code **PL** for plain language

WEBSITE GUIDE ADVISES	CANDIDATE'S SCRIPT	CORRECTOR'S CODES EXPLAINED
Spend your opening paragraph taking the critical quotation apart and explaining, in your own words, what each of its claims actually means.	On the surface, Bishop's poetry *is* very simple and straightforward. The language she uses consists almost entirely of ordinary, everyday terms, without obscure references, and she hardly ever uses difficult symbols or images to recreate experiences. It is – to use her own expression – a 'plain language', clear, uncomplicated, lucid, unadorned. In addition, the situations that she *does* feature in her work are all very familiar, such as visiting a dentist or pulling into a petrol station for a refill. At the same time, one can return time after time to her poems, enjoying them again, and getting a little more out of them each time. So, they're not shallow by any means. They're very deep, in fact. I think this is what she meant by 'difficult thoughts' in her description of her own work – reflections on the complexities of ordinary human experiences, explorations of the problematic choices and challenges that life can offer. It makes Bishop's poetry intriguing, that she can suggest so much underneath such an ordinary surface.	**PL** (will occur each time the candidate addresses 'plain language' either by using the phrase itself or one of its synonyms) **DT** (will occur each time the candidate addresses 'difficult thoughts' either by using the phrase itself or one of its synonyms)
You might like to take a single aspect of the critical quotation – in this case 'plain language' – and discuss its meaning and relevance with the aid of quotations and references …	It's very easy to demonstrate <u>the clear surface of Bishop's poetry</u>, the ordinary conversational language she uses. We just need a few short quotations. *I caught a tremendous fish* *and held him beside the boat* *half out of water, with my hook* *fast in a corner of his mouth.* 'The Fish' *In Worcester, Massachusetts,* *I went with Aunt Consuelo* *to keep her dentist's appointment* 'In the Waiting Room'	The corrector has underlined a topic that has been introduced and the corrector expects this topic to be focused on and developed over a paragraph before the introduction of any additional topics **PL**

WEBSITE GUIDE ADVISES	CANDIDATE'S SCRIPT	CORRECTOR'S CODES EXPLAINED
… before moving to the other aspect of the quotation – 'difficult thoughts' – and discussing, with the aid of quotations and references, examples of what these might be …	In the first extract – the opening of 'The Fish' – all the words are among the most ordinary in the English language and very few of them are longer than a single syllable. There's nothing at all complicated here, including the rhythm, which moves smoothly along in a matter-of-fact way. But the word that really stands out is 'tremendous'. It's a word that children use – 'tremendous' – when they want to express something really important to them. It's not in the least a conventional 'poetic' word. It's not even very precise. But it's perfect for capturing the simple excitement of the catch. In the same way, nothing could be plainer than the everyday language of the opening of 'In the Waiting Room,' which just reports, in the deadest manner possible, one of the most boring experiences of all – waiting for someone. There's no hint at all of the fireworks to come, or that this dull waiting room is actually 'the inside of a volcano'.	**PL** **PL** **PL**
	This visit to the dentist's waiting room is typical of the kind of <u>ordinary situations</u> that Bishop describes so plainly, but so effectively. As well as this and catching a fish, there's also a birthday in 'The Bight', travel abroad in 'Questions of Travel', a South American carnival in 'Armadillo', a child's unhappy drawing in 'Sestina', a top-up at a petrol station in 'Filling Station' and a child's first fairly bewildered experience of death in 'First Death in Nova Scotia'. These are private, everyday experiences.	The corrector has underlined a topic **PL**
… for instance, the dawning of self-awareness in a girl …	All the same, even though the language is always conversational and the situations are always recognisable, there's also a great deal going on in these poems, <u>a great deal that is suggested by the words</u>. I don't just mean the girl's change in 'In the Waiting Room' from boredom to surprise when she sees the photographs of dead men, half-naked women,	**PL** The corrector has underlined a topic

WEBSITE GUIDE ADVISES	CANDIDATE'S SCRIPT	CORRECTOR'S CODES EXPLAINED
… and in a woman …	'horrifying' breasts and 'light bulb' heads in a copy of the *National Geographic*, and then through embarrassment to dizziness when it dawns on her that she's 'one of *them*' too, a human, a woman, like her 'foolish aunt'. There's *obviously* a great deal going on in *this* poem, if not on the surface, then inside the girl, inside her head, inside the waiting room – 'inside' is a plain but vital word, with a great many meanings, in this poem. As is stressed, 'nothing stranger could ever happen' than this 'difficult' moment of self-awareness, which is the most commonplace experience of all, of course, since it happens to all of us, and shapes all our lives forever afterwards. At least in this poem, you *know* what happens to the narrator. But what happens to the narrator in 'Filling Station'? She opens on a note of disgust when she pulls into the station – 'Oh, but it is dirty!' – and she holds on to that revulsion for a while – she uses the rather childish word 'dirty' three more times, to describe an overalls, a dog and the whole scene – but by the end of the poem she is self-conscious and making embarrassed jokes to laugh off her discomfort – the cans of oil 'softly say: ESSO—SO—SO—SO.' What has happened? We're not told, but we can *feel* the shifts through what the words suggest. Firstly, there are all those questions – 'Why the taboret?/Why, oh why, the doily?' Once you start asking questions about people, you're expressing an interest; and once you express an interest, you become involved with them, they're not just objects any more. Then there are all the domestic details – the 'comic books', the 'begonia', the 'doily' – that reveal to us that this is a family, not just a man in a 'monkey suit' and his 'greasy sons'. The narrator never admits her prejudices, or her mistakes, but by the end of the piece, we can all see them clearly, and the wonderful thing is that it's the plain language and the ordinary details – a dog, comics, a napkin – that achieve this.	**PL** **DT** **PL** **DT** **PL**

WEBSITE GUIDE ADVISES	CANDIDATE'S SCRIPT	CORRECTOR'S CODES EXPLAINED
… the process of change …	This <u>change</u>, from one condition to another, inside a person, is very common in Bishop's poetry. And surely change is the most 'difficult thought' of all, to hold and to describe? The most obvious examples – 'In the Waiting Room' and 'Filling Station' – have already been mentioned, but probably the most dramatic, and the most revealing, of those on the course is 'The Fish', where the narrator goes from a sense of 'tremendous' achievement in catching the fish to letting the same fish go in the last line. What happens in between? Firstly, through looking at the fish, and being vaguely reminded of home – 'his brown skin hung in strips/like ancient wallpaper' – and then through imagining the inside of the fish – 'the frightening gills' and 'his shiny entrails' – and again being reminded of home – 'tinfoil' is what the fish's eyes remind her of – she begins to identify more and more with this creature, until, as a friend once remarked in class, 'the fish becomes a human being like herself'. The 'victory' of the fisherwoman becomes the 'victory' of the fish, and she accepts its right to a separate existence. Bishop once described her poetry as 'not a thought, but a mind thinking', and where she recreates the process of a mind thinking, of a person responding to others, to another living thing, or to specific experiences, her work is at its most positive. Where there	The corrector has underlined a topic **DT** **DT** **DT**
… and the tragedy of paralysis …	is none of that movement in a poem, where everything is static, the people are always unhappy, always weighed down by a sense of being trapped. This is true of the little girl in the tear-filled world of 'Sestina', where everybody cries, including the little figures she draws. It's true of 'The Bight', where Bishop marks her birthday, alone, in Key West, Florida, reflecting on life and death, on how everything is 'awful but cheerful'. And it's true of 'The Prodigal', who lives in 'brown enormous odor', until his final decision 'to go home', to leave behind the	

Poetry

212

WEBSITE GUIDE ADVISES	CANDIDATE'S SCRIPT	CORRECTOR'S CODES EXPLAINED
	stupor of the drink. A person who is not fully alive, Bishop seems to suggest. Change may be a 'difficult thought' to capture in plain language, but paralysis is a difficult, or troubling, state to contemplate.	**DT/PL** **DT**
… and the tension of opposites …	I think this is why <u>opposites</u>, the last of the 'difficult thoughts' I want to consider, are so important to Bishop and her poetry. The tension between them keeps us alive, keeps us on the move. When we are abroad, we think of home. When we are home, we think of being abroad. And, as 'Questions of Travel' puts it, 'it would have been a pity' to miss out on the experience of being lured from one to the other. Most of Bishop's poems explore opposites, but the one I enjoy best in this respect is 'First Death in Nova Scotia'. The whole poem is a fascinating series of contrasts – between the colours red, white and black; between movement and stillness, between speech and silence, between childish expressions and adult expressions – all coming, of course, from the central complex contrast between life and death. The whole effect, contained in the poem's simple language, is of a moment frozen in time, of a life frozen in that moment – Arthur is 'laid out'; the loon is 'stuffed' and unmoving; the figures in the chromographs are eternally static; the lake is frozen, so the water doesn't even ripple; Arthur is like a 'doll' lying there, and finally, 'clutching his tiny lily', incapable of doing anything else with it, he can't go anywhere, not even when the royal couples seem to invite him. By contrast, there are only two movements in the poem, although both are highly significant. The child speaker is lifted up and places a lily in the dead boy's hand. He doesn't accept it. She places it. She is alive, mobile, active. He is dead. The only other movement suggests a violent burst of energy that leads to death, and it's very striking: Arthur's father once 'fired	The corrector has underlined a topic **DT** **DT** **PL** **DT**

WEBSITE GUIDE ADVISES	CANDIDATE'S SCRIPT	CORRECTOR'S CODES EXPLAINED
Finally, bring all the parts of the critical quotation together again and give your overall assessment.	a bullet' into the now stuffed loon. It is fascinating also to examine the tension between silence and speech in the poem. The dignified figures in the chromographs never open their mouths and the loon 'hadn't said a word' since Arthur's father shot it. Did it speak before that? When words are finally spoken, they break into the silence like intruders, almost violently: '"Come," said my mother,/"Come and say good-bye'. But the girl doesn't 'say' anything. Why would she? The dead can't hear or respond. Silence dominates, overwhelms this poem. How can silence dominate a poem of words, particularly if that poem is spoken aloud? It's a 'difficult thought', one of many prompted, rather than described, by Bishop's uncomplicated, unadorned language, that is so like the sea she loved so much – a contrast between clear surface and concealed depths. So yes, in her own phrase, Bishop's poetry succeeds in expressing 'difficult thoughts in plain language'.	DT PL PL/DT DT/PL

CORRECTOR'S USE OF MARKING SCHEME

P – Clarity of Purpose – consistently focused on the terms of the question, relevant points, terms explained and explored, well-illustrated opinions – excellent

C – Coherence of Delivery – well organised, focused introduction, separate treatment of distinct points, good paragraphing, fluid links between paragraphs, smooth development of argument, clear conclusion – excellent

L – Efficiency of Language Use – accurate expression, appropriate vocabulary, effective discursive register, impresive vocabulary and terminology – excellent

M – Mechanics – devoid of spelling or gammatical errors – excellent

Prescribed Poets

Elizabeth Bishop

Elizabeth Bishop was born on 8 February 1911, in Worcester, Massachusetts, USA. She was an only child. Her father died in October 1911 and her mother was admitted to a psychiatric institution in 1916. Bishop was moved between her maternal grandparents in Nova Scotia and her paternal grandparents in Worcester. Many of her poems dramatise important experiences from these times. In 1930, she entered Vassar College in New York, where her problems with alcohol began. After a trip

to Europe – she would always love travel and particularly to exotic places – she settled in Key West, Florida, in 1939. 1946 saw the publication of her first book of poems, *North & South*, but also the beginning of an unhappy period living in New York. In 1951, she made her first visit to Brazil, where she met again with a young Brazilian woman named Lota Soares. They took the decision to live together as a couple. She won the Pulitzer Prize in 1956 and the National Book Award in 1959, but her personal life deteriorated as her literary success grew. She was sometimes criticised in Brazil as a patronising foreigner. She moved back to New York in 1967. Lota Soares joined her, but died from an overdose of sleeping pills that she took on her first night there with Bishop. For the remainder of her life, Bishop travelled, taught and wrote. She died on 6 October 1979.

Prescribed Poems

'Students at Higher Level will be required to study a representative selection from the work of eight poets: a representative selection would seek to reflect the range of a poet's themes and interests and exhibit his/her characteristic style and viewpoint. Normally the study of at least six poems by each poet would be expected.' (DES English Syllabus, 6.3)

Themes and Interests

explores what she herself called **A SENSE OF HOME**, explaining 'I've never felt particularly homeless, but, then, I've never felt particularly at home. I guess that's a pretty good description of a poet's sense of home. He carries it within him.'

explores the complexities of **ESTRANGEMENT** and **SUFFERING**

The Poetry of Elizabeth Bishop

explores what a critic has described as the 'human experiences of **GRIEF** and **LONGING**'

dramatises **THE PROCESS OF CHANGE** in living things, including people, and is therefore more concerned with questions than with answers

Style and Viewpoint

The Poetry of Elizabeth Bishop

uses what she described as a 'plain' style, which means that its **LANGUAGE** is clear on the surface, but contains subtle depths, like the sea she so much loved

dramatises the process of change and therefore uses incident as significant metaphor and draws its **IMAGERY** from a mastery of precise descriptive detail

captures the character of people through voice and the character of places through other intricate **SOUND** patterns

holds the often unsettling complexities of life within strict poetic **FORMS**, some popular, such as the sonnet, some less frequently used, such as the villanelle and the sestina

Poetry

217

READ

Poetry

The Fish

I caught a tremendous fish
and held him beside the boat
half out of water, with my hook
fast in a corner of his mouth.
He didn't fight.   5
He hadn't fought at all.
He hung a grunting weight,
battered and venerable
and homely. Here and there
his brown skin hung in strips   10
like ancient wallpaper,
and its pattern of darker brown
was like wallpaper:
shapes like full-blown roses
stained and lost through age.   15
He was speckled and barnacles,
fine rosettes of lime,
and infested
with tiny white sea-lice,
and underneath two or three   20
rags of green weed hung down.
While his gills were breathing in
the terrible oxygen
—the frightening gills,
fresh and crisp with blood,   25
that can cut so badly—
I thought of the coarse white flesh
packed in like feathers,
the big bones and the little bones,
the dramatic reds and blacks   30
of his shiny entrails,
and the pink swim-bladder
like a big peony.
I looked into his eyes
which were far larger than mine   35
but shallower, and yellowed,
the irises backed and packed
with tarnished tinfoil
seen through the lenses
of old scratched isinglass.   40
They shifted a little, but not
to return my stare.

—It was more like the tipping
of an object toward the light.
I admired his sullen face,   45
the mechanism of his jaw,
and then I saw
that from his lower lip
—if you could call it a lip—
grim, wet, and weaponlike,   50
hung five old pieces of fish-line,
or four and a wire leader
with the swivel still attached,
with all their five big hooks
grown firmly in his mouth.   55
A green line, frayed at the end
where he broke it, two heavier lines,
and a fine black thread
still crimped from the strain and snap
when it broke and he got away.   60
Like medals with their ribbons
frayed and wavering,
a five-haired beard of wisdom
trailing from his aching jaw.
I stared and stared   65
and victory filled up
the little rented boat,
from the pool of bilge
where oil had spread a rainbow
around the rusted engine   70
to the bailer rusted orange,
the sun-cracked thwarts,
the oarlocks on their strings,
the gunnels—until everything
was rainbow, rainbow, rainbow!   75
And I let the fish go.

Glossary

[9] **homely:** North American English, plain, unattractive

[33] **peony:** a shrub with splendid flowers

[40] **isinglass:** transparent gelatine made from fish, used as glue

[52] **leader:** length of heavy fishing line attached to the main line

[68] **bilge:** curved bottom of boat or ship

[72] **thwarts:** crosspiece seats for a rower in a boat

[73] **oarlocks:** parts holding the oars in place

[74] **gunnels:** upper edges of a boat's sides

ANALYSE

This is one of two poems on your course that recreate Bishop's experiences after she had moved to Key West in Florida in 1939.

The narrator, presumably Bishop herself, since she was very keen on fishing, describes catching 'a tremendous fish'. The catch is usually the completion of the experience when fishing; here it is only the beginning. Bishop contemplates her catch, until it is no longer a mere catch, but a breathing, struggling, separate being, whose life is, literally, in her hands. She releases it, back into the water.

The fish is first perceived as masculine and natural (I 'held him', 'half out of water') and then associated through simile with the domestic and the feminine (his skin is 'like ancient wallpaper', 'roses', 'tinfoil'). Consequently, the creature is at once hard and ugly ('grunting … battered … sullen … coarse') and soft and beautiful ('rainbow … roses … peony').

So what is this creature, this catch, this fish? As usual with Bishop, answers are not important, and certainties are not important. Like so many of Bishop's works, the poem dramatises the process of discovery, where the questions, the suggestions, are far more important than the presumptions. You cannot start a process with an assertion; you start a process with wonder, with a question. If there is any conclusion at all here it is that you can never fully comprehend the essence of another being. This is why there are so many comparisons in the poem: curiously, the fish brings wallpaper to mind along with tinfoil and gel and battles. In reality, such comparisons are not at all accurate. And so, in the poem, they are all somehow incomplete, somehow inexact: the tinfoil is 'tarnished', which means dirty, not bright; the wallpaper is 'stained', so not clean or clear; the isinglass is scratched, and as a result not clear either.

Poetry

So what *is* this fish? Is it a Christ-like figure, possibly suggested by the five wounds it bears, by its association with fishermen, by the possible biblical reference to oil on troubled waters? Is it a symbol of the brute strength of nature? Of death? Of life? Of the spiritual, the other world? Of the indifference of nature to man, since the fish does not 'return my stare' and lacks any curiosity about this odd creature who has captured it? All these are suggested by the imagery of the poem. All these come to the mind of the person contemplating that fish. But they are not answers. They are thoughts, possibilities, images. What is the fish? Study the final line: 'And I let the fish go.' Not 'him' any more, although at the beginning she lifted 'him' from the water, but simply 'the fish'.

The poem dramatises a process; in this case, the process of seeing – of really seeing, not just looking at – of understanding, of recognition, of acceptance, of celebration. It opens with a simple statement, a straightforward description of an event: 'I caught a tremendous fish.' But the event is not enough. Maybe it should be. Isn't that why people fish? But it isn't. In fact, it's somewhat disappointing, a bit of a letdown, since the fish 'didn't fight./He hadn't fought at all.' Perhaps dissatisfied because of that, she continues gazing at its exterior, at its 'brown skin', which is difficult to describe, 'like ancient wallpaper'. It's when she gets to the gills 'breathing in/the terrible oxygen' that she imagines beneath the surface. Let's concentrate on that tiny preposition 'in'. Inside. The journey has become an internal one, a trip to the 'entrails', perhaps to the essence, of the fish. Well, take the obvious route and try the eyes first: 'I looked into his eyes'. But the eyes don't admit anything: they only 'shifted a little, but not/to return my stare'. It's when she finally sees the hooks in the fish's mouth that she can imagine its life, its struggles, its previous escapes. And what she sees then, imagining the 'victory' of the fish, is not her catch any more, but the oil on the bilge water in the boat, coloured like a rainbow, reflecting the colours of life, of nature, which both the fish (ugly or beautiful, masculine or feminine, or all together) and herself are parts of. And so: 'I let the fish go.'

(i) Elizabeth Bishop has said of her own work, 'I like to present complicated or mysterious ideas in the simplest way possible.' In this poem, 'the simplest way possible' is obvious – a detailed description of a fish – but what, in your opinion, is the 'complicated or mysterious idea'?

(ii) As accurately as you can, trace the feelings and thoughts of the speaker, from the triumphant opening 'I caught a tremendous fish' to the downbeat ending 'And I let the fish go', noting where the shifts occur.

MAKE

Poetry

READ

The Bight
[On my birthday]

At low tide like this how sheer the water is.
White, crumbling ribs of marl protrude and glare
and the boats are dry, the pilings dry as matches.
Absorbing, rather than being absorbed,
the water in the bight doesn't wet anything,   5
the color of the gas flame turned as low as possible.
One can smell it turning to gas; if one were Baudelaire
one could probably hear it turning to marimba music.
The little ocher dredge at work off the end of the dock
already plays the dry perfectly off-beat claves.   10
The birds are outsize. Pelicans crash
into this peculiar gas unnecessarily hard,
it seems to me, like pickaxes,
rarely coming up with anything to show for it,
and going off with humorous elbowings.   15
Black-and-white man-of-war birds soar
on impalpable drafts
and open their tails like scissors on the curves
or tense them like wishbones, till they tremble.
The frowsy sponge boats keep coming in   20
with the obliging air of retrievers,
bristling with jackstraw gaffs and hooks
and decorated with bobbles of sponges.
There is a fence of chicken wire along the dock
where, glinting like little plowshares,   25
the blue-gray shark tails are hung up to dry
for the Chinese-restaurant trade.
Some of the little white boats are still piled up
against each other, or lie on their sides, stove in,
and not yet salvaged, if they ever will be, from the last bad storm,   30
like torn-open, unanswered letters.
The bight is littered with old correspondences.
Click. Click. Goes the dredge,
and brings up a dripping jawful of marl.
All the untidy activity continues,   35
awful but cheerful.

Poetry

Glossary

[title and 5] **bight:** curve or recess in coastline

[2 and 34] **marl:** lime-rich mud

[7] **Baudelaire:** French poet (1821–1867)

[8] **marimba:** African xylophone

[10] **claves:** cylindrical sticks used as percussion instruments

[16] **man-of-war birds:** predatory tropical birds, frigate birds

[20] **frowsy:** scruffy, dingy

[20 and 23] **sponge:** aquatic invertebrate animal

ANALYSE

On her birthday, Bishop sees only 'crumbling' earth, 'dry' boats and 'unanswered letters' in the bay that she contemplates. All this activity she sums up as 'awful but cheerful'. Failure, connections lost, relationships lapsed – the sense of being washed up is what the low tide in the bay brings to her.

From the subtitle onwards – 'On my birthday' – the reader is aware of a mind reflecting on and interpreting the sights that are described. The poem is dated 8 February 1948, when Bishop was thirty-seven years old. It recreates a scene from her time in Key West in Florida and is a perfect example of her understated, indirect exploration of a theme, which in this case might be expressed as the 'bight' of middle age, life at low tide. Nothing is explicitly stated about 'life' or 'living'. The language captures the scene itself. And yet, because we are always conscious of the human spectator, we get the impression of a mood throughout. That mood, and everything else about the poem, can be pinpointed with reference to the final line – 'awful but cheerful' – which Bishop chose as an epitaph on her grave stone.

Re-read the opening line – 'At low tide like this how sheer the water is.' – and you can feel the presence of a human mind assessing the scene; 'like this' and 'how sheer' both indicate an individual perspective. The human perspective is made explicit in line 7: 'One can smell it turning to gas'. Apart from the general pronoun 'one', the 'gas' is an image in someone's head, not an objective part of the scene. And then the perspective is individualised in line 13 – 'it seems to me' – but that light little touch is enough; there is no further direct reference to the human. Read the rest of it to experience how subtle this is, how, without hammering home the message, Bishop keeps you aware of a human responding – 'with humorous elbowings' to describe the jostling of the pelicans, 'open their tails like scissors' or 'tense them like wishbones' to describe the flight of the man-of-war birds, 'the obliging air of retrievers' to describe the movement of the froth on the tide, a froth formation which puts the viewer in mind of 'boats', 'decorated with bobbles of sponge', 'like little plowshares' to describe the shark tails, 'like torn-open, unanswered letters' to describe the fishing boats, at which point we are very, very close to the human mind offering us these perspectives, because only humans write letters, only humans receive and don't answer them – all making inevitable the interpretation of the final line – 'awful but cheerful' – as applying as much to the life of the human as to the 'untidy activity' in the bay.

It's worth going back over it again and again, because the more you read 'The Bight', the more you become aware of an individual behind the surface of the poem repeatedly making comparisons in their mind. From the opening image of the gas flame – the low tide reminds the viewer of a flame turned down to its lowest setting, the minimum of existence, life and energy – there are at least eight further similes and metaphors; and the more you become conscious of these, the more the human voice comes into the foreground and the scene recedes into the background, until you start reading the poem again, when the scene comes into the foreground once more. It's a wonderful achievement to manage this so delicately, and 'The Bight' is a perfect example of Bishop's understated art.

The final thing to notice is how, in lines 7–8, that human mind briefly wanders off on a little fantasy – imagining if it were the French poet Baudelaire, it might hear jazz music in the lowering of the gas – before returning to the scene in front of it with the most ordinary of all the details in the poem – 'The little ocher dredge at work off the end of the dock'. These lines dramatise the entire movement of the poem, between the mind and the scene, the scene and the mind, back and forth, like waves falling in a bay.

MAKE

(i) A former student of Elizabeth Bishop's said of her teaching of poetry, 'To her, the images and the music of the lines were primary.' This poem contains many images of sounds – claves, crash, click, and so on – as well as its own intricate sound patterns. Pick out some examples and comment on how they express the poem's theme, 'awful but cheerful'.

(ii) The poem is very rich in similes – 'like pickaxes' – and metaphors – 'old correspondences' – and colour. Pick out the most impressive of each of these three forms of imagery, in your opinion, and comment on why you think Bishop selected them.

READ

Poetry

At the Fishhouses

Although it is a cold evening,
down by one of the fishhouses
an old man sits netting,
his net, in the gloaming almost invisible,
a dark purple-brown,   5
and his shuttle worn and polished.
The air smells so strong of codfish
it makes one's nose run and one's eyes water.
The five fishhouses have steeply peaked roofs
and narrow, cleated gangplanks slant up   10
to storerooms in the gables
for the wheelbarrows to be pushed up and down on.
All is silver: the heavy surface of the sea,
swelling slowly as if considering spilling over,
is opaque, but the silver of the benches,   15
the lobster pots, and masts, scattered
among the wild jagged rocks,
is of an apparent translucence
like the small old buildings with an emerald moss
growing on their shoreward walls.   20
The big fish tubs are completely lined
with layers of beautiful herring scales
and the wheelbarrows are similarly plastered
with creamy iridescent coats of mail,
with small iridescent flies crawling on them.   25
Up on the little slope behind the houses,
set in the sparse bright sprinkle of grass,
is an ancient wooden capstan,
cracked, with two long bleached handles
and some melancholy stains, like dried blood,   30
where the ironwork has rusted.
The old man accepts a Lucky Strike.
He was a friend of my grandfather.
We talk of the decline in the population
and of codfish and herring   35
while he waits for a herring boat to come in.
There are sequins on his vest and on his thumb.
He has scraped the scales, the principal beauty,
from unnumbered fish with that black old knife,
the blade of which is almost worn away.   40

Down at the water's edge, at the place
where they haul up the boats, up the long ramp
descending into the water, thin silver
tree trunks are laid horizontally
across the gray stones, down and down   45
at intervals of four or five feet.

Cold dark deep and absolutely clear,
element bearable to no mortal,
to fish and to seals . . . One seal particularly
I have seen here evening after evening.   50
He was curious about me. He was interested in music;
like me a believer in total immersion,
so I used to sing him Baptist hymns.
I also sang "A Mighty Fortress Is Our God."
He stood up in the water and regarded me   55
steadily, moving his head a little.
Then he would disappear, then suddenly emerge
almost in the same spot, with a sort of shrug
as if it were against his better judgment.
Cold dark deep and absolutely clear,   60
the clear gray icy water . . . Back, behind us,
the dignified tall firs begin.
Bluish, associating with their shadows,
a million Christmas trees stand
waiting for Christmas. The water seems suspended   65
above the rounded gray and blue-gray stones.
I have seen it over and over, the same sea, the same,
slightly, indifferently swinging above the stones,
icily free above the stones,
above the stones and then the world.   70
If you should dip your hand in,
your wrist would ache immediately,
your bones would begin to ache and your hand would burn
as if the water were a transmutation of fire
that feeds on stones and burns with a dark gray flame.   75
If you tasted it, it would first taste bitter,
then briny, then surely burn your tongue.
It is like what we imagine knowledge to be:
dark, salt, clear, moving, utterly free,
drawn from the cold hard mouth   80
of the world, derived from the rocky breasts
forever, flowing and drawn, and since
our knowledge is historical, flowing, and flown.

Glossary

[4] **gloaming:** twilight, dusk

[6] **shuttle:** a bobbin used in weaving

[24 and 25] **iridescent:** rainbow-like play of colours in light

[28] **capstan:** revolving cylinder for winding rope

[32] **Lucky Strike:** brand of cigarette

[37] **sequins:** small shiny discs

[52] **total immersion:** baptism by immersing body in water

[74] **transmutation:** changing form

[77] **briny:** salty

ANALYSE

On the surface, Bishop's art seems merely descriptive, accurate and beautiful in its detail. The opening of 'At the Fishhouses' seems to capture a static scene as a painter would, a moment frozen in time … the evening light, the fishhouses by the sea, the old man mending nets. But if you look closely at the language, you'll notice immediately that this is a poem about the process of change, not about a particular moment. The time is twilight, the transition between day and night, neither one nor the other, but a passage between the two. All the visible details are changed, mostly decayed, from what they once were: the old man's 'shuttle' is worn from age and use; the 'capstan' is 'cracked'; the ironwork is 'rusted'. The old man is a figure from the past as well as the present – 'He was a friend of my grandfather.' – he, too, was once young. When they talk, the poet and the old man speak of 'decline'. Further, there are images of damage and death everywhere: 'flies' and 'dried blood' and 'unnumbered fish'. Finally, whereas a painting is merely visual, here the sensory detail draws on more transitory sensations: the 'smells' of codfish, the taste of cigarettes, the feel of fish scales.

But even the poem itself moves on. Its gaze changes – in line 41, after the break between sections – shifting from the fishhouses and the old man down to 'the water's edge'. Nothing stays the same. Life is an unending process. This is the first great perception of the poem, the first aspect of its theme. Although the scene on land contains elements of this unending change, its accurate, 'absolutely clear', *symbol* is the sea itself, the form of which is always the same in one sense, and always changing in another: 'forever, flowing' as the paradox of the penultimate line puts it.

The awareness that nothing lasts, that everything is in a state of flux, that even the 'dignified tall firs' in the background are simply 'waiting for Christmas', or waiting for death, in other words … this awareness is chilling, frightening, for any human being to contemplate. This is why the sea, the symbol of this knowledge, is twice described as 'cold dark deep and absolutely clear'. This is why it is an 'element bearable to no mortal'. Only fish and seals can bear 'total immersion' in such truth; humans, the poem seems to suggest, need to invent something more comfortable to keep themselves warm, suggested by the faith in 'Baptist hymns'. Leaving the comfort of faith behind brings pain – 'if you should dip your hand in,/your wrist would ache immediately' – destruction – 'your hand would burn' – bitterness, and isolation.

Poetry

But ultimately, the sea is only a poetic symbol of knowledge – 'it is like what we imagine knowledge to be'. This is two removes away from actual knowledge – '*like* what we *imagine*'. It is not knowledge itself, which is 'historical, flowing, and flown' – gained from and containing our past, always changing, always eluding us. It is an image of knowledge, a metaphor. That is all poetry, and perhaps life, can offer.

We cannot know anything or fix anything in a permanent form; like the sea, our individual lives are 'dark, salt, clear, moving, utterly free'. We can, however, create magic, create beauty – captured in the rainbow image of 'creamy iridescent coats of mail' – through our work, through the process of living, just as the old man mending his nets at the opening of the poem does: 'He has scraped the scales, the principal beauty,/from unnumbered fish with that black old knife'.

MAKE

(i) Elizabeth Bishop has said of her own work, 'I like to present complicated or mysterious ideas in the simplest way possible.' In this poem, 'the simplest way possible' is obvious – a detailed depiction of a scene at a fishing harbour – but what, in your opinion, is the 'complicated or mysterious idea'?

(ii) The imagery of change dominates the poem – time, light, history, decline, water, nature, tools. Identify some examples and comment on how the sea – the ultimate symbol of change – affects these, such as rusting the 'ironwork'.

READ

The Prodigal

The brown enormous odor he lived by
was too close, with its breathing and thick hair,
for him to judge. The floor was rotten; the sty
was plastered halfway up with glass-smooth dung.
Light-lashed, self-righteous, above moving snouts,   5
the pigs' eyes followed him, a cheerful stare—
even to the sow that always ate her young—
till, sickening, he leaned to scratch her head.
But sometimes mornings after drinking bouts
(he hid the pints behind a two-by-four),   10
the sunrise glazed the barnyard mud with red;
the burning puddles seemed to reassure.
And then he thought he almost might endure
his exile yet another year or more.

But evenings the first star came to warn.   15
The farmer whom he worked for came at dark
to shut the cows and horses in the barn
beneath their overhanging clouds of hay,
with pitchforks, faint forked lightnings, catching light,
safe and companionable as in the Ark.   20
The pigs stuck out their little feet and snored.
The lantern—like the sun, going away—
laid on the mud a pacing aureole.
Carrying a bucket along a slimy board,
he felt the bats' uncertain staggering flight,   25
his shuddering insights, beyond his control,
touching him. But it took him a long time
finally to make his mind up to go home.

Glossary

[title] **Prodigal:** in the Christian Bible the Prodigal Son wasted his inheritance before finally returning home in repentance

[10] **two-by-four:** length of wood, two inches thick and four inches wide

[20] **the Ark:** in the Christian Bible, the boat built by Noah to save his family from the Flood that covered the earth

[23] **aureole:** circle of light surrounding something

In 'The Prodigal', a man lives and works amidst the 'brown enormous odor' of a pig-sty, in exile, tugged towards home as a bat is guided by its own radar, but reluctant to leave, drinking heavily to avoid the conflict inside him, so that 'it took him a long time/finally to make his mind up to go home'.

The poem is based on the biblical parable of The Prodigal Son, as told in St Luke's gospel, which describes a son who wastes his inheritance with loose living in a foreign country, ends up feeding pigs to stay alive, but eventually returns home to be forgiven by his father. Bishop concentrates on the lowest point of the man's life, his existence among the pigs, and the poem is generally taken as an exploration of her own problems with alcoholism and her experience of being an outsider herself. While it's helpful to know the last point, it's not essential; the poem concerns itself with the figure of the outsider.

In form, the poem is a double sonnet – two stanzas of fourteen lines each, with an irregular pattern of rhyming in each.

The imagery of the first four lines captures the disgusting squalor outside – 'brown enormous odor … rotten … plastered … with … dung' – the way it enters the prodigal's being, through nose ('enormous odor'), ear ('breathing'), eye ('brown') and skin (the touch of 'thick hair'), and the overwhelming effect it has on him, making him incapable of clear thought ('too close … for him to judge'), as if the mess was inside as well as out.

The pigs are largely indifferent to him – 'self-righteous', which is a strange way of describing an animal, means having an exaggerated awareness of one's own rights and virtues, and suggests that the pigs know that this is their home, not his – and it is the prodigal who rather pathetically reaches out for the comfort of contact ('he leaned to scratch her head'). His relationship is with another type of outcast, another 'prodigal' who wasted her inheritance, in this case, the sow who ate her own young ones.

The next section of the poem doesn't tell us that the prodigal drank to escape his loneliness; it tells us that drink helped the prodigal cope. There's a great difference between these two. In the morning after a drinking bout, the world is brighter and more colourful – 'the sunrise glazed the barnyard mud with red', a beautiful image of dawn, and 'the burning puddles seemed to reassure', and equally beautiful image of warmth. It is also a more comfortable and more forgiving place. This is surprising, because you expect a hangover after a drinking bout. The key word is 'seemed', however, which is reinforced by the triple hesitation of 'he thought he almost might' in the next line. The booze offers no more than the illusion of comfort and escape. It's an illusion that's obviously very welcome, because a fantasy is a form of escape, but the prodigal has to return home, his 'exile' is something he 'might endure … another year', but which he probably won't.

The second stanza opens with the poem's second 'But' – the first was at the beginning of line 9, introducing the consolations of drink – and also replaces 'mornings' with 'evenings'. I suppose the latter are lonelier times for solitary humans; they're certainly darker, lit only by that single 'star', which suggests so many things – home, the star guiding the wise men to Bethlehem for Christ's birth, the North Star, orientation, a compass. As the animals settle for the night, only the prodigal is alone. No species is solitary – 'cows and horses … pigs' and all are 'companionable'. But night awakens another creature – the bat – just as it awakens in the prodigal an instinctive ('beyond his control') but disturbing ('shuddering insights') homing urge that ends up 'touching him', which obviously means affecting him, but which also reminds us of the beginning of the poem, where 'thick hair' brushes against him and he 'leaned to scratch' the head of the sow.

The poem's third 'But' – 'But it took him a long time' – introduces the final, dramatic shift, from the illusion of consolation, to the pull of home, to the decision 'to go home'. He has passed through suffering, escape, acceptance, before finding outrage and resolve; and the poem ends with an echo of the 'brown' that began it on the warm relief of the sound 'home'. In this context, 'home' is not merely family, but human society.

MAKE

(i) 'In 'The Prodigal', exile and homecoming are explored in terms of removal from and return to the human community.' To what extent would you agree with this assessment of the poem? Give reasons for your answer.

(ii) Bishop is often praised for the power of her sensory detail. Pick out examples here, identifying which of the five senses are used in the imagery, and since such detail in poetry is not there merely as ornament, comment on why the poem's imagery is so rich in this way.

Poetry

Questions of Travel

There are too many waterfalls here; the crowded streams
hurry too rapidly down to the sea,
and the pressure of so many clouds on the mountaintops
makes them spill over the sides in soft slow-motion,
turning to waterfalls under our very eyes.   5
—For if those streaks, those mile-long, shiny, tearstains,
aren't waterfalls yet,
in a quick age or so, as ages go here,
they probably will be.
But if the streams and clouds keep travelling, travelling,   10
the mountains look like the hulls of capsized ships,
slime-hung and barnacled.

Think of the long trip home.
Should we have stayed at home and thought of here?
Where should we be today?   15
Is it right to be watching strangers in a play
in this strangest of theatres?
What childishness is it that while there's a breath of life
in our bodies, we are determined to rush
to see the sun the other way around?   20
The tiniest green hummingbird in the world?
To stare at some inexplicable old stonework,
inexplicable and impenetrable,
at any view,
instantly seen and always, always delightful?   25
Oh, must we dream our dreams
and have them, too?
And have we room
for one more folded sunset, still quite warm?

But surely it would have been a pity   30
not to have seen the trees along this road,
really exaggerated in their beauty,
not to have seen them gesturing
like noble pantomimists, robed in pink.
—Not to have had to stop for gas and heard   35
the sad, two-noted, wooden tune
of disparate wooden clogs
carelessly clacking over
a grease-stained filling-station floor.
(In another country the clogs would all be tested.   40
Each pair there would have identical pitch.)
—A pity not to have heard

the other, less primitive music of the fat brown bird
who sings above the broken gasoline pump
in a bamboo church of Jesuit baroque: 45
three towers, five silver crosses.
—Yes, a pity not to have pondered,
blurr'dly and inconclusively,
on what connection can exist for centuries
between the crudest wooden footwear   50
and, careful and finicky,
the whittled fantasies of wooden footwear
and, careful and finicky,
the whittled fantasies of wooden cages.
—Never to have studied history in   55
the weak calligraphy of songbirds' cages.
—And never to have had to listen to rain
so much like politicians' speeches:
two hours of unrelenting oratory
and then a sudden golden silence   60
in which the traveller takes a notebook, writes:

"Is it lack of imagination that makes us come
to imagined places, not just stay at home?
Or could Pascal have been not entirely right
about just sitting quietly in one's room?   65

Continent, city, country, society:
the choice is never wide and never free.
And here, or there … No. Should we have stayed at home,
wherever that may be?"

Glossary

[1] **here:** Brazil

[34] **pantomimists:** actors using mime

[45] **Jesuit baroque:** ornamental building style of the Roman Catholic missionary order the Jesuits, long active in South America

[64] **Pascal:** Blaise Pascal (1623–1662), the French mathematician and philosopher who remarked that all human evil derived from man's inability to sit quietly in his room

The poem opens, not with a sightseer's description of waterfalls, but with the strange observation of a questioning mind: 'There are too many waterfalls here'. The crowded clouds 'spill over' the mountains, turning to water in their contact with the colder earth, becoming streams and waterfalls, always changing, always 'travelling, travelling', and as a consequence distorting the mountain tops, which look like 'capsized ships'. Doesn't too much travel always distort the scenery? Look at something with a tourist's eye and what you see is not what those who live there see.

These thoughts, these observations, lead to a series of questions. When we're away, we think of home. So why bother going away? If we're so attached to home, shouldn't we stay there? But, of course, we humans are forever thinking simultaneously about what we have and what we don't have, or, as Bishop puts it, 'must we dream our dreams/and have them, too?' Doesn't this divided attention of ours, with one eye on what we can see and the other on what we can't, actually distort what we're looking at while we're away? We want to package it and take it home, we always have room in our wallets or purses for 'one more folded sunset'. Take a snapshot and get out of here, get another step closer to home, where, of course, we will immediately start dreaming of being away again.

The poem dramatises Bishop having an argument with herself: 'think', she insists; 'should we …?'. she asks; 'surely', she points out. The language is that of debate. There are always two sides to a debate, of course, and we want to hear them both, just as we want to see both sides of the sun, from home and from the other side of the world: 'to see the sun the other way around.'

To be able to see 'the other way around' is surely an advantage, a gift. To be incapable of doing so would be a loss, a pity. Who would want to miss out on the beautiful sights and experiences described in the third section of the poem; although, as always in Bishop's poetry, the descriptions are technically inaccurate. Trees that are 'gesturing/like noble pantomimists'? Whoever heard of such a thing? The 'two-noted, wooden tune' of clogs? The 'fat brown bird' singing away? The baroque (it means ornate, or profusely ornamented in a Renaissance style) Jesuit church, with its towers and crosses? These are the things she saw in Brazil? Of course they are. If you go there, of course, you will see something different, as everyone must. But the real pity would have been 'not to have pondered'. Experience provokes thought. The richer and more varied the experience, then the richer and more varied the thought. Here, the wooden clogs and bamboo church lead to confused and deliberately confusing thoughts – 'blurr'dly [what a very confused word] and inconclusively' – about the uses of wood, to create clogs and to make cages. Never to have entertained this thought would be an incalculable loss. Even the similarities in sound and sense between the two words – clogs/cages – cages also clog – is enlightening. As she also reflects on noise, natural and human, rain and speeches, and on its absence, which is silence, the poem distils its thinking into the questions in the final, italicised sections.

Is it the poverty of our imagination, the first question asks, that makes us travel to see places, because we can't imagine them realistically enough. Or was the seventeenth-century French philosopher Blaise Pascal wrong when he insisted that only evil came from leaving one's own room? But such questions – questions of travel? – have already been answered in the poem, not directly, but by implication: real living is in the interaction between mind and experience, imagination and travel. Return to the clouds that the poem opens with: they exist in the sky, on mountain tops, as waterfalls, as streams, as evaporation, as clouds again. Which is their natural element? Sky? Mountain? River? Land? Sky, mountain, river, land … continent, city, country, society. The choice may never be 'wide', but if water was to stay in one state, it wouldn't be water, would it? If humans were to stay in one 'place', they wouldn't be human.

MAKE

(i) Elizabeth Bishop has said of her own work, 'I like to present complicated or mysterious ideas in the simplest way possible.' In this poem, 'the simplest way possible' is obvious – a detailed description of waterfalls – but what, in your opinion, is the 'complicated or mysterious idea'?

(ii) It has been said that Bishop's work is more concerned with questions than with answers, something that may be evident from the very title of this poem. Count the number of actual questions in the poem, pick the one you consider to be the core question, the central theme, and explain your choice.

The Armadillo
For Robert Lowell

This is the time of year
when almost every night
the frail, illegal fire balloons appear.
Climbing the mountain height,

rising toward a saint   5
still honored in these parts,
the paper chambers flush and fill with light
that comes and goes, like hearts.

Once up against the sky it's hard
to tell them from the stars—   10
planets, that is—the tinted ones:
Venus going down, or Mars,

or the pale green one. With a wind,
they flare and falter, wobble and toss;
but if it's still they steer between   15
the kite sticks of the Southern Cross,

receding, dwindling, solemnly
and steadily forsaking us,
or, in the downdraft from a peak,
suddenly turning dangerous.   20

Last night another big one fell.
It splattered like an egg of fire
against the cliff behind the house.
The flame ran down. We saw the pair

of owls who nest there flying up   25
and up, their whirling black-and-white
stained bright pink underneath, until
they shrieked up out of sight.

The ancient owls' nest must have burned.
Hastily, all alone,   30
a glistening armadillo left the scene,
rose-flecked, head down, tail down,

and then a baby rabbit jumped out,
short-eared, to our surprise.
So soft!–a handful of intangible ash   35
with fixed, ignited eyes.

Too pretty, dreamlike mimicry!
O falling fire and piercing cry
and panic, and a weak mailed fist
clenched ignorant against the sky!   40

Glossary

[3] **illegal fire balloons:** celebratory fire balloons floated, illegally, on feast days in Brazil
[13] **the pale green one:** the planet Uranus
[16] **Southern Cross:** four bright stars in the southern hemisphere in the shape of a cross

Like 'Questions of Travel', 'The Armadillo' is a reflection inspired by Bishop's experiences in Brazil, this time by the Brazilian custom of floating celebratory fire balloons during the St John's Day Carnival (24 June) and other festivals. The event is both beautiful and ugly, a celebration and a cruelty – these tensions are in Bishop's work again – because, as well as providing a magnificent spectacle, these fire balloons sometimes fall to earth, destroying wild life: owls, rabbits, even the armour-plated armadillo.

Simple enough on the surface, the poem offers a fascinating study of how Bishop uses intricate sound patterns and the selection of detail to control the reader's responses.

At the beginning, as the poem concentrates on neutral description of the fire balloons, the rhythm and the metre are both very regular, hardly noticeable. The rhyming scheme is ABAB – and you can't get anything more conventional than that – and the stresses in each line form a pleasing, untroubled pattern. In addition, notice how it is the balloons themselves that are described as vulnerable – they are 'frail'.

In the second stanza, the first thing that begins to wobble is the rhyming scheme – it's now CDBD – although the metre and the rhythm remain smooth, and the images associated with the balloons are quite soft and beautiful – 'flush', 'fill with light' and 'like hearts'. The balloons, carried on the breeze, may shake a little in their ascent, but they are still magnificent, attractive.

Things begin to break up in the poem from the third stanza onwards. No longer clearly visible because of the heights they've climbed to, the balloons are blurred, indistinct. The uncertainty of their status is captured in the irregular rhyming scheme, in the now fractured rhythm – 'planets, that is—the tinted ones:/Venus going down' – where the increasingly intrusive punctuation of commas, dashes and colons disrupt – and in the increasingly treacherous possibilities suggested by the descriptive details – 'they flare and falter', 'receding … forsaking us', 'turning dangerous'.

The sudden shift from the general to the specific in the sixth stanza – from 'this … time of year' to 'last night' – is dramatic and filled with tension. The balloons that drifted out of sight, apparently harmless, now explode in the middle of one's life. That's not the only change. The language moves from neutral and general and distant – 'they' – to personal and close – 'We saw'. The violence and destruction suddenly erupt in the extreme verbs and images – 'splattered like an egg of fire', 'whirling', 'shrieked', 'glistening' – and in the tense rhythm capturing the horror of the spectacle: 'The flame ran down. We saw the pair'. The rhyming scheme, of course, disintegrates, scattering like the doomed animals in front of the fire.

The destruction, the horror, the power of the technique … all reach their culmination in the penultimate stanza. The cuteness of the creature is shown to us in the imagery – 'baby rabbit', 'short-eared', 'So soft!' – only so that we can witness it being fried, or 'ignited', in the wonderful but paradoxically chilling image, 'a handful of intangible ash'.

Such is the absolute control of sound and image that we are now appalled. That horror and rage is openly expressed in the final italicised stanza, which draws back from the description of the events to respond morally to them, with a 'fist clenched … against the sky'.

But wait. Isn't this destruction and suffering caused by humans? Isn't that the point of the image 'a handful of intangible ash' in the penultimate stanza? Shouldn't we be railing at ourselves, really, rather than at the heavens, which is where the fire comes from, admittedly, but only because we put it there?

MAKE

(i) A critic has remarked, 'Bishop's style of writing, though it sometimes involved sparse details from her personal life, was known for its highly detailed and objective, distant point of view.' This poem is 'highly detailed', but – with particular reference to the final stanza – do you agree that it has an 'objective, distant point of view'?

(ii) This is a wonderful poem for studying Bishop's intricate use of sound patterns – rhyme, rhythm, metre, alliteration, assonance, and so on. Pick out some examples, but in each case make an effort to explain *why* you think Bishop selected that particular effect.

Sestina

September rain falls on the house.
In the failing light, the old grandmother
sits in the kitchen with the child
beside the Little Marvel Stove,
reading the jokes from the almanac,   5
laughing and talking to hide her tears.

She thinks that her equinoctial tears
and the rain that beats on the roof of the house
were both foretold by the almanac,
but only known to a grandmother.   10
The iron kettle sings on the stove.
She cuts some bread and says to the child,

It's time for tea now; but the child
is watching the teakettle's small hard tears
dance like mad on the hot black stove,   15
the way the rain must dance on the house.
Tidying up, the old grandmother
hangs up the clever almanac

on its string. Birdlike, the almanac
hovers half open above the child,   20
hovers above the old grandmother
and her teacup full of dark brown tears.
She shivers and says she thinks the house
feels chilly, and puts more wood in the stove.

It was to be, says the Marvel Stove.   25
I know what I know, says the almanac.
With crayons the child draws a rigid house
and a winding pathway. Then the child
puts in a man with buttons like tears
and shows it proudly to the grandmother   30

But secretly, while the grandmother
busies herself about the stove,
the little moons fall down like tears
from between the pages of the almanac
into the flower bed the child   35
has carefully placed in the front of the house.

READ

Poetry

Time to plant tears, says the almanac.
The grandmother sings to the marvellous stove
and the child draws another inscrutable house.

Glossary

[4] **Little Marvel Stove:** brand name stove, which is an apparatus for cooking and heating by burning solid fuels

[5] **almanac:** annual calendar containing tides and astronomical data

[7] **equinoctial:** equinox, when the day and night are of equal length, happens each September and March; equinoctial is the adjective

[39] **inscrutable:** impossible to interpret

ANALYSE

'Sestina' recreates a situation from Bishop's early life. A grandmother and child are together in 'failing light', as the year itself fades, drifting through September. The only other figure is that of a little man that the girl draws with her crayons. It's a sad poem, a recreation of a sad time, in which everything turns to tears: the rain, the steam from the kettle, the buttons on the drawn man …

A sestina is a verse form, and quite an artificial one, too, which is rarely used successfully, although Bishop manages to create something subtle and quietly effective here. A sestina consists of seven stanzas; the final words in each line of the first stanza are repeated in a different sequence each time in the next five; and then repeated in their final order in the three-line envoi that ends the poem. That amount of repetition can either be tiresome (this is what makes the form difficult) or significantly monotonous, sadly stressing the same sense of loss or failure. In Bishop's 'Sestina', the recurring words are: house, grandmother, child, stove, almanac and tears. The repetitions emphasise the absences (mother and father) from the house and mark each stanza with weeping.

In the first stanza it is September (the year is declining) and the light is failing (the day is declining), so the immediate impression is of a gloomy sadness. But, as always in a Bishop poem, there is a play between opposites here, because the scene is also cosy and warm and intimate, a grandmother reading jokes to her grandchild beside the heat of the stove. The sadness is on the inside of the old woman – she is 'laughing and talking to hide her tears' – but the tenderness and the love on the outside are just as real. Once again, Bishop captures a complex situation with the simplest of words: the inevitable sadness of a child without parents, and of a grandmother without her own children. No matter how much they love each other, there's an emptiness lying between them; and that emptiness has been created by the absence of the father and the mother.

Just as September is inevitable, just as autumn is inevitable, so the grandmother thinks that her tears were inevitable, which is why she imagines them 'foretold by the almanac', a calendar that provides statistical information on the seasons, the phases of the moon, and anniversaries – so perhaps September is a special anniversary for the old woman, which is why her tears were

Poetry

'foretold' by the almanac, because it foretold September, but only 'known to' or understood by the grandmother.

In the third stanza, the poem shifts from the grandmother's knowledge of the world to the child's attempts to make sense of the world. Because she can see that the grandmother is holding back the tears, it seems to the child as if the tears are everywhere, in the steam rising from the boiling kettle, in the rain dancing on the outside of the house.

The old woman tries to contain or disguise all this sorrow that the child can see, by tidying up – a brilliant image of her trying to sweep away tears – and by putting the revealing almanac away. But there's no escape. The tears reappear in her teacup – perhaps literally, since she may be crying quietly while drinking – and then crop up in the child's drawing of 'a man with buttons like tears,' and then the almanac, hanging over the stove, starts to lose its moon-shaped drawings, which 'fall down like tears' into the child's drawing.

In these sections, the poem moves beautifully between the child's inner world and the grandmother's inner world. The saddest aspect is that they're both thinking of the same thing – a house with a 'proper' family, including a mother and father. And in a touching image to end the poem – *Time to plant tears*, says the almanac' – we see that in the garden of the house without parents, nothing grows except tears. The poem finishes with the prospect of recurrence, as inevitable as the seasons listed in the almanac, with the grandmother making another pot of tea and the child drawing another house that can't be entered into ('inscrutable').

MAKE

(i) A critic has remarked of Bishop's poetry: 'her underlying themes include the struggle to find a sense of belonging, and the human experiences of grief and longing'. To what extent do you find aspects of each of these three themes – belonging, grief and longing – in 'Sestina'?

(ii) The sestina is a particularly strict and rather artificial verse form, as described in the ANALYSE panel above. Why, in your opinion, did Bishop use it for this subject matter, and do you consider it successful?

First Death in Nova Scotia

In the cold, cold parlor
my mother laid out Arthur
beneath the chromographs:
Edward, Prince of Wales,
with Princess Alexandra,   5
and King George with Queen Mary.
Below them on the table
stood a stuffed loon
shot and stuffed by Uncle
Arthur, Arthur's father.   10

Since Uncle Arthur fired
a bullet into him,
he hadn't said a word.
He kept his own counsel
on his white, frozen lake,   15
the marble-topped table.
His breast was deep and white,
cold and caressable;
his eyes were red glass,
much to be desired.   20

"Come," said my mother,
"Come and say good-bye
to your little cousin Arthur."
I was lifted up and given
one lily of the valley   25
to put in Arthur's hand.
Arthur's coffin was
a little frosted cake,
and the red-eyed loon eyed it
from his white, frozen lake.   30

Arthur was very small.
He was all white, like a doll
that hadn't been painted yet.
Jack Frost had started to paint him
the way he always painted   35
the Maple Leaf (Forever).
He had just begun on his hair,
a few red strokes, and then
Jack Frost had dropped the brush
and left him white, forever.   40

The gracious royal couples
were warm in red and ermine;
their feet were well wrapped up
in the ladies' ermine trains.
They invited Arthur to be   45
the smallest page at court.
But how could Arthur go,
clutching his tiny lily,
with his eyes shut up so tight
and the roads deep in snow?   50

Glossary

[3] **chromographs:** pictures

[4-6] **Edward, Alexandra, George, Mary:** British royalty; Edward became king when his father George died in 1936; Princess Alexandra was King George V's mother

[8] **loon:** diving bird that feeds on fish

[36] **Maple Leaf:** emblem of Canada

[42] **ermine:** a fur used in heraldry, consisting of a white background flecked with black tails

[46] **page:** young attendant on a person of rank

ANALYSE

'First Death in Nova Scotia', as the title indicates, grows out of the early years of Bishop's life, when she went to live with her maternal grandparents in Nova Scotia. The poem recreates a child's perception of and experience of death. The suggestive title – 'First Death in Nova Scotia' – obviously can't be taken literally, in the sense of meaning the first death that happened in the area, although it holds many other possibilities: first death in that family, first death experienced by the child who is speaking, and so on.

We can sense that the poem recreates a distant time from the use of the old-fashioned word 'chromographs' in the third line. A chromograph, or chromo-lithograph, was a coloured print or reproduction of an original photograph. It suggests an image of reality, a representation of the real thing rather than the reality itself, just as the stuffed bird is a representation of life, although the symbol, the bird, was once living itself. A chromograph also suggests something duller than the original, something faded, something lacking the vibrant colours of a photograph. If you take up this point and follow the colours in the poem, you get some fascinating results. There is white, the colour of death on the human skin, 'like a doll/that hadn't been painted yet,' and also the colour of ice, on the 'white, frozen lake' that the stuffed bird will never sink into, and also the colour of Jack Frost, who starts to paint all living things as soon as they breathe. Contrasted with the white there is vivid red, in the 'red glass' eyes of the stuffed bird and in the 'few red strokes' in the hair of the dead boy. Curiously, both reds, although vivid, are completely lifeless: one is glass, the other is in hair that will never grow. It's not a living red, in other words, but rather like frozen blood. Red also appears in the fur worn by the couples in the chromographs, where it appears beside ermine (white, again, this time with black spots). If white is the colour of death and stillness – Arthur can go nowhere because the roads are 'deep in snow' – then black is the colour of human mourning.

Or, instead of chasing the unchanging colours through the poem, you could contrast movement and stillness within it. The piece is dominated by stillness. Arthur is 'laid out'; the loon (a diving, fishing bird) is 'stuffed' and unmoving; the figures in the chromographs are eternally static; the lake is frozen, so the water doesn't even ripple; Arthur is like a 'doll' lying there, and finally, 'clutching his tiny lily', incapable of doing anything else with it, he can't go anywhere, not even when the royal couples seem to invite him. The entire effect is of a moment frozen in time, of a life frozen in that moment. By contrast, there are only two movements in the poem, although both are highly significant. The girl – I get the *impression* of a girl – the child speaker, is lifted up and places a lily in the dead boy's hand. He doesn't accept it. She places it. She is alive, mobile, active. He is dead. The only other movement suggests a violent burst of energy that leads to death, and it's very striking: Arthur's father once 'fired/a bullet' into the now stuffed loon.

Or you could examine the play between silence and speech, which in reality is only a variation on the tension between stillness and movement, since speech requires motion and silence doesn't. The dignified figures in the chromographs never open their mouths and the loon 'hadn't said a word' since Arthur's father shot it. Did it speak before that? A childish question. And quite appropriate, because what we have here is a child's perspective. When words are finally spoken, they break into the silence like intruders, almost violently: '"Come," said my mother,/"Come and say good-bye'. But the girl doesn't 'say' anything. Why would she? The dead can't hear or respond. And it's not meant literally, not 'say', you don't 'say' things to the dead that you might to the living, or even to a favourite doll, or at least to one that had been painted to make it look lifelike. Silence dominates, overwhelms this poem. Even the royal couples' invitation to Arthur is not real, not audible, only in the imagination of the speaker. They can't speak. The only words in the poem are harsh, cold, intrusive – 'Come' – apart, of course, from the words of the poem itself, for the poem is nothing but words.

And reflecting on those words, consider the contrast between childish and adult expressions throughout the poem, because, of course, the poem was written by an adult, from the perspective of a child, so that there are two minds thinking simultaneously here. Examples? The repetitions strike me as childlike: 'the cold, cold parlor', 'Uncle/Arthur, Arthur's father' – because they sound like childish riddles and games – as do the references to 'Jack Frost' and the stuffed bird not saying a word and the comparison between Arthur and an unpainted doll. On the other hand, the phrases 'cold and caressable', 'kept his own counsel' and 'gracious royal couples' sound like the expressions of adults, possibly overheard by that same child.

The fundamental contrast in the poem, of course, is that between death and life. This is the source of all the other contrasts. For all the stillness, silence and lack of colour associated with it, death, it is suggested, may actually be a journey to a better place, a passing to a better existence, as adults would have children believe. After all, the royal couples 'invited Arthur to be the smallest page at court'. But that invitation, no matter how attractive, cannot be accepted; the promise of death as an improvement cannot be fulfilled. For 'how could Arthur go' when he cannot see and the snow makes movement impossible? Death is a glass eye, a photograph, an unfinished doll. It is forever white, or forever red, or forever incompletely one or the other. It can never develop. It is a condition, not a promise.

MAKE

(i) Elizabeth Bishop said of her own work, 'The greatest challenge, for me, is to try and express difficult thoughts in plain language.' Do you think she succeeded with both ambitions – difficult thoughts, plain language – in 'First Death in Nova Scotia'?

(ii) The dominant imagery of the poem draws on colours, particularly red, white and black. Pick out some examples, commenting on what each might mean to the child speaker and what each might mean to the adult poet behind the child speaker.

Filling Station

Oh, but it is dirty!
—this little filling station,
oil-soaked, oil-permeated
to a disturbing, over-all
black translucency.   5
Be careful with that match!

Father wears a dirty,
oil-soaked monkey suit
that cuts him under the arms,
and several quick and saucy   10
and greasy sons assist him
(it's a family filling station),
all quite thoroughly dirty.

Do they live in the station?
It has a cement porch   15
behind the pumps, and on it
a set of crushed and grease-
impregnated wickerwork;
on the wicker sofa
a dirty dog, quite comfy.   20

Some comic books provide
the only note of color—
of certain color. They lie
upon a big dim doily
draping a taboret   25
(part of the set), beside
a big hirsute begonia.

Why the extraneous plant?
Why the taboret?
Why, oh why, the doily?   30
(Embroidered in daisy stitch
with marguerites, I think,
and heavy with gray crochet.)

Somebody embroidered the doily.
Somebody waters the plant,   35
or oils it, maybe. Somebody
arranges the rows of cans
so that they softly say:
ESSO—SO—SO—SO
to high-strung automobiles.   40
Somebody loves us all.

Glossary

[title] **Filling Station:** petrol station, American English

[5] **translucency:** allowing light, but not detail, to pass through

[8] **monkey suit:** work uniform, American English

[24] **doily:** small ornamental lace or paper mat

[27] **hirsute begonia:** also known as hairy begonia, a tropical plant with thick hairy stems

[29] **taboret:** low stool or small table

[32] **marguerites:** daisies

[39] **ESSO:** trade name for ExxonMobil, and trading name at the time of Standard Oil (SO), hence the phonetic name

ANALYSE

Somebody pulls in to a filling station, needing to fill up the car with gas during a journey, and the poem expresses her reactions to the scene.

At first the voice is queasy, fussy, judgemental, rather disgusted: 'Oh, but it is dirty!' She is disturbed and appalled by the 'black' appearance of the place, by the oil. She is nervous and anxious: 'Be careful with that match!' This place is dangerous, potentially explosive, threatening. Clearly, she wants to get out of there as quickly as possible.

She is most appalled, we suspect, by the fact that this, on first sight, is an all-male world: a father and 'several' sons. Several? Can't she count? Or are they too quick for her? After all, they are 'greasy', slippery. Or is it that she looks at them, but doesn't see them, like a tourist seeing something other than what's there. She herself uses the term 'family' – '(it's a family filling station)' – but she doesn't mean it in the accepted sense; she means just father and sons. In fact, she fussily observes that they're 'all quite thoroughly dirty', as if there was no mother to force them to wash, as if she herself is tempted to clean them up.

As so often with Bishop, the experience leads to questions, and the questions then alter the speaker, and with her the course of the poem: 'Do they live in the station?' Now, a question is more attentive, more human, more *concerned* than a dismissive statement like 'Oh, but it is dirty!' A question starts to open your eyes, invites you to see more than what was merely obvious to your prejudices, just as the narrator here begins to see beyond her first impression – 'It has a cement porch/behind the pumps' – and indeed as all the other characters in the previous poems began to see more. She now notices a dog, which is also 'dirty,' but – crucial addition – 'quite comfy' as well. These people can't be all bad, then, if they're treating the dog properly. The observation comes as a slightly surprised and rather slight approval.

Then, finally, she begins to notice the human details of these human lives. There are children's comic books. Their illustrations provide 'the only note of colour'. But why didn't she notice the colour first, instead of the dirt? It was there all the time. There's also a doily, which is a decorative mat, laid on or under a serving plate. And now that she's looking, she also sees a taboret (a low stool shaped like a drum) and a begonia, which is a flowering plant, and which surely must have a little colour as well. These are domestic details. This is, after all, a real family.

Why are these things there, she asks. She calls the plant 'extraneous', which means unnecessary. She persists with her questions. 'Why, oh why,' she laments critically. They are immensely silly questions. The proper response is 'why not?' What's it got to do with her? She's a visitor.

In the final section, the narrator tries to make fun of the scene and the family. 'Somebody waters the plant,/or oils it, maybe.' Ha, ha. The oil cans are arranged in such a way that the last two letters of the manufacturer's name, ESSO, are visible on each can, giving a funny sequence: 'ESSO—SO—SO—SO' which is soothingly called out to 'high-strung automobiles.' And, the last suggestion is – 'Somebody loves us all' – that only a mother could love this lot. Slightly mocking as it is, it's a long way from the anxious disgust at the beginning: 'Oh, but it is dirty!' I get the impression that the humour is self-defensive. The woman-narrator, with her superior tone and obsession with cleanliness, has been caught out treating a family of humans as rather unattractive creatures – 'Father wears a dirty,/oil-soaked monkey suit' – and now covers her own shame with the haughty, 'Somebody loves us all', even these creatures.

The 'somebody' never physically appears in the poem, but is visible through the doily, the begonia, the 'daisy stitch' embroidery with 'marguerites', a type of daisy. It is, of course, the family's mother. Her colourful, delicate additions to the grimy world of the filling station express tenderness, affection, care, attentiveness, delicacy – all the qualities the narrator lacks.

MAKE

(i) The critic, Robert Dale Parker said of this poem: 'Much depends on how we take the ending' as a 'charming little appreciation of motherhood' or by reading it 'with a sarcastic accent on somebody'. Which reading do you favour, and why?

(ii) In capturing a narrator's voice, and particularly the shifting responses of a narrator, the control of sound effects is essential. Pick out the shifts in tone in the narrator's voice in this poem, from 'Oh, but it is dirty!' to 'Somebody loves us all', commenting on what words in particular carry the emotions.

In the Waiting Room

In Worcester, Massachusetts,
I went with Aunt Consuelo
to keep her dentist's appointment
and sat and waited for her
in the dentist's waiting room.   5
It was winter. It got dark
early. The waiting room
was full of grown-up people,
arctics and overcoats,
lamps and magazines.   10
My aunt was inside
what seemed like a long time
and while I waited I read
the *National Geographic*
(I could read) and carefully   15
studied the photographs:
the inside of a volcano,
black, and full of ashes;
then it was spilling over
in rivulets of fire.   20
Osa and Martin Johnson
dressed in riding breeches,
laced boots, and pith helmets.
A dead man slung on a pole
—"Long Pig," the caption said.   25
Babies with pointed heads
wound round and round with string;
black, naked women with necks
wound round and round with wire
like the necks of light bulbs.   30
Their breasts were horrifying.
I read it right straight through.
I was too shy to stop.
And then I looked at the cover:
the yellow margins, the date.   35
Suddenly, from inside,
came an *oh!* of pain
—Aunt Consuelo's voice—
not very loud or long.
I wasn't at all surprised;   40
even then I knew she was
a foolish, timid woman.

I might have been embarrassed,
but wasn't. What took me
completely by surprise
was that it was *me*:
my voice, in my mouth.
Without thinking at all
I was my foolish aunt,
I—we—were falling, falling,
our eyes glued to the cover
of the *National Geographic*,
February, 1918.

I said to myself: three days
and you'll be seven years old.
I was saying it to stop
the sensation of falling off
the round, turning world.
into cold, blue-black space.
But I felt: you are an *I*,
you are an *Elizabeth*,
you are one of *them*.
Why should you be one, too?
I scarcely dared to look
to see what it was I was.
I gave a sidelong glance
—I couldn't look any higher—
at shadowy gray knees,
trousers and skirts and boots
and different pairs of hands
lying under the lamps.
I knew that nothing stranger
had ever happened, that nothing
stranger could ever happen.

Why should I be my aunt,
or me, or anyone?
What similarities—
boots, hands, the family voice
I felt in my throat, or even
the *National Geographic*
and those awful hanging breasts—
held us all together
or made us all just one?
How—I didn't know any

45

50

55

60

65

70

75

80

word for it—how "unlikely" …   85
How had I come to be here,
like them, and overhear
a cry of pain that could have
got loud and worse but hadn't?

The waiting room was bright   90
and too hot. It was sliding
beneath a big black wave,
another, and another.

Then I was back in it.
The War was on. Outside,   95
in Worcester, Massachusetts,
were night and slush and cold,
and it was still the fifth
of February, 1918.

Glossary

[1] **Worcester, Massachusetts:** where Bishop was born

[9] **arctics:** waterproof overshoes

[14] *National Geographic*: official magazine of the National Geographic Society, first published in 1888

[21] **Osa and Martin Johnson:** American adventurers and documentary film-makers

[23] **pith helmets:** lightweight sun helmets made from the pith of tropical plants

[25] **Long Pig:** translation of term formerly used in some Pacific Islands for human flesh prepared as food

[95] **The War:** the First World War (1914–1918)

ANALYSE

'In the Waiting Room' presents a young girl at a later stage of development than the child character in either 'First Death in Nova Scotia' or 'Sestina'. Whereas in 'Sestina' the child is executing a crude drawing and in 'First Death in Nova Scotia' the child has no language, here the girl is advanced – 'I could read' – capable of analysis – 'carefully/studied the photographs' – and on the verge of self-conscious independence. Indeed, the poem dramatises a moment of awareness. The girl is almost seven – 'three days/and you'll be seven years old' – traditionally considered the age of reasoning in humans.

The girl has accompanied her aunt – 'a foolish, timid woman' – to the dentist, and while waiting in the waiting room reads a copy of *National Geographic*, where she suddenly encounters another world through the photographs of African explorers published in the magazine. It is the world of adulthood that she really encounters, of being a woman … the world of her 'foolish, timid' aunt and millions of other adult women.

The poem can be enjoyably approached through its contrasts, which have their source in the tension between being a child and a woman, a tension that suddenly erupts in the girl's consciousness.

Look at the disturbing clash between the ordinary and the bizarre in the poem. On the one hand, we have the everyday details of the dentist's waiting room, the crowd of patients, the winter overcoats. On the other, there are 'Babies with pointed heads' and 'black, naked women with necks/wound round and round with wire.' Half of these images are familiar, half of them are strange. Of course, which is which depends entirely on your perspective, doesn't it? The black African women would find the dentist bizarre and the babies with pointed heads ordinary. Although the poem doesn't say so – it doesn't *say* anything – this is clearly part of the experience being explored.

But let's continue for the moment with the poem's contrasts: that between what the girl finds comforting, for instance – the dentist, the room, the 'grown-up people', the whites, and even winter and the dark, neither of which is frightening, and also the cry of pain from her aunt – and what the girl finds terrifying, giving her a 'sensation of falling off' the world – first, the 'horrifying' breasts of the black women, and then, most extraordinarily, the sound of her own voice, and then, in a reversal of her earlier experience, the other people in the waiting room, or at least the bits of them that she dare look at, the 'gray knees,/trousers and skirts and boots'. Similarly, there is a contrast between order – the patients waiting (patiently), the queue, even the appointment itself – and loss of control – the cry of pain, 'the sensation of falling off', the War. As the poem begins, 'inside' is presented as cosy, because it's winter and dark outside; but this, too, is quickly reversed, because one of the photographs in the magazine is 'inside' a volcano, and then the cry of pain, her own voice, is 'inside' her mouth. Clearly, the mind that entered the waiting room is the unreflecting mind of a child, untroubled by anything more serious than boredom; the mind that leaves is in turmoil, more like that of an adult's.

It was said above that these tensions *erupt* in the girl's mind, because that is the very image that the poem introduces us to and advises us to use: 'the inside of a volcano … spilling over', 'rivulets of fire.' What causes this eruption? Rather than trying to answer this question, it is better to note that the poem itself insists on offering us more questions, not answers. There is a cascade of questions in the second half of the poem – '*Why* should you be one, too?' – 'Why should I be my aunt?' – 'How had I come to be here?' – before it settles back, into the calm world where it started, although everything has changed in the meantime, because the girl has changed in the meantime. The poem does not offer answers. It does not even attempt to *approach* answers. The poem dramatises the questions, dramatises the moment of self-awareness, of self-consciousness, in a young girl. I, too, am one of *them*, she suddenly realises, one of these women, with 'horrifying' breasts, one of the same family as my aunt, with 'the family voice', related to 'a foolish, timid woman'. Why? Why, indeed. Why should each of us be what we are? Why am I a member of the human race? Why am I, at the same time, distinct from all other members of the human race?

Such questions will bring on a panic attack. Which is what happens in the waiting room: it was 'too hot. It was sliding/beneath a big black wave'. Such questions have no answers. We have to live with them. And the final section of the poem begins that life-long process of living with them.

MAKE

(i) The critic Judith Merrin observed that 'In the Waiting Room' 'carries simplicity of language to its extreme in an extremely unnerving situation'. Pick out some examples of this 'simplicity of language' and comment on what you think is 'extremely unnerving' about the situation.

(ii) In capturing a narrator's voice, and particularly the shifting responses of a narrator, the control of sound effects is essential. Pick out the shifts in tone in the narrator's voice in this poem, from the matter-of-fact opening through the turbulence in the centre to the mixture of confusion and relief at the end, commenting on what words in particular carry the emotions.

Poetry

The Poetry of Elizabeth Bishop

Themes and Interests

- The poetry of Elizabeth Bishop explores what she herself called **A SENSE OF HOME**, explaining 'I've never felt particularly homeless, but, then, I've never felt particularly at home. I guess that's a pretty good description of a poet's sense of home. He carries it within him.'

Biographical details, for once, may be relevant here, as Bishop spent many of her early years between two sets of grandparents and two locations – Worcester in the USA and Nova Scotia in Canada – and wrote about these experiences in 'Sestina', where a child sadly draws a home she can never have, 'First Death in Nova Scotia', where a child tries to imagine what home an infant might go to after its death, and 'In the Waiting Room', where a girl struggles with the sense of belonging. In one sense or another, all the poems on your course contain this theme. 'The Prodigal' is an obvious example, since the character is in exile and drinks to avoid 'home', though he knows that he will return. 'Questions of Travel' explores, openly and philosophically, the conflicting concepts and experiences of 'home' and 'away'. In 'Filling Station', the figures, originally found repulsive – 'Oh, but it is dirty!' – are experienced as more human after the recognition that the gas station is a 'home'. But it is not only humans who inhabit homes, of course. Other creatures do, too. Sometimes these creatures' homes are destroyed by human insensitivity and cruelty, as in 'The Armadillo', and sometimes humans understand enough to return such creatures to their home, as in 'The Fish'. 'At the Fishhouses' uses the metaphor of the sea as home, to fish and seals at least, to explore the nature of human knowledge, and in 'The Bight' the poet, on her birthday, settles for inhabiting a home that is 'awful but cheerful'.

- The poetry of Elizabeth Bishop explores what a critic has described as the 'human experiences of **GRIEF** and **LONGING**'

Poetry Foundation (www.poetryfoundation.org/) says of Bishop's poetry: 'Her verse is marked by precise descriptions of the physical world and an air of poetic serenity, but her underlying themes include the struggle to find a sense of belonging, and the human experiences of grief and longing.' A 'sense of belonging' refers back to the theme of home discussed above. Grief, longing, yearning – human awareness of loss, generally – is the new theme introduced here. One might start with 'The Prodigal' – with its unflinching depiction of human misery – or with 'Sestina', which is dominated by tears, and the repetitive form of which represents people caught in an endless cycle of grief. In both these poems, the central character yearns for release. The girl in 'In the Waiting Room', who enters the room as a child and leaves it, a short time later, with a newly acquired self-awareness, has lost her carefree innocence. Her mourning takes the forms of bewilderment and anger, expressed by all those outraged questions she asks of herself, and of life. A similar bewilderment is experienced by the child in 'First Death in Nova Scotia', as she struggles, in her childish way, to make sense of death. 'Questions of Travel' is a philosophical reflection on loss and gain, and on the perverse inability of humans to be satisfied, regardless of where they are. A sense of loss and a contained grief also mark the narrator's voice in 'The Bight' and 'At the Fishhouses'.

- The poetry of Elizabeth Bishop explores the complexities of **ESTRANGEMENT** and **SUFFERING**

    George S. Lensing has summed up Bishop's concerns as: 'Shunning self-pity, the poems thinly conceal her estrangements as a woman, a lesbian, an orphan, a geographically rootless traveler, a frequently hospitalized asthmatic, and a sufferer of depression and alcoholism.' Both 'estrangements' – which means alienation, exile – and 'a geographically rootless traveller' refer back to the earlier theme of a 'sense of home' or a 'sense of belonging'. The additional theme is suffering, generally. A consistent form of that suffering is the experience of death. The two early poems, of course – 'First Death in Nova Scotia' and 'Sestina' – deal with physical death – the loss of a child and a parent, respectively – but different forms of death are present in other poems, particularly in 'The Prodigal', a portrait of a man who is spiritually and emotionally dead. The suffering of owls, rabbits and an armadillo, inflicted by humans celebrating a religious festival, is the subject of 'The Armadillo'. Both 'The Bight' and 'At the Fishhouses' are suffused with discomfort, emotional and intellectual, while 'Questions of Travel' explores a similar discomfort as the restlessness that characterises human beings.

- The poetry of Elizabeth Bishop dramatises **THE PROCESS OF CHANGE** in living things, including people, and is therefore more concerned with questions than with answers

    One of most distinctive features of Bishop's poems is that they frequently dramatise the process of change. She tells how she read, as a student, that 'baroque [seventeenth-century] sermons attempted to dramatise the mind in action rather than in repose' and how this influenced her poetry. 'The Fish', for instance, opens with 'I caught a tremendous fish' and closes with 'And I let the fish go'. Clearly, something profound has happened between these stages inside the human who caught the fish. Similarly, 'Filling Station', opens with 'O, but it is dirty!' and closes with 'Somebody loves us all', and again, some profound change in attitude, or in the expression of attitude, has occurred, although it's never quite clear how profound the change is here. A detailed exploration of 'In the Waiting Room' will also illustrate this point, since it dramatises the arrival of self-awareness in a girl. The last thoughtless act the girl does is picking up a copy of *National Geographic*; after that, she will be blessed, and cursed, with the self-consciousness that empowers and afflicts all humans. Perhaps the most profound change of all in human life has occurred. When Bishop recreates the process of a mind thinking, of a person responding to other living things, her work is at its most positive. When there is none of that movement in a poem, when everything is static, the people are always unhappy, always weighed down by a sense of being trapped. This is true of 'The Bight', a poem dated 8 February 1948, when Bishop was thirty-seven years old, and subtitled 'On my birthday'. It recreates a scene from her time in Key West, Florida, and is a perfect example of her understated exploration of a theme, which in this case might be expressed as the 'bight' of middle age, life at low tide. Nothing is openly stated about 'life' or 'living', everything captures the scene itself, and yet we get the impression of a mood throughout. That mood, and everything else about the poem, can be pinpointed with reference to the final line – 'awful but cheerful' – which Bishop chose as an epitaph on her grave stone.

Style and Viewpoint

- The poetry of Elizabeth Bishop uses what she described as a 'plain' style, which means that its **LANGUAGE** is clear on the surface, but contains subtle depths, like the sea she so much loved

On the surface, Bishop's poetry is very simple and straightforward. The language she uses consists almost entirely of ordinary, everyday terms, without obscure references, and she hardly ever uses difficult symbols or images to recreate experiences. As well as that, the situations that she does feature in her work are all very familiar, like visiting a dentist or pulling into a petrol station for a refill. At the same time, you can return time after time to her poems, enjoy them again, and get a little more out of them each time. So, they're not shallow by any means. They're very deep, in fact. It's very easy to demonstrate the clear surface of Bishop's poetry, the ordinary conversational language she uses. You just need a few short quotations. In the opening of 'The Fish', for instance, all the words are among the most ordinary in the English language and very few of them are longer than a single syllable. There's nothing at all complicated here, including the rhythm, which moves smoothly along in a matter-of-fact way. But the word that really stands out is 'tremendous'. It's a word that children use – 'tremendous' – when they want to express something really important to them. It's not in the least a 'poetic' word. It's not even very precise. But it's perfect for capturing the simple excitement of the catch. In the same way, nothing could be more everyday than the opening of 'In the Waiting Room', which just reports, in the deadest manner possible, one of the most boring experiences of all – waiting for someone. There's no hint at all of the fireworks to come, or that this dull waiting room is actually 'the inside of a volcano'. All the same, even though the language is always conversational and the situations are always recognisable, there's also a lot going on in Bishop's poems, a great deal that is *suggested* by the words.

- The poetry of Elizabeth Bishop dramatises the process of change and therefore uses incident as significant metaphor and draws its **IMAGERY** from a mastery of precise descriptive detail

Poetry as drama involves the use of incident as significant metaphor. This is the technique of the classic short story, where an event is not isolated, but defines an entire life. Such defining events or incidents feature in almost all the poems by Bishop on your course, from the very specific timing of her birthday in 'The Bight', through the crucial few minutes in 'Filling Station', the few minutes in 'In the Waiting Room', the few minutes in 'The Armadillo', to the excitement of the catch in 'The Fish'. Of course, a good literary story works because it operates on two different levels at the same time: what the characters can see, and what the reader can see. In her innocence, the child in 'First Death in Nova Scotia' fantasises that the 'drama' of the situation consists of the bird trying to get at the 'cake'. We know that it is provided by death. The two layers of meaning – the use of dramatic irony, in other words – is the key to reading the poem. Similarly, poetry as narrative requires the mastery of precise descriptive detail. In an interview with Bishop, J. Bernlef remarked that her 'work has often been compared with that of painters: her preference for minute description … her endless attention to detail'. Quotations from any of Bishop's poems will illustrate the truth of this. For example, a close reading of 'The Fish' will reveal how eloquent and how precise the descriptions are, including as they do colours – white, reds, blacks, pink; shapes – big bones, little bones, entrails, bladder; the tactile – coarse, flesh, feathers; and the visual – shiny, peony. Similarly, a study of the sensory detail – derived from smell [olfactory], hearing [auditory] and touch [tactile], as well as sight [visual] – in 'At the Fishhouses' and 'The Bight' and many other poems, will be rewarding.

- The poetry of Elizabeth Bishop captures the character of people through voice and the character of places through other intricate **SOUND** patterns

In literature, characters are created through voice, appearance and behaviour. Bishop is adept at all three. Look how the character in 'The Prodigal', for instance – like all guilty creatures – is restless at night, is shaken, but affected emotionally, by his own thoughts, and inhabits a dark, 'slimy' world, in the company of bats whose flight is as 'uncertain' as his own path in life. The same mastery is evident in other poems. In terms of sound, however, the ability to capture a character's voice is the most important. Bishop's control of voice, through such sound effects as rhythm, tone, assonance, sibilance, and so on, is obvious throughout, since almost all the poems employ narrators. The voices range from childish innocence in 'First Death in Nova Scotia', through the unsettling dawn of self-awareness in 'In the Waiting Room', outrage in 'The Armadillo', contemplation in 'Questions of Travel', prejudice in 'Filling Station', to a sense of emptiness and dislocation in 'The Bight' and 'At the Fishhouses'. The rhythms of living things is also beautifully recreated in the sound patterns of Bishop's poems – the stillness of the fish in 'The Fish', the terrified scurrying of the doomed creatures in 'The Armadillo', the ease of the seal in 'At the Fishhouses', the sloth of the pigs in 'The Prodigal', even the mechanism of the dredger in 'The Bight'. Bishop also uses sound effects to capture the character of places and things – for instance, the sound of the waterfalls in 'Questions of Travel', the sound of the fish-processing activities in 'At the Fishhouses', the stuffiness of the room in 'In the Waiting Room', the grime of the gas station in 'Filling Station', the interior of a boat in 'The Fish'.

- The poetry of Elizabeth Bishop holds the often unsettling complexities of life within strict poetic **FORMS**, some popular, such as the sonnet, some less frequently used, such as the villanelle and the sestina

In terms of the beauty and perfection of its forms, Bishop's poetry has attracted much praise, including 'craft-like accuracy', the observation that she spent many years on a single poem 'working towards an effect of spontaneity', 'she gives us maps', and 'the organisation is smooth'. Bishop herself remarked, 'what really appeals to me is scenery and architecture'. One key is her observation: 'I like to present complicated or mysterious ideas in the simplest way possible.' An essential ingredient of 'the simplest way possible' is her choice of poetic forms – particularly strict and traditional forms, such as the sonnet and the sestina. An equally important key, however, is her belief that form cannot control chaos. The revealing symbol here is that of the sea, present in much of her work, but particularly significant in 'At the Fishhouses', where it is always 'the same sea', but also always changing, 'forever, flowing'. We have to put some shape on our lives, but each shape is temporary. We have to put some shape on our words, but each shape is specific to the particular experience. The formulaic repetitions in 'Sestina' are skilfully monotonous – they express the dullness of loss. The double sonnet of 'The Prodigal' captures the double bind of the character. The long, flowing, uninterrupted form of 'The Fish' perfectly expresses the suspended drama of a decision. The changing form of the stanzas in 'The Armadillo' – smooth and regular, then jagged and

irregular – mirror the beautiful ascent of the fire balloons and their terrifyingly destructive descent to earth. Similarly, the form of 'Questions of Travel' is reflective, that of 'Filling Station' hurried and then uncertain, that of 'The Bight' flat. In each case, the form expresses the experience and the experience is expressed by the form; there is no clear division in poetry between content and shape. To use a quotation from earlier, each of Bishop's poems is like a map, beautifully drawn, but applicable only to a specific time, as well as a specific place. The first poem in her first published collection of poetry is called 'The Map'.

Eavan Boland

Eavan Boland was born in Dublin in 1944. When she was six, her family moved to London, where her father worked as a diplomat. Growing up as an outsider in England raised questions about identity and the past that would later feature heavily in her poetry. She returned to Ireland to attend secondary school and then Trinity College, Dublin, where she studied Latin and English. She published her first poetry pamphlet soon after her graduation. She married in 1969 and has two children, and has written much about the complexities of love and motherhood and the beauty of the every day. She has lectured at a number of universities, including Trinity College.

Prescribed Poems

'Students at Higher Level will be required to study a representative selection from the work of eight poets: a representative selection would seek to reflect the range of a poet's themes and interests and exhibit his/her characteristic style and viewpoint. Normally the study of at least six poems by each poet would be expected.' (DES English Syllabus, 6.3)

Poetry

Themes and Interests

explores and dramatises different forms of **LOVE** – particularly romantic and parental love – and the gestures of love, such as the kiss and the gift

explores the complexities of **FEMALE EXPERIENCE**, including **MOTHERHOOD**, and particularly the tension between a mother's need to protect her child and the child's struggle for independence

The Poetry of Eavan Boland

presents **HISTORY** and the past as forces that shape the present, particularly in the connections between different generations of women

examines how we try to contain life within a **DOMESTIC** order and how the forces of nature can threaten, disrupt or destroy this

Style and Viewpoint

The Poetry of Eavan Boland

is cerebral, which means that its **LANGUAGE** deliberately engages the intelligence rather the emotions or the instincts

employs landscape and everyday items as symbolic **IMAGERY** to express the complexity of experience, and uses mythology and history as metaphor

balances detailed descriptions of objects or dramatic scenes with reflective passages, using intricate **SOUND** patterns to recreate emotions

employs unusual and unconventional **FORMS**, such as two-line stanzas and irregular rhyming schemes, to represent the complexities of human experience

Poetry

READ

The War Horse

This dry night, nothing unusual
About the clip, clop, casual

Iron of his shoes as he stamps death
Like a mint on the innocent coinage of earth.

I lift the window, watch the ambling feather   5
Of hock and fetlock, loosed from its daily tether

In the tinker camp on the Enniskerry Road,
Pass, his breath hissing, his snuffling head

Down. He is gone. No great harm is done.
Only a leaf of our laurel hedge is torn –   10

Of distant interest like a maimed limb,
Only a rose which now will never climb

The stone of our house, expendable, a mere
Line of defence against him, a volunteer

You might say, only a crocus, its bulbous head   15
Blown from growth, one of the screamless dead.

But we, we are safe, our unformed fear
Of fierce commitment gone; why should we care

If a rose, a hedge, a crocus are uprooted
Like corpses, remote, crushed, mutilated?   20

He stumbles on like a rumour of war, huge
Threatening. Neighbours use the subterfuge

Of curtains. He stumbles down our short street
Thankfully passing us. I pause, wait,

Then to breathe relief lean on the sill   25
And for a second only my blood is still

With atavism. That rose he smashed frays
Ribboned across our hedge, recalling days

Of burned countryside, illicit braid:
A cause ruined before, a world betrayed.   30

Poetry

Glossary

[7] **tinker:** a once common, now discredited, term for Travellers

[7] **Enniskerry Road:** a road linking the suburbs of south Dublin to the town of Enniskerry in County Wicklow

[27] **atavism:** recurrence of a trait typical of one's ancestors

[29] **braid:** literally cord, perhaps on a soldier's uniform; figuratively gold and silver bullion

ANALYSE

'The War Horse', one of Boland's first major poems, was written when she was twenty-seven years old, and it introduces many of the major themes and subjects of her work.

A horse, represented in the title as a military animal, a fiercesome battle horse, has broken away from its tether in the nearby Travellers' camp. Travellers were commonly known as 'tinkers' at the time. The horse threatens the domestic order of suburbia. It stamps 'death' with its great hooves, destroying a hedge, a rose bush and a flower, all those things of nature that civilised people cultivate to tame their environment, or to pretend to themselves that the environment can be tamed. In capturing the brutality of war and the violence of nature, and the destruction that both can bring to a previously calm civilisation, the language is particularly extreme – 'maimed ...

screamless dead ... crushed, mutilated'. The hedges and flowers, the walls and houses, the 'subterfuge/Of curtains', are man's 'line of defence' against such destructive forces. They are inadequate. They are rather pathetic, really. What could a curtain, or a rose, do to keep the horse at bay?

Although the gender is not specified in the poem, it is, most likely, a woman inside the house, lifting the window curtains, peering out, leaning with relief on the sill when the danger is past. The poem emerges directly from the experiences of Boland's life. As she writes in her autobiographical book *Object Lessons*: 'I married in my mid-twenties and went to live in a suburban house at the foothills of the Dublin mountains. The first winter in the suburb was harsh ...'

But there is a broader background, because this 'was the early 70s, a time of violence in Northern Ireland', when nightly images of riots in Belfast and Derry could be seen on television.

Poetry

Sectarian violence between Catholics and Protestants had erupted a few years earlier, the British army had been called in to restore order, and now these soldiers were seen as an occupying force by some, bringing to mind the history of England's long military occupation of Ireland over previous centuries. This explains the opening out of the poem in the final three stanzas, as it looks backwards, to reflect on power and destruction and violence, and people's responses to them, in the past. The experience is 'atavistic' for Boland, which means that it reminds her of her own resemblance to distant ancestors. The smashed rose puts her in mind of the Irish countryside destroyed by occupying troops (many on horseback, obviously) and of the 'cause' (of Irish freedom) which was destroyed so many times throughout the country's history, a cause, and a dream, that was always 'betrayed'.

Let's also admire the technique of 'The War Horse', and in particular how the intricate sound patterns of the poem recreate the anxiety at the appearance of the horse – 'I lift the window … I pause, wait,' – and the relief at its departure – 'He is gone. No great harm is done.' While the woman is constricted with nervousness, the horse roams about freely (the two are related, obviously), and the verse also expresses in its freer movement the untethered movement of the animal: 'loosed from its daily tether/In the tinker camp on the Enniskerry Road'.

The form of the poem is unusual – tight two-line stanzas and a rhyming scheme that's sometimes strict and sometimes loose – and it is interesting to examine how the lines move within these restrictions, at times leisurely – 'You might say, only a crocus, its bulbous head/ Blown from growth' – at others, tensely – 'Thankfully passing us. I pause, wait'. The regular/ irregular form represents both how the animal moves and how the spectators respond to it.

MAKE

(i) In the poem, the horse has both personal and historical/political associations. Identify each and comment on how they relate to each other within the poem itself.

(ii) Trace the pattern of sounds in the poem as it moves through the speaker's anxiety at the threat of the horse, her relief at its departure, and her sense of loss for the destruction it leaves behind. Refer to the two-line stanza form, the rhyming scheme, and other sound effects.

Poetry

Child of our Time
(for Aengus)

Yesterday I knew no lullaby
But you have taught me overnight to order
This song, which takes from your final cry
Its tune, from your unreasoned end its reason;
Its rhythm from the discord of your murder   5
Its motive from the fact you cannot listen.

We who should have known how to instruct
With rhymes for your waking, rhythms for your sleep,
Names for the animals you took to bed,
Tales to distract, legends to protect   10
Later an idiom for you to keep
And living, learn, must learn from you dead,

To make our broken images, rebuild
Themselves around your limbs, your broken
Image, find for your sake whose life our idle   15
Talk has cost, a new language. Child
Of our time, our times have robbed your cradle.
Sleep in a world your final sleep has woken.
17 May 1974

Glossary

[1] **lullaby:** a gentle song to send a child to sleep

[11] **idiom:** a language, a mode of expression

On 17 May 1974, at the height of the conflict in Northern Ireland between the Republican and Unionist communities, three bombs exploded in the centre of Dublin and a fourth in Monaghan town. Thirty-three people were killed as a result. A photograph of a dead boy being carried from the scene by a fireman appeared in the newspapers the next morning, and inspired this poem.

Boland is interested in her own response to his death, and specifically in her own response as a *writer*, and through that in the relationship between language and events. Look at the opening line: 'Yesterday I knew no lullaby'. It's focus is on the writer's perception of the inadequacy of her words. The day before the death of the boy, she had no song to accompany a child to rest, presumably because it had not occurred to her that she might ever need one; but now, the death has forced her into a response. Of course, 'lullaby' in the ordinary sense is completely inappropriate – it usually soothes a *sleeping* child – and so the song that is made is not at all sweet or pleasant or shapely. Instead, it contains the boy's 'final cry', it is marked by the 'discord' of his murder, and it addresses a boy who 'cannot listen'.

Language should be an enrichment of life, the second stanza suggests, and particularly of a child's life. It should provide rhyming sounds to make the child's waking joyful – nursery rhymes and songs – and soothing rhythms to lull him back into sleep at the end of the day. It should provide the magic of names for the child's toys, stories to entertain, legends to learn from (and therefore to 'protect'), and finally a form in which life itself is both understood and lived (an 'idiom for you to keep/And living, learn'). The adult world should have bestowed all these gifts of language on the child, but since the child is dead, such gifts are useless, the final line of the stanza suggests, and so the world has to learn new uses for its language. Since it could not protect the child's life, it must create a response to the child's death.

This point is made obvious at the opening of the third stanza. The images, or pictures that language creates – the rhymes, the legends, the tales of the previous stanza – are now 'broken', shattered and useless, by the broken limbs of the boy, and specifically by the picture, or 'image', of those broken limbs that Boland saw in the newspapers and is responding to. What good are words if they cannot preserve life? Or worse. What good are words if they help to destroy life? This is the startling question posed by lines 15 and 16: 'find for your sake whose life our idle/Talk has cost, a new language'. Careless talk costs lives. Why? Because the breakdown of communication leads to violence. Because chatter distracts from real issues. Because thoughtless words hurt, and hurt provokes retaliation. Because violence, a form of communication in itself, is a rejection of dialogue. A 'new language' is required. Poetry? Certainly the world needs to be 'woken' to the need for real communication through language, to the horrible consequences of failing to sustain that communication, and the child's death should be the impetus to that awareness: 'Sleep in a world your final sleep has woken.'

MAKE

(i) The terms that are used throughout will tell you that this is a poem about expression and communication – 'lullaby … cry … names … idiom … talk … language'. Working from the details in the poem, what do you think are the differences between using sounds to 'express' (such as 'cry') and using sounds to 'communicate' (such as 'talk')?

(ii) To a large extent, the poem is deliberately built on apparent contradictions, known as paradoxes – unreason and reason, rhythm and discord, sleep and woken. Explain each of these contradictions and comment on why you think Boland has very obviously chosen this device.

The Famine Road

'Idle as trout in light Colonel Jones
these Irish, give them no coins at all; their bones
need toil, their characters no less.' Trevelyan's
seal blooded the deal table. The Relief
Committee deliberated: 'Might it be safe,   5
Colonel, to give them roads, roads to force
from nowhere, going nowhere of course?'

> *one out of every ten and then*
> *another third of those again*
> *women – in a case like yours.*   10

Sick, directionless they worked fork, stick
were iron years away; after all could
they not blood their knuckles on rock, suck
April hailstones for water and for food?
Why for that, cunning as housewives, each eyed –   15
as if at a corner butcher – the other's buttock.

> *anything may have caused it, spores,*
> *a childhood accident; one sees*
> *day after day these mysteries.*

Dusk: they will work tomorrow without him.   20
They know it and walk clear. He has become
a typhoid pariah, his blood tainted, although
he shares it with some there. No more than snow
attends its own flakes where they settle
and melt, will they pray by his death rattle.   25

> *You never will, never you know*
> *but take it well woman, grow*
> *your garden, keep house, good-bye.*

'It has gone better than we expected, Lord
Trevelyan, sedition, idleness, cured   30
in one; from parish to parish, field to field;
the wretches work till they are quiet worn,
then fester by their work; we march the corn
to the ships in peace. This Tuesday I saw bones
out of my carriage window. Your servant Jones.'   35

> *Barren, never to know the load*
> *of his child in you, what is your body*
> *now if not a famine road?*

Glossary

[title] **The Famine:** the Great Irish Famine, the Great Hunger, caused initially by potato blight, occurred in Ireland between 1845 and 1848, though its effects lasted until 1851, and reduced the population by 25 per cent

[1] **Colonel Jones:** Chairman of the Irish Board of Works

[3] **Trevelyan:** Charles E. Trevelyan was Secretary for Ireland during the Great Famine, with overall political responsibility; he described the famine as 'a direct stroke of an all-wise Providence'

[4–5] **Relief Committee:** government organisation set up with the initial intention of helping famine victims

[22] **typhoid:** infectious bacterial fever, often fatal

[22] **pariah:** outcast

[30] **sedition:** rebellion

ANALYSE

Poetry

As with much of Boland's poetry, 'The Famine Road' has a context in Irish history. The reader needs to familiarise themselves with the background in order to appreciate fully the worlds created by the poem.

There are actually *two* famine roads in the poem: one printed in regular type and the other in italics, one from the past and the other in the present, one describing the destitution of the population between 1845 and 1851 and the other capturing the despair of an infertile woman in contemporary Ireland. The form of the poem consists of switching back and forth between the two. We'll consider each separately and then combine them again.

The poem opens with the sound of the callous, indifferent voice of Trevelyan, instructing one of his military commanders, Colonel Jones, who sits on the Relief Committee. Comparing the Irish to trout lazing in sunny waters – the image is not only of creatures rather than humans, but also of something to be caught and put to use – he insists that they should not be given any charity, that hard labour – 'toil' – is the only cure for idleness. Boland imagines him sitting at a wooden table – 'deal' is a type of wood – on which a dead seal bleeds, an obvious image of mass slaughter. Instead of charitable relief, Trevelyan insists that the Irish must work for their assistance, and since there is no productive work available, they can work just for the sake of working, by building roads 'from nowhere, going nowhere'.

The second section of the 1845–1851 narrative describes the poor wretches who were forced to slave on these absurd roads. Physically ill, without direction and without proper tools, they are reduced to subsisting on 'hailstones' for both food and water. Here, Boland takes the callous voice of the opening stanza and deliberately exaggerates it, imagining it declaring, 'could/they not blood their knuckles on rock …?' – in other words, even if they lack the necessary tools, surely they could use their hands, their knuckles, to break the rock. It goes on to speculate that they will survive on rainwater, and therefore won't need fresh water carried to them, and that they're so greedy and vicious, that they'll inevitably descend to cannibalism, eyeing the backsides of those around them as if they were picking a cut of meat in a butcher's.

In the third section of the Great Famine narrative, there is an exploration of how cruelty breeds cruelty, how extreme suffering strips away the humanity and compassion of its victims. One of the work party becomes infected with typhoid. The others 'know it' – they recognise the symptoms – and they 'walk clear', which literally means that they avoid the sufferer, but the word 'clear' holds many suggestions, including cleanliness, health and a clear conscience, none of which any of the others could possibly have in reality. He becomes a 'pariah', a social outcast, ironically among social outcasts. Some of those who shun him are his blood relatives – 'he shares it [his blood] with some there' – but still, they treat him with the indifference that melting, or dying, snowflakes have for each other.

In the final section, Colonel Jones reports to Trevelyan on the success of the scheme. According to him, it achieves all its original objectives, in fact goes 'better than we expected'. You might think that in a famine, the primary objective is to feed people. Not among those English who governed Ireland at the time. The aims of the project were to eliminate rebellion, to punish the local population for the 'idleness' that brought about their starving in the first place, to eliminate unwanted and not very useful people, and, by all of this, to create the conditions whereby food could be exported from the country for profit instead of being used to feed the starving. All these aims are splendidly realised, although the speaker seems completely unaware that they have turned Ireland into a mass graveyard, which is what is suggested by the final image: 'This Tuesday I saw bones/out of my carriage window.'

A sterile project eliminates the possibility of a future. Such is the concept that links the two narratives in the poem.

In the second narrative, in the italicised stanzas, a woman visits a gynaecologist and is rather coldly informed that she is infertile and is told to keep her mind off it by keeping herself busy with gardening and housework. The parallels between the two narratives are obvious enough. In both, the male voice is callous, indifferent, uncaring. Both are unconcerned about the fate of the victims. It was estimated that one in ten of the population died during the Great Famine, and it is estimated that '*one out of every ten*' women is infertile. In both narratives, the experts are completely uninterested in discovering the *causes* of the problem – '*anything may have caused it*', the gynaecologist says with impatient indifference. In both, the 'solution' is pointless work – building the road going nowhere or preoccupation with repetitive domestic chores. The final lines offer a direct analogy between the infertile woman and the victims of the Great Famine – '*what is your body/now if not a famine road?*'

MAKE

(i) Visually, the form of the poem is very clear, as it alternates between past and present. However, Boland has been criticised for this analogy between the mass suffering of famine victims and the private suffering of an infertile woman. The question is not whether the comparison is justified, outside the terms of the poem itself, but whether it illuminates something about each form of suffering. What is your opinion? Does the analogy work?

(ii) The imagery of sickness dominates the poem – physical, psychological, spiritual, social. Identify the examples. Trevelyan was certain that this sickness was caused by laziness – 'idle' is the opening word – but what, in your opinion, is the poem's suggestion?

READ

The Shadow Doll

(This was sent to the bride-to-be in Victorian times,
by her dressmaker. It consisted of a porcelain doll,
under a dome of glass, modelling the proposed
wedding dress.)

They stitched blooms from the ivory tulle
to hem the oyster gleam of the veil.
They made hoops for the crinoline.

Now, in summary and neatly sewn –
a porcelain bride in an airless glamour –   5
the shadow doll survives its occasion.

Under glass, under wraps, it stays
even now, after all, discreet about
visits, fevers, quickenings and lusts

and just how, when she looked at   10
the shell-tone spray of seed pearls,
the bisque features, she could see herself

inside it all, holding less than real
stephanotis, rose petals, never feeling
satin rise and fall with the vows   15

I kept repeating on the night before –
astray among the cards and wedding gifts –
the coffee pots and the clocks and

the battered tan case full of cotton
lace and tissue-paper, pressing down, then   20
pressing down again. And then, locks.

Glossary

[1] **tulle:** a very fine netting used for veils and dresses

[3] **crinoline:** a stiffened petticoat used to make a long dress stand out

[11] **seed pearls:** very small pearls

[12] **bisque:** unglazed, biscuit-coloured porcelain

[14] **stephanotis:** a Madagascan climbing plant with waxy white flowers

As in many of Boland's poems, the contemplation of an object from history leads here to comparisons between present and past, to reflections on women's experiences and to considering the object as a symbolic image offering a meaning deeper than the one originally intended.

The first stanza concentrates on the techniques used to create and arrange the doll's wedding dress, which, as the author's note explains, was a miniature version of the dress that the actual bride would wear. The dressmakers stitched flowers from the white silk to make a decorative hem for the veil over the bride's head and made hoops to fit inside the crinoline dress, so that it would hang properly, billowing outwards. The emphasis is on two things: prettiness and constriction.

Consider the images of restriction for a moment, as they appear at the beginning, innocently enough, and as they are developed through the poem: 'stitched … hem … hoops … neatly sewn … Under glass, under wraps … pressing down, then/pressing down again … And then, locks.' The doll is encased, trapped inside its little glass dome, where light and life cannot tarnish it; and the obvious suggestion is that the actual bride, because she can 'see herself/inside it all', is trapped inside her little marriage, obliged only to look good and not live, certainly not stray outside the cage. The prettiness is artificial. It is certainly there for everyone to see – the material is 'tulle', or fine silk, the veil gleams, there are 'pearls' and flowers, and everything is beautifully detailed and 'neatly sewn' – but none of it is real. The 'glamour' is 'airless'. That is, it survives only because it is not allowed to breathe, because no contaminating air is allowed into the chamber. The bride doll is mere 'porcelain'. The flowers are 'less than real'. The whole thing is a 'shadow'. But the greatest price that the doll/bride pays for preserving her prettiness is that she is struck dumb, she is mute, she is denied a voice of her own. Now, for a woman writer, this is clearly the most significant deprivation, and clearly far too high a price to pay for male approval of visual female beauty. The doll is 'discreet'. That is, she keeps her mouth shut, says nothing. She is unable to use language to express or explore her own emotional life, her illnesses, or 'fevers', her pregnancy, or 'quickenings', when she feels the child move inside her, her desires, or 'lusts', and her 'visits', which must be a polite word, a euphemism, for menstruation.

The doll's muteness, and by extension the inability of the middle-class Victorian woman to describe and thereby to control her own life, is brilliantly contrasted with Boland's own independence as a modern woman, since the doll never felt 'satin rise and fall with the vows/I kept repeating on the night before' – she never felt her clothes move with the breathing

required to consciously and voluntarily articulate a commitment to a lover, or husband. These are the thoughts and emotions that Boland herself can give voice to on the eve of her own wedding, as she sits among the other wedding gifts and good luck cards, where the shadow doll, in its battered old case and still protectively wrapped, is also visible, until Boland closes the lid, pressing it down, and then locking it. The gesture, the *choice*, indicates the fundamental difference between the Victorian woman and the modern woman in the poem. One was inside the glass dome, let us say; the other was outside. One was treated as a doll, the other laid claim to her independence.

MAKE

(i) Throughout the poem, there's an implied contrast between the life of the Victorian bride and the life of the modern bride who is the author. Work out some of the details.

(ii) This poem is a detailed description of an historical object. But the language chosen to describe something can either be neutral or thought-provoking. Pick out some of the intentionally thought-provoking expressions in this poem and comment on what they're designed to make the reader think about.

Poetry

White Hawthorn in the West of Ireland

I drove West
in the season between seasons.
I left behind suburban gardens.
Lawnmowers. Small talk.

Under low skies, past splashes of coltsfoot,   5
I assumed
the hard shyness of Atlantic light
and the superstitious aura of hawthorn.

All I wanted then was to fill my arms with
sharp flowers,   10
to seem, from a distance, to be part of
that ivory, downhill rush. But I knew,

I had always known
the custom was
not to touch hawthorn.   15
Not to bring it indoors for the sake of

the luck
such constraint would forfeit –
a child might die, perhaps, or an unexplained
fever speckle heifers. So I left it   20

stirring on those hills
with a fluency
only water has. And, like water, able
to re-define land. And free to seem to be –

for anglers,   25
and for travellers astray in
the unmarked lights of a May dusk –
the only language spoken in those parts.

Glossary

[5] **coltsfoot:** plant of the daisy family with yellow flowers, used in herbal medicine

[8] **aura:** distinctive atmosphere generated by something

ANALYSE

Like many of Boland's poems, this one is an exploration of making connections with the past, with the history of Ireland, its authentic heritage, its richer, more mysterious life that is threatened by modernity. The exploration is expressed in the poem as a physical journey: 'I drove West', it opens. In Ireland, the West – Galway, the Gaeltacht, Kerry and the rest – has a particular social and historical significance, since it is where native Irish culture is still at its strongest. Boland then travels from the tame, bland world of modern Ireland in which she normally resides – 'suburban gardens./Lawnmowers. Small talk' – towards … well, let's discover what.

Not only is its destination significant, but the timing of the journey is vitally important. She sets out 'in the season between seasons', that is, the period between spring and summer, or the festival of Bealtaine (May) in Irish, when the arrival of summer was heralded by bonfires and celebrations. The hawthorn tree is one of the sacred trees of witchcraft and in Irish folklore is also referred to as the fairy bush. It was considered bad luck to cut it for fear of offending the fairies that inhabit the tree. However, during the May Day celebrations the collecting of the sprigs and flowers was allowed for use in the festivities, after which they were placed in the home to banish all evil influences.

As she travels West – 'under low skies' and past 'coltsfoot' – it is this tradition that she is reaching towards. The meaning of 'the … aura of hawthorn' is obvious from the explanations above, and the 'Atlantic light' is the unique appearance of the sea on the West coast, which she tries to capture with the phrase 'hard shyness', suggesting a combined strength and delicacy.

Her enthusiasm almost overcomes her and her inclination is to throw herself into the hawthorn, 'to seem, from a distance, to be part' of it. But she is not just an ignorant tourist. She is aware of the customs, and of the removal of luck that such mistreatment would bring, the death of a child, the sickness of a herd of cattle. The suggestion seems to be that luck is a natural condition and can only be damaged by evil human behaviour, which is a nice thought. So she leaves the hawthorn as it is, untouched, untainted by her 'suburban' arms. And surely that is the only authentic way to re-enter one's historical heritage, by leaving it intact and respecting it?

The final two stanzas offer a celebration of the hawthorn in its element, the symbol of the real 'West' of Ireland, of the real Ireland. Blossoming white on the hillsides, it seems to flow down them like water, 'with a fluency/only water has'. Like water, it too changes or redefines land, a natural force moulding the very shape of the country. It is 'free to seem to be', to represent something greater and deeper than what it actually is. This is the point of selecting the hawthorn as a metaphor in the first place: it represents the 'West'. It represents it in a way that only an image, a symbol, a metaphor can, that is, in a way that is superior to ordinary, rational language. That is why it is 'the only language spoken in those parts'. It is a type of poetry, in other words; the poetry of the landscape of Ireland.

Poetry

MAKE

(i) Many of Boland's poems, including this one, use the term 'language' in relation to things that cannot actually speak, such as the hawthorn here. What do you think she intends by this, specifically in relation to the hawthorn?

(ii) It has been said that Boland 'employs landscape to express the complexity of experience'. Here she uses it to contrast two parts of Ireland, maybe even two types of Ireland – suburban Dublin and the West. Pick out the details.

READ

Outside History

There are outsiders, always. These stars –
these iron inklings of an Irish January,
whose light happened

thousands of years before
our pain did: they are, they have always been   5
outside history.

They keep their distance. Under them remains
a place where you found
you were human, and

a landscape in which you know you are mortal.   10
And a time to choose between them.
I have chosen:

out of myth into history I move to be
part of that ordeal
whose darkness is   15

only now reaching me from those fields,
those rivers, those roads clotted as
firmaments with the dead.

How slowly they die
as we kneel beside them, whisper in their ear.   20
And we are too late. We are always too late.

Glossary

[18] **firmaments:** the heavens, the sky

ANALYSE

This poem is quite difficult to 'explain', but if it's read with any attention, it gives rise to fascinating questions about what the past means to us and how we should look at the past. For the sake of clarity, its theme can be reduced to this: the stars are outside history, inhuman, indifferent to the suffering of man; Boland chooses to be inside history, human, responding to the suffering of man.

The first part of the poem is clearly about outsiders: 'There are outsiders, always.' But surely there's more than one type of outsider – there are rebels, for instance, who *want* to be outsiders; and social outcasts, who don't; and the neglected, who don't either; and those who deliberately remain aloof from the needs of others – and the poem has yet to show us which types it will explore.

Poetry

'These stars' seems to suggest that they will be considered first as 'outsiders'. Boland describes them as 'inklings' – intimations or suggestions – 'of an Irish January', because when they were born, long, long ago, the January night on which she sees them didn't yet exist; in other words, their 'light happened', or they were born, 'thousands of years before'. For two reasons, they are therefore indifferent to the 'pain' of human existence: the pain didn't yet exist when they were born, and they're already dead by the time the pain comes into being. They are therefore 'outside' human history. They simply don't exist at the same time as humans. Their light takes thousands of years to reach us, and when it does, the stars are already dead; so their light is a false image. There's no point looking to them for guidance, is there? 'They keep their distance.'

They have nothing to say to us, but still, there is a life 'under them' – man's life on earth – which Boland startlingly presents as two possibilities: discover your own humanity, or die – 'a place where you found/you were human, and/a landscape in which you know you are mortal'. Each human being has a choice between these two, making contact with the wider human community, which is presented as a discovery you must make at some particular point in your life, and staying aloof, to extinguish alone, like the stars, which is presented as a continuous knowledge of your own isolation. Boland asserts: 'I have chosen'.

The language of the next stanza makes her decision explicit. She rejects the false light of 'myth', of standing outside history, of distorting the past. Now, the Irish have many ways of distorting the past, whether by romanticising the 'national struggle', venerating the supposedly 'Celtic', suppressing the voices of victims, or whipping up hatred for the supposedly brutal English … and one imagines that many of these are included, by suggestion, in that term 'myth'. Instead of 'myth', she opts for 'history', for making the effort to know and understand what actually happened, to attend to the 'darkness' of what was suppressed rather than to the things that were officially illuminated. That darkness contains the 'ordeal', or struggles, of countless people – as numerous as the stars, actually, or 'clotted as/firmaments', as packed as the skies – whose voices reach us only now, when it is too late, when we cannot help them – the 'kneel beside them, whisper in their ear' is a gesture of assistance, of comfort. But even if we cannot comfort them, if we 'are always too late' for that, at least we can attend to them. Boland's way of attending to the past, of course, is by writing about it. And it does feature as a central theme in many of her poems. She does, indeed, write 'history' and not 'myth'.

(i) Boland writes here, 'I have chosen: out of myth into history'. Examine what she means by 'myth' and 'history' and then take any other Boland poem that, in your opinion, supports or questions her claim.

(ii) This poem largely consists of a series of literal statements, but it is also very rich in suggestiveness. Take any of the statements – 'they have always been/outside history', for instance, or 'We are always too late' – and explore its possible meanings.

READ

The Black Lace Fan my Mother Gave me

It was the first gift he ever gave her,
buying it for five francs in the Galeries
in pre-war Paris. It was stifling.
A starless drought made the nights stormy.

They stayed in the city for the summer.   5
They met in cafés. She was always early.
He was late. That evening he was later.
They wrapped the fan. He looked at his watch.

She looked down the Boulevard des Capucines.
She ordered more coffee. She stood up.   10
The streets were emptying. The heat was killing.
She thought the distance smelled of rain and lightning.

These are wild roses, appliqued on silk by hand,
darkly picked, stitched boldly, quickly.
The rest is tortoiseshell and has the reticent,   15
clear patience of its element. It is

a worn-out, underwater bullion and it keeps,
even now, an inference of its violation.
The lace is overcast as if the weather
it opened for and offset had entered it.   20

The past is an empty café terrace.
An airless dusk before thunder. A man running.
And no way now to know what happened then –
none at all – unless, of course, you improvise:

The blackbird on this first sultry morning,   25
in summer, finding buds, worms, fruit,
feels the heat. Suddenly she puts out her wing –
the whole, full, flirtatious span of it.

Glossary

[2] **Galeries:** a network of historical shopping arcades in Paris

[9] **Boulevard des Capucines:** one of the four 'grands boulevards' of Paris, subject of a wonderful painting by the impressionist Claude Monet in 1873.

[13] **appliqued:** literally 'put on', from the French for 'stitch on'

[17] **bullion:** gold and silver before coining

ANALYSE

If you read the opening line – 'It was the first gift he ever gave her' – immediately after reading the title – 'The Black Lace Fan my Mother Gave me' – the insights, reflections and experiences of this poem are instantly revealed: the connections through personal history between one generation and another, and between present and past; the different forms of love; the different gestures of love; the significance of objects; the meaning of gifts; the passing of time.

A woman contemplates a delicate object that holds the key to her existence, perhaps even the key to her personality and character.

It is a black lace fan, the first gift that her father gave to her mother in the early days of their courtship in pre-1939 Paris after buying it for five francs, not a small sum at the time, in a store called Galeries Lafayette. Looking at it, she imagines the circumstances in which the gift was bought, offered and accepted, and she dramatises the events of that distant day. She uses the weather as imagery to create an oppressive, intense atmosphere – 'stifling' heat and 'stormy' nights – and the staccato sound patterns of very short sentences – 'That evening he was later./ They wrapped the fan.' – to capture the tension, the urgency, the uncertainty of the moment.

The stages of the little drama are very easy to understand, and might be somewhat amusing, except for the sense of a larger threat looming over the lovers, a sense of impending disaster created by the imagery of the overhanging storm, and particularly by the line 'She thought the distance smelled of rain and lightning.' We are suddenly reminded that this is 'pre-war Paris'. We remember that the German word for their army's offensive strategy in the Second World War was 'Blitzkrieg', literally 'lightning war'. The city, and the lovers, are threatened with annihilation. How fragile life, and love, are.

As if prompted by this reflection, the poem now returns from recreating the past to considering the fan again. The imagery is highly suggestive. The 'wild roses' that are 'appliqued' into the silk material of the fan capture the apparently wild romance of that summer in Paris; and even the technique that the embroiderer used – 'stitched boldly, quickly' – reflects the intense, hurried nature of the affair. The handle of the fan is made from the shell of a tortoise and retains the reticence, or restraint, and 'patience' of that creature. How do restraint and patience sit with intense and hurried? Well, think about it. Two people under pressure because of events beyond their control, and yet gentle, even a little shy with each other.

Poetry

The fan is old – 'worn-out' – but treasured, because, like an 'underwater bullion' it holds the treasures of the past, although it also holds the troubles of that past, a suggestion – or 'inference' – of the violence both in its original manufacture, because a tortoise had to die to make it, and in the circumstances surrounding its purchase as a gift, when Paris was threatened by war. The cloud of war hanging over the city is retained in the blackness of the lace pattern, which looks like 'overcast … weather'.

The fan speaks of the past, but only of that particular moment and not of what happened afterwards: 'And no way now to know what happened then'. What happened afterwards can only be imagined by the daughter of those two lovers, and through her and her poem, by us. That is what is meant by 'improvise' here, to imagine, to guess. As a poet, Boland offers us, not an analysis, but a metaphor. The metaphor comes to her through the sight of a blackbird cooling itself by spreading its wing … rather like the opening of a fan, rather like the opening of a woman's heart to the possibility of love, the possibility of a future together, the possibility of marriage, the possibility of children: 'Suddenly she puts out her wing – the whole, full, flirtatious span of it.' Who is the 'she' here? The blackbird? The lover in Paris? The fan? Well, all three together. That's why metaphor is better than analysis; it can hold much, much more at the one time.

MAKE

(i) Romantic love is the central subject of this poem. Taking the blackbird, the weather, the gift and the approaching war into account, discuss how it is presented.

(ii) The fan holds the notions of delicacy, shyness, romance, threat and violence. Pick out the images that suggest each of these.

READ

This Moment

A neighbourhood.
At dusk.

Things are getting ready
to happen
out of sight.   5

Stars and moths.
And rinds slanting around fruit.

But not yet.

One tree is black.
One window is yellow as butter.   10

A woman leans down to catch a child
who has run into her arms
this moment.

Stars rise.
Moths flutter.   15
Apples sweeten in the dark.

ANALYSE

'This Moment', as the title suggests, freezes a moment in time – as if a snapshot was taken, or a movie paused – and then releases it again. Because the moment is so beautiful – at its centre is the tender embrace of mother and child – the effect is complex; it makes one feel both appreciative and sad. Appreciative, because the stilled image holds much of what is best in human beings – gentleness, protectiveness, affection, innocence, warmth. Sad, because – as the poem records – such moments do not last. Perfection cannot be preserved. Happiness cannot be safeguarded. Innocence cannot be kept. Time keeps moving on. Time ages everything. Although the final image – 'Apples sweeten in the dark' – is one of growth and fertility, it contains the germ of its own decay, since those same apples will soon ripen and fall. The three images in the final stanza are very interesting, because they offer different concepts of time – the 'stars' which rise in the sky come to us from a long time ago and are already extinguished, they are 'outside history', as another Boland poem puts it; 'moths' are far more fragile, suggested by the precarious sound of 'flutter', and also have far briefer life spans; the 'apples' are seasonal and extend over a portion of a year, from buds in spring to fall in autumn. Each thing has a different time scale; and, of course, if you look back at the two humans in the previous stanza – one adult, one child – you will notice now that each has a different length of time ahead of them. So the poem brilliantly captures a perfect moment – this moment – but in the full awareness that such perfection is fleeting.

Poetry

The brilliance of the poem's snapshot is in the everyday detail selected and in the sense of anticipation, almost of suspended tension, created by the form of the poem, particularly in the first two stanzas. The short lines contribute to the drama. So does the setting, the half-light transition from day to 'dusk'. So does the general air of vague mystery – it's 'a neighbourhood' rather than a specific place, and the splendidly imprecise and slightly worrying 'things' are about to happen. Night-time movement, a little menacing, cloaked in darkness – 'rinds slanting around fruit' – is promised, but then suspended: 'But not yet.'

The final details are sketched in to complete the landscape – a tree in darkness, a lighted window, as homely as 'butter' – and that wonderful, central image of the child running from darkness towards light, from the street to home, from concrete into her mother's soft arms. The pair are frozen in mid-movement – the woman leaning down, the child running upwards – for a moment. It's a beautiful, but artificial, moment, that only a poem, or a photograph, or a painting, or some artistic representation, can capture. And this poem does immortalise it, while at the same time noting that life itself has moved beyond it – 'Stars rise …'

(i) The 'moment' occurs at dusk. Describe the character of this period between day and night, as captured in the poem, and comment on its significance.

(ii) Boland has been praised for her ability to capture a dramatic scene. Identify any feature in this poem that helps to create drama or tension.

MAKE

READ

Poetry

The Pomegranate

The only legend I have ever loved is
the story of a daughter lost in hell.
And found and rescued there.
Love and blackmail are the gist of it.
Ceres and Persephone the names.   5
And the best thing about the legend is
I can enter it anywhere. And have.
As a child in exile in
a city of fogs and strange consonants,
I read it first and at first I was   10
an exiled child in the crackling dusk of
the underworld, the stars blighted. Later
I walked out in a summer twilight
searching for my daughter at bed-time.
When she came running I was ready   15
to make any bargain to keep her.
I carried her back past whitebeams
and wasps and honey-scented buddleias.
But I was Ceres then and I knew
winter was in store for every leaf   20
on every tree on that road.
Was inescapable for each one we passed.
And for me.
                  It is winter
and the stars are hidden.   25
I climb the stairs and stand where I can see
my child asleep beside her teen magazines,
her can of Coke, her plate of uncut fruit.
The pomegranate! How did I forget it?
She could have come home and been safe   30
and ended the story and all
our heart-broken searching but she reached
out a hand and plucked a pomegranate.
She put out her hand and pulled down
the French sound for apple and   35
the noise of stone and the proof
that even in the place of death,
at the heart of legend, in the midst
of rocks full of unshed tears
ready to be diamonds by the time   40
the story was told, a child can be
hungry. I could warn her. There is still a chance.
The rain is cold. The road is flint-coloured.
The suburb has cars and cable television.
The veiled stars are above ground.   45
It is another world. But what else
can a mother give her daughter but such

beautiful rifts in time?
If I defer the grief I will diminish the gift.
The legend will be hers as well as mine.   50
She will enter it. As I have.
She will wake up. She will hold
the papery flushed skin in her hand.
And to her lips. I will say nothing.

Glossary

[5] **Ceres:** Roman goddess of agriculture; see ANALYSE panel

[5] **Persephone:** daughter of Ceres; see ANALYSE panel

[18] **buddleias:** a cultivated shrub with fragrant flowers

[48] **rifts:** breaks, splits, openings in the ground

ANALYSE

This poem both illustrates and explains Boland's use of myths and legends as metaphor and explores many of the recurring themes of her work, such as our doomed efforts to control life's natural forces within a domestic order, the relationships between different generations of women, and motherhood.

Ceres, the goddess of the earth, was the mother of Persephone. After Persephone was abducted by her uncle, Hades, Ceres wandered the world in search of her. Life on earth came to a standstill during this period, until she pleaded with Zeus, the father of the gods, who instructed Hades to return Persephone. But before she was released, Hades tricked Persephone into eating pomegranate seeds, which forced her to return to the underworld for one month each year for every seed that she ate. It was summer on earth when she was with her mother, and winter when she was underground again.

It's clear that this 'story of a daughter lost in hell' holds a deep personal significance for Boland. It weaves through her entire life, offering different reflections at different times, from when she was a child with a mother, to when she was a mother with a daughter. This is why she can 'enter it anywhere'.

Her own first contact with the legend was 'as a child' in London – 'city of fogs' because it was notoriously foggy, mainly from burning coal in the old days. She immediately identified with it, seeing herself as Persephone in the underworld. Being Irish, she was exiled in London, trapped, and unable to see home. At a much later stage in her life, when she was a mother and worried about her daughter being out, she, again, easily identified with the legend, although this time as Ceres, the distraught mother searching for her missing daughter. She is relieved and overjoyed when the girl comes 'running' and she protectively carries the child back home, past the few, rather ironically presented dangers that modern suburbia holds – the whitebeam trees, the stinging wasps, the ornamental shrubs. But, as Ceres, she knows that a child cannot be protected forever by her mother. She knows that growth is inevitable. Change is the essence of life, and indeed the central theme of this poem: 'I knew/winter was in store for every leaf … Was inescapable … for me'.

When it comes, the change is quite sudden. The next section begins: 'It is winter'. Present tense. It has already arrived. Time flies. The child is already a teenager. Already on the verge of growing up, and growing away from her mother. And what represents that inevitable departure? The pomegranate, of course, lying on a plate, not yet cut, so not yet eaten, but inescapable.

For a moment, the protective mother imagines her daughter always remaining a child, never growing away from her. The child could have returned home safely, and stayed at home safely, but somewhere along the way, she plucked the fruit. Boland presents the symbol of the fruit, not as knowledge itself, but as a hunger for knowledge, a hunger for experience. That much is obvious from lines 34–42, although some of the details can be a little difficult to grasp here. As I see it, the child, in pulling down the pomegranate, destroys walls and barriers and dwellings, hence 'the noise of stone', kills off her own innocent childhood in the act, sheds tears for the loss, but will be grateful for it later – so the 'unshed tears' will turn into 'diamonds'.

Again, the mother thinks that she could protect her child from growing up: 'I could warn her.' The images of winter and the comforts of suburbia combine to represent both the dangers and the protection: 'rain ... cold' and 'flint-coloured' wet roads on the one hand, 'cars and cable television' on the other. The child is not yet in the underworld, she is still on the earth, still within protected distance, so the 'stars' that she sees are 'above ground' while the underground is 'another world,' a world there is no need to visit.

But the natural desire to protect is overcome by a realisation, expressed as a question. What else do you rear children for except to be independent human beings, like yourself? What can you do, except give them the benefit of your experiences? The poem expresses it, far better, as, 'But what else/can a mother give her daughter but such/beautiful rifts in time?' where 'rifts' means, literally, gaps or breaks, but also, much more suggestively, a backwash from a wave that has just broken. The reason is stated explicitly in the next line, which is one of the most important in the poem: 'If I defer the grief I will diminish the gift.' Growing up brings its own pains along with it, but if you try to protect someone from those pains, then you will prevent them from growing up, from the 'gift' of full humanity. You can't have one without the other. This is reinforced by the image of the daughter, Eve-like, eating the fruit in the final lines – 'She will hold/the papery flushed skin in her hand./And to her lips' – where the sensuality of the pomegranate and of the act of eating it are obvious. And the mother's role at that stage? None. Her role is finished. She has nothing to say. She is silent. 'I will say nothing.' Each daughter must find her own particular way into womanhood.

(i) There are two children featured in the poem – Boland herself as a child in London and her daughter as a child in Dublin. Can you see any differences between the two?

(ii) It was claimed earlier in the textbook that the poetry of Eavan Boland 'employs landscape and everyday items as symbolic imagery to express the complexity of experience, and uses mythology and history as metaphor'. Pick out relevant examples here.

Love

Dark falls on this mid-western town
where we once lived when myths collided.
Dusk has hidden the bridge in the river
which slides and deepens
to become the water   5
the hero crossed on his way to hell.

Not far from here is our old apartment.
We had a kitchen and an Amish table.
We had a view. And we discovered there
love had the feather and muscle of wings   10
and had come to live with us,
a brother of fire and air.

We had two infant children one of whom
was touched by death in this town
and spared: and when the hero   15
was hailed by his comrades in hell
their mouths opened and their voices failed and
there is no knowing what they would have asked
about a life they had shared and lost.

I am your wife.   20
It was years ago.
Our child was healed. We love each other still.
Across our day-to-day and ordinary distances
we speak plainly. We hear each other clearly.

And yet I want to return to you   25
on the bridge of the Iowa river as you were,
with snow on the shoulders of your coat
and a car passing with its headlights on:

I see you as a hero in a text –
the image blazing and the edges gilded –   30
and I long to cry out the epic question
my dear companion:

Will we ever live so intensely again?
Will love come to us again and be
so formidable at rest it offered us ascension   35
even to look at him?

But the words are shadows and you cannot hear me.
You walk away and I cannot follow.

Glossary

[1] **this mid-western town:** Iowa City, USA
[6] **hero:** Odysseus; see ANALYSE panel
[8] **Amish:** a strict Mennonite sect, living mostly in Pennsylvania and Ohio

ANALYSE

The poem opens in a particular moment, on Boland's return to the 'mid-western town' of Iowa City in the United States, where she once lived and worked at the university. It is dusk, the closing of the day, the onset of night, a time of transition. The words are addressed to someone else, or are silently formed in the presence of someone else: 'where we once lived', they say. Born out of one particular moment, the poem recalls another particular time in the history of the same lives, 'when myths collided'. Myths are stories about superhuman beings or wondrous events. We have no idea yet what stories are involved, or how they collided. We are about to find out. In the real town, the descending dusk obscures the bridges over the river, and in Boland's imagination the shadowy river slips, or 'slides', into 'the water/the hero crossed on his way to hell'. The 'hero' here is Odysseus, from Greek legend. After the long siege of Troy, Odysseus was condemned to wandering the earth instead of returning home directly to his beloved wife, Penelope. At one stage, he braves the terrors of the underworld, known as Hades, in an effort to shorten his journey home. Hades was approached by way of the River Styx, hence the reference here to 'the water/the hero crossed on his way to hell'.

It is a poem of love and heroes, and of the passing of time, of long years of separation, of struggle for reunion, of a journey. In it, the mythological love between Odysseus and Penelope intersects with the everyday love between Boland and her husband.

Boland recalls their life together in Iowa and also their love for each other, which she describes as something as graceful, as tender and as powerful as a bird's wings – it had 'the feather and muscle of wings' – something as elemental, as natural and as necessary as 'fire and air'.

It needed to be all of those things to withstand the challenge that life threw at it. While the couple lived in Iowa, one of their two children was 'touched by death' – that is, contracted meningitis, a potentially fatal, life-threatening disease – but was not taken, was 'spared'. In a continuation of the same sentence, the poem now returns to the myth of Odysseus. While in the underworld, the hero tried to communicate with his old dead comrades, but because they had not taken a special potion, they were unable to speak to him. Quite clearly, the anecdote illustrates a breakdown in communication at a certain point between people who had 'shared' a life, but who had drifted apart in some way. But what is its significance here? What does it mean?

In the next stanza, Boland is obviously addressing her husband, just as Odysseus was addressing his comrades: 'I am your wife … We love each other still.' Just as obviously, there is not a breakdown of ordinary communication between them. The lines are quite explicit: 'we speak plainly. We hear each other clearly.' They even stress that 'ordinary', 'day-to-day' communication is healthy.

'And yet' …

Something vital has been lost from that period in the past. 'And yet I want to return …' Something so precious that she would exchange the present for the past, this present moment for that past moment, when her husband stood 'on the bridge of the Iowa river … with snow on the shoulders' of his coat, a figure brilliantly illuminated by the headlights of a passing car, and brilliantly caught in the vivid imagery of the description. Recalling it, she sees him 'as a hero in a text', a man of extraordinary strength and courage and beauty, the offspring of a god. Why? Because he faced down death when it threatened his child? Because he loved as passionately as Odysseus did? But what does it matter? He was, then, a hero. And now? Now, years later, when they have lived together 'day-to-day' and have no more than 'ordinary distances' between them, when they speak, not in the wildness of love, but 'plainly' to each other? What now? Now she longs to 'cry out the epic question': 'Will we ever live so intensely again?'

Threatened by danger, strengthened by love, alert each moment of the day, intently alive to every sensation. Will they ever recapture that? Will they ever again be visited by a love that was so 'formidable', like the heroes of the legends, that even while it was at rest it offered them elevation, flight, 'ascension', just to contemplate it?

But questions of heroic proportions are for heroes to answer; and heroes are things of the past. Many things no longer exist from a golden past, including the intense communication that was possible between the lovers in the early days of their life together. Now, Boland's words, like the words of Odysseus's dumb comrades in hell when they try to speak with him, are mere 'shadows', existing only in the mind. Odysseus turns and walks out of hell, and his comrades, condemned to stay there, cannot follow him. The hero turns and walks out of Boland's presence: 'You walk away and I cannot follow.'

Constructed as eight stanzas of diminishing substance, the form of the poem is wonderful. It opens with the closing of the day and it ends in 'shadows'. It opens with a couple and it ends with two individuals: 'You walk away and I cannot follow.' It opens with a voice holding the present and the past together at once – 'Dark falls … where we once lived' – and it ends with the past having slipped away, leaving only the present. Perhaps the passing of time makes everything 'ordinary' – even heroes, even love, even intensity.

MAKE

(i) This is undoubtedly a poem about love. But is it about the power of romantic love or the power of parental love?

(ii) Consider two things in relation to the form of the poem – the fact that the stanza length decreases from six lines at the beginning to two at the end, and the fact that the past tense and the present tense keep merging into one another throughout – and comment on why you think Boland decided to use them.

The Poetry of Eavan Boland

Themes and Interests

- The poetry of Eavan Boland explores and dramatises different forms of **LOVE** – particularly romantic and parental love – and the gestures of love, such as the kiss and the gift

Sometimes, usually in the early stages of a relationship, romantic love is presented by Boland as intense. Two memorable descriptions are 'feather and muscle of wings … a brother of fire and air' from 'Love' and the very simple 'a man running' from 'The Black Lace Fan my Mother Gave me'. The first metaphor brilliantly captures everything about romantic love in its early stages: its vigour, its energy, but its tenderness too, its danger, its ability to lift you up as if on wings. In the second poem, Boland imagines her mother and father when they were young. Their meeting is on the point of failure. And then, suddenly, 'a man running'. One can see the scene perfectly – the urgency, the beginning of an argument, the acceptance of the gift – and one can imagine the rest, which is what the poem allows us to do. Both poems blend and contrast a woman's relationship with her lover and a woman's relationship with her children. Originally intended as an expression of sexual love, the black lace fan is now valued as an expression of maternal love. In poems such as 'This Moment' and 'The Pomegranate', as well as 'Love', parental love is, above all, protective. Darkness is descending, or illness is threatening, or the complexities of growing up are encroaching … but in each case the parent takes up a position that is in the child's best interest. It is dusk in 'This Moment', 'things are getting ready to happen out of sight' and a child is not yet home, until 'a woman leans down to catch' it and gather it into safety.

- The poetry of Eavan Boland presents **HISTORY** and the past as forces that shape the present, particularly in the connections between different generations of women

A great deal of Boland's poetry seems to suggest a kind of unbroken thread linking one generation of women with another. In 'The Famine Road', which deals with the project of constructing useless roads to keep the starving people occupied during the Great Famine of 1845–1848, a barren woman is compared to the famine road itself, a life going nowhere, with no one to take up its thread in the future. The poem that most explicitly makes this link between generations of women its main theme is 'The Pomegranate'. This is why history is so vital in Boland's poetry. To know who you are, you need to know where you came from, who your people are. If you are 'outside history', as in the poem of that title, you are like a star, solitary, indifferent, without identity. So, poems such as 'Love', 'The Pomegranate' and 'The Black Lace Fan my Mother Gave me' explore personal history, 'The Shadow Doll' blends personal history with the social history of women, and 'The Famine Road', 'White Hawthorn in the West of Ireland', 'The War Horse' and 'Child of our Time' draw on Irish national history.

- The poetry of Eavan Boland explores the complexities of **FEMALE EXPERIENCE**, including **MOTHERHOOD**, and particularly the tension between a mother's need to protect her child and the child's struggle for independence

In 'The Pomegranate', although she knows that 'winter was in store for every leaf on every tree on that road', in other words that time has its own unavoidable rhythm, the mother is tempted to try to prevent her child growing away from her. 'I could warn her', she prompts herself. A similar protective instinct is explored in the short poem 'This Moment'. But Boland knows that things will inevitably move on, that each girl will in time become a woman. In the poetry, female experience is by no means confined to motherhood, although this is a central element. Both 'The Shadow Doll' and 'The Famine Road' explore the experience of women in a male-dominated society. The former dramatises the constrictions of women who were treated as dolls, objects of visual beauty, while the latter dramatises the callousness of treating women merely as reproductive machines. The woman as lover and daughter is featured in both 'Love' and 'The Black Lace Fan my Mother Gave me'. Boland's poetry therefore explores themes and describes situations that are part of every modern woman's life, but that are not really part of traditional poetry. They include reflections on what life is like for a woman in modern Ireland and what life was like for Irish women in earlier times, on the relationships between different generations of women, and on domesticity.

- The poetry of Eavan Boland examines how we try to contain life within a **DOMESTIC** order and how the forces of nature can threaten, disrupt or destroy this

Boland knows that no matter what we build, the natural forces of life will eventually disrupt it. This awareness prevents her poetry from ever becoming sentimental. It is present in much of her work on the Leaving Certificate course. Even the fan she was given by her mother, in 'The Black Lace Fan my Mother Gave me', 'keeps ... an inference of its violation', because the death of a creature was required to make its tortoiseshell. Death itself threatens the family in 'Love' and the horror of modern violence is captured through the senseless death of a child in 'Child of our Time'. The poem that most directly explores it is 'The War Horse'. In a new Dublin suburb, a stray horse tramples over a carefully sown domestic garden, stirring comparisons with English destruction of Irish land in the past, while the anxious neighbours 'use the subterfuge of curtains'. The horse, 'loosed from its daily tether', is presented as a destructive force, threatening suburbia, like a war threatening civilisation. Against it stand the flimsy defences of flowers and hedges. And that is how vulnerable, how fragile, and how precious, civilised human life is. Famine destroys it in 'The Famine Road', bombs shatter it in 'Child of our Time', and time threatens it in 'The Pomegranate'.

Style and Viewpoint

- The poetry of Eavan Boland is cerebral, which means that its **LANGUAGE** deliberately engages the intelligence rather than the emotions or the instincts

Because Boland always critically examines the experiences featured in her poems, instead of simply responding to them emotionally, her style of writing can be quite demanding. Sometimes, it's like watching a complex mind concentrating. It's not that her vocabulary is obscure or her expression deliberately difficult; rather that her language invites contemplation, deliberation. 'The War Horse' is a good example to start with. The reflections in the poem, particularly of the horse symbolising the English destruction of Irish homesteads, could hardly have popped into her mind as she was nervously watching the animal. They must be the result of days, months, even years of absorbing and considering the experience.

You might notice that many of the personal experiences in some of the other poems occurred in a distant past. 'The Black Lace Fan my Mother Gave me' has layers of historical time, going right back to 1939, when her parents were in Paris, and five years before her own birth. 'The Famine Road' is set in both mid-nineteenth century Ireland and modern Ireland, 'The Shadow Doll' in Victorian England and modern Ireland, 'Love' in a return visit to Iowa years after a traumatic event that occurred there. In all of these, there's a deliberate attempt to distance the material, so that it can be contemplated. Although always grounded in real and very common experiences, and often those that are highly charged emotionally, the subject matter of her poetry is the *significance* of these experiences, sometimes only discovered years after the events themselves. Her reflections, particularly on so-called ordinary events, make us more aware of the depth of meaning in them. Her use of language is intended to promote that awareness.

- The poetry of Eavan Boland employs landscape and everyday items as symbolic **IMAGERY** to express the complexity of experience, and uses mythology and history as metaphor

'The Pomegranate' both illustrates and explains Boland's use of myths and legends as metaphors and symbols, which is one of the most characteristic features of her work. It illustrates it because it uses the story of Ceres and Persephone to explore a theme. It explains it because it is obvious that from a very early age Boland drew on the classical legends as a means of interpreting, understanding and ordering her own experiences. 'Love' employs the Odysseus myth to similar effect, and mythology, legend and folklore are also present in both 'The War Horse' and 'White Hawthorn in the West of Ireland'. The use of mythology is one of her main devices for revealing the profound in the ordinary, in the act of bending down to look into a washing machine or going out to call her children home at dusk, in 'my ordinary future as a woman', as she puts it in her autobiographical book *Object Lessons*, from which the two examples are taken. 'White Hawthorn in the West of Ireland' uses landscape to contrast modern suburban Dublin with the wilder country west of the Shannon, and to suggest differences in value systems and philosophies; and landscape is also an essential symbolic feature of almost all the poems on the Leaving Certificate course, particularly 'The War Horse', 'The Famine Road', 'The Black Lace Fan my Mother Gave me', 'This Moment' and 'Love'. Throughout her work, the detailed descriptions of ordinary objects and everyday events make us more aware of the depths of meaning in them. Does it spoil the beauty of the fan or the value of the gift to wonder about its history? Quite the opposite, really. Among the symbolic objects captured in beautiful detail are the black lace fan, the windows of a home at night, a doll, fruit, clothing, and flowers and shrubs.

- The poetry of Eavan Boland balances detailed descriptions of objects or dramatic scenes with reflective passages, using intricate **SOUND** patterns to recreate emotions

Boland's poetry is adept at using intricate sound patterns to capture the drama or tension in a particular situation or moment. The control of rhythm is wonderful throughout – to recreate the anxious intake and then release of breath in 'The War Horse', to represent the tangled, difficult response to a child's murder and senseless death in 'Child of our Time', to dramatise the callous voices in 'The Famine Road', to represent the suffocating constrictions that women were subjected to in Victorian times in 'The Shadow Doll', to symbolise the opening out of a journey, from cramped suburbia to clear countryside, in 'White Hawthorn in the West of Ireland', to echo a sense of solitary distance in 'Outside History', to capture the drama of a hurried, intense war-time meeting of lovers in 'The Black Lace Fan my Mother Gave me', to express the anxiety and then relief of a mother watching out for her child's return home as darkness descends in 'This Moment', to express the anxiety and then acceptance of a mother watching her daughter growing up and becoming independent in 'The Pomegranate', and to dramatise the trauma of parents threatened with the potentially fatal illness of one of their children in 'Love'.

- The poetry of Eavan Boland employs unusual and unconventional **FORMS**, such as two-line stanzas and irregular rhyming schemes, to represent the complexities of human experience

There are two features of poetic form that are worth paying close attention to in the work of Boland, because each is an integral part of her technique and contributes to the power of her poetry. Firstly, looking at her poems on the page, one immediately notices the variations in the line lengths and sentence lengths. Some lines are quite long complete sentences, for instance, 'She looked down the Boulevard des Capucines' from 'The Black Lace Fan my Mother Gave me'. Some lines are short, sharp, very crisp complete sentences, for example, 'One tree is black' and 'Stars rise' from 'This Moment'. Some complete sentences wander over three or more lines, such as 'We had two infant children one of whom/was touched by death in this town/and spared' from 'Love'. In each case, the technique expresses the thought and the thought is expressed by the technique; there is no clear division in poetry between content and style. More specifically, however, because Boland characteristically combines drama with reflection in her poetry, you can see, generally, how the shorter sentences are used to generate dramatic tension and the longer ones employed to slow the rhythm down to a more thoughtful beat. Secondly, again from looking at her poems on the page, you notice that Boland uses a great variety of stanza lengths – sometimes with great consistency, such as the four-line stanzas (quatrains) throughout 'The Black Lace Fan my Mother Gave me' and the terse two-line stanzas (couplets) throughout 'The War Horse'; sometimes with apparent inconsistency, such as the following sequence of lines per stanza in 'Love': 6-6-7-5-4-4-4-2. Once again, the choice is always deliberate and always has a role in exploring an experience. 'Love', for instance, deals with the fading of intensity.

John Donne

Donne was born a Roman Catholic, in London in 1571 (or 1572), at a time when Catholicism was officially banned by Elizabeth I, and remained one until 1598, when he considered it necessary to convert to the Anglican religion, probably as the only way of prospering socially. He studied at Oxford and took Law at Lincoln's Inn, and he was an adventurer in Lord Essex's expeditions to attack the Spanish at Cadiz (1596) and the Azores (1597). When he returned to England, he was appointed private secretary to Lord Keeper Egerton, but in 1601 he married and eloped with Egerton's seventeen-year-old niece. Done out of love, obviously – a love which seemed to have sustained him for much of his life – it was not a good career move. He was sacked and the couple lived in considerable poverty for a long time because Donne was unable to get another decent appointment, until James I heard him preaching and was instrumental in persuading him to become an Anglican priest. He was ordained in 1615, but his wife died in 1617, after which Donne devoted himself to the church and to his religious writings. He died in 1631.

Prescribed Poems

'Students at Higher Level will be required to study a representative selection from the work of eight poets: a representative selection would seek to reflect the range of a poet's themes and interests and exhibit his/her characteristic style and viewpoint. Normally the study of at least six poems by each poet would be expected.' (DES English Syllabus, 6.3)

Note: spellings have been modernised throughout.

Themes and Interests

> is a deep celebration of **CONTENTED SEXUAL LOVE**, never presenting it as a disruptive force, but as a bond, a source of satisfaction, health and stability

> dramatises the similarities and differences between **DIVINE LOVE** and sexual love

The Poetry of John Donne

> is a **REALISTIC DEPICTION OF LOVE** in all its aspects, physical, psychological, emotional, spiritual

> is **SELF-CONSCIOUS AND ANALYTIC**, addressing the mind rather than the heart over an extensive range of human experience

Style and Viewpoint

The Poetry of John Donne

> is argumentative and logical in character, which means that its **LANGUAGE** calls the mind into play rather than appeals to the senses

> draws its **IMAGERY** from science, politics, exploration, and other areas of the social world of his time, employing far-fetched comparisons, known as conceits

> is alive with the **SOUND** effects of the speaking voice, including repetition, emphasis, stress, alliteration, rhyme, and so on, all designed to present or carry an argument

> uses poetic **FORMS** as logical structures for delivering the drama of a debate, with another or with oneself

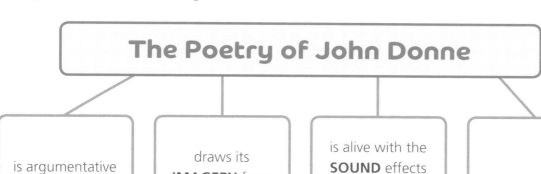

Poetry

The Sun Rising

Busy old fool, unruly sun,
    Why dost thou thus,
Through windows, and through curtains call on us?
Must to thy motions lovers' seasons run?
    Saucy pedantic wretch, go chide   5
    Late school-boys, and sour prentices,
  Go tell court-huntsmen, that the King will ride,
  Call country ants to harvest offices;
Love, all alike, no season knows, nor clime,
Nor hours, days, months, which are the rags of time.   10

    Thy beams, so reverend, and strong
    Why shouldst thou think?
I could eclipse and cloud them with a wink,
But that I would not lose her sight so long:
    If her eyes have not blinded thine,   15
    Look, and tomorrow late, tell me,
  Whether both th'Indias of spice and mine
  Be where thou left'st them, or lie here with me.
Ask for those kings whom thou saw'st yesterday,
And thou shalt hear, All here in one bed lay.   20

    She'is all states, and all princes, I,
    Nothing else is.
Princes do but play us; compared to this,
All honour's mimic; all wealth alchemy.
    Thou sun art half as happy as we,   25
    In that the world's contracted thus;
  Thine age asks ease, and since thy duties be
  To warm the world, that's done in warming us.
Shine here to us, and thou art everywhere;
This bed thy centre is, these walls, thy sphere.   30

Glossary

[7] **court-huntsmen:** indicates that this poem was written during the reign of King James I, who had a passion for early-morning stag hunts and who obviously favoured those of his court staff who accompanied him

[8] **call country ants to harvest offices:** call hard-working farmers to the duties of the harvest

[17] **both th'Indias of spice and mine:** refers to two of the greatest trading regions for England in the seventeenth century, the East Indies, land of precious spices, and the West Indies, where gold was mined; so **mine** here as in 'gold mine'

[24] **alchemy:** predecessor of chemistry that sought to change base metals (such as copper, lead and tin) into gold; also anything flashy, but fake

ANALYSE

As an expression of contented, satisfied love, this piece has few equals. 'She'is all states, and all princes, I,/Nothing else is.' In our rare moments of perfect union, the rest of us capture the same sentiment, much less beautifully, but just as authentically: *She means the world to me.* This imagery of states and princes is taken up and developed from imagining the sun circling the earth, passing countries and rulers in its orbit. Although Donne's poems are always superbly finished, they always *feel* like the responses of a mind reacting to a particular situation. In the first stanza, 'the King' is merely a peripheral detail, attached to the 'court-huntsmen', who are only one of many groups of people – schoolboys, apprentices, farmers – that the sun would be better off pestering. Late in the second stanza, 'those kings' return, again at the tail of a long list of people and places the sun will observe in its orbit, but by the third stanza, as if finally realising the worth of it, Donne makes royalty the central metaphor and develops it in detail – states, princes, honours conferred by monarchs, wealth possessed by rulers.

Overall, though, the poem is dominated by two concepts, both natural developments from the initial irritation at the sun's intrusion: time and space.

In its orbit, the sun traverses the entire earth. Notice how the poem starts in the bedroom where the lovers have been woken – 'windows' and 'curtains' – and then gradually extends outwards – school, workplace, court, countryside – and keeps travelling until the entire globe – 'both th'Indias' – has been covered. Such vast distances are considered only for the sake of dismissing their attractions. What's the point of leaving the bedroom when it contains everything of value, everything of interest? And contains it all at the same time, since 'She'is all states, and all princes, I', whereas if you were abroad you could visit only one state, only one prince, at a time. In any case, that world of politics is not real, is only 'play' when compared with the reality of love; it only imitates honours and forges wealth. By the end of the poem, Donne has argued himself into the belief that the lover's bed *is* the world – 'Shine here to us, and thou art everywhere;/This bed thy centre is' – and that the bedroom walls should therefore define the orbit of the sun – 'these walls, thy sphere'.

The poem which opened with playfully dismissing the sun – calling it a 'fool', a busybody and a disturber of the peace, while ordering it to push off and pester others who might appreciate its attentions a bit more – now ends with an enthusiastic invitation to the same sun to stay forever. Pity for the lonely old sun, who is only 'half as happy' as the two lovers because it has no one to share with, has replaced irritation. Donne's poems are wonderful at dramatising shifts in thoughts and attitudes, and 'The Sun Rising' is a fabulous example of this.

The second shaping aspect of the poem is time, which the sun regulates – daylight and darkness, morning and night, the seasons, the years. The sun regulates everything. Or rather, it *imagines* that it regulates everything. But it's mistaken – 'Must to thy motions lovers' seasons run?' – because love, which is 'all alike', or the same at all times, is not subject to the vagaries or the ravages of time. It's constant, without seasonal or climatic changes – 'no season knows, nor clime' – and in fact exists outside time, without 'hours, days, months'. Donne's phrase for these divisions is 'the rags of time', which is contrasted here with a timeless condition, or eternity. So, the sun is mistaken about its ability to regulate everything. The sun overestimates its own power, an observation that is mischievously developed in the second stanza, where Donne reminds the sun that he could blot it out simply by closing his eyes. He doesn't want to close his eyes, because then he would have to stop gazing at his lover as well, who gives off a far brighter light, in any case. All-powerful? Far from it. The sun is actually a lonely old busybody, worn out from useless travelling – 'Thine age asks ease' – and more to be pitied than scolded.

(i) Donne is a poet of love. Referring closely to the details of the poem, what *kind* of love do you think is captured here?

(ii) In separate treatments, trace the imagery of time and then the imagery of space through the poem, commenting on what you consider the most suggestive examples of each.

Song: Go, and catch a falling star

Go, and catch a falling star.
    Get with child a mandrake root,
Tell me, where all past years are,
    Or who cleft the Devil's foot,
Teach me to hear mermaids singing,   5
    Or to keep off envy's stinging,
        And find
        What wind
Serves to advance an honest mind.

If thou be'est born to strange sights,   10
    Things invisible to see,
Ride ten thousand days and nights,
    Till age snow white hairs on thee,
Thou, when thou return'st, wilt tell me
All strange wonders that befell thee,   15
        And swear
        No where
Lives a woman true, and fair.

If thou find'st one, let me know,
    Such a pilgrimage were sweet,   20
Yet do not, I would not go,
    Though at next door we might meet,
Though she were true, when you met her,
And last, till you write your letter,
        Yet she   25
        Will be
False, ere I come, to two, or three.

Glossary

[2] **mandrake:** a plant with purple flowers and a forked root – the roots looked like human beings

[4] **cleft:** split

[5] **hear mermaids singing:** to hear them singing was to hear what could not be heard, except by yourself

[12] **Ride ten thousand days and nights:** specifically refers to the Squire of Dames from Edmund Spenser's poem *The Fairie Queene*, who found only three women who refused to have sex with him: a prostitute he couldn't afford to pay for, a nun who couldn't get him to swear an oath of secrecy, and 'a plain country gentlewoman, that of good honest simplicity denied him'

[18] **true, and fair:** faithful, *and* attractive.

ANALYSE

This is one of six poems under the heading in an early manuscript *Songs which were made to certain airs that were made before* – in other words, lyrics made to fit existing tunes – and the rhythm of the little piece is definitely easier to appreciate if you approach it from that point of view. In particular, you might note how each verse reaches out desperately, grasping for the impossible – 'Go, and catch a falling star' and 'If thou be'est born to strange sights' – before being tugged back by the two short lines towards the end, where the abruptness of the lines and the clanging of the rhymes mock and destroy the optimism. You can imagine the accompanying music: a rambling, tripping little melody, broken up by two sharp chords.

Although it's not clear precisely how Donne wrote his poems on the page, the punctuation in these versions is considered reliable and always worth close attention. In particular here, the comma after 'Go' in the opening line subtly determines the emphasis and even the meaning of the command – 'Go, and catch a falling star' is a completely different instruction to 'Go and catch a falling star', which sounds dismissive and mocking rather than forlornly hopeful – and the comma between 'true' and 'and fair' in line 18 suggests that you might find a faithful woman all right, but she's not going to be good-looking, an entertaining cynicism that would be completely lost if the lines read 'No where/Lives a woman true and fair'.

In 'The Flea', Donne makes a desperate, but fruitless assault on his lover's chastity; in 'Song', he sighs forlornly about women's lack of chastity. Isn't he being inconsistent? Of course. Jilted by a lover, a man may believe in the immediate aftermath that all women are cruel and unfaithful. Sitting beside a desirable woman who refuses all advances, a man may convince himself that all women are cold and impregnable. Inconsistency testifies to the variety of life, and to the abundant variety of Donne's poetry. In any case, poems attempt to capture the truth of a moment or a situation, which is the only truth that's available in life. Furthermore, in many instances, the truth captured by a poem is an imagined truth, not an autobiographical one.

Go (Donne instructs some imaginary, sympathetic listener), and catch a star falling from the sky, make the root of the mandrake plant

Poetry

pregnant, tell me where the time goes, or who split the devil's cloven foot, teach me to hear the singing of mermaids or to avoid the stinging sensation of envying others, and tell me how to find a circumstance that rewards honesty.

If you have the gift of seeing what's not there (Donne gently mocks), then ride for thirty years, until your hair is white, and when you return you can describe to me the wonders that you saw, and confirm that you couldn't find a woman who was both faithful and attractive.

If you do find one, though (Donne concludes), inform me immediately, because to travel to meet her would be sweet; but no, don't bother … I wouldn't actually go, even if you were only next door, because even though she might really be faithful as you were writing to me, that never lasts long with women and she'd have deceived me before I got there, before I could even count to two or three.

MAKE

(i) In your opinion, is the tone here entirely humorous and playful, or is the song also trying to make a serious point? Give reasons for your answer, referring to the language and imagery of the poem.

(ii) This poem is called a 'song'? What features, if any, do you think it shares with contemporary songs? Identify similarities or differences, as appropriate.

READ

Poetry

The Anniversary

All kings, and all their favourites,
    All glory of honours, beauties, wits,
The sun itself, which makes times, as they pass,
Is elder by a year, now, than it was
When thou and I first one another saw: 5
All other things, to their destruction draw,
    Only our love hath no decay;
This, no tomorrow hath, nor yesterday,
Running it never runs from us away,
But truly keeps his first, last, everlasting day.   10

    Two graves must hide thine and my corse,
    If one might, death were no divorce,
Alas, as well as other princes, we
(Who prince enough in one another be,)
Must leave at last in death, these eyes, and ears,   15
Oft fed with true oaths, and with sweet salt tears;
    But souls where nothing dwells but love
(All other thoughts being inmates) then shall prove
This, or a love increased there above,
When bodies to their graves, souls from their graves remove.   20

    And then we shall be throughly blessed,
    But we no more, than all the rest.
Here upon earth, we are kings, and none but we
Can be such kings, nor of such subjects be;
Who is so safe as we? where none can do   25
Treason to us, except one of us two.
    True and false fears let us refrain,
Let us love nobly, and live, and add again
Years and years unto years, till we attain
To write threescore, this is the second of our reign.   30

Glossary

[2] **wits:** the term used for what we would call intellectuals, although the wits of the time were expected to be sparkling intelligences; the seventeenth-century meaning survives in *keeping your wits about you* and *having the wit to do something*

[11] **Two graves must hide thine and my corse:** refers to the Christian belief that body and soul separate at death; the suggestion being that, because they love one another so much, if they were buried in the same grave then the souls would never want to leave

[17] **where nothing dwells but love:** where nothing other than love has a home

[18] **inmates:** lodgers or temporary dwellers

[27] **True and false fears let us refrain:** let us banish any fears we might have about one another, whether those fears are justified ('true') or not ('false')

[30] **threescore:** three by twenty (a score); hence sixty years

ANALYSE

If 'The Sun Rising' expressed delight in love, this poem captures something broader and deeper – contentment, security, serenity, fulfilment in love. It's not an expression of love; it's a *celebration* of loving commitment. It's not a promise of fidelity; it's a celebration of *certainty*. We can never be sure who Donne addressed any of his poems to, because the evidence hasn't survived, but this feels very much like a celebration of his relationship with Anne More, who eloped to marry him when she was seventeen and he was thirty.

The feeling of assurance in the poem comes from the measured development of the thought and the measured control of the rhythm. To get a fuller appreciation of these qualities, you might like to contrast this piece with 'The Flea', where the poet's mind is lively, throwing in points as they occur to him, and the rhythm is correspondingly uneven, full of stops and starts, commands, pleas, entreaties, sighs … Here, the calm, stately opening, as he parades the splendours of the world in slow procession before us – 'All

kings … all … favourites … all glory' – is sustained and built on as the poem develops. It's not a poem without energy or excitement, though. Their love is 'running', which means that it's alive, energetic, that it sets the blood racing. But it's also running on the spot, as we might express it, because 'it never runs from us away'. It's a marvellous image to capture both the vigour and the stability of their love. In the final stanza, there is also excitement, communicated in the quickening rhythm – 'Let us love nobly, and live, and add again/Years and years unto years' – but, once again, it's an excitement generated by constancy, an excitement which is contained within the steadiness of the relationship, and which is given a final expression in the calm assurance of the last line: 'this is the second of our reign'.

In this poem, Donne manages to capture the contradiction of genuine love: it's simultaneously wild and calm, makes your heart beat faster and makes you feel more assured at the same time. Consider how he manages this by combining images of movement – 'they pass', 'to their destruction', 'running', 'remove' – with images of stability – 'never runs', 'dwells' – and images of

Poetry

time passing – 'elder by a year', 'tomorrow', 'yesterday', 'Years and years unto years' – with images of eternity – 'everlasting day'.

As with 'The Sun Rising', though, the unifying metaphor of 'The Anniversary' is that of the court, introduced immediately – 'All kings' – since the king would be leading any procession, including this one; and then leisurely, logically developed as the poem advances. All royalty must die, is the contemplation in the second stanza. All those magnificent parades are winding majestically towards the grave. But lovers are a different kind of royalty, because death doesn't take away their kingdom, as it does with other princes, it only shifts it to a better location. 'And then', the third stanza opens, 'we shall be throughly blessed'. Even here on earth, lovers are a different kind of royalty. All kings fear treachery and treason. Love offers far greater security – 'Who is so safe as we?' – and by implication far greater wealth too. All other monarchs are diminished by the passing of time – 'All other things, to their destruction draw' – but the 'kings' of love are made more prosperous by the passing of the years. In fact – 'Let us … add again/Years and years unto years' – time is the gift that life bestows on them. Time gives when you are in love, and takes away when you are not.

MAKE

(i) The poem's imagery is derived from contrasts, for instance, that between the constancy of love and the movement of all other things passing it by. Pick out some other contrasts in the imagery and comment on their effectiveness.

(ii) The dominant mood here is one of assurance. Comment on some of the technical features – for instance, repetition, assertion, punctuation, pace, sound effects – that create and express this mood, illustrating your remarks with examples from the poem.

Poetry

Song: Sweetest love, I do not go

Sweetest love, I do not go,
    For weariness of thee,
Nor in hope the world can show
    A fitter love for me;
      But since that I   5
Must die at last, 'tis best,
To use my self in jest
    Thus by feigned deaths to die.

Yesternight the sun went hence,
    And yet is here today,   10
He hath no desire nor sense,
    Nor half so short a way:
      Then fear not me,
But believe that I shall make
Speedier journeys, since I take   15
    More wings and spurs than he.

O how feeble is man's power,
    That if good fortune fall,
Cannot add another hour,
    Nor a lost hour recall!   20
      But come bad chance,
And we join to it our strength,
And we teach it art and length,
    Itself o'er us to advance.

When thou sigh'st, thou sigh'st not wind,   25
    But sigh'st my soul away,
When thou weep'st, unkindly kind,
    My life's blood doth decay.
      It cannot be
That thou lov'st me, as thou say'st,   30
If in thine my life thou waste,
    Thou art the best of me.

Let not thy divining heart
    Forethink me any ill,
Destiny may take thy part,   35
    And may thy fears fulfil;
      But think that we
Are but turned aside to sleep;
They who one another keep
    Alive, ne'er parted be.   40

Glossary

[8] **feigned:** pretended, false

[33] **divining heart:** heart that anticipates the future

[34] **Forethink me any ill:** feel badly about any ill that might befall me *before* it actually happens

ANALYSE

This is one of six poems under the heading in an early manuscript *Songs which were made to certain airs that were made before* – in other words, lyrics made to fit existing tunes – and the rhythm of this piece is definitely easier to appreciate if you approach it from that point of view. In this case, an actual air survives.

Over the five stanzas, five fairly conventional consolations or recommendations are offered to the partner who must stay behind.

Firstly, there's the assurance that the departure is enforced, done reluctantly, and not prompted by any failing in either lover. He is not leaving because he has tired of his lover, or because he hopes to find a better lover elsewhere.

I'll be back, is the assurance of the second stanza; and as so often in Donne, the progress of the sun offers him a comparison, a metaphor. Yesterday the sun left us, but is back again today. And unlike me, he really had no desire to return, or any ability to find the quickest way. I'll be even faster. The 'wings and spurs' here are easy to understand – 'wings' for speedy flight, 'spurs' to quicken a horse – and they seem to be attached to 'desire' and 'sense'. Perhaps desire will be his spur and his homing sense will be his wings.

We tend to ignore our good luck and dwell on the bad, the third stanza argues. When something good happens, we can't manage to stretch it out and make it last; but when something bad happens – a 'bad chance' – then we brood on it, we add to it with our misery ('we join to it our strength'), and we show it clever and long drawn-out ways to get us down even further.

Don't cry, is the request in the fourth stanza; don't grieve; you'll only make us both feel worse. This stanza makes use of a very common concept in Donne: that two true lovers are really one. It is beautifully expressed in the final line here: 'Thou art the best of me.' Because they are one, when she sighs, it is his soul that feels the sadness; when she cries, she's shedding a part of him from inside her. That is the meaning of that other beautiful line, 'in thine my life thou waste' – by wearing yourself down with sorrow, you're tearing me apart as well.

Don't anticipate anything bad happening to me, the final stanza recommends; your fears may find themselves coming true, or be fulfilled. Better to think that we are parted only as lovers in their bed part from each other when they turn away to fall asleep. And the song ends with the tender assurance that those who give life to each other, as lovers do, can never really be parted, no matter what physical distance is between them.

MAKE

(i) In this poem, five recommendations are offered to the partner who must stay behind. Take each in turn and comment on how consoling you think each is or might be.

(ii) This poem is called a 'song'? What features, if any, do you think it shares with contemporary songs? Identify similarities or differences, as appropriate.

The Dream

Dear love, for nothing less than thee
Would I have broke this happy dream,
      It was a theme
For reason, much too strong for phantasy,
Therefore thou waked'st me wisely; yet   5
My dream thou brok'st not, but continued'st it;
Thou art so true, that thoughts of thee suffice,
To make dreams truths, and fables histories;
Enter these arms, for since thou thought'st it best,
Not to dream all my dream, let's act the rest.   10

As lightning, or a taper's light,
Thine eyes, and not thy noise waked me;
      Yet I thought thee
(For thou lov'st truth) an angel, at first sight,
But when I saw thou saw'st my heart,   15
And knew'st my thoughts, beyond an angel's art,
When thou knew'st what I dreamed, when thou knew'st when
Excess of joy would wake me, and cam'st then,
I must confess, it could not choose but be
Profane, to think thee anything but thee.   20

Coming and staying showed thee, thee,
But rising makes me doubt, that now,
      Thou art not thou.
That love is weak, where fear's as strong as he,
'Tis not all spirit, pure, and brave,   25
If mixture it of fear, shame, honour, have.
Perchance as torches which must ready be,
Men light and put out, so thou deal'st with me,
Thou cam'st to kindle, goest to come; then I
Will dream that hope again, but else would die.   30

Glossary

[11] **taper:** thin candle, one of the few sources of interior lighting available at the time

[16] **knew'st my thoughts, beyond an angel's art:** refers to the belief, common at the time, that God can see into your mind and read your thoughts, but that angels don't have this ability, or this 'art'; the implication is that his mistress, who *can* read his thoughts, is therefore more elevated than an angel, which explains why Donne, in line 20, describes his conclusion as **profane**, or irreverent

[27–28] **torches which must ready be,/Men light and put out:** torches which need to be quickly available are first lit and put out, because a torch that has already been lit flares up more quickly when relit

ANALYSE

As another poem of engrossed passion, intense and intensely absorbed in the pleasures of love and loving, this belongs with 'The Sun Rising' and 'The Anniversary', and yet it is different from these two, because here there is no consciousness of anything other than the couple. In fact, there is hardly any consciousness at all, because the poem occurs in a state somewhere between sleep and waking and, as such moments always are, is full of blurred images, doubts, questions and drowsy pleasures. At the same time, the argument of this poem is quite involved.

The most consistent of the drowsy pleasures, and the central conceit of the poem, is the confusion between his dream and reality, which is set up in lines 3 and 4: 'It was a theme/For reason, much too strong for phantasy' – and played on throughout. He has been dreaming of his mistress – a 'happy dream' – is woken by his mistress gazing at him – 'Thine eyes, and not thy noise waked me' – and wakes up to see his mistress beside him, which is precisely what he had been dreaming of. She is so 'true' – steadfast, strong, honest, powerful, faithful, virtuous, real – that she is capable of transforming dreams into reality, of making fantasies ('fables') come true ('histories').

The poem opens on a gentle, loving note – 'Dear love' – and then it reverses the usual consequence of waking from a dream, which is to find the reality grim and disappointing by comparison. In this case, he is delighted to exchange his dream for the reality. On second thoughts – 'yet' – it occurs to him that his dream hasn't been broken at all, because he is still contemplating the same sight, that of his mistress' face. She is so magically real, he reflects, that she is capable of entering his dreams and turning them into reality, and since he was obviously dreaming of making love with her, now he invites her to 'Enter these arms' and make the completion of his dream come true: 'let's act the rest', he suggests.

And the mood is right, as the opening of the second stanza makes clear, because it was no disturbing noise that jolted him from his sleep – 'not thy noise waked me' – but the passionate flash, like 'lightning' of her eyes, and then the gentler light, of the 'taper' or candle, of her eyes gazing on him as he woke. He thinks he's in heaven when he wakes and, 'at first sight', that she is an angel. But this thought, touching in itself, is really too conventional for Donne. It's the beginning of his exploration of what his mistress means to him, not the completion. But if she was *only* an angel, he reflects, then she wouldn't have been able to read his mind, to enter his dream, to wake him at the moment when he was about to dream of making love with her, to make his dream reality, because mere angels don't have the 'art' to do that. So, she must be greater than an angel, which is … herself.

The thought is particularly knotty in the third stanza; deliberately so, presumably, as the half-conscious, or half-unconscious, lover struggles to come to terms with his sensations and reflections. He is, I think, arguing with, or demonstrating to, himself. It has the feel of someone thinking aloud about a very involved issue. It goes something like this. Coming to bed, or into my arms, was physical proof that it was really you; but when you left, I wondered if I was dreaming again. It's a weak kind of love that is dominated by fear; it's not a spiritual, perfect love, if it is adulterated with fear and shame and concerns for honour. Maybe you come and go, rousing my desire and dampening it again, for the same reason that torches are lit and then blown out, so that they can immediately burst into flame when lit again … maybe you came to bed to prepare me, and went away only to make your return more passionate, while I had been dreaming hopefully of fulfilment. Then I'll dream that dream again, until I die. (It adds to your appreciation of the poem's humorous logic to know that 'to die' was also a common euphemism at the time for reaching a sexual climax.)

MAKE

(i) Donne's poems are often praised for the logical development of an argument, and that is undoubtedly a virtue of 'The Dream'. In your opinion, however, is there also the expression of emotion in this poem? Identify examples to support your point of view.

(ii) A poem emerging from sleep to wakefulness must surely rely on references to darkness and light for much of its imagery. Pick out some examples from 'The Dream' and comment on their effectiveness.

READ

A Valediction: forbidding Mourning

As virtuous men pass mildly away,
    And whisper to their souls, to go,
Whilst some of their sad friends do say,
    The breath goes now, and some say, no:

So let us melt, and make no noise,   5
    No tear-floods, nor sigh-tempests move,
'Twere profanation of our joys
    To tell the laity our love.

Moving of th' earth brings harms and fears,
    Men reckon what it did and meant,   10
But trepidation of the spheres,
    Though greater far, is innocent.

Dull sublunary lovers' love
    (Whose soul is sense) cannot admit
Absence, because it doth remove   15
    Those things which elemented it.

But we by a love, so much refined,
    That our selves know not what it is,
Inter-assured of the mind,
    Care less, eyes, lips, and hands to miss.   20

Our two souls therefore, which are one,
    Though I must go, endure not yet
A breach, but an expansion,
    Like gold to aery thinness beat.

If they be two, they are two so   25
    As stiff twin compasses are two,
Thy soul the fixed foot, makes no show
    To move, but doth, if th' other do.

And though it in the centre sit,
    Yet when the other far doth roam,   30
It leans, and hearkens after it,
    And grows erect, as that comes home.

Such wilt thou be to me, who must
    Like th' other foot, obliquely run;
Thy firmness makes my circle just,   35
    And makes me end, where I begun.

Poetry

Glossary

[8] **the laity:** adapts an expression used in a religious context for those members of the congregation who are not priests themselves; in this case, it describes those who do not have the experience or learning to understand such spiritual love

[9] **Moving of th' earth** means earthquakes and [11] **trepidation of the spheres** means, roughly, disturbances among the orbiting hollow globes that ancient astronomers believed circled the earth; the whole meaning is that people are worried by earthquakes but not troubled at all by the far greater collision of spheres

[13] **sublunary:** literally, under the moon and so **sublunary lovers** describes those who are conventional lovers, relying on the inconstancy of the moon for their inspiration

[15–16] **it doth remove/Those things which elemented it:** in the case of ordinary, dull lovers, absence separates the bodies, and since the bodies were the very things that made the love what it was (**elemented it**) then the love dies from the separation.

[24] **Like gold to aery thinness beat:** the practice of beating gold to make the refined gold leaf, which the perfect lovers will equal, even surpass, because their thinness will be **aery**, having no corruptible substance at all

[26] **twin compasses:** the compass was a popular metaphor for stability within change.

The first sentence extends leisurely over two whole verses, very relaxed, unflustered by the impending departure, very sure of itself. The composure is expressed through the selection of soft sounds – 'virtuous', 'mildly' and 'whisper', for example, which have equally soft meanings – combined with the precise punctuation, which dictates how the lines should be read. Again, it's worth taking a specific example to demonstrate how this subtle technique works. Have a look at the comma after 'souls' and before 'to go' at the end of the second line. It stops you reading it as 'whisper to their souls to go', which is beginning to sound anxious, hurried. It forces a slight pause after 'souls', so that 'to go' is then said gently, as the beginning of an easeful voyage. In the second stanza, Donne's word for this gentle movement is 'melt': 'So let us melt, and make no noise.' You don't have to analyse all the punctuation, although that's fun in itself. You do have to attend to it throughout the poem, and let your ear notice its effects.

After this beautifully assured opening, Donne then advances his argument in three measured stages, in much the same way as you would present your supporting points if you were proposing or opposing a motion in a debate. Without the reassurance of the opening, however, much of the material would lose its strength to convince. The three stages of the argument all reinforce a single point: that the separation of the bodies of true lovers does not also mean the separation of their souls.

Firstly, Donne introduces an engaging illustration. The physical movements of the earth, when one piece becomes detached from another, cause danger, destruction and fear. But by contrast, the far greater physical movements of the spheres, which oscillate much more extremely and much more constantly, cause no harm at all. The illustration establishes the dual nature of human beings, having both body and soul. It also establishes the two levels on which true love exists: physical and spiritual.

Donne now applies his illustration to love. Those for whom love is merely physical, those 'Whose soul is sense', or whose spiritual dimension is the senses, are 'dull' lovers. It's worth pausing to consider the meanings of 'dull'. They include unintelligent and unexciting and lacking in colour. For Donne, intelligence is exciting and sexy and colourful; excitement is intellectual, as well as physical and emotional. These dull types can't sustain physical separation, because the only dimension they have is the physical. By contrast, Donne and his wife know a love which is 'of the mind', although, paradoxically, it is so refined that they 'know not what it is'. Because of it, they are 'Inter-assured', which has many beautiful meanings, among them 'mutually convinced' and 'mutually comforted' and 'equally safe'. Because of it, they 'Care less,' – 'less,' take note, because they do still suffer from physical separation – about missing the physical attributes of the other.

Donne now rounds off his argument in brilliant style, drawing his conclusion – 'Our two souls therefore … endure not yet/A breach', meaning that the souls cannot be separated, no matter where the bodies are – and, like all effective debaters, providing the clinching detail as well as the general argument. In this case, the detail is that now famous metaphor of the compass. It should be noted again, as with all of Donne's language, how the image, which expresses love, appeals to the mind and not to the emotions or the senses. It should also be noted, however, that the tone of the entire poem remains dominated by the gentle expression of assuring love at the opening; so the appeal is to the mind of a living, loving woman, not to a dry, detached mind, if you could have such a thing. The metaphor requires little explanation, other than to remark how brilliantly it captures the two levels that the poem has always concerned itself with – it is always joined at the top, no matter how far apart the feet at the base may be – and how much incidental riches Donne manages to tease from it along the way – how the woman is the 'centre' of the compass, therefore the source of stability; how 'leans, and hearkens' captures the yearning of parted lovers; how the subsidiary image of the 'circle just' (true circle) created by the compass contains suggestions of perfection, of completion, of true love, and of the wedding band.

Poetry **MAKE**

(i) The final conceit here is that of the comparison between the parting lovers and a compass. Examine the other comparisons that preceded it and comment on what features they all have in common.

(ii) This is a reassuring poem. Show how the sound effects – starting with the gentle sibilance of the opening – hold this tone of softness throughout.

READ

The Flea

Mark but this flea, and mark in this,
How little that which thou deny'st me is;
Me it sucked first, and now sucks thee,
And in this flea, our two bloods mingled be;
Confess it, this cannot be said   5
A sin, or shame, or loss of maidenhead,
  Yet this enjoys before it woo,
    And pampered swells with one blood made of two,
    And this, alas, is more than we would do.

Oh stay, three lives in one flea spare,   10
Where we almost, nay more than married are.
This flea is you and I, and this
Our marriage bed, and marriage temple is;
Though parents grudge, and you, we'are met,
And cloistered in these living walls of jet.   15
  Though use make you apt to kill me,
    Let not to this, self murder added be,
    And sacrilege, three sins in killing three.

Cruel and sudden, hast thou since
Purpled thy nail, in blood of innocence?   20
In what could this flea guilty be,
Except in that drop which it sucked from thee?
Yet thou triumph'st, and say'st that thou
Find'st not thyself, nor me the weaker now;
  'Tis true, then learn how false, fears be;   25
    Just so much honour, when thou yield'st to me,
    Will waste, as this flea's death took life from thee.

Glossary

[4] **our two bloods mingled be:** it was believed at the time that sexual intercourse involved the mingling of blood from the participants

ANALYSE

Raunchy love poems on fleas were very common in sixteenth-century England. This is Donne's distinctive version, an entertaining exercise in logic – proposition, deduction, conclusion – which is deliberately flippant and ingenious.

Notice how, from the very first word, the poem addresses the mind of both mistress and reader. 'Mark', which means 'take note of', is repeated and refined almost immediately – 'and mark in this'. The rest of the poem continues in the style of its opening line, trying to persuade, to convince, to sway. The purpose is the same as in more conventional love poetry, but this is an *intellectual* seduction; it wants to conquer the mind before it turns its attentions to having the body. It's one of the great pleasures of Donne's love poetry that he starts from the acceptance that women, too, have minds and celebrates them as just as subtle and complex and witty as the minds of men.

Follow the argumentative, persuasive phrasing, addressed directly to the lover – 'Mark', 'Confess it', 'Oh stay', 'Let not' and 'then learn'. Notice the language and techniques of debate: the outrageous exaggeration, for instance, in the phrase 'Cruel and sudden' to describe the woman as she cold-heartedly slaughters the flea that was biting her; or the playful but effective use of repetition – 'Mark but this flea, and mark in this' and the measured reuse of 'this' in the first stanza – and of commands, pleas and rhetorical questions.

But perhaps the greatest achievement of the poem, and of much of Donne's work, is that it doesn't simply present a finished argument; it recreates for us the argument in progress, the to-and-fro of a real debate, the interaction between two people, although one never actually speaks. The emotions in a poem, and indeed the progress of the poem itself, are both shaped by the logical reasoning of the poet's mind. The poem is a *process*, not a statement or a declaration.

The fact is, that *everything* in a Donne poem serves the argument, including the imagery, which is never there just for adornment. Religion, for instance, is dragged into 'The Flea' – 'temple', 'cloistered' and 'sacrilege' in the second stanza – not because Donne or the poem has, at this time, any regard for or interest in religion, but as emotional blackmail and intellectual weight; merely to make the argument more effective and powerful, in other words.

As for the argument itself …

Consider this flea (Donne urges his reluctant mistress) and try to understand just how trifling what you're refusing me actually is. It sucked my blood first, then it sucked yours; so our two bloods are mixed inside it. You could hardly call this a sin, or in any way shameful. You certainly couldn't claim that you'd lost your virginity. And yet it has had its fun. Which is more than we've managed to do.

No, don't kill it! (Donne pleads). You'll be saving three lives if you spared it. Inside this flea, we're almost … no, we're *actually* married. It's our *sacred* marriage bed, our temple. No matter how much your parents resent it, or you, the fact is that we're joined together in there, in religious seclusion, cut off from the outside by the walls of the flea's body. You mightn't be too worried about killing me while crushing this flea but, really, you'd also be committing suicide, wouldn't you, and sacrilege, for that matter, destroying a temple – three separate sins, in other words.

Poetry

So, you've done it anyway (Donne accepts). Your thumbnail is covered in the blood of the innocent insect. Except for the little drop of blood it sucked from you, it did nothing to you. And yet you proclaim your victory over it, and you tell me that it hasn't done any harm, that neither of us is any weaker, even though I said earlier that you were killing both of us. Well … you're right, actually. And what's more, you should learn from this. When we have sex, it'll be no more fatal, no more serious, than the flea-bite. So …

MAKE

(i) The argument is deliberately outrageous here, but would you agree that it has energy, wit and, ultimately, appeal? Comment on each in turn, paying close attention to the language of the poem.

(ii) Technically, this is an exercise in rhetoric. Identify some standard rhetorical devices – such as repetition, emphasis, exaggeration, humour, address to an audience – and comment on their use and effectiveness.

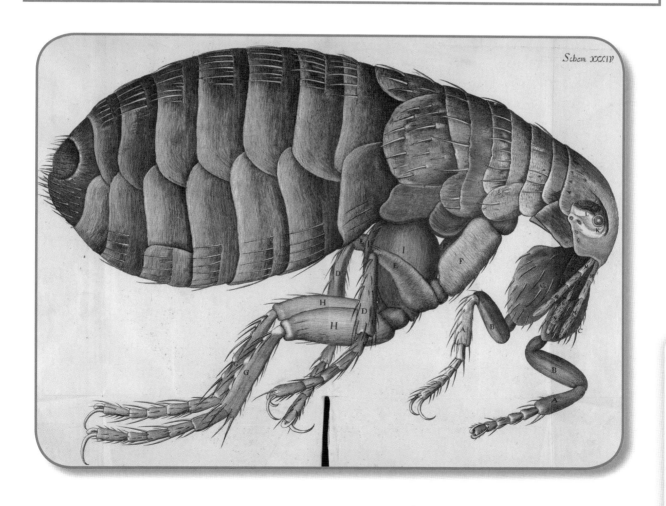

READ

Batter my heart

Batter my heart, three-personed God; for, you
As yet but knock, breathe, shine, and seek to mend;
That I may rise, and stand, o'erthrow me, and bend
Your force, to break, blow, burn, and make me new.
I, like an usurped town, to another due,   5
Labour to admit you, but oh, to no end,
Reason your viceroy in me, me should defend,
But is captived, and proved weak or untrue,
Yet dearly I love you, and would be loved fain,
But am betrothed unto your enemy,   10
Divorce me, untie, or break that knot again,
Take me to you, imprison me, for I
Except you enthral me, never shall be free,
Nor ever chaste, except you ravish me.

Glossary

[5] **an usurped town:** a town that has been occupied by an enemy

[5] **to another due:** the occupied town owes allegiance, or belongs to, someone else, someone other than the occupying enemy

[9] **would be loved fain:** eagerly wishes to be loved

[11] **Divorce me, untie, or break that knot again:** dissolve the bond between the occupier and myself, annul it, or destroy it by force

[13] **enthral:** to enslave or capture, but also to captivate, as a lover is enthralled by his mistress

ANALYSE

The theme is easy to comprehend – Donne prays that God will take complete control of him and drive out all others – but the expression of it is profoundly subtle. Three quite separate conceits are working simultaneously; and miraculously, they seem to be working in unison; just as three separate entities work together in the 'three-personed God' of Christian belief (God the father, the Son and the Holy Ghost).

Firstly, Donne presents himself as something manufactured by God that needs to be radically overhauled. As yet, Donne complains, God is only breathing on him and shining him up, a kind of cosmetic, surface polishing that doesn't get to the core of the problem. Quite the contrary. He needs to be broken apart, reshaped ('blow' and 'burn' suggest working with metal that has been softened by intense heat), so that he can be made anew.

Now Donne extends the conceit and specifically defines the object. He is not just any old simple piece of metal, but something as complex as a town. This metaphor provides rich possibilities, all marvellously explored over the next four lines. He is a town that has been occupied by the enemy (the devil) and though he tries to open the gates to admit God ('I ... Labour to admit you'), he's unsuccessful, not because he doesn't want to, but because reason, which is God's representative in human beings, is in itself too weak, a prisoner itself, or else too easily seduced or bought by the enemy, to properly resist. And yet, Donne cries, despite the betrayals of the mind, Donne's heart – 'Batter my heart, three-personed God' – is still faithful, still loves.

And this leads to the most startling conceit of all, for that love of Donne for his God is now described in sexual terms, in much the same way as sexual love in the secular poems was often described in spiritual or religious terms. The language becomes dominated by the terms of sexual love, with Donne presenting himself as the mistress and presenting God as the ardent suitor – Donne is 'betrothed' to the devil, he needs to be divorced or have the arrangement annulled or otherwise destroyed. He needs to be taken and ravished. Most successful of all, perhaps, is the expression 'enthral' – 'I/Except you enthral me, never shall be free' – because it contains both of the poem's major conceits, that of Donne as a captive of the devil who needs to become God's prisoner, and that of Donne as a straying lover.

MAKE

(i) The power of this sonnet depends a great deal on sound effects – starting and ending with the forceful words 'Batter' and 'ravish' – and on the recurring images of confinement, such as 'an usurped town'. Examine some other examples of each device and comment on their effectiveness.

(ii) Love is the theme of many of Donne's poems. What *kind* of love is expressed and explored here?

READ

At the round earth's imagined corners

At the round earth's imagined corners, blow
Your trumpets, angels, and arise, arise
From death, you numberless infinities
Of souls, and to your scattered bodies go,
All whom the flood did, and fire shall o'erthrow,   5
All whom war, dearth, age, agues, tyrannies,
Despair, law, chance, hath slain, and you whose eyes,
Shall behold God, and never taste death's woe,
But let them sleep, Lord, and me mourn a space,
For, if above all these, my sins abound,   10
'Tis late to ask abundance of thy grace,
When we are there; here on this lowly ground,
Teach me how to repent; for that's as good
As if thou hadst sealed my pardon, with thy blood.

Glossary

[1] **the round earth's imagined corners:** the conflict between the description of the earth in the Bible as being flat and four-cornered and the scientific knowledge of the earth's roundness

[1–2] **blow your trumpets:** the biblical description of the last day, announced by angels blowing their trumpets

[4] **to your scattered bodies go:** the Christian belief that the soul separates from the body at death; the bodies, turned to dust, become **scattered** throughout the world by the winds

[5] **the flood:** refers to the biblical story of the flood engulfing the earth, survived only by Noah and his family in the ark

[5] **the fire:** the biblical story of the final destruction of the earth by fire

[6] **dearth:** famine, but written as 'death' in most manuscript versions of the poem

[6] **agues:** old word for illnesses

[14] **sealed:** to authorise an official document with the official's seal

[14] **my pardon, with thy blood:** the Christian belief that Christ sacrificed himself to save man; so **pardon** here means forgiveness, absolution, salvation

ANALYSE

The grandeur of this sonnet's octave – anticipating the final day of judgement – is very similar to the majestic processional opening of 'The Anniversary'. The muscular, energetic verbs, stressed in ascending rhythm – 'blow … arise, arise … go' – have a cumulative effect. The repetition of 'All … All …' at the beginnings of lines 5 and 6 provides a grandeur in the sound. The lists have a high, formal feel to them, as if a grand official was reading them from a scroll – 'war, dearth, age, agues, tyrannies,/Despair, law, chance'. The sounds are of military triumph – 'trumpets' – and the imagery of triumph of life's abundance – 'numberless infinities'. And then the opening word of the sestet suspends all that and puts it on hold – 'But'. It strikes an anxious note, a negative note. Whereas the love poem 'The Anniversary' concluded on an enjoyment of the moment and the happy expectation of its annual recurrence, this divine poem asks for the imagined grandeur to be delayed, to give Donne time to prepare his soul. The sounds become heavier, more cowed – 'mourn', 'late', 'lowly'. The imagery of abundance reverses to become something negative, like a weight – 'my sins abound'. The feeling of elevation, of lift-off, from the octave is now replaced by the notions of crime, imprisonment, dungeon – 'this lowly ground', 'repent', 'pardon'.

For all the similarities in technique, the divine sonnets are entirely different in character from the love poems. The joyous contentment is gone, the pleasure, the mischief. The reason for this is obvious enough: in the love poems, Donne was playing with an equal; here, and in the other two sonnets, he is struggling with a master. Mischief and rebellion would be out of place. Although love is possible, it is not a love between equals and it lacks a physical consummation. The sense of fun that characterised the love poems has been replaced by a sense of need in the divine poems: 'But let them sleep, Lord' and 'Teach me how to repent'. The sense of satisfaction has been replaced by a sense of unease.

MAKE

(i) How would you describe the dominant tone of this poem – celebratory, fearful, anxious, contrite? Give reasons for your choice, supporting your points with close reference to the language of the sonnet.

(ii) In terms of style, the following list identifies recurring features in the poetry of John Donne: the debating technique; the rhythms of the speaking voice; the extraordinary images or conceits; political or scientific imagery; the humour; the sound effects, the word play, such as pun, paradox and oxymoron. Pick two that, in your opinion, particularly apply to 'At the round earth's imagined corners' and with the aid of quotations discuss their use in the poem.

READ

Thou hast made me

Thou hast made me, and shall thy work decay?
Repair me now, for now mine end doth haste,
I run to death, and death meets me as fast,
And all my pleasures are like yesterday,
I dare not move my dim eyes any way,   5
Despair behind, and death before doth cast
Such terror, and my feeble flesh doth waste
By sin in it, which it towards hell doth weigh;
Only thou art above, and when towards thee
By thy leave I can look, I rise again;   10
But our old subtle foe so tempteth me,
That not one hour I can myself sustain;
Thy Grace may wing me to prevent his art,
And thou like adamant draw mine iron heart.

Glossary

[11] **our old subtle foe:** Satan, the devil

[14] **adamant:** a magnetic stone, which draws the 'iron heart' of Donne towards it; the word also has suggestions of adamantine, or hard, rock

ANALYSE

One of the first things to notice about this sonnet is how similar in style and technique it is to the love poems.

For one thing, the piety here is just as witty as the *amour* had been, employing a series of unusual comparisons or metaphors to express the thought, among them: (i) the soul as an iron entity manufactured by God which gets worn by use and needs to be drawn back to its source by the magnet that is God and then repaired; (ii) the geometry of sight (looking backwards over the past, forwards towards the future, downwards towards the devil, upwards towards God – the four points of the compass, really); and (iii) the possible movements of man, running towards death, weighed down under his own sins and the temptations of the devil, flying with the assistance of God.

Secondly, it is *thought* that Donne is still concerned with expressing. For him, faith is an experience that engages the mind as well as the body and the soul, just as sexual love did in the other poems.

Thirdly – and obviously a related point – notice how this poem is also presented as an argument, an address, a dramatic exchange, an attempt to persuade or convince, just as most of the love poems were. From the opening line, with its rhetorical question – 'shall thy work decay?' – to the possibility contained in the conclusion – 'Thy Grace may wing me' – the poem offers a dramatic tension, a conflict of opposites, any number of possible outcomes.

Poetry

You who made me, now that my end is near, don't let me waste into decay, Donne pleads. I'm hurrying towards death, but daren't look towards it. I'm dragged towards hell. Only you can lift me upwards and draw me towards you.

Nevertheless, for all the similarities in technique, these divine poems are entirely different in character to the love poems. The joyous contentment is gone, the pleasure, the mischief. The reason for this is obvious enough: in the love poems, he was playing with an equal; here, and in the other two sonnets, he is struggling with a master. Mischief and rebellion would be out of place. Although love is possible – and sexual love is a surprising metaphor in 'Batter my heart' – it is not a love between equals and it lacks a physical consummation. The sense of fun that characterised the love poems has been replaced by a sense of need in the divine poems: 'Repair me now', 'Teach me how to repent' and 'Batter my heart'. The sense of satisfaction has been replaced by a sense of unease.

(i) In this and the other two divine sonnets, there is a sense of something broken – 'repair' here, 'mend' in 'Batter my heart'. What is it that is broken, and – drawing on the details from 'Thou hast made me' – how can it be fixed?

(ii) Donne's poems, secular and divine, are argumentative in style. Identify any features of argumentative or persuasive writing in this sonnet and comment on their effectiveness.

MAKE

Poetry

The Poetry of John Donne

Themes and Interests

- The poetry of John Donne is a deep celebration of **CONTENTED SEXUAL LOVE**, never presenting it as a disruptive force, but as a bond, a source of satisfaction, health and stability

From the Romantic writers of the mid-nineteenth century to those of the present day, sexual love has been equated with passion in our culture, and passion has invariably been presented as anarchic, dangerous, destructive and wild, if desirable. For Donne, sexual love may be playful, as in 'The Flea', or more deeply committed, as in many other poems, but, though intense, it is always a source of stability rather than disruption, a source of contentment rather than anguish. In Donne's sometimes outrageous conceits, love is a compass in 'A Valediction', offering the same structure and permanence no matter how far apart the separate arms are, and a pleasurable dream that finds physical and, again, permanent, substance in 'The Dream', and self-contained and contented in 'The Sun Rising' and 'The Anniversary'. Any combination of these will provide varied and comprehensive illustrations of love as security in Donne's poetry, and there are revealing quotations from each: 'inter-assured of the mind', 'not yet/A breach', 'fixed foot' and 'Thy firmness' from 'A Valediction'; 'a theme/For reason', ''Tis not all spirit, pure, and brave,/If mixture it of fear' from 'The Dream'; 'Love ... no season knows', 'All here in one bed lay', 'Nothing else is' from 'The Sun Rising'; 'Only our love hath no decay', 'Running it never runs from us away', 'Who is so safe as we?' 'The Anniversary'. These are serene poems of assured love, whether the occasion is sad in itself, as in 'A Valediction', because the lovers are parting temporarily, or playful, as in 'The Flea', or joyous, as in 'The Sun Rising' and 'The Anniversary'. Technically, the effect is achieved by a combination of a calm, stately rhythm and a measured development of the argument.

- The poetry of John Donne is a **REALISTIC DEPICTION OF LOVE** in all its aspects, physical, psychological, emotional, spiritual

Love, these days, is located in the heart, in the emotions. If you ask someone for a phrase describing their love, they will tell you that their heart belongs to another, and if you ask for a phrase describing the loss of love, they will tell you that their heart is broken. We live in an age in which the dominant criterion is subjective feeling – if it doesn't make *you* feel good, there's something wrong with it. But humans are intellectual, physical and spiritual, as well as emotional beings. More than any other poet, Donne recognised, utilised and celebrated this. In Donne's poetry, an essential aspect of romantic love is physical and sensual pleasure, particularly tactile and visual pleasure – 'enjoys', 'pampered', 'these living walls of jet' are expressive quotations from 'The Flea'; 'Enter these arms', 'let's act the rest', 'Excess of joy' are from 'The Dream'; 'I would not lose her sight', 'that's done in warming us' from 'The Sun Rising'; 'these eyes, and ears', 'When thou and I first one another saw' from 'The Anniversary'; 'eyes, lips, and hands', 'Thy firmness' from 'A Valediction'. But for Donne, an equal part of romantic love is intellectual engagement, the marriage of minds, as Shakespeare put it in one of his sonnets. A seduction is always persuasive, always aiming at the mind –

'Mark', 'Oh stay', 'In what could this flea guilty be …?' from 'The Flea' – and sensual pleasure is always accompanied by an even more refined intellectual pleasure – 'thou saw'st my heart,/ And knew'st my thoughts' is from 'The Dream'; 'none can do/Treason to us, except one of us two' from 'The Anniversary'; 'a love, so much refined,/That our selves know not what it is' from 'A Valediction'. Donne's poems, appealing as much to the reader's mind as to the lovers, are structured on the logic of an argument – proposition, deduction, conclusion. It makes the poetry unusual, but should not constitute a difficulty. An intelligent reader will pride themselves on their ability to follow such logic. Nor is man's spiritual dimension ever absent in Donne's treatment of romantic love – 'souls where nothing dwells but love' is from 'The Anniversary'; 'I thought thee … an angel, at first sight' is from 'The Dream'; 'Our marriage bed, and marriage temple' from 'The Flea'; 'my soul' from 'Song: Sweetest love, I do not go'; and 'Thy soul the fixed foot' from 'A Valediction'. The heart is certainly not neglected in Donne's poetry – the word itself is often used in titles and text – but one gets the impression that mere emotions – fleeting, superficial – are the minor elements of love for Donne, when compared with the riches of the intellect, the senses and the soul.

- The poetry of John Donne dramatises the similarities and differences between **DIVINE LOVE** and sexual love

The sonnets on your course are usually numbered 1 ('Thou hast made me'), 7 ('At the round earth's imagined corners') and 14 ('Batter my heart') in *Divine Meditations*, a sequence of nineteen sonnets on devout subjects, including death and judgement (7), man's relationship with Christ (14) and penitence (1). No one knows when they were written, but some foremost scholars on Donne maintain that these meditations belong to 1610, long before the death of Donne's wife and long before his ordination. There are two standard portraits of Donne: one depicting him as a dashing, mischievous adventurer; the other offering him as a respected clergyman. He was both these things, often at the same time. If you look closely enough, you'll see that the eyes have the same devilish glint in all portraits. By and large, the poems by Donne on your course also fall into neat categories – love poems and divine poems – although, as with the man's eyes, there is much that is common to both styles. The bulk of his love poems seem to have been written before his wife's death, and the bulk of the divine poems afterwards. Keep in mind, however, that, in the spring of 1613, he seems to have written both a sexy poem for St Valentine's Day and a devout poem for Good Friday. He was a complex man. In the divine poems, the manner is just as witty – in the sense of intellectual – as it is in the love poems, similarly employing a series of unusual comparisons or metaphors to express the thought. Secondly, it is *thought* that Donne is still concerned with expressing. For him, faith is an experience that engages the mind as well as the body and the soul, just as sexual love did in the other poems. Technically, the divine poems are also presented as arguments, attempts to persuade or convince, just as most of the love poems were. Nevertheless, for all the similarities in manner and technique, these divine poems are entirely different in character from the love poems. The joyous contentment is gone, the pleasure, the mischief. The reason for this is obvious enough: in the love poems, he was playing with an equal; in the divine sonnets, he is struggling with a master. The sense of fun that characterised the love poems has been replaced by a sense of need in the divine poems. The sense of satisfaction has been replaced by a sense of unease.

- The poetry of John Donne is **SELF-CONSCIOUS AND ANALYTIC**, addressing the mind rather than the heart over an extensive range of human experience

  As mentioned above, the intelligent reader will pride themselves on their ability to follow the logic of an argument – proposition, deduction, conclusion. This is the manner of a Donne poem. It dramatises the process of thought, rather than starting from a ready-made conclusion. In 'The Flea', notice how the rhythm of the lines captures the movements of a mind thinking on the spot, almost making it up as it goes along. It's present in the first stanza – 'Confess it, this cannot be said/A sin, or shame, or loss of maidenhead,' – where Donne seems to be adding to, even improving on, his argument, as new points occur to him: *this isn't a sin, or you couldn't call it shameful, could you? And it certainly doesn't amount to losing your virginity* … Best of all is 'Where we almost, nay more than married are' in the second stanza, where Donne actually interrupts himself after coming up, in mid-sentence, with something better than what he started with. The first stanza consists of a witty lecture on a captured flea, but the second stanza opens with an urgent plea, as the woman is obviously about to crack the insect with her nail; the third stanza opens on a note of mock sadness and disappointment – the woman is cruel and impetuous because she's obviously executed the poor flea – but Donne soon recovers his optimism, when it occurs to him that the dead flea provides him with as strong a case to make as did the living flea. The same applies to all the other poems. In each, the thought twists and turns and responds to events as they happen. 'The Sun Rising' opens with an exasperated dismissal of the sun shining in one's eyes early in the morning. 'The Dream' also opens on a moment of waking, caught between sleep and consciousness, the thoughts blurred and confused, and only gradually clearing up. 'A Valediction' opens on the sadness of parting and works its way through the reassurance of reunion.

Style and Viewpoint

- The poetry of John Donne is argumentative and logical in character, which means that its **LANGUAGE** calls the mind into play rather than appeals to the senses

  Wits – the word used in the second line of 'The Anniversary': 'All glory of honours, beauties, wits' – were expected to be sparkling intelligences, capable of using unexpected associations between words and ideas in order to be illuminating or humorous. Donne's poetry is often described as displaying *wit* in this sense. The seventeenth-century meaning of the word lingers on in our colloquial expressions *keeping your wits about you* and *having the wit to do something*. It is possible, of course, that the modern reader may find Donne's terminology – the scientific terms, and so on – fairly challenging. But Donne never indulges in a private language; his references are always to the widely held ideas of his time. In 'The Flea', for instance, the phrase 'our two bloods mingled be' relies for its effect on the belief, common at the time, that sexual intercourse involved the mingling of blood from the participants, a notion that was derived from an ancient Greek philosopher called Aristotle, but that we may find merely amusing today. Of course, one has to research the contemporary references to get the most from Donne's poems. But surely that makes his language accessible, since the information is so easily available, rather than obscure. Donne's language is that of a proposition presented to the mind for consideration – 'All other things, to their destruction draw,/Only our love hath no decay' ('The Anniversary'); 'Repair me now, for now mine end doth haste' ('Thou hast made me') – a development or reason advanced in support of the proposition – 'As lightning, or a taper's light,/Thine eyes, and not thy noise waked me' ('The Dream'); 'This flea is you and I, and this/Our marriage bed' ('The Flea') – or a conclusion, again presented to the mind as logical – 'True and false fears let us refrain' ('The Anniversary'); 'I/Except you enthral me, never shall be free' ('Batter my heart'). The appeal of the language is always to the mind – as in a court of law, for instance – and never to the distractions of the senses or the emotions. This does not at all mean that it is dull. It displays wit, in the sense described above, and is sparkling and humorous.

- The poetry of John Donne draws its **IMAGERY** from science, politics, exploration, and other areas of the social world of his time, employing far-fetched comparisons, known as conceits

A conceit is a startling comparison between two unlikely, or previously unlikely, ideas or things, usually developed at greater length than most comparisons in poetry, and, in Donne, functioning as a device within an argumentative structure. In 'The Flea', during a long seduction, the insect humorously becomes, not only the place where the lovers lie together – 'Our marriage bed, and marriage temple' – but the embodiment of their love. The poem draws on the legal notions of guilt, innocence and murder, and on the medical beliefs at the time. 'The Sun Rising' uses the contemporary belief that the sun orbited the earth to advance the notion that the lovers are the centre of the universe. It draws on references from social life at home (schools, court, farming), exploration abroad (the East Indies, just opened up for trade by English adventurers), politics (states and princes) and astrology. Geometry and exploration are at the heart of the extended comparison in 'A Valediction', which also draws on contemporary religious belief, astrology and anatomy, to reassure that true lovers never actually part, because their union is beyond the merely physical. In both 'Batter my heart' and 'Thou hast made me', the soul is treated as something manufactured by God, and therefore requiring maintenance, something subject to malfunction, misuse and destruction over time, and in need of constant adjustment. Among other conceits, 'The Dream' compares a passionate man to a previously lit torch, which flares up more quickly than a brand new one – 'torches which must ready be,/Men light and put out'. 'The Anniversary' compares true lovers to a kingdom, inclusive of rulers, ruled and territory – 'none can do/Treason to us, except one of us two.' – and 'Song: Sweetest love, I do not go' compares the lover's heart to a diviner, a person who searches for water underground with a divining rod or uses special powers to foresee the future, with a further pun on 'divine', or godlike, angelic.

- The poetry of John Donne is alive with the **SOUND** effects of the speaking voice, including repetition, emphasis, stress, alliteration, rhyme, and so on, all designed to present or carry an argument

In the divine sonnets, the speaking voice is that of the supplicant. It is not, however, a quiet or subdued voice. It rages with emotion and need; it argues, accuses, cajoles. Consider the sound effects in 'Batter my heart', for instance. It opens with that hammer blow of an imperative command – 'Batter'. The first line ends on the accusatory 'you' – which you have to stress heavily, because of the punctuation, with the two pauses before it, and because it

brings the line to a thundering close. The dissatisfaction, bordering on rebellion, accumulates in the second line with the repeated stresses on the tame activities 'knock, breathe, shine', a rhythm that's echoed in line 4 with the much more radical and more violent 'break, blow, burn', where the consistent alliteration of the 'bs' adds to the destructive tempo. That's the violent complaint of the first quatrain. The second quatrain strikes a more reasonable note, as if the resentment had exhausted itself. The rhythm slows, tempered by the fractured punctuation in line 5, the more involved thought, the more clogged language – try saying 'like an usurped town' quickly – and the softer 'u' and 'o' sounds of the words, by contrast with the harder 'a', 'e', 'i' sounds of the first quatrain – 'I, like an usurped town, to another due'. The sounds control the rhythm, and the rhythm expresses the changes in thought and feeling. The sestet opens on an uncertainty, a hesitation, markedly different from the furious demand of the poem's beginning – 'Yet' – and this is followed by two of the most gentle, most mellow sounds in the English language – 'dearly' and 'love' – with the latter being immediately echoed in the repetition, 'loved'. The line ends on a positive rhyme – 'fain', which means eagerly and chimes with the hopeful 'again' – the uncertainly and need are continued in 'But' at the beginning of the next line, and the list that follows is closer to prayer in its rhythms and sounds and punctuation than to the angry insistence at the start of the sonnet – 'Divorce me, untie, or break that knot again'. In the secular poems, the speaking voice is that of the lover – playful, celebratory, or, as in 'A Valediction: forbidding Mourning', reassuring. In this poem, the opening sounds, as the lovers prepare to part, are soft and gentle – the quiet sibilance of 'virtuous … pass … whisper … souls …' and the assonance in the repetition of the broad vowel sounds – 'sad … say … say', 'go … now … no' – and the controlling influence of the adverb 'mildly' in the first line. The way the punctuation controls the rhythm is particularly interesting in this poem. The voice is gentle, reassuring, consoling, and above all patient – 'Such wilt thou be to me, who must/Like th'other foot, obliquely run'. It's impossible to read this without quietly emphasising certain key words – 'Such … must … other … obliquely' – and without pausing softly after 'me … must … foot … run', because of the punctuation and line ending. The overall effect is of deeply affectionate persuasion.

- The poetry of John Donne uses poetic **FORMS** as logical structures for delivering the drama of a debate, with another or with oneself

In poetry, the traditional way to greet the morning sun was with reverence, welcoming it as life-giving, as a warming god, or – depending on your inclination at the time – a warming goddess. In 'The Sun Rising', Donne takes this conventional form and makes something more mischievous out of it. He dismisses the sun as a busybody, an intruder, and then gradually comes to pity it as a loner. This is typical of Donne's approach. He takes traditional, even overused or clichéd forms, and freshens them in unexpected ways. The form of love poem in which the poet dreams or daydreams of his mistress, for instance, was extremely common at the time Donne was writing but, in 'The Dream', he makes something distinctive out of the conventional form, creating a work that *recreates* in sound and imagery the confusion we often feel on waking from a dream. It is possible that the 'Song: Sweetest love, I do not go' and 'A Valediction' were both written for his wife, Anne More, when Donne left for France in 1611 in the service of Sir Robert Drury. The former was set to an existing popular tune, but goes far beyond the standard versions in terms of sensibility and imagination, while the latter is part of a very long, very fine tradition of love poems inspired by parting and absence, but employs a very unusual metaphor – that of the compass – which is not part of the tradition at all. Similarly, the divine sonnet – in which the poet addresses or prays to God – was and still is a popular poetic form, since it allows for a contained and highly structured expression of devotion. Donne, however, who always adds vitality and individuality, used it as much to berate, hassle and provoke his God – 'Repair me now, for now mine end doth haste' ('Thou hast made me'); 'But let them sleep … Teach me how to repent' ('At the round earth's imagined corners'); 'Take me to you, imprison me' ('Batter my heart') – as to worship Him.

A Note on the Metaphysical Poets

John Donne is one of a group of seventeenth-century writers known as the Metaphysical Poets. The description was first used by a later poet and critic called John Dryden, sixty-two years after Donne's death. 'He affects the metaphysics,' Dryden wrote of Donne, 'not only in his satires, but in his amorous verses, where nature should only reign; and perplexes the minds of the fair sex with nice speculations of philosophy, when he should engage their hearts, and entertain them with the softnesses of love.' Dryden complains that Donne is aiming too high when wooing a woman – at the head instead of the heart – and therefore ends up muddling rather than seducing the object of his love. In itself, this criticism offers a handy introduction to the key elements of Donne's poetry, which is analytical and self-conscious, which is structured as a logical argument rather than a declaration, and which uses language that calls the mind into play rather than appeals to the senses. Such features are no longer assumed to be faults in writing. In any case, Dryden's use of the word 'metaphysics' was taken up by a writer from the next generation, Samuel Johnson remarked in his essay 'Life of Cowley', which appeared in his *Lives of the Poets*: 'About the beginning of the seventeenth century, appeared a race of writers that may be termed the metaphysical poets … [who] were men of learning, and to show their learning was their whole endeavour' – and the term has stuck ever since.

The word 'metaphysical' literally means 'after, or beyond, the physical', suggesting some sort of philosophical analysis of the nature of the universe, and as such it's really a misleading description of Donne's work, giving a wrong impression if taken on face value. You should note its origin. You should be aware of what it is trying to capture in the distinctive style of these writers: the play of ideas. But you should also be wary of its limitations.

Paul Durcan

Paul Durcan was born in Dublin in 1944 and grew up in Turlough, County Mayo. His father, John, was a circuit court judge. While Durcan was studying at University College Dublin, he was committed against his will to a psychiatric hospital and given electric shock treatment. He moved to London in 1966 and married in 1968. He and his wife Nessa had two daughters. They separated in 1984. Durcan has written many books of poetry, his first was published in 1967, his most recent in 2012.

Prescribed Poems

'Students at Higher Level will be required to study a representative selection from the work of eight poets: a representative selection would seek to reflect the range of a poet's themes and interests and exhibit his/her characteristic style and viewpoint. Normally the study of at least six poems by each poet would be expected.' (DES English Syllabus, 6.3)

Poetry

Themes and Interests

is **AUTOBIOGRAPHICAL**, drawing on personal experiences from childhood, boyhood, youth, marriage, fatherhood, divorce, living alone, becoming a grandfather, and so on

explores the complexities of, and tensions within, the modern Irish **FAMILY**, including love, security, control and disintegration, using his own family of origin and created family as starting points

The Poetry of Paul Durcan

is **SATIRICAL**, commenting critically on Irish hypocrisy, bureaucracy, consumerism, middle-class culture, religious failures, and other social ills

utilises the persona of the well-meaning man who often struggles with the demands of life and with the burdens of a traumatised past, often employing a **SELF-DEPRECATING** portrait

Style and Viewpoint

The Poetry of Paul Durcan

is literal, because its **LANGUAGE** rarely contains more than its surface meaning and is therefore close to conversational prose, a style particularly suited to the satiric public pieces

draws its **IMAGERY** from the everyday events of late twentieth-century and early twenty-first-century Ireland, from Irish landscape, and from painting, an art form with which Durcan has a particular affinity

relies heavily on the **SOUNDS** and rhythms of the speaking voice, a quality that makes it particularly effective when spoken in performance, by Durcan himself

is unorthodox in its use of poetic **FORMS**, employing idiosyncratic versions of prayers, ballads, couplets, dramatic monologues, and so on

Poetry

Nessa

I met her on the first of August
In the Shangri-La Hotel,
She took me by the index finger
And dropped me in her well.
And that was a whirlpool, that was a whirlpool,   5
And I very nearly drowned.

Take off your pants, she said to me,
And I very nearly didn't;
Would you care to swim? she said to me,
And I hopped into the Irish Sea.   10
And that was a whirlpool, that was a whirlpool,
And I very nearly drowned.

On the way back I fell in the field
And she fell down beside me,
I'd have lain in the grass with her all my life   15
With Nessa:
She was a whirlpool, she was a whirlpool,
And I very nearly drowned.

O Nessa my dear, Nessa my dear,
Will you stay with me on the rocks?   20
Will you come for me into the Irish Sea
And for me let your red hair down?
And then we will ride into Dublin City
In a taxi-cab wrapped up in dust.
Oh you are a whirlpool, you are a whirlpool,   25
And I am very nearly drowned.

Glossary

[title] **Nessa:** Nessa O'Neill, who married Durcan

[2] **Shangri-La:** fictional country symbolic of earthly paradise, invented by James Hilton in his 1933
novel *Lost Horizon*, filmed in 1937 and 1973

ANALYSE

The theme is falling in love – figuratively and, apparently, literally also, since 'On the way back I fell in the field'. The loss of balance and self-control suggested by such common descriptions as 'falling in love' and 'head over heels' are contained here in the central metaphor of the 'whirlpool', a rotating mass of water into which things can be drawn.

The first meeting is a whirlpool. The first sexual encounter – 'Take off your pants' – is a whirlpool. The woman was and still is a whirlpool. Durcan's use of language relies on taking colloquial, everyday expressions and reusing them in poetry. Here we have dropping 'in her well', for getting lost, or descending into the underworld. We have the implicit sink or swim, for failing or succeeding, in the line 'Would you care to swim? she said to me'. Line 22 refers to the familiar expression letting your hair down, to suggest ease, relaxation and a good time.

And finally, there is the phrase 'on the rocks', representing bad times, when you're down on your luck, but when those who love you stick with you ('Will you stay with me on the rocks?'). Other notable images are those of perfection – 'the first of August' and 'Shangri-La'. The form of the poem is that of a light-hearted ditty or ballad, and the playful form and tone are intended to capture the brightness and lightness of the relationship.

MAKE

(i) Taking the 'whirlpool' as the central metaphor of the poem, trace and analyse any other related references; for example, to water, drowning, loss of control, spinning, whirling, and so on.

(ii) This is a celebration of the loved one. Would you consider it successful?

The Girl with the Keys to Pearse's Cottage
to John and Judith Meagher

When I was sixteen I met a dark girl;
Her dark hair was darker because her smile was so bright;
She was the girl with the keys to Pearse's Cottage;
And her name was Cáit Killann.

The cottage was built into the side of a hill;   5
I recall two windows and cosmic peace
Of bare brown rooms and on whitewashed walls
Photographs of the passionate and pale Pearse.

I recall wet thatch and peeling jambs
And how all was best seen from below in the field;   10
I used sit in the rushes with ledger-book and pencil
Compiling poems of passion for Cáit Killann.

Often she used linger on the sill of a window;
Hands by her side and brown legs akimbo;
In sun-red skirt and moon-black blazer;   15
Looking towards our strange world wide-eyed.

Our world was strange because it had no future;
She was America-bound at summer's end.
She had no choice but to leave her home –
The girl with the keys to Pearse's Cottage.   20

O Cáit Killann, O Cáit Killann,
You have gone with your keys from your own native place.
Yet here in the dark – El Greco eyes blaze back
From your Connemara postman's daughter's proudly mortal face.

Glossary

[title] **Pearse's Cottage:** a small restored cottage in Connemara, County Galway, used by nationalist, writer and leader of the 1916 Rising, Patrick Pearse (1879–1916), as a summer home

[23] **El Greco:** painter (1541–1614) who regarded colour as the most important element in painting

ANALYSE

This is a statement of anger and pain, arising from the disillusioned recognition that the Ireland of the 1970s had failed miserably to live up to the splendid visions of the state's self-sacrificing founders, particularly Patrick Pearse. It's a country that cannot even offer its own young a home.

The central character here is the symbolic girl of the title – dark-haired, like so many female representations of Ireland in the past; named Cáit, the Irish form of Kate or Cathleen, like Cathleen Ní Houlihan, the mythical symbol of Irish nationalism; and the holder of keys to Pearse's Cottage, and therefore the keeper of the vision that inspired the 'passionate and pale' Pearse. That she has to emigrate means that the idealism she is minder of also has to depart the country. She is from Connemara – perhaps representing the most 'authentic' Ireland, because it was never fully occupied by foreign powers, since its land was predominantly poor. She is also dressed in the traditional 'sun-red skirt' of Connemara women. Cáit looks at modern Ireland – our 'strange' world that has 'no future' – with astonishment, and then she has to leave it all – the keys, the cottage, Patrick Pearse and his idealism – behind her, as she emigrates, 'America-bound'.

Apart from the imagery, the most effective technical aspect is the alliteration of stanza two, particularly in the final line – 'Photographs of the passionate and pale Pearse' – where the explosive sounds capture the intensity of the man. The form of the poem is based on the traditional ballad, which in Ireland was routinely used as a vehicle for bemoaning Ireland's occupation by the English and imagining the perfection that would materialise once the country was 'free'. Its use here is heavily ironic.

MAKE

(i) In the poem, 'Pearse's Cottage' stands for a vision of an Ireland that never became real. Pick out other aspects of this imagined Ireland and, from the details of the poem, contrast the Ireland that actually came into being.

(ii) The work 'dark' occurs in both the opening and closing stanzas, but it has changed its meaning from one to the other. What do you think it suggests in each location?

READ

The Difficulty that is Marriage

We disagree to disagree, we divide, we differ;
Yet each night as I lie in bed beside you
And you are faraway curled up in sleep
I array the moonlit ceiling with a mosaic of question marks;
How was it I was so lucky to have ever met you?   5
I am no brave pagan proud of my mortality
Yet gladly on this changeling earth I should live for ever
If it were with you, my sleeping friend.
I have my troubles and I shall always have them
But I should rather live with you for ever   10
Than exchange my troubles for a changeless kingdom.
But I do not put you on a pedestal or throne;
You must have your faults but I do not see them.
If it were with you, I should live for ever.

Glossary

[7] **changeling:** in folklore, a child, usually ugly, left by fairies as a substitute for one they've taken away

ANALYSE

This poem has fourteen lines, but little else of the elegantly tight structure that is a sonnet. It doesn't hold to a regular rhyming scheme, but instead employs a rather random recurrence of certain words – 'you' ends lines 2 and 5, for instance; 'ever' ends lines 7, 10 and 14; 'them' ends lines 9 and 13. The sound effects throughout are somewhat ungainly – 'troubles' echoes around inside the poem like a pebble in a tin can; and the repeated use of 'I should' and 'I do not' sounds like alternating declarations and retractions of the marriage vows. Nevertheless, the use of alliteration throughout is powerful and effective. This is particularly true of the opening line – 'We disagree to disagree, we divide, we differ' – where the hard, clashing 'd' sounds replicate the conflicts and tensions between two people who are living together.

The verse is a statement that life, and therefore marriage, can be difficult at times, but also magical at times, a combination nicely captured in the image of the moonlight on the ceiling providing the background for question marks. The picture is of dark marks on a clear canvas, contorted forms cut into smooth space, hard questions on a soft texture. Moonlight is associated with romance, questions with difficulties. The poem is also a declaration of undying love – 'If it were with you, I should live for ever.'

MAKE

(i) In the poem, the woman is 'curled up in sleep' and the poet is awake asking questions. It is something that happens 'each night'. Confining yourself only to the details in the poem, what does this suggest to you about the relationship, and about the two individuals involved in it?

(ii) The poet says he was 'lucky to have ever met you'. What evidence, if any, does he provide to illustrate this?

Poetry

READ

Wife Who Smashed Television Gets Jail

"She came home, my Lord, and smashed in the television;
Me and the kids were peaceably watching *Kojak*
When she marched into the living room and declared
That if I didn't turn off the television immediately
She'd put her boot through the screen;   5
I didn't turn it off, so instead she turned it off –
I remember the moment exactly because Kojak
After shooting a dame with the same name as my wife
Snarled at the corpse – Goodnight, Queen Maeve –
And then she took off her boots and smashed in the television;   10
I had to bring the kids round to my mother's place;
We got there just before the finish of *Kojak*;
(My mother has a fondness for *Kojak*, my Lord);
When I returned home my wife had deposited
What was left of the television into the dustbin,   15
Saying – I didn't get married to a television
And I don't see why my kids or anybody else's kids
Should have a television for a father or mother,
We'd be much better off all down in the pub talking
Or playing bar-billiards –   20
Whereupon she disappeared off back down again to the pub."
Justice O'Brádaigh said wives who preferred bar-billiards to family television
Were a threat to the family which was the basic unit of society
As indeed the television itself could be said to be a basic unit of the family
And when as in this case wives expressed their preference in forms of violence   25
Jail was the only place for them. Leave to appeal was refused.

Glossary

[2] *Kojak:* an American detective series on television between 1973 and 1978, very popular in Ireland, where people widely borrowed American expressions from it

[9] **Maeve:** the name of the shot character in the TV episode, the name of the speaker's wife, and **Queen Maeve,** a character from Irish legend who was famous for the number of lovers she had

[20] **bar-billiards:** a form of billiards played in pubs, on a small table in which balls are struck into holes guarded by pegs

This poem, published in the mid-1970s, shows the destructive influence of television. It suggests that an addiction to television damages the family. Perhaps we would replace television with the internet now as the greatest danger to healthy communication between people, but back in the 1970s in Ireland, television was the dominant technology.

The poem imagines a court case in which a judge has to decide between husband and wife. At the beginning, the husband is speaking and giving evidence. He says that his wife came home when he and their kids were 'peaceably' watching television. She 'marched' into the room and 'declared' that she would destroy the television if it wasn't turned off. The husband's language suggests that he was doing no harm and that his wife – who is aggressive and violent – was in the wrong. We immediately learn, though, that she simply turned the television off. She wasn't destructive. Not yet, in any case. The violence, actually, is on the television, where the detective Kojak is just after 'shooting a dame'. Notice the contemptuous attitude to women – 'dame' – and to death – 'Snarled at the corpse'. It's at this stage that the wife 'took off her boots and smashed in the television'. Why? In response to the contempt? Possibly.

In any case, the husband, according to his own testimony, didn't even ask. He just took the kids and went to his mother's place, where she was also watching *Kojak*. Obviously, catching the end of the episode was far more important to him than anything else. When he came back home, his wife had thrown the broken television set into the dustbin.

Now we hear the wife's side, although not directly from her but as reported by her husband. The language that she uses shows how much damage television has done. Television has taken her husband from her life. Television has deprived her children of their parents. It is, she says, like a monster, destroying everything in its path.

Finally, the judge speaks. It is his role to decide between the two. As a judge, of course, he represents the entire society. On behalf of society, his decision is that the wife was in the wrong. Television is more important than anything else. It is 'a basic unit of the family'. Without it, the family would disintegrate. So he sends the wife to jail, thereby breaking up the family. This is a particularly dramatic example of irony. The judge insists he's doing one thing – protecting the family – but is actually doing the opposite. This irony is also present in the husband's evidence. The final message of the poem itself is clear, though. What destroys the family is television and those who defend it.

(i) The poem works by using a number of different voices. For instance, the husband's voice is self-justifying. Identify each voice, describe it, and select quotations to justify your description.

(ii) Though the internet and more modern devices have long replaced television in the centre of our culture, do you think the poem still has relevance? Explain.

READ

Parents

A child's face is a drowned face:
Her parents stare down at her asleep
Estranged from her by a sea:
She is under the sea
And they are above the sea: 5
If she looked up she would see them
As if locked out of their own home,
Their mouths open,
Their foreheads furrowed –
Pursed-up orifices of fearful fish –   10
Their big ears are fins behind glass
And in her sleep she is calling out to them
     Father, Father
     Mother, Mother
But they cannot hear her: 15
She is inside the sea
And they are outside the sea.
Through the night, stranded, they stare
At the drowned, drowned face of their child.

Glossary

[3] **Estranged:** no longer on friendly terms with, alienated

[10] **Pursed-up:** contracted, tightened, wrinkled

[10] **orifices:** openings, particularly ones in the body such as the mouth or nostril

ANALYSE

According to the poem, parents looking down on their sleeping child are like people looking at a sea creature in water. This is the central metaphor of 'Parents', the figurative comparison that controls the entire poem. As you know from your science classes, light refracts, or bends, as it passes from one medium through another. So, you get a visual distortion if you're out of water and looking at something that is in water. The metaphor of the poem suggests that neither the child nor the parents can see each other as they really are, without distortion. They inhabit different worlds. Perhaps they are different creatures.

The opening line seems to suggest that the child is in trouble: 'A child's face is a drowned face'. Of course, we understand from the next line that the child is only drowned in sleep and that this is a good image for describing the difference between those who are awake and those who are asleep – they seem to inhabit separate elements: 'She is under the sea/And they are above the sea'. The most important word in the opening section is probably 'estranged', though. It doesn't mean only 'separated'. Because it shares the same root and much of the same meaning with 'strange' and 'stranger', it also means alienated. We should also note that it is the parents who are 'estranged' from the child, not the other way round, as if they have left their natural element and wandered off into the wrong one.

This idea is confirmed and developed in the imagery of the next section. The parents are out of the water, but they are described as 'fearful fish'. Fish out of water are dying fish, which is why they are 'fearful', of course. The notion that they are out of their element is reinforced by the simile 'As if locked out of their own home', which is how the child sees them. Their 'home' is water. They have 'fins'. Their mouths are like the 'pursed-up' mouths of fish trying to breathe out of water.

When the child calls to them, therefore – 'Father/Mother' – she is not calling because she is frightened for herself, but because she is anxious about them. They can't hear this cry, of course. All parents listen only for the cry of the child who is in trouble. They can never hear the cry of the child who says the parents are in trouble. And yet, in the poem, the parents are the ones who are 'stranded', which literally means left aground on a shore, as in the phrase *a stranded whale*.

In the final line, the poem returns to repeat the word 'drowned' from the opening line. It does so twice – 'drowned, drowned'. But by now we understand that is the opposite of danger and death. A fish is more alive when it is 'drowned' than when it is 'stranded'.

What does it all mean? Perhaps that childhood is the natural element of human beings and that when we leave it, we are 'stranded' in adulthood. Even worse, we don't quite understand our own loss. We think the child is the one who is 'drowned' and needs to be rescued.

MAKE

(i) Would you agree that the mood of this poem is quite bleak or dark? Use quotations to support your points.

(ii) Relationships between parents and children is still among the hottest topics in today's world. Would you consider that the poem has continuing relevance? Explain.

"Windfall", 8 Parnell Hill, Cork

But, then, at the end of the day I could always say –
Well, now, I am going home.
I felt elected, steeped, sovereign to be able to say –
I am going home.
When I was at home I liked to stay at home;   5
At home I stayed at home for weeks;
At home I used sit in a winged chair by the window
Overlooking the river and the factory chimneys,
The electricity power station and the car assembly works,
The fleets of trawlers and the pilot tugs,   10
Dreaming that life is a dream that is real,
The river a reflection of itself in its own waters,
Goya sketching Goya among the smoky mirrors.
The industrial vista was my Mont Sainte-Victoire.
While my children sat on my knees watching TV   15
Their mother, my wife, reclined on the couch
Knitting a bright-coloured scarf, drinking a cup of black coffee,
Smoking a cigarette – one of her own roll-ups.
I closed my eyes and breathed in and breathed out.
It is ecstasy to breathe if you are at home in the world.   20
What a windfall! A home of our own!
Our neighbours' houses had names like "Con Amore",
"Sans Souci", "Pacelli", "Montini", "Homesville".
But we called our home "Windfall".
"Windfall", 8 Parnell Hill, Cork.   25
In the gut of my head coursed the leaf of tranquillity
Which I dreamed was known only to Buddhist Monks
In lotus monasteries high up in the Hindu Kush.
Down here in the dark depths of Ireland,
Below sea level in the city of Cork,   30
In a city as intimate and homicidal as a Little Marseilles,
In a country where all the children of the nation
Are not cherished equally
And where the best go homeless, while the worst
Erect block-house palaces – self-regardingly ugly –   35
Having a home of your own can give to a family
A chance in a lifetime to transcend death.

At the high window, shipping from all over the world
Being borne up and down the busy, yet contemplative, river;
Skylines drifting in and out of skylines in the cloudy valley;   40

Firelight at dusk, and city lights;
Beyond them the control tower of the airport on the hill –
A lighthouse in the sky flashing green to white to green;
Our black-and-white cat snoozing in the corner of a chair;
Pastels and etchings on the four walls, and over the mantelpiece   45
"Van Gogh's Grave" and "Lovers in Water";
A room wallpapered in books and family photograph albums
Chronicling the adventures and metamorphoses of family life:
In swaddling clothes in Mammy's arms on baptism day;
Being a baby of nine months and not remembering it;   50
Face-down in a pram, incarcerated in a high chair;
Everybody, including strangers, wearing shop-window smiles;
With Granny in Felixstowe, with Granny in Ballymaloe;
In a group photo in First Infants, on a bike at thirteen;
In the back garden in London, in the back garden in Cork;   55
Performing a headstand after First Holy Communion;
Getting a kiss from the Bishop on Confirmation Day;
Straw hats in Bois de Boulougne, wearing wings at the seaside;
Mammy and Daddy holding hands on the Normandy Beaches;
Mammy and Daddy at the wedding of Jeremiah and Margot;   60
Mammy and Daddy queueing up for *Last Tango in Paris*;
Boating on the Shannon, climbing mountains in Kerry;
Building sandcastles in Killala, camping in Barley Cove;
Picnicking in Moone, hide-and-go-seek in Clonmacnoise;
Riding horses, cantering, jumping fences;   65
Pushing out toy yachts in the pond in the Tuileries;
The Irish College revisited in the Rue des Irlandais;
Sipping an *orange pressé* through a straw on the roof of the Beaubourg;
Dancing in Père Lachaise, weeping at Auvers.
Year in, year out, I pored over these albums accumulating,   70
My children looking over my shoulder, exhilarated as I was,
Their mother presiding at our ritual from a distance –
The far side of the hearthrug, diffidently, proudly.
Schoolbooks on the floor and pyjamas on the couch –
Whose turn is it tonight to put the children to bed?   75

Our children swam about our home
As if it was their private sea,
Their own unique, symbiotic fluid
Of which their parents also partook.
Such is home – a sea of your own –   80
In which you hang upside down from the ceiling

With equanimity, while postcards from Thailand on the mantelpiece
Are raising their eyebrow markings benignly:
Your hands dangling their prayers to the floorboards of your home,
Sifting the sands underneath the surfaces of conversations,   85
The marine insect life of the family psyche.
A home of your own – or a sea of your own –
In which climbing the walls is as natural
As making love on the stairs;
In which when the telephone rings   90
Husband and wife are metamorphosed into smiling accomplices,
Both declining to answer it;
Initiating, instead, a yet more subversive kiss –
A kiss they have perhaps never attempted before –
And might never have dreamed of attempting   95
Were it not for the telephone belling.
Through the bannisters or along the bannister rails
The pyjama-clad children solemnly watching
Their parents at play, jumping up and down in support,
Race back to bed, gesticulating wordlessly: 100
The most subversive unit in society is the human family.

We're almost home, pet, almost home …
Our home is at …
I'll be home …
I have to go home now …   105
I want to go home now …
Are you feeling homesick?
Are you anxious to get home? …
I can't wait to get home …
Let's stay at home tonight and …   110
What time will you be coming home at? …
If I'm not home by six at the latest, I'll phone …
We're nearly home, don't worry, we're nearly home …

But then with good reason
I was put out of my home: 115
By a keen wind felled.
I find myself now without a home
Having to live homeless in the alien, foreign city of Dublin.
It is an eerie enough feeling to be homesick
Yet knowing you will be going home next week;   120
It is an eerie feeling beyond all ornithological analysis

To be homesick knowing that there is no home to go home to:
Day by day, creeping, crawling,
Moonlighting, escaping,
Bed-and-breakfast to bed-and-breakfast;   125
Hostels, centres, one-night hotels.

Homeless in Dublin,
Blown about the suburban streets at evening,
Peering in the windows of other people's homes,
Wondering what it must feel like   130
To be sitting around a fire –
Apache or Cherokee or Bourgeoisie –
Beholding the firelit faces of your family,
Beholding their starry or their TV gaze:
Windfall to Windfall – can you hear me?   135
Windfall to Windfall …
We're almost home, pet, don't worry anymore, we're almost home.

Glossary

[title] **Windfall:** figuratively, an unexpected gain or piece of good fortune; literally, the name of Durcan's house

[13] **Goya:** Spanish painter (1746–1828)

[14] **Mont Sainte-Victoire:** mountain in southern France, often painted by Paul Cézanne (1839–1906)

[22 and 23] the house names are 'With Love', 'Carefree', the surnames of two Italian Popes

[28] **Hindu Kush:** great mountain system of Central Asia

[53–69] the references are to Irish, English and French holiday locations

[61] *Last Tango in Paris:* 1972 film directed by Bernardo Bertolucci, once notorious for its depiction of alienated sexuality

[69] **Auvers:** Vincent Van Gogh (1853–1890), whose grave is mentioned in line 46, is buried here

[121] **ornithological:** relating to the study of birds

[132] **Apache** and **Cherokee** are North American native tribes, now almost extinct; **Bourgeoisie** is the dominant European tribe, still flourishing

ANALYSE

This monologue has five sections.

In the first section (lines 1–37), home is depicted as a miraculous gift, the 'windfall' of the title. The word 'dream' is used a number of times to describe the experience of having a home of one's own. Similar terms suggesting an elevated state of living are 'ecstasy' and 'elected' – which has the religious connotation of God's chosen – 'steeped' – which means extremely lucky – 'sovereign' and 'winged chair'. Home offers an exalted condition, a 'tranquillity' that can 'transcend death'.

In section two (lines 38–75), this notion of home as earthly paradise is reinforced and reflected by images – the prints that hang in the interior of the house and the photographs taken of family activities, all suggesting togetherness and contentment in the day-to-day activities of

ordinary life or holidays. Photographs are ambivalent, though. They also record departures from home and the passing of time. Nevertheless, the questions in this section are still untroubled – 'Whose turn is it tonight to put the children to bed?'

Section three (lines 76–101) is particularly effective. It offers rich metaphor to contrast with the direct expression of the remainder of the poem. Interestingly, home is compared to a sea – an image also used in 'Parents' – in which the dullness, or unnaturalness, of routine social behaviour is reversed – 'you hang upside down' and spend your time 'climbing the walls' and 'making love on the stairs'. This is why, in the final line of the section, the family is described as 'subversive'. *Happy* family is implied.

Section four (lines 102–112) collects a list of everyday expressions to reveal how essential, comforting and nourishing home is to us.

The final section (line 113–136) opens with the revelation that the poet was 'put out of my home'. The reason for this is described as 'good', or justified, but not otherwise explained. Clearly, however, the poet accepts the blame or the responsibility for his eviction, which was undertaken 'with good reason'. If you look back sympathetically over the poem, you might notice indications of a certain powerlessness throughout, a helplessness in the face of forces that are not quite under control. Even the title of the poem, and the name of the house – 'Windfall' – carries suggestions of an accidental gift, of something that somehow or another drops into a person's lap. Equally mysteriously, and now tragically in this section, it is somehow taken away. In any case, everything from the earlier sections is now reversed for the poet – he's 'homeless' and 'homesick' rather than 'at home'; his feelings are 'eerie' rather than ecstatic; he's 'creeping, crawling' rather than sitting in a 'winged chair'; and he's on the outside 'peering in the windows' rather than on the inside 'at the high window' looking out.

MAKE

(i) The notion that beauty creates reflections of itself is present throughout the poem. It starts in the lines containing 'Goya sketching Goya'. Can you find other examples? And comment on how it is present or absent in the final section of the poem.

(ii) A 'windfall' is an unexpected gift. Is this how home is understood throughout the poem? Or are there exceptions, in your opinion.

Six Nuns Die in Convent Inferno

To the
happy memory of six Loreto nuns
who died
between midnight and morning of
2 June 1986

I

We resided in a Loreto convent in the centre of Dublin city
On the east side of a public gardens, St Stephen's Green.
Grafton Street – the *paseo*
Where everybody *paseo*'d, including even ourselves –
Debouched on the north side, and at the top of Grafton Street,   5
Or round the base of the great patriotic pebble of O'Donovan Rossa,
Knelt tableaus of punk girls and punk boys.
When I used to pass them – scurrying as I went –
Often as not to catch a mass in Clarendon Street,
The Carmelite Church in Clarendon Street   10
(Myself, I never used the Clarendon Street entrance,
I always slipped in by way of Johnson's Court,
Opposite the side entrance to Bewley's Oriental Café),
I could not help but smile, as I sucked on a Fox's mint,
That for all the half-shaven heads and the martial garb   15
And the dyed hair-dos and the nappy pins
They looked so conventional, really, and vulnerable,
Clinging to warpaint and to uniforms and to one another.
I knew it was myself who was the ultimate drop-out,
The delinquent, the recidivist, the vagabond,   20
The wild woman, the subversive, the original punk.
Yet, although I confess I was smiling, I was also afraid,
Appalled by my own nerve, my own fervour,
My apocalyptic enthusiasm, my other-worldly hubris:
To opt out of the world and to   25
Choose such exotic loneliness,
Such terrestrial abandonment,
A lifetime of bicycle lamps and bicycle pumps,
A lifetime of galoshes stowed under the stairs,
A lifetime of umbrellas drying out in the kitchens.   30

I was an old nun – an agèd beadswoman –
But I was no daw.
I knew what a weird bird I was, I knew that when we
Went to bed we were as eerie an aviary as you'd find
In all the blown-off rooftops of the city: 35

Scuttling about our dorm, wheezing, shrieking, croaking,
In our yellowy corsets, wonky suspenders, strung-out garters,
A bony crew in the gods of the sleeping city.
Many's the night I lay awake in bed
Dreaming what would befall us if there were a fire: 40
No fire-escapes outside, no fire-extinguishers inside;
To coin a Dublin saying,
We'd not stand a snowball's chance in hell. Fancy that!
It seemed too good to be true:
Happy death vouchsafed only to the few.   45
Sleeping up there was like sleeping at the top of the mast
Of a nineteenth-century schooner, and in the daytime
We old nuns were the ones who crawled out on the yardarms
To stitch and sew the rigging and the canvas.
To be sure we were weird birds, oddballs, Christniks,   50
For we had done the weirdest thing a woman can do –
Surrendered the marvellous passions of girlhood,
The innocent dreams of childhood,
Not for a night or a weekend or even a Lent or a season,
But for a lifetime.   55
Never to know the love of a man or a woman;
Never to have children of our own;
Never to have a home of our own;
All for why and for what?
To follow a young man – would you believe it –   60
Who lived two thousand years ago in Palestine
And who died a common criminal strung up on a tree.

As we stood there in the disintegrating dormitory
Burning to death in the arms of Christ –
O Christ, Christ, come quickly, quickly –   65
Fluttering about in our tight, gold bodices,
Beating our wings in vain,
It reminded me of the snaps one of the sisters took
When we took a seaside holiday in 1956
(The year Cardinal Mindszenty went into hiding   70
In the US legation in Budapest.
He was a great hero of ours, Cardinal Mindszenty,
Any of us would have given our right arm
To have been his nun – darning his socks, cooking his meals,
Making his bed, doing his washing and ironing.)   75
Somebody – an affluent buddy of the bishop's repenting his affluence –
Loaned Mother Superior a secluded beach in Co. Waterford –

Ardmore, along the coast from Tramore –
A cove with palm trees, no less, well off the main road.
There we were, fluttering up and down the beach,   80
Scampering hither and thither in our starched bathing-costumes.
Tonight, expiring in the fire, was quite much like that,
Only instead of scampering into the waves of the sea,
Now we were scampering into the flames of the fire.

That was one of the gayest days of my life,   85
The day the sisters went swimming.
Often in the silent darkness of the chapel after Benediction,
During the Exposition of the Blessed Sacrament,
I glimpsed the sea again as it was that day.
Praying – daydreaming really –   90
I became aware that Christ is the ocean
Forever rising and falling on the world's shore.
Now tonight in the convent Christ is the fire in whose waves
We are doomed but delighted to drown.
And, darting in and out of the flames of the dormitory,   95
Gabriel, with that extraordinary message of his on his boyish lips,
Frenetically pedalling his skybike.
He whispers into my ear what I must do
And I do it – and die.
Each of us in our own tiny, frail, furtive way   100
Was a Mother of God, mothering forth illegitimate Christs
In the street life of Dublin city.
God have mercy on our whirring souls –
Wild women were we all –
And on the misfortunate, poor fire-brigade men   105
Whose task it will be to shovel up our ashes and shovel
What is left of us into black plastic refuse sacks.
Fire-brigade men are the salt of the earth.

Isn't it a marvellous thing how your hour comes
When you least expect it? When you lose a thing,   110
Not to know about it until it actually happens?
How, in so many ways, losing things is such a refreshing experience,
Giving you a sense of freedom you've not often experienced?
How lucky I was to lose – I say, lose – lose my life.
It was a Sunday night, and after vespers   115
I skipped bathroom so that I could hop straight into bed
And get in a bit of a read before lights out:
Conor Cruise O'Brien's new book *The Siege*,
All about Israel and superlatively insightful

For a man who they say is reputedly an agnostic –   120
I got a loan of it from the brother-in-law's married niece –
But I was tired out and I fell asleep with the book open
Face down across my breast and I woke
to the racket of bellowing flame and snarling glass.
The first thing I thought was that the brother-in-law's married niece   125
Would never again get her Conor Cruise O'Brien back
And I had seen on the price-tag that it cost £23.00:
Small wonder that the custom of snipping off the price
As an exercise in social deportment has simply died out;
Indeed a book today is almost worth buying for its price,   130
Its price frequently being more remarkable than its contents.

The strange Eucharist of my death –
To be eaten alive by fire and smoke.
I clasped the dragon to my breast
And stroked his red-hot ears.   135
Strange! There we were, all sleeping molecules,
Suddenly all giving birth to our deaths,
All frantically in labour.
Doctors and midwives weaved in and out
In gowns of smoke and gloves of fire.   140
Christ, like an Orthodox patriarch in his dressing gown,
Flew up and down the dormitory, splashing water on our souls:
Sister Eucharia; Sister Seraphia; Sister Rosario;
Sister Gonzago; Sister Margaret; Sister Edith.
If you will remember us – six nuns burnt to death –   145
Remember us for the frisky girls that we were,
Now more than ever kittens in the sun.

II

When Jesus heard these words at the top of Grafton Street
Uttered by a small, agèd, emaciated, female punk
Clad all in mourning black, and grieving like an alley cat,   150
He was annulled with astonishment, and turning round
He declared to the gangs of teenagers and dicemen following him:
"I tell you, not even in New York City
Have I found faith like this."

That night in St Stephen's Green,   155
After the keepers had locked the gates,
And the courting couples had found cinemas themselves to die in,
The six nuns who had died in the convent inferno,
From the bandstand they'd been hiding under, crept out

> And knelt together by the Fountain of the Three Fates, 160
> Reciting the Agnus Dei: reciting it as if it were the torch song
> Of all aid – Live Aid, Self Aid, Aid, Aids, and All Aid –
> *Lord, I am not worthy*
> *That thou should'st enter under my roof;*
> *Say but the word and my soul shall be healed.* 165

Glossary

[passim] **St Stephen's Green, Grafton Street, Clarendon Street, Johnson's Court**, and so on, are place names in central Dublin

[3] *paseo:* Spanish, a leisurely stroll, a path designed for such

[5] **Debouched:** emerged from confined to open space

[7] **punk:** aggressive counter-cultural style, movement, music, popular in late 1970s

[20] **recidivist:** repeat offender

[72] **Cardinal Mindszenty:** József Mindszenty (1892–1975), leader of Catholic Church in Hungary, opponent of fascism and communism

[118] **Conor Cruise O'Brien:** Irish diplomat, politician, writer (1917–2008)

[161] **Agnus Dei:** literally Lamb of God, an invocation forming a set part of the Roman Catholic mass

ANALYSE

In part I, which is fittingly in six sections, one of the victims, representing all the nuns, reflects on the religious life and on her own death.

Lines 1–30 introduce the order and the group, and then distinguishes the individual voice – 'scurrying as I went'. And it *is* the voice of a unique individual. That's the point here. The contrast is with society's apparent rebels, the punks on Grafton Street, who are actually lacking freedom and individuality – they are 'conventional', they wear 'uniforms', they cling 'to one another'. The nun, on the other hand, made a conscious, free, self-aware choice 'to opt out of the world' and to embrace 'exotic loneliness'.

That first claim may be startling. The second claim, in lines 31–62, made after a few graphic details are provided to give us a physical impression – 'old nun … weird bird … wheezing … wonky suspenders' – is even more so. The prospect of death is briefly described as 'too good to be true', before the nun turns to consider the mystery that is a religious vocation, the voluntary relinquishing of 'love … children … home' to follow a man 'who died a common criminal'.

Lines 63–84 return briefly to the notion of a welcomed death – 'come quickly, quickly' – before the beauty of life interposes itself one last time. The point here is that death is not welcomed as a rejection of life. The nun remembers 'a secluded beach' in County Waterford, a holiday, a high point, a 'Scampering hither and thither', and it occurs to her, again, that death – 'scampering into the flames' – is another such high point.

It is only in lines 85–108 that the meaning of this is developed. The religious life is devoted to God – figuratively, the ocean that washes against the earth – and full union with God is only possible in death. All deaths, even by fire, are therefore a kind of drowning. This image is one of the oldest in Christian literature: rebirth through drowning.

It's not because their life was barren that they welcome death – 'Wild women were we all' – but because death is the ultimate life.

Lines 109–131 develop this notion of death as 'marvellous', since 'losing things' – particularly one's life – 'is such a refreshing experience'. The circumstances of the nun's death, and her humorous regret that her 'brother-in-law's married niece' will never get her expensive book back, all humanise her, and touch us with sympathy.

The final section of part I (lines 132–147) celebrates the 'Eucharist', or sacrament, of her death, and asks for the nuns to be remembered as they were in the peak of life, 'frisky girls'.

Part II imagines two events in the aftermath of the deaths. In the first (lines 148–154), Jesus is astonished at the expression of faith we have just heard from an 'agèd ... female punk' and celebrates and welcomes her. In the second (lines 155–165), the nuns are resurrected in Christ, as is the belief in Christian religions, and, figuratively, kneel by the Fountain of the Three Fates in St Stephen's Green, Dublin. They become the symbols of comfort and help – both are contained in 'Aid' – for the rest of us.

MAKE

(i) It has been said that 'Six Nuns Die in Convent Inferno' 'transforms the details of the incident into an extended exercise in spiritual and physical contemplation'. Would you agree with this assessment? Give reasons for your answer.

(ii) There are images associated with rebellion throughout the poem – punk, Cardinal Mindszenty, wild, freedom, and so on. Pick out as many as you can find, and comment on their role in relation to the poem's themes.

READ

Sport

There were not many fields
In which you had hopes for me
But sport was one of them.
On my twenty-first birthday
I was selected to play   5
for Grangegorman Mental Hospital
In an away game
Against Mullingar Mental Hospital.
I was a patient
In B Wing.   10
You drove all the way down,
Fifty miles,
To Mullingar to stand
On the sidelines and observe me.

I was fearful I would let down   15
Not only my team but you.
It was Gaelic football.
I was selected as goalkeeper.
There were big country men
On the Mullingar Mental Hospital team,   20
Men with gapped teeth, red faces,
Oily, frizzy hair, bushy eyebrows.
Their full forward line
Were over six foot tall
Fifteen stone in weight.   25
All three of them, I was informed,
Cases of schizophrenia.

There was a rumour
That their centre-half forward
Was an alcoholic solicitor   30
Who, in a lounge bar misunderstanding,
Had castrated his best friend
But that he had no memory of it.
He had meant well – it was said.
His best friend had had to emigrate   35
To Nigeria.

To my surprise,
I did not flinch in the goals.
I made three or four spectacular saves,

354

Diving full stretch to turn 40
A certain goal around the corner,
Leaping high to tip another certain goal
Over the bar for a point.
It was my knowing
That you were standing on the sideline 45
That gave me the necessary motivation –
That will to die
That is as essential to sportsmen as to artists.
More than anybody it was you
I wanted to mesmerise, and after the game – 50
Grangegorman Mental Hospital
Having defeated Mullingar Mental Hospital
By 14 goals and 38 points to 3 goals and 10 points –
Sniffing your approval, you shook hands with me.
"Well played, son." 55

I may not have been mesmeric
But I had not been mediocre.
In your eyes I had achieved something at last.
On my twenty-first birthday I had played on a winning team
The Grangegorman Mental Hospital team. 60
Seldom if ever again in your eyes
Was I to rise to these heights.

Glossary

[6] **Grangegorman Mental Hospital:** psychiatric hospital in north Dublin city

[8] **Mullingar Mental Hospital:** psychiatric hospital in the Midlands of Ireland

[17] **Gaelic football:** team sport, fifteen against fifteen, in which points and goals are scored

[27] **schizophrenia:** mental disorder

[32] **castrated:** removed the testicles of

[50] **mesmerise:** dazzle or hypnotise; to succeed in doing so is to be **mesmeric**

ANALYSE

This poem deals with the relationship between Durcan and his father, using a particular event to dramatise the nature of that relationship. Significantly, the event occurs on Durcan's twenty-first birthday. Traditionally in Ireland, you reach full independence at the age of twenty-one. The irony is that Durcan is not free at twenty-one. He is a patient in a psychiatric hospital. Although it is not mentioned in the poem itself, we know that Durcan was put there by his father, against his will.

The opening three lines establish the relationship. The father thinks the son is generally hopeless, but might accomplish something in sport. It's funny, and ironic, therefore, that Durcan is playing for one psychiatric hospital in a weird match against another. The standard must be really poor, as demonstrated by the fantastic score of 14–38 for one side to 3–10 for the other. Only players with mental disorders are qualified to play. And they're not allowed to play against anyone other than people who also have mental disorders. Nevertheless, the father drives fifty miles from Dublin to Mullingar to attend the match. This sounds caring, but the poet carefully selects one word to give us a more subtle insight. The father has come 'to stand/On the sidelines and observe me'. Now, if he had travelled to support or cheer or encourage, we might applaud him. But to observe his son? It sounds distant, doesn't it? It sounds judgemental. It sounds distrustful. More than anything else in the opening section, that revealing word defines the attitude of the father to the son.

Nevertheless, the son – like any son – wants to impress and please his father. This, too, sounds natural enough. But again, the choice of words is revealing. The son is 'fearful' – full of fear – that he won't live up to his father's expectations. The poem comically captures the ordeal he has to go through. It's as if he's a hero in an old tale, battling monsters – 'Men with gapped teeth, red faces … Cases of schizophrenia … castrated his best friend'.

That need to impress his father gives Durcan 'the necessary motivation' in the game. He performs brilliantly as goalkeeper, making some outstanding saves and helping his team to a decisive victory. The father congratulates him: 'Well played, son.' But again, the language describing this is very revealing. The father doesn't 'beam' his approval, or even 'express' his approval; he 'sniffs' it; he draws air through his nose, as if he was detecting a bad smell, as if he was *disapproving*. He's not generous in his praise. This is why the opening to this section reads 'To my surprise' rather than 'To my father's surprise'.

As far as we can tell from the final section, this was the first, and last, time that Durcan's father said anything positive to him. Before this, according to the father, the boy had done nothing worthy of praise. After it, he never did anything again that was worthy of praise.

Poetry

MAKE

(i) 'The setting of this poem is bizarre, and the mood is sad, but accepting.' Would you agree with each of these claims? Select quotations to support your views.

(ii) 'Apart from the hilarious descriptions of the monsters he has to play the match against, the most impressive thing about the language in this poem is the words chosen to describe the father's actions and reactions.' Would you agree with this assessment? Give reasons for your answer.

Father's Day, 21 June 1992

Just as I was dashing to catch the Dublin–Cork train,
Dashing up and down the stairs, searching my pockets,
She told me that her sister in Cork wanted a loan of the axe;
It was late June and
The buddleia tree in the backyard   5
Had grown out of control.
The taxi was ticking over outside in the street,
All the neighbours noticing it.
"You mean that you want me to bring her down the axe?"
"Yes, if you wouldn't mind, that is – "   10
"A simple saw would do the job, surely to God
She could borrow a simple saw."
"She said that she'd like the axe."
"OK. There is a Blue Cabs taxi ticking over outside
And the whole world inspecting it,   15
I'll bring her down the axe."
The axe – all four-and-a-half feet of it –
Was leaning up against the wall behind the settee –
The fold-up settee that doubles as a bed.
She handed the axe to me just as it was,   20
As neat as a newborn babe,
All in the bare buff.
You'd think she'd have swaddled it up
In something – if not a blanket, an old newspaper,
But no, not even a token hanky   25
Tied in a bow round its head.
I decided not to argue the toss. I kissed her goodbye.

The whole long way down to Cork
I felt uneasy. Guilt feelings.
It's a killer, this guilt.   30
I always feel bad leaving her
But this time it was the worst.
I could see that she was glad
To see me go away for a while,
Glad at the prospect of being   35
Two weeks on her own,
Two weeks of having the bed to herself,
Two weeks of not having to be pestered
By my coarse advances,
Two weeks of not having to look up from her plate   40
And behold me eating spaghetti with a knife and fork.

Our daughters are all grown up and gone away.
Once when she was sitting pregnant on the settee
It snapped shut with herself inside it,
But not a bother on her. I nearly died.   45

As the train slowed down approaching Portarlington
I overheard myself say to the passenger sitting opposite me:
"I am feeling guilty because she does not love me
As much as she used to, can you explain that?"
The passenger's eyes were on the axe on the seat beside me.   50
"Her sister wants a loan of the axe …"
As the train threaded itself into Portarlington
I nodded to the passenger "Cúl an tSúdaire!"
The passenger stood up, lifted down a case from the rack,
Walked out of the coach, but did not get off the train.   55
For the remainder of the journey, we sat alone,
The axe and I,
All the green fields running away from us,
All our daughters grown up and gone away.

Glossary

[5] **buddleia:** shrub with fragrant flowers
[46] **Portarlington:** town in County Laois, a railway stop between Dublin and Cork
[53] **Cúl an tSúdaire:** Irish for Portarlington, literally translated as 'the tanner's nook'

ANALYSE

The poem catches the speaker, presumably the poet, at a particularly useless stage of his life, no longer needed by his adult daughters, no longer wanted by his wife in the absence of children to rear, and condemned to the pointless chore of delivering an unnecessary axe to a destination 270 kilometres away, a task that makes him appear dangerously unbalanced in the eyes of others. It may strike you as funny, and there are certainly amusing absurdities in the anecdote – the axe as a naked, newborn babe; the wary passenger on the train – or it may strike you as self-pitying. As mentioned in the comments on other poems, one gets the impression that things simply happen to the speaker in many of Durcan's poems – some bad things, some good, some ridiculous – and he's as helpless as a child in the face of them. Of course, this is the classic fate of the clown in our culture – life is a series of accidents, all of which make him look … a victim of circumstances, put-upon, absurd; tragic and funny at the same time.

Ironically, the poem opens with a sense of purpose – 'I was dashing to catch the … train' – before the wife's mad request introduces an element of the absurd that sabotages purpose and comes to dominate the journey he undertakes. Already, before he embarks, he is becoming an object of laughable curiosity, a figure of fun – a 'taxi ticking over outside/And the whole world inspecting it' – something that stays with him throughout and culminates in the wary distance of the train passenger, who looks anxiously at the axe and leaves the carriage.

Poetry

In any case, he takes the ridiculous axe from Dublin to Cork. Presumably, it's what his role in relation to his wife has been reduced to – comic, useless, laughable. Otherwise – as detailed in lines 28–44, which are definitely more self-pitying than humorous – he's just a liability, an irritation, redundant, unnecessary, in the way. No doubt he was a fine father – this is implicit – but now that 'Our daughters are all grown up and gone away', he's just a pest, 'coarse', a man whose once-quaint habits – 'eating spaghetti with a knife and fork' – and once-attractive attentiveness – 'my … advances' – have simply become tiresome.

The defining image of this tragic joker is that of a man travelling to Cork in the company of an axe, unable to do anything about the accidents that have befallen him – 'For the remainder of the journey, we sat alone,/The axe and I'.

MAKE

(i) 'It may strike you as funny, or it may strike you as self-pitying.' What is your judgement of 'Father's Day, 21 June 1992'? Give reasons for your answer.

(ii) Durcan's poetry has been praised for its 'satire, humour and melancholy, in a language that is lively and colloquial.' Would you agree that all five terms – satire, humour, melancholy, lively, colloquial – apply to 'Father's Day, 21 June 1992'? Give reasons for your answer.

Poetry

The Arnolfini Marriage
after Jan Van Eyck

We are the Arnolfinis.
Do not think you may invade
Our privacy because you may not.

We are standing to our portrait,
The most erotic portrait ever made,   5
Because we have faith in the artist

To do justice to the plurality,
Fertility, domesticity, barefootedness
Of a man and a woman saying "we":

To do justice to our bed   10
As being our most necessary furniture;
To do justice to our life as a reflection.

Our brains spill out upon the floor
And the terrier at our feet sniffs
The minutiae of our magnitude.   15

The most relaxing word in our vocabulary is "we".
Imagine being able to say "we".
Most people are in no position to say "we".

Are you? Who eat alone? Sleep alone?
And at dawn cycle to work   20
With an Alsatian shepherd dog tied to your handlebars?

We will pause now for the Angelus.
Here you have it:
The two halves of the coconut.

Glossary

[title] *The Arnolfini Portrait* is a painting in oils on a panel, dated 1434, by Jan Van Eyck

[22] **Angelus:** Roman Catholic devotion commemorating the incarnation of Jesus

ANALYSE

This is Durcan's interpretation of a famous painting, *The Arnolfini Portrait*, by Jan Van Eyck. Although it is delivered in the voice of the couple in the portrait and addresses a viewer, presumably the poet himself, to give the impression that this is what the painting itself says, nevertheless, it remains Durcan's interpretation.

Durcan has the couple speak as one, and the first word of the poem – 'We' – is the key to Durcan's interpretation. For him, the portrait is an 'erotic' declaration of unity and wholeness – 'two halves of the coconut'. It is unlikely that this was the painting's original intention, but we can accept it as a lonely modern Irishman's understanding of it. For Durcan, the portrait says 'we' – a shared domesticity, sexuality, fertility, property – the small things of daily life, the 'minutiae', that go to make the life itself, the 'magnitude'. Moreover, it assertively says 'we', in a poignant way, to the solitary viewer, who sleeps 'alone' and whose relationship with his 'Alsatian shepherd dog' is so different from the couple's relationship with their own integrated 'terrier', not least because there is obviously no one else at home to mind the dog while he cycles to work 'at dawn'.

MAKE

(i) The poem is based on a contrast between solitariness and a shared enterprise, between the individual looking at the painting and the couple in the painting. Pick out the details capturing each state and comment on the implied emotions attached to each.

(ii) From the opening line – 'We are the Arnolfinis' – the tone is one of assurance and self-confidence. Find other examples of this assurance and self-confidence throughout the poem, in the language, the imagery, the sounds, the opinions.

Rosie Joyce

I

That was that Sunday afternoon in May
When a hot sun pushed through the clouds
And you were born!

I was driving the two hundred miles from west to east,
The sky blue-and-white china in the fields   5
In impromptu picnics of tartan rugs;

When neither words nor I
Could have known that you had been named already
And that your name was Rosie –

Rosie Joyce! May you some day in May   10
Fifty-six years from today be as lucky
As I was when you were born that Sunday:

To drive such side-roads, such main roads, such ramps, such roundabouts,
To cross such bridges, to by-pass such villages, such towns
As I did on your Incarnation Day.   15

By-passing Swinford – Croagh Patrick in my rear-view mirror –
My mobile phone rang and, stopping on the hard edge of P. Flynn's highway,
I heard Mark your father say:

"A baby girl was born at 3.33 p.m.
Weighing 7 and a 1/2 lbs in Holles Street.   20
Tough work, all well."

II

That Sunday in May before daybreak
Night had pushed up through the slopes of Achill
Yellow forefingers of Arum Lily – the first of the year;

Down at the Sound the first rhododendrons   25
Purpling the golden camps of whins;
The first hawthorns powdering white the mainland;

The first yellow irises flagging roadside streams;
Quills of bog-cotton skimming the bogs;
Burrishoole cemetery shin-deep in forget-me-nots;   30

The first sea pinks speckling the seashore;
Cliffs of London Pride, groves of bluebell,
First fuchsia, Queen Anne's Lace, primrose.

I drove the Old Turlough Road, past Walter Durcan's Farm,
Umbrella'd in the joined handwriting of its ash trees;   35
I drove Tulsk, Kilmainham, the Grand Canal.

Never before had I felt so fortunate.
To be driving back into Dublin city;
Each canal bridge an old pewter brooch.

I rode the waters and the roads of Ireland,   40
Rosie, to be with you, seashell at my ear!
How I laughed when I cradled you in my hand.

Only at Tarmonbarry did I slow down,
As in my father's Ford Anglia half a century ago
He slowed down also, as across the River Shannon   45

We crashed, rattled, bounced on a Bailey bridge;
Daddy relishing his role as Moses,
Enunciating the name of the Great Divide

Between the East and the West!
We are the people of the West,   50
Our fate to go East.

No such thing, Rosie, as a Uniform Ireland
And please God there never will be;
There is only the River Shannon and all her sister rivers

And all her brother mountains and their family prospects.   55
There are higher powers than politics
And these we call wildflowers or, geologically, people.

Rosie Joyce – that Sunday in May
Not alone did you make my day, my week, my year
To the prescription of Jonathan Philbin Bowman –   60

Daymaker!
Daymaker!
Daymaker!

Popping out of my daughter, your mother –
Changing the expressions on the faces all around you –   65
All of them looking like blue hills in a heat haze –

But you saved my life. For three years
I had been subsisting in the slums of despair,
Unable to distinguish one day from the next.

III

On the return journey from Dublin to Mayo   70
In Charlestown on Main Street
I meet John Normanly, organic farmer from Curry.

He is driving home to his wife Caroline
From a Mountbellew meeting of the Western Development Commission
Of Dillon House in Ballaghadereen.   75

He crouches in his car, I waver in the street,
As we exchange lullabies of expectancy;
We wet our foreheads in John Moriarty's autobiography.

The following Sunday is the Feast of the Ascension
Of Our Lord into Heaven: 80
Thank You, O Lord, for the Descent of Rosie onto Earth.

Glossary

[15] **Incarnation:** simply, birth, or form; in religious belief, the embodiment of a god

[17] **P. Flynn:** Pádraig Flynn, born 1939, Irish politician, resigned in disgrace from Fianna Fáil in 2012, once Minister of State at the Department of Transport, with responsibility for roads

[23] **Achill:** large island off County Mayo, also gives its name to a village and [25] **Sound** in the same county, the starting point of the journey from west to east across Ireland, which also includes

[30] **Burrishoole** in County Mayo, [43] **Tarmonbarry** in County Roscommon and [36] **Kilmainham** in Dublin city

[24] **Arum Lily:** common name for *Zantedeschia*, it begins a list of Irish flora, such as rhododendrons, irises, and so on

[48] **Great Divide:** usually, the partition of British India; used comically here for the supposed differences between the west and east of Ireland

[60] **Jonathan Philbin Bowman:** Irish journalist and broadcaster (1969–2000)

[72] **John Normanly:** organic farmer from Curry, County Sligo, married to Caroline

[78] **John Moriarty:** Kerry writer, whose autobiography is entitled *Nostos* (1938–2007)

[79] **Ascension:** in Roman Catholic belief, the taking up to heaven of the resurrected Jesus

Poetry

ANALYSE

This is a celebration of the birth of Durcan's granddaughter, Rosie Joyce.

Part I reports how, when and where Durcan heard the news.

Part II fancifully locates the child's birth within a sudden flowering of new life all along the route Durcan, a kind of Solitary Wise Man, was travelling, from Achill to Dublin, for the event – the first lilies of the year conveniently spring up, the 'first rhododendrons', the 'first yellow irises', and so on. Along the way, he's reminded of his own childhood travelling the same road. A darker time, a less functional family, a less fortunate child – 'We crashed'. It leads to the contemplation that we're all part of the same human family, really – '*We are the people*' – and to an appreciation that this new life has dragged him out the oppressions of his old life – 'For three years/I had been subsisting in the slums of despair'. The verb 'subsisting' here suggests merely existing rather than joyously living, and the image of the 'slums' is contrasted with the scenes of natural beauty described earlier.

Part III describes the return journey after the child's birth. It is characterised by the celebration of new life – 'organic farmer', 'expectancy', 'Ascension'. Birth, growth, fruition.

MAKE

(i) The landscape of Ireland is used throughout to express the joy and celebration at the birth of a new human life. Pick out some of the details and comment on their effectiveness.

(ii) A critic has remarked, scathingly, that 'Paul Durcan is the subject of almost every poem Paul Durcan has written'. Comment on this view, with reference to 'Rosie Joyce'.

READ

The MacBride Dynasty

What young mother is not a vengeful goddess
Spitting dynastic as well as motherly pride?
In 1949 in the black Ford Anglia,
Now that I had become a walking, talking little boy,
Mummy drove me out to visit my grand-aunt Maud Gonne   5
In Roebuck House in the countryside near Dublin,
To show off to the servant of the Queen
The latest addition to the extended family.
Although the eighty-year-old Cathleen Ni Houlihan had taken to her bed
She was keen as ever to receive admirers,   10
Especially the children of the family.
Only the previous week the actor MacLiammóir
Had been kneeling at her bedside reciting Yeats to her,
His hand on his heart, clutching a red rose.
Cousin Séan and his wife Kid led the way up the stairs,   15
Séan opening the door and announcing my mother.
Mummy lifted me up in her arms as she approached the bed
And Maud leaned forward, sticking out her claws
To embrace me, her lizards of eyes darting about
In the rubble of the ruins of her beautiful face.   20
Terrified, I recoiled from her embrace
And, fleeing her bedroom, ran down the stairs
Out onto the wrought-iron balcony
Until Séan caught up with me and quieted me
And took me for a walk in the walled orchard.   25
Mummy was a little but not totally mortified:
She had never liked Maud Gonne because of Maud's
Betrayal of her husband, Mummy's Uncle John,
Major John, most ordinary of men, most
Humorous, courageous of soldiers,   30
The pride of our family,
Whose memory always brought laughter
To my grandmother Eileen's lips. "John,"
She used cry, "John was such a gay man."
Mummy set great store by loyalty; loyalty   35
In Mummy's eyes was the cardinal virtue.
Maud Gonne was a disloyal wife
And, therefore, not worthy of Mummy's love.
For dynastic reasons we would tolerate Maud,
But we would always see through her.   40

Glossary

[title] **MacBride Dynasty:** Major John MacBride (1868–1916) was an Irish republican, executed for his role in the 1916 Rising; husband to Maud Gonne; father of Séan MacBride, Irish politician and international civil rights campaigner. A **dynasty** is a succession of people from the same family who play a prominent role in a society and its politics

[5] **Mummy:** Durcan's mother, Sheila MacBride, niece of John MacBride

[5] **Maud Gonne:** (1866–1953) Irish revolutionary republican, feminist and actress; muse to W.B. Yeats; married John MacBride

[7] **the servant of the Queen:** the ironic title of Maud Gonne's autobiography is *A Servant of the Queen*, although it also contains a reference to the symbolic emblem of Irish nationalism [9] Cathleen Ní Houlihan

[12] **MacLiammóir:** Micheál MacLiammóir (1899–1978), English-born Irish actor

[15] **Cousin Séan and his wife Kid:** Séan MacBride, who married Catalina (Kid) Bulfin

ANALYSE

Durcan's quite understandable reluctance to embrace, as a child, an 'eighty-year-old' reptilian bed-ridden aunt, equipped with 'claws' and lizard eyes, is turned symbolically into a family's rejection of a 'disloyal' woman, and thereby a family's embrace of more noble values, though they would always be civil to 'Maud'. Of course, the reluctance is that of a frightened child, who knows nothing and reacts to appearances.

The poem, on the other hand, is written by a mature man, no longer relying on appearances or the judgements of others. Implicit in it is a criticism of the family's rejection of Maud Gonne. They sided with one of their own, Maud's husband, John MacBride, 'The pride of our family'. In real life, Maud Gonne had petitioned for divorce from John MacBride, citing his drunkenness and cruelty, but none of these charges was upheld in court and the divorce was not granted. Similarly, the family refuses to seriously consider the charges. They are more interested in preserving the myth of MacBride as 'such a gay man'. They're more interested in holding the family together through 'loyalty' and silence – the values of a Mafia 'family' – than they are in the truth.

MAKE

(i) 'The MacBride Dynasty' is from a 2007 collection that has been described as paying 'tribute to the life of his mother'. In your view, is the poem a 'tribute' to his mother? Give reasons for your answer.

(ii) Comment on the portrait of Maud Gonne presented in the poem, paying particular attention to the images selected to describe her.

Poetry

READ

En Famille, 1979

Bring me back to the dark school – to the dark school of childhood:
To where tiny is tiny, and massive is massive.

Madman

Every child has a madman on their street:
The only trouble about *our* madman is that he's our father.

Ireland 2002

Do you ever take a holiday abroad?
No, we always go to America.

ANALYSE

A two-line poem is a couplet, most popular in Chinese poetry, where it is ideally profound yet concise. Durcan's couplets are concise and aspire to profundity on, respectively, the comfortingly familiar terrors of childhood, the novelty of having a madman as a father, and the loss of Ireland's identity in the twenty-first century.

MAKE

(i) The couplet is a very compressed form which can carry intense emotions. Comment on any of the above couplets in light of this description.

(ii) In terms of theme, relate any of the couplets above to any other poem or poems by Durcan on your course.

Poetry

The Poetry of Paul Durcan

Themes and Interests

- The poetry of Paul Durcan is **AUTOBIOGRAPHICAL**, drawing on personal experiences from childhood, boyhood, youth, marriage, fatherhood, divorce, living alone, becoming a grandfather, and so on

'The MacBride Dynasty' features Durcan as a child, brought by his mother to visit the famous feminist revolutionary, Maud Gonne, and running away in terror from the 'claws' and lizard eyes, as he saw them, of the old woman. It sets a perspective – entirely subjective – and a motif – inability to cope – that continues in almost all the other Durcan poems on your course. 'The Girl with the Keys to Pearse's Cottage' has lovesick Durcan at sixteen, besotted by the dark-haired vision of a romantic Ireland; a dalliance that ends badly. 'Nessa', 'The Difficulty that is Marriage' and '"Windfall"' chart Durcan's love of, marriage to, and separation from his wife. 'Father's Day, 21 June 1992', captures Durcan, in the final stages of his marriage, in the company of a pointless implement, a heavy-handed axe, that has to travel half the country to crudely chop a mere shrub. 'The Arnolfini Marriage' accosts Durcan, the painting's viewer, as a sad failure, dragging his dog to work with him instead of having a home to leave it in. 'Sport' finds Durcan in a psychiatric hospital as a young man, having been put there by his father, hoping for his father's approval while playing as goalkeeper in an absurd game of Gaelic football. The couplet 'Madman' identifies his father as the one who should have been in the psychiatric hospital. 'Rosie Joyce' finds Durcan rescued from depression at the age of fifty-six by the birth of his granddaughter. All poets draw on personal and subjective experiences, of course. In many of the poems on your course, however, there's an ironic distance between the voice in the finished poem and the original experience. Sometimes this is achieved by means of a distinct persona, such as Prufrock in Eliot's 'The Love Song of J. Alfred Prufrock'. Sometimes it is attained by means of implicit judgement, as in Bishop's 'Filling Station'; sometimes in the contemplation of universal human truth, as in Plath's 'Elm'. In each of these cases, the individual ego drops away to nothing in the face of something far more profound. Durcan chooses not to establish that distance. His poetry is a very direct confrontation with his own experiences. This undoubtedly gives it power, particularly when he dramatises it in his accomplished public readings, but whether or not it can provide depth and complexity is a question that each reader and critic must address.

- The poetry of Paul Durcan is **SATIRICAL**, commenting critically on Irish hypocrisy, bureaucracy, consumerism, middle-class culture, religious failures, and other social ills

In fairness to Durcan, it should be noted that his best verse, which is satirical, is not well represented by the selection on your course, which heavily favours the personal material. There are fine examples of satire, nonetheless. The most humorous is 'Wife Who Smashed Television Gets Jail', which successfully ridicules a society that claims to protect the family, but ends up destroying it by imprisoning mothers, and successfully exposes a self-destructive tendency in modern humans to seek refuge in entertainment at the expense of everything else. The most accomplished of these poems is 'Six Nuns Die in Convent Inferno', which contrasts the values of society's best-known rebels at the time, the punks, and the

conventional values of mainstream society itself, children and a home, with the extreme, self-denying values of the religious life, an 'exotic loneliness' and 'terrestrial abandonment' that includes 'apocalyptic enthusiasm' and 'other-worldly hubris'. There are elements of satire also in 'The Girl with the Keys to Pearse's Cottage' and 'The MacBride Dynasty', both of which explore the decay of idealism in modern Ireland – the beautiful contemporary girl has to emigrate to America to survive and the once-upon-a-time girl, Maud Gonne, is now an octogenarian. America is also featured in 'Ireland 2002', where it *is* Ireland, which no longer exists, even in its own people's heads. The trouble with satire is that things quickly move on, particularly in the modern world – fashions change, times change, causes change – thus making the poetry outdated and irrelevant. Nevertheless, the best satire always targets *human* failings, rather than the specific failings of a particular time and place, and in this respect Durcan's satires are accomplished examples of the genre.

- The poetry of Paul Durcan explores the complexities of, and tensions within, the modern Irish **FAMILY**, including love, security, control and disintegration, using his own family of origin and created family as starting points

In one way or another, all Durcan poems on your course deal with the family, whether that is Durcan's family of origin, Durcan's created family of wife and two daughters, or the religious family of nuns in 'Six Nuns Die in Convent Inferno'. 'Sport' in particular explores the difficult relationship between Durcan and his father. While Durcan was studying at University College Dublin he was committed against his will to a psychiatric hospital and given electric-shock treatment, experiences that form the background to 'Sport'. Durcan moved to London in 1966 and married in 1968. He and his wife, Nessa, had two daughters. 'Parents' describes the relationship between a sleeping child and her parents, 'Nessa' the first meeting with his future wife, '"Windfall"' and 'Father's Day' the disintegration of the marriage, 'The Arnolfini Marriage' the contrast between a perfect family (painted on a panel) and a lonely viewer, presumably in the aftermath of his own failed relationships. 'Rosie Joyce' celebrates the renewal of family in the birth of Durcan's granddaughter. For Durcan, the family seems to be an inescapable failure, the success of which he is granted occasional glimpses of, in paintings and in his grandchild.

- The poetry of Paul Durcan utilises the persona of the well-meaning man who often struggles with the demands of life and with the burdens of a traumatised past, often employing a **SELF-DEPRECATING** portrait

Things happen to the speaker in a Durcan poem. There's always a banana skin somewhere in his path. The most revealing quotation is from '"Windfall"', his record of the miraculous appearance – there's hardly any other way to describe a 'windfall' – of his home in Cork with his wife and kids: 'But then with good reason/I was put out of my home'. It's an extraordinary way of phrasing it. One thinks of putting a dog or a cat out. The acceptance of responsibility – 'with good reason' – saves it from self-pity. But it's also a very revealing way of phrasing it. The more you read of Durcan's poetry, the more you discover him as a victim of life's vicissitudes, always unable to *control*, and mostly unable to *influence*, the forces that shape his life. This powerlessness begins in childhood, of course, when he had a 'madman' as a father, and where he was once caught in the 'claws' of an old woman in 'The MacBride

373

Dynasty'. It continues into his late teens and early adulthood, where we find him caught between the posts playing goalkeeper for a psychiatric institution that he didn't choose in 'Sport'. Elsewhere, he is caught in the 'whirlpool' of love in 'Nessa', depicted carrying a useless implement all the way from Dublin to Cork in 'Father's Day', and caught in the solitary fantasy of immortal companionship while staring at the ceiling with his wife sleeping beside him in 'The Difficulty that is Marriage'. Things happen to this tragic character, both good and bad – 'She took me by the index finger/And dropped me in her well' ('Nessa'); 'She had no choice but to leave her home' ('The Girl with the Keys to Pearse's Cottage'); 'I was put out of my home' ('"Windfall"'); 'I decided not to argue the toss' ('Father's Day'); 'I was selected to play … I was a patient/In B Wing … I was selected as goalkeeper' ('Sport').

Style and Viewpoint

- The poetry of Paul Durcan is literal, because its **LANGUAGE** rarely contains more than its surface meaning and is therefore close to conversational prose, a style particularly suited to the satiric public pieces

The critic Alan Dent remarked on Durcan's 'prose-like style' and commented that it's 'a way of keeping in check … deeper feelings'. Comparing two quotations, one from the earliest Durcan poem on your course, 'Nessa', published in 1975 – 'On the way back I fell in the field/And she fell down beside me,/I'd have lain in the grass with her all my life/With Nessa' – and the second from the most recent Durcan poem on your course, 'The MacBride Dynasty', published in 2007 – 'Terrified, I recoiled from her embrace/And, fleeing her bedroom, ran down the stairs/Out onto the wrought-iron balcony/Until Séan caught up with me and quieted me' – is a revealing exercise. Both are statements, presumably of facts. They're not evocations, or reflections, or dramatisations, or descriptions, or expressions of feeling. They're bald statements. Secondly, if you removed the line endings in each case, nothing in the subsequent patterns of the text would suggest poetry. Most importantly, however, not one of the words or phrases in either quotation is figurative, metaphoric or symbolic. Each word or phrase is functional, literal, meaning what it says on the surface and not suggesting any depth or complexity. For instance, the verb 'recoiled' in 'I recoiled from her embrace' is a fine word in the context, expressive of the boy's horror, but it remains a mere statement about an event. As with his treatment of autobiographical material, mentioned above, his choices in relation to language are conscious and purposeful, as they are with any poet. Just like his material, his language, too, gives great directness and impact to his poetry, certainly on a first hearing or reading. The style is forceful and uncomplicated. Once again, however, whether or not it can provide depth and complexity is a question that each reader and critic must address.

- The poetry of Paul Durcan draws its **IMAGERY** from the everyday events of late twentieth- and early twenty-first-century Ireland, from Irish landscape, and from painting, an art form with which Durcan has a particular affinity

There are references to Irish emigration, Irish history, Irish politics, the courts and judiciary, and contemporary events, such as the fire at the Loreto Convent in Stephen's Green in 1986, scattered throughout the work. The poems draw on and explore contemporary Ireland. The Irish landscape has a recurring presence, usually literal – such as the journey from west to east and back again in 'Rosie Joyce', the train journey from Dublin to Cork in 'Father's Day', and the location of the house in '"Windfall"' – but very occasionally symbolic – such as the Connemara of dark-haired, red-skirted cailíní in 'The Girl with the Keys to Pearse's Cottage'. Colour is a recurring motif – the 'red hair' of 'Nessa', the 'dark hair' and 'sun-red skirt and moon-black blazer' of Cáit, the 'dyed hair-dos' and 'yellowy corsets' of 'Six Nuns Die in Convent Inferno', the 'red faces' of 'Sport', the 'blue hills' and 'yellow irises' and 'sky blue-and-white china' of 'Rosie Joyce'. Paintings or prints or photographs feature centrally in many poems, particularly 'The Arnolfini Marriage' and '"Windfall"'.

- The poetry of Paul Durcan relies heavily on the **SOUNDS** and rhythms of the speaking voice, a quality that makes it particularly effective when spoken in performance, by Durcan himself

Durcan's poetry is far more effective when performed, as you can experience for yourself by checking out the link in Further Material. It's something he readily acknowledges himself. In fact, the subtitle of his collected poems, *Life is a Dream*, published in 2009, was *40 Years Reading Poems 1967–2007*, in the Foreword of which he writes: 'I have spent forty years giving readings of my poetry' and quotes T.S. Eliot to the effect that, 'The chief value of the author's recording, then, is as a guide to the rhythms.' Eliot, however, didn't write for reading, but recorded his poems to elucidate the writing. Durcan's verse is written for the speaking voice. In fact, Durcan's verse usually features a speaking voice or voices – the wife, husband and judge in 'Wife Who Smashed Television Gets Jail'; the nun in 'Six Nuns Die in Convent Inferno'; a couple in a painting in 'The Arnolfini Marriage', and Durcan himself in most other poems. When performed aloud, the dramatic rhythms of it become obvious and enjoyable, and the jokes take off, such as, for instance, 'The passenger's eyes were on the axe on the seat beside me' from 'Father's Day'. On the page, they're not as impressive. All the voices sound somewhat the same. There's no variation in rhythm, or tone, or feeling. But in fairness, if you transcribed the most brilliant stand-up comedy routine to mere words on a page, you'd end up with more or less the same result. Durcan's poems are at their best heard in performance.

- The poetry of Paul Durcan is unorthodox in its use of poetic **FORMS**, employing idiosyncratic versions of prayers, ballads, couplets, dramatic monologues, and so on

Durcan's verse is structurally loose, intentionally so. His most popular form is the long dramatic monologue, usually delivered by himself. '"Windfall"', 'Rosie Joyce' and 'Father's Day' fall into this category. The occasion is usually a journey, through time in the first example, through space across the country, west to east or north to south, in the other two. The form is more successful when the speaker is not himself, when there is room for the expression of something positive rather than self-defeating, as in 'Six Nuns Die in Convent Inferno'. By sharp contrast, three of the poems on your course are in the form of couplets – each merely two lines – where the objective is to be terse and vigorously expressive, to make a strong point with a single elegant stroke. The remaining poems are formed as anecdotes – that is, they take a particular incident or event, real or invented, and describe it in dramatic terms. Examples include the real visit Durcan paid as a child to Maud Gonne, the imagined prosecution of a wife for destroying the family television, the real first meeting between Durcan and his future wife, the imagined interaction between himself and a painting, the real Gaelic football match he played in as a young man.

Thomas Stearns Eliot

Thomas Stearns Eliot was born in 1888, in St Louis, Missouri, of an old New England family. He was educated at Harvard and did graduate work in philosophy at the Sorbonne, Harvard and Oxford University. He settled in England, where he was for a time a schoolmaster (1915–1916) and a bank clerk (1917–1925). In 1915, he married Vivienne Haigh-Wood. It was an unhappy marriage, leading to nervous breakdowns in both husband and wife. Vivienne's illness turned out to be permanent. They legally separated in 1933. In 1925, Eliot joined the publishing house Faber & Faber as literary editor, and later became its director. In 1927, Eliot became a British citizen and about the same time entered the Anglican Church. He was awarded the Nobel Prize for Literature in 1948 and died on 4 January 1965.

Prescribed Poems

'Students at Higher Level will be required to study a representative selection from the work of eight poets: a representative selection would seek to reflect the range of a poet's themes and interests and exhibit his/her characteristic style and viewpoint. Normally the study of at least six poems by each poet would be expected.' (DES English Syllabus, 6.3)

Themes and Interests

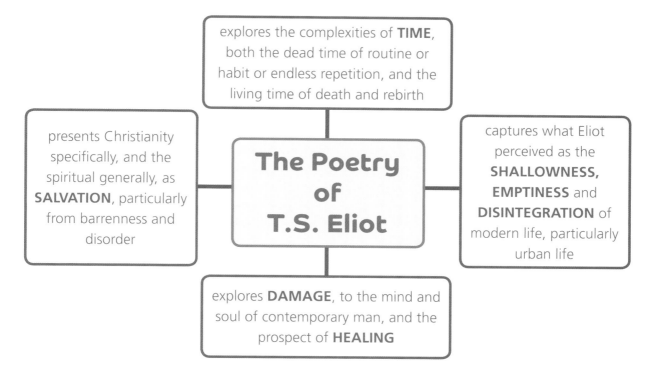

explores the complexities of **TIME**, both the dead time of routine or habit or endless repetition, and the living time of death and rebirth

presents Christianity specifically, and the spiritual generally, as **SALVATION**, particularly from barrenness and disorder

The Poetry of T.S. Eliot

captures what Eliot perceived as the **SHALLOWNESS, EMPTINESS** and **DISINTEGRATION** of modern life, particularly urban life

explores **DAMAGE**, to the mind and soul of contemporary man, and the prospect of **HEALING**

Style and Viewpoint

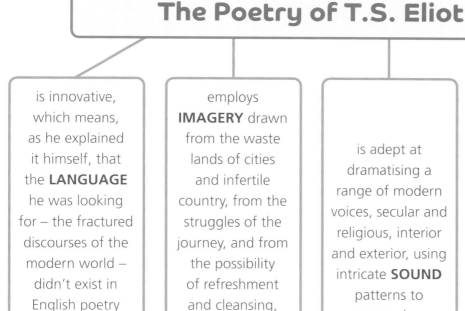

The Poetry of T.S. Eliot

is innovative, which means, as he explained it himself, that the **LANGUAGE** he was looking for – the fractured discourses of the modern world – didn't exist in English poetry before he brought it in, mainly from French poets

employs **IMAGERY** drawn from the waste lands of cities and infertile country, from the struggles of the journey, and from the possibility of refreshment and cleansing, to express the complexity of his vision

is adept at dramatising a range of modern voices, secular and religious, interior and exterior, using intricate **SOUND** patterns to capture them

'bursts out of any recognisable poetic shape', as the writer Jeannette Winterson puts it, 'just as the world had burst out of any recognisable order', and so invents new poetic **FORMS**

The Love Song of J. Alfred Prufrock

S'io credessi che mia risposta fosse
a persona che mai tornasse al mondo,
questa fiamma staria senza più scosse.
Ma per ciò che giammai di questo fondo
non tornò vivo alcun, s'i'odo il vero,
senza tema d'infamia ti rispondo.

Let us go then, you and I,
When the evening is spread out against the sky
Like a patient etherised upon a table ;
Let us go, through certain half-deserted streets,
The muttering retreats   5
Of restless nights in one-night cheap hotels
And sawdust restaurants with oyster-shells :
Streets that follow like a tedious argument
Of insidious intent
To lead you to an overwhelming question ...   10
Oh, do not ask, 'What is it?'
Let us go and make our visit.

In the room the women come and go
Talking of Michelangelo.

The yellow fog that rubs its back upon the window-panes,   15
The yellow smoke that rubs its muzzle on the window-panes,
Licked its tongue into the corners of the evening,
Lingered upon the pools that stand in drains,
Let fall upon its back the soot that falls from chimneys,
Slipped by the terrace, made a sudden leap,   20
And seeing that it was a soft October night,
Curled once about the house, and fell asleep.

And indeed there will be time
For the yellow smoke that slides along the street,
Rubbing its back upon the window-panes ;   25
There will be time, there will be time
To prepare a face to meet the faces that you meet ;
There will be time to murder and create,
And time for all the works and days of hands
That lift and drop a question on your plate ;   30
Time for you and time for me,
And time yet for a hundred indecisions,
And for a hundred visions and revisions,
Before the taking of a toast and tea.

In the room the women come and go   35
Talking of Michelangelo.

    And indeed there will be time
To wonder, 'Do I dare?' and, 'Do I dare?'
Time to turn back and descend the stair,
With a bald spot in the middle of my hair—   40
(They will say: 'How his hair is growing thin!')
My morning coat, my collar mounting firmly to the chin,
My necktie rich and modest, but asserted by a simple pin—
(They will say : 'But how his arms and legs are thin!')
Do I dare   45
Disturb the universe?
In a minute there is time
For decisions and revisions which a minute will reverse.

    For I have known them all already, known them all—
Have known the evenings, mornings, afternoons,   50
I have measured out my life with coffee spoons ;
I know the voices dying with a dying fall
Beneath the music from a farther room.
    So how should I presume?

    And I have known the eyes already, known them all— 55
The eyes that fix you in a formulated phrase,
And when I am formulated, sprawling on a pin,
When I am pinned and wriggling on the wall,
Then how should I begin
To spit out all the butt-ends of my days and ways? 60
    And how should I presume?

    And I have known the arms already, known them all—
Arms that are braceleted and white and bare
(But in the lamplight, downed with light brown hair!)
Is it perfume from a dress   65
That makes me so digress?
Arms that lie along a table, or wrap about a shawl.
    And should I then presume?
    And how should I begin?

           .....

    Shall I say, I have gone at dusk through narrow streets 70
And watched the smoke that rises from the pipes
Of lonely men in shirt-sleeves, leaning out of windows? ...

    I should have been a pair of ragged claws
Scuttling across the floors of silent seas.

.....

And the afternoon, the evening, sleeps so peacefully!   75
Smoothed by long fingers,
Asleep ... tired ... or it malingers,
Stretched on the floor, here beside you and me.
Should I, after tea and cakes and ices,
Have the strength to force the moment to its crisis?   80
But though I have wept and fasted, wept and prayed,
Though I have seen my head (grown slightly bald) brought in upon a platter,
I am no prophet—and here's no great matter ;
I have seen the moment of my greatness flicker,
And I have seen the eternal Footman hold my coat, and snicker,   85
And in short, I was afraid.

And would it have been worth it, after all,
After the cups, the marmalade, the tea,
Among the porcelain, among some talk of you and me,
Would it have been worth while,   90
To have bitten off the matter with a smile,
To have squeezed the universe into a ball
To roll it towards some overwhelming question,
To say: 'I am Lazarus, come from the dead,
Come back to tell you all, I shall tell you all'—   95
If one, settling a pillow by her head,
  Should say : 'That is not what I meant at all.
  That is not it, at all.'

And would it have been worth it, after all,
Would it have been worth while,   100
After the sunsets and the dooryards and the sprinkled streets,
After the novels, after the teacups, after the skirts that trail along the floor—
And this, and so much more?—
It is impossible to say just what I mean!
But as if a magic lantern threw the nerves in patterns on a screen :   105
Would it have been worth while
If one, settling a pillow or throwing off a shawl,
And turning toward the window, should say :
  'That is not it at all,
  That is not what I meant at all.'   110

.....

No! I am not Prince Hamlet, nor was meant to be ;
Am an attendant lord, one that will do
To swell a progress, start a scene or two,

Advise the prince ; no doubt, an easy tool,
Deferential, glad to be of use,   115
Politic, cautious, and meticulous ;
Full of high sentence, but a bit obtuse ;
At times, indeed, almost ridiculous—
Almost, at times, the Fool.

   I grow old ... I grow old ...   120
I shall wear the bottoms of my trousers rolled.

   Shall I part my hair behind? Do I dare to eat a peach?
I shall wear white flannel trousers, and walk upon the beach.
I have heard the mermaids singing, each to each.

I do not think that they will sing to me.   125

I have seen them riding seaward on the waves
Combing the white hair of the waves blown back
When the wind blows the water white and black.

We have lingered in the chambers of the sea
By sea-girls wreathed with seaweed red and brown   130
Till human voices wake us, and we drown.

ANALYSE

(epitaph) The Italian epigraph is from Canto 27 of the first book – *Inferno* or *Hell* – of *The Divine Comedy*, in which Dante (1265–1321), having strayed from the true path of virtue into a life of worldly pleasures, describes a vision in which he travelled through Hell, Purgatory and Paradise. The classical poet Virgil is his initial guide, although it is his love Beatrice, symbolic of the Virgin Mary and representing faith, who finally leads him to God, because Virgil, representing only the summit of human knowledge, is not allowed to enter into Paradise. While in Hell, Dante met many of the damned, and it is one of these, Guido da Montefeltro (1223–1298) – who is roasting within a single flame in hell because, he claims, he was corrupted by Pope Boniface VIII and used his abilities as a warrior to evil effect – whose words are quoted in the epigraph. Here is an English version from Northern Irish poet Ciaran Carson's modern translation of *The Inferno*, a work that has won many prizes and which is strongly recommend to those of you interested in reading a little more Dante:

  If I supposed that any word of this
    were heard by one who might return to review
    the world, my flame would stay forever voiceless.

  But since none, if what I hear is true,
    has from this deep returned alive, I fear
    no ignominy when I answer you.

In one sense, the significance of the epigraph is transparent, because the connections between Guido da Montefeltro and Prufrock are obvious enough. Both are damned, both are in hopeless situations, both are stuck, both are oppressed by regret, and both insist on indulging in an utterly pointless confession. But why bother making the same point twice, once in English and once in Italian? What does the epigraph *add* to the poem? Perhaps Eliot was wary that the poem, without the epigraph, would not be capable of carrying his full meaning, which is not only that contemporary man is hopelessly lost but also that the path to salvation, although neglected, is still available. The most important reference point in the epigraph is not the speaker, Guido da Montefeltro, who is so like Prufrock, but the listener, Dante, who will discover the true path to Paradise, and who is so like … whoever is listening to Prufrock's confession, perhaps.

The other supposedly difficult part of the poem is Prufrock's curious invitation in the opening line: 'Let us go then, you and I'. Who is he talking to? You will come across suggestions that Prufrock is divided against himself, that the 'you' stands for the timid, public Prufrock and the 'I' stands for the passionate inner man. Such an interpretation can't be sustained through the poem without giving rise to nonsense. For instance, in line 122 – 'Shall I part my hair behind? Do I dare to eat a peach?' – why should the strong inner man worry about such trivialities? If you return to the epigraph, you will note that the extract ends with a 'you and I' – *ti rispondo*, 'I answer you' – just before the 'Love Song' opens with a 'you and I'. Isn't it just as possible that Prufrock is copying *The Divine Comedy*, that he is fantasising about accompanying Dante, or fantasising about *being* Dante? After all, the entire poem is one long, debilitating fantasy, in which he dreams about a crisis, women, Michelangelo, a cat-like fog, social engagements, women, Michelangelo, a crisis, social engagements, making conversation, escape, a crisis, John the Baptist, death, a crisis, Lazarus, rejection, a crisis, rejection, Hamlet, Polonius, social engagements, the Fool, ageing, appearance, loneliness, futility, social engagements, death. This sequence of barely connected thoughts, returning time and time again to a central worry, is typical of fretful day dreaming. So does it matter what he means by 'you and I'? Neither of them ever leaves the room. 'Let us go', he begins; but they don't. The entire experience happens in Prufrock's mind, including the 'you and I', whatever he means by that phrase.

What kind of a mind is it? What kind of world are we in? These are far more important questions.

Actually, it's quite an educated mind, stocked with classical names: Michelangelo (1475–1564), the Italian painter and sculptor, who created powerful, heroic figures and reflected on great religious themes; Lazarus, the biblical character who was restored to life when Jesus came across his family mourning; Hamlet, the hero of a Shakespeare play, who must avenge his father's murder and who, in the process of doing so, deals decisively with women; the wise Fool, again found in Shakespeare's plays; all combined with allusions to the works of unnamed English poets: Geoffrey Chaucer ('Full of high sentence' – line 117 – or full of educated talk, is how a character is described in the Prologue to *The Canterbury Tales*) and John Donne (line 124, 'I have heard the mermaids singing' echoes Donne's 'Teach me to hear mermaids singing' from his poem 'Song: Go, and catch a falling star', which, as both the title and the line indicate, explores a wish to capture the extraordinary and the beautiful).

All the references are to men of accomplishment, men of elegance, men of purpose, but all the imagery evokes exhaustion, squalor and uncertainty. In this way, the magnificence of the past is contrasted with the grubbiness of the modern world, and the achievements of heroic men are contrasted with the pathetic inability of Prufrock to even ask a question. Prufrock is a modern, educated man: his mind is crowded with examples of splendour, but he himself is condemned to insignificance, to a living death. Unlike Dante, he will never emerge from this hell, he will never reach Paradise. He is Guido da Montefeltro, eternally repeating his own useless apology for himself.

(lines 1–12) At the beginning of the poem, Prufrock readies himself for a journey. 'Let us go', he says to himself. All great quests and adventures begin with a journey – from *The Divine Comedy* to *The Lord of the Rings*, to another of Eliot's poems on your course, 'Journey of the Magi' – but this particular journey, like everything else in 'The Love Song of J. Alfred Prufrock', is doomed before it begins. Prufrock imagines the world outside his room as drugged ('etherised'), indistinct, grubby, sordid ('sawdust restaurants'), dangerous ('insidious') and boring ('tedious'). Why the hell would you want to step out there? He doesn't, of course. That's the point of those images in his head. The outside world is unappealing.

Prufrock's journey, if he embarks on it, will lead him to 'an overwhelming question'. What is that question? A proposal of marriage? An invitation to sex? The meaning of life? We don't know. The evidence to identify the question is never provided in the poem, which means that it's not in the least an important issue. The important point is that the timid, uncertain Prufrock immediately draws back from confronting the issue: 'Oh, do not ask. "What is it?"'. He is no hero, no truth-seeker, no spiritual adventurer. He is, as he says himself, 'afraid'. And his fear makes his life meaningless. 'Let us go and make our visit', he urges himself again; but, if the purpose of the journey is to arrive at a question, and he won't face the question, what *is* the purpose of the journey? Why go out at all?

(lines 13–14) Instead, he stays where he is, imagining his destination, a room where women move about, discussing the renaissance painter Michelangelo, creator of heroic figures, indeed an artistic giant himself, and the exact opposite of Prufrock. 'Come and go' probably describes their movements relative to Prufrock (if you imagine him static, which would be consistent with his character), and it seems to suggest that Prufrock himself is the centre, the axis, the point of reference. It's a joke, of course. The women apparently ignore him. Later in the poem, he will imagine others talking about him, but in a contemptuous manner.

(lines 15–22) Perhaps Prufrock is standing at the window, looking out, bracing himself for his journey. But the 'yellow fog' outside envelops and obscures everything, inducing him to sleep rather than inspiring him to action. Notice how everything mimics the lazy self-indulgence of a sleepy cat in this wonderful description – 'rubs its back … rubs its muzzle … Lingered … Slipped … Curled … fell asleep' – and ends up overpowering the initial resolution – 'Let us go then' – that the love song opened with. Sleep is more attractive to him. Compare this with Dante, a real hero, a real traveller, indeed a real lover.

(lines 23–34) You get the impression that if Prufrock could curl up and fall asleep, then he would. But he can't. Because he is human, and has a mind, a conscience, his unfinished task keeps nagging at him. It's his own consciousness – or self-consciousness, if you like – that nags him throughout, to such an extent that he longs to be rid of it at one stage – 'I should have been a pair of ragged claws/Scuttling across the floors of silent seas' (lines 73–74) – because it becomes so tiresome. Aware that he's not getting anywhere, that he's slipping backwards, in fact, he now reassures himself: 'There will be time'. But even the manner of this reassurance – repetitious, meandering, irrelevant – is time wasting in itself. He is, in fact, daydreaming. Some of his thoughts are wandering and pointless, although derived from his situation. The idea, for instance, that 'there will be time/For the yellow smoke' is more or less meaningless. Most of them return to his neurotic anxiety about his inevitable, impending journey. Again, he remarks that he must prepare himself, must put on a 'face' to meet others. There's nothing remarkable about this. We all do it, all the time. It's Prufrock's intense anxiety that makes it *seem* like something significant. In fact, he briefly spends the central section of this passage striving for significance. When he acts, what he does will be as appalling as murder, as profound as creation. But, as always, he immediately falls back again – 'drop a question on your plate' puts him in the position of a beggar, a charity collector, a waiter or an ill-at-ease, ignored party guest; and that damned question is back again to terrify him – and the lines quickly wrap themselves around themselves, strangling any possibility of forward movement – 'a hundred indecisions,/ And for a hundred visions and revisions'.

(lines 35–36) So, instead of going forward, we're back again, along with Prufrock's agitated mind: in that room, with those women, talking of that fellow Michelangelo.

(lines 37–48) And instead of going forward, Prufrock's mind goes around in circles again, utterly pointless circles at that, since he is now wondering if there will be time to wonder. Apart from wondering about wondering, what *does* he wonder about? What does he worry about? Well, he worries about worrying, of course. He asks himself if he will ask the question: 'Do I dare?' You see now how the poem recreates the folding in on itself of a mind that is paralysed by consciousness, a very modern type of mind. (Why does it turn in on itself? Because it has nothing outside itself that it can seek: no faith, no religion, no vision, no quest. Again, contrast Dante.) This folding in is again perfectly captured in one of the many images of withdrawal – 'Time to turn back and descend the stair' – and the debilitating self-consciousness is represented by the image of the 'bald spot in the middle' of his hair. Baldness – before shaved heads became a symbol of virility among men – was a sign of impotency, weakness, lack of sexual prowess. (Remember, the world's very first Strongest Man – Samson – lost his hair and his strength simultaneously – the demon barber was a woman, of course.) Now, he imagines others talking about him, not in the admiring, respectful manner of the women talking about Michelangelo, but pitying him, perhaps even mocking him. He imagines himself tastefully dressed, but that won't save him. People won't compliment his clothes; they'll just deride his skinny limbs. Thinness, of course, is another sign of weakness; although that, too, has become dangerously fashionable since Eliot wrote his poem.

(lines 49–54) He's been here before, he now reminds himself: 'I have known them all already.' That's why he knows what to expect. He's been here before. In fact, he's lived here all his life, in these rooms, with these women, at these breakfast parties or dinner parties. He has measured out his life 'with coffee spoons', meaning that he drifts from one little social gathering to the next, one cup of coffee to the next. He has heard it all before – the comments of others, the derision, the whispered mockery – so why should he presume that it's going to be any different this time?

(lines 55–61) And he has seen it all before, the eyes that stare at him and that mentally deride him, fixing him like a dead insect that's pinned to a display board. How, he asks himself, can he pop a question in a dignified manner if he is pinned like an insect and looking idiotically incompetent? How could he manage to look imposing and heroic and impressive, like those gangster film heroes spitting cigarette butts from their mouths before they start a job (that's what 'spit out all the butt-ends' suggests).

(lines 62–69) He has been there before. The room. The woman. The question. He has never asked the question, though. It's not the woman's face or her eyes that he remembers, presumably because he never had the courage to look in her eyes. What he recalls is her arms, because that's what he spent his time staring at; arms that he can now describe in minute detail, their colour, their ornaments, their hairs. He recalls the woman's perfume as well, although significantly he remembers smelling it, not from her body, but from her dress. So, he's been there before. And he's never even approached the question, never mind had a positive answer. So how can he presume that it might be any different this time?

(lines 70–72) Maybe if he approached it another way. Maybe if he looked at her and said to her, in an impressive way, that he had wandered through the city's narrow streets at twilight and watched lonely working men smoking their pipes at their windows … Would that impress her? Oh, don't be ridiculous!

(lines 73–74) It would be better to be a mindless crustacean, a crab, living in the silent ocean, than to endure these idiotic voices inside his head, outside his head, human voices ….

(lines 75–86) Prufrock, of course, because he is human, cannot be mindless, cannot be a creature without consciousness. He contemplates again, briefly this time, the next most attractive escape, which is sleep – 'sleeps so peacefully' – but the way he presents this indulgence to himself – 'Smoothed by long fingers' – has the opposite effect, because it inevitably reminds him again of the woman, her longed-for caresses, the question, the crisis. Should he – the phrasing includes both will he be able to and will it be appropriate – after the refreshments, be able to force the issue? He's pessimistic. Although he has prepared himself rigorously, like any saintly hero, having 'wept and fasted, wept and prayed' – he's joking again, at his own expense – although he's been martyred, like John the Baptist – joking again, bald head and platter mocking himself once more – he hasn't really suffered or been martyred, because he's only joking, he's no prophet. That word – 'prophet' – is a useful example for understanding the technique of the poem, and indeed the workings of Prufrock's mind, which is the same thing. On the one hand, Prufrock is aware of the past significance of the word – a prophet was a visionary, a saint – but on the other, when he applies it himself, it becomes ridiculously diminished – he simply wants to know what will happen if he puts the 'overwhelming question' to the woman, or indeed if he'll be able to put it at all. So, 'I am no prophet' has two meanings, and 'here's no great matter' indicates Prufrock's awareness of the triviality of his own quest. He has, he says, seen the moment of his triumph threatened, like a flame flickering in the wind – all his mind again, of

course – and he has seen the threat of death (magnificently presented, not as a terrifying figure with a scythe, but as a sniggering servant), and he was simply too afraid.

(lines 87–98) At this point, Prufrock has accepted that he will never ask that 'overwhelming question'. He will not begin his heroic journey, his quest. 'Would it have been worth it' indicates that the agonising is over, that the decision has been made, because otherwise he would say, 'Will it be worth it?' After all, he says to himself, would it have been worth the daredevil risk ('bitten off the matter with a smile'), worth the heroic effort ('squeezed the universe into a ball'), worth the profound pose and gesture ('I am Lazarus, come from the dead'), if the woman was simply bored, indifferent and condescending ('That is not what I meant at all').

(lines 99–110) Would it even have been worth the journey, never mind the big heroic gestures, he wonders then. Would it have been worth going there, putting up with the chit-chat, the refreshments, the company, enduring the awful agony of trying to express oneself (throwing 'the nerves in patterns on a screen'), worth all the rest of the nonsense, if the woman was simply bored, indifferent, condescending?

(lines 111–119) After one acceptance, comes another – 'I am not Prince Hamlet' – expressed very plainly and directly, much more plainly and directly than the earlier sections of the poem, with their interminable twistings and turnings. Although there are many references here that you may have to research – Hamlet is the Shakespearean hero, set the task of revenging his father's murder by the old man's restless ghost, the 'attendant lord' is Polonius from the same play, a long-winded political adviser to the man who murdered Hamlet's father, and 'the Fool' is also from Shakespeare, the visionary clown, who sees deeply into the nature of things, as the character of the Fool does in *King Lear* – nevertheless the language and the phrasing are very plain, almost factual. He is no noble prince like Hamlet, torn between the ugliness and the beauty of existence, Prufrock accepts. He is more like the lackey Polonius, neither noble nor powerful himself, a victim of fate (Polonius was killed when he was mistaken for someone else) rather than its ally.

(lines 120–131) In sharp contrast to this, but maybe arising from it – for where else is there to go once you have come to accept your fatal inadequacies, your smallness? – the final sections of the poem drift off into sheer fantasy. We're still in Prufrock's mind, of course, but now it's a mind that has given up hope, or given up the illusion and pretence of hope, which is possibly all he ever had. It's a mind that is inhabited by sadness and loss ('I grow old'), by self-mockery (parting your hair behind was once considered slightly scandalous in America, and Eliot himself once caused a small sensation when he returned from Europe sporting the style, but the 'daring' of doing this is here presented as about as 'daring' as eating a peach. Who cares?), and by loneliness and yearning (he has heard mermaids singing, but 'I do not think that they will sing to me' and he has watched them 'riding … on the waves'). There are intimations of a world that is graceful, beautiful and satisfying … but the world is under water, a sea world, and humans cannot live there. The human voices that he hears recalls Prufrock to the human world, of sawdust restaurants, fog, novels, teacups, arms, rooms, questions … It's supposed to be the 'real' world, but we can now understand him when he suggests that it is merely a living death, that the recall to this world 'drowns' him.

Additional Glossary

Prufrock's mind, which is an educated mind, is cluttered with knowledge of the past, particularly of the literary past. As mentioned in relation to the word 'prophet' earlier, all these references both retain their original dignity and are diminished by their residence inside Prufrock's mind. Apart from the ones already dealt with in the above discussion, you might also like to know the following:

[23] **there will be time:** passage from Ecclesiastes in the Christian Bible: 'To everything there is a season and a time, a time to be born, and a time to die.' (It's quite often chanted by insane, religiously twisted serial killers in modern crime stories.)

[29] **works and days:** the Greek poet Hesiod wrote *Works and Days* on rural lifestyles

[52] **dying fall:** Shakespeare's *Twelfth Night*, the opening lines of which have the lovesick Orsino demanding a particular piece of music because it has 'a dying fall', which means a diminishing cadence

[82] **brought in upon a platter:** the head of John the Baptist was given to Salome on a platter, when she asked for it as a reward for her dancing

[92 and 93] **squeezed the universe into a ball/To roll it:** from a poem called 'To His Coy Mistress' by the English poet Andrew Marvell (who lived in the same period as John Donne), where the poet urges his mistress to roll their 'sweetness up into one ball'

MAKE

(i) Identify the images of numbness, tiredness, exhaustion and debility through the poem from 'etherised' in line 3 to 'drown' in line 131 and then identify the expressions of uncertainty or confusion – from 'Let us go then' in line 1 to 'Do I dare to eat a peach?' in line 122. Comment on how one relates to the other – is it the exhaustion that creates the uncertainty or the confusion that is responsible for the debility?

(ii) Prufrock's voice is one of unease, fear and hesitation. Identify any features – rhythm, rhyme, repetition, imagery, and so on – that express these feelings.

READ

Poetry

Preludes

I

The winter evening settles down
With smell of steaks in passageways.
Six o' clock.
The burnt-out ends of smoky days.
And now a gusty shower wraps   5
The grimy scraps
Of withered leaves about your feet
And newspapers from vacant lots ;
The showers beat
On broken blinds and chimney-pots,   10
And at the corner of the street
A lonely cab-horse steams and stamps.

And then the lighting of the lamps.

II

The morning comes to consciousness
Of faint stale smells of beer   15
From the sawdust-trampled street
With all its muddy feet that press
To early coffee-stands.

With the other masquerades
That time resumes,   20
One thinks of all the hands
That are raising dingy shades
In a thousand furnished rooms.

III

You tossed a blanket from the bed,
You lay upon your back, and waited ;   25
You dozed, and watched the night revealing
The thousand sordid images
Of which your soul was constituted ;
They flickered against the ceiling.
And when all the world came back   30
And the light crept up between the shutters,
And you heard the sparrows in the gutters,
You had such a vision of the street
As the street hardly understands ;
Sitting along the bed's edge, where   35
You curled the papers from your hair,

Or clasped the yellow soles of feet
In the palms of both soiled hands.

IV

His soul stretched tight across the skies
That fade behind a city block,   40
Or trampled by insistent feet
At four and five and six o' clock;
And short square fingers stuffing pipes,
And evening newspapers, and eyes
Assured of certain certainties,   45
The conscience of a blackened street
Impatient to assume the world.

I am moved by fancies that are curled
Around these images, and cling :
The notion of some infinitely gentle   50
Infinitely suffering thing.

Wipe your hand across your mouth, and laugh ;
The worlds revolve like ancient women
Gathering fuel in vacant lots.

Glossary

[19] **masquerades:** a false show or pretence

[22] **shades:** American English, blinds on the windows

[36] **curled the papers:** before the availability of manufactured curlers, women used paper strips to curl their hair

[54] **vacant lots:** unoccupied or undeveloped building sites

---

ANALYSE

The opening two sections, with their dreary atmosphere, sordid detail and sense of pointlessness, of time passing uselessly, are typical of Eliot's early work. Evening, which should be so full of promise after a day's labour, brings only dreariness: food smells, the sound of rain, the sight of horse steam and lamp light. But there's always the next morning, isn't there? Morning, emblem of new beginnings, fresh starts, alertness, life's possibilities. It brings the stale odour of spilled beer, sawdust, mud, the first ritual drink of coffee, 'masquerades', and the raising of shades to admit the daylight. Another day, bringing us to another evening, leading to another day, bringing us another evening … Time passes, pointlessly.

This is an exhausted, fragmented, colourless world.

Let's take exhausted first. The evening 'settles down', the days are 'burnt-out' – a wonderful image that compares a day to a smoked cigarette, its energy gone up in smoke, leaving only ashes – the leaves are 'withered', the morning, instead of being a vibrant wake-up call, 'comes to consciousness' as if it's too weak to do anything but limp in.

The world is fragmented, broken, lacking anything to make it coherent or whole. The days are butt-ends, the leaves are 'scraps', newspaper pages are blown by the wind, the blinds are 'broken', and, above all, the humans (in Section II) are experienced as body parts, as feet, as mouths ('coffee'), as noses, as masks, as hands.

And finally, there is no colour in this world. Eliot lays on the dullness: 'winter', the grey ash of the cigarette ends, 'grimy', 'chimney-pots', 'sawdust', 'muddy', 'dingy'. There are two sources of light, of course – the lamps and the morning – but neither manages to break through the smoke and the gusting rain, or lift the gloom of the sawdust and mud.

The final two sections expose the human inhabitants of this exhausted, fragmented, grimy world. The lines of forensic poetry give one the impression of a roof being peeled back, like the lid of a tin can, so that we can peer into the rooms at the trapped animals in their cages.

Section III, which deals with a woman, opens on a note of weariness, languor, reluctance to move. The woman seems about to get up, since she tosses 'a blanket from the bed', but then she continues lying there, dozing, dreaming. Her dreams are far from profound or noble. They are, in fact, 'sordid', because they reflect her soul, and in turn feed her soul, which is itself 'sordid'. The morning light and sounds finally rouse her – 'And when all the world came back' – but notice how everything is demeaned, how the light 'crept up' rather than blazed and even the sparrows chirrup in 'gutters' rather than trees or hedges. The woman sits on the edge of her bed and looks through the window at the street. They reflect one another, woman and street: her hands are 'soiled', her feet are 'yellow' and she has bits of paper (as curlers) in her hair. Remember those newspapers from Section I blowing about the vacant lots? Her view of the street is described in the poem as a 'vision', another example of Eliot's characteristically grim irony. A vision is a profound spiritual insight.

Section IV opens with a male, although other than gender there is no difference between him and the woman in Section III. His soul, too, has become simply a part of the city that he dwells in, since it is now part of the skyline, 'stretched tight across the skies/That fade behind a city block'. The image also suggests an animal skin, dried and stretched, tied between poles, which is rather grotesque. The human soul as a skinned animal? The other image of the battered soul – 'trampled by insistent feet' – is equally disturbing; the suggestion here is that the masses in the city – those same feet that are 'muddy' and that tread 'a thousand furnished rooms' in Section II – pummel a man's soul, on the hour, every hour, 'At four and five and six o' clock', because that's what time is in the urban modern world, regulated, deadening, time that is useless, good for nothing except destruction.

'Preludes' is, pre-eminently, a piece about time, about dead time: winter, evening, six o'clock, days, morning, early, time resumes, the night, light crept up, four and five and six o'clock, evening newspapers …

In the city, all time is dead, there is no fundamental difference in human experience between night and day, morning and evening, all bring the same futility and dreariness. And yet the man in Section IV is 'Impatient'. 'Impatient' means that you are weary of present time and want to move on to future time. He is 'Impatient to assume the world', an absolutely brilliant phrase, because 'assume' can mean to accept without proof, to take the responsibility on oneself, to pretend, to adopt or to appropriate. In the context of the world's dreariness and futility that so dominate the poem, both his 'impatience' and his resolve – 'eyes/Assured of certain certainties' – are rather pathetic.

This is why the poem's speaker is 'moved', not so much emotionally, as the word might suggest, not so much moved to compassion or pity, but roused to slight excitement by the 'notion' or idea ('fancies' suggests 'fanciful') that man is a gentle creature, made noble by his suffering in this grey world.

The 'notion' is raised only to be laughed at – 'Wipe your hand across your mouth, and laugh' – because the 'worlds' that have been described through the poem, of joyless urban squalor in streets and furnished rooms and bedrooms, worlds of infinite futility – captured by that timeless image of poor women gathering firewood in deserted sites – simply recreate themselves, one giving way to the next, just as, at the beginning of 'Preludes', another day gives way to another evening, leading to another day, bringing on another evening … Time passes, uselessly.

MAKE

(i) *Preludes* has been read as a condemnation of modern, urban life. Would you agree with this reading? Give reasons for your answer.

(ii) The tone is quite detached in the opening lines, but commentators have also found expressions of scorn, disgust, ridicule, sarcasm and pity in 'Preludes'. Identify the words and phrases containing each of these attitudes.

Poetry

READ

Aunt Helen

Miss Helen Slingsby was my maiden aunt,
And lived in a small house near a fashionable square
Cared for by servants to the number of four.
Now when she died there was silence in heaven
And silence at her end of the street.   5
The shutters were drawn and the undertaker wiped his feet—
He was aware that this sort of thing had occurred before.
The dogs were handsomely provided for,
But shortly afterwards the parrot died too.
The Dresden clock continued ticking on the mantelpiece,   10
And the footman sat upon the dining-table
Holding the second housemaid on his knees—
Who had always been so careful while her mistress lived.

Glossary

[1] **maiden aunt:** unmarried aunt

[10] **Dresden clock:** porcelain clock made in the German city of Dresden, which was famous for its production of fine china

[11] **footman:** male servant whose duties include admitting visitors and waiting at table

[12] **housemaid:** female servant whose duties include cleaning

ANALYSE

For light relief in Eliot's poetry, and a wry rather than a grim reflection on disintegration and decline in the modern world, one can turn to the freakish, stunted, thirteen-line sonnet, 'Aunt Helen'.

An old-fashioned spinster, representative of a fading old-fashioned world, has died. She had shared her life with some dogs, a parrot, a Dresden clock and four servants. Other than the Dresden clock, which 'continued ticking on the mantelpiece', nothing survives her death unchanged. The dogs 'were handsomely provided for', a phrase which may indicate where Miss Slingsby's wealth ended up after her death or which may be using the English language with the same irony as the Mafia do when they promise to make you an offer you can't refuse. The parrot dies. The servants' behaviour deteriorates.

The world changes with the passing of Aunt Helen. It seems a change for the worse, a loosening of morals and etiquette, a fracturing of what was once coherent and self-contained and whole. Clearly, though, Aunt Helen's death did not cause these changes, since it is presented, jokingly, as something so common as to pass without much notice: the undertaker 'was aware that this sort of thing had occurred before', which sounds more like mild disapproval of the servants than a response to an old woman's death. Though Aunt Helen's passing and the footman loosening the housemaid's caution are both minor and rather comically sad events, they are also part of a wider and more serious social disintegration.

In fact, the language of the poem is so quaint – 'servants to the number of four' and 'this sort of thing had occurred before' and 'always been so careful' – that the poem itself seems to be throwing its hands up despairingly at how times have changed.

MAKE

(i) The speaker is Helen Slingsby's niece or nephew. They're careful not to express any feelings directly. What feelings, in your view, are implied by the selection of details?

(ii) We can infer from the description that Aunt Helen was both extravagant in some areas ('handsomely provided for') and small-minded in others ('small house'). In your opinion, which was the more dominant characteristic? Give reasons and use quotations.

READ

from The Waste Land II. A Game of Chess

The Chair she sat in, like a burnished throne,
Glowed on the marble, where the glass
Held up by standards wrought with fruited vines
From which a golden Cupidon peeped out   80
(Another hid his eyes behind his wing)
Doubled the flames of sevenbranched candelabra
Reflecting light upon the table as
The glitter of her jewels rose to meet it,
From satin cases poured in rich profusion.   85
In vials of ivory and coloured glass
Unstoppered, lurked her strange synthetic perfumes,
Unguent, powdered, or liquid—troubled, confused
And drowned the sense in odours ; stirred by the air
That freshened from the window, these ascended   90
In fattening the prolonged candle-flames,
Flung their smoke into the laquearia,
Stirring the pattern on the coffered ceiling.
Huge sea-wood fed with copper
Burned green and orange, framed by the coloured stone,   95
In which sad light a carvèd dolphin swam.
Above the antique mantel was displayed
As though a window gave upon the sylvan scene
The change of Philomel, by the barbarous king
So rudely forced ; yet there the nightingale   100
Filled all the desert with inviolable voice
And still she cried, and still the world pursues,
'Jug Jug' to dirty ears.
And other withered stumps of time
Were told upon the walls ; staring forms   105
Leaned out, leaning, hushing the room enclosed.
Footsteps shuffled on the stair.
Under the firelight, under the brush, her hair
Spread out in fiery points
Glowed into words, then would be savagely still.   110

  'My nerves are bad to-night. Yes, bad. Stay with me.
Speak to me. Why do you never speak? Speak.
    What are you thinking of? What thinking? What?
I never know what you are thinking. Think.'

  I think we are in rats' alley   115
Where the dead men lost their bones.

'What is that noise?'
                    The wind under the door.
'What is that noise now? What is the wind doing?'
                    Nothing again nothing.   120
                                        'Do
You know nothing? Do you see nothing? Do you remember
'Nothing?'

          I remember
Those are pearls that were his eyes.   125
'Are you alive, or not? Is there nothing in your head?'
                                        But
O O O O that Shakespeherian Rag—
It's so elegant
So intelligent   130
'What shall I do now? What shall I do?
I shall rush out as I am, and walk the street
With my hair down, so. What shall we do tomorrow?
What shall we ever do?'
                    The hot water at ten.   135
And if it rains, a closed car at four.
And we shall play a game of chess,
Pressing lidless eyes and waiting for a knock upon the door.

   When Lil's husband got demobbed, I said—
I didn't mince my words, I said to her myself,   140
Hurry up please its time
Now Albert's coming back, make yourself a bit smart.
He'll want to know what you done with that money he gave you
To get yourself some teeth. He did, I was there.
You have them all out, Lil, and get a nice set,   145
He said, I swear, I can't bear to look at you.
And no more can't I, I said, and think of poor Albert,
He's been in the army four years, he wants a good time,
And if you don't give it him, there's others will, I said.
Oh is there, she said. Something o' that, I said.   150
Then I'll know who to thank, she said, and give me a straight look.
Hurry up please its time
If you don't like it you can get on with it, I said.
Others can pick and choose if you can't.
But if Albert makes off, it won't be for lack of telling.   155
You ought to be ashamed, I said, to look so antique.
(And her only thirty-one.)
I can't help it, she said, pulling a long face,

It's them pills I took, to bring it off, she said.
(She's had five already, and nearly died of young George.)   160
The chemist said it would be all right, but I've never been the same.
You *are* a proper fool, I said.
Well, if Albert won't leave you alone, there it is, I said,
What you get married for if you don't want children?
HURRY UP PLEASE ITS TIME   165
Well, that Sunday Albert was home, they had a hot gammon,
And they asked me in to dinner, to get the beauty of it hot—
HURRY UP PLEASE ITS TIME
HURRY UP PLEASE ITS TIME
Goonight Bill. Goonight Lou. Goonight May. Goonight.   170
Ta ta. Goonight. Goonight.
Good night, ladies, good night, sweet ladies, good night, good night.

The complete poem of 'The Waste Land' is in five sections – *The Burial of the Dead*, *A Game of Chess*, *The Fire Sermon*, *Death by Water* and *What the Thunder Said* – and it comes with seven pages of notes by Eliot himself, in which he explains the source material for the various references to literary works and historical events within the text. It is 434 lines in length, of which *A Game of Chess* is ninety-six lines, slightly less than a quarter.

The poem is a terrifying vision of Europe at the end of the First World War and it marks the climax of Eliot's early period of social, satiric poetry. After this, he would turn almost exclusively to the religious vision implicit in the final section of the poem, *What the Thunder Said*, where it is clear that man cannot save himself from the 'arid plain' of the Waste Land, the modern world. 'Waste', when applied to land, describes a land that is devastated or ruined, but it is also interesting to note that the American military and mobsters use the verb 'wasted' as a synonym for 'dead'. The poem is very concerned with the dead – both the living dead and the literally dead.

As with the rest of 'The Waste Land', section II *A Game of Chess* hops from one location to another, in this case from a rich, privileged world to a poorer, more ordinary one. There is no attempt to establish logical or sequential connections between the locations. The poem simply jumps from one to the other at the end of line 138 (the line numbers refer to the entire poem, 'The Waste Land'). But the decision to place them side by side is obviously significant and the reader will be conscious of contrasts and similarities because of it.

A Game of Chess opens, as Eliot informs us in his notes, with an echo from Shakespeare's play *Anthony and Cleopatra* (Act II, Scene ii), where Enobarbus describes Cleopatra's arrival:

The barge she sat in, like a burnished throne,
Burned on the water. The poop was beaten gold;
Purple the sails and so perfuméd that
The winds were lovesick with them; the oars were silver

This lavish, stately and composed world is mimicked or recreated in the opening of *A Game of Chess*. The movement of the verse outdoes the original for pomp. The phrasing is deliberately old-fashioned: 'wrought with fruited vines' and 'Doubled the flames'. The vocabulary is obscure and archaic: 'Cupidon' is a kind of mini-Cupid, the Roman God of love, a beautiful young man and 'laquearia', is an ornate ceiling, specifically, according to Eliot himself, a ceiling described in Virgil's *Aeneid*, under which Dido welcomed Aeneas to Carthage.

Put into crude prose, this first, stately, nine-line sentence (down to 'profusion') means: The chair she was sitting in, like a polished throne, glowed on the marble floor, where the mirror in her dressing table – held up by supports in the shape of vines, from which a little Cupid peered out, while another hid himself behind his wing – where this mirror reflected the flames of a seven-branched candlestick, throwing the light on to the dressing table, where the light from her jewels, in satin cases, came to meet it.

The atmosphere changes from line 86 onwards, however, and, as so often in Eliot's poetry, a nervous, troubled atmosphere is carried by polluted air, here, the woman's 'strange synthetic perfumes'. They 'troubled' the nose, 'confused' the brain, 'drowned' the sense in odours and wafted upwards, joining the candle flames, which they fattened or corrupted, to reach the 'coffered', or sunk panelled, ceiling. It is towards that ceiling that our gaze is now directed. Painted on it is a depiction of the scary Greek myth of Philomel and her strange family. Philomel was raped by her sister's husband, Tereus, who cut off her tongue afterwards, so that she couldn't tell anyone. But Philomel weaved a tapestry to tell the story to her sister, Procne, who then killed her young son, chopped him up and served him cooked to her husband as revenge. Tereus chased the two women, but the gods turned them all into birds. Philomel became a nightingale. It is this nightingale that is represented as still singing on the ceiling. 'Jug Jug' was how the poets of Shakespeare's time represented the song of birds, but it also crudely suggested the sexual act, hence 'to dirty ears'.

The poem has wandered rather languidly, rather like the smoke and perfume drifting upwards, into violence, rape and death. But associations of death have always clung to this woman sitting in the 'Chair'. Cleopatra killed herself with a poisonous snake when she heard of Anthony's death, and Dido threw herself into fire when Aeneas left Carthage. For all the grandeur of the Chair, she is surrounded by 'withered stumps of time' – the decayed remnants of old tragedies.

Someone else now approaches – 'Footsteps shuffled on the stair' – and, in a wonderful image, the woman's neurotic, wired condition finds expression in the hair she is trying to brush, which becomes spiky, testy and overheated.

One half of what happens next is startlingly clear. The woman complains and pleads, all in a fractured, highly strung, neurotic voice. It is the voice of someone on the edge of a breakdown: neurotic ('My nerves are bad to-night'), desperate ('Stay with me./Speak to me'), accusing ('Why do you never speak?'), paranoid ('What is that noise?') and lost ('What shall I do now?'). The way that the verse creates the rhythms of this broken voice, and broken woman, is quite brilliant.

On the other hand, we are never told who the second person is, although it's most likely a male lover/husband. It's not clear whether he responds verbally to the woman, or whether it's his unspoken thoughts that are represented. His words are not enclosed within quotation marks, unlike the woman's. Of course, this technique sharpens the distance between the two. His voice, in any case, whether it's inner or outer, is certainly calmer, more composed. It's not any more positive, however. While the woman seems rattled by her hopeless situation, the man seems deadened by his sense of hopelessness:'I think we are in rats' alley/Where the dead men lost their bones.' His musings are completely disconnected from the woman's anxieties (so it doesn't really matter whether he's actually talking to her or not; they're not having a conversation). A scrap of Shakespeare's *The Tempest* – 'Those are pearls that were his eyes', another image of a dead, drowned man, following the 'dead men' in rats' alley – pops into his mind, and then another scrap, now of a ragtime tune – 'that Shakespeherian Rag' – which *The Tempest* reminds him of. The only time he seems to respond directly to the woman is with the bitter indifference of his answer to her desperate: 'What shall we ever do?' His reply offers only hopeless perseverance: we'll go on, doing the same things we always do, with the same regularity, having a bath at ten, taking a cab at four if it rains, whiling away the time with chess, pressing our thumbs into our unprotected eyes, and waiting for the summons ('a knock upon the door' obviously suggests death). As Eliot explained in his notes, the most important of the references here, not least because it is also the title of this section of 'The Waste Land', is to the game of chess. In a play called *Women Beware Women*, by Thomas Middleton, who was writing around the same time as Shakespeare, a woman is kept busy playing a game of chess in one room while her daughter is being raped next door. In the context in which it occurs, therefore, the reference to the game of chess suggests idling away the time while the world is disintegrating around you. 'What shall we ever do?' Find something to entertain ourselves with while the world collapses.

By comparison with the complexity of the opening, the final section of *A Game of Chess* is straightforward, although perhaps more powerful, and in its way more suggestive. A working-class woman is talking to her friend in a pub at closing time. As she gossips away, amid constant interruptions from the barman calling time, her voice is magnificently captured. She tells a sordid little story of working-class life, of a woman whose husband has just been demobbed (discharged from the army), a woman whose teeth are bad, whose husband can't bear to look at her mouth, who's had five kids, and one home-made abortion on the advice of the local chemist, whose health is damaged as a result, who doesn't want sex any more but has it more or less forced on her …

What a life! Is it any better, or any worse, than the life of the woman sitting in the Chair in the first section? There are so many similarities – the nerves, the ill-health, the dissatisfaction, the uncommunicative husband, the anxieties – that the obvious differences in class and wealth seem trivial somehow.

We're not told what happens to either woman. There's no answer to the first woman's question, 'What shall we ever do?' and the story of the second woman is terminally interrupted by the pub closing and the gossipers finding themselves outside, bidding one another goodnight. But we know what happens to them, really. They simply go on with their desperate, despairing lives. Until death takes them – the 'knock upon the door' in the first section, and the final 'good night, sweet ladies' in the second section, which is said, not by the gossipy drinker, but by the sweet Ophelia, tragic lover of Hamlet in Shakespeare's play, who was driven mad by the cruelties of the world and committed suicide shortly after uttering those words. One more connection, incidentally, between the women in *A Game of Chess*: Cleopatra, Dido and Ophelia all killed themselves, for love.

MAKE

(i) The title of this extract from 'The Waste Land' is *A Game of Chess* and it has been said that chess is the most appropriate activity for this waste land, a game that is without feeling or human contact. Read back through the extract, attempting to identify any expression of feeling *for others* expressed by the characters and then comment again on the appropriateness of the title.

(ii) Identify and comment on any sound effects that you can locate in the extract – for instance, onomatopoeia, rhyme, rhythm, voice, and so on.

READ

Journey of the Magi

'A cold coming we had of it,
Just the worst time of the year
For a journey, and such a long journey :
The ways deep and the weather sharp,
The very dead of winter.'   5
And the camels galled, sore-footed, refractory,
Lying down in the melting snow.
There were times we regretted
The summer palaces on slopes, the terraces,
And the silken girls bringing sherbet.   10
Then the camel men cursing and grumbling
And running away, and wanting their liquor and women,
And the night-fires going out, and the lack of shelters,
And the cities hostile and the towns unfriendly
And the villages dirty and charging high prices :   15
A hard time we had of it.
At the end we preferred to travel all night,
Sleeping in snatches,
With the voices singing in our ears, saying
That this was all folly.   20

Then at dawn we came down to a temperate valley,
Wet, below the snow line, smelling of vegetation,
With a running stream and a water-mill beating the darkness,
And three trees on the low sky.
And an old white horse galloped away in the meadow.   25
Then we came to a tavern with vine-leaves over the lintel,
Six hands at an open door dicing for pieces of silver,
And feet kicking the empty wine-skins.
But there was no information, and so we continued
And arrived at evening, not a moment too soon   30
Finding the place ; it was (you may say) satisfactory.

All this was a long time ago, I remember,
And I would do it again, but set down
This set down
This : were we led all that way for   35
Birth or Death? There was a Birth, certainly,
We had evidence and no doubt. I had seen birth and death,
But had thought they were different ; this Birth was
Hard and bitter agony for us, like Death, our death.
We returned to our places, these Kingdoms,   40
But no longer at ease here, in the old dispensation,
With an alien people clutching their gods.
I should be glad of another death.

Poetry

Glossary

[title] **Magi:** the plural form of 'magus', a sorcerer, magician or astrologer of ancient times. In Christian literature, the Gospel of Matthew describes how three magi, usually translated as 'three wise men' – Balthazar, Gaspar and Melchior – came from the east to honour the birth of Jesus Christ. They are also usually described as 'kings'

ANALYSE

'Journey of the Magi' is a useful poem for illustrating the transition in Eliot's poetry from early satire to later devotion. For a start, it is itself a poem about transition, from the old, pre-Christian world to the opening of the new era with the birth of Christ. It is a poem that celebrates a new birth, although it focuses more on the harshness of the journey towards it. But it is also a poem that takes with it much of Eliot's earlier technique. For instance, the speaking voice here – 'And I would do it again, but set down/This set down/This : were we led all that way for/Birth or Death?' – is remarkably similar at times to the speaking voice in 'Prufrock'. Both poems also end in death. But there's a crucial difference, of course. Prufrock is no Lazarus and will never be restored to life; the death here, of 'the old dispensation', is also a glorious birth. It's also important to note that the year in which the poem was composed, 1927, was also the year in which Eliot converted to the Church of England and left the Unitarian Church. 'Journey of the Magi' was written for a Christmas pamphlet that year at the request of his publisher.

Perhaps Eliot's vision hasn't changed, really. The true believer always hovers between relinquishing this world and embracing the next, and while Eliot's early poetry explored the former, the later material simply turns over the same coin and displays the other side of it. 'Journey of the Magi' lets the old world go – painfully, reluctantly – and while it doesn't exactly embrace or celebrate the new Christianity, it does recognise that this is where the future lies.

The first five lines of the poem are borrowed from a sermon delivered on Christmas Day 1622 before King James I by Lancelot Andrewes, a writer and cleric Eliot was particularly attached to. The extract from Andrewes' sermon offered Eliot both a perspective on Christ's birth that mirrored his own situation – Eliot is journeying towards the discovery of Christ – and the key note of harsh struggle that is involved in such an undertaking.

After the quotation – it is as if one of the Magi is hearing it from another or reading it aloud to himself – the poem is a litany of remembered discomforts: and this, and that, and the other thing … Five separate lines begin with 'And', a sequence broken only by a line beginning with 'Then', which has more or less the same meaning and effect. Memories that have obviously stuck clearly in the mind are echoed and repeated: 'A cold coming we had of it … A hard time we had of it.' The images are of pain and exhaustion: 'the camels galled', which means made sore by the rubbing of the saddles, 'sore-footed', 'cursing', 'hostile', 'dirty'. Anything pleasant – the girls bringing sherbets, or cold drinks made from fruit juices – is presented as a distraction from the task, almost a temptation, which the 'camel men' succumb to, but the Magi don't. All the time there is doubt and uncertainty, loss of faith, voices whispering in their ears that 'this was all folly'. What drove them on, resisting temptation, stopping their ears to despair, enduring pain? What kept them going? Faith? Hope?

Poetry

Perhaps the answer is suggested in the next section of the poem, not so much by what is stated directly in the description of the scene at Bethlehem – which was, in fact, no more than 'satisfactory', an extraordinarily downbeat word – as by the selection of the details, all of which anticipate events in the subsequent life of Christ. The 'three trees on the low sky' suggest the Crucifixion and the three crosses on the hill at Calvary. The 'old white horse' is mentioned in Revelations, another book of the New Testament. The 'pieces of silver' clearly anticipate Judas' betrayal of Christ for thirty of these, and 'dicing' is what the soldiers did for Christ's clothes. The Magi are travelling towards the future, in other words. What else can one do?

Hence, in the third section: 'I would do it again'. Almost as if it was not a matter of personal choice. Even though there was no joy in either the journey or the discovery – the former being 'hard' and the latter no more than 'satisfactory' – even though, after all those years, the speaker remains uncertain about the purpose or meaning of the journey – 'were we led all that way for/Birth or Death?' – and even though the event destroyed the old world that he was familiar with, made him 'no longer at ease' in these old, outdated 'Kingdoms', the Magus 'would do it again', would indeed 'be glad of another death'. Why? Because he has at least understood that death, agonising though it may be, is a necessary event before rebirth, rejuvenation. It is a religious consciousness that speaks. It is the consciousness of a man who has discovered his salvation and who does not need to rationally understand such a mystery. It is, in other words, the consciousness of Eliot himself during that year of 1927 when he made the journey to be received into the Church of England.

(i) Despite the fact that the images are of 'pain and suffering', T.S. Eliot said that 'Journey of the Magi' was 'obviously a subject suitable for the Christmas season', which is clearly a time of celebration for Christians. Identify the images of discomfort – physical, intellectual, spiritual – and comment on whether or not you can also find any evidence of celebration in the poem.

(ii) Like many Eliot poems, this is a monologue, the sound of a single voice speaking. Describe this voice – starting with something as basic as optimistic or pessimistic – and say who you think it is speaking *to*, if anyone.

READ

from Landscapes *III. Usk*

Do not suddenly break the branch, or
Hope to find
The white hart behind the white well.
Glance aside, not for lance, do not spell
Old enchantments. Let them sleep.   5
'Gently dip, but not too deep',
Lift your eyes
Where the roads dip and where the roads rise
Seek only there
Where the grey light meets the green air   10
The hermit's chapel, the pilgrim's prayer.

Glossary

[title] **Usk:** small town in Monmouthshire, southeast Wales

[3] **hart:** adult male deer

[6] **'Gently dip …':** quotation from *The Old Wives' Tale* (1595) by George Peele

ANALYSE

Usk is from a series of five short poems called 'Landscapes' and is one of two in the series using British locations, the other being *Rannoch*.

Written at the time of transition in Eliot's life, when his life and poetry were shifting from social to religious concerns, *Usk* advises a rejection of superstitions and enchantments, of the old folklore still present in such ancient locations as the Roman town of Usk, in pursuit of the true spiritual path. Don't go for the superstitious ritual ('break the branch'). Don't look for the superstitious vision ('the white hart behind the white well'). Don't look back to the medieval knights ('lance') or their magicians ('Old enchantments'). After quoting a line from *The Old Wives' Tale*, which is also about superstition, he points towards the true path – acceptance of the real world ('Where the roads dip … and … rise'), individual devotion, symbolised both by the lone 'hermit' and the communal 'pilgrim'.

MAKE

(i) Each poem in 'Landscapes' has been described as a 'sketch' of a perception or theme. What, in your opinion, is the perception or theme of *Usk*?

(ii) In a 'sketch' a painter quickly selects significant detail. but provides only a rough impression of the whole. Do you think it's an appropriate term to describe the technique of *Usk*? Give reasons for your answer, paying particular attention to the use of repetition and alliteration in the sound effects.

Poetry

READ

from Landscapes *IV. Rannoch, by Glencoe*

Here the crow starves, here the patient stag
Breeds for the rifle. Between the soft moor
And the soft sky, scarcely room
To leap or soar. Substance crumbles, in the thin air
Moon cold or moon hot. The road winds in   5
Listlessness of ancient war,
Languor of broken steel,
Clamour of confused wrong, apt
In silence. Memory is strong
Beyond the bone. Pride snapped,   10
Shadow of pride is long, in the long pass
No concurrence of bone.

Glossary

[title] **Rannoch:** part of Glencoe in the Highlands of Scotland, site of an infamous massacre in 1692

[7] **languor:** oppressive stillness, inactivity

ANALYSE

Rannoch, by Glencoe is from a series of five short poems called 'Landscapes' and is one of two in the series using British locations, the other being *Usk*.

Written at the time of transition in Eliot's life, when his life and poetry were shifting from social to religious concerns, *Rannoch* laments the persistence of old and bitter rivalries, the inability to synthesise conflicting elements ('No concurrence of bone') and move on more strongly.

The landscape still holds the deprivation and violence of its history – 'the crow starves', the stag is born to be shot. In a wonderful image – 'scarcely room' – the barren and mountainous terrain offers no space for rising above history, or indeed the worst in nature. The air is 'thin', the roads narrow, the atmosphere heavy with the old violence of 'ancient war' and 'broken steel' and 'confused wrong'. The sounds are destructive – 'Clamour' or 'silence' – not pleasing or productive. This is because people hold on grimly to old grievances – 'Memory is strong' and 'Shadow of pride is long'.

MAKE

(i) Each poem in 'Landscapes' has been described as a 'sketch' of a perception or theme. What, in your opinion, is the perception or theme of *Rannoch*?

(ii) In a 'sketch' a painter quickly selects significant detail, but provides only a rough impression of the whole. Do you think it's an appropriate term to describe the technique of *Rannoch*? Give reasons for your answer, concentrating in particular on how the atmosphere is quickly established through the violent imagery and alliteration.

Poetry

from Four Quartets *East Coker IV*

The wounded surgeon plies the steel
That questions the distempered part ;
Beneath the bleeding hands we feel
The sharp compassion of the healer's art
Resolving the enigma of the fever chart.   5

Our only health is the disease
If we obey the dying nurse
Whose constant care is not to please
But to remind of our, and Adam's curse,
And that, to be restored, our sickness must grow worse.   10

The whole earth is our hospital
Endowed by the ruined millionaire,
Wherein, if we do well, we shall
Die of the absolute paternal care
That will not leave us, but prevents us everywhere.   15

The chill ascends from feet to knees,
The fever sings in mental wires.
If to be warmed, then I must freeze
And quake in frigid purgatorial fires
Of which the flame is roses, and the smoke is briars.   20

The dripping blood our only drink,
The bloody flesh our only food :
In spite of which we like to think
That we are sound, substantial flesh and blood—
Again, in spite of that, we call this Friday good.   25

Glossary

[title] **East Coker:** village in Somerset, England. Eliot's ancestors travelled from there to America in 1669 and Eliot's ashes are now buried there

For many readers, 'Four Quartets', written and published between 1935 and 1942, is the finest expression of Eliot's Christianity.

The full poem, which is in four parts – *Burnt Norton*, *East Coker*, *The Dry Salvages* and *Little Gidding* – with each part divided into several sections, is a very complex exploration of Christian belief. You might be interested to know that there is no hell in it, even though visions of hell characterised Eliot's early poems, but that the writer's reflections on time are sustained. The opening lines of 'Four Quartets' – 'Time present and time past/Are both perhaps present in time future/And time future contained in time past' – may also be helpful in coming to terms with the experience of time in 'Journey of the Magi'.

The small section of 'Four Quartets' on your course – *East Coker IV* – presents us with a portrait of Christ as a 'wounded surgeon'. It's a very challenging idea, to say the least. How can a surgeon successfully operate on his patients if he himself is wounded? But, of course, in religious terms, the surgeon *must* be wounded in order to save. It was through Christ's death, his wounds, that man was saved. This is the central vision, metaphor and paradox of the poem, which is sustained and repeated and developed throughout.

The wounded surgeon vigorously wields the scalpel ('the steel') that probes the diseased ('distempered') part of our being. Underneath his bleeding hands (the obvious reference is to the nailed hands of Christ on the cross), we feel love of and sympathy for the healer's ability to solve the riddle of the medical chart (in other words, correctly diagnose what is wrong with us).

The disease we suffer from is the necessary stage to health (this is the same Christian paradox as explored in 'Journey of the Magi': death is essential to rebirth). Provided we obey the dictates of the Church, here metaphorically presented as 'the dying nurse', whose constant care is not to make us comfortable, but rather to remind us of original sin ('Adam's curse' is a reference to the Christian belief in Adam as the first sinner when he took the apple of knowledge from Eve in Paradise), and of the fact that we must get worse, die, before we can be restored, or reborn.

Continuing and sustaining the metaphor he has introduced, Eliot now presents the world as a 'hospital'. It's worth reflecting on this, because it's quite a brilliant image. Why are you in hospital? How do you behave while in hospital? The world is a hospital, where we must be treated, because it was created like that ('endowed') by a millionaire who ruined his perfect inheritance (Adam again). If we behave as we should do in a hospital, the 'paternal' or fatherly care we get in there, which will never desert us, will bring us to death, wherein we shall be reborn healthy (same paradox again).

The chill of approaching death rises up through the body, the fever rages in the brain ('mental wires'), in order to come alive ('warmed'), one must die ('freeze') and shiver in the purifying flames of purgatory (place of cleansing in Christian faith), where the flames bear flowers (instead of destroying, same paradox) and the smoke is Christ's suffering for us ('briars' is a reference to the crown of thorns he had to wear when he was mocked as King of the Jews).

The only drink we will be allowed is blood (of Christ, obviously – Communion in the Christian faith), the only food the body of Christ (Communion again), even though we humans like to think that we can take other nourishment, earthly nourishment ('substantial flesh and blood'), the fact is that the only good that is on offer to us is Christ's death from the Crucifixion, which happened on Good Friday ('Friday good').

(i) This extract from 'Four Quartets' works by employing and developing a number of paradoxes – for instance, that we must die in order to live. Identify some of the other paradoxes in the extract and comment on their meaning.

(ii) There are many abstract ideas expressed in *East Coker*, all of them relating to Christian belief. Do you think the poem succeeds in making them clear?

The Poetry of T.S. Eliot

Themes and Interests

- The poetry of T.S. Eliot explores the complexities of **TIME**, both the dead time of routine or habit or endless repetition, and the living time of death and rebirth

  Of all the complex features of Eliot's poetry, perhaps his treatment of time is the most fascinating. It's one of the first things one notices as a recurring thematic element in the work. The word is used on thirteen occasions in 'The Love Song of J. Alfred Prufrock' alone, for instance, on seven in the extract from 'The Waste Land' and four in 'Journey of the Magi'. The poetry seems obsessed with or dominated by time. 'There will be time', Prufrock claims repeatedly. But even the manner of this reassurance – repetitious, meandering, irrelevant – is actually wasting time. In 'Preludes' one day follows another to the same empty pattern. Even Aunt Helen's clock now ticks away uselessly after her death. And the barman's cry – 'Hurry up please its time' – in ('The Waste Land') *A Game of Chess* symbolically represents the loss of time, and opportunity. In all of these poems, everybody is always conscious of and concerned about time. But time never brings them anything, never goes anywhere. In the city of the early poems, all time is dead. Mostly, this is explicitly expressed: 'the other masquerades/That time resumes' is from 'Preludes', and 'other withered stumps of time' from *A Game of Chess*. In the imagery, time is associated with falsity and decay. In both these short quotations, 'other' – meaning 'the same' – is used to suggest pointless repetition. 'Journey of the Magi' is also concerned with time, but in a different way. Because it *is* a journey, it is part of a process, not something atrophied, or wasted away, in itself. Any given point on a journey has a past, a present and a future. Time here is man's time ('the old dispensation'), death (the end of time) and eternity (the beginning of Time). Through the separate treatments of time, we can understand how the two periods of Eliot's poetry – secular and religious – are related. Time is experienced as endless repetition in the early work – where the use of repetition has a vital technical role – but time is experienced as death/rebirth in the later work.

- The poetry of T.S. Eliot captures what Eliot perceived as the **SHALLOWNESS**, **EMPTINESS** and **DISINTEGRATION** of modern life, particularly urban life

  In an essay entitled 'Christianity and Culture', Eliot advanced the following opinion:

  > There is no doubt that in our headlong rush to educate everybody, we are lowering our standards … destroying our ancient edifices to make ready the ground upon which the barbarian nomads of the future will encamp in their mechanised caravans.

  Our immediate task is not to debate the rights and wrongs of Eliot's position on mass education, but to respond to his poetry. Nevertheless, the above quotation offers a reliable guide to the *type* of work Eliot created. In other words, we can expect a poetry that does not lower its own 'standards', a poetry that celebrates and sustains 'ancient edifices' (the high culture of the past), a poetry that has no appeal to and no meaning for 'the barbarian nomads'.

Poetry

The biographical note prepared for the Nobel Prize award in 1948 had this to say:

> Eliot has been one of the most daring innovators of twentieth-century poetry. Never compromising either with the public or indeed with language itself, he has followed his belief that poetry should aim at a representation of the complexities of modern civilization in language and that such representation necessarily leads to difficult poetry. Despite this difficulty his influence on modern poetic diction has been immense.

However, don't run away with the notion that Eliot wrote poetry that tried to preserve the 'ancient edifices' in some kind of time warp, a poetry that was nostalgic and that wallowed in a distant and mostly forgotten past. In his own words, what he sought was 'to apply the language of poetry to contemporary life', where 'contemporary' (at the time he was writing it) meant the urban, industrialised, commercialised life of the early twentieth century. It's the seedy, banal world of 'cheap hotels', 'sawdust restaurants' and 'vacant lots' that is captured – 'pinned' to use Eliot's own word – in 'Prufrock' and 'The Waste Land' and the other early poems. He always maintained that the language he was looking for did not exist at the time in English poetry, and so he turned to the French symbolist poets, particularly Baudelaire and Laforgue, for inspiration.

- The poetry of T.S. Eliot presents Christianity specifically, and the spiritual generally, as **SALVATION**, particularly from barrenness and disorder

Let's return to Eliot's views on mass education, which were quoted earlier. Two basic values are contained in his judgement: (1) the modern world is somehow below 'standard'; and (2) humans are capable of something better. Eliot explored both of these in his poetry and criticism. Indeed the early poems – from 'Prufrock', begun in 1910 and published in 1915, to 'The Waste Land', written in 1921 – are essentially satires on modern culture, where the literary term 'satire' indicates a work in which the inadequacies of an age are held up to scorn by means of humour, ridicule and irony. There are always hints of the something better that humans are capable of – Michelangelo and Dante represent the glories of an ancient culture, Miss Helen Slingsby represents a more recently lost social order, and the 'soul' survives, barely, as a continuing spiritual potential – but the essential focus of the poems is a savage mockery of the pettiness and presumptions of modern life. At first sight, the devotional later poetry – 'Journey of the Magi' (1927), 'Landscapes' (1936) and 'Four Quartets *East Coker IV*' (1940) – seems a radical departure from this, but a little reflection will convince you that it is only a logical development. Humans are capable of something better, and that 'something better', Eliot believed, was spiritual, faith, religion. The glories of the past, including Michelangelo and Dante, were the glories of Christianity, and it is the decay and destruction of that religious culture that has cheapened the modern world. This is how Eliot put it in another of his essays:

> What is a Classic? … this restriction of religious sensibility itself produces a kind of provinciality: the provinciality which indicates the disintegration of Christendom, the decay of common belief and a common culture.

Eliot's two styles of writing poetry, the satiric and the devotional, are therefore complementary rather than conflicting, merely two sides of the same coin. Both, of course, emerge from the particular circumstances of his life. While you should be wary of poetry that can be understood *only* by reference to the poet's life, biographical detail is always interesting and illuminating.

- The poetry of T.S. Eliot explores **DAMAGE**, to the mind and soul of contemporary man, and the prospect of **HEALING**

For Eliot, there were three possible responses to this 'unreal world' of shadows, where people live inauthentic lives and, in another of Dante's phrases from *The Divine Comedy*, treat 'shadows as a solid thing': (1) one can live in it mindlessly, without realising that one is actually dead; (2) one can recognise its unreality and try to lift oneself upwards, towards some sort of honest, authentic life; or (3) one can fully understand that this is hell. Responses (2) and (3) involve some sort of spiritual dimension, some sort of genuine religious faith or belief. Prufrock, for instance, would like to be Lazarus – 'I am Lazarus, come from the dead' – but he has no contact with the kind of power that could perform such miracles; he's a modern man, without faith. He is selfish, obsessed with his own personality, his ego, concerned about his natural needs, with an aggressive, acquisitive relation to society and culture. Eliot's phrase is 'each in his prison'.

Style and Viewpoint

- The poetry of T.S. Eliot is innovative, which means, as he explained it himself, that the **LANGUAGE** he was looking for – the fractured discourses of the modern world – didn't exist in English poetry before he brought it in, mainly from French poets

In Eliot's earlier poetry, characters talk to themselves or each other, rarely communicating or fully expressing anything, rarely finishing a sentence, drawing on scraps of knowledge but never creating any meaning. Their language is fractured, just like their world. It consists of bits and pieces, mostly broken. Out of these, Eliot created the language of his poetry. The word 'muttering' is applied to city streets and appears early in 'The Love Song of J. Alfred Prufrock'. By and large, it's what Prufrock spends the rest of the poem doing. He repeats himself a great deal, going round in pointless circles – 'there will be time' – asks himself meaningless questions – 'Do I dare/Disturb the universe?' – plays silly jingles with words – 'In a minute there is time/For decisions and revisions which a minute will reverse' – and wanders off the point, if there *is* a point, into strange digressions – 'I am not Prince Hamlet'. In 'Preludes', the most eloquent expression is not words at all, but a contemptuous gesture and sound – 'Wipe your hand across your mouth, and laugh'. In the section from 'The Waste Land', the first woman's language is clipped, neurotic – 'My nerves are bad to-night. Yes, bad' – and the second woman's is rambling, inconsequential, grating – 'You *are* a proper fool, I said.' Some of the same confusion and uncertainty appears even in the language of 'Journey of the Magi', with its stuttering 'but set down/This set down/This'. It is only in the extract from 'Four Quartets' that the language becomes authoritative. Here, at last, are statements of faith and belief, replacing the endless questions and nervous tics of the characters from the earlier poems.

- The poetry of T.S. Eliot employs **IMAGERY** drawn from the waste lands of cities and infertile country, from the struggles of the journey, and from the possibility of refreshment and cleansing, to express the complexity of his vision

  In 'The Love Song of J. Alfred Prufrock', follow the images of numbness, tiredness, exhaustion and debility through the poem: 'etherised', 'Curled', 'fell asleep', 'How his hair is growing thin', 'how his arms and legs are thin', 'sleeps so peacefully', 'tired', 'it malingers', 'Stretched on the floor', 'settling a pillow by her head', 'lingered' and finally 'drown'. Then follow the images of uncertainty and confusion, firstly as these are represented by the sounds in the poem: 'muttering retreats', 'a tedious argument', 'do not ask, 'What is it?', 'Talking of Michelangelo', 'indecisions', 'revisions', 'Do I dare?', 'voices dying', 'digress', 'silent seas', 'That is not what I meant at all', 'It is impossible to say just what I mean', 'obtuse', 'human voices'. Then follow these same images of uncertainty and confusion, but now as they are represented by the visual elements in the poem. You will notice that almost everything lacks clarity: 'certain half-deserted streets', the 'yellow fog', 'yellow smoke', 'the faces', 'the voices', 'the eyes', 'Arms that are … white and bare', 'Arms that lie along a table', 'one, settling a pillow by her head', 'as if a magic lantern threw the nerves in patterns on a screen'. And finally, follow the rhythms and images of unease and fear and hesitation, firstly through the wonderful movement of the poem, which captures the contortions of an internal voice constantly urging itself forward – 'Let us go then, you and I' – but always falling back on itself in fear – 'Shall I say', 'would it have been worth it' – and then through the metaphors of agitation and indignity: 'restless nights', 'insidious intent', 'there will be time … there will be time … there will be time' (the repetition seeking reassurance), 'They will say', 'When I am pinned and wriggling on the wall', 'I have seen the eternal Footman hold my coat, and snicker', 'Almost, at times, the Fool', 'I grow old'. These images of waste, in all its senses, are continued through 'Preludes' – the days are 'burnt-out', the soul is 'stretched tight across the skies' – *A Game of Chess* – 'Those are pearls that were his eyes' – and 'Journey of the Magi' – 'the camels galled', 'hostile', 'dirty'. Imagery of nourishment and new hope and health is rarer, but occurs in 'Journey of the Magi' – 'at dawn we came down to a temperate valley' – and the extract from 'Four Quartets' – 'The sharp compassion of the healer's art' and 'we call this Friday good'.

- The poetry of T.S. Eliot is adept at dramatising a range of modern voices, secular and religious, interior and exterior, using intricate **SOUND** patterns to capture them

  One of the most striking features of Eliot's poetry is its dramatisation of a range of modern voices, sometimes inside the head, like Prufrock's, sometimes outside it, like the women in ('The Waste Land') *A Game of Chess*, but always voices that are talking to themselves, as if communication was not a possibility. Prufrock speaks to no one – that's the ironic joke of 'you and I' – but hears voices all the time inside his head – the women in the room 'Talking of Michelangelo', the onlookers scoffing at him, saying 'But how his arms and legs are thin!', the snickering Footman, the dismissive woman with her contemptuous 'That is not what I meant at all'. For him, this cacophony of human voices inside his head is hell. In the extract from 'The Waste Land', the highly strung, neurotic female voice, the composed voice of the distant male character, the voices of the nattering woman and impatient barman in the pub, are all brilliantly created. Unusually, nobody speaks in 'Preludes', although theirs is the silence of loneliness and alienation. 'Journey of the Magi' is another monologue, brilliantly recounting in grim and tedious detail the narrative of a journey – 'Then the camel men … And the night-fires … And the cities … And the villages …' – and then expressing the uncertainty in relation to what has been witnessed: 'were we led all that way for/Birth or Death?'

- The poetry of T.S. Eliot 'bursts out of any recognisable poetic shape', as the writer Jeanette Winterson puts it, 'just as the world had burst out of any recognisable order', and so invents new poetic **FORMS**

Eliot wanted to capture the fragmented nature of the modern world – as Jeanette Winterson, again, puts it, he understood 'that the first world war had devastated consciousness – the inside of people's heads, as well as their world order'. Since form and content are one in the greatest poetry, it follows that the traditional poetic forms were now just as outdated as the traditional social world. Eliot had to create new forms that somehow or other mirrored and gave shape to the fragmentation of life. Just as the language of his characters consists of disjointed bits and pieces, mostly broken – as illustrated above – so his poems contain bits and pieces of older forms, mostly broken, and are themselves intentionally disjointed. 'The Love Song of J. Alfred Prufrock' is shaped, if that's the word, as the rambling, repetitious voice of a neurotic. The structure of the poem is inside Prufrock's head, and therefore unique. Nevertheless, Eliot also uses traditional forms, though always in fragments – the rhyming scheme is highly irregular, but expressive; the refrains are essential; the three-line stanzas at the end of the poem are, in technical terms, bits of a Petrarchan sonnet. Similarly, 'Aunt Helen' is a truncated, thirteen-line sonnet. ('The Waste Land') *A Game of Chess* uses detached fragments from many standard sources – a Shakespeare play, an epic poem, classical epics, a Jacobean play – to make a new creation, an assembly of separate forms and separate voices. 'Journey of the Magi' has a form similar to that of 'Prufrock', in that it's a monologue, structured by the inner voice. 'Landscapes' uses the unusual technique of allowing a location to represent a reflection.

Gerard Manley Hopkins

Hopkins was born in 1844 at Stratford, now part of Greater London. He won a prize at secondary school for his earliest surviving poem and continued to write poetry after entering Balliol College, Oxford, in 1863. A student of great academic ability, he obtained a first-class degree. He converted to Catholicism in 1866, became a Jesuit novice, and was ordained a priest in 1877. The editors of the Jesuit journal *The World* rejected his poetry, considering it too difficult for its readers. In 1884, he was appointed Professor of Greek at University College, Dublin, but was overwhelmed by his responsibilities there and became ill and depressed, a state of desolation expressed in the so-called 'terrible sonnets'. He died of typhoid fever in 1889, without publishing any of his poems.

Prescribed Poems

'Students at Higher Level will be required to study a representative selection from the work of eight poets: a representative selection would seek to reflect the range of a poet's themes and interests and exhibit his/her characteristic style and viewpoint. Normally the study of at least six poems by each poet would be expected.' (DES English Syllabus, 6.3)

Poetry

Themes and Interests

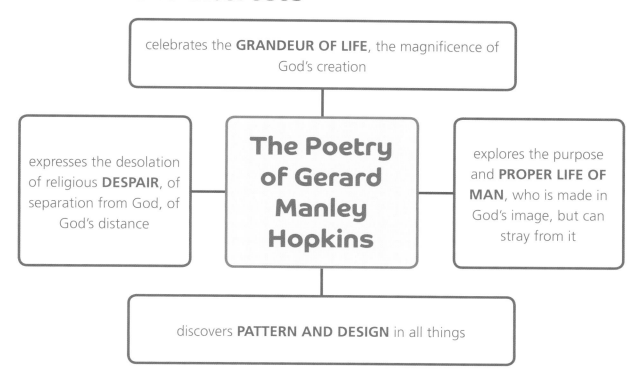

celebrates the **GRANDEUR OF LIFE**, the magnificence of God's creation

expresses the desolation of religious **DESPAIR**, of separation from God, of God's distance

The Poetry of Gerard Manley Hopkins

explores the purpose and **PROPER LIFE OF MAN**, who is made in God's image, but can stray from it

discovers **PATTERN AND DESIGN** in all things

Style and Viewpoint

The Poetry of Gerard Manley Hopkins

is unconventional and exciting in its **LANGUAGE**, which is used, not for self-expression or communication, but in an attempt to capture the essence of living things

employs the **IMAGERY** of nature, its darkness as well as its beauty, to create 'inscape', a term Hopkins used to describe the uniqueness of each living thing

employs vigorous and unusual **SOUND** patterns, particularly in its verbs and metre, to create 'instress', a term Hopkins used to describe the energy of a living thing

holds the intensity and the energy within strict poetic **FORMS**, particularly the sonnet

Poetry

READ

God's Grandeur

The world is charged with the grandeur of God.
  It will flame out, like shining from shook foil;
  It gathers to a greatness, like the ooze of oil
Crushed. Why do men then now not reck his rod?
Generations have trod, have trod, have trod;   5
  And all is seared with trade; bleared, smeared with toil;
  And wears man's smudge and shares man's smell: the soil
Is bare now, nor can foot feel, being shod.

And for all this, nature is never spent;
  There lives the dearest freshness deep down things;   10
And though the last lights off the black West went
  Oh, morning, at the brown brink eastward, springs —
Because the Holy Ghost over the bent
  World broods with warm breast and with ah! bright wings.

Glossary

[2] **foil:** 'Shaken goldfoil gives off broad glares like sheet lightning.' (Hopkins, *Letters*)

[4] **reck:** pay heed to

[13] **Holy Ghost:** Holy Spirit; for most Christians, the third divine person of the Trinity, Father, Son and Holy Ghost

ANALYSE

The first three lines celebrate, in the most intense of language, Hopkins' perception of the magnificence of God's creation. That magnificence he describes as 'grandeur', a grand word in itself, combining beauty, nobility and power. Listen to the explosions of the verbs in these lines. The world is 'charged' with God's magnificence, as objects are charged with electricity; it will burst out in flames, 'shining' like shimmering pieces of gold foil, with all the particles, all the beauties of creation, attracted by the electrical current, all flowing like the oil of crushed olives into a rich liquid ooze. 'Charged … flame out … shining … shook … gathers … ooze': the verbs are powerful, muscular, strengthened even further by the multiple alliterations – 'grandeur of God … shining from shook … gathers to a greatness'.

At the beginning of the fourth line, however, the word 'Crushed', although it's the completion of a sentence started on the previous line – 'like the ooze of oil/Crushed' – has the effect of *actually* crushing this celebration. It pulls the poem up short, before the despairing question that then forces us to reflect: why don't humans therefore recognise God's authority? If God's creation is so magnificent: 'Why do men then now not reck his rod?' And now the clashing sounds, 'men then', and the alliteration, 'now not', work against the flow, so that it's impossible to say this line without stammering. When the vigour of the verbs returns – 'trod … seared … bleared … smeared' – it is to capture how dreadfully men have wasted God's gift and to express

Hopkins' weariness at this. Now the sounds are mean and nasty – all those *es* in 'seared, bleared, smeared' – whereas before they were joyous – those *ahs* and *ays* in 'charged' and 'flame' – and the alliteration is based on the hissing *s* sound – 'smudge, shares, smell, soil'. Man's industry, Hopkins claims, takes man away from intimate contact with nature, God's creation; our feet are 'shod', and so we can no longer feel the earth on our flesh. When applied to humans, the word 'shod' is a provocative choice, since it usually describes what's done to workhorses.

The second section of six lines – the sestet of the Petrarchan sonnet – opens nevertheless on a note of comfort, of relief and gratitude, building back slowly to celebration. In spite of man's industry and his crushing of the earth, nature is never exhausted, or weakened, or sold off (all meanings of 'spent'). It is like an inexhaustible well of freshness, 'deep down', beyond the reach of man, it constantly renews itself, just as the day renews itself when the first light of morning follows the setting of the sun, 'the last lights off the black West'. But notice the vigour of the language again. The light doesn't simply emerge each morning; it 'springs', a word that suggests renewed energy, and not only morning, of course, but the freshness of the season of spring as well. Such life, the last two lines remind us, is because God, in the form of the Holy Ghost, protects both man and nature, brooding like a bird. The last image is startling. The Holy Ghost, normally represented as an angel – 'bright wings' – here becomes a part of nature itself, a bird brooding in the nest of the world.

MAKE

(i) This is a poem about the sparkle and energy and lightness of nature, but also about the heaviness of man, which can do damage to nature. Pick out some of the sounds that express each aspect.

(ii) This is a poem about the sparkle and energy and lightness of nature, but also about the heaviness of man, which can do damage to nature. Pick out some of the images that capture each aspect.

READ

Spring

NOTHING is so beautiful as Spring –
　When weeds, in wheels, shoot long and lovely and lush;
　Thrush's eggs look little low heavens, and thrush
Through the echoing timber does so rinse and wring
The ear, it strikes like lightnings to hear him sing; 　　　5
　The glassy peartree leaves and blooms, they brush
　The descending blue; that blue is all in a rush
With richness; the racing lambs too have fair their fling.

What is all this juice and all this joy?
　A strain of the earth's sweet being in the beginning 　　　10
In Eden garden. – Have, get, before it cloy,
　Before it cloud, Christ, lord, and sour with sinning,
Innocent mind and Mayday in girl and boy,
　Most, O maid's child, thy choice and worthy the winning.

Glossary

[11] **Eden:** the Garden of Eden, Paradise in Christian belief
[13] **Mayday:** traditionally a holiday in many cultures, celebrating spring

ANALYSE

This is a Petrarchan sonnet of octave and sestet, in which the first eight lines attempt to capture in sound and colour the energy of spring and the final six lines preach that, if man hadn't fallen from God's grace by sinning, then life would be eternal spring.

From the confident assertion of the opening line, with its heavy stresses on 'Nothing' and 'beautiful' – '*Noth*ing is so *beau*tiful as spring' – the poem hurtles forward, celebrating energy with the language and colour with the images. As always with Hopkins, the strength and vigour of the verbs carry most of the effect. Here, 'wheels … shoot … rinse … wring … strikes … brush … rush' give the poem its hectic momentum. As is usual, again, the frequent alliteration adds to this effect, in particular the tumbling *r* sounds in the final two lines of the octave, 'rush … richness … racing'. As for the colours, some are prominent, in particular the 'blue' of the clear, spring sky, some are suggested, such as the green of 'weeds' and 'leaves', the brown of 'timber' and 'thrush' and the yellow and red of 'lightnings'. Behind the sound effects, the words simply select features of spring's abundant new life: the shooting weeds, the tiny eggs of the thrush, the singing of that thrush in the trees, the blooming of the pear tree, all against the backdrop of the clear, blue sky. The final image in the octave is of lambs darting about the place, a fairly conventional image of spring, but one whose function in this poem is not fully apparent until later.

Hopkins' favourite technique in his earlier poems is to rush headlong into an enthusiastic celebration of nature, dragging us readers along with him, and then to bring us up short, sometimes, as here, with a stark question: 'What is all this juice and all this joy?' The question is not meant to make us reflect, but to listen to Hopkins' preaching. Your first task as a critic, however, is to notice how the rhythm has been slowed, initially by the framing of the question, which you can't avoid pausing after, and then by the selection of heavier and thicker words that have to be enunciated separately: 'strain of the earth's sweet being in the beginning'. Try saying that quickly and you'll find that the alliteration here – the two *b*s – is slowing you down. As for the content, these splendours

of spring, Hopkins claims, are a 'strain' of the 'sweet beginning' of life in the Christian Paradise of Eden, where 'strain' – an interesting, complex word – holds suggestions of a musical note that was once part of a larger melody and of a trace of something that remains from a lost purity. He then prays to Christ, his 'lord', to 'get' and hold that freshness, before it 'cloy', which means *is made weary*, and 'cloud', which means *is darkened*, and goes 'sour with sinning'. That freshness, he maintains, lives in the innocent minds of the young, where innocence is symbolised by 'Mayday', the spring festival, and youth is represented by 'girl and boy', Notice how, as well as slowing the rhythm, all the words now have negative or worrying associations – 'cloud … sour … sinning'. In the final line, the 'maid's child' is Christ, born of a young virgin according to Christian belief. Young people are the 'Most', the 'choice' of Christ, or the pick of Christ's creations, and they are 'worthy the winning', or worthy of Christ's efforts to preserve them. The references to Christ, lamb of God in the Gospel of John in the Christian Bible, and to the 'girl and boy', echo and develop 'racing lambs' from the final line of the octave.

MAKE

(i) The poetry of Hopkins often explores the belief that man is born in God's image, but can easily stray from this. Examine how this theme is presented in 'Spring'.

(ii) Spring/Winter – freshness/decay – are common contrasts in poetry. Pick out the images Hopkins uses to capture each state – freshness and decay – and see if you can experience his attitude to each in the sounds as well as the images he uses.

Poetry

READ

As kingfishers catch fire, dragonflies draw flame

As kingfishers catch fire, dragonflies draw flame;
As tumbled over rim in roundy wells
Stones ring; like each tucked string tells, each hung bell's
Bow swung finds tongue to fling out broad its name;
Each mortal thing does one thing and the same: 5
Deals out that being indoors each one dwells;
Selves – goes itself; *myself* it speaks and spells,
Crying *Whát I dó is me: for that I came.*

Í say móre: the just man justices;
Keeps gráce: thát keeps all his goings graces;   10
Acts in God's eye what in God's eye he is –
Chríst – for Christ plays in ten thousand places,
Lovely in limbs, and lovely in eyes not his
To the Father through the features of men's faces.

Glossary

[7] **Selves:** this operates as a verb and means 'asserts their own nature and individuality'

[10] **gráce:** in the Christian sense, 'the love and mercy given to us by God'

[14] **Father:** God the Father; for most Christians, the first divine person of the Trinity, Father, Son and Holy Ghost

ANALYSE

This sonnet – a Petrarchan one of octave and sestet – is a simple article of Christian faith expressed with extraordinary complexity. Just as each thing is both unique in itself and also part of a species, so each man is unique in himself but also made in the image of Christ. That's the simple article of Christian faith. As for the complexity of expression …

The language of the opening lines attempts to capture, through sound and rhythm, the nature of each thing being described. In 'As tumbled over rim in roundy wells/Stones ring' – just as stones made a distinctive sound when pushed into a well – the slight sound of 'rim' is amplified by the alliterative 'roundy' and finished off by the sharp 'ring', a sequence that attempts to recreate the sound of a stone scratching off the top of the well, echoing as it falls, and splashing at it lands. And 'each tucked string tells' actually sounds like the plucking of guitar or violin strings, while 'each hung bell's/Bow swung' recreates the dee-dah-ding-dong of a peeling bell.

So much for the sounds; what about the sense? Just as the brilliant flash of the kingfisher bird, the fiery glimmer of the dragonfly, the ping of a stone dropped in a well, the plucking of a string and the swing of a bell all expressed what they uniquely are – 'Deals out' what is 'indoors' or within them, their 'Selves' – so it is with me, '*myself*', I, too, am unique, but I too have a purpose, '*for that I came*', for which I was born.

Poetry

The sestet expands on this notion that man, like everything else, has an essence and a purpose. 'Í say móre', it opens assertively, before declaring that the *good* man 'justices', a verb which means acts in a godly way, and the good man 'Keeps gráce', which means keeps safe or intact the grace or favours or blessings granted him by God, which in turn will keep all his action, his 'goings', graceful and therefore pleasing to God, and therefore Christ-like. The idea is simple, really. If man accepts Christ as the example to follow, he will remain in Christ's image. The idea is simple; but the expression is tortured, and it seems that Hopkins himself was somewhat dissatisfied by this poem.

The final lines repeat a common observation of Hopkins' that the splendour of God is reflected in the splendour of his creations, in particular here in the splendour of man, in 'the features of men's faces'.

MAKE

(i)   The stress mark (´) used by Hopkins in this poem is known as an acute accent. He deliberately uses it on some words and not on others. Why, in your opinion, did he select those words? Examine each in turn.

(ii) It was said earlier that Hopkins' poetry discovers 'pattern' – the form of something in itself – and 'design' – the form given to it by another – in all things. How does he apply this to man in this poem?

READ

The Windhover

To Christ our Lord

I CAUGHT this morning morning's minion, king-
   dom of daylight's dauphin, dapple-dawn-drawn Falcon, in his riding
   Of the rolling level underneath him steady air, and striding
High there, how he rung upon the rein of a wimpling wing
In his ecstasy! then off, off forth on swing,   5
   As a skate's heel sweeps smooth on a bow-bend: the hurl and gliding
   Rebuffed the big wind. My heart in hiding
Stirred for a bird, – the achieve of, the mastery of the thing!

Brute beauty and valour and act, oh, air, pride, plume, here
Buckle! AND the fire that breaks from thee then, a billion   10
Times told lovelier, more dangerous, O my chevalier!

No wonder of it: shéer plód makes plough down sillion
Shine, and blue-bleak embers, ah my dear,
Fall, gall themselves, and gash gold-vermillion.

Glossary

[title] **Windhover:** kestrel, small hawk

[1] **minion:** favourite, darling

[2] **dauphin:** prince, eldest son of French king

[4] **wimpling:** rippling

[11] **chevalier:** knight

[12] **sillion:** thick wet soil turned over by a plough

ANALYSE

Poetry

A 'windhover' – literally, a bird that hovers in or on the wind – is an old English dialect name for a kestrel, which is a small hawk.

The octave – the first eight lines of this irregular sonnet – attempts to recreate the flight and movement of the bird as it hunts in the air. For the most part, Hopkins uses sound effects – rhythm, rhyme, half-rhyme, alliteration, assonance, stress, repetition – to create his impression of the bird. The description is given from his point of view – he is watching the kestrel – and is contained within the opening four words, 'I caught this morning' (meaning, *I caught sight of this morning*) and the final sixteen, which openly express his admiration and awe at the grace and grandeur ('achieve of') and perfection ('mastery') of the creature ('thing').

The language describing the kestrel is so dense in suggestiveness that it's better to take the words individually and then fling them back together again while re-reading. The bird is the darling ('minion') of the morning, because that's when it hunts. It is the prince ('dauphin') of the kingdom of daylight, visible at dawn against the cloud-spotted sky ('dapple-dawn-drawn'), as it glides along the calm air ('underneath him steady air') and circles at the top of its flight ('striding/ High there') like a horse on a rein circling its trainer ('rung upon the rein'). Then it swoops on a downward curve, hurtling through the air ('Rebuffed the big wind'), no doubt in pursuit of its prey.

For all the splendour and variety of these images, though, it's the control of rhythm and sound, as the poem imitates the bird's movements, that has the major effect.

The sestet, which is divided into two sections, is different in intention. It draws back from immersion in the bird's movements to contemplate the significance, for Hopkins, of what he has just witnessed and described. Part of the separation, the drawing back, is achieved by the change in verb tense. What happened in the octave happened in the past – 'I caught this morning' – whereas the reflections in the sestet are ongoing, in the present tense – 'Buckle … breaks'.

Line 9 simply lists the attributes of the creature, which are buckled, or joined together, in that one bird. After that, interpretation becomes a little more difficult. Hopkins imagines 'fire', which is energy, breaking from the kestrel; and then imagines a fire that is 'a billion/Times' more beautiful and masterful ('dangerous'). In other words, he imagines the creator of this creature. He imagines Christ, to whom the poem is dedicated. And when he imagines Christ, the image of a knight on horseback ('my chevalier') comes to his mind. This movement in Hopkins from the power and beauty of creation to the power and beauty of the creator is a common one, occurring in many of his poems.

The final three lines present us with two images – that of ploughed land and that of a collapsing coal or wood fire. From both comes brightness: the 'Shine' of the earth when the sunlight hits the moist sods turned over by the plough (that's what 'sillion' is, these sods) and the golden-red 'gash' of sparks when the fire collapses in on itself. The meaning of the images? Simple enough, really. In Christian belief, Christ's sacrifice, or death, gave life and fire, or hope, to man. The kestrel is one small flicker of God's great fire, one aspect of the splendour of His creation.

MAKE

(i) It is obvious that Hopkins is brilliant at 'describing' the grandeur of life. But in what sense, in your opinion, does this poem manage to *celebrate* the grandeur of life, as is often claimed for Hopkins' work? Pick out the language that is celebratory.

(ii) It was said above that Hopkins uses the following sound effects – rhythm, rhyme, half-rhyme, alliteration, assonance, stress, repetition – to create his impression of the bird. Can you pick out an example of each effect?

Poetry

READ

Pied Beauty

GLORY be to God for dappled things –
    For skies of couple-colour as a brinded cow;
      For rose-moles all in stipple upon trout that swim;
Fresh-firecoal chestnut-falls; finches' wings;
    Landscape plotted and pieced – fold, fallow, and plough;   5
      And áll trádes, their gear and tackle and trim.

All things counter, original, spare, strange;
    Whatever is fickle, freckled (who knows how?)
      With swift, slow; sweet, sour; adazzle, dim;
He fathers-forth whose beauty is past change: 10
      Praise him.

Glossary

[title] **Pied:** having two or more colours

[1] **dappled:** marked with spots

[2] **couple-colour:** having colours in twos, in couples

[3] **stipple:** dots or specks

[5] **fallow:** ploughed land left for a period before sowing

[7] **counter:** contrasting

[8] **fickle:** subject to change

[10] **He:** God the Father; for most Christians, the first divine person of the Trinity, Father, Son and Holy Ghost

ANALYSE

Poetry

This little poem expresses simply, in its first line, the central theme of most of Hopkins' early work: 'Glory be to God for dappled things'. The remainder of the opening section merely offers examples of those 'dappled things', those objects and images that are multicoloured and capture in themselves the variety of God's creation, such as the two-tone sky ('skies of couple-colour'), the rose-like speckles ('rose-moles') on a swimming trout, the chestnuts that fall in the autumn winds ('chestnut-falls') looking like glowing coals in a fire ('Fresh-firecoal'), all kinds of land, enclosed ('pieced' and 'fold'), ploughed or unploughed ('fallow'), and all kinds of work ('áll trádes') on that land.

In fact – as the second section expands – *everything* that is contrasting ('counter'), unique or unusual, everything that changes ('is fickle') all things that are beautiful and whose beauty is the one aspect of them that doesn't change ('whose beauty is past change') have been created by God the Father ('He fathers-forth'). The poem ends as it began, with an explicit prayer to God: 'Praise him'.

This is one of Hopkins' experiments in the shortened sonnet form. Instead of the standard fourteen lines, it has ten-and-a-half. The number of lines is arrived at by making the shortened sonnet exactly three-quarters of the structure of a Pertrarchan sonnet, which is eight lines plus six lines. Three-quarters of eight is six, and three-quarters of six is four and a half. His name for these reduced forms was 'curtal sonnets', where 'curtal' means shortened, abridged or curtailed. What they achieve by abbreviating the verse form has been a matter of debate, but Hopkins' intention seems to have been to make the expression of thought and feeling more intense by concentrating it. The intended effect is probably most visible in the final half-line.

(i) Hopkins' distinctive use of sound is very evident in this poem, where, for example, four stresses occur together without a break in 'swift, slow; sweet, sour'. Pick out a few examples and comment on their effect.

(ii) Compression – increasing the volume while reducing the space – is a characteristic of Hopkins' style. Pick out some examples of it here – in individual words and phrases, and indeed in the reduced sonnet form he invented – and comment on their effectiveness.

Poetry

READ

Felix Randal

FELIX RANDAL the farrier, O is he dead then? my duty all ended,
Who have watched his mould of man, big-boned and hardy-handsome
Pining, pining, till time when reason rambled in it, and some
Fatal four disorders, fleshed there, all contended?

Sickness broke him. Impatient, he cursed at first, but mended   5
Being anointed and all; though a heavenlier heart began some
Months earlier, since I had our sweet reprieve and ransom
Tendered to him. Ah well, God rest him all road ever he offended!

This seeing the sick endears them to us, us too it endears.
My tongue had taught thee comfort, touch had quenched thy tears,   10
Thy tears that touched my heart, child, Felix, poor Felix Randal;

How far from then forethought of, all thy more boisterous years,
When thou at the random grim forge, powerful amidst peers,
Didst fettle for the great grey drayhorse his bright and battering sandal!

Glossary

[1] **farrier:** blacksmith
[6] **anointed:** rubbed with oil, as part of the Christian ceremony of the Last Rites for the dying
[7] **ransom:** literally, money paid for the release of a captive; figuratively here, prayers for the release of Felix's soul
[14] **fettle:** trim the rough edges of
[14] **sandal:** figuratively, horseshoe

ANALYSE

Poetry

Felix Randal, real name Felix Spencer, was a parishioner of Hopkins', a blacksmith, or farrier, who died of consumption at the age of thirty-one on 21 April 1880. This sonnet was completed by Hopkins seven days later.

In many editions, the opening reads 'Felix Randal the farrier, O is he dead then?' but in some, 'Felix Randal the farrier, O he is dead then?' Either way, the opening is dominated by that exclamation 'O', which is an expression of sadness, because a man has passed away, but also of relief, because the man was suffering and because, in Hopkins' belief, he has gone to a better carer than Hopkins himself could be. The first line ends with a note of acceptance in the face of death, 'my duty all ended'. It is still an acceptance tinged with relief, because the priest had watched the powerful Felix – 'big-boned', 'hardy-handsome' – wasting away with his illness, both physically and mentally, since his mind 'rambled'. The word Hopkins chooses for the blacksmith's decline is 'pining', which suggests not only physical deterioration, but also a longing (as in, when you *pine* for something you can't have or something you have lost). By the end, four fatal diseases were erupting in his body ('fleshed there'), so perhaps the pining is a longing for release as well as a nostalgia for his lost health.

That sigh of acceptance is heard again in the second quatrain: 'Ah well. God rest him …' It is the acceptance of a religious man, who believes that the farrier is now more comfortable with God, and it echoes the acceptance of Felix Randal himself, who quite naturally cursed his sickness at first but then, after being administered the Sacrament of the Sick ('anointed' or blessed with holy oils), was comforted in his faith. The tension in the language here is between 'broke' and 'mended'. It means that the illness broke him physically and mentally, but that faith mended him spiritually, enabling him to accept his illness and the 'sweet reprieve', or sweet relief, of the Christian sacraments administered by the priest.

As always with Hopkins, the recreation of some specific experience leads to a more general observation, and in the first section of the sestet, the poem opens out to a reflection on the nature of the relationship between the dead man and the priest. It is a mutually beneficial relationship, a mutually endearing one: the priest administers comfort and consolation ('touch had quenched thy tears') and in return is spiritually enriched himself ('Thy tears that touched my heart').

The poem ends with an interesting perspective, though; not with an image of the dead man, or of the saved soul, but with a resurrection of Felix at the height of his physical powers, before a hint of the illness that struck him ('How far from then forethought of'), hammering away at his anvil in the forge, powerful, skilled, impressive. All of Hopkins' earlier poems celebrate life. Usually, it is the vigour and the beauty of the natural world that is praised. Here, the vigour and beauty of humanity is sung, ringing out as strikingly as the blows of the blacksmith's hammer are recreated in the sounds of the final line: 'great grey dray…' And that explains the quiet sadness of the opening, 'O is he dead then?' Such a loss, this 'boisterous', 'powerful' man.

MAKE

(i) Although its subject is the death of a once-powerful blacksmith, this poem is a celebration of two robust forms of life – physical energy and spiritual energy. Pick out the details capturing each.

(ii) The tone of the poem, beginning with the sound of 'O is he dead then?' in the first line, is one of acceptance rather than grief. Pick out the other sounds that express this acceptance.

Poetry

READ

Inversnaid

THIS darksome burn, horseback brown,
His rollrock highroad roaring down,
In coop and in comb the fleece of his foam
Flutes and low to the lake falls home.

A windpuff-bonnet of fáwn-fróth   5
Turns and twindles over the broth
Of a pool so pitchblack, féll-frówning,
It rounds and rounds Despair to drowning.

Degged with dew, dappled with dew
Are the groins of the braes that the brook treads through,   10
Wiry heathpacks, flitches of fern,
And the beadbonny ash that sits over the burn.

What would the world be, once bereft
Of wet and of wildness? Let them be left,
O let them be left, wildness and wet;   15
Long live the weeds and the wilderness yet.

Glossary

[title] **Inversnaid:** a waterfall on the shore of Loch Lomond in the Scottish Highlands

[1] **burn:** stream

[2] **rollrock:** literally rolling down rocks

[3] **coop:** 'enclosed hollow' (according to Hopkins' notebook)

[5] **bonnet:** brimmed hat tied under the chin

[6] **twindles:** twirls

[9] **Degged:** watered (northern English dialect)

[9] **dappled:** marked with spots

[10] **braes:** steep hillsides

[11] **flitches:** streaks, but also slabs, sides

[12] **beadbonny:** 'bonny' is beautiful; here, beautiful with beads

[13] **bereft:** deprived

ANALYSE

'Inversnaid' is a hymn to nature and a plea for nature to be left unpolluted – 'Long live the weeds and the wilderness yet' – but unusually for Hopkins, the creation is celebrated here without reference to the creator. Unlike many of the other poems on your course, 'Inversnaid' does not feature God.

Inversnaid is on the shore of Loch Lomond in the Scottish Highlands. The poem was written in 1881, following a visit to Scotland.

As is usual with Hopkins, the sounds and suggestiveness of the words and the intricacies of the rhythm recreate the feel and look of the place he is recapturing, here a 'burn' or stream that is 'darksome' from flowing through 'brown' bogs and 'roaring' down the 'highroad' of the mountain side, sometimes getting trapped or cooped up ('coop'), sometimes rushing through the rocks like a comb through hair ('comb'), bubbling up so that its 'foam' looks like sheep on the mountain side ('the fleece of his foam'). If you pick all the images apart and then put them back together again, you get a marvellous visual impression of the flow of the stream. And if you then read the stanza aloud, you get a marvellous aural impression as well.

The second stanza gets trapped in a whirlpool, as it pauses to consider the frothy swirl of a pool formed by the rushing stream, where the 'fáwn' coloured froth rotates and spatters ('Turns and twindles') like boiling water in a cauldron, a place so grim ('pitchblack'), so fiercely frowning ('féll-fyfring'), that despair itself would drown in it.

Poetry

427

And then, on we go, released from the dread pool and its eternal circular motion, through the banks of the hillside ('groins of the braes'), through packed heather ('heathpacks'), through tufts ('flitches') of ferns, past the mountain-ash or rowan tree ('beadbonney' = full of beautiful (bonny), berries (beads)).

The final stanza is a characteristic withdrawal from such hectic beauty to a contemplation of its significance, and here of the vital importance of man not spoiling nature with his interminable development and expansion. This poem was written in 1881, remember; so even then the sense of nature being threatened by civilisation was a worry. Destroy this – the wet, the wilderness, the weeds – and we destroy life itself. 'Let them be', Hopkins pleads.

MAKE

(i) This poem attempts to represent both the appearance and the sound of the waterfall. Pick out the images and the sound patterns Hopkins uses to capture its appearance and its music.

(ii) Offer a personal response to the theme of this poem – a hymn to unpolluted nature – with particular reference to the repetition of 'let them be' in the final stanza.

READ

I wake and feel the fell of dark, not day

I WAKE and feel the fell of dark, not day.
What hours, O what black hoürs we have spent
This night! what sights you, heart, saw; ways you went!
And more must, in yet longer light's delay.
   With witness I speak this. But where I say   5
Hours I mean years, mean life. And my lament
Is cries countless, cries like dead letters sent
To dearest him that lives alas! away.

   I am gall, I am heartburn. God's most deep decree
Bitter would have me taste: my taste was me;   10
Bones built in me, flesh filled, blood brimmed the curse.
   Selfyeast of spirit a dull dough sours. I see
The lost are like this, and their scourge to be
As I am mine, their sweating selves; but worse.

Glossary

[1] **fell:** skin, hide, pelt (see ANALYSE panel)

[5] **witness:** in a religious sense, a public affirmation of faith

[9] **gall:** bile, bitterness; biblical reference to vinegar offered to Christ when he was crucified

[11] **curse:** misfortune, evil, doom; also Christian reference to the loss of the Garden of Eden

ANALYSE

This terrified poem wakes up in the middle of the night.

It comes to consciousness abruptly – 'I wake' – and has the creepy experience – communicated by those two hissing alliterative *fs* in 'feel the fell' – of being stalked and surrounded by the darkness. The word 'fell' is rich, because the image carries suggestions of a blow (as in *to fell a tree*), something fierce or terrible (as in *one fell swoop*) and the hide or pelt of an animal (an old meaning of the word, used by Macbeth in Shakespeare's play, who speaks of his *fell of hair* standing on end with fright). Which is the correct interpretation? As many as you can hold in your mind simultaneously, though perhaps the last mentioned is the most powerful. Can you imagine waking and feeling suffocated by animals' hides pressing against you?

If 'fell' suggests so many images, notice how the sound of 'What hours, O what black hoürs', with the heavy stresses on 'hours', 'O', 'black' and 'hoürs' again, communicate both the horror of the experience and the interminable nature of the suffering, going on for 'hours … hoürs', through 'sights' and 'ways', so that all the senses are equally tortured. And as if this drawn-out suffering wasn't enough, there is more – 'And more must', the opening of line 4 insists. Neither is there any prospect of relief, because the day, and the light, which might be expected to lift the nightmare, bring only an extension of the agony.

Poetry

This disturbing claim that daylight is yet another 'delay', a deferring of relief, ends the first quatrain on a troubled note, and on an implied question. If day brings no release from the nightmare, what can?

There is no answer in the second quatrain. There is no answer in the poem.

For the rest of this sonnet, there is only an increasingly desperate insistence on the reality of the suffering. 'With witness I speak this' is more than just an assertion that what he says is true; it is also a plea to be heard, not to be ignored, a plea for some response. 'With witness I speak this' is a man crying out, *It's true! What I tell you is true!* But who is he talking to? The repeated pleas and expressions of pain – 'cries countless' – seem to fall on deaf or absent ears, 'like dead letters' sent to someone who no longer lives at the old address. Is the 'dearest him' a man or God? Both, one supposes. Hopkins is fond of holding as many references as possible within the single phrase.

The sestet begins by beating out his worthlessness, like a penitent beating his chest in guilt and despair – 'I am gall, I am heartburn' – meaning that he is all bitterness, all burning. God's decree, or authority, has made Hopkins bitter to himself. The imagery is quite extraordinary here. Can you imagine the self-loathing involved in tasting sourness off your own flesh? Every time being disgusted by the taste: 'my taste was me'.

Hopkins is always comprehensive when describing the human body – look above to how the nightmare is felt *and* heard *and* seen *and* tasted – so here the 'curse' of alienation, of absence from God, of God's disapproval, of sinfulness, inhabits the skeleton ('Bones built in me'), the flesh ('flesh filled') and the bloodstream ('blood brimmed'). The image in the next line is just as startling. If you make bread with bad ingredients, with milk that's gone off, then the dough will be sour. The 'yeast' of his self is incapable of making anything palatable enough to enjoy. He's worthless, in other words.

Worthless to God, he feels himself to be one of the damned – 'The lost are like this' – whose agony and self-disgust are captured in 'sweating selves' – they sweat out what they are, which is sourness – until it occurs to him, in the only faint note of comparative hope or consolation in the entire poem, that the damned are worse off than he is. At least he is not yet permanently 'lost', only 'dull' and 'Bitter'.

Any poem that ends on the word 'worse', however, is not a poem of consolation.

This is one of a group of poems by Hopkins that have become known as 'the terrible sonnets', from a phrase coined by his friend Canon Dixon, 'the terrible crystal', meaning that the works in question 'crystallised' the terrible dejection of Hopkins when he was desolate during his latter years in Ireland.

(i) Identify and comment on the experiences – emotions and thoughts – that could be described as 'terrible' here.

(ii) Identify and comment on the effectiveness of the images and the sounds that, in your opinion, best express the 'terrible' nature of the experience.

No worst, there is none. Pitched past pitch of grief

No worst, there is none. Pitched past pitch of grief,
More pangs will, schooled at forepangs, wilder wring.
Comforter, where, where is your comforting?
Mary, mother of us, where is your relief?
My cries heave, herds-long; huddle in a main, a chief   5
Woe, wórld-sorrow; on an áge-old anvil wince and sing –
Then lull, then leave off. Fury had shrieked 'No ling-
ering! Let me be fell: force I must be brief'.

 O the mind, mind has mountains; cliffs of fall
Frightful, sheer, no-man-fathomed. Hold them cheap   10
May who ne'er hung there. Nor does long our small
Durance deal with that steep or deep. Here! creep,
Wretch, under a comfort serves in a whirlwind: all
Life death does end and each day dies with sleep.

Glossary

[1] **pitch:** the steepness of a slope, the highest point of a sound
[4] **Mary:** in Christian belief, the mother of Christ, traditionally a comforter
[6] **wórld-sorrow:** in Christian belief, the Fall of Man, the loss of Eden
[8] **fell:** decisive, ruthless

Judging by the lines that follow, the opening sentence, 'No worst, there is none', means that there is no such thing as 'the worst', because there is always something even more agonising.

Let's concentrate initially, however, on the *impact* of the words, with the repeated negatives – 'No worst … none' – and the heavy stresses giving the *feeling* of unbearable, unending suffering. Notice how in the following sentence the language recreates the impression of cuts ('Pitched … pitch … grief'), of blows ('pangs … –pangs') and of being crushed ('wring'). He is thrown, or pitched, he cries, past his present high point, or pitch, of suffering, into further suffering, so that he cries out, in vain, with two desperate pleas, for comfort, for relief. 'Comforter, where, where is your comforting?/Mary, mother of us, where is your relief?' Again, notice how the very sounds of 'Comforter', which is soft and cushioning, and of 'relief', which is like an easeful release of a sigh, convey in themselves his longing to be spared the pain.

This is a false lull, however. His pleas remain unanswered. There is no help on offer. And the second quatrain vividly captures the nature and extent of his pain in three quite startling images. His cries of pain are like terrified animals huddling together in a herd, and as always in Hopkins, the words themselves both demonstrate the sensations – look how the alliterative 'heave … herds … huddle' are huddling together on the line – and put them in a wider context: his sorrow is part of a 'wórld-sorrow', which suggests the fall of man in Christian belief. The second image is of being hammered on an anvil, the blow itself carried by 'wince', the reverberation by 'sing', the fading echo by 'lull' and the momentary silence by 'leave', before the cycle begins again, like spasms of pain. The third image is of a mythological creature of vengeance, the 'Fury', shrieking, insisting, that the pain must be immediate ('No ling-/gering!') and cruel ('fell') and swift ('brief'),

The sestet opens on a somewhat different note, that of exhaustion rather than pain or complaint, beginning with that initial expression of endurance: 'O the mind, mind has mountains'. Once again, notice how the sounds – the stretching out of the vowels in that half line – both expresses the feeling and informs our reading. *Listen* to a Hopkins poem and you will experience what it is. The image here is easy enough to understand. The human mind has mountains and chasms, terrifying drops and overwhelming gradients, so steep, so high, so deep, that we cannot endure such extremes for long. The only small consolation we can find ('a comfort' that 'serves in a whirlwind', just as a hovel served Shakespeare's King Lear in a storm) is that it will eventually end, ultimately with death ('all/Life death does end') and temporarily with sleep ('each day dies with sleep'). Not much of a consolation, you'll have to admit, more the release of exhaustion than of assistance, and exhaustion wonderfully expressed in the fading energy of the last line: 'all/Life death does end and each day dies with sleep'.

MAKE

This is one of a group of poems by Hopkins that have become known as 'the terrible sonnets', from a phrase coined by his friend Canon Dixon, 'the terrible crystal', meaning that the works in question 'crystallised' the terrible dejection of Hopkins when he was desolate during his latter years in Ireland.

(i)   Identify and comment on the experiences – emotions and thoughts – that could be described as 'terrible' here.

(ii) Identify and comment on the effectiveness of the images and the sounds that, in your opinion, best express the 'terrible' nature of the experience.

Poetry

Thou art indeed just, Lord, if I contend

Justus quidem tu es, Domine, si disputem tecum; verumtamen
justa loquar ad te: Quare via impiorum prosperatur? &c.

THOU art indeed just, Lord, if I contend
With thee; but, sir, so what I plead is just.
Why do sinners' ways prosper? and why must
Disappointment all I endeavour end?
   Wert thou my enemy, O thou my friend,   5
How wouldst thou worse, I wonder, than thou dost
Defeat, thwart me? Oh, the sots and thralls of lust
Do in spare hours more thrive than I that spend,
Sir, life upon thy cause. See, banks and brakes
Now, leavèd how thick! lacèd they are again   10
With fretty chervil, look, and fresh wind shakes
Them; birds build – but not I build; no, but strain,
Time's eunuch, and not breed one work that wakes.
Mine, O thou lord of life, send my roots rain.

Glossary

[epigraph] **Justus …:** Latin, from the Bible, meaning: *You are righteous, Lord, when I dispute with you, but I will still put my case. Why do the ways of the evil ones flourish?*

[1] **contend:** struggle, argue

[7] **sots:** habitual drunkards

[7] **thralls:** slaves, servants

[9] **brakes:** group of bushes or shrubs close together

[11] **chervil:** parsley plant

[13] **eunuch:** in this sense, ineffectual creature

Of the three 'terrible sonnets' on your course, this is the least extreme, the most composed. You can hear the note of acceptance in the reasonableness of the opening, which concedes superiority to God – 'Thou art indeed just, Lord' and is then respectful – 'but, sir' – when challenging, or seeking an explanation. That little 'sir' is quite a complex form of address. It is obviously a respectful address to a superior, but it is also a demand that the superior show respect in return. It is simultaneously deferential and severe. In the opening to this poem, however, the dominant note is one of accommodation. Even the questions are phrased in a rational, patient way. In studying Hopkins' techniques, particularly his use of sound, it's interesting to note the differences between this and the earlier sonnets. Here the words are neither extreme nor clogged together. Instead, the language is quite ordinary for a Hopkins

poem, quite simple to comprehend, and the words are quite distinct from each other, as if Hopkins is being careful to express himself as plainly as possible, to give God no excuse for evasion. What adds to the sense of reasonableness is the manner of the address: conciliation – 'O thou my friend' – combined with respect – 'sir' is used twice.

Halfway through, however, in line 7, it's as if Hopkins' patience starts to fray and the poem begins generating the excitement of indignation, initially with that same exclamation of 'Oh'. Whereas the first one expresses affection – 'O thou my friend' – the second sounds exasperated. The first is written 'O' without a comma, the second 'Oh,' with the comma, making it into a more abrupt, sharper expression. It's amazing what a little punctuation and variation in spelling can achieve. In any case, Hopkins starts to get annoyed that his dedicated service to the Lord doesn't seem to be getting any recognition, never mind any reward. Notice how his increasing anger is communicated by the loss of reasonableness in the language: 'sots' means drunkards and carries with it a wonderfully strong tone of disgust, and 'thralls', meaning slaves, which is a word you can't help drawing out, again in disgust, as you say it. Those who enjoy the pleasures of life, he points out, seem to be getting on better than those who are virtuous. 'See', he insists indignantly, jabbing a finger at God, everything else is flourishing, river banks, thickets, birds building nests – and notice how the alliteration and the heavy emphases kick in again as his indignation rises – everything except him.

He comes back down from his mounting annoyance, though, and the poem ends on a note of supplication, on a request, a prayer, a tone of acceptance – 'Mine, O thou lord of life, send my roots rain' – marked by a return to the original form of the exclamation 'O'.

MAKE

This is one of a group of poems by Hopkins that have become known as 'the terrible sonnets', from a phrase coined by his friend Canon Dixon, 'the terrible crystal', meaning that the works in question 'crystallised' the terrible dejection of Hopkins when he was desolate during his latter years in Ireland.

(i) Identify and comment on the experiences – emotions and thoughts – that could be described as 'terrible' here.

(ii) Identify and comment on the effectiveness of the images and the sounds that, in your opinion, best express the 'terrible' nature of the experience.

The Poetry of Gerard Manley Hopkins

Themes and Interests

- The poetry of Gerard Manley Hopkins celebrates the **GRANDEUR OF LIFE**, the magnificence of God's creation

Even in the depths of personal dejection, in the 'terrible sonnets', Hopkins can celebrate the abundance and beauty of natural life, using its energy and fertility as images in contrast with what he experiences as his own barrenness; 'send my roots rain', he prays. He is, of course, praying to his God – 'Thou art indeed just, Lord' – who is the creator of all this grandeur. The point is explicit even in the title of 'God's Grandeur', which is dominated by the energetic image of fire and the concept of 'greatness' in nature. The word 'beautiful' or its variants occurs in 'Spring' ('Nothing is so beautiful as Spring'), in 'Pied Beauty' ('He fathers-forth whose beauty is past change'), in 'As kingfishers catch fire' ('Lovely in limbs'), 'The Windhover' ('Brute beauty') and even in 'Felix Randal' ('hardy-handsome'), which is echoed in the adjective used to capture the splendour of the stream that makes the waterfall in 'Inversnaid' ('This darksome burn'). Whether it is the natural world generally that is being celebrated, or a recurring feature of it, such as 'dappled things' in 'Pied Beauty', or individual instances of it, such as the kestrel and the blacksmith, the focus in the detail is always on the magnificence of life, the splendour, the handsomeness that is a mirror image of the beauty of its creator, God.

- The poetry of Gerard Manley Hopkins explores the purpose and **PROPER LIFE OF MAN**, who is made in God's image, but can stray from it

In Hopkins' belief, men are born pure and beautiful, in the image of their creator, God. Mankind was created pure and beautiful – 'in Eden garden' as he puts it in 'Spring' – and after that each 'girl and boy' is born with an 'Innocent mind'. Unlike other features of the natural world, however – birds, fish, flowers, rivers – man can stray from his own nature, and thereby stray from his creator. Human beings can turn 'sour with sinning', as 'Spring', again, phrases it. Unlike other creatures, each man has a choice. He can remain true to his nature, and therefore beautiful – 'the just man ... Keeps gráce ... Acts in God's eye what in God's eye he is' ('As kingfishers catch fire') – or he can rebel, like Felix Randal – 'Impatient, he cursed at first'. 'Felix Randal' charts the course of a man's natural beauty, ugliness through rebellion, and recapturing of grace through acceptance of God's will. Felix was once splendid – 'powerful amidst peers' and 'hardy-handsome' – and becomes splendid again once he ceases cursing his fate and accepts it instead – 'mended/Being anointed and all'. The consequences of man straying from his own nature, and therefore from God, are dramatised in the 'terrible sonnets' – alienation, bitterness, darkness, sorrow, suffering, bewilderment, resentment – but the relief, as always, is again in the acceptance of God's word – 'Mine, O thou lord of life, send my roots rain'.

- The poetry of Gerard Manley Hopkins expresses the desolation of religious **DESPAIR**, of separation from God, of God's distance

In the natural world, only man experiences desolation. Kingfishers don't, hawks don't, shrubs don't, waterfalls don't. Or more exactly, they *can't*. Wherever these living things appear in Hopkins' poetry, they appear splendidly as themselves; they cannot be otherwise. They may fade and die, but that decay is also part of the natural process. Wherever humans appear in Hopkins' poetry, on the other hand, they appear as splendid beings made in God's image, certainly, but also wretchedly as alienated from God, and therefore alienated from themselves. Men don't simply die in body, as all other living things do; they decay in their souls. In several poems, Hopkins refers to the original Fall of Man – the 'curse', the 'world-sorrow' – the loss of 'Eden garden' through sin. It's a loss, an exile, that keeps repeating itself in man's life. In 'Felix Randal' a young blacksmith falls ill, is 'broken' by sickness, and then becomes broken in spirit as he curses his fate. It is only when he accepts his fate, returns to God by 'Being anointed' that he is 'mended' again. The same pattern is evident in 'As kingfishers catch fire' – man is truly himself only when he 'Acts in God's eye' – and in the 'terrible sonnets'. 'No worst, there is none' dramatises the extreme suffering of alienation, capturing it in terrifying images of shrieking in a storm and plunging from a cliff. 'I wake and feel the fell of dark' uses the symbolic image of waking in the middle of the night, terrified, disorientated, sickened by sourness in the stomach. 'Thou art indeed just, Lord' angrily expresses resentment and uses unsettling images of barrenness to dramatise the same theme.

- The poetry of Gerard Manley Hopkins discovers **PATTERN AND DESIGN** in all things

There is a unique pattern, a form, to all individual living things – a hawk, a trout, a blacksmith – and Hopkins delights in using language to capture and celebrate that uniqueness. Do keep in mind, however, that he's not attempting to paint portraits. Motion is as much the essence of anything as is appearance, and so Hopkins is always trying to capture the nature of a thing in movement – a hawk in flight in 'The Windhover', a waterfall hurtling downwards in 'Inversnaid', a blacksmith at work in 'Felix Randal', and so on. As well as being unique, however, each living thing is also part of a species, part of a group. All hawks have attributes in common – that's what makes each a hawk. All waterfalls share common features, all blacksmiths have something that define them as blacksmiths, as distinct from tailors. This is part of the pattern of all living things. So, in Hopkins, one always finds both the individual thing – Felix Randal, *the* windhover, *this* 'darksome burn' – and the species – 'men', 'generations', 'dappled things', 'áll tráses', 'the weeds and the wilderness', 'kingfishers', 'dragonflies', 'the features of men's faces'. But living things not only have 'pattern'; they also have 'design'. The latter word – 'design' – suggests a creator, a designer. So, the beauty of each individual thing in Hopkins' poetry originates in the beauty of the creator. This is best expressed in 'As kingfishers catch fire', where the individuality of the poet – '*Whát I dó is me*' – is recognised as being dependent on God – 'Acts in God's eye what in God's eye he is' – but the same belief is present in all the poems.

Style and Viewpoint

- The poetry of Gerard Manley Hopkins is unconventional and exciting in its **LANGUAGE**, which is used, not for self-expression or communication, but in an attempt to capture the essence of living things

Keeping in mind all the time that Hopkins' intention is to use language to capture the essence of living things – their movement as well as their appearance – it's instructive, as well as enjoyable, to consider closely some of the innovative and unconventional techniques and devices he used. These include:

1. **condensed language**, including ellipsis, which is the omission of words – 'blood brimmed (*with* omitted) the curse' ('I wake'); 'Selves (*many words* omitted) – goes itself' ('As kingfishers'); 'Thrush's eggs look (*like* omitted) little low heavens' ('Spring')

2. **unusual words** – 'He fathers-forth' ('Pied Beauty'); 'fretty chervil' ('Thou art'); 'the sots' ('Thou art')

3. **obscure language** – 'Selfyeast of spirit a dull dough sours' ('I wake'); 'the fleece of his foam/Flutes' ('Inversnaid'); 'just man justices' ('As kingfishers'); 'force I must be brief' ('No worst'); 'a comfort serves in a whirlwind' ('No worst')

4. **unusual colloquial words** – 'Degged' ('Inversnaid'); 'all road' ('Felix Randal');

5. **word play, pun, multiple meaning** – 'The world is *charged* with the grandeur of God' ('God's Grandeur'); 'Pitched past *pitch* of grief' ('No worst'); 'dapple-dawn-drawn Falcon' ('The Windhover'); '*Buckle*' ('The Windhover')

6. **invented words** – 'the achieve of' ('The Windhover'); 'twindles' ('Inversnaid'); 'fleshed' ('Felix Randal'); 'forepangs' ('No worst')

7. **compound words** – 'rollrock highroad' ('Inversnaid'); 'A windpuff-bonnet of fáwn-fróth' ('Inversnaid'); 'féll-frówning' ('Inversnaid'); 'big-boned and hardy-handsome' ('Felix Randal')

8. **unusual syntax (word order)** – 'He fathers-forth whose beauty is past change' ('Pied Beauty'); 'till time when reason rambled in it, and some/Fatal four disorders, fleshed there, all contended?' ('Felix Randal'); 'Selfyeast of spirit a dull dough sours' ('I wake'); 'Bones built in me, flesh filled, blood brimmed the curse' ('I wake').

- The poetry of Gerard Manley Hopkins employs the **IMAGERY** of nature, its darkness as well as its beauty, to create 'inscape', a term Hopkins used to describe the uniqueness of each living thing

Hopkins' imagery is characterised by its daring, for example in the metaphors 'O thou lord of life, send my roots rain' ('Thou art'); 'Time's eunuch' ('Thou art'); 'horseback brown' ('Inversnaid'); 'the fire that breaks from thee' ('The Windhover'); in the simile 'cries like dead letters' ('I wake'); the synecdoche: 'My tongue had taught thee comfort' ('Felix Randal'); and the examples of hyperbole '…a billion/Times told lovelier, more dangerous, O my chevalier!' ('The Windhover'); 'for Christ plays in ten thousand places' ('As kingfishers catch fire'). Most of the imagery is drawn from the natural world, however, because he found in nature both his subject matter and the means of expressing it. 'God's Grandeur' is alive with images of fire, light and fecundity; 'Spring' draws on a similar range of abundance and freshness; fire and flame occur again in 'As kingfishers catch fire', as well as music, language and features. 'The Windhover' draws again on fire – a Hopkins favourite – light, music and the movements of the wind to capture the majesty of the bird. The ploughed land, which appears in many poems, is a central image in 'Pied Beauty', which also draws on fire, colour and light. Colour and light shine through the description of the waterfall in 'Inversnaid'. Even the 'terrible sonnets', expressions of personal desolation, draw on nature imagery for their meaning and power: the starved soul is a dry root in 'Thou art indeed just, Lord'; the hide of an animal and soured milk are used to depict the nightmare of alienation from God in 'I wake and feel the fell of dark'; animal herds and treacherous cliffs and storms are employed in 'No worst, there is none' to describe the extremity of separation from one's maker.

- The poetry of Gerard Manley Hopkins employs vigorous and unusual **SOUND** patterns, particularly in its verbs and metre, to create 'instress', a term Hopkins used to describe the energy of a living thing

'Sprung rhythm', the term Hopkins himself used to describe his sound patterns, was a system of metre used in Old English poetry and in Welsh poetry long before Hopkins adopted it. It's easy enough to understand. If you read the following line from a poem by Tennyson, another Victorian English poet – 'The woods decay, the woods decay and fall' – you'll automatically stress it as 'The *WOODS deCAY*, the *WOODS deCAY* and *FALL*' and your reading will automatically fall into sections of one unstressed syllable and one stressed syllable, / the *WOODS* /. Each of these sections containing a stress is called a foot, which is marked off by using forward slashes (/). In Tennyson's line, there are five feet because there are five stresses: / The *WOODS* / *deCAY* / the *WOODS* / *deCAY* / and *FALL* /. By contrast with this, in 'sprung rhythm' one stressed syllable can make up an entire foot and doesn't need to be accompanied by an unstressed syllable. If you read the following line from 'Pied Beauty' – 'With swift, slow; sweet, sour; adazzle, dim' – you'll automatically stress it as 'With *SWIFT, SLOW; SWEET, SOUR; aDAZZle, DIM*'; giving a line of six stresses, or six feet – / *With SWIFT,* / *SLOW;* / *SWEET,* / *SOUR;* / *aDAZZle,* / *DIM* / – three of which in the middle are not accompanied by other unstressed syllables, or, as Hopkins referred to them, 'hangers' or 'outrides'. You don't necessarily have to mention 'sprung rhythm' when you're discussing Hopkins' poetry, but you *do* have to mention that Hopkins forces you to read the lines in very unusual and challenging ways, and that his purpose in doing so is to capture the essence, particularly the movement, the *feel*, of whatever he is describing, whether that's a bird, a waterfall, a fish, a storm, a man, an emotion, or an experience.

- The poetry of Gerard Manley Hopkins holds the intensity and the energy within strict poetic **FORMS**, particularly the sonnet

The greater the riches you have, the more securely you'll keep them. Interestingly, this seems to apply to poetry as much as it does to ordinary life. Poets like Hopkins, whose language is very rich and unconventional, tend to favour strict poetic forms – standard schemes of rhyme, metre and length – to hold and compress the beauty, and thereby make it shine more intensely. As mentioned above, beauty for Hopkins was in the design and pattern of individual things. Strict poetic forms are all about design and pattern, and so Hopkins' attraction to them is easily understood. He had a particular fondness for the sonnet form, a Hopkins poem of fourteen lines with a regular rhyming scheme, so much so that nine of the ten poems on your course are exercises in the sonnet. Although he experimented a great deal, his preference was for the Petrarchan sonnet – called after the Italian Renaissance poet Francesco Petrarca – which is usually split into two sections: one of eight lines, known as an octave, and one of six lines, known as a sestet. It usually rhymes A-B-B-A-A-B-B-A in the octave and varies the rhyming scheme in the sestet. In itself, it has a great formal beauty – and Hopkins celebrated the beauty of things in themselves – but depending on the arrangement of the lines, it can also be used as a subtle expression of complex thought processes. In the 'terrible sonnets' in particular, the layout of the poems tends to represent shifts in feeling or intensity – for example, the final six lines of 'No worst, there is none' reaches a pitch of despair, and the final six lines of 'I wake and feel the fell of dark' a pitch of self-loathing, whereas the first four lines of 'Thou art indeed just, Lord' introduces an argument that is developed in the remaining ten. In many instances – 'God's Grandeur', 'Spring' and 'Felix Randal' among them – the sestet is used for a change of mood or a subtle change of direction, which is the classic form of the Petrarchan sonnet.

John Keats

John Keats was born in London on 31 October 1795. His early life seems to have been modestly comfortable and happy, until the deaths of his father in a riding accident in April 1804 and of his mother from tuberculosis in March 1809. As is obvious from his letters, these early losses contributed to his later faith in the power of art to ease human suffering, a major theme in his poetry. While increasingly viewing poetry as both a vocation and a profession, he also qualified as a 'surgeon' in 1816 – the equivalent of a doctor's assistant now – and practised in Margate and London. Against scathing conservative criticism, he devoted himself to poetry and to developing his unique voice. But his time was limited. In 1818, his brother Tom died from tuberculosis and Keats himself was showing signs of the same illness. This awareness of approaching death gave an intensity to all his experiences, including his love for Fanny Brawne. Advised by doctors to travel to Italy for his health, Keats died in Rome in 1821, aged twenty-five, and was buried there in the Protestant cemetery.

Prescribed Poems

'Students at Higher Level will be required to study a representative selection from the work of eight poets: a representative selection would seek to reflect the range of a poet's themes and interests and exhibit his/her characteristic style and viewpoint. Normally the study of at least six poems by each poet would be expected.' (DES English Syllabus, 6.3)

Themes and Interests

uncovers the **PAIN** and **DISCONTENT** at the heart of human life, what he describes as 'The weariness, the fever, and the fret'

presents the **ENCHANTMENT OF ART** as a release from human suffering and as the creation of beauty, ease and immortality

The Poetry of John Keats

presents the enchantments of **LOVE** and **BEAUTY** and **NATURE** as consolations for and escapes from human suffering

dramatises the **IRONIC PARADOX** that imagining beauty, since we cannot sustain it, makes the ordinary world even more painful

Style and Viewpoint

The Poetry of John Keats

is sensuous, which means that its **LANGUAGE**, although remaining colloquial, is descriptively luxuriant, rich, lush

employs nature, art, music, song and sensory detail as symbolic **IMAGERY** to capture the intense experience of living, and uses mythology and fable as reference

uses intricate and at times luxuriant **SOUND** patterns to recreate intense emotions and feelings

employs a wide range of traditional poetic **FORMS**, such as the sonnet, the ballad and the ode, and always brings something new and distinctive to each

Poetry

READ

'To one who has been long in city pent'

To one who has been long in city pent,
  'Tis very sweet to look into the fair
  And open face of heaven—to breathe a prayer
Full in the smile of the blue firmament.
Who is more happy, when, with heart's content,   5
  Fatigued he sinks into some pleasant lair
  Of wavy grass, and reads a debonair
And gentle tale of love and languishment?
Returning home at evening, with an ear
  Catching the notes of Philomel – an eye   10
Watching the sailing cloudlet's bright career,
  He mourns that day so soon has glided by:
E'en like the passage of an angel's tear
  That falls through the clear ether silently.

Glossary

[1] **pent:** pent-up, confined
[4] **firmament:** the heavens or sky
[7] **debonair:** gentle, gracious [the meaning of the time]
[10] **Philomel:** the name means 'lover of song' and is used here as a synonym for 'nightingale'
[14] **ether:** sky

Poetry

ANALYSE

Poems evoking the countryside as a release from the grim servitude of the city were common in the nineteenth century, although this early sonnet, written when he was a twenty-year-old medical student in London, already shows signs of Keats' distinctive take on human discomfort – 'pent' and 'Fatigued' – and on the nature of human fulfilment – 'love and languishment'. It is also interesting to note that the fulfilment is achieved through art, in this case a book, a theme that would dominate much of his later poetry. Similarly, although the particular sonnet form, and even the opening line, are modelled on the work of an earlier poet, John Milton – Milton's sonnet opens 'As one who long in populous city pent' – Keats' characteristic style – sensory detail, luxuriant language – is already evident.

The opening lines, capturing the contrast between the confinement of the city and the freedom of the country, use rhythm, other sound effects, colour and imagery in rich combinations. The cramped rhythm of the opening line opens out into the looser flow of the next line and a half; the pinched sound of 'city' and 'pent' give way to the more pleasing 'sweet', 'breathe' and 'smile'; the darkness suggested by 'pent' gives way to the 'blue' of the sky; and the personification of the sky – it has a 'face' and a 'smile' while the city is anonymous – makes it a more pleasant companion for a human.

In the second quatrain, the contentment of flopping down and chilling out is recreated by one long, flowing rhetorical question – 'Who is more happy …?' – and in the broad, rich vowel sounds in the end rhymes like 'lair/debonair' and in the internal echoes of 'wavy' and 'tale'. The thing to note, however, is that happiness is not passive. It doesn't automatically arrive simply from being in the country and taking our ease. Keats was a dynamic man and an energetic poet. In his personal life, he found meaning and purpose and comfort in art, and this sonnet contains one of the earliest expressions of that aesthetic in his poetry. The 'one' of the poem finds happiness through reading a 'tale of love and languishment', in other words a story that

Poetry

somehow holds passion and ease together in the one experience. Note also that the tale, in its style, is both dashing ('debonair') and sensitive ('gentle'). This, too, is one of the earliest expressions of Keats' sense of the contrarieties of experience, the contradictions and tensions of life.

The final section of the poem is also an early expression of another of Keats' great themes – the transitory nature of things. The day ends, the light fades, the nightingale falls silent. Nothing lasts. And therefore, happiness, contentment and pleasure are also temporary. The 'one' returns to the confinement of the city – although he is 'Returning home', it is important to note – with a heavy enough heart, mourning the death of the day, although again it is important to note that it is an easeful passing, the day 'has glided by', like the delicate falling of 'an angel's tear'. The melancholy, in other words, seems genuine, but light, in this sonnet, in contrast to some of his later work.

MAKE

(i) The word 'pent' defines the constrictions of the city. Identify the opposing attractions and pleasures of the country as they are described in this sonnet.

(ii) The atmosphere that the sonnet wants to capture is one of easy pleasure – 'sweet'. Identify either the sounds or the images that are effective in expressing this.

Poetry

Ode to a Nightingale

I

My heart aches, and a drowsy numbness pains
  My sense, as though of hemlock I had drunk,
Or emptied some dull opiate to the drains
  One minute past, and Lethe-wards had sunk:
'Tis not through envy of thy happy lot,   5
  But being too happy in thine happiness —
    That thou, light-wingèd Dryad of the trees,
      In some melodious plot
  Of beechen green, and shadows numberless,
    Singest of summer in full-throated ease.   10

II

O, for a draught of vintage! that hath been
  Cooled a long age in the deep-delvèd earth,
Tasting of Flora and the country green,
  Dance, and Provençal song, and sunburnt mirth!
O for a beaker full of the warm South,   15
  Full of the true, the blushful Hippocrene,
    With beaded bubbles winking at the brim,
      And purple-stainèd mouth,
  That I might drink, and leave the world unseen,
    And with thee fade away into the forest dim –   20

III

Fade far away, dissolve, and quite forget
  What thou among the leaves hast never known,
The weariness, the fever, and the fret
  Here, where men sit and hear each other groan;
Where palsy shakes a few, sad, last grey hairs,   25
  Where youth grows pale, and spectre-thin, and dies;
    Where but to think is to be full of sorrow
      And leaden-eyed despairs;
  Where Beauty cannot keep her lustrous eyes,
    Or new Love pine at them beyond to-morrow.   30

IV

Away! away! for I will fly to thee,
  Not charioted by Bacchus and his pards,
But on the viewless wings of Poesy,
  Though the dull brain perplexes and retards.
Already with thee! tender is the night,   35
  And haply the Queen-Moon is on her throne,

Clustered around by all her starry Fays;
    But here there is no light,
Save what from heaven is with the breezes blown
    Through verdurous glooms and winding mossy ways.   40

V
I cannot see what flowers are at my feet,
    Nor what soft incense hangs upon the boughs,
But, in embalmèd darkness, guess each sweet
    Wherewith the seasonable month endows
The grass, the thicket, and the fruit-tree wild –   45
    White hawthorn, and the pastoral eglantine;
        Fast fading violets covered up in leaves;
            And mid-May's eldest child,
    The coming musk-rose, full of dewy wine,
        The murmurous haunt of flies on summer eves.   50

VI
Darkling I listen; and, for many a time
    I have been half in love with easeful Death,
Called him soft names in many a musèd rhyme,
    To take into the air my quiet breath;
Now more than ever seems it rich to die,   55
    To cease upon the midnight with no pain,
        While thou art pouring forth thy soul abroad
            In such an ecstasy!
    Still wouldst thou sing, and I have ears in vain—
        To thy high requiem become a sod.   60

VII
Thou wast not born for death, immortal Bird!
    No hungry generations tread thee down;
The voice I hear this passing night was heard
    In ancient days by emperor and clown:
Perhaps the self-same song that found a path   65
    Through the sad heart of Ruth, when, sick for home,
        She stood in tears amid the alien corn;
            The same that oft-times hath
    Charmed magic casements, opening on the foam
        Of perilous seas, in faery lands forlorn.   70

VIII

Forlorn! the very word is like a bell
  To toll me back from thee to my sole self!
Adieu! the fancy cannot cheat so well
  As she is famed to do, deceiving elf.
Adieu! adieu! thy plaintive anthem fades   75
  Past the near meadows, over the still stream,
    Up the hill-side; and now 'tis buried deep
    In the next valley-glades:
  Was it a vision, or a waking dream?
    Fled is that music—Do I wake or sleep?   80

Glossary

[2] **hemlock:** highly poisonous plant of the parsley family

[4] **Lethe:** Greek mythology, the river of forgetfulness

[7] **Dryad:** Greek mythology, a woodland nymph

[13] **Flora:** Roman mythology, the goddess of flowers

[14] **Provençal:** relating to Provence, France

[16] **Hippocrene:** Greek mythology, fountain on Mount Helicon that was the source of poetic inspiration

[32] **Bacchus:** Greek and Roman mythology, the god of wine

[32] **pards:** leopards

[37] **Fays:** fairies

[66] **Ruth:** Christian Bible, a Moabite woman who accompanied her mother-in-law into exile in Bethlehem

ANALYSE

The ode opens on the poet's awareness and expression of the heartache and dullness of ordinary life. The first words are a cry of existential pain – 'My heart aches' – and then the rhythm of the lines drags across heavy, elongated sounds – 'drowsy numbness', 'hemlock', 'opiate' – before collapsing into the depression of 'sunk'. Contrasted with this is the lightness, splendour, energy, elevation and music of the nightingale. The bird both belongs to the world – it's in a shady plot of beech trees – and transcends it – it's a 'light-wingèd Dryad', a nymph that can fly.

So, the poet's dilemma is beautifully and economically established in the first stanza. How can you simultaneously inhabit the world and transcend it? How can you get from 'drowsy numbness' to 'full-throated ease'?

Keats yearns first for alcohol, that time-honoured escape from the burdens of life. 'O, for a draught of vintage!' he gasps. Wine, after all, comes from the earth and is of the earth, it, too, is derived from 'country green', and it, too, tastes of the joys of summer, of 'sunburnt mirth', all similar to the nightingale earlier. Doesn't it, too, promise and provide lightness, splendour, energy, elevation and music? Its promise is wonderfully captured in the luxuriance of the rich sounds – 'beaded bubbles winking' – and the lush imagery – 'purple-stainèd mouth'.

Poetry

But can wine actually *provide* escape? Possibly, but in posing the question, Keats can't avoid dwelling on 'The weariness, the fever, and the fret' that he wants to flee from. That's the point and meaning of the line, 'Where but to think is to be full of sorrow'. The repetitions in this section fall like dull blows, pounding in the head – 'Here … hear … Where … Where … Where …'. The broad vowel sounds articulate suffering – 'groan … palsy … grey … pale … leaden'. Everything is heavy. The images are of disease and decline – 'palsy … grey hairs … spectre-thin'. One is conscious that wine, for all its temporary transfusion of joy and energy, leaves one debilitated afterwards.

So Keats grasps for something superior to 'Bacchus and his pards', for the uplifting power of poetry, product of the elevating, though invisible – hence 'viewless wings' – human imagination. He strives to project himself into the mood – a poetic moon, poetic stars – but again, as with wine, the very act of forcing the issue reminds him of what he lacks. He's thinking of being inspired, instead of actually being so, and this, remember, is a world 'Where but to think is to be full of sorrow'. Hence the darkness that envelops stanza five and that symbolises the darkness in his own being. The pain of knowing what you want and not being able to have it, of being so close, is magnificently captured in the imagery of this stanza, where the poet can smell the beauties of nature – 'guess each sweet' – but can't see them. Because of this failure, the stanza ends, not with transcending the conscious mind, but with an increased awareness of decay – the 'murmurous' buzzing of flies, those noisy reminders of waste and death.

Keats then thinks of death itself as a means of escape. The rhythm slows, the stresses soften, the sounds become more seductive – 'love', 'easeful', 'soft', 'quiet' – as 'Death' is presented as a lover, a sweet liberator, a wealthy benefactor – 'Now more than ever seems it rich to die'. But again the mind intervenes with a harsh but obvious truth – death is going to remove him from the 'ecstasy' of the bird's song, not bring him into it. Ironically the bird's song would become a 'requiem' – music for the repose of the dead – and Keats himself no more than an insensible 'sod' of earth.

As the opposite of death, the nightingale and its song – 'immortal Bird' – come to symbolise immortality in the poem. In a final reach for escape, Keats yearns for this immortality, forcing himself once more into the mood, convincing himself that because the same song was

heard in 'ancient days' by kings and commoners and biblical characters, then it can be a portal, opening out on any time and into the 'magic' of another world, another existence, represented again, as in stanza four, by 'faery' creatures. The phrase 'Charmed magic casements' is particularly expressive, because it holds the prospects of the enchantment, sorcery and escape – a 'casement' is a window – that Keats is yearning for; but the word 'Perhaps' in the middle of the stanza is equally eloquent, because it carries all the doubt and uncertainty that have been present throughout the poem.

It's the double sound and double meaning of another word – 'Forlorn' is both long ago and sad, and can sound both mysterious and miserable – that brings it home to Keats that he's been trying to fool himself, imagining an escape without managing it. As the actual bird flies away and its song fades, Keats accepts that the imagination offers only the illusion of immortality and permanent beauty. The 'fancy' cheats, but can't manage it completely. The bird's song becomes a fading 'plaintive anthem', a mournful tune. In the end, the uncertainty that has marked the poem throughout comes to dominate entirely, leaving Keats in a state of confused and painful self-consciousness – 'Do I wake or sleep?'

MAKE

(i) This ode opens, literally, on heartache – 'My heart aches' – and it ends in obvious confusion – 'Do I wake or sleep?' Work through the stanzas, identifying the dominant emotion in each and commenting on how one develops from another.

(ii) 'Sensuous language attempts to capture sensation.' Select some examples of Keats' language that, in your opinion, capture the sensations in this ode and comment on how you think they achieve this effect.

READ

On First Looking into Chapman's Homer

Much have I travelled in the realms of gold,
   And many goodly states and kingdoms seen;
   Round many western islands have I been
Which bards in fealty to Apollo hold.
Oft of one wide expanse had I been told   5
   That deep-browed Homer ruled as his demesne;
   Yet did I never breathe its pure serene
Till I heard Chapman speak out loud and bold:
Then felt I like some watcher of the skies
   When a new planet swims into his ken;   10
Or like stout Cortez when with eagle eyes
   He stared at the Pacific – and all his men
Looked at each other with a wild surmise –
   Silent, upon a peak in Darien.

Glossary

[title] **Chapman:** George Chapman (1559–1634), English poet and translator of Homer's *Iliad* and *Odyssey*

[title] **Homer:** Greek epic poet, author of *Iliad* and *Odyssey*

[4] **fealty:** loyalty

[4] **Apollo:** Greek mythology, god of music, poetry

[11] **Cortez:** Hernán Cortez (1485–1547), Spanish conquistador and leader of the expedition to the Americas that brought about the fall of the Aztecs

[14] **Darien:** former name of Panama, central America

ANALYSE

Keats wrote this sonnet in a single morning in October 1816 after returning to his lodgings following a late-night reading of George Chapman's translation of the fifth book of *The Odyssey* at a friend's lodgings. The reading was something of a revelation to Keats and a huge influence on his own work. As is stated, what appealed about Chapman's translation was that the style was 'loud and bold' – confident, masculine, energetic, vigorous, muscular. These qualities would feature in Keats' own poetic language subsequently. Ironically, the effect of first encountering it left him temporarily speechless – 'Silent' – as often happens when we are profoundly moved by some deep experience.

George Chapman

The controlling metaphor of the poem is that of exploration. The opening line presents the poet as an experienced explorer, much-travelled 'in the realms of gold', which stands both for the legendary city of fabulous riches believed by sixteenth-century Spanish explorers to exist in South America and known by them as El Dorado (literally, 'the gilded one') and for books, which

Poetry

were embossed on the cover and spines using gold leaf. From there, the double meaning of territory – land and literature – is sustained throughout. The 'western islands', owned by poets who are bound by the feudal obligation of fidelity to Apollo, the Greek god of music and poetry, stand for European literature. The work of Homer, the greatest of these European writers, is described as a 'wide expanse' – a vast body of rich work – and as a 'demesne'– a region. It is, of course, only the experienced explorer, having dedicated a life to the search, who can fully appreciate the discovery of a legendary location, in this case Chapman's translation into English of Homer's epic. Keats describes it as encountering the fresh air of a perfectly clear sly – 'breathe its pure serene' – and in two extended similes derived from the sonnet's controlling metaphor, compares it to someone who routinely studies the skies suddenly catching sight of a new planet coming into view, and then to a Spanish conquistador, Cortez, reaching the top of a mountain in Panama and looking out on the other side of the country, into a vast new ocean beyond. The effect is breath-taking, leaving the viewer speechless with awe.

The dominant images in the sonnet – of gold, the ocean, stars and planets – are taken directly from the section of Chapman's *Odyssey* translation he had heard the night before, and the poem dramatises his own sense of himself standing on the edge of discovery, like the astronomer and the conquistador, with a new poetic life opening up in front of him.

This is a Petrarchan or Italian sonnet form, that is, the fourteen lines are divided into two sections, the octave of eight lines with an A-B-B-A-A-B-B-A rhyming scheme and a sestet of six lines with a C-D-C-D-C-D rhyming scheme. The division is usually used to carry a shift in thought or perspective, but Keats subtly adapts the entire form to dramatise the moment of change and opportunity itself, so that the revelation seems simultaneously both startling and inevitable.

MAKE

(i) This sonnet metaphorically equates the discovery of a new translation of Homer with the discovery of a new planet or ocean. Is the comparison an effective one, in your opinion?

(ii) The sonnet depends a great deal on the imagery of territory for its effect – 'realms', 'states', and so on. Pick out as many examples as you can find, commenting on what each suggests to you.

READ

Poetry

Ode on a Grecian Urn

I

Thou still unravished bride of quietness,
  Thou foster-child of silence and slow time,
Sylvan historian, who canst thus express
  A flowery tale more sweetly than our rhyme:
What leaf-fringed legend haunts about thy shape   5
  Of deities or mortals, or of both,
    In Tempe or the dales of Arcady?
  What men or gods are these? What maidens loth?
What mad pursuit? What struggle to escape?
    What pipes and timbrels? What wild ecstasy?   10

II

Heard melodies are sweet, but those unheard
  Are sweeter; therefore, ye soft pipes, play on;
Not to the sensual ear, but, more endeared,
  Pipe to the spirit ditties of no tone:
Fair youth, beneath the trees, thou canst not leave   15
  Thy song, nor ever can those trees be bare;
    Bold Lover, never, never canst thou kiss,
Though winning near the goal – yet, do not grieve:
  She cannot fade, though thou hast not thy bliss,
    For ever wilt thou love, and she be fair!   20

III

Ah, happy, happy boughs! that cannot shed
  Your leaves, nor ever bid the Spring adieu;
And, happy melodist, unwearièd,
  For ever piping songs for ever new;
More happy love! more happy, happy love!   25
  For ever warm and still to be enjoyed,
    For ever panting, and for ever young –
All breathing human passion far above,
  That leaves a heart high-sorrowful and cloyed,
    A burning forehead, and a parching tongue.   30

IV

Who are these coming to the sacrifice?
  To what green altar, O mysterious priest,
Lead'st thou that heifer lowing at the skies,
  And all her silken flanks with garlands dressed?
What little town by river or sea shore,   35
  Or mountain-built with peaceful citadel,

Is emptied of this folk, this pious morn?
And, little town, thy streets for evermore
  Will silent be; and not a soul to tell
    Why thou art desolate, can e'er return.   40

V
O Attic shape! Fair attitude! with brede
  Of marble men and maidens overwrought,
With forest branches and the trodden weed;
  Thou, silent form, dost tease us out of thought
As doth eternity: Cold Pastoral!   45
  When old age shall this generation waste,
    Thou shalt remain, in midst of other woe
Than ours, a friend to man, to whom thou say'st,
  'Beauty is truth, truth beauty,—that is all
    Ye know on earth, and all ye need to know.'   50

Glossary

[3] **Sylvan:** rural, pastoral

[7] **Tempe:** a valley in Greece, between Mounts Olympus and Ossa

[7] **Arcady:** from Greek *Arkadia*, a region; in mythology and poetry, a rural paradise, the home of Pan

[41] **Attic:** relating to ancient Athens, or Attica

[41] **brede:** old spelling of braid

[45] **Pastoral:** a work of art portraying a rural paradise

ANALYSE

The urn in question is a two-handed ceramic pot used in ancient Greece for carrying food or oil and decorated with paintings and drawings. Keats was familiar with many examples from his visits to the British Museum and from his study of engravings in contemporary books such as Henry Moses' *A Collection of Antique Vases*, from which he traced a particular drawing. In the poem, this work of art becomes a beautiful but troubling image of permanence, a magnificent creation of humans, aesthetically representing human life, which is energetic and abundant, and yet not at all accurately representing human life, which is finite and subject to decay.

All these contradictions and tensions are implicit in the language of the opening lines addressing the urn. The object is 'still unravished', which simply means 'not yet damaged'. It seems like a celebratory image of permanence, but 'still' implies more luck than anything else and even suggests the inevitability of destruction over time. The word 'unravished' has a wealth of possible meanings, since 'ravish' can mean, variously, to fill someone with joy, to carry away, to seize, to overcome with emotion, to force sexually. If the urn is 'unravished' does it mean that it is untouched by joy and emotion, as is echoed in 'Cold Pastoral' in the fifth stanza? Of course it does. This is an object. If the urn is an 'unravished bride' does it mean that it cannot procreate, or create, by itself, as is suggested by 'never canst thou kiss' in the second stanza? Of course it

does. The word 'still' contains the meaning 'static' – as in 'keep still' – as well as the intimation of permanence. How can something static express the vitality of human life? How can something that is silent express anything? And yet the urn does have something to say to us – its art is even more expressive than poetry – which is why it's the adopted child, or 'foster-child', of silence. The natural children of silence would be dumb. The natural children of time – humans – live a small span of time. The urn is much older, and so is also a foster-child of 'slow time'.

What is implicit in all these tensions in the opening lines is what becomes the theme and the meaning of the entire ode – humans can fulfil themselves only in the process of doing something, which involves the passage of time, which involves inevitable loss and death, and any attempt to stop this process, no matter how desirable, no matter how magnificent, is unnatural.

In the opening stanza, which on the surface is an ecstatic exclamation of admiration and wonder for the beauty of the object, these tensions are really concealed within the extraordinary subtleties of the language, as explored above. They become more overt, and troubled, as the ode progresses. The admiration is expressed in a series of awe-struck questions as the viewer focuses on the details on the urn, which clearly depicts a procession accompanied by music, religious in intention but also allowing occasion for lovers to meet. You might notice that alternating questions and statements dominate the poem and are used to carry its development.

The second stanza, for instance, following the series of hectic questions in the first, opens with the arresting claim, 'Heard melodies are sweet, but those unheard/Are sweeter'. The music natural instruments can produce is beautiful, but the music produced by the imagination is more perfect. This is true. As humans, we can imagine a perfection that we cannot live. Art enables us to capture that perfection. For six lines or so, it seems a miracle – eternal song, eternal youth, eternal greenery – until we hit 'never canst thou kiss', which no longer strikes us as a gain, but rather as a loss, a deprivation. This is why the poet immediately hurries towards consolation, compensation – 'yet, do not grieve' – assuring the youth that both his love and his loved one can never fade. But there's a problem with this. The youth on the urn can no more hear than he can speak or kiss. Why is Keats addressing him? Or isn't it the case that Keats' plea – 'do not grieve' – is addressed to himself and to the reader, in an effort to convince both?

This pleading becomes desperate in the third stanza, a frenzied attempt to hold on to the notion that art can offer us permanence and happiness. The insistent, over-the-top repetition of 'happy' – the word is used six times, three in one line alone – is revealing. Keats is trying too hard, protesting too much. And while he's hammering away with this word, the imagery slips, almost unnoticed, one might say, from the signs of robust health – 'cannot shed/Your leaves', 'For ever warm' – to the symptoms of disease – 'A burning forehead, and a parching tongue'. The artificial passions of art may be more perfect than, or 'Far above', 'breathing human passion', but they are lifeless, and therefore unfulfilling – the youth will be 'for ever panting', where 'panting', in this sense, primarily meanings 'longing'.

Stanza four draws out of this cul-de-sac, back from these painful contradictions, away from the lovers, and apparently to another section of the scene depicted on the urn. In effect, it seems to start the process all over again. Notice how the questions reassert themselves and replace the frenetic assertions of the previous stanza. Notice how their composed interest contrasts with the hectic excitement of the questions in the opening stanza. Notice also how the rhythm slows to something more deliberate and thoughtful, created by the longer sentences, the sibilance, the

more restrained punctuation and the dropping of the frantic repetition. Consequently, although the implied conclusion is the same – the people depicted on the urn are all, in reality, long dead, and this is why 'not a soul … can e'er return' – the tone is more sad than fevered, more accepting than desperate.

This sad, but necessary acceptance is what allows the urn, in the final stanza, to 'tease us out of thought', to release us from the frantic need to search for meaning in and control of life, to release us from the frantic questions that plague us. It becomes 'a friend to man' – not an illusionary escape from life, but a gentle reminder of the truths of life, as would be provided by a genuine friend. The last two lines of the ode have been endlessly debated, but the basic sense is obvious if one has followed the tensions in the poem: there is no absolute truth that somehow sits outside the process of living and that one can reach; it's found in the beauty of living, a beauty that contains, for humans, its own decline inside itself. 'Beauty is truth, truth beauty'. The beauty of the Grecian urn is not something outside human endeavour; it is the result of human endeavour.

MAKE

(i) This ode consists of a great many excited questions – ten in all – and a categorical statement at the end – 'Beauty is truth, truth beauty'. In your opinion, which of these two – question or statement – more accurately captures the experience of contemplating the work of art that is the urn? Give reasons for your answer.

(ii) The ode relies on visual imagery for much of its effect – the urn can be seen, but its melodies are 'unheard'. Pick out what you consider the most successful visual images and give reasons for your choice.

'When I have fears that I may cease to be'

When I have fears that I may cease to be
    Before my pen has gleaned my teeming brain,
Before high-pilèd books, in charactery,
    Hold like rich garners the full-ripened grain;
When I behold, upon the night's starred face,   5
    Huge cloudy symbols of a high romance,
And think that I may never live to trace
    Their shadows, with the magic hand of chance;
And when I feel, fair creature of an hour!
    That I shall never look upon thee more,   10
Never have relish in the faery power
    Of unreflecting love! – then on the shore
Of the wide world I stand alone, and think
Till love and fame to nothingness do sink.

Glossary

[3] **charactery:** the art of characterising by symbols

The inevitability of death is considered here, not as something powerful or interesting in itself – 'cease to be' is a quiet and gentle end – but as the loss of life's abundant riches. As is usual in Keats, these riches are the enchantments of love and beauty and nature, and the enchantment of art. The notion of abundance is maintained in the language throughout – 'teeming' means both overflowing with and swarming with; 'high-pilèd' is stacked high; the granaries, or 'garners' are 'rich'; the cloudy symbols are 'Huge' – until everything is shrunk to 'nothingness' by the thought of death in the final line. The imagery of nature represents creativity and productivity – the harvest of 'full-ripened grain'; the stars and clouds moving in the sky like stories – but also destruction – the final two lines contemplate the sea, that featureless 'nothingness' devouring everything on land, just as time devours life. Similarly, the imagery of magic and fairies, as in many other poems by Keats, captures the enchantments of love and poetry – 'the magic hand of chance', 'the faery power/Of unreflecting love'.

This is a Shakespearian sonnet, that is, the fourteen lines are divided into three quatrains and a couplet, with an A-B-A-B/C-D-C-D/E-F-E-F/G-G rhyming scheme. The rhythm of the first three quatrains is cumulative, like three waves breaking in sequence on a shore. They reinforce the same thought or feeling by repeating it from different angles or in different ways. The final couplet usually offers the conclusion of the thought, the release of the feeling. If you reduce the current sonnet to the opening phrases in each section, you'll easily see both the pattern itself and the point of it: 'When I … When I … And when I … then'. You'll notice that Keats, like all great poets, uses a structure but never gets trapped in a formula – the conclusion begins in the middle of line 12, because this creates a more natural flow of thought.

The first quatrain imagines death ending life before its fulfilment, before Keats has expressed himself fully in writing. The image of an interrupted harvest is used, where the crop is not fully gathered, or 'gleaned', and the grain never ripens.

The second quatrain imagines the same, but with subtle variations. The imagery shifts from the earth to the sky – stars and clouds – and the role of the poet changes from self-expression to recording – the 'shadows' of the moving clouds are traced, not invented. There are stories inside us and stories outside us. The poet must garner both. This quatrain also offers an insight into Keats' mode of writing poetry; a friend reported him as saying 'he never sits down to write, unless he is full of ideas – and then thoughts come about him in troops'.

The third quatrain explores the same idea of unfulfilled promise, but with reference to love rather than poetry. Apparently, the 'fair creature of an hour' was actually a young woman Keats had glimpsed at Vauxhall Gardens in the summer of 1814, almost four years before this sonnet was written in January 1818, but obviously she represents 'the faery power/Of unreflecting love'.

The final two and a half lines capture the sad consequence of all these sad thoughts in a wonderful image of a solitary human standing on the edge of life – 'the shore/Of the wide world' – contemplating the approaching emptiness of the sea.

MAKE

(i) This sonnet opens on an evocation of fear, but do you think this emotion dominates the poem? Consider in particular the structure of the sonnet – three quatrains and a couplet – in tracing its emotions.

(ii) The sonnet speaks of leaving things behind – art, imagination, love. In your opinion, are all three equally important to Keats or is one more important than the other two? Give reasons for your answer.

READ

La Belle Dame Sans Merci

I
O what can ail thee, knight-at-arms,
    Alone and palely loitering?
The sedge has withered from the lake,
    And no birds sing.

II
O what can ail thee, knight-at-arms,   5
    So haggard and so woe-begone?
The squirrel's granary is full,
    And the harvest's done.

III
I see a lily on thy brow,
    With anguish moist and fever-dew,   10
And on thy cheeks a fading rose
    Fast withereth too.

IV
I met a lady in the meads,
    Full beautiful – a faery's child,
Her hair was long, her foot was light,   15
    And her eyes were wild.

V
I made a garland for her head,
    And bracelets too, and fragrant zone;
She looked at me as she did love,
    And made sweet moan.   20

VI
I set her on my pacing steed,
    And nothing else saw all day long,
For sidelong would she bend, and sing
    A faery's song.

VII
She found me roots of relish sweet,   25
    And honey wild, and manna-dew,
And sure in language strange she said –
    'I love thee true'.

VIII
She took me to her elfin grot,
    And there she wept and sighed full sore,   30
And there I shut her wild wild eyes
    With kisses four.

Poetry

IX

And there she lullèd me asleep,
    And there I dreamed – Ah! woe betide! –
The latest dream I ever dreamt
    On the cold hill side.   35

X

I saw pale kings and princes too,
    Pale warriors, death-pale were they all;
They cried – 'La Belle Dame sans Merci
    Hath thee in thrall!'   40

XI

I saw their starved lips in the gloam,
    With horrid warning gapèd wide,
And I awoke and found me here,
    On the cold hill's side.

XII

And this is why I sojourn here   45
    Alone and palely loitering,
Though the sedge is withered from the lake,
    And no birds sing.

Glossary

[title]: French, meaning 'the beautiful woman without mercy'

[3] **sedge:** plant that grows in wet ground

[13] **meads:** meadows

[26] **manna:** sweet substance derived from plants; in the Christian Bible, the miraculous food that saved the Israelites from starvation

[29] **elfin:** belonging or relating to elves

[29] **grot:** grotto, cave

[41] **gloam:** twilight

[45] **sojourn:** temporary stay

ANALYSE

This strangely powerful ballad – in which a knight-at-arms is seduced by a fairylike woman, wakes alone from a warning nightmare, but finds no joy in his escape – has been interpreted, variously, as expressing Keats' ambivalent feelings about an individual woman (Fanny Brawne), about love in general and about poetry. Actually, the full force of the ballad depends on mystery and uncertainty – Who is talking to the knight? What historical period are we in? Where? Who is the lady? Real or imagined? Human or elfin? Where does she go? – and any simple 'explanation' merely takes away from it. One thing is obvious: the ballad deals with enchantment and its hollow aftermath. If you have read Keats' other poems, you'll already be familiar with this recurring theme. In any case, the poem was written by Keats in April 1819, four months after the death of his brother Tom, two months after he himself suffered a severe

haemorrhage, and just two years before his own death, all caused by tuberculosis, some of the symptoms of which – fatigue, chills, fever – form the imagery of this ballad. This context alone offers an understanding of the ballad's life-in-death narrative.

The introductory first three stanzas quiz the knight, describe him and set the scene. The tone is unsettled, baffled. The knight, conventionally a symbol of strength and of life's quest, is here feeble – 'ail … palely … haggard … woe-begone … fever' – and distracted – 'loitering'. The world he inhabits is a waste land – post-apocalyptic in our terms – where everything is 'withered' and silenced by the ravages of winter. Ironically, the flowers of nature don't bloom in the landscape, but symbolically on the knight's face – the 'lily' on his forehead is the emblem of death and the 'fading rose' on his cheeks the flushed hue of ill-health.

The remaining stanzas provide the knight's description of what happened to him. The repetitive rhythm of the ballad is incantatory, resembling the bewildered chant of a man drugged or hypnotised. The imagery brilliantly mimics that of the ballad's opening stanzas, first as contrast, and then as reflection. When the knight first encounters the 'lady' it's in the 'meads', or lush meadows, of splendid summer. The woman's face is 'beautiful', her movement 'light', her eyes alive with promise. The flowers that wither on the knight's face are here used to adorn the woman's. Perhaps the most eloquent phrase, though, is 'sweet moan'. The knight's experience is indeed 'sweet' at this stage – he feeds on it in stanza VII, gorging himself on 'relish sweet' and 'honey wild' and 'manna-dew' – and the word 'moan' suggests the ecstasy of love and pleasure, although it also holds connotations of discomfort and pain and loss. And from this point on, it's the pain and loss that overwhelm the knight. In the next stanza, the woman's expressions are already entirely sorrowful – the 'sweet moan' has become 'wept and sighed full sore'. He closes her eyes, and yet it is he who is lullèd asleep, as if his dependence on her is so absolute that his own life and energy fade with hers. As we often do, he dreams of the last thing he saw while awake, which in this case is death – of humans in 'pale kings … death-pale', of the day and the season in 'gloam', and of enchantment in 'in thrall', which is slavery. He wakes alone to the cold, empty, meaningless aftermath, to the chilling awareness that everything – love, enchantment, ecstasy, life itself perhaps – is a mere 'sojourn', or temporary stay.

(i) Part of the unsettling effect of this ballad is created by the chanting use of repetition. Pick out some examples of recurring words or phrases and comment on their effect.

(ii) In your opinion, is this ballad about the emptiness of love, the emptiness of dreaming, or the emptiness of ecstasy? Give reasons for your answer.

To Autumn

I

Season of mists and mellow fruitfulness,
    Close bosom-friend of the maturing sun,
Conspiring with him how to load and bless
    With fruit the vines that round the thatch-eves run;
To bend with apples the mossed cottage-trees,   5
    And fill all fruit with ripeness to the core;
        To swell the gourd, and plump the hazel shells
    With a sweet kernel; to set budding more,
And still more, later flowers for the bees,
Until they think warm days will never cease,   10
        For summer has o'er-brimmed their clammy cells.

II

Who hath not seen thee oft amid thy store?
    Sometimes whoever seeks abroad may find
Thee sitting careless on a granary floor,
    Thy hair soft-lifted by the winnowing wind;   15
Or on a half-reaped furrow sound asleep,
    Drowsed with the fume of poppies, while thy hook
        Spares the next swath and all its twinèd flowers;
And sometimes like a gleaner thou dost keep
    Steady thy laden head across a brook;   20
    Or by a cider-press, with patient look,
        Thou watchest the last oozings hours by hours.

III

Where are the songs of Spring? Ay, where are they?
    Think not of them, thou hast thy music too –
While barrèd clouds bloom the soft-dying day,   25
    And touch the stubble-plains with rosy hue:
Then in a wailful choir the small gnats mourn
    Among the river sallows, borne aloft
    Or sinking as the light wind lives or dies;
And full-grown lambs loud bleat from hilly bourn;   30
    Hedge-crickets sing; and now with treble soft
    The redbreast whistles from a garden-croft;
        And gathering swallows twitter in the skies.

Glossary

[4] **eves:** eaves, part of a building's roof that overhangs the walls

[7] **gourd:** fleshy, edible fruit

[18] **swath:** a row or line of crops

ANALYSE

Poetry

This is the third of Keats' great odes on your course, but whereas 'Ode to a Nightingale' and 'Ode on a Grecian Urn' reach unsuccessfully for permanence, this perfectly structured poem is, at last, an ode to transience – the beauty of autumn can occur only in that specific season and is actually dependant on the passing of time.

The first stanza evokes the abundance and ripeness of autumn before the harvest, focuses on the world of vegetation, and uses predominantly tactile imagery. The second stanza captures the reaping of the harvest itself, focuses on human activity, and employs predominantly visual imagery. The final stanza describes the bareness of the autumn landscape after the harvest but before winter, focuses on wildlife, and uses predominantly auditory imagery. The form of the poem is similar to the earlier odes, but is more tightly structured – the poem also moves from the morning of 'maturing sun' to the evening of 'gathering swallows' – with each stanza containing eleven lines, including a rhyming couplet.

The opening stanza evokes the ripeness and abundance – 'swell', 'plump', 'budding', 'o'er-brimmed' – of the vegetable world – 'fruit', 'vines', 'apples', 'gourd', 'hazel', 'flowers'. The effect is of a ripe fullness poised in the moment before it pops. The sounds are of languor and indolence – the rotund alliteration of 'mists … mellow … maturing'; the muggy feel of 'mossed cottage-trees' and 'clammy'. Nothing moves. Everything is suspended. The rhythm of the lines is of accumulation – 'With … To bend … And fill … To swell … With … And still more'.

The second stanza is all about human activity, gathering the harvest. It opens with a question, and questions, even rhetorical ones like this, suggest movement, responses. The first word – 'Who' – introduces the human into the scene, and this is sustained throughout the stanza, specifically by personifying autumn itself, as a female figure reclining in the granary, a labourer resting in the fields, a gleaner steadily watching cider being pressed from apples. It is important to note, however, that the frantic energy of work is only suggested by the details; what we actually see is autumn resting after effort – 'sitting careless', 'asleep', 'Drowsed', 'Steady', 'patient'. The sounds are of rest – the consistent sibilance of 'seeks … careless … soft … asleep' and the rhythm is measured, slowing bit by bit until it reaches the languidness of 'last oozings hours by hours'.

The final stanza wakes with another question, but more sharply delivered – 'Where are the songs of Spring?' The implication is that the songs of spring are full of gaiety and vitality, obviously lacking in autumn, as already captured. Autumn has its own 'music', however – the 'choir' of gnats, the bleating of sheep, the singing of crickets, the whistling of birds. The details are of the fading of the day and the approach of winter – both the robin and the 'gathering swallows' are associated with this season – and the references are to decline, and ultimately to death – 'soft-dying day', 'stubble', 'wailful', 'sinking'.

All four seasons are either mentioned – 'summer', 'Spring' – or suggested – autumn and winter – in the poem, which therefore celebrates the cycle of life, not just a single period of the year, although autumn is the most perfect symbolically, because it holds the entire process – birth, growth, maturation and approaching death – within itself.

MAKE

(i) Select examples of the sensuous imagery in each stanza – respectively, tactile, visual and auditory – and comment on its effectiveness in evoking an aspect of the autumn season.

(ii) It has been said that in this ode Keats achieved ease and acceptance. What features, in your opinion – sounds, images, thoughts, feelings – communicate this ease and acceptance?

Poetry

READ

Bright star! would I were steadfast as thou art

Bright star! would I were steadfast as thou art—
    Not in lone splendour hung aloft the night
And watching, with eternal lids apart,
    Like nature's patient, sleepless Eremite,
The moving waters at their priestlike task   5
    Of pure ablution round earth's human shores,
Or gazing on the new soft-fallen mask
    Of snow upon the mountains and the moors—
No—yet still steadfast, still unchangeable,
    Pillowed upon my fair love's ripening breast,   10
To feel for ever its soft swell and fall,
    Awake for ever in a sweet unrest,
Still, still to hear her tender-taken breath,
And so live ever—or else swoon to death.

Glossary

[4] **Eremite:** Christian hermit or recluse
[6] **ablution:** cleansing, ceremonial washing

ANALYSE

This sonnet is perhaps the best known of Keats' poems, particularly since it provided the title for Jane Campion's stimulating 2009 film on the poet's life, *Bright Star.* The date of its composition is much disputed. We know that Keats' love, Fanny Brawne, transcribed it into her copy of Dante's poems in November 1819, and that therefore the poem is associated with her, but an earlier version also exits from October 1818, probably before Keats met Fanny.

In the opening of the first section of the sonnet, the octave, Keats yearns to be 'steadfast', thinking of the North Star in the skies as an image of permanence. It's a wish that is familiar from other Keats poems – the desire to hold the moment, to hold the beauty, to freeze the ecstasy. The North Star has the disadvantage of being solitary – it hangs there 'in lone splendour' – but otherwise it seems the perfect symbol of the eternally fortunate spectator, forever gazing from an unchanging distance on all that is beautiful about earth, the purity of its waters and its snow – 'pure ablution' – the magnificence of its landscape. Significantly, there are no humans visible in this ideal picture of our world, since the perspective is too distant to include them. Equally significantly, there are intimations of dissatisfaction in all this celebration of splendour, quite

Poetry

apart from the fact that the star is alone. For instance, surely a form that is 'sleepless' is actually lifeless, in any human sense; and surely something that is merely watching is not a participant in life?

These implied inadequacies in using the star as an image of permanence are developed more openly in the second section of the sonnet, the sestet, which begins with the bold negative 'No'. That 'No' is a rejection of the drawbacks, the solitariness, the distance, the lack of engagement, the absence of emotion, merely watching life; but it is followed by a restating of the desire for permanence – 'yet still steadfast'. Permanence in what, though? In human love, beautifully captured in the tender, sensual imagery of 'Pillowed upon my fair love's ripening breast'. You can't have life without breath. You can't have love without heartbeat. You can't have either without the knowledge that both will fade, and die. You can't have life without motion. You can't have movement without change. You can't have change without decline. That's why it's all a 'sweet unrest', even at its most gentle – 'ripening breast … soft swell and fall … tender-taken breath'. You can't have life without death. You can't be unmoving, like the North Star, without being unmoved. You can't have permanence in human love – 'And so live ever—or else swoon to death'. We are not stars, no matter how bright. We are not watchers, but participants, actors; loving, breathing, dying forms.

MAKE

(i) The contrast in the imagery is between the stillness of the star – 'steadfast' – and the movements of the earth – 'moving waters'. Isn't it impossible for Keats to have the former without leaving the latter? Give reasons for your response.

(ii) The sound effects are dominated by sibilance here – the hissing *s* sound. Pick out some examples and comment on how you believe they contribute to the atmosphere of the sonnet.

The Poetry of John Keats

Themes and Interests

- The poetry of John Keats uncovers the **PAIN** and **DISCONTENT** at the heart of human life, what he describes as 'The weariness, The fever, and the fret'

Most of the suffering expressed or explored in Keats' poetry emerges directly from the acute awareness of life's transience, a not unexpected note in the work of a young poet whose immediate family fell victim to tuberculosis, a lingering illness that doesn't arrive suddenly or finish you off quickly, and who succumbed to the disease himself at twenty-five. Even in the midst of joy and pleasure and celebration, Keats never loses sight of time passing. In 'To one who has been long in city pent', the 'one' who has spent a blissful day of ease and escape in the country 'mourns' at the end of it 'that day so soon has glided by'. Of course, such awareness can give a peculiar intensity to your engagement with life, but it can also find expression in deep despair, gloom and alienation. The consciousness of it in 'Ode to a Nightingale' inspires one of the greatest and most terrifying visions of life's troubles – 'Here, where men sit and hear each other groan' – and in 'La Belle Dame Sans Merci' gives rise to a nightmare of horror – 'I saw their starved lips in the gloam,/With horrid warning gapèd wide'. In 'Ode on a Grecian Urn', 'breathing human passion' – that is, the intensity of living, of human engagement with life – leaves 'a heart high-sorrowful and cloyed'. The repeated use of words such as 'sorrow', 'sorrowful', 'sad' and 'mourn' is notable in the poetry. It's only in 'To Autumn' that the passing of time is accepted, not only as natural, but as necessary. The ripeness of autumn is a stage in the cycle of life; or to put it another way, without the cycle there would be no ripeness, no fertility. Elsewhere, though, the unavoidable ticking of the clock brings fear – 'When I have fears that I may cease to be/Before my pen has gleaned my teeming brain' – and heartache – 'My heart aches, and a drowsy numbness pains/My sense' – and frustration – 'And so live ever—or else swoon to death' – and despair – 'And on thy cheeks a fading rose/Fast withereth too'.

- The poetry of John Keats presents the enchantments of **LOVE** and **BEAUTY** and **NATURE** as consolations for and escapes from human suffering

The escape from the imprisonment of the city in 'To one who has been long in city pent' is to the country, or nature, a common enough notion in nineteenth-century life and literature, and indeed still popular in contemporary life. It's interesting to note, though, that such an escape is described as breathing with ease – 'to breathe a prayer' – because to breathe, in one form or another, occurs in a number of poems, including 'On First Looking into Chapman's Homer' ('breathe its pure serene'), 'Ode on a Grecian Urn' ('All breathing human passion far above'), 'Ode to a Nightingale' ('to take into the air my quiet breath') and 'Bright Star' ('Still, still to hear her tender-taken breath'). It's not irrelevant that tuberculosis, the disease Keats suffered from and died of, is caught by breathing in infected air and manifests itself afterwards as shortness of breath. In most of the poems, nature therefore offers air that is fresh and nourishing and healthy, and thereby an escape from the pains and burdens of life, the exception being 'To Autumn', where the season's ripeness is also the beginning of the season's decay, unless the fruits are harvested and used, although even here the death of autumn also heralds the approaching freshness of winter – 'gathering swallows twitter in the skies'. Love offers the purest air in the beautiful imagery of 'Bright Star' ('To feel for ever its soft swell and fall') but also an atmosphere so rarefied that men cannot stay awake in it in 'La Belle Dame Sans Merci' ('And there she lullèd me asleep'). Enchantment, as always in Keats, is both intoxicating and sapping.

- The poetry of John Keats presents the **ENCHANTMENT OF ART** as a release from human suffering and the creation of beauty, ease and immortality

Art is explicitly the subject of 'On First Looking into Chapman's Homer', which features the classical epics of Homer, 'Ode on a Grecian Urn', which takes as its symbolic object a classical urn, and 'When I have fears that I may cease to be', which reflects on Keats' own writing. In all three, art is experienced as the opening out and discovery of new and magical worlds. 'On First Looking into Chapman's Homer' explicitly uses as a metaphor the discovery of new worlds by the Spanish explorer Cortez, 'when with eagle eyes/He stared at the Pacific'. The image here is of a vast, uncharted, spectacular ocean. Keep in mind that Cortez and his men are sailors. To discover new *lands* may please the statesman and merchants. To discover a new ocean, for a sailor, is to open out new journeys, new adventures, a renewal of life. The same magical feeling is present in the other metaphor in this sonnet, that of an astronomer discovering a new planet. In 'Ode on a Grecian Urn', the figurative exploration is not through space, but through time – the urn comes to us from a distant past as a 'foster-child of … slow time' – and through the soul – the urn doesn't speak of or to the physical world, but pipes 'to the spirit ditties of no tone'. It's a mysterious, magical world – count the number of … increasingly baffled questions about it – which draws the poem into itself, from the opening contemplation of the entire object to the minute details on the illustration, and then back out again – 'O Attic shape' – to consider the object from a distance once more, and to reflect on its significance. Art, the final stanza suggests, 'dost tease us out of thought'. And indeed, that is what has actually happened in the progress of the poem itself. Its enchantment releases us from absorption in our own woes and enables us to touch, at least for a while, both beauty and immortality. It also reminds us, however, that we can touch these things only for a while. A similar notion of art as exploration, discovery, magic and teasing us out of thought is clearly captured in the expressive description 'Huge cloudy symbols of a high romance' that are traced 'with the magic hand of chance' in 'When I have fears that I may cease to be', which compares Keats' own writing to a harvest and worries that it may not be gathered before death, or winter, comes. In a sense, the nightingale's song in 'Ode to a Nightingale' is obviously also a symbolic representation of art, although in the same poem the imagination fails because 'the dull brain perplexes and retards' and Keats is unable to take flight on 'the viewless wings of Poesy', although we may well ask how the imagination can be failing in the actual composition of a poem. But this is the inherent paradox that informs all of Keats' work. Art is both ease and struggle at the one time. It is the magical country of the soul in a physical world, a perfection in the midst of defect, a stillness caught in the process of living, a symbol of immortality in the midst of decay.

- The poetry of John Keats dramatises the **IRONIC PARADOX** that imagining beauty, since we cannot sustain it, makes the ordinary world even more painful

The ironies of existence could not have been lost on a man for whom oxygen was both life and death – his tuberculosis, which killed him at twenty-five, was contracted by breathing, an activity to which the only alternative is not breathing. In a sense, we're all trapped in the same paradox, of course; it was just a lot more acute with Keats. In his celebration of the magic of art, 'On First Looking into Chapman's Homer', when he is describing the awe-struck Cortez looking out as the first European on the Pacific Ocean, it is surely not without an awareness of what subsequently happened in the Spanish colonisation of Mexico – the destruction of the Aztec empire and civilisation, the long history of imperial occupation and suppression. When he imagines love, tenderly and beautifully, in 'Bright Star', it is while listening to the soft, but finite, breathing of his beloved. The ironies of life are inescapable. Love, for all its enchantments, ultimately reminds us of our own mortality. We cannot attain in love the steadfastness, or permanence, of the North Star. The star is indifferent, inactive, distant, uninvolved – it is unmoving because it is unmoved – and these things are the antithesis of love. The nightingale in 'Ode to a Nightingale' is audible but elusive, apparently within reach but actually out of reach, as are the qualities it represents – beauty, melody, expression, ease, immortality. Similarly, the illustrations on the urn in 'Ode on a Grecian Urn' apparently depict the intensity of life – love, ritual, music – but are actually lifeless. This is the paradox of art. This is the paradox of contemplating beauty – it sharpens awareness of the opposite. In most of the poems, the attempt to escape the limitations of the self – 'The weariness, the fever, and the fret' – leaves the poet with a much more acute sense of himself – the pronoun 'I' anchors every stanza of 'Ode to a Nightingale', forbidding flight; the insistent questions of 'Ode on a Grecian Urn' keep the striving human spectator in constant view; the opening address to the star in 'Bright Star' quickly rejects its 'lone splendour' and closes with the awareness of love's mortality. It's only in 'To Autumn' that nothing is reached for, that no escape is sought, that the ironies of life are accepted and celebrated; and as a result this is the only poem where, ironically, ease is absolutely achieved.

Style and Viewpoint

- The poetry of John Keats is sensuous, which means that its **LANGUAGE**, although remaining colloquial, is descriptively luxuriant, rich, lush

Sensuous language attempts to capture the sensation of an experience, physical, emotional and psychological. It therefore has an immediacy that is quite different from the distance required in reflective or analytical language. The expression is richer and more complex, appealing to all five senses as well as to the mind and articulating intense emotions. As readers of Keats, we are always *in* the experience itself – catching the song of the nightingale as it happens, turning the Grecian urn to follow its details, questioning the doomed knight in 'La Belle Dame Sans Merci', observing the North Star in 'Bright Star'. 'Ode to a Nightingale', for instance, opens *in* pain, not just with the awareness of pain or with a description of pain – 'My heart aches' – drawing on tactile sensations for its evocation of dullness and sluggishness – 'a drowsy numbness pains/My sense' – and then using sparkling auditory and visual images – 'Singest', 'beechen green' – to contrast the joy of the bird. The second stanza jumps immediately to yearning – quite understandably – and again it is the *sensation* of longing that is expressed, through predominantly gustatory detail this time, evoking the cool taste of wine drawn from the earth to quench an acute thirst. After a despairing insight into man's lot in the third stanza, this yearning is given more desperate voice in the next stanza – 'Away! away!' – a move that blunders into darkness and thoughts of 'easeful Death', before we hear, simultaneously with the poet, the fading song of the departing nightingale 'buried deep/In the next valley-glades'. Throughout, the language has *been* the experience, if we can put it like that, not merely describing or evoking it. There is no distance between the expression and the sensation at any stage; they are always one – 'My heart aches … O, for a draught of vintage! … Away! away! … I cannot see … I listen … Forlorn!' The same is true of all Keats' poems on your course – the language *is* the experience – but one more example will be useful. 'Ode on a Grecian Urn' opens on a rather quiet contemplation of an art object – 'Sylvan historian' – but quickly becomes excited by the drama on the urn – 'What mad pursuit? What struggle to escape?' – until there is no longer any gap between poet and object, By stanza two, Keats is more or less on the urn himself, intimately addressing its figures – 'Fair youth, beneath the trees'. The poem is dramatising the sensation of absorption in a work of art, creating the experience itself through its sensuous language – sounds, tactile feelings, sights – and not merely describing the experience.

- The poetry of John Keats employs nature, art, music, song and sensory detail as symbolic **IMAGERY** to capture the intense experience of living, and uses mythology and fable as reference

As mentioned above, nature for Keats symbolically represents freedom from constriction, as well as beauty and, ultimately, in 'To Autumn', the rhythm and cycle of life itself, including human life. It occurs throughout Keats' work as dominant imagery, most literally in 'To one who has been long in city pent', where it is described as the 'open face of heaven'. The bird in 'Ode to a Nightingale' is both part of and an expression of nature; the sea becomes a metaphor for mystery and imagination in 'On First Looking into Chapman's Homer' and a symbol of purity in 'Bright Star'; landscape is apocalyptic in 'La Belle Dame Sans Merci'; and the Grecian urn depicts a rural scene and is a 'Sylvan historian'. There is hardly an aspect of nature – sea, sky, landscape, fruit, crops, birds – that is not celebrated and used symbolically in Keats' poetry. Art, of course, offers the deepest enchantment for Keats, and, significantly, art often depicts a scene from nature, as in the details from 'Ode on a Grecian Urn', or else is depicted by means of nature imagery, as in 'On First Looking into Chapman's Homer', where the wonder of reading is compared to an explorer contemplating new territory, and in 'When I have fears that I may cease to be', where writing is understood in terms of the harvest. Song and music are obviously artistic expressions and also features of harvest celebrations, and so, for Keats, they link art and nature in his imagery, most notably in the bird's song in 'Ode to a Nightingale'. The figures on the Grecian urn include the youth serenading his love and the celebrants at the sacrifice playing 'pipes and timbrels'. The knight's blindness in 'La Belle Dame Sans Merci' is in part induced by song – 'For sidelong would she bend, and sing/A faery's song.' In 'To Autumn', the seasons are distinguished by their music, the jaunty 'songs of Spring' contrasting with the more sombre notes of autumn, the 'wailful choir' of gnats,

the singing of the 'Hedge-crickets', the twittering of the 'gathering swallows'. Song and music appeal to the ear, but all the other senses also provide rich imagery for Keats – taste in 'roots of relish sweet,/And honey wild, and manna-dew' ('La Belle Dame Sans Merci'); sight in 'Watching the sailing cloudlet's bright career' ('To one who has been long in city pent'); touch in 'To feel for ever its soft swell and fall' ('Bright Star'); and smell in 'guess each sweet … grass … the fruit-tree … violets … musk-rose' from the blinded fifth stanza of 'Ode to a Nightingale', where vision is closed off – to mention a few examples. Classical literature and reference books were part of the standard reading of an educated person in Keats' time, so there is nothing forced about the classical allusions in the poet's work; they are as natural a point of reference as nature itself. They are present in almost every poem, from the use of Philomel as a synonym for a nightingale in 'To one who has been long in city pent', through Apollo, Homer and Cortez in 'On First Looking into Chapman's Homer', and Bacchus and Ruth in 'Ode to a Nightingale', to the Grecian urn itself as the central object in the poem that it gives its name to.

- The poetry of John Keats uses intricate and at times luxuriant **SOUND** patterns to recreate intense emotions and feelings

By far the best and most enjoyable approach here is to take specific examples. Consider, for instance, how the repeated and varied use of *ee* sounds in 'To one who has been long in city pent' communicates a sense both of weariness and of rest, expressing the thematic tensions of the sonnet – 'sweet … breathe … Fatigued … evening … ear … career … E'en … tear … clear ether'. Explore the use of repetition in 'La Belle Dame Sans Merci', first in the incantatory metre that imprisons you within its beat and then in the recurrence of certain phrases, a recurrence that expresses bewilderment and captivity – 'I met … I made … I set'; 'She found … She took … she lullèd'; 'I saw … I saw'. Examine the effectiveness of sibilance in 'Bright Star', beginning with the soft and mysterious sound of 'star' itself and following the echoes in 'steadfast … splendour … sleepless … priestlike task … gazing', and so on, appreciating how it perfectly captures that yearning for ease that so dominates the sonnet and that comes so close to a death-wish in the final sibilance of 'or else swoon to death'. Consider the subtleties of rhyme in 'When I have fears that I may cease to be'. End rhyme is not just a system for creating pleasing sound patterns, although it does that, but also a way of associating hitherto unrelated words in imaginative ways, whether to contrast or compare, and also a way of stressing important images or thoughts. In this sonnet, 'brain' and 'grain' are drawn together by rhyme, for instance, reinforcing the metaphor that creative literary work has the character and rhythm of a harvest, and though the sentences containing them run on without punctuation, the fact that 'trace' in line 7 and 'power' in line 11 rhyme with earlier sounds forces us to stress them more than we would otherwise do. Finally, explore rhythm in the fifth stanza of 'Ode to a Nightingale', where the sensation of groping blindly and being entangled in lush vegetation is replicated by the laboured movement of the verse, created in part by the clogging sounds of individual words such as 'embalmèd' and 'Wherewith', in part by gluing words together that are difficult to enunciate in sequence, such as 'seasonable month endows', and in part by punctuation and line endings, as in 'The grass, the thicket, and the fruit-tree wild'.

- The poetry of John Keats employs a wide range of traditional poetic **FORMS**, such as the sonnet, the ballad and the ode, and always brings something new and distinctive to each

There are four sonnets by Keats on your course, three odes, and one ballad. Two of the sonnets – 'To one who has been long in city pent' and 'On First Looking into Chapman's Homer' – are predominantly Petrarchan (also called Italian) sonnets. The Petrarchan sonnet consists of two distinct sections, an octave, setting a 'question', and a sestet, providing a 'resolution', with a volta, or turn in thought, mood or tone, in line 9. It also has a regular rhyming scheme, usually A-B-B-A-A-B-B-A for the two-quatrain octave, and C-D-C-D-C-D for the sestet. By and large, Keats follows the rules, but since he's not interested in just an intellectual exercise, not interested in advancing an 'argument', but more interested in capturing human experience, he also bends those rules. In neither sonnet is the sestet quite distinct from the octave, with the result that the poems are more fluid, more naturalistic, and more tuned to the irregularities of human feeling and thought than more standard models. 'When I have fears that I may cease to be' is predominantly a Shakespearean (also called Elizabethan or English) sonnet. This type of sonnet usually consists of three quatrains and a couplet, with the volta occurring in the couplet. Again with Keats, though, the fluid movement of the feelings and thoughts overrides the strict adherence to the form. 'Bright Star' combines elements of the two sonnet forms to handle the complexities of both wanting to be like and not like the North Star, the 'sweet unrest' of line 12. The ballad is a narrative verse form, often set to music, and therefore with its own strict schemes of metre and rhyme. 'La Belle Dame Sans Merci' uses these conventions, but manages to create an incantatory rhythm that is quite spooky and an atmosphere of dread and mystery that is way beyond the capabilities of the standard ballad. It's in the odes, however, that Keats found his fullest expression as a poet. As practised in England, the ode has certain conventions – it's a lyrical celebration of something or someone, with a standard rhyming scheme – but beyond these general requirements, it's not restrictive. This combination of shape and freedom seems to have inspired Keats more than any other poetic form, and his five great odes written in 1819, three of which are on your course, are not only among the best in the language, but also the last major examples of this form in English poetry. Each of the odes is beautifully structured in a formal way – 'Ode to a Nightingale', for instance, consists of eight stanzas of ten lines each and uses a standard A-B-A-B-C-D-E-C-D-E rhyming scheme – but each also reads as an utterly spontaneous expression of feeling and thought.

471

Sylvia Plath

Sylvia Plath was born in 1932, in Boston, Massachusetts, USA. As was customary, her mother relinquished her career as an educator when she married. Her father died in 1940. On the surface, Plath was an enviable high achiever – talented, academically successful, attractive, popular – but she was also prone to depression and attempted suicide in August 1953, by swallowing sleeping pills. In 1955, she won a scholarship to study in Cambridge, where she met a young English poet named Ted Hughes. They married in 1956 and lived and worked together in Cambridge, America, London and Devon, where

they finally parted. In mid-December 1962, Plath moved back to London with her two children, Frieda and Nicholas. On 11 February 1963, ill with flu, unable to cope, she sealed off a room so that her children would not be harmed by the fumes and then she gassed herself to death. She was thirty years old. She considered her life, personally and professionally, a failure. She is now one of the most important – certainly one of the most debated – of modern poets.

Prescribed Poems

'Students at Higher Level will be required to study a representative selection from the work of eight poets: a representative selection would seek to reflect the range of a poet's themes and interests and exhibit his/her characteristic style and viewpoint. Normally the study of at least six poems by each poet would be expected.' (DES English Syllabus, 6.3)

Themes and Interests

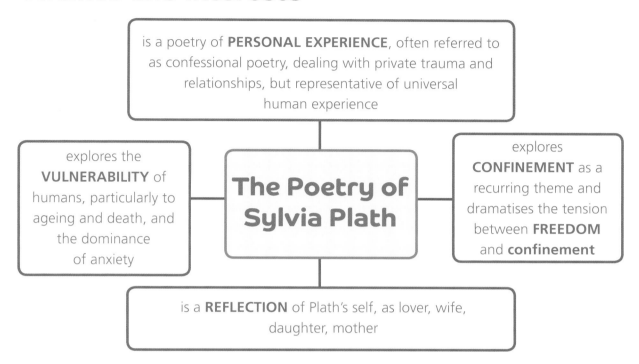

is a poetry of **PERSONAL EXPERIENCE**, often referred to as confessional poetry, dealing with private trauma and relationships, but representative of universal human experience

explores the **VULNERABILITY** of humans, particularly to ageing and death, and the dominance of anxiety

The Poetry of Sylvia Plath

explores **CONFINEMENT** as a recurring theme and dramatises the tension between **FREEDOM** and **confinement**

is a **REFLECTION** of Plath's self, as lover, wife, daughter, mother

Style and Viewpoint

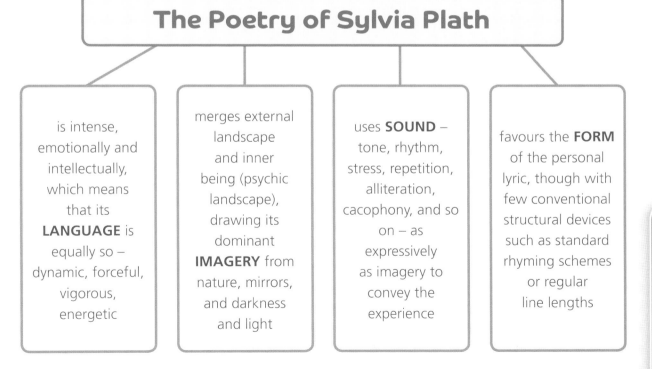

The Poetry of Sylvia Plath

is intense, emotionally and intellectually, which means that its **LANGUAGE** is equally so – dynamic, forceful, vigorous, energetic

merges external landscape and inner being (psychic landscape), drawing its dominant **IMAGERY** from nature, mirrors, and darkness and light

uses **SOUND** – tone, rhythm, stress, repetition, alliteration, cacophony, and so on – as expressively as imagery to convey the experience

favours the **FORM** of the personal lyric, though with few conventional structural devices such as standard rhyming schemes or regular line lengths

Poetry

READ

Poetry

Black Rook in Rainy Weather

On the stiff twig up there
Hunches a wet black rook
Arranging and rearranging its feathers in the rain.
I do not expect a miracle
Or an accident   5

To set the sight on fire
In my eye, nor seek
Any more in the desultory weather some design,
But let spotted leaves fall as they fall,
Without ceremony, or portent.   10

Although, I admit, I desire,
Occasionally, some backtalk
From the mute sky, I can't honestly complain:
A certain minor light may still
Lean incandescent   15

Out of kitchen table or chair
As if a celestial burning took
Possession of the most obtuse objects now and then—
Thus hallowing an interval
Otherwise inconsequent   20

By bestowing largesse, honor,
One might say love. At any rate, I now walk
Wary (for it could happen
Even in dull, ruinous landscape); skeptical,
Yet politic; ignorant   25

Of whatever angel may choose to flare
Suddenly at my elbow. I only know that a rook
Ordering its black feathers can so shine
As to seize my senses, haul
My eyelids up, and grant   30

A brief respite from fear
Of total neutrality. With luck,
Trekking stubborn through this season
Of fatigue, I shall
Patch together a content   35

Of sorts. Miracles occur,
If you care to call those spasmodic
Tricks of radiance miracles. The wait's begun again,
The long wait for the angel,
For that rare, random descent.   40

Glossary

[8] **desultory:** random, without a pattern

[10] **portent:** sign or omen, usually of the future

[15] **incandescent:** shining brilliantly

[17] **celestial:** heavenly

[18] **obtuse:** dull, stupid or insensitive

[19] **hallowing:** making holy

[21] **largesse:** generosity, great gifts

[25] **politic:** cautious, cagey, practical

[37] **spasmodic:** in fits and starts

When describing a landscape, Plath always focused on those features of the external world that expressed her own inner turmoil, and the opening scene here is a good introduction to this aspect of Plath's poetry, usually referred to as psychic landscape.

Everything about the scene is gloomy: wet, rain, the colour black and even the posture – 'Hunches' – of the bird, which suggests a life curled up, suffering, more or less defeated. Only more or less, though, because the bird still puts in an effort, arranging and rearranging its feathers; in other words, getting ready for flight, if and when flight is possible again.

On one level, lines 6–10 sound fatalistic and gloomy: nothing will change for the better, probably, and even if the weather improves it doesn't mean anything for me. On another level, it indicates a calm acceptance. First, there is the presence of 'Any more', suggesting that previously Plath drove herself to despair searching for insights, visions ('set the sight on fire/In my eye'), illuminations and the rest. She will not punish herself any more by expecting miracles. Secondly, there is the calm, measured rhythm of the lines and the relaxed tone. Both tone and rhythm are sustained throughout the poem, indicating that this is really a hopeful piece, for all its gloomy opening. Not optimistic, because optimism is active, whereas the mood of this poem is one of waiting – note the phrases throughout that indicate uncertainty: 'Although', 'may still', 'Wary', 'I only know', 'With luck'.

Notice how the hesitancy, the uncertainty, is expressed through the punctuation and structure in lines 11–13. It's impossible to say the lines quickly, with any energy. And, in fact, you could say that lack of energy, listlessness, is the poem's real theme. It may be difficult to understand how the sky, or a kitchen chair in the next section, can talk back or suddenly become a source

ANALYSE

Poetry

of light. But we all freely use the expressions 'life is good at the moment', 'life is dull at the moment', 'things are brightening up'. Life always contains possibilities of illumination.

The mood of the poem is a balance between hope and a kind of gloomy uncertainty. This is the first section where they occur together. The uncertainty is present in the phrasing – 'may still', 'As if' and 'One might say' – and in the words suggesting lack of importance, such as 'obtuse objects' and 'inconsequent'. The hope is captured through images of spiritual brightness and energy – the most complex of which is 'celestial burning' because 'burning' involves both energy and light – and in the qualities 'largesse', 'love'.

Again, you will notice the combination of a listless uncertainty – 'At any rate', 'Wary', 'skeptical', 'politic' – with the hope of sudden release, sudden elevation from the dull and mundane ('ruinous landscape') to an intense, spiritual experience. The word 'flare' continues the imagery of intense energy expressed through burning, and of course 'angel' continues the spiritual strain.

The theme of the poem – the possibility that gloom can always be lifted – now returns to the starting point, the rook, for a final expression. The rook is hunched and wet, but can still change, still shine. It is the sudden flap of the wings – the angel at her elbow also has wings? – that captures her interest and sustains her hope. However – most important – the bird has not yet flown. 'I only know that … [it] can', she writes. The poem is about possibility, not achievement.

What continues to dominate is the hope, although an uncertain hope. The phrases 'With luck' and 'Of sorts' stress this mood again. Even the phrase 'Trekking stubborn', which means going doggedly on, not giving up, indicates this. It's not optimism, as you can see. It's hope, the reason for which is explored in the final stanza.

This final stanza perfectly illustrates the hopeful uncertainty that dominates the poem. First there is the definite statement: 'Miracles occur'. But this is immediately qualified. Well, she says, you can hardly call what I experience a real miracle. It's good, it's welcome, but it's also something less than a miracle, which does, after all, restore life to the dead, and I'm only talking about restoring light to the gloomy. The poem ends, not with this uncertainty, however, but with hope. And perhaps patience. Waiting, obviously, is not a pleasant experience, but it is better than nothing, better, in other words, than 'neutrality'.

MAKE

(i)   What, in your opinion, is the theme of this poem – depression, loss of inspiration, hope, despair? Support your choice with reasons and with relevant quotations.

(ii) The atmosphere of this poem is dominated, as the title suggests, by the weather. Pick out the imagery relating to the weather and comment on the meaning and effectiveness of each example.

The Times Are Tidy

Unlucky the hero born
In this province of the stuck record
Where the most watchful cooks go jobless
And the mayor's rôtisserie turns
Round of its own accord.   5

There's no career in the venture
Of riding against the lizard,
Himself withered these latter-days
To leaf-size from lack of action:
History's beaten the hazard.   10

The last crone got burnt up
More than eight decades back
With the love-hot herb, the talking cat,
But the children are better for it
The cow milks cream an inch thick.   15

Glossary

[2] **stuck record:** before the dominance of CDs and downloads, people listened to music on vinyl records, on which the playing needle sometimes got stuck in a damaged groove and played the same bar of music over and over

[4] **rôtisserie:** revolving roasting spit

[13] **love-hot herb:** a witch's potion for lovers

This little satire on the triviality and inconsequence of the modern world is not one of Plath's best poems and comes from a pretty unproductive period of her writing life, between the energy of her first efforts and the maturity of the later material. The ironic contempt inherent in the title is amusing, because 'tidy' is what every conscientious housewife and mother of the time (1958) required her home to be. It's a specifically domestic word and Plath had her problems with domesticity.

The interesting features from the first stanza that can be related to the other poems include the use of the word 'province' for the modern world – a province is on the periphery, away from the centre of activity. It anticipates other places of isolation such as 'Finisterre' – and the various images of futility and pointless motion – the record stuck in the groove and the rôtisserie revolving by itself – because futility became such a personal issue for this writer, and being stuck in a groove became such a personal fear.

The second stanza suggests that modern life is no longer heroic – a very, very common complaint among twentieth-century poets – represented by the idiocy of riding out like a knight

READ

ANALYSE

Poetry

of old to save ladies from dragons. There are no dragons any more, as Cervantes' Don Quixote discovered a long time ago. In the humorously ironic vocabulary of the poem, the dragon is reduced to the indignity of 'the lizard'. There are no knights either. And possibly, although this is more controversial, no ladies. History – rational progress – has removed all the dangers (the 'hazard') of the old world.

Rational it may be, the final stanza suggests, but it is progress. Women may not be rescued by knights any more, but neither are they burned as witches ('The last crone got burnt up/More than eight decades back'). Nobody believes in magic potions ('the love-hot herb') and magical animals ('the talking cat') and, by and large, people are better for the loss of all that superstition ('The cow milks cream an inch thick'). Perhaps women, no longer concerned about being burned as witches, have devoted their spare time to tidying. The times *are* tidy, after all, as the savagely satiric tone reminds us throughout.

(i) The poem suggests that our modern lives are richer in some respects – the 'cream' has replaced mere milk – and poorer in others – 'Unlucky the hero'. Which side of the argument do you think it favours – richer or poorer – and why?

(ii) The tone here is largely humorous and ironic. Pick out some of the wording or phrasing that expresses Plath's humour and comment on what you consider her intention was.

MAKE

Poetry

Morning Song

Love set you going like a fat gold watch.
The midwife slapped your footsoles, and your bald cry
Took its place among the elements.

Our voices echo, magnifying your arrival. New statue.
In a drafty museum, your nakedness   5
Shadows our safety. We stand round blankly as walls.

I'm no more your mother
Than the cloud that distills a mirror to reflect its own slow
Effacement at the wind's hand.

All night your moth-breath   10
Flickers among the flat pink roses. I wake to listen:
A far sea moves in my ear.

One cry, and I stumble from bed, cow-heavy and floral
In my Victorian nightgown.
Your mouth opens clean as a cat's. The window square   15

Whitens and swallows its dull stars. And now you try
Your handful of notes;
The clear vowels rise like balloons.

Glossary

[title] Frieda, the daughter of Sylvia Plath and Ted Hughes, was born on 1 April 1960 in London. Later the same year, Plath became pregnant again, but she had a miscarriage on 6 February 1961. 'Morning Song' was written shortly after the miscarriage.

[1] **you:** Frieda

[11] **flat pink roses:** describes the wallpaper in the bedroom

Comparisons are the basic building material of poetry, and most of them are unlikely, yanking two things together that have little in common in the 'real' world – even the opening of most Valentine's Day verse, 'My love is like a red, red rose,' is pretty stupid if taken literally – for the very good reason that obvious comparisons are clichés and don't stimulate feeling or thought. Even so, the simile in the first line here, which describes the newly born infant as 'like a fat gold watch', is, at the very least, thought-provoking. You can appreciate its compliments – the child as a gift, as precious, as an independent but still dependant life – but the image is of something cold, mechanical, something that is admired but not warmly loved. An odd image for a young mother to use for her newly born infant, you might think. In any case, it introduces a whole series of images suggesting something vibrant and beautiful, but also cold and rather distant: 'elements', 'New statue', 'drafty museum', 'cloud' and 'mirror'. And yet, as the second part of the poem demonstrates, Plath is a loving, tender, attentive, delighted mother: 'I wake to listen' anxiously to the baby's regular breathing; 'One cry, and I stumble from bed'. What is the meaning of this divided attitude, this apparent contradiction? Is it a tension that all exhausted new mothers feel? Or is it another expression of Plath's peculiarly divided attitude to herself, and through herself to her baby, a division that is captured even in the title of Anne Stevenson's biography of Plath: *Bitter Fame*?

There are two key passages. One is a difficult three-line section – 'I'm no more your mother/ Than the cloud that distills a mirror to reflect its own slow/Effacement at the wind's hand' – which, paraphrased, means: 'I'm no more your mother than a cloud shedding rain is the creator of the resulting pool of water on the ground below, a pool that reflects the clouds as it disappears in the process of shedding the rain.' The cloud gives birth to the pool of water at its own expense. The pool of water is a reflection of the cloud. The cloud doesn't exist any more, except as a reflection. Both the distance and interdependence between the two are terrifying. The woman gives birth to the child at her own expense. The child is a reflection of the mother. The mother doesn't exist any more as a separate person. The central image is that of the mirror. As with everything else, when Plath looked at her own child, she saw only herself, or worse, her own 'Effacement', which means rubbing out or elimination. In other words, Plath saw herself, and saw herself as nothing.

The second key passage refers to the child's 'handful of notes', a lovely phrase for the presumably happy babbling of an infant, its 'clear vowels', rising 'like balloons'. This seems a positive,

Poetry

affirmative, celebratory ending. It opens the possibility of escape, not least for Plath herself. The balloons that are the child's little communications will rise into the air and float to freedom ... until we recall that we are in a bedroom, 'among the flat pink roses', and that the balloons will only hit the ceiling and descend again. They are trapped. And we are drawn back to the other images of dark confinement in the poem – 'a drafty museum', which is the world where the new child, the 'New statue', must take its place; and 'We stand round blankly as walls.'

Like so many of Plath's poems, particularly those dealing with her children – see 'Child' – it reaches out lovingly, hopefully, only to find itself groping in darkness.

MAKE

(i) The word 'Effacement' is at the centre of this poem's reflections. Similar terms occur in other poems, for instance 'neutrality' in 'Black Rook in Rainy Weather' and 'the voice of nothing' in 'Elm'. What is your understanding of its meaning here?

(ii) The central section of this poem, lines 7–9, is very contorted and difficult in its expression, starting with a negative comparison – 'I'm no more' – rather than a clear statement. Identify any other evidence of uncertainty in the poem – phrasing, imagery, hesitant rhythm, and so on – and comment on how it expresses Plath's sense of inadequacy as a new parent.

READ

Finisterre

This was the land's end: the last fingers, knuckled and rheumatic,
Cramped on nothing. Black
Admonitory cliffs, and the sea exploding
With no bottom, or anything on the other side of it,
Whitened by the faces of the drowned.   5
Now it is only gloomy, a dump of rocks—
Leftover soldiers from old, messy wars.
The sea cannons into their ear, but they don't budge.
Other rocks hide their grudges under the water.

The cliffs are edged with trefoils, stars and bells   10
Such as fingers might embroider, close to death,
Almost too small for the mists to bother with.
The mists are part of the ancient paraphernalia—
Souls, rolled in the doom-noise of the sea.
They bruise the rocks out of existence, then resurrect them.   15
They go up without hope, like sighs.
I walk among them, and they stuff my mouth with cotton.
When they free me, I am beaded with tears.

Our Lady of the Shipwrecked is striding toward the horizon,
Her marble skirts blown back in two pink wings.   20
A marble sailor kneels at her foot distractedly, and at his foot
A peasant woman in black
Is praying to the monument of the sailor praying.
Our Lady of the Shipwrecked is three times life size,
Her lips sweet with divinity.   25
She does not hear what the sailor or the peasant is saying—
She is in love with the beautiful formlessness of the sea.

Gull-colored laces flap in the sea drafts
Beside the postcard stalls.
The peasants anchor them with conches. One is told: 30
'These are the pretty trinkets the sea hides,
Little shells made up into necklaces and toy ladies.
They do not come from the Bay of the Dead down there,
But from another place, tropical and blue,
We have never been to.   35
These are our crêpes. Eat them before they blow cold.'

Glossary

[title] **Finisterre** is the extreme western tip of Brittany in France, which Sylvia Plath and Ted Hughes had visited in 1960

[3] **Admonitory:** both criticising and warning, as in 'admonish'

[10] **trefoils:** three-leaved plants

[13] **paraphernalia:** bits and pieces, but **ancient paraphernalia** is guesswork, perhaps the accumulated bits and pieces of the dead past carried by the mists

[19] **Our Lady of the Shipwrecked:** a statue of the Virgin Mary, prayed to on behalf of shipwrecked sailors

[36] **crêpes:** dessert pancakes, originally from France

ANALYSE

When describing a landscape, Plath invariably described herself; or, if you prefer, Plath always focused on those features of the external world that expressed her inner turmoil. Whichever way you put it, 'Finisterre' is the best example on your course of this aspect of Plath's poetry, usually referred to as psychic landscape. 'Finisterre' literally means the land's end, the end of solid ground, the end; and it is similar to 'bottom', the image of extremity and finality used in 'Elm'. Let's examine first the various words and images used to describe this landscape: it is 'knuckled and rheumatic,' meaning old, deformed and diseased; it is pointlessly grasping at the ever-changing, ever-elusive emptiness of the sea, 'Cramped on nothing', where 'Cramped' also contains suggestions of confinement and deformity, of being stunted; it is 'Black' and 'Admonitory', full of that dark, brooding threat that one becomes familiar with in Plath's work; 'gloomy'; a 'dump' where 'Leftover soldiers' who can't 'budge' are discarded; it is shrouded in 'mists'; it is 'without hope'. We are, of course, already familiar with this dark, overwhelming emptiness, that is nonetheless crowded with the ghosts of the past, for – as always in her work – it is Plath herself.

This place is swarming with the dead, enveloped with a sense of death. The cliff face acquired its pale colour from 'the faces of the drowned' being dashed up against it. The land on top is a graveyard of old soldiers mutilated by 'messy wars'. Even the living vegetation, the three-leaved plants, seem to Plath to have been formed by fingers 'close to death', an embroidery that an old lady might pass the time with. The sighs of the dead – their hopelessness disturbingly captured by the image of them throwing their own insubstantiality against the rocks – swirl around in the mists, eternally dashing against the cliff, rising into the air, falling back again to the sea, to dash against the cliff … a vision of pointless circularity, of hell.

Given such bleakness, what can we humans, standing with Plath on the land's end, which is the earth itself, look to for comfort, for support? What can we pray to? The poem's perspective shifts in stanza three to the huge statue of the Virgin Mary, Our Lady of the Shipwrecked, that dominates the cliff top. Another smaller figure of a marble sailor is praying desperately to her, but she is not even aware of him, she is 'striding' towards the sea, in love with its 'beautiful formlessness', in other words, with the very thing that she is supposed to be protecting the

Poetry

sailor from. Significantly, therefore, the old peasant woman is not praying to the distant, uncaring, uninterested giant that is 'Our Lady', but to the pleading sailor, a human like herself. That this sailor is himself praying to the indifferent Lady captures the absurdity and futility of it all. Given such bleakness, what can we look to for comfort? Not to the gods, in any case.

The poem's final stanza withdraws from all this bleakness at the edge of the cliff and returns to what is basically the tourist town behind it. How are we to read this? The place is cheap and tacky, full of 'trinkets' and 'postcard' versions of the landscape, offering 'necklaces' made from shells that come from some beach other than the 'Bay of the Dead', shells that suggest a prettified life, 'tropical and blue', that the inhabitants of this place have never visited or experienced. In other words, the touristy town survives by ignoring the reality of the 'Bay of the Dead', by trivialising everything, by pretending. We do this all the time, of course, since we cannot devote ourselves to living if we are constantly obsessed with death. But is it a good or a bad thing, this make-believe life of ours? In the final line of the poem, Plath is offered the local crêpes, a small, warming nourishment – 'Eat them before they blow cold.' – to drive away the chill of contemplating the dead. Does she accept it? There's no answer. Not in this poem, anyway.

MAKE

(i) 'Plath hardly ever devotes an entire poem to something that looks like mere description of a scene in nature. There is always a metaphorical touch or dimension to the realistic composition.' Do you agree with this assessment of Plath's landscape poetry with reference to 'Finisterre'? Give reasons for your answer.

(ii) Explore the use of sound, as effects and as imagery, in the description of the landscape here. Pay particular attention to cacophony in the opening stanza and onomatopoeia and assonance in subsequent stanzas (see Glossary on page 195).

Mirror

I am silver and exact. I have no preconceptions.
Whatever I see I swallow immediately
Just as it is, unmisted by love or dislike.
I am not cruel, only truthful –
The eye of a little god, four-cornered.   5
Most of the time I meditate on the opposite wall.
It is pink, with speckles. I have looked at it so long
I think it is a part of my heart. But it flickers.
Faces and darkness separate us over and over.

Now I am a lake. A woman bends over me,   10
Searching my reaches for what she really is.
Then she turns to those liars, the candles or the moon.
I see her back, and reflect it faithfully.
She rewards me with tears and an agitation of hands.
I am important to her. She comes and goes.   15
Each morning it is her face that replaces the darkness.
In me she has drowned a young girl, and in me an old woman
Rises toward her day after day, like a terrible fish.

Glossary

[1] **preconceptions:** ideas conceived beforehand

[11] **reaches:** depths

[14] **an agitation of hands:** a wringing of hands, showing anxiety

A mirror speaks, with apparent modesty, but actual smugness. 'I am a mirror,' it says. 'I am silver in colour and I am accurate in what I do, which is to reflect. I have no prejudices about anything that appears in front of me. Whatever comes in front of me, I take in immediately. It could be said that I kill it ('I swallow immediately'), although I do not put it as directly as this. In any case, I take in only what is there. I never distort ('unmisted') things either by loving them' (in which case, you would flatter them) 'or by hating them' (in which case, you would be unfair to them). 'In that sense, I'm completely honest and I'm not cruel' (human beings, by implicit comparison, are both dishonest and cruel). 'I am the eye of a small, rectangular god' (so many people worship mirrors that this seems a reasonable description of itself). 'Most of the time, though, I look only across to the opposite wall, which is pink and speckled, the colour and pattern of the wallpaper there. I have looked at it for so long that it really seems a part of me now; it seems to have grown into my heart. Sometimes, however, others stand in front of me and come between us. Darkness, too, also comes between us.'

'I am also a lake.' (Before glass was invented, people used water to look at their own reflections; the most famous, in the Greek myth, being Narcissus, the beautiful youth who fell in love with his own image and drowned while trying to embrace it. Perhaps the theme of the Narcissus

myth, and therefore of the poem 'Mirror', is that self-absorption is self-destruction.) 'Like Narcissus in the story, a woman bends over me to consider her reflection, searching for what she really is in her reflection. I tell her the truth, of course. I am exact, truthful. I shed light on things. I am not like those creators of shadows and half-light, candles and the moon, both used by lovers when they meet, both unreliable. When she turns away from me, it is to them that she looks. Just as I do with everything else that appears in front of me, I record this movement accurately and show her back. When she returns to me, of course, she is always crying, always wringing her hands in anguish. The candles and the moon, the hope of love, of flattery – these are such disappointments for a woman. Once again I accurately show her to herself. This is why she relies on me so much, this is why I am so important to her. Many things change as time passes. Sometimes she is in front of me, sometimes not. Every morning, though, hers is the first face I see after the darkness of the night. Many things change, as I've said. Once the woman was a young girl, maybe not as beautiful as Narcissus, but as youthful. This young girl she has given to me and I have swallowed it up. Now she is a woman. Every day she gets older, loses more and more of her youth. Every day, when she looks in me, she sees the terrible prospect of being an old woman staring back at her.'

The mirror is represented as neutral ('exact', 'truthful', 'unmisted by love or dislike'), as essential ('I am important to her', worshiped as 'a little god'), as having dangerous depths ('I am a lake', 'Searching my reaches') and as recording the passing of time ('moon', 'morning', 'day after day'). What it reflects is hope of love ('she turns to ... the candles or the moon'), pain (although 'not cruel' itself, it sees the woman's 'tears and an agitation of hands'), the ageing process (from 'young girl' to 'old woman') and death ('drowned a young girl'). Mostly what it reflects is a barrier, though ('Most of the time I meditate on the opposite wall'). All of these concerns are the central themes of Plath's poetry – identity, particularly that of a woman in Western society; love, ageing, death, pain, truth and accuracy, particularly in poetry ('Art,' as Shakespeare wrote, 'holds a mirror up to nature'); and confinement.

MAKE

(i) 'I am … exact,' the mirror claims at the beginning of the poem, meaning 'precise'. Is this claim borne out by the remainder of the poem, in your opinion? Do you think that the mirror is 'exact' and truthful in the poem?

(ii) 'I am silver', the mirror says, claiming riches and illumination, perhaps. Concentrating on the images in the poem, do you think that this claim is borne out? Can the mirror be a source of comforting pleasure and light?

READ

Pheasant

You said you would kill it this morning.
Do not kill it. It startles me still,
The jut of that odd, dark head, pacing

Through the uncut grass on the elm's hill.
It is something to own a pheasant,   5
Or just to be visited at all.

I am not mystical: it isn't
As if I thought it had a spirit.
It is simply in its element.

That gives it a kingliness, a right.   10
The print of its big foot last winter,
The tail-track, on the snow in our court—

The wonder of it, in that pallor,
Through crosshatch of sparrow and starling.
Is it its rareness, then? It is rare.   15

But a dozen would be worth having,
A hundred, on that hill—green and red,
Crossing and recrossing: a fine thing!

It is such a good shape, so vivid.
It's a little cornucopia.   20
It unclaps, brown as a leaf, and loud,

Settles in the elm, and is easy.
It was sunning in the narcissi.
I trespass stupidly. Let be, let be.

Glossary

[title] This poem was written in April 1962, at Court Green in Devon, where Sylvia Plath,
Ted Hughes and their baby daughter, Frieda, had come to live the previous August

[1] **You:** most likely, Ted Hughes

[12] **our court** Court Green, which had a courtyard and a pheasant

[20] **cornucopia:** from the horn of plenty in mythology, meaning abundance

[23] **narcissi:** in spring, apparently, Court Green was covered with beautiful daffodils and narcissi,
which is the plural of narcissus, which is the name of the youth who killed himself when he fell in love
with his own reflection in the water

Poetry

ANALYSE

At times, Plath seemed incapable of celebration without a simultaneous anxiety. Anxiety dominates the two love poems to her children that are on your course, and it is present again here, from the very beginning: 'Do not kill it.'

That 'Pheasant' is a celebration of living beauty, of nature, if you like, and of its powerful effect on Plath herself, is obvious enough. The bird is so impressive that it 'startles' her, an interesting choice of word because it contains elements of fright as well as those of pleasant surprise. It is no conventional, tame beauty, however, since its head is 'odd' – and Plath seemed to enjoy the oddness, the uniqueness of living things, including her own children – and 'pacing', another interesting word, containing not so much suggestions of elegance and grace, but of powerful, purposeful movement. This bird is no cuddly pet. It is its own master and comes to 'visit' the owner of the house, rather than trotting up dutifully when summoned. It is this quality, this independence, this self-sufficiency – and you can understand why the troubled young woman who was Plath would so admire that – that leads to the description of 'kingliness' that the bird possesses, of being just 'right', or of having the 'right' to exist (again the word 'right' here has at least two shades of meaning). Plath is at pains to explain that she is not investing any outside meaning, not forcing her own interpretation on the creature, not distorting it into some spiritual symbol – 'I am not mystical', she says, an echo of a similar reluctance to read 'portents' or 'design' into nature in 'Black Rook in Rainy Weather' – it is just that the thing in itself is so magnificent, 'a good shape', 'vivid', a 'cornucopia'. Magnificent enough and grand enough to give the spectator an uneasy feeling of intruding on so wonderful a life: 'I trespass stupidly.' Magnificent enough to desire more, 'a dozen', a 'hundred', rather than this single one, which is actually threatened. And then we are reminded of the context of all this celebration, of the opening of the poem – 'You said you would kill it this morning./Do not kill it.' The poem now closes with the anxious, repeated plea: 'Let be, let be.' One suspects that this final plea is as much for herself as for the bird. Look back to the sentence that preceded it on the same line – 'I trespass stupidly.' – and think back to all the other poems when the contemplation of something beautiful outside herself was inevitably corrupted by Plath's sudden awareness of her own inadequacy: 'I trespass stupidly.'

MAKE

(i) Basing your answer on a close reading of the details in the poem, what, in your opinion, does the pheasant represent for Plath?

(ii) There are two experiences implicit in the opening lines – being 'startled' by life and being repelled by killing. In your opinion, which of these two tones comes to dominate the poem?

READ

Elm
For Ruth Fainlight

I know the bottom, she says. I know it with my great tap root:
It is what you fear.
I do not fear it: I have been there.

Is it the sea you hear in me,
Its dissatisfactions?   5
Or the voice of nothing, that was your madness?

Love is a shadow.
How you lie and cry after it
Listen: these are its hooves: it has gone off, like a horse.

All night I shall gallop thus, impetuously,   10
Till your head is a stone, your pillow a little turf,
Echoing, echoing.

Or shall I bring you the sound of poisons?
This is rain now, this big hush.
And this is the fruit of it: tin-white, like arsenic.   15

I have suffered the atrocity of sunsets.
Scorched to the root
My red filaments burn and stand, a hand of wires.

Now I break up in pieces that fly about like clubs.
A wind of such violence   20
Will tolerate no bystanding: I must shriek.

The moon, also, is merciless: she would drag me
Cruelly, being barren.
Her radiance scathes me. Or perhaps I have caught her.

I let her go. I let her go   25
Diminished and flat, as after radical surgery.
How your bad dreams possess and endow me.

I am inhabited by a cry.
Nightly it flaps out
Looking, with its hooks, for something to love.   30

I am terrified by this dark thing
That sleeps in me;
All day I feel its soft, feathery turnings, its malignity.

490

Clouds pass and disperse.
Are those the faces of love, those pale irretrievables? 35
Is it for such I agitate my heart?

I am incapable of more knowledge.
What is this, this face
So murderous in its strangle of branches?—

Its snaky acids hiss. 40
It petrifies the will. These are the isolate, slow faults
That kill, that kill, that kill.

Glossary

[title] Like 'Pheasant', this poem was also written in April 1962, at Court Green in Devon, where Sylvia Plath, Ted Hughes and their baby daughter, Frieda, had come to live the previous August; the elm, a wych elm, which is a rough, tough old tree, the name of which is close to 'witch', grew on a mound outside the house

[1] **tap root:** main root, that grows straight downwards

[15] **arsenic:** a strong poison

[18] **filaments:** both the thin wires inside light bulbs, and also strands of fibre, both meanings are suggestive in the context

[23–26] the **moon** is first described as **barren**, like a sterile woman who can't give life to another, and then as **flat, as after radical surgery**, like a woman without breasts after their surgical removal in the operation known as mastectomy

[33] **malignity:** the noun from 'malign', evil

[40] **Its snaky acids:** the allusion is to the mythical Greek female monster Medusa, who had living venomous snakes instead of hair and whose eyes turned onlookers to stone

ANALYSE

Like so much of Plath's work, 'Elm' is a poem of unease, of agitation, of anxiety, of suffering, except that in this case there is no relief, no celebration, no appreciation of vulnerable beauty, no hope, no sense of waiting for the suffering to lift. The poem ends with the awareness of Plath's own self-destructive 'faults'. It is also a perfect example of how Plath uses external landscape to express an inner state, because, after the first stanza it is impossible, and unhelpful, to distinguish between elm and woman. Indeed, the effect of that opening verse is to make tree and woman one. 'I've hit the bottom,' the tree warns the woman. The woman is unimpressed: 'So have I,' she replies. The remainder of the poem is then an exploration of what that experience of hitting and inhabiting rock 'bottom' means and is, for the tree, for the woman.

Is it longing, the 'dissatisfactions' expressed in the eternal sighing of the sea? Is it the sound of emptiness, of hollowness, of 'nothing', referring us back to Plath's suicide attempt as a young woman, her 'madness', when life must have seemed devoid of meaning?

491

Is that 'bottom' the inevitable, aching disappointment of the search for love, because love is merely a fleeting 'shadow', not real, not substantial, perhaps imaginary, an invention of the desperate mind, as elusive as a horse galloping away?

Is the 'bottom' reached by chasing insanely after love, in one's dreams, until the 'head' is so addled that it can no longer think, is mere 'stone', until the 'pillow' it lies on turns to dead, coarse 'turf', with the promise of love still echoing away mockingly inside that stone of a head?

Or instead, would the release of 'poisons', be better, the 'arsenic' of acid rain, the sound of a hail-storm? Peculiar associations these – of arsenic, poison – for water and the tree, for is water not supposed to bring life and nourishment to the tree? But perhaps if life is all suffering, all bitter, then it is merely a poison in itself.

And life *is* suffering. Like Plath, the tree has been 'Scorched' by life, in its case by the sun burning its fibres, in Plath's case by the electric shock treatment she was subjected to while in a mental institution as a young woman. The word 'filaments', as mentioned in the glossary, contains a reference to electricity as well as to natural fibres.

This scorching, understandably, leads to dehydration and disintegration, wonderfully captured in the image of the scattered dead leaves for the elm, and suggesting a truly horrible image of a broken, fractured being when applied to a human, a disintegration caused by a frantic internal wind, a sustained 'shriek', or scream, of pain.

The scream becomes the entire life – 'I am inhabited by a cry', which is not only a cry of pain, but also a cry for comfort, for relief – a life which is pointlessly, obsessively devoted to 'Looking … for something to love'.

What, then, is the malign, soft, dark thing that sleeps inside the tree or the woman, and that so terrifies both? Is it the need for love? A child? The hunger for comfort itself?

Probably love, since everything – including the passing clouds – might be the real thing, might be 'the faces of love', although we are back here to the insubstantiality of love, its elusiveness, its fleeting nature, its own mocking suggestion that it may not exist at all, terrible possibilities that were previously captured in the image of love as a 'shadow'? Is this what all the suffering is in aid of? A shadow?

And whose is the face, the 'murderous' face, that Plath sees in the branches of the elm at the end of all these despairing thoughts, that serpent of a face, full of destructive and self-destructive acid, the face that turns the mind, the 'will' to stone again, the face that will 'kill … kill … kill'? Whose face is that? It is the same face that Plath sees in 'Mirror' and that she reflects in her baby's eye in 'Child'. Her own, of course. 'Elm', as with most Plath pieces, ultimately captures, as she put it herself, the 'stigma' of selfhood, where 'stigma' means a distinguishing mark, a scar, a sign of disease, a sign of mental deficiency or emotional upheaval.

MAKE

(i)   The language in 'Elm', which is about being at rock bottom, is particularly extreme in its references to pain and mutilation – 'shriek', 'surgery'. Pick out further examples and discuss their meaning and purpose.

(ii) Despite the extremity of the language, the tone at the beginning is one of almost cold acceptance – 'I do not fear it: I have been there.' In your opinion, is this same tone maintained throughout the poem. Deal with each stanza individually.

Poppies in July

Little poppies, little hell flames,
Do you do no harm?

You flicker. I cannot touch you.
I put my hands among the flames. Nothing burns.

And it exhausts me to watch you   5
Flickering like that, wrinkly and clear red, like the skin of a mouth.

A mouth just bloodied.
Little bloody skirts!

There are fumes that I cannot touch.
Where are your opiates, your nauseous capsules?   10

If I could bleed, or sleep!——
If my mouth could marry a hurt like that!

Or your liquors seep to me, in this glass capsule,
Dulling and stilling.

But colorless. Colorless.   15

Glossary

[title] **Poppies:** usually red, with at least two standard symbolic associations: with death and violence, from the poppy fields germinated by the human slaughter on French and Belgian battlefields during the First World War; and with sleep, escape and addiction from opium poppies, which are actually white

[10] **opiates:** narcotics

[10] **capsules:** small containers made of gelatine, round or bullet-shaped, containing medicine

[13] **glass capsule:** bell-shaped glass cover used to protect a flower arrangement or to cover a scientific experiment

By mid-1962, while they were living in Devon, the marriage of Sylvia Plath and Ted Hughes was in serious trouble. She suspected him of having an affair. In July, while he was away, she confirmed her fears by reading his letters, which she then burned in the vegetable garden. Afterwards, she wrote 'Poppies in July'.

It's a poem about being in hell, emotionally speaking.

It moves rapidly from an apparently relaxed appreciation of the flowers – that gentle 'Little' in the first line misleads, although its immediate repetition is a bit harsher – through a disturbing confession of hopelessness – 'Nothing burns', she says creepily of her hands when she plunges them into the flowers – and exhaustion, into anger and extreme violence, first towards her rival, then, in despair, towards herself, until it finally collapses into a longing for a drug-induced escape. Along the way, the image of the vivid red poppy has marvellously managed to contain everything – flames that do not burn physically, but burn internally, in the heart and soul, and so are 'hell flames', because the tortures of hell are psychological, dominated, in Christian belief, by a horrible awareness of loss; an existence, a 'Flickering' that she can have no influence over and that still compels her, although observing it exhausts; the wrinkled red of lips, the lips of the rival kissing her husband; those lips that she would like to smash, blood-red, like crushing a poppy; and finally, as the exhaustion and hopelessness take over, the longing for death ('If I could bleed') or the oblivion ('sleep') that is processed from the poppies in opium.

You will notice again that word 'flicker', which is so frequent in Plath's poetry. How fragile life is as it is presented in that image, as if the most it can manage is a flicker. Here the flicker is tormenting, as if the field of poppies blowing in the wind is taunting her. The flicker turns into a dance – 'Little bloody skirts' – her rival's dance of triumph. You will also notice again how the poem reaches out, as so many of Plath's poems do, only to recoil in exhaustion, or terror. Here the poem reaches out in anger, and then in desperation – in forlorn questions ('Where are your opiates …?') and groping repetition ('If I could bleed … If my mouth') – lashing out violently at first and then with decreasing strength and assurance, until it finally folds into weariness ('Dulling and stilling') and listlessness, in the despairing repetition of 'colorless. Colorless.'

MAKE

(i) Images associated with the poppy are used here to flick rapidly, almost chaotically, through the complex emotions of the situation – contempt, rage, self-accusation, guilt and so on – before the final exhaustion. Identify as many images and emotions as you can find.

(ii) In the last line, 'colorless' is obviously the antithesis, or opposite, of the vivid red of the poppies. But why does the speaker long for it?

The Arrival of the Bee Box

I ordered this, this clean wood box
Square as a chair and almost too heavy to lift.
I would say it was the coffin of a midget
Or a square baby
Were there not such a din in it.   5

The box is locked, it is dangerous.
I have to live with it overnight
And I can't keep away from it.
There are no windows, so I can't see what is in there.
There is only a little grid, no exit.   10

I put my eye to the grid.
It is dark, dark,
With the swarmy feeling of African hands
Minute and shrunk for export,
Black on black, angrily clambering.   15

How can I let them out?
It is the noise that appalls me most of all,
The unintelligible syllables.
It is like a Roman mob,
Small, taken one by one, but my god, together!   20

I lay my ear to furious Latin.
I am not a Caesar.
I have simply ordered a box of maniacs.
They can be sent back.
They can die, I need feed them nothing, I am the owner.   25

I wonder how hungry they are.
I wonder if they would forget me
If I just undid the locks and stood back and turned into a tree.
There is the laburnum, its blond colonnades,
And the petticoats of the cherry.   30

They might ignore me immediately
In my moon suit and funeral veil.
I am no source of honey
So why should they turn on me?
Tomorrow I will be sweet God, I will set them free.   35

The box is only temporary.

Glossary

[title] Plath's father was a beekeeper and she retained an enthusiasm for it throughout her life, even persuading her husband, Ted Hughes, to attend the local bee meeting in Devon in 1962 and discussing with him the prospect of breeding them, an idea obviously scuppered by their separation later that year

[1] **box:** bee box, used for transporting bees

[10] **a little grid:** a wire mesh, too fine for the bees to escape through but sufficient to allow in air

[22] **Caesar:** the title of the supreme ruler in ancient Rome, the best known of whom was Julius

[29] **colonnades:** branches of the laburnum tree, growing like columns

[32] **moon suit:** protective bee-keeper suit, which resembles an astronaut's when walking on the moon

ANALYSE

The poem opens on a relaxed, matter-of-fact descriptive note, telling us about the origin and appearance of the box. It looks ordinary, in one sense. Like a kitchen chair. Note that this is the second time we have seen Plath use the kitchen chair as a metaphor for the ordinary, the everyday. The mood shifts abruptly, though, with the introduction of 'coffin' in the imagery – suggesting death, of course – and then 'midget' and 'square baby' – bringing the grotesque, the unformed, the tragic to mind – and with the shift in sound from the neutral opening to the uncertainty of 'I would say' and the unsettling discomfort of 'din'.

The note of anxiety intensifies in the second stanza, with the edgy, insistent repetitive rhythm – 'I have to … I can't … I can't' – and the imagery of dangerous confinement and disability – 'locked … I can't see … no exit'. You might ask why, if the box is locked, it is also dangerous. What's dangerous about a secure box? It goes back to the speculations in the opening stanza, of course: midgets and square babies. Open the box and you never know what you're releasing.

And yet you can't not open it: 'I can't keep away from it'. Apart from the stressed curiosity, there's also the awareness that you'll never know what's in there if you don't look and that ignorance is an even more fearful state.

The language is at its most intense in the third stanza, as it summons up dread of the box's contents. The repetition of 'dark' and 'black' conjure up an unknown and unseen terror, and the physical imagery of 'swarmy' and 'clambering' evoke the notion of a dense group of creatures, overwhelming and desperate. Perhaps the most disturbing image is that of 'African hands', with its implied reference to the nineteenth-century slave trade, when Africans were kidnapped and shipped to the New World in the overcrowded holds of sailing ships. The grotesque notion of the insects as miniature slaves 'shrunk for export' is particularly unnerving.

In the fourth stanza, however – no doubt prompted by that extreme image of exploitation and suffering – the poem turns on the central question: 'How can I let them out?' Two meanings are possible, one pointing backwards towards the fear of the previous stanzas, one pointing forwards towards something superior to anxiety:

 (i) Could I bring myself to release them? Would it be dangerous to do so? and

(ii) What would I have to do to release them?

The first meaning remains focused on herself, her own concerns and her fears. The second meaning considers the welfare of the bees in the box. So the whole poem shifts from the matter-of-fact neutrality of the opening to an expression of consideration. There is still great personal fear – the exclamation 'my god', the heavy sound of 'appalls' and the frightening image of the 'mob' all communicate this – but at least the distance of the opening has been replaced by the possibility of involvement, the possibility of seeing the individuality of 'one by one'.

The fifth stanza begins to explore the possibilities of this involvement. The thing to note here is how much the tone of the speaker's voice has changed: from the neutral lack of concern in the poem's opening lines to the almost frantic searching around here for clues as to what to do ('They can be sent back./They can die') and the desperate need for reassurance ('I am not a Caesar'). Notice how the rhythm of the short, sharp statements in this stanza convey all this. Each line ends abruptly with a full stop, and the longer final line is chopped into three terse statements, separated by commas. There is a final attempt to evade responsibility in the extreme image of 'a box of maniacs'. Though she has 'ordered' the box, clearly 'maniacs' is not what she requested, and therefore not what she is obliged to take care of.

In the opening line of the sixth stanza, Plath's agitation, which had been concerned with herself, turns into a gentle expression of concern: 'I wonder how hungry they are.' The line starts with 'I' and progresses to 'they'. The expression 'I wonder' is thoughtful, composed, reflective; much different from the aggressively assertive expressions of repulsion, reluctance and anxiety earlier.

And the image of hunger – their hunger – introduces the notion of a need other than her own. Although Plath's poetry is often violent and despairing, it also has many gentle moments – here, and notably in the two poems on her children, 'Child' and 'Morning Song'. Even the verb tenses in this stanza – the conditional 'if' – are softer and more considerate than the aggressive interrogatives ('How can I let them out?') and imperatives ('I have to live with it') of the earlier sections. Similarly, the imagery softens from the dark and grotesque metaphors of midgets, square babies, miniature slaves, violent mobs and maniacs to the more delicate, more colourful and more nourishing pictures of trees and flowers – 'laburnum', 'blond colonnades', 'cherry' – and to the particularly delicate feminine image of the 'petticoats'.

The poem ends with the prospect ('might … why should they … Tomorrow') of the speaker being in control ('sweet God') and being a generous benefactor, a bestower of life and freedom ('I will set them free'). It is finally recognised that the bees – let us imagine that they represent life itself – are no danger to the well-protected beekeeper in her 'moon suit and funeral veil' – literally, the standard white protective clothing and face mask – and that they are not interested in exploiting her any more than they are in attacking her: 'I am no source of honey.'

The famous last line of the poem seems confident and assured: 'The box is only temporary.' It suggests that whatever black nightmares of dread and anxiety are symbolically represented by that box – confinement, imprisonment, suffering, depression – they are merely temporary jails that don't last forever. These disabilities can be controlled and ended by the self-possessed individual. Life, let us say, is to be released, celebrated and embraced, not neurotically locked away and dreaded.

It *seems* confident. It *seems* assured. But look again at the details of the previous stanza – 'might … Tomorrow'. It is not achieved yet, that opening out of life, that opening out to life.

MAKE

(i) 'In the box imagery, with its rampant life, Plath begins to develop a familiar situation in her poetry: inner turmoil and outer form.' Would you agree with this assessment of 'The Arrival of the Bee Box'? Give reasons for your answer.

(ii) "The Arrival of the Bee Box' exceeds the five-line stanza pattern. It closes with an extra line – significantly, a line about form that the form of the poem is not able to contain.' Discuss this interesting comment on the ultimately irregular form of this poem, but read the entry at the end of this chapter on poetic form in Plath's poetry before embarking on your response.

READ

Child

Your clear eye is the one absolutely beautiful thing.
I want to fill it with color and ducks,
The zoo of the new

Whose names you meditate—
April snowdrop, Indian pipe,   5
Little

Stalk without wrinkle,
Pool in which images
Should be grand and classical

Not this troublous   10
Wringing of hands, this dark
Ceiling without a star.

Glossary

[title] **Child:** Nicholas, the second child of Sylvia Plath and Ted Hughes, was born on 17 January 1962; Plath wrote this poem a few days after his first birthday, on 28 January 1963

[5] **April snowdrop:** plant with drooping, white, bell-shaped flowers

[5] **Indian pipe:** white woodland plant with a solitary long flower that resembles a pipe

[9] **classical:** here means stately, noble

[10] **troublous:** full of troubles

ANALYSE

At last, apparently, Plath has found perfection in life. At last, apparently, she has found a source of light that does not cloud over even as she looks at it. At last, apparently, she has found a clear surface that she can see through. Looking down at her one-year-old son in his cot, or his pram, or in her arms, she judges the innocent brightness of his eyes as 'the one absolutely beautiful thing'. Perhaps 'judges' is the wrong word; it's too rational, and her response here is full of feeling, full of enthusiasm, full of care and attentiveness. She wants to fill her child's world – what he sees around him – with vibrant colours, and toys, all the splendid spectacle of a brave new world. The images of perfection continue. The child is associated with whiteness, with flowers, with a young plant without imperfections.

And then, the first hint of darkness, of disappointment, of withdrawal into her own depression, that is so characteristic of Plath's poems, in that little word that opens the ninth line … 'Should'. This is how things *should* be, magnificent, orderly, stately, dignified, colourful, controlled. That's how life *should* be. Or maybe, for those who already know Plath's poetry well, the warning came with the word 'Pool' to describe her son's 'clear eye', because we know the depths to which pools and mirrors drag Plath. Or maybe the disappointment began as early as the second

Poetry

line, with 'I want', since everything that follows is a mother's wish, a dream, not reality at all.

Wherever you place the beginning of the recoil into melancholy, what happens is extremely sad. Declaring that a world of joy should fill her son's eye, Plath bends down, closer to her child, and sees … her own reflection, her own agitation, her own 'Wringing of hands', her own misery and imprisonment. This, it seems to her suddenly, is all that she can offer her own child. It is an awful moment in Plath's poetry, when her son, whom she obviously loves, turns into yet another torturing mirror, and the room they are in becomes no more than a prison cell. The poem, which opened so brightly, ends with a combined image of confinement and darkness – 'this dark/ Ceiling without a star' – the combination that perhaps overwhelmed Plath a fortnight later, when she killed herself.

MAKE

(i) This short poem opens on light, space and beauty. It ends on darkness, constriction and unpleasantness. Write a short description of how the change of mood makes you feel as a reader, supporting your exploration with detailed references to the sounds and imagery of the poem.

(ii) Referring to any other poems by Sylvia Plath on your course, but using 'Child' as a core reference, discuss one of the following: (a) the theme of motherhood in Plath's poetry; (b) the imagery of reflective surfaces in Plath's poetry; (c) the use of colour in Plath's poetry.

Poetry

The Poetry of Sylvia Plath

Themes and Interests

- The poetry of Sylvia Plath is a poetry of **PERSONAL EXPERIENCE**, often referred to as confessional poetry, dealing with private trauma and relationships, but representative of universal human experience

With some poets, it can be helpful to link their experiences directly to the poems, to see their works as explorations of particular stages in their lives. It's helpful, for instance, to adopt a biographical approach to the Durcan poems on your course. The same holds for Plath. But while Durcan described and responded to the events of his life, the outer circumstances, Plath's poetry is an expression of an inner life, a description of internal events. It's true that most of her poems can be located in specific events or situations. 'Child' was written two weeks before her suicide, 'Poppies in July' in direct response to the discovery of her husband's infidelity, 'Pheasant' in direct opposition to her husband's game hunting when they lived in Devon, 'Elm' at a particularly low point after the couple's separation, and so on. There are two very important points to note, however. Firstly, each poem captures what is happening, emotionally and psychologically, within Plath, and few make any reference at all to specific external events, although we can now fill in the details from our knowledge of her biography. This focus on the complexity of the inner life, more or less to the exclusion of everything else, is what makes her work so incredibly intense. Listen to a few brief quotations – 'I must shriek … a brief respite from fear/Of total neutrality … I put my hands among the flames … A mouth just bloodied … It is the noise that appalls me most … the atrocity of sunsets … I am inhabited by a cry … the last fingers, knuckled and rheumatic'. It is a poetry of **personal experience**, not a poetry of personal record, which is entirely different and far less intense. Plath's life, and her poetry, were both *very* intense. She once described her life as 'magically run by two electrical currents: joyous positive and despairing negative'. The phrase offers you an insight into her writing, also. She also wrote: 'The blood jet is poetry/There is no stopping it.' Secondly, however – and this is vitally important – Plath's work transcends specific events and is a poetry of **universal human experience**. 'Poppies in July' is a magnificent expression of sexual jealousy – that awful mix of rage, resentment, guilt and despair – and not just a description of *her* sexual jealousy; 'Elm' is a terrifying depiction of hitting rock bottom; 'Child' and 'Morning Song' are painfully honest about the complexities of motherhood; 'Mirror' looks back coldly at the little god most of us worship every morning.

- The poetry of Sylvia Plath explores **CONFINEMENT** as a recurring theme and dramatises the tension between **FREEDOM** and **confinement**

The experience of confinement is at the core of Plath's work. Her poetry is constantly troubled by images of containment and constantly reaches for images of liberation: the wall in 'Mirror', the box in 'Arrival of the Bee Box', the stuck record in 'The Times Are Tidy', walls again in 'Morning Song', the 'strangle of branches' in 'Elm', the 'dark/Ceiling' in 'Child'; and to struggle against these restrictions, the rook arranging its feathers in readiness for flight in 'Black Rook in Rainy Weather', 'riding' out in 'The Times Are Tidy', the balloons in 'Morning Song', the pheasants in open country – 'A hundred, on that hill' – in 'Pheasant', release in 'Arrival of the Bee Box', where the laburnum and cherry await and 'The box is only temporary', and finally the zoo – 'color and ducks' – in 'Child'. Sometimes the confinement is presented as exhaustion, either through weariness or being drugged, but in any case an inability to act, a listlessness, characteristic of depression. And sometimes freedom is seen as dangerous, as having the depths of a lake, the sting of a bee, the violence of the sea or the fascination of witchcraft. It is possible that Plath also began to experience the mirror as confinement. It encloses us within its frame. Because of the close connection between mirror and poetry in her work, it is possible that she also began to experience poetry as confinement. Most of the poems feature either a sudden swoop of depression in the midst of joy – in 'Child', after a tender opening full of love for her one-year-old son Nicholas, she sees her own depression in the baby's open eye – or else the hope of release, of light, or flight, in the depths of depression – both 'The Arrival of the Bee Box' and 'Black Rook in Rainy Weather' begin in an edgy, depressed state, full of gloom, seeing danger in life, but both use the image of flight (bird and bee) to suggest a lifting of the depression. Her poetry, then, tries to keep the warring opposites in balance. Note in particular the sharp contrasts in 'Black Rook in Rainy Weather': where 'desultory', 'mute', 'dull', 'ruinous', 'stubborn' and 'fatigue' are opposed by 'fire', 'light', 'incandescent', 'celestial', 'hallowing', 'flare' and 'shine' in the imagery. There are exceptions to this. When they are written as immediate responses to a painful situation, as 'Poppies in July' was written in 1962 while her husband Ted Hughes was having an affair with Assia Wevill, they tend to be unbalanced, dominated by the negative. Deeply depressed, Plath can associate only negatives with the beautifully vivid red of the poppies: blood, violence, pain, betrayal, the bloody skirt that took her man, and opium. Her only forms of release are also entirely negative: violence inflicted on her (better than being ignored, is the suggestion), sleep, drugs and death.

- The poetry of Sylvia Plath is a **REFLECTION** of Plath's self, as lover, wife, daughter, mother

Reading the poetry of Plath forces us to struggle with the individual herself. Each starting point inevitably brings us back to Plath herself. This is because each poem is a reflection of Plath. She could not escape from herself, a point most touchingly illustrated by the short lyric 'Child', which opens with her son's beauty and ends with her own despair. For a writer whose poetry always reflects herself and for whom everything in nature also offers a reflection, the most appropriate, and most complex, symbol is that of the mirror. Of the poems on your course, the most appropriate starting point here is 'Mirror', written in 1961 during the week before Plath's twenty-ninth birthday. The mirror is represented as neutral ('exact', 'truthful', 'unmisted by love or dislike'), as essential ('I am important to her', worshiped as 'a little god'), as having dangerous depths ('I am a lake', 'Searching my reaches') and as recording the passing of time ('moon', 'morning', 'day after day'). What it reflects is hope of love, but not love itself ('she turns to … the candles or the moon'), pain (although 'not cruel', it sees the woman's 'tears and an agitation of hands'), the ageing process (from 'young girl' to 'old woman') and death ('drowned a young girl'). Mostly what it reflects is a barrier, though ('Most of the time I meditate on the opposite wall'). All of these concerns are the central themes of Plath's poetry: identity, particularly that of a woman; the forlorn hope of love; the certainty of ageing and death and pain; and, of course, confinement. The most unsettling of all Plath's poems, though, is 'Elm', which ends with the awareness of Plath's own self-destructive 'faults'. Who owns the 'murderous' face that she sees in the branches of the

elm at the end of all her despairing thoughts about love and dreams, that serpent of a face, full of destructive and self-destructive acid, the face that turns the mind, the 'will' to stone again, the face that will 'kill … kill … kill'? Isn't it the same face that Plath saw in 'Mirror' and reflected in her baby's eye in 'Child'. Whatever Plath looked at, she saw, in the end, only her own reflection.

- The poetry of Sylvia Plath explores the **VULNERABILITY** of humans, particularly to ageing and death, and the dominance of anxiety

Death is the ultimate release from pain, and it undoubtedly becomes an attraction in some of Plath's poetry. 'They can die', she writes of the bees in 'The Arrival of the Bee Box' – where she is dressed in a 'funeral veil' – 'I need feed them nothing'. It's always an option. She had to keep pushing more positive alternatives: 'laburnum' and 'cherry' in the same poem, 'Miracles', 'radiance' and 'the angel' in 'Black Rook in Rainy Weather', the 'handful of notes' that 'rise like balloons' and that represent a child's potential in 'Morning Song', the 'zoo of the new' in 'Child', and the pheasants in the poem of that name. One major difference between 'Black Rook in Rainy Weather' and 'The Arrival of the Bee Box' that should be noted is that she is passive in the former, waiting for gloom to lift – 'The wait's begun again' – while in the latter she is in total control, she is 'sweet God', capable of freeing the bees by her own actions. She only rarely felt in control, however, and 'The Arrival of the Bee Box' is an unusually positive piece. Closely linked to the exploration of death is the fear of ageing. There is a constant awareness of the passing of time in her poetry, from 'this season/Of fatigue' in 'Black Rook in Rainy Weather', where she longs for a 'brief respite from fear', through the 'moth-breath' of a child that just 'Flickers' with life in 'Morning Song' and the old woman in 'Mirror', to the repeated use of the words 'wrinkly' and 'wrinkle'. Fear is more than the fear of death or growing old, however. Fear dominates the poetry. A nervousness. Not only as a theme, but also as a tone. 'Pheasant' opens: 'You said you would kill it this morning./Do not kill it.' 'It is the noise that appalls me most of all', the narrator of 'The Arrival of the Bee Box' exclaims. The 'Wringing of hands' that recurs so often is a gesture of anxiety as well as pain and agitation. An infant's nakedness, or vulnerability, 'Shadows our safety' – in other words throws a shadow over our own illusions of safety, making us realise just how vulnerable we are – in 'Morning Song'. And, most significant of all, the opening lines of 'Elm': 'I know the bottom … It is what you fear.' This has the same meaning as the common phrase *hitting rock bottom*. It's what we all fear.

Style and Viewpoint

- The poetry of Sylvia Plath is intense, emotionally and intellectually, which means that its **LANGUAGE** is equally so – dynamic, forceful, vigorous, energetic

Random quotations will immediately illustrate how dynamic and intense Plath's language is. The third last line in 'Elm', describing the wonderfully evocative 'strangle of branches' in the tree, is 'Its snaky acids kiss.' Packed into this spitting four-word line are allusions to Christian belief, Greek mythology, science and the study of reptiles. In other words suggestions of the devil who, in the form of a serpent, tempted and destroyed Adam and Eve in Paradise, of Medusa, the snake-headed woman who turned onlookers to stone, of poisonous acid rain that destroys instead of fertilises, of aggressive predators. This is language at its most alive, most intense. This is Plath's language. A quick selection of verbs from the same poem –

'gallop … suffered … Scorched … inhabited … terrified … petrifies' – will illustrate what is meant by the terms 'vigorous' and 'energetic'. Pick more or less at random from another poem, say, 'Poppies in July': 'A mouth just bloodied./Little bloody skirts!' In a sharp, savage movement, using the multiple uses and associations of 'blood', the language jumps from bleeding lips – Caused by a blow? A passionate kiss? A bite? – to an enraged curse, which is uttered by a mouth, of course; and the red mouth – Lipstick? Blood? – transforms into a provocative red skirt. 'Dynamic' means characterised by constant change, activity or progress, full or energy and new ideas. These are accurate expressions to describe Plath's language: its associations are rich, its transformations are swift and imaginative. One more example, from 'The Arrival of the Bee Box': 'It is dark, dark,/With the swarmy feeling of African hands/ Minute and shrunk for export,/Black on black, angrily clambering.' Crowded into these few lines are thoughts of slavery – Africans transported in slave ships to America – imprisonment, being overwhelmed, being overcome, fainting, trade, commerce, profit, miniature people, rage, rebellion, repulsion … No commentary can 'explain' lines of Plath's poetry – the poetry itself is far richer and far more subtle than any commentary – but it's always a pleasure to follow the suggestiveness of her incredibly wealthy language.

- The poetry of Sylvia Plath merges external landscape and inner being (psychic landscape), drawing its dominant **IMAGERY** from nature, mirrors, and darkness and light

The imagery of darkness dominates the poetry of Plath. From the 'dark, dark' interior of the box in 'The Arrival of the Bee Box', through 'this dark thing/That sleeps in me' in 'Elm', and on to 'this dark/Ceiling without a star' in 'Child', darkness threatens, envelops and suffocates her entire world. And it is not only the external world that is always 'dark'. It's not merely a question of waking without light, alone, disorientated, fearful and blinded – all of which are contained in the imagery of darkness. For Plath, the darkness is inside her as well as outside. In 'Elm', she is 'terrified by this dark thing/That sleeps in me', a malign, evil creature, bird-like, with 'hooks' that 'flaps out' nightly, looking for prey; and in 'Mirror', the only thing the mirror has of its own, aside from the objects it reflects, is 'darkness' – 'it is her face that replaces the darkness'. Both the elm and the mirror are projections of Plath herself, of course. Occasionally a poem, such as 'Child', for instance, will open on a bright, positive note, offering the image of a source of light that doesn't cloud over even as she looks at it. In this case – 'Your clear eye is the one absolutely beautiful thing' – it's the innocent, transparent eye of her infant son, not yet dulled or soiled by life. Occasionally a poem, such as 'Black Rook in Rainy Weather', will hope for the descent of 'fire', of 'A certain minor light', of 'spasmodic/Tricks of radiance' – all suggesting illumination and energy. But 'Child' ends with 'this dark/Ceiling without a star' – a metaphor of confinement as well as of bleakness – and in the end all 'Black Rook in Rainy Weather' has to offer *is hope*; it's a poem about waiting for brightness, not about brightness itself. Plath also had an intense involvement with nature. Trees, flowers, landscapes, birds, insects, creatures recur throughout her poetry. The titles of six out of the ten Plath poems on your course contain references to things in nature – a rook, a landscape in Brittany, a pheasant, an elm, poppies and bees – but each description of some natural thing is also a description of Plath herself. This is the unique merging of external landscape and internal state of being – where the elm and the woman are one, Finisterre and the woman are one, the bees and the woman are one, and so on – that is known as psychic landscape, where everything mirrors the poet's state of being.

- The poetry of Sylvia Plath uses **SOUND** – tone, rhythm, stress, repetition, alliteration, cacophony, and so on – as expressively as imagery to convey the experience

Let's look at two quotations to illustrate Plath's use and control of sound.

The first is from 'Finisterre': 'This was the land's end: the last fingers, knuckled and rheumatic,/Cramped on nothing. Black/Admonitory cliffs.' Of course, it's impossible to ignore the extraordinary image of the land as fingers clutching air, but let's focus on how the sound effects contribute to creating a sense of the place. The colon (:) after 'end' abruptly brings the opening line up short, long before it has a chance to develop any momentum. The effect is of immediately running out of land, which is what Finesterre feels like. One more step and you're over the cliff. The heavy stresses on 'last fingers' prepare for the even heavier stresses on the hard, distorted knuckles and on the ill, defective sound of 'rheumatic', before the extraordinarily constricted stress on 'Cramped' and the release into emptiness of 'nothing'. The sounds contribute to the sense of the place and to the reader's experience of the place, as described by Plath.

The second quotation demonstrates Plath's control of tone in a speaking voice and is from 'The Arrival of the Bee Box': 'The box is locked, it is dangerous./I have to live with it overnight/ And I can't keep away from it.' The thing to note here is how the anxiety and uncertainty are created through the rhythm of the terse, clipped statements, through the use of abrupt monosyllables (a favourite technique of Plath's), and the repetitive patterns. All contribute to creating a voice that is anxious, almost neurotic. This is maintained for three more stanzas, reaching an apparently indifferent 'They can die, I need feed them nothing, I am the owner', before changing sound, and therefore tone, and therefore feeling, with the more considerate, inquisitive, potentially caring: 'I wonder how hungry they are./I would if they would …' where the rhythm has eased out and the words have softened.

- The poetry of Sylvia Plath favours the **FORM** of the personal lyric, though with few conventional structural devices such as standard rhyming schemes or regular line lengths

In poetry, the lyric expresses personal emotion and is usually written in the present tense. It was the dominant form of poetry in the early twentieth century, fell out of favour somewhat following the criticism of, among others, T.S. Eliot that it was more interested in melody than complexity, but returned to dominance in the mid-twentieth century, particularly in America, in the hands of such confessional poets as Plath. It is, of course, easy to demonstrate that Plath's lyrics express personal emotion – love for her children, anxiety about her own identity, fear of confinement, jealousy, despair, and so on. It's equally easy to show her use of the present tense, something that gives a striking immediacy to the best lyric poetry and to all of Plath's work – the opening lines of the earliest of her poems on your course are 'On the stiff twig up there/Hunches a wet black rook', and the opening line of the last of her poems on your course is: 'Your clear eye is the one absolutely beautiful thing.' What is somewhat unusual about the form of Plath's lyric poetry is its absence of regular schemes – rhyming schemes, metrical schemes. In the same poem, the line length can go from fourteen syllables to two syllables – from 'Your clear eye is the one absolutely beautiful thing' to 'Little' in 'Child' – or from sixteen to four, as in 'The Arrival of

the Bee Box'. In neither of these poems, or in any of the others, is there a concerted attempt at consistent end-rhyme – 'midget' half-rhymes with 'in it' and 'me' is echoed by 'tree' and 'free' in 'The Arrival of the Bee Box'. It's obvious that Plath has a fondness for stanzas of unevenly numbered lines – particularly stanzas of three lines and five lines – but even this is not always held to. Clearly, it's a deliberate choice. But what's the reason? For Plath, rhythm was more expressive than metre, the irregularity of emotional articulation more real than any controlling scheme. In 'Elm', when she wrote such a line as 'Or shall I bring you the sound of poisons?', she wanted to capture the taunting of the tree; and when she wrote: 'Are those the faces of love, those pale irretrievables?/Is it for such I agitate my heart?' she wanted to capture the exhaustion of hopelessness; and when she wrote: 'That kill, that kill, that kill', she wanted to capture the destructive ferocity of the 'slow faults' that are fatal for us. The irregular forms of her lyric poetry express the irregularities of life.

PERMISSION ACKNOWLEDGEMENTS

The publisher and author gratefully acknowledge the following for granting permission to reproduce the following photographs:

© AF Archive/Alamy: 8, 11, 14, 18, 20, 22, 23, 24, 25, 31, 33, 41, 48, 49, 51, 52, 54, 60, 61, 63, 66, 67, 72 (*Rear Window* poster, *The King's Speech* poster) 79, 91, 93, 118, 124, 126, 128, 129, 132, 162, 166, 167 • © Classic Image/Alamy: 9 • © Geraint Lewis/Alamy: 12, 81, 83, 84, 86, 87, 154 • © The Art Archive/Alamy: 13 • © Moviestore collection Ltd/Alamy: 16, 36, 57, 58, 89, 90, 96, 115, 117, 119 • © Pictorial Press Ltd/Alamy: 28, 42 (Fitzgerald), 121, 130 • © Vehbi Koca/Alamy: 35 • © The Granger Collection/TopFoto: 42 (book cover) • © Lordprice Collection/Alamy: 44 • © Photos 12/Alamy: 46, 47, 53, 55. 59, 62, 65, 69, 165, 170 • © United Artists/TopFoto: 68 • THE FAULT IN OUR STARS by John Green (Penguin Books, 2012). Cover reproduced in its entirety with permission from Penguin Books Ltd: 72 • *Foster* cover: Reprinted by kind permission of Faber and Faber Ltd: 72 • sjtheatre/Alamy: 72 (*A Doll's House*) • © Robert Herrett/Alamy: 72 (*All My Sons*) • *The Uncommon Reader* cover: Reprinted by kind permission of Faber and Faber Ltd: 72 • © enrem images/Alamy: 103 • © Andre Jenny/Alamy: 140 • © Johan Persson/Arena PAL: 159, 161 • © Jeff Morgan/Alamy: 171 • © Paul Thompson Images/Alamy: 173 • © Stan Kujawa/Alamy: 177 • © HG Delaney/Alamy: 179 • © Howard Davies/Alamy: 194 • © Peter van Evert/Alamy: 198 • © Photo Alto/Alamy: 206 • © Topham Picturepoint: 216 • © Dwayne Fuller: 220 • © Tom Salyer/Alamy: 223 • © Christopher Bailey/Alamy: 231 • © B.A.E.Inc./Alamy: 232 • © Imagebroker/Alamy: 244 • © Visions of America, LLC/Alamy: 252 • © Juniors Bildarchiv GmbH/Alamy: 267 • © Keystone Pictures USA/Alamy: 269 • © Marc Tielemans/Alamy: 275 • © Filatova Natalia/Alamy: 282 • © Masterpics/Alamy: 299 • © Florilegius/Alamy: 302 • © Heritage Image Partnership Ltd/Alamy: 311 • © British Library Board/TopFoto: 317 • © Giles Angel/Alamy: 333 • © David Robertson/Alamy: 335 • © Andreas von Einsiedel/Alamy: 346 • © Zuma Press, Inc./Alamy: 355 • © Bryn Bache/Alamy: 356 • © Urban Zone/Alamy: 371 • © World History Archive/TopFoto: 376 • © Lebrecht Music and Arts Photo Library: 393 • © Bygone Collection/Alamy: 427 • © Falkensteinfoto/Alamy: 443 • © Walker Art Library/Alamy: 451 • © Lindsay Constable/Alamy: 497 • Other images from Shutterstock and Wikicommons (public domain)

The publisher and author gratefully acknowledge the following for granting permission to reproduce the following copyrighted works:

COMPARATIVE STUDY: text from *All My Sons*: Reprinted by kind permission of The Wylie Agency (UK) Limited • text from *Foster*: Reproduced with permission of Curtis Brown Group Ltd, London on behalf of Claire Keegan. Copyright © Claire Keegan 2010 • text from *The Fault in Our Stars* by John Green (Penguin Books, 2012, 2013). Reproduced with permission from Writers House • text from *The Uncommon Reader*: Reprinted by kind permission of Faber and Faber Ltd

POETRY: THE BACK YARD by Carl Sandburg, courtesy of The Carl Sandburg Family Trust and The Barbara Hogenson Agency, Inc. • Dream Song #14: "Life, friends" from THE DREAM SONGS by John Berryman. Copyright © 1969 by John Berryman. Copyright renewed 1997 by Kate Donahue Berryman • Katie Donovan 'Yearn On' from *Rootling: New & Selected Poems* (Bloodaxe Books, 2010). Reproduced with permission of Bloodaxe Books on behalf of the author, www.bloodaxebooks.com • Li-Young Lee, "A Story" from *The City In Which I Love You*. Copyright © 1990 by Li-Young Lee. Reprinted with the permission of The Permissions Company, Inc., on behalf of BOA Editions, Ltd., www.boaeditions.org • Elizabeth Bishop: "Armadillo," "At the Fishhouses," "The Bight," "Filling Station," "First Death in Nova Scotia," "The Fish," "In the Waiting Room," "The Prodigal," "Questions of Travel," and "Sestina" from THE COMPLETE POEMS 1927–1979 by Elizabeth Bishop. Copyright © 1979, 1983 by Alice Helen Methfessel. Reprinted by permission of Farrar, Straus and Giroux, LLC • Eavan Boland: 'The War Horse', 'Child of our Time', 'The Famine Road', 'The Shadow Doll', 'White Hawthorn in the West of Ireland', 'Outside History', 'The Black Lace Fan my Mother Gave me', 'This Moment', 'The Pomegranate', 'Love' by Eavan Boland from *New and Selected Poems* (2013), reprinted by permission of Carcanet Press • Paul Durcan: "Nessa", "The Girl with the Keys to Pearse's Cottage", 'The Difficulty that is Marriage', 'Wife Who Smashed Television Gets Jail", "Parents", "Windfall", "Six Nuns Die in Convent Inferno", "Sport", "Father's Day, 21 June 1992", "The Arnolfini Marriage", "Rosie Joyce", "The MacBride Dynasty", "En Famille 1979", "Madman", and "Ireland 2002" from the collection LIFE IS A DREAM: 40 YEARS READING POEMS by Paul Durcan. Acknowledgement is made as follows: Copyright © Paul Durcan. Reproduced by permission of the author c/o Rogers, Coleridge & White Ltd., 20 Powis Mews, London W11 1JN • T.S. Eliot: 'The Love Song of J. Alfred Prufrock', 'Preludes', 'Aunt Helen', 'The Waste Land' *II. A Game of Chess*, 'Journey of the Magi', 'Landscapes' *III. Usk*, 'Landscapes' *IV. Rannoch, by Glencoe*, 'Four Quartets *East Coker IV* from *Collected Poems 1909–1962*. Reprinted by kind permission of Faber and Faber Ltd • Sylvia Plath: 'Black Rook in Rainy Weather', 'The Times Are Tidy', 'Morning Song', 'Finisterre', 'Mirror', 'Pheasant', 'Elm', 'Poppies in July', 'The Arrival of the Bee Box', 'Child' from *Collected Poems*. Reprinted by kind permission of Faber and Faber Ltd

The author and publisher have made every effort to trace all copyright holders. If any have been overlooked we would be happy to make the necessary arrangements at the first opportunity.

Excellence in **English** *Paper 1 Language*
and
Excellence in **English** *Paper 2 Literature 2017*
Higher Level English for Fifth and Sixth Year

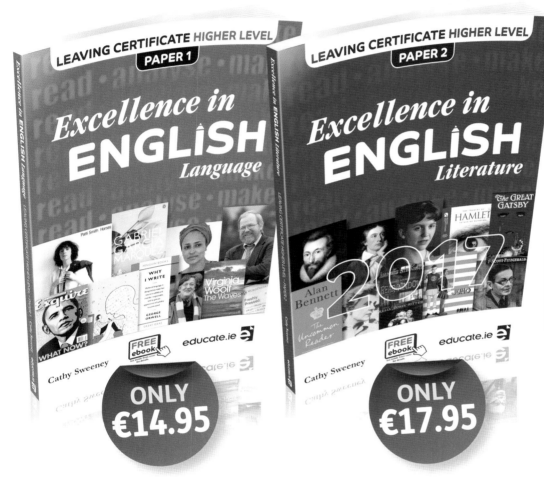

Excellence in English Language is a comprehensive package (textbook, ebook and digital resources) that helps students toward success in Leaving Certificate Higher Level English Paper 1.

- **Lively and engaging** comprehension pieces and composing tasks
- The unique READ – ANALYSE – MAKE method helps students to develop essential skills for Paper 1
- **Downloadable worksheets** enable students to test their knowledge and progress at regular intervals

Excellence in English Literature (Higher Level 2017) is a comprehensive package (textbook, ebook and digital resources) that helps students towards success in the Leaving Certificate Higher Level English Paper 2.

- Uses a unique READ – ANALYSE – MAKE method to develop the **essential skills required for understanding and discussing texts**
- Provides **all of your poetry**
- Offers **outstanding choice in all three sections of Paper 2**, covering two Single Texts and three different groups of the Comparative Texts prescribed for Higher Level in 2017 and all of the poems set for each of the 2017 prescribed poets
- Provides students with lively and engaging **audio lectures** on each of the 2017 prescribed poets and **downloadable guides** to answering exam questions

To order: Freephone: 1800 613 111   Email: sales@educate.ie   www.educate.ie

Notes

Notes

Notes

Notes

Notes